W9-AAH-303

ROADS to SUCCESS

ROADS to SUCCESS

ROBERT HELLER

A Dorling Kindersley Book

LONDON, NEW YORK, SYDNEY, DELHI, PARIS,
MUNICH & JOHANNESBURG

Project Editor Mark Wallace
US Editor Gary Werner
Senior Art Editor Tracy Miles
DTP Designer Julian Dams
Production Controller Michelle Thomas

Managing Editor Adèle Hayward
Senior Managing Editor Stephanie Jackson
Senior Managing Art Editor Nigel Duffield

First published in the United States in 2001
by Dorling Kindersley Publishing, Inc.
95 Madison Avenue
New York, New York 10016

2 4 6 8 10 9 7 5 3 1

Published in Great Britain by Dorling Kindersley Limited.

A CIP record for this book is available from the Library of Congress.

ISBN 0-7894-7845-5

Reproduced by Colourpath, London
Printed in Slovakia by TBB

Contents

Introduction

The eight famed individuals whose lives and thoughts are described in these pages fall at first sight into two distinct groups: the doers and the educators. The doers have done great things. Jack Welch's spectacular creation of value at General Electric, Bill Gates' building of Microsoft into the enabling software force of the electronic revolution, Andy Grove's parallel driving of Intel's magnificent microprocessor machine, and Warren Buffett's achievement of by far the greatest fortune ever derived from straight investment.

But the educators are no mean achievers themselves. Peter Drucker created management writing as a genre, and used his great skill to change the ways in which managers manage. Stephen R. Covey, with his 10 million sales of *The Seven Secrets of Highly Effective People* and his own business services empire, is only rivaled by Tom Peters, whose seven million sales of *In Search of Excellence* helped launch a successful consultancy group. Charles Handy (like Drucker) is not an entrepreneur, but his gentle philosophy has changed the debate about management and society on both sides of the Atlantic.

Similar approaches

In fact, the divide between doers and educators is less important than the similarities. All eight men have thought long and deeply about management, and their views have been set down in powerful words. Among the doers, both Grove and Gates have written important books based on their experiences of the electronic revolution and their insights into its dynamics and its management. While heading Intel, Grove has also been a part-time teacher, developing his unique theories on strategy at Stanford University. Welch has used everything from annual statements to innumerable interviews to expound his highly potent ideas, and the wit and wisdom of Buffett's chairman's reports for Berkshire Hathaway made them treasured classics.

Likewise, the educators have kept their feet firmly planted in management realities. Drucker has been a highly valued consultant for America's leading companies, including GE, both before and during Welch's amazing regime. The *Excellence* study, which established Peters' early reputation, sprang from work at McKinsey (where he was a practicing management consultant) on the attributes that distinguish highly successful companies. Handy came from an industrial background and based his highly original thought on direct observation of management practice. Covey left academic posts precisely to help make American management more effective by every means in his power.

Management teachings

There are bridges between the teachings, too. Thus, Handy's "Sigmoid Curve" is blood brother to Grove's "strategic inflection point." Indeed, the eight

Masterminds offer a strikingly consistent set of analyses, precepts, and rules, even though their starting points and major themes differ so greatly. Where Covey is inspired by his belief in underlying, unchanging moral laws, Welch has devoted much of his work and teaching to generating high-class individual contributions within the framework of a corporate giant. Where Grove is "paranoid" about the management of rapid change (fully understandable in the context of Silicon Valley), Handy is deeply concerned about the impact of long-term socioeconomic change on organizations.

Gates has become increasingly occupied with the revolutionary implications and forces of the internet, which his friend Buffett prefers to pass by, stressing the eternal verities of investment and management. Peters is excited and enthused by the discontinuities, rather than the continuities, and preaches all-around managerial revolution. Drucker, authoritative about both the unchanged and the fast-changing, sets a farseeing but pragmatic study of management in a broad social, political, and economic context.

Lessons for managers

The eight Masterminds thus make a rich combination from which all managers and would-be managers can learn important lessons. For this book, their teachings on key issues have been distilled into two dozen highly practical Masterclasses which contain invaluable advice on the best ways to become a master manager. Like the writings from which they spring, the classes aim at achieving higher levels of personal and organizational effectiveness – a keynote of the entire octet. They deal with theory in masterly fashion, but just as importantly convert ideas into activity and devise programs for action.

Thinking managers do the same. This book is food for their thoughts and deeds. Its rich diversity emphasizes that there is no one right path to managerial achievement, no universal panacea. But there are universal ideas, which the Masterminds exemplify in words (and deeds) that offer universal inspiration.

Robert Heller

warren BUFFETT

Biography

Warren Buffett was born on August 30, 1930, in Omaha, Nebraska, where he lives and works to this day, earning for himself the affectionate title of "The Sage of Omaha." Though by no means a recluse, he believes that his Midwest location shields him from the frenzy of Wall Street. He came by his profession naturally enough: his father was an investment banker, who also served as a congressman in Washington, DC.

Applying Graham's ideas

Buffett learned the fundamentals of finance at the Wharton School of Finance, Pennsylvania, and then earned an economics degree from the University of Nebraska. Studying for his master's at Columbia Graduate Business School, Buffett came under the influence of Benjamin Graham. After working as an investment salesman for the family firm in Omaha from 1951 to 1954, Buffett moved to New York to work for Graham's investment company – Graham-Newman Corporation – as a securities analyst.

From 1956 to 1969, Buffett ran a private investment partnership in Omaha for well-to-do Nebraskans, including family and friends. He was very successful at applying Graham's ideas, searching for businesses whose intrinsic value – their real worth as going concerns – was greater than the stock price. The partnership was eventually liquidated to the great profit of the investors – and of Buffett. From 1970, he transcended that success, having acquired control in 1965 of Berkshire Hathaway, a textile company which, curiously, was one of his poorest investments (see p. 86).

Berkshire's meteoric rise

That hardly mattered, though, when Buffett began using Berkshire as a vehicle for other interests, including brilliant stock purchases. Over 34 years, the company achieved an astonishing 24.7 percent compound annual return for its shareholders. Buffett has been its chairman and chief executive officer from the start, working with a small staff and shunning almost all the trappings of great riches and executive eminence. But his wry personality, enormous success, and mounting billions in personal wealth have made him a legend – and the hero of his shareholders.

Any of them who bought shares in 1965 have seen spectacular results. Had they invested $10,000, it would now be worth $51 million. The chief beneficiaries from this miracle of investment have, of course, been Buffett and his family. His wife of 47 years, Susan, sits on the board, as do his daughter, also Susan, and Howard, one of his two sons. But neither these two nor Peter, the third child, play any management role. Buffett's right-hand man for many years was his vice-chairman, Charlie Munger. Regularly praised by Buffett, who gives his old friend a great share of the credit for Berkshire's success, Munger retired to the sidelines in 1999 at the age of 75.

Personal style

Some 15,000 shareholders flock to Omaha for Berkshire's annual general meeting. Throwing out the first ball for the local minor league baseball team has become one of Buffett's rituals for this weekend event. Investors can shop for jewelry at a company-owned store, vie for reservations at Gorat's, where Buffett likes to dine, and line up for the autographs of Buffett and Munger.

The personal touch and the homeyness are genuine; to an unusual extent, Buffett is what he seems. What the *Financial Times* once called his "wisecracks and folksy wisdom" accurately measure the man. It is characteristic of Buffett that virtually all of his wealth (an astounding $40 billion in May 1999, second only to that of Bill Gates) is invested in Berkshire. This, of course, gives him a tremendous spread, both in the share portfolio and in the company's wholly owned businesses. These range from Dairy Queen ice-cream parlors, bought for $590 million in 1998, to auto insurance and shoe manufacturing.

Being a contrarian investor

Berkshire also owns General Re, America's largest re-insurance company, which cost $22 billion in 1998, and all in stocks. Using stocks for investment purposes was something of a departure for Buffett, who had previously made a point of being a cash purchaser on almost every occasion. Such a preference is one of his several distinctive "contrarian" characteristics. As a contrarian, he has never followed the herd, and the herd has never followed him. In fact, his career has been built on a paradox. If everybody searched for and bought undervalued shares, their prices would rise rapidly until they were fully valued. Therefore, Buffett's unique success as an investor has depended on others not following his ideas.

In another paradox, the past success of his theories has now made it much harder for him to apply them. As the Berkshire wealth has boomed, so each new investment has had to be increasingly gigantic to make any impact on the whole. With a net worth of $57.4 billion in May 1999, his company faced a situation that Buffett described frankly:

"Our future rates of gain will fall far short of those achieved in the past. Berkshire's capital base is now simply too large to allow us to earn truly outsized returns. If you believe otherwise, you should consider a career in sales but avoid one in mathematics."

Because of the technical bookkeeping consequences of the General Re transaction, the gain in Berkshire's book value (see p. 52) in 1998 was 48.3 percent. Buffett has only bettered that annual increase once in his company's history. But the special contribution of General Re hid the fact that the stock market grew 10 times faster than Berkshire's $37.3 billion portfolio of shares. That was weighed down by three of Buffett's favorite holdings: Coca-Cola, Gillette, and Walt Disney, which all had a miserable 1998.

It appeared equally uncharacteristic of Buffett to invest heavily in copper in 1997, prompting memories of an earlier attempt to corner the market in metal, which ruined the super-rich Hunt brothers. No disaster attended Buffett's plunge into copper, but it was not a great success. In fact, Buffett has had some conspicuous failures, about which he talks more bluntly than anybody else. The worst episode was probably the scandal at Salomon Brothers Inc., the largest Wall Street investment bank; Buffett had to take the chair, and spend more time than he wanted away from Omaha, to save the bank and rescue his huge investment.

Accumulating businesses

But Buffett has not made a truly large investment in stocks since buying 4.3 percent of McDonald's in 1995. Since that purchase, Buffett has been busily converting Berkshire into a different kind of company. The purchase of General Re marked another stage in this process. In 1996,

Investing in brand power
Coca-Cola, an outstandingly successful investment, typifies the kind of company Buffett most favors: one focused on a single powerful brand that has a dominant share in an easily understood market.

74 percent of Berkshire's assets consisted of shares in other companies. Now stock market investments account for under a third of the Berkshire total worth. Buffett presides over $82 billion in wholly owned operating companies, which employ no less than 47,566 workers.

There is no pattern to this accumulation of businesses, except for the predominance taken by insurance, enhanced by the General Re purchase. Buffett's collection of insurers has sales of some $14 billion, and far outweighs the other sectors. The three largest of these, however, are still substantial: home furnishings bring in $793 million of sales, "flight services" produce over $850 million, and Scott Fetzer, a highly varied bundle of products, from vacuum cleaners to encyclopedias, has $1 billion in revenues.

Creating a conglomerate

Scott Fetzer is a typical example of a now unfashionable corporate breed – the "conglomerate," less flatteringly called a "ragbag." The noun fits Berkshire as a whole. Conglomerates as a corporate form are a long way removed from "value investing"; notoriously, most conglomerates have subtracted rather than added to the value of their subsidiaries. Buffett has always greatly favored investments in exactly the opposite kinds of company: those focused on powerful single brands, like Coca-Cola. But he is striving to build a company that will outlast him; a portfolio of stock market investments would not serve that purpose.

Whether a sprawling conglomerate will do so without its creator's magic touch is another, more difficult question. Few of the conglomerates built in their great era, the 1960s, survived their founders' departures. Buffett is in a new game. His rise to fabulous riches was built on the strong theoretical foundations learned from Benjamin Graham. But that theory governed picking stocks. Provided the buy was right, no further action was required, except collecting the dividends; the management decisions were taken by the company concerned, not by Buffett.

So far, Buffett has applied a similar approach to management, trusting the operating executives to deliver profits in suitable quantities. Now the old master needs to demonstrate that his management theories and practice, which have been applied very successfully so far, can be as effective as his investment ideas. That is a tall order.

1

Assessing the value of companies

How market values diverge from the "intrinsic value" of businesses • **Three non-financial criteria for identifying an outstanding company** • Four financial criteria that specifically relate to managerial excellence • **Having the courage and conviction to put all your eggs in one basket** • Following probability theory in the choice and timing of investments • **Being indifferent to the day-to-day movement of stock prices** • How to value a business and think about market prices

Buffett's ability to choose undervalued stocks is a living and amazingly successful denial of the academic theory that markets are "efficient," that is, the price of a security accurately sums up all the information available on the company and its stock. On the contrary, Buffett maintains (and, more significantly, has proved) that market values diverge, often markedly, from the "intrinsic value" of a business, which represents the real and lasting worth of its economic attributes.

Buffett looks for companies that have a history of stability as well as above-average performance. This seems a rational enough approach, and it has certainly been a successful one for him. Yet the theory appears to be founded on the fallacy that the past is a good guide to the future. Obviously, there can never be any certainty that either the stability or the superior performance will continue. But, in Buffett's view, it is simply more probable that a company with a good history will remain good than that a bad company, based on its historical record, will become good.

Focus investing

Buffett therefore proceeds with total confidence to implement an investment policy which, as explained by Robert G. Hagstrom, Jr., in *The Warren Buffett Portfolio* (1999), looks like simplicity itself: "Choose a few stocks that are likely to produce above-average returns over the long haul, concentrate the bulk of your investments in those stocks, and have the fortitude to hold steady during any short-term market gyrations."

This policy of what is termed "focus investing" belongs to neither of the two warring schools of thought that actually dominate modern stock market investment. Most investment funds, from pensions to mutual funds, are actively run by their managers, whose employment, rewards, and reputations rest on their ability to pick shares that out-perform the market. They typically buy a great number of stocks in order to "spread the risks."

The fund managers, in effect, use a shotgun rather than a rifle – although they claim to be sharpshooters, of course. As Buffett has often pointed out, the more stocks they buy, the more likely they are, at best, only to match the performance of the market as a whole. That being so, argue proponents of the second school of thought, why not simply invest in the whole market? Instead of picking individual stocks, index funds "track" a popular stock market index. The problem here, however, is that, by definition, it is impossible to "outperform" the market.

Meeting non-financial criteria

Buffett recommends index funds for the uninformed investor; but that choice only makes sense for those who truly believe that stock market performance is entirely random and not susceptible to human reasoning. That is not Buffett's view. He believes that rationality rules in all matters, including, first, how you identify an outstanding company. He applies three non-financial criteria:

- It is simple and understandable.
- It has a consistent operating history.
- It has favorable long-term prospects.

The first criterion bars Buffett from high-technology, gee-whiz investment and therefore from participating in phenomenal growth sagas such as that of Microsoft, the creation of his friend Bill Gates. The argument is that if you cannot understand the business, you cannot make a rational judgment of its investment value. Given that so many other opportunities exist, why go into situations where one arm is tied behind your back?

The "consistent operating history" speaks for itself; Buffett no more wants volatile management than volatile technology. But the next insistence, on "favorable long-term prospects," ventures into futurology. He is again extrapolating the past into the future. When investing in Coca-Cola, for example, he is not betting on some

The billionaire buddies
Warren Buffett and Bill Gates, the two richest men in America, are close personal friends. Despite that, Buffett will not buy Microsoft shares because he only invests where he understands the technology.

marvelous new drink yet to be born. He is assuming that existing markets for existing beverages will continue to expand steadily, that further new markets will generate further rapid growth, that Coca-Cola's marketing skills will still sustain its share, and that its financial management will optimize profitability.

Any of these propositions might be falsified by events, as actually happened to Coca-Cola from 1998 to 1999. But once again Buffett is betting on the probabilities and on the "long term." Over several years, he reckons, the chances are that reverses will be more than corrected. The proviso is that the company must enjoy a management that follows three requirements: it must be rational; it must be candid with shareholders; and it must resist the "institutional imperative," that is, the irrational tendency of corporate leaders to imitate other managements' practices and policies, irrespective of their suitability or sense.

Meeting financial criteria

Naturally, Buffett expects financial benefits to flow from this good managerial behavior. His financial criteria, though, are not those used by most investment analysts. Because excellent profits are the result of good management, Buffett watches indicators that specifically relate to managerial excellence. He looks at:

- Return on equity (not earnings per share)
- "Owner earnings" (the share of profits that belongs to investors)
- Profit margins (which must be high)
- Return on reinvested profits (which must create at least $1 of market value for every dollar reinvested)

The majority of public companies will fail on at least one of Buffett's three non-financial and four financial criteria, thus narrowing his field of choice substantially. If a company has passed muster on all these counts, Buffett can proceed to the two crucial issues: First, what is the business truly worth, that is, what is its "intrinsic value"? And, second, is the market value significantly lower than that true worth? Of course, by insisting that the chosen investment should be within your area of personal knowledge, Buffett narrows the field still further.

Putting your eggs in one basket

This insistence on a restricted area of investment paves the way toward investing in only five to ten securities, as Buffett recommends. His argument is that the risk actually increases when investments are spread too thinly. Instead, he commands: "Put all your eggs in one basket – and watch that basket."

Buffett can quote substantial authority for this line of reasoning, not only Philip Fisher, the famous American investment adviser who put his eggs in very few baskets, but also the great Cambridge economist John Maynard Keynes. In 1934, Keynes wrote: "One's knowledge and experience are definitely limited and there are seldom more than two or three enterprises at any given time in which I personally feel myself entitled to put *full* confidence."

The logic behind Keynes's argument and Buffett's practice is unassailable. However, it is incomplete. The investor is being asked to put total faith in his or her own judgment, even though the three, or five, or 10, or 15 stocks chosen are unlikely to be the very best choices available. Each decision to buy excludes other investments that may perform better. The diversified investors prefer a wider choice to reduce dependence on their judgment and thus reduce the risk of being wrong. Accepting that risk is not so much a matter of logic as of courage, Buffett is very clear on this vital point: "With each investment you make, you should have the courage and the conviction to place at least 10 percent of your net worth in that stock."

Judging the probabilities

If you trust your own judgment, the courage and the conviction are rational. Yet the stock market is irrational. So, how can this apparent contradiction be resolved? Here mathematics enters the picture. To Buffett, investment is a matter of judging the "probabilities." Probability theory is a very important and respectable branch of mathematics, and it is essential to Buffett's theory of investment: "Take the probability of loss times the amount of possible loss from the probability of gain times the amount of possible gain. That is what we're trying to do. It's imperfect, but that's what it is all about."

Probabilities are basic to the art of arbitrage, at which Buffett is a master. The principle of arbitrage is to estimate the probable result if a given event occurs, for example,

"Our goal is to find an outstanding business at a sensible price, not a mediocre business at a bargain price. Charlie and I have found making silk purses out of silk is the best that we can do; with sows' ears we fail."
The Essays of Warren Buffett

if an announced takeover bid succeeds. If it looks as though the stock in the company concerned can be bought for a value lower than the probable outcome, Buffett becomes interested. To illustrate the point, one year Berkshire made a very easy $64 million after the announcement of a takeover bid by Kohlberg Kravis & Roberts (KKR), the investment specialists, for the food and tobacco giant RJR Nabisco.

Buffett's approach to arbitrage is essentially the same as his investment strategy. In both cases, he buys into situations where the probability is that the stocks are undervalued and that this undervaluation will be corrected. The difference is time-scale; the arbitrage position will be closed out as soon as possible, while the investment will be kept "indefinitely so long as we expect the business to increase in intrinsic value at a satisfactory rate." That answers the question about how long Buffett believes a stock should be held: possibly forever.

Calculating value

Buffett makes the crucial point that he and Munger have invested "as business analysts – not as market analysts, not as macroeconomic analysts, and not even as security analysts." The basic task is calculating value, for instance, that of the Washington Post Company in mid-1973. Buffett says that the general estimate of WPC's "intrinsic business value" would have been $400–500 million, even though it was valued on the stock market at only $100 million. So Buffett bought and, following another of his principles, bought big. A quarter of a century later, Berkshire still holds the stock, which continues to satisfy Buffett's requirements for keeping shares:

- The prospective return on equity capital of the underlying business is satisfactory.
- Management is competent and honest.
- The market does not overvalue the business.

The third requirement raises a difficulty. Buffett says flatly that sometimes "the market may judge a business to be more valuable than the underlying facts would indicate it is. In such a case, we will sell our holdings." Yet his practice and his words suggest that he is a very reluctant seller. He refers to "primary holdings" (including WPC) that "we expect to keep permanently." As he explains: "Even if these securities were to appear significantly overpriced, we would not anticipate selling them, just as we would not sell See's [the candy business] or *Buffalo Evening News* if someone were to offer us a price far above what we believe those businesses are worth."

This statement demonstrates that Buffett makes no distinction between two investment activities: buying part of a company through the stock market and buying all of a company by private treaty. On the same analogy, he is indifferent to the stock market behavior of the stocks he purchases: "We don't need a daily quote on our 100 percent position in See's... to validate our well-being. Why, then, should we need a quote on our 7 percent interest in Coke?"

"Consciously paying more for a stock than its calculated value... should be labeled speculation (which is neither illegal, immoral, nor – in our view – financially fattening)."
The Essays of Warren Buffett

Irresistible business strength

The value of Buffett's primary holdings, using his own approach, lies not in the stock market quotation but in the calculable, irresistible business strength of companies like those he calls "The Inevitables":

> "Is it really so difficult to conclude that Coca-Cola and Gillette possess far less business risk over the long term than, say, any computer company or retailer? Worldwide, Coke sells about 44 percent of all soft

A base in Nebraska
Buffett believes that working from his home town, Omaha, insulates him from the frenetic activity of the Wall Street financial houses, whose sophisticated knowledge, he says, is not needed by investors.

drinks, and Gillette has more than a 60 percent share (in value) of the blade market. Leaving aside chewing gum, in which Wrigley is dominant, I know of no other significant businesses in which the leading company has long enjoyed such global power."

Buffett adds that "both Coke and Gillette have actually increased their worldwide shares of market in recent years." He argues correctly that these companies, through "the might of their brand names, the attributes of their products, and the strength of their distribution systems," have "an enormous competitive advantage."

But how reliable is the consequent "protective moat around their economic castles"? The rational answer is that no company is an "Inevitable." Emotionally, though, Buffett feels deeply attached to those investments that have served him so well. It is unlike the rational Buffett to make irrational judgments about inevitability. Nevertheless, it is as difficult to find any chinks in Buffett's investment armor as it is to fault the success of his strategies. Their strength lies in their simplicity.

Unnecessary knowledge

Sophisticated knowledge of markets and finance, he says, is not vital, or even necessary: "You may, in fact, be better off knowing nothing" about "efficient market theory," or modern portfolio theory, option pricing, or emerging markets. Buffett observes caustically that this "of course, is not the prevailing view at most business schools, whose finance curriculum tends to be dominated by such subjects." In Buffett's view, investment students need only two courses ("well-taught," naturally): how to value a business and how to think about market prices.

These business courses would be short ones, too, judging by Buffett's summary of what the goal for an investor should be: "to purchase, at a rational price, a part interest in an easily understandable business whose earnings are virtually certain to go intrinsically higher five, 10, and 20 years from now." There are three important missing pieces from this formula, however: what is a "rational" price?; how certain is "virtually certain"?; and what is the meaning of "intrinsically higher" earnings?

Obviously, an "over-priced" purchase – one made at an irrational price exceeding the intrinsic business value – will not deliver the next leg of Buffett's strategic intent. He assumes that if a company's intrinsic earnings (those from its underlying business) grow materially, say, by 20 percent a year, the stock price will rise correspondingly. Pay too much at the outset and the likelihood of future advances in earnings will be seriously diminished.

Time may help to correct your error, provided you let it. Buffett says firmly that "if you aren't willing to own a stock for 10 years, don't even think about owning it for 10 minutes. Put together a portfolio of companies whose aggregate earnings march upward over the years, and so also will the portfolio's market value." Buffett adds in his best self-deprecating manner that "lethargy bordering on sloth remains the cornerstone of our investment style." In one year, for instance, Berkshire neither bought nor sold a share in five of its six major holdings. That is the final building block of his investment strategy. If you can't find anything worth buying, don't.

The strategy is a minority one. Many investors, especially professionals, not only buy many stocks but change them often, thus generating, as Buffett observes, nothing except commissions for stockbrokers. However, he rejects the label (which he is often given) of "contrarian," one who goes against the crowd, even though that, very obviously, is what he does. He observes that adopting a contrarian approach for its own sake is "just as foolish as a follow-the-crowd strategy." Rather, Buffett approvingly quotes Bertrand Russell: "Most men would rather die than think. Many do." If thinking long and hard before investing makes Buffett a contrarian, that is fine by him.

Ideas into action

- Look for companies with a history of stability and above-average performance.
- Only make investments that are within your own area of knowledge.
- Put all your eggs in one basket – and proceed to watch that basket.
- Make your investments as a business analyst, not as a security analyst.
- Regard the buying of a stock as if you were buying the whole company.
- Do without a sophisticated knowledge of markets and finance.
- Always be willing to own a stock for a minimum of 10 years.

Sitting at the feet of the master

Warren Buffett was a student at the University of Nebraska when he discovered a book that, more than anything else, launched his career as a radical investment thinker and a sensationally successful practitioner.

The book was *The Intelligent Investor* by Benjamin Graham (right), who taught at Columbia Graduate Business School. Enormously impressed by Graham's writings, Buffett went to graduate school at Columbia specifically to sit at the master's feet.

His own mathematical talents made him highly responsive to Graham's central teaching: that the "intrinsic value" of a company could be worked out quite accurately, and that its stock should only be purchased when its price was below the calculated value. The degree of that undervaluation he termed the "margin of safety." Graham also taught Buffett the right "mental attitude" toward market fluctuations. That mind-set was built around "a remarkably accommodating fellow named Mr. Market who... appears daily and names a price at which he will either buy your interest [in a private business] or sell you his." Mr. Market has "incurable emotional problems" that cause his named prices to fluctuate wildly between optimism and pessimism. But you are not interested in anything but that price and whether it interests you. Mr. Market is there to serve you, not to guide you. It is his wallet, not his wisdom, that concerns you.

Theory into practice

Buffett bore Graham's advice in mind when he worked for his father's stockbroking company, starting in 1952. He kept up the relationship with Graham, and after two years accepted his invitation to join the Graham-Newman Corporation in New York. The firm specialized in arbitrage – taking advantage of the differences in price between quotations for securities and what they were worth if, for example, an announced takeover deal went through.

While working for Graham-Newman, Buffett calculated that its earnings from arbitrage averaged 20 percent annually over the whole period from 1926 to 1956 – which bridged the Great

"The key to successful investing was the purchase of shares in good businesses when market prices were at a large discount from underlying business values." *The Essays of Warren Buffett*

Crash. This analysis of winning returns, not from inside information but from "highly publicized" events, convinced Buffett that Grahamite theories worked – that "Mr. Market" often got it wrong.

Having mastered and proved Graham's theories, Buffett was ready to apply them in practice. Using $100 of his own money, the 25-year-old Buffett set up an investment partnership in Omaha. The seven partners were personal friends who trusted Buffett to handle their investments, and contributed $100,000 between them. With $100,100 thus at his disposal, Buffett's target was high: to beat the market, as measured by the Dow Jones Industrial Average, by 10 points a year. By the time Buffett closed the partnership in 1969, he had easily beaten the target, topping the Dow by 22 points – with an average annual return of 30.4 percent. Graham's "margin of safety" had worked for the disciple even more wonderfully than the master would have expected.

Investing in stocks

Buffett's teachings on investment sound deceptively simple. But there is no deception. They truly are simple. Do not allow investment advisers to persuade you that investment is a complex matter needing great expertise. Instead, learn how to assess the fundamental and financial values of a business yourself, and invest according to your convictions.

Ignoring convention

To invest well you must be prepared to go against the prevailing wisdom and ignore conventional investment guidelines. So:

- Do not put your eggs in many baskets.
- Do not place small amounts in each basket.
- Do not switch holdings frequently.
- Do not avoid holding cash.
- Do not rely on outside analysis.
- Do not often act on a hunch.
- Do not follow the crowd.
- Do not watch the market intently.
- Have fixed investment principles.

Contrarian principles

The conventional approach, Buffett believes, makes it difficult to beat the market and easy to do worse. Increase your chances of finding winning stocks by adhering to Buffett's contrarian principles.

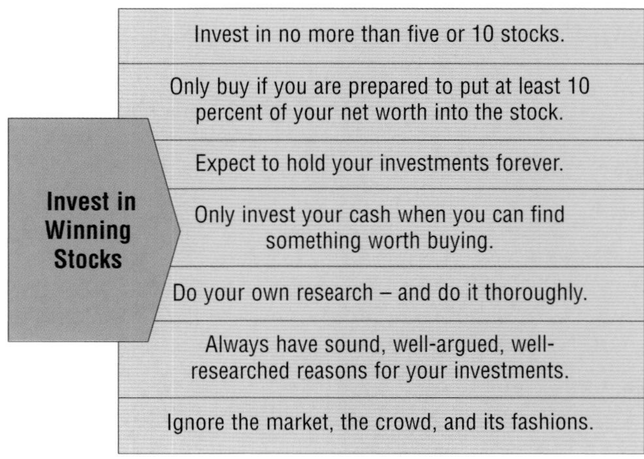

1 Assessing value

All investors hope to find a bargain. Conventional investors measure value by looking at factors relating to the market price. Buffett urges you to look only at the fundamental worth of the business.

Investigating the business

Valuing a business involves assessing the quality of its customer franchise and management, about which market rating tells nothing.

Valuing a Business
Make sure you understand the business thoroughly.
Ask whether the business has consistently increased sales and operating profits over time.
Determine if it is reasonable to expect this consistent performance to continue into the distant future.

Are you able to rate management's quality? You have a better chance of judging how well a business is run, and its likely future performance, if you focus on firms that are within your personal knowledge – including any that you know well through direct personal contact. Do all the research you can:

- Buy a few shares in any business that interests you and attend the annual general meeting to get a look at the management.
- Read all you can about the business, especially its management, in press clippings, on the Internet, in its annual reports, etc.
- If possible, use its products and services, rate them against competitive products and services, inspect its premises, and test its responsiveness to customers.

Assessing financial value

When you are as confident as possible that the business you have studied has good long-term prospects, you move on to the next stage. How does your assessment translate into financial value? And how does that valuation compare with the market price? Remember that unless the latter is markedly below your judgment of the true, or intrinsic, value, you should not buy.

2 Measuring the financials

Before investing in a business that you judge to have favorable prospects, you must assess whether its true, or intrinsic, value promises you a large enough return on your capital in the longer term. To be sure of your assessment, take Buffett's advice and thoroughly investigate the financial standing of the business before making any decision to buy.

Calculating intrinsic value

Your self-confidence should be increased by Buffett's insistence that sophisticated financial knowledge is not required. The definition of intrinsic value does rest on a mathematical concept – and there are technicalities involved. Putting them on one side, the basic proposition is simple: compare your proposed stock-market investment, which carries an element of risk, with a risk-free alternative. The argument is as follows:

- A top-rated government bond is as near to a risk-free investment as you will ever find.
- If the annual interest is 9 percent, its return over 100 years is 900 percent of a purchase price of 100.
- Unless the shares in an organization can beat this return, they are plainly not worth buying.

So Buffett looks for companies where the net cash coming into the business can be expected to grow, for all intents and purposes forever, at a percentage appreciably above the interest on long-term government bonds. The difference between these two future streams of money determines the present-day "intrinsic value" of the shares and, therefore, whether they are worth buying.

Predicting future profits

Buffett always does these calculations before investing. You will see that they rest on prediction, which is always a risky business. But you must also turn your favorable view of the company's prospects into hard numbers. What are you actually hoping for, and how realistic is that hope? Buffett's concept carries a powerful lesson you dare not ignore:

Always do your math before investing.

Finding the figures

Some of the figures that you need to assess a company's financial prospects must be dug out of the published accounts. Buffett seeks the answers to four critical questions:

Four Key Financial Questions
1 What percentage is the company earning on the shareholders' capital (or equity)?
2 How much are the earnings that belong to the shareholders?
3 What are the profit margins?
4 Does the company create at least $1 of market value for every $1 of shareholder funds that it keeps in the business?

Earnings to equity ratio

The first question is the easiest to answer; many companies publish the figure. Equity is the company's capital minus its long-term debt. Divide that into the profits after tax to find the percentage return. This must be significantly higher than the return on long-term bonds. As a rule-of-thumb, a company with a 15-percent return on equity can be expected to grow its value by 15 percent per annum.

Shareholder earnings

Working out "owner-earnings" means adding to after-tax profits the funds set aside for financial reasons – above all, depreciation. While the company must allow for the eventual replacement of its plant and equipment, etc., the cash is not being spent now. Adding back depreciation, plus the company's share of any profits from interests in other companies, gives you a truer picture of its earning power.

Profit margins

To answer the third question, you need to measure the strength of the company's "franchise" (its customer base) and its business model (in other words, the relationship between its costs and its prices). Look at operating profits as a percentage of sales. Analyze the results carefully; too low a figure (under 5 percent) is a discouraging sign, while too high a figure (over 20 percent) could be unsustainable.

Market value

The fourth question is absolutely vital to your overall assessment of the fundamental value of the business. Add back the "retained" profits that were not paid out in tax and dividends over, say, three years. Compare the company's market value at the start of the period with that at the end. Does the difference add up to more than the retained profits? That is the only way in which management can demonstrate its ability to use shareholders' money wisely and well.

Exercising caution

You are of necessity relying on published accounts. Buffett warns that these often contain misleading figures, sometimes deliberately so. Look carefully at the cashflow. If it is heading down when the profit is going up, be very wary. Remember that a company's accounts will nearly always juggle profits upward rather than downward. That being the case, discouraging answers to the four key questions are even more worrying than they seem at first sight.

Buying below market value

There is another rule-of-thumb that will help you to evaluate a business. In the case of Mrs. Blumkin and the Nebraska Furniture Mart (see p. 48), Buffett bought a successful business with capable management for substantially less than the value of its annual sales. Unless there is a sinister explanation, a low ratio of market value to sales is an encouraging sign.

Misleading figures

You cannot bank the profits shown in the accounts. You can only bank the cash coming in. If that is less than the cash going out, bankruptcy may result.

Rolls-Royce, Britain's most famous company, announced decent profits year after year, despite heavy spending on aero-engine research and development. The spending, however, was not charged in the accounts against profits, but added to them as "the value of R&D recoverable from sales resulting from existing orders." The company still had to find the cash to pay for all the R&D. Re-examination of the accounts showed that the cashflow was negative, and Rolls-Royce could only pay the dividend by raising money from the shareholders! Eventually, the company ran out of cash and just went bankrupt.

3 Managing the investment

If your research indicates that the shares are available below their intrinsic value, you have a "margin of safety." You can make the investment. Now you have to manage it successfully.

Holding stocks

Buffett has no use for investment management in the usual sense: the active buying and selling of stocks across a large number of holdings on a day-to-day basis. Rather, he points out the advantages of investing so wisely that you never have to sell a share.

The Advantages of Not Selling

No dealing costs

No taxation on your capital gains

The magic of compound interest

The third advantage is the most important in the argument for keeping stocks long-term. In *The Warren Buffett Portfolio*, Robert G. Hagstrom illustrates these advantages by setting out two outcomes from a brilliant $1,000 investment that doubles in value every year.

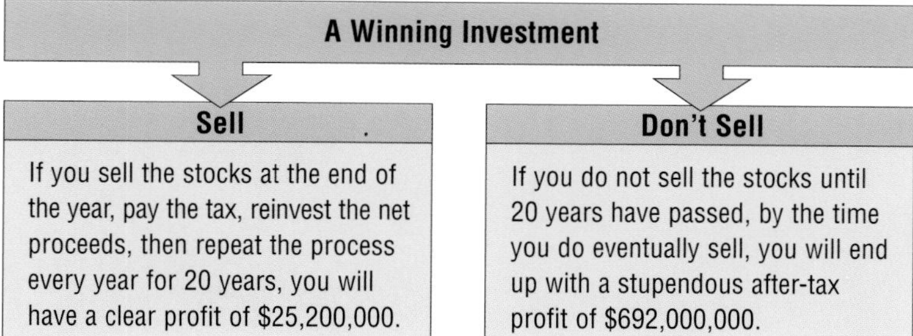

This, of course, is a fairy-tale exercise. But the principle is absolutely real. Never forget it. Remember "Mr. Market," who is always ready to buy or sell. You are only interested in him when he wants to sell to you at well below market value or to buy well above it. In the first case, you buy. In the second, you seriously consider taking your profit.

2

Making acquisitions pay

Why, in most acquisitions, it is better to be the target • **The importance of being active, interested, but never in a hurry** • Understanding that a managerial kiss will not turn a toadlike business into a princely one • **How issuing stocks in acquisitions amounts to a partial sale** • Ensuring that the opportunity's value matches or surpasses any alternative • **Paying careful attention to the post-acquisition management of the buy** • Concentrating on two tasks: capital allocation and the top appointment

Most mergers and acquisitions take place at a premium above the current stock market price. To Buffett, this is seldom justifiable. Sometimes, especially able managers buy apparently fully valued businesses whose greater, unrecognized worth they proceed to unlock. But Buffett does not play this game; he is interested in one factor alone: the intrinsic value of a company, not its stock market value.

He accepts that mergers are often motivated by sound strategic consideration, and that "there truly are synergies in a great many mergers." But the existence and exploitation of these synergies – the savings and other benefits from combining the two forces – are not the sole driving force. Managers are activated more by the desire to enhance the size of their corporation or by the excitement of acquisition. That is why Buffett is certain that mergers will continue:

> "You don't get to be the CEO of a big company by being a milquetoast. You are not devoid of animal spirits. And it gets contagious. I've been a director of 19 different public companies over the years, and I can tell you that the conversation turns to acquisitions and mergers much more when the competitors of the particular company are engaging in those."

The animal spirits and the bandwagon effect are stronger when stock markets are generally buoyant, which "tends to encourage mergers, because everybody's currency [their stocks] is more useful in those circumstances." But Buffett is in no doubt that the advantage usually lies with the seller: "In most acquisitions, it's better to be the target than the acquirer. The acquirer pays for the fact that he gets to haul back to his cave the carcass of the conquered animal." That payment helps to make Buffett "suspicious of people who just keep acquiring almost by the week."

Hunting for acquisitions

Buffett prefers to see organic growth, and notes that outstanding companies – "a Microsoft or an Intel or a Wal-Mart," for example – have relied overwhelmingly on internal expansion, as opposed to companies that are "on a real acquisition binge." Frequently, "they feel they're using funny money, and it has certain aspects of a chain-letter game." The "funny money" is often followed by funny accounting, which Buffett would like to see countered by instituting "a period where merged companies just run by themselves after a deal" without any financial changes.

This has always been Berkshire Hathaway's approach to its own purchases, of which there have been many. In fact, Buffett regards acquisition as "the most exhilarating" of all the activities in which he and Charlie Munger have participated. They seek only businesses that have "excellent economic characteristics and a management that we like, trust, and admire." Buffett is constantly on the hunt, but never "acquisition-hungry," rather adopting "the same attitude one might find appropriate in looking for a spouse. It pays to be active, interested, and open-minded, but it does not pay to be in a hurry."

Characteristically, this view is based on experience and observation, and not on theory. Buffett has "observed that many acquisition-hungry managers were apparently mesmerized by their childhood reading of the story about the frog-kissing princess [whose kiss turned the frog into a handsome prince]":

> "Remembering her success, they pay dearly for the right to kiss corporate toads, expecting wondrous transfigurations. Initially, disappointing results only deepen their desire to round up new toads… Ultimately, even the most optimistic manager must

face reality. Standing knee-deep in unresponsive toads, he then announces an enormous 'restructuring' charge... the CEO receives the education but the stockholders pay the tuition."

Good businesses at fair prices

Buffett has, characteristically, made his own mistakes in buying businesses and learned from them. He recalls his early days as a manager: "I, too, dated a few toads. They were cheap dates... but my results matched those of acquirers who courted higher-priced toads. I kissed and they croaked." His conclusion "after several failures of this type" was to follow the advice of a golf pro: "Practice doesn't make perfect; practice makes permanent." So, Buffett revised his strategy "and tried to buy good businesses at fair prices rather than fair businesses at good prices."

To put this another way, Buffett aims his acquisition strategy at maximizing real economic benefits. His positive thoughts on how you achieve this end, however, are built on avoiding the negative steps taken by other managements. Many of the latter are mesmerized by size for its own sake and deceived into believing that "their managerial kiss will do wonders for the profitability of Company T(arget)." Buffett acknowledges that some "managerial superstars" have the ability to turn toads into princes, but remarks that both changeable toads and kissing superstars are rarities.

On the other hand, Buffett recounts that: "We have done well with a couple of princes – but they were princes when purchased. At least our kisses didn't turn them into toads. And, finally, we have occasionally been quite successful in purchasing fractional interests in easily identifiable princes at toadlike prices."

Growing organically
Buffett cites Wal-Mart as an example of an outstanding company that has relied on internal expansion for growth, unlike many businesses that embark on doomed acquisition binges.

Full business value

Buffett has strong views on the "currency" that should be used in acquisitions: either stocks or cash. His "simple basic rule" is that "we will not issue shares unless we receive as much intrinsic business value as we give." He notes that "such a ploy might seem axiomatic," as anything else prompts the obvious question, "Why… would anyone issue dollar bills in exchange for fifty-cent pieces?" The

CEO, Buffett allows, may initially prefer to use cash or debt. But his "cravings" may "outpace cash and credit resources."

The CEO's problem arises because the purchased company will usually sell for its "full business value." The purchaser could itself receive this full value if it sold out completely: "But when the buyer makes a partial sale of itself – *and that is what the issuance of stocks to make an acquisition amounts to* – it can customarily get no higher value set on its shares than the market chooses to grant it." That value, so Buffett's investment philosophy argues, is often below intrinsic value. The acquirer is paying more in value than is being received.

"Under such circumstances," Buffett observes, "a marvelous business purchased at a fair sales price becomes a terrible buy." He has no difficulty in demolishing the three rationalizations used by the managements who place themselves in this fix. The arguments are:

- *The company we're buying is going to be worth a lot more in the future.*
  BUT the value of the buyer will also presumably increase, so the imbalance in price will remain.
- *We have to grow.*
  BUT who is the "we" who have to grow? "For present shareholders, the reality is that all existing businesses shrink when shares are issued." That is, the shareholders' interest in the "old" businesses is automatically reduced.
- *Our stock is undervalued and we've minimized its use in this deal – but we need to give the selling shareholder 51 percent in stock and 49 percent in cash so that certain of those shareholders can get the tax-free exchange they want.*
  BUT the purchaser should put the interests of his own shareholders first.

Destruction of value

Buffett dismisses the irrational policies that result from such management rationalizations in a phrase that is his anathema: "destruction of value." A true business-value-for-business-value merger (Buffett's own speciality) is the exception. "It's not that acquirers wish to avoid such deals; it's just that they are very hard to do," he says. Exceptions also arise when the acquirer's stock is selling above its intrinsic value. In these cases, "the shareholders of the acquired company receive an inflated currency (frequently pumped up by dubious accounting and promotional techniques)."

Buffett was writing long before the age of the Internet and its stratospheric stock market valuations. The securities concerned, however, have been used mainly to buy other hype-inflated stock. In that case, the actual values being exchanged may be the same, although nobody can possibly know that for a fact. But Buffett's major conclusion still stands. If the issue of shares dilutes the value of the acquirer's equity, the initial destruction of shareholders' wealth will be compounded by a relative decline in the acquirer's share price. He points out: "Other things being equal, the highest stock market prices relative to intrinsic business value are given to companies whose managers have demonstrated their unwillingness to issue shares at any time on terms unfavorable to the owners of the business."

"Most major acquisitions... are a bonanza for the shareholders of the acquiree... But, alas, they usually reduce the wealth of the acquirer's shareholders...."
The Essays of Warren Buffett

It is abundantly clear that Buffett and Munger are extremely skeptical about acquisitions: "We believe most deals do damage to the shareholders of the acquiring company." This raises a question that Buffett himself poses. All of Berkshire's wholly owned companies, of course, have been acquired, so how have the two men avoided the traps? The first answer is that they never look at earnings

Inflated Internet stock

Many runaway Internet stock market stars are using their inflated stocks as cheap currency to purchase other hype-inflated companies whose intrinsic business value is impossibly difficult to determine.

projections prepared by sellers: "[We] never give them a glance, but instead keep in mind the story of the man with an ailing horse. Visiting the vet, he said: 'Can you help me? Sometimes my horse walks just fine and sometimes he limps.' The vet's reply was pointed: 'No problem – when he's walking fine, sell him.'"

Deciding to buy

Buffett and Munger do not have a strategic plan when it comes to making acquisitions: "We feel no need to proceed in an ordained direction (a course leading almost invariably to silly purchase prices)." They simply compare any proposed buy with the dozens of other opportunities available, including "the purchases of small pieces of the best businesses in the world via the stock market." They only proceed when they are satisfied that the acquisition opportunity matches or surpasses the value of any alternative. That means the buys will:

- Be large purchases (unless after-tax earnings are very large, Buffett will not consider the buy)
- Have demonstrated consistent earning power ("future projections are of little interest to us, nor are 'turnaround' situations")
- Be businesses earning good returns on equity while employing little or no debt
- Have management in place ("we can't supply it")
- Be simple businesses ("if there's lots of technology, we won't understand it")
- Have an offer price ("we don't want to waste our time or that of the seller by talking, even preliminarily, about a transaction when price is unknown")

But Buffett is, above all, not a financial wheeler-dealer. Since he buys for the long term, expecting to hold his purchases for ever, Berkshire is obliged to pay careful attention to an issue that seldom engages corporate acquirers – that is, how to manage the buy after acquisition, or rather, in Berkshire's case, how to not manage them.

Admitting to error
Buffett departed from his own expectation of holding stocks forever when he sold McDonald's in 1998, after only three years – and just before a large rise: "My decision to sell was a very big mistake."

Post-acquisition autonomy

Buffett's objective after the purchase is to secure the best possible performance from the acquired company. Presumably, other buyers share the same aim, but the great majority seek to reach that objective by intervention in the affairs of the new company. Buffett does not, and this allows him to claim that:

> "Berkshire offers something special. Our managers operate with extraordinary autonomy. Additionally, our ownership structure enables sellers to know that when I say we are buying to keep, the promise means something. For our part, we like dealing with owners who care what happens to their companies and people. A buyer is likely to find fewer unpleasant surprises dealing with that type of seller."

This preferred type of seller will "care about placing the companies in a corporate home that will both endure and provide pleasant, productive working conditions for the managers." That is also greatly in Buffett's interest. What advantage can there be in a transient purchase whose management, after acquisition, suffers unpleasant and counterproductive treatment?

Of all the various aspects of Buffett's acquisition theory, this emphasis on the performance and contentment of the acquired management is the simplest and hardest to fault. You may be able to argue (rightly or wrongly) that a "strategic" acquisition is justified, despite its excessive price, because it extends the reach of the corporation or prevents a competitor from seizing a real advantage. But it is impossible to argue a case for post-acquisition management that does not encourage and enable the acquired managers to give of their best in conditions of security and stability.

Avoiding intervention

Buffett emphasizes that an owner-manager sells the business "only once – frequently in an emotionally charged atmosphere with a multitude of pressures coming from different directions." As he says, "mistakes made in the once-in-a-lifetime sale of a business are not reversible." Post-acquisition management, he argues, is so often ineffective for two reasons:

- If the buyer is in much the same business, it "will usually have managers who feel they know how to run your business operations and, sooner or later, will want to apply some hands-on 'help'."
- The buyer's management "will have their own way of doing things and, even though your business record undoubtedly will be far better than theirs, human nature will at some point cause them to believe that their methods of operating are superior."

Berkshire is saved from the second temptation, partly because it is less likely to operate in the same business, even more because "we don't have, and don't expect to have, operating people in our parent organization." This has a simple yet powerful consequence: "When we buy a business, the sellers go on running it just as they did before the sale; we adapt to their methods rather than *vice versa*."

This leaves Buffett to concentrate on just two tasks: allocating capital and selecting and "compensating the top man." Other personnel decisions, operating strategies, etc., are that top man's bailiwick. "Some Berkshire managers talk over some of their decisions with me; some don't. It depends on their personalities and, to an extent, upon their own personal relationship with me."

Buffett does, however, believe in imposing one condition when buying a family business: he leaves 20 percent of the stocks in the hands of the operating members of the family. "Very simply, we would not want to buy unless we felt key members of present management would stay on as our partners. Contracts cannot guarantee your continued interest; we would simply rely on your word." The language, as always with Buffett, is crystal-clear and homespun. But it goes to the heart of acquisition success – and failure.

Ideas into action

- Look for organic growth first before you consider acquisitions.
- Be prepared to wait until a satisfactory deal comes along.
- Buy good businesses at fair prices, not fair businesses at good prices.
- Seek only a true exchange of business value for business value.
- Never look at earnings projections that have been prepared by sellers.
- Don't spend time on discussion unless a price is already known.
- Give management an ownership interest in the success of the business.

Buying and retaining Mrs. Blumkin

Buffett has, from the early days, preferred buying 100 percent of businesses to investing in only part of their equity. He loves the personal involvement with these businesses and their managements.

Their attractions are exemplified in an acquisition made in 1983: Nebraska Furniture Mart. As a local, Buffett knew this discount business well. It had been created and developed by Mrs. Rose Blumkin, who started with only $500. By the time Buffett took an interest, sales were $100 million-plus, generated from one 200,000 sq-ft store. Buffett found that Nebraska Furniture Mart outperformed any other US home furnishings store, and that the store's sales of furniture, carpets, and appliances exceeded those of all competitors in Omaha (right) put together.

The Blumkins easily passed a favorite Buffett test: "One question I always ask myself in appraising a business is how I would like, assuming I had ample capital and skilled personnel, to compete with it. I'd rather wrestle grizzlies than compete with Mrs. B and her progeny." Buffett regarded it as an ideal business – "one built upon exceptional value to the customer that in turn translates into exceptional economics for its owners." When he bought control, leaving 10 percent with the managing owners and making another 10 percent available as options, Mrs. Blumkin was 90. She continued to work full-time for the business.

Long-term growth

While the Blumkin business was by no means Buffett's first such purchase, it is a model Berkshire acquisition: run by the management that created its success, capable of sustained growth (in the first year sales rose by $14.3 million), low in operating costs, concentrated on an easily understandable business – and cheap. A dollar per dollar of sales is a common rough guide to a buying price: Buffett paid half that much. Growth makes his low prices seem ridiculous: See's Candy Stores, bought in 1972 for $25 million, had operating profits of $62 million in 1998.

The growth in these wholly owned businesses has not been uninterrupted. Every now and

"We have no one – family, recently recruited MBAs etc. – to whom we have promised a chance to run businesses we have bought from owner-managers. And we won't have." *The Essays of Warren Buffett*

again, Buffett has had to tell shareholders of disappointing years. But his long-term view embraces the possibilities of short-term difficulties and set-backs. Only rarely have long-term trends moved against good buys, as with the *Buffalo Evening News*, bought in 1977, which could not escape the adverse change in newspaper economics two decades later. Even the *News*, though, has continued to perform well by most standards, enhancing Buffett's belief in his ability not only to pick but ultimately to manage good acquisitions.

Through his experiences, Buffett developed a strong and simple philosophy for the control and direction of subsidiary companies. The American term for these – "affiliates" – better describes the relationship. As he wrote in 1994, "We achieved our gains through the efforts of a superb corps of operating managers who get extraordinary results from some ordinary-appearing businesses."

3

Avoiding the accounting trap

Using book value and intrinsic business value as accounting tools • **How both conventional and "creative" accounting can be misleading** • Using high earnings on equity capital as the main managerial test • **Calculating "look-through" earnings as the true measure of "economic well-being"** • Why "economic goodwill" matters more than goodwill in balance sheets • **The folly of wrapping up silly purchases with accounting niceties** • "Whatever the merits of options... their accounting treatment is outrageous"

Much of Berkshire Hathaway's remarkable creation of wealth has been built on Buffett's iconoclastic approach to accounting. His unorthodox attitude centers around the use of two concepts: "book value" and "intrinsic business value." As Buffett defines them:

> "Book value is an accounting concept, recording the accumulated financial input from both contributed capital and retained earnings. Intrinsic business value is an economic concept, estimating future cash output discounted to present value. Book value tells you what has been put in; intrinsic business value estimates what can be taken out."

Using book value as a yardstick

Buffett's reports to shareholders always emphasize the annual increase in Berkshire's book value, even though he states that "We never take the one-year figure very seriously." He asks rhetorically, "Why should the time required for a planet to circle the sun synchronize precisely with the time required for business actions to pay off?" He recommends that no less than a five-year view should be taken as "a rough yardstick" of the economic performance of a business.

Buffett calculates this progress in terms of book value "because in our case (although not, by any means, in all cases) it is a conservative but reasonably adequate proxy for growth in intrinsic business value – the measurement that really counts." Although Buffett does not go so far as to claim that his "proxy" gives an accurate figure, book value is very easy to calculate and it also avoids "the subjective (but important) judgments employed in calculation of intrinsic business value."

He explains the difference with a simple analogy. Two students go to college. The book value of their education – the amount spent on fees, and so on – is identical. "But the present value of the future payoff (the intrinsic business value) might vary enormously – from zero to many times the cost of the education." The accountants measure only the first of these figures, although the second is far more important in assessing the worth of the enterprise.

Criticizing the accountants

Unsurprisingly, Buffett is deeply skeptical about conventional accounting – both its use and its misuse. Here he cites a brilliant passage from an unpublished satire by his mentor Benjamin Graham. In 1936, Graham showed how the finances of a real corporation, US Steel, could be utterly transformed by adopting so-called "creative" accounting, operating within the conventions of the profession, but exploiting them to present the company's performance in the most favorable light. Graham wrote:

> "Our company has lagged somewhat behind other American business enterprises in utilizing certain advanced bookkeeping methods, by means of which the earning power may be phenomenally enhanced

"Clearly, investors must always keep their guard up and use accounting numbers as a beginning, not an end, in their attempts to calculate true 'economic earnings' accruing to them."
The Essays of Warren Buffett

without requiring any cash outlay or any changes in operating or sales conditions. It has been decided not only to adopt these newer methods but to develop them to a still higher stage of perfection."

Among other devices, plant would be carried on the books at a negative figure, everybody would be paid in stock (thus eliminating the wage bill), and inventory would be valued at virtually nothing. The corporation would thus have "an enormous competitive advantage... We shall be able to sell our products at exceedingly low prices and still show a handsome margin of profit." If competitors sought to imitate its methods, US Steel would devise still more advanced bookkeeping methods and reinforce its "unique prestige... as the originator and pioneer in these new fields of service to the user of steel."

Determining real value

The US Steel satire drives home Buffett's view that accounts and accountants often diverge sharply from the realities of industry and commerce. Even conventional, uncreative accounting can be deeply misleading. It does not provide the two financial yardsticks that Buffett applies when valuing a company:

- Roughly speaking, how much is the business worth? This relates not to its balance sheet but to its intrinsic value.
- How great is its ability to meet future obligations? (For this purpose, it is not enough to calculate cashflow in the orthodox manner. You have to subtract from profits, etc. the amount of the reinvestment in the business that you must make "to fully maintain its long-term competitive position and its unit volume.")

There is a third yardstick, which is non-financial: how effective are the company's managers at operating the business? Buffett argues as follows: "The primary test of managerial economic performance is the achievement of a high earnings rate on equity capital employed (without undue leverage, accounting gimmickry, etc.) and *not the achievement of consistent gains in earnings per share*" [my italics]. The latter criterion has been the prime measure used by stock market analysts and the investors who they serve. As Buffett points out, however, while the "term 'earnings' has a precise ring to it... in reality... earnings can be as pliable as putty when a charlatan heads the company reporting them."

The implication is that there are many charlatans around. "Indeed, some important American fortunes have been created by the monetization of accounting mirages." Excesses similar to those that Graham lampooned in the US Steel satire "have many times since found their way into the financial statements of major American corporations and been duly certified by big-name auditors." Berkshire, naturally, is innocent of these devices. Nevertheless, its own reported earnings are also misleading, although "in a different but important way."

Reporting accurate earnings

What Buffett calls "look-through earnings" give a much more accurate picture of what Berkshire actually earns. The company owns some businesses fully, so all their earnings come into the corporate total. The same is true of Berkshire's share of earnings in all holdings of 50 percent or more and most of those above 20 percent. Below that level, only dividends can be counted. "But while our reported operating earnings reflect only the dividends received, our economic well-being is determined by [the] earnings, not [the] dividends." Conventional accounting allows less than half of Berkshire's earnings "iceberg" to "appear above the surface, in plain view."

"I believe the best way to think about our earnings is in terms of 'look-through' results, calculated as follows: Take $250 million, which is roughly our share of the 1990 operating earnings retained by our investees; subtract $30 million, for the incremental taxes we would have owed had that $250 million been paid to us in dividends; and add the remainder, $220 million, to our reported operating earnings of $371 million. Thus our 1990 'look-through earnings' were about $590 million."

Any practitioner of creative accounting, as deplored by Buffett, would be proud of that piece of multiplication. But he introduces an important qualification. The underlying earnings concerned have been reinvested in the businesses. Their value "is not determined by whether we own 100 percent, 50 percent, 20 percent or 1 percent of the businesses in which they reside". Rather, the value is determined "by the use to which they [the earnings] are put and the subsequent level of earnings produced by that usage." As Buffett admits, this attitude is rather unconventional:

"Many businesses would be better understood by their shareholder owners... if managements and financial analysts modified the primary emphasis they place upon earnings per share, and upon yearly changes in that figure."
The Essays of Warren Buffett

"But we would rather have earnings for which we did not get accounting credit put to good use in a 10 percent-owned company by a management we did not personally hire, than have earnings for which we did get credit put into projects of more dubious potential by another management – even if we are that management."

Creating economic benefit

He is proud of the fact that shareholders in Berkshire have "benefited economically in full measure from your share of our retained earnings, no matter what your accounting system." However, in "a great many capital-intensive businesses," retained earnings that were "credited fully and with painstaking precision... under standard accounting methods have resulted in minor or zero economic value." Buffett stresses that "managers and investors alike must understand that accounting numbers are the beginning, not the end, of business valuation."

Although Buffett comes across as a severe critic of standard accounting procedures, he is at pains to soften this attitude: "We would not like to have the job of designing a better system," and "it's much easier to criticize than to improve... accounting rules. (The inherent problems are monumental.)" His point is rather to stress that investors (and companies) should seek to maximize "economic" earnings, whatever the impact on "accounting" earnings, and to show that focusing on "look-through earnings" is one way to achieve that maximization.

"An approach of this kind will force the investor to think about long-term business prospects rather than short-term stock market prospects, a perspective likely to improve results. It's true, of course, that, in the long run, the scoreboard for investment decisions is market price. But prices will be determined by future earnings. In investing, just as in baseball, to put runs on the scoreboard one must watch the playing field...."

Goodwill accounting

Buffett has occasionally changed his mind about accounting concepts, for example, "goodwill." There are two varieties of goodwill in Berkshire's accounts. One is financial: the difference in value between the market price of shares owned by the company and their value stated under standard accounting principles. The other and more important goodwill is "economic": the difference between the tangible and intrinsic values of a business. When a business is purchased for more than its accounting or book value, the difference appears in the accounts as goodwill. But Berkshire owns "several businesses that possess economic goodwill... far larger than the accounting goodwill that is carried on our balance sheet."

Although Buffett says that "you can live a full and rewarding life without ever thinking about goodwill and its amortization," in his early days he thought about the subject to considerable effect. Graham taught him "to favor tangible businesses whose value depended largely upon economic goodwill," which caused Buffett "to make many important business mistakes of omission, though relatively few of commission." Buffett quotes John Maynard Keynes to explain his error: "The difficulty lies not in the new ideas but in escaping from the old ones."

Loyalty to Graham and his teachings delayed Buffett's escape, which when it came was complete. "Ultimately, business experience, direct and vicarious, produced my

From customer to owner
Buffett was at first a customer for Executive Jet's "fractional aircraft ownership," which is akin to timeshare villas. He thinks it will be the fastest-growing of all the firms in the Berkshire empire.

present strong preference for businesses that possess large amounts of enduring goodwill and that utilize a minimum of tangible assets." Buffett had come to understand that "the traditional wisdom – long on tradition, short on wisdom" made you believe, wrongly, that you were best protected against inflation by investing in businesses "laden with natural resources, plant and machinery, or other tangible assets."

The value of intangible assets

On the contrary, such corporations tend to have low rates of return, which, at times of inflation, can often only just fund the need of the existing business to keep up with rising prices. Consequently, nothing is "left over for real growth, for distribution to owners, or for acquisition of new businesses." In contrast, many owners of intangible assets of lasting value, which needed little in the way of tangible assets, enjoyed earnings that bounded upward during inflation, enabling them to finance acquisitions with ease. Buffett cites communications as an example of enduring business franchises and little tangible investment.

"During inflation," he concludes, "goodwill is the gift that keeps giving." Once again, however, he refers only to true economic goodwill, and not to spurious accounting goodwill, of which there is plenty around and which is another matter entirely:

> "When an overexcited management purchases a business at a silly price, the... accounting niceties... are observed. Because it can't go anywhere else, the silliness ends up in the goodwill account. Considering the lack of managerial discipline that created the account, under such circumstances it might better be labeled 'No-Will'."

"Businesses logically are worth far more than net tangible assets when they can be expected to produce earnings on such assets considerably in excess of market rates of return. The capitalized value of this excess return is economic goodwill." *The Essays of Warren Buffett*

Buffett notes that these businesses still typically observe "the 40-year ritual" of amortizing, or writing off, the goodwill: "the adrenalin so capitalized," he says acidly, "remains on the books as an 'asset' just as if the acquisition had been a sensible one." Berkshire itself follows this 40-year rule, deducting an equal annual amount from its profits to depreciate the accounting goodwill created by takeover. But the consequences depart very significantly from economic reality. For instance, Buffett paid $25 million for See's Candy Stores in 1972. That was $17 million more than the net tangible assets, but very much below the economic value.

Scorning stock options

When attacking conventional accounting, Buffett reserves most scorn for the subject of stock options. You can see why from an unusual item in the Berkshire accounts after the buy in 1997 of General Re, the largest US reinsurer. Compensation (or executive pay) jumped by $68 million after Berkshire bought control. Buffett emphasized that nobody had been paid any more: "the item does not signal that either Charlie [Munger] or I have experienced a personality change. (He [Munger] still travels coach [economy class].)" Rather, that large sum was the cost of replacing General Re's stock option plan with cash incentives linked to managers' operating results.

The crucial point is that there was no actual cost. Under the conventions, however, cash rewards have to be accounted for, while stock options do not figure in the accounts at all. In effect, "accounting principles offer management a choice: pay employees in one form and count the cost, or pay them in another form and ignore the cost." As Buffett comments, their choice of the latter course of action comes as no great surprise. But options do cost real money. When the holder cashes in the option by buying the shares, he pays the old "at-the-market" price, which dates back to the time of issue. He will "exercise" the option (buying the shares at the old price) only if he can now sell them at a significantly higher price.

Counting the true cost of options

The true cost of stock options to the company is, therefore, the difference (often huge) between the price it receives from the option-holders, and the price for which the company could have sold the same shares at-the-market on the day when the option is exercised. Buffett thinks that properly structured options are an "appropriate, and even ideal, way to compensate and motivate top managers." But he has no doubt that "Whatever the merits of options may be, their accounting treatment is outrageous." He justifies his outrage with a clear analogy:

> "Think for a moment of that $190 million we are going to spend for advertising at GEICO [the insurance business] this year. Suppose that, instead of paying cash for our ads, we paid the media in 10-year, at-the-market Berkshire options. Would anyone then care to argue that Berkshire had not borne a cost for advertising, or should not be charged this cost in its books?"

Buffett's question is unlikely to get any more of an answer than the three he asked a few years earlier: "If options aren't a form of compensation, what are they? If compensation isn't an expense, what is it? And if expenses shouldn't go into the calculation of earnings, where in the world should they go?" The reality is that top managements have a vested interest in a system that boosts their profit figures and conceals the fact that their rewards are costing the shareholders great sums of money.

But Buffett finds even more reason for scorn in "restructurings and merger accounting," where "the behavior of managements has been even worse." He finds the "attitude of disrespect that many executives have today for accurate reporting" to be "a business disgrace." His own insistence on getting as near as humanly possible to the financial realities, however, has not held back Berkshire's progress at all. Rather, that insistence has been a cornerstone of its success.

Ideas into action

- Take at least a five-year view of economic performance.
- Work out the present value of the future payoffs of the business.
- Ask whether the business can meet its future obligations.
- Make each dollar of retained earnings create at least a dollar of market value.
- Focus on long-term business prospects, not on short-term share gains.
- Invest in intangible assets that promise to have lasting tangible value.
- Insist on getting as near as you possibly can to financial reality.

Buying companies

Whether or not you will ever purchase a business, or sell one, the principles, as taught by Warren Buffett, are valuable because you can apply them equally to investing in stocks and to valuing a company as a prospective employee.

Helping managers to win

Buffett has developed a highly effective approach to business management through buying companies and helping their managers to win outstanding results. As with his investing in stocks, Buffett rarely diverts from three clearly articulated principles:

Three Key Principles of Business Purchase
1 Buy good businesses at fair prices.
2 Insist on the seller offering a price.
3 Look for evidence of consistent earning power.

Investment in the broadest sense

Even if you do not become a strict follower of Buffett, always have clear, effective criteria for your investment decisions, and always stick to those guidelines. If you are considering buying part of a business – that is, investing in stocks – study this Masterclass in conjunction with that on pages 28–33 to enhance your abilities and success as an investor.

The principles are also a good guide to whether you should join a particular company. You are, in effect, an investor. You are investing part of your life – your most valuable possession – in the employer. Use the Buffett approach to see whether the company is likely to give you full value in return. Unless it can, look for a better "investment" elsewhere.

When looking for a new employer, people are naturally anxious. Be just as cautious when making any decisions about the value of a company. Buffett, a superb acquirer, has written: "we face the inherent problem that the seller of a business practically always knows far more about it than the buyer." Remember that.

Stick to guidelines

Most managers who buy other companies do far worse than Buffett. That is because they depart from his guidelines, despite their crystal-clear logic. Buffett's advice adds up to a series of "don'ts."

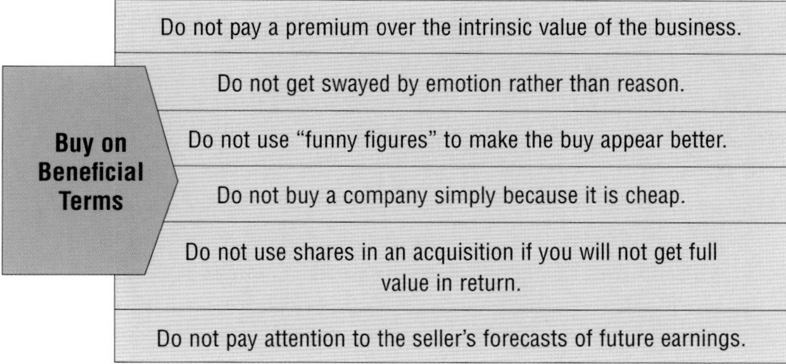

Full obedience to these "don'ts" would prevent most mergers and acquisitions from taking place; Buffett would welcome this. He believes that, however seductive the "strategic" motives, you should buy only on terms that benefit you financially. But truly beneficial deals are hard to find and execute, which is why you should be especially careful.

Measuring motives

There will always be more companies available than you can buy, whatever you can afford. You must also consider management capability; it is all too easy to "bite off more than you can chew." You will rarely find that mergers and acquisitions go as smoothly as you hoped, or yield all the financial benefits that were expected by the time they were expected. So, what are your motives?:

- Do you find making this deal more fun than running the business, and is that why you are interested?
- Are you pursuing the deal because you have a strategic purpose in mind?
- If so, how exactly will achieving that purpose enhance the intrinsic value of the business?
- If not, why are you considering the deal at all?

1 Assessing management

When considering whether to buy a business, Buffett, not surprisingly, looks for managers who are much like himself. That naturally makes it much easier for him to "like, trust, and admire" them, which he regards as three necessities.

Essential qualities of a manager

To earn Buffett's liking, trust, and respect, managers must show that they possess three essential qualities, all of which are exemplified by Buffett. They must be able to live up to the following statements:

- "I am candid with everybody with whom I have dealings – shareholders, colleagues, employees, customers, and others."
- "I am rational in all my management decisions and actions, analyzing every situation dispassionately before deciding on what is best."
- "I resist the 'institutional imperative' – I do what I think is right, rather than what others are doing."

Can you honestly say the same? If not, why not? Write down the reasons, and consider what changes you can make to pass the triple standard. There is no excuse for falling short.

Producing results

When considering a potential purchase, rule out any company with top managers who do not tell the whole truth, who do not think and act logically, or who follow the herd. Then look at the company's track record. Good management should produce good results.

Characteristics of Good Management
Always puts the owners' interests before management's.
Shows consistent increases in sales and profits from operations.
Achieves above-average returns.
Reinvests profits very effectively.
Acts to ensure that long-term growth prospects are favorable and will be achieved.

The quality issue

The quality of financial results is all-important. How were the high return on equity and superior profit margins achieved? Was it through heavy debt? Buffett prefers companies with minimal borrowings, and so should you. Do high margins result from good management or from a monopoly? Assess where the business fits on the price/quality matrix:

The Price/Quality Matrix		
High price/ high quality	Medium price/ high quality	Low price/ high quality
High price/ medium quality	Medium price/ medium quality	Low price/ medium quality
High price/ low quality	Medium price/ low quality	Low price/ low quality

Only take an interest in companies in which quality is high. High price plus high quality should be profitable, although it is inherently unstable, since it invites competition and narrows the market.

A winning combination

Mrs. Blumkin (see p. 48), with her high quality and low prices, followed a far superior course, widening the market, delighting the customers, and making life very difficult for her competitors. High profits from this valuable combination can flow only from excellent management that follows three golden policies.

The Three Golden Policies		
1 Minimize costs	**2** Maximize sales	**3** Optimize ratio of sales to capital

Following these three golden policies is a sign of well-focused management, guaranteeing a company a high return on equity, high owner-earnings, good margins, and a good return on reinvested capital. Such results all point to a company that will be a good potential investment; it takes good management to mine so much gold, and a good investor to share the mining.

2 Managing managers

How well managers run a business before acquisition must be less important than how they run the company afterward, when it has become your property. To make the most of your purchase, learn the most effective ways of managing the managers.

Establishing trust

When you buy a business, in effect you hire the managers in place. You can take one of three attitudes toward them:

Three Possible Attitudes
1 I do not trust these people to do a proper job, and will replace them with my own nominees.
2 I do not trust these people to do a proper job, but will control them tightly to ensure that they do.
3 I do trust these people to do a proper job, and will let them get on with it in their own way.

For Buffett, the first two attitudes would rule out the acquisition. It rarely makes sense to buy a company whose managers you cannot trust. Ask yourself the following three questions:

- Is this person competent to do the job?
- If "no," why did I keep them?
- If "yes," why am I refusing to let them show their competence?

A policy of non-interference

Buffett does not interfere with a manager's work, *even when he thinks he knows better*. This is crucial. There are two quite separate jobs: running the business, and running the people who do it. Buffett restricts the latter to a very few vital functions, including approval of capital expenditure, approval of top management rewards, and making the top appointments. The key word here is "approval": the managers come up with the plans and you, after due questioning, agree to the idea, revised or not. Ensure your managers tell you bad news as soon as they know it; otherwise they should be free to seek your advice as much or as little as they like.

3 Building the business

Buffett judges a business on its ability to sustain superior organic growth, developing the existing business and markets powerfully, and expanding into new products and geographic areas continuously in ways that enhance the intrinsic value.

Link reward to responsibility

Buffett allows his business managers so much room in which to manage because he wants them to build the business as if it were their own. Top managers often pay lip-service to this idea, but the reality is very different. Rewards, like stock options and bonuses, tend to be linked to the performance of the whole company. Buffett argues that nobody should be rewarded for results that are outside his or her control. If people create greater wealth from their direct responsibilities, share that wealth with them directly, giving both due reward and the incentive to optimize "organic growth."

Organic growth

Your business can grow in several ways. Does it:

- Sell more year-by-year to existing customers by:
  (a) increasing demand for existing products and/or services?
  (b) improving existing products and/or services?
  (c) introducing new products and/or services?
- Sell more year-by-year to new customers by:
  (a) widening the demand for existing products and/or services?
  (b) cashing in on the appeal of improved products and/or services?
  (c) introducing new products and/or services?

Supervise growth by insisting on full, regular financial reports that tell you how the company is performing on the same clear criteria that persuaded you to buy. Never be fuzzy. If everyone knows what is expected of them, then you can safely expect that what you want will be achieved.

Analysis

If you have not answered YES to every part of the above questions, something is wrong. Draw up plans for filling the gaps these answers reveal in your organic growth strategy. It is possible to fill gaps by acquisition, but that only makes sense if you follow Buffett's strict rules of purchase.

4

Managing the managers

Why boards of directors should make managers think and act like owners • **Applying owner-related principles to the management of a business** • The company as a conduit through which shareholders own the assets • **Why the word "long-term" gives directors "a lot of wiggle room"** • The supreme irony of inadequate CEOs who keep their jobs • **The triple test for CEOs and other corporate seniors** • Controlling managers by getting people to swim purposefully forward in the same direction

Buffett's approach to management, like his theories on investment, is based on elementary, commonsense principles, such as being rational and candid with shareholders. Berkshire Hathaway's own annual reports have long been prized for their candor, as well as their wisdom and wit. Buffett even seems to find an ironic pleasure in owning up to his failures in these reports, and also at shareholders' meetings. That is explained partly by his belief that confession is good for both the soul and for the company; the public disclosure of error encourages managements to avoid its repetition.

Observation and the laws of probability alike confirm that making mistakes, both large and small, is an inevitable fact of business life. Trying to hide those mistakes, though, can and must be avoided. An error that Buffett especially condemns is the mishandling of the company's funds, which belong not to managers but to shareholders. The prime responsibility of management is looking after the shareholders' capital. That being so, the correct course of action for boards of directors is to make managers think and act like owners themselves.

Buffett believes that such managerial behavior cannot be achieved by regulation. Although he recognizes that on occasions the interests of shareholders and managers will

"We won't 'smooth' out quarterly or annual results: If earnings figures are lumpy when they reach headquarters, they will be lumpy when they reach you… I try to give shareholders as much value-defining information as can be conveyed…." *The Essays of Warren Buffett*

clash, he does not agree that legal constraints are effective ways of resolving the conflict. The effective solution is to select the right CEOs in the first place – those who are able, honest, and hard-working – and to reward them only for genuine achievement.

Measuring achievement

Buffett measures genuine achievement primarily by return on capital, arguing that managements with higher-than-average ability will prove their ability by earning higher-than-average returns. This justifies the reinvestment of those earnings in ways that give the shareholders more for their money than they could expect to earn by their own efforts. If management cannot pass this acid test, there are only three theoretical options for the management to consider:

- Invest the profits at inferior rates of return.
- Acquire other businesses to enhance performance.
- Give back the money to shareholders and allow them to seek a better, more rewarding home for their funds.

The first option is a nonstarter as it mistreats the shareholders and their money. The second route is, of course, only another way of investing the shareholders' capital; and why should shareholders expect a management that earns lower-than-average returns on its own business to have any success at picking, buying, or running higher-than-average companies? That leaves only the third option. Buffett totally agrees with the management guru Peter Drucker that companies have no right to retain funds that they cannot put to excellent use.

The "Owner's Manual"

Managements will more effectively focus on giving shareholders better returns on their investment if they master what Buffett calls "owner-related business principles." These appear in what he terms the "Owner's Manual," which, while clearly relating specifically to Berkshire, also establishes a dozen general principles:

- Think of shareholders as owner-partners, and of yourselves as managing partners.
- Have a major portion of your net worth invested in the company ("We eat our own cooking").
- Aim to maximize the average annual rate of gain in intrinsic business value on a [growth in value] per-share basis.
- For preference, reach your goal by directly owning a diversified group of businesses that generate cash and consistently earn above-average returns on capital.
- Ignore conventional accounting, with its insistence on consolidating the earnings of individual companies, and concentrate on their individual earnings.
- Do not let accounting consequences influence your decisions on operations or allocating capital.
- Use debt sparingly and, when you do have to borrow, try to structure your loans over a long term at a fixed rate of interest.
- Never ignore long-term economic consequences for the shareholders when buying businesses. (Buffett refers to the sinful opposite as "filling a managerial wish list at shareholder expense.")
- Check noble intentions periodically against results – does every dollar of retained earnings over time deliver at least a dollar of market value?

- Only issue shares when you receive as much in business value as you give.
- Regardless of the price you may be offered, never sell any good businesses.
- Be candid in reporting to shareholders, emphasizing the plusses and minuses that are important in appraising business value.

Learning from the great
Buffett is a follower of the great Cambridge economist and investor John Maynard Keynes, who seldom invested at any one time in more than two or three companies in which he had full *confidence.*

There is a 13th principle established in the "Owner's Manual": "We would rather see Berkshire Hathaway's stock at a fair level than a high level."

Like the others, this principle is full of common sense and the lessons of experience. There is a weakness to the 13 principles, however, which is that few managers are in the same fortunate position as Buffett and Munger (Buffett's long-time friend), who were not only managing partners but also controlling partners thanks to the size of their shareholdings. Massive stock options and other means of making managers into multimillionaire shareholders still leave these hired hands with minute fractions of the total equity. They have a tendency to think of these holdings as stakes in the company itself, and fail to grasp a central point stressed by Buffett: "We do not view the company itself as the ultimate owner of our business assets but instead view the company as a conduit through which our shareholders own the assets."

Providing information

Buffett and Munger, after all, could have owned these assets directly, instead of placing them in Berkshire. Hired-hand executives, however large their fortunes may be, clearly never have this option. But the mind-set recommended by Buffett has an important consequence and benefit. The owner of a private company managed by other people expects regular and full information about what is going on and how the management evaluates the business, currently and prospectively: "you should expect no less in a public company." The shareholders are entitled to the same sort of reporting that "we feel is owed to us by managers of our business units."

This full provision of full information is not the norm for the majority of publicly owned companies. Buffett points out, however, that such companies differ from each other in fundamental ways that are not acknowledged by most commentators. According to Buffett, there are three categories: first, and by far the most common, is where the corporation has no controlling shareholder; second, as in Berkshire's case, where the controlling owner is also the manager; and, in the third case, where the controlling owner is not involved in the management.

The last two cases are so rare that little can be said of great general value. As Buffett says, where somebody has both ownership and management control, even if he is "mediocre or worse – or is overreaching – there is little a director can do about it except object." The third case, however, should logically be the most effective in ensuring first-class management:

> "... the owner is neither judging himself nor burdened with the problem of garnering a majority. He can also ensure that outside directors are selected who will bring useful qualities to the board. These directors, in turn, will know that the good advice they give will reach the right ears, rather than being stifled by a recalcitrant management. If the controlling

"The management failings that Charlie and I have seen make us thankful that we are linked with the managers of our three permanent holdings. They love their business, they think like owners, and they exude integrity and ability."
The Essays of Warren Buffett

owner is intelligent and self-confident, he will make decisions in respect to management that are meritocratic and pro-shareholder. Moreover – and this is critically important – he can readily correct any mistake he makes."

As the passage above suggests, Buffett is by no means optimistic about getting similar responses in a company that does not have a controlling shareholder. He believes that "directors should behave as if there is a single absentee owner, whose long-term interest they should try to further in all proper ways." But what if they behave otherwise? As Buffett points out, the word "long-term" gives directors "a lot of wiggle room":

"If they lack either integrity or the ability to think independently, directors can do great violence to shareholders while still claiming to be acting in their long-term interest. But assume the board is functioning well and must deal with a management that is mediocre or worse. Directors then have the responsibility for changing that management, just as an intelligent owner would do if he were present. And if able but greedy managers overreach and try to dip too deeply into the shareholders' pockets, directors must slap their hands."

Criticizing the CEO

Buffett remarks that there are companies where "CEOs clearly do not belong in the jobs" although "their positions, nevertheless, are usually secure." But security should depend on performance. Buffett places very highly the attraction and retention of outstanding executives; and at Berkshire, he observes, this task "hasn't been all that difficult." Buffett compares the performance of CEOs in his own businesses with that of "many CEOs" elsewhere, and finds that it "contrasts vividly."

The "supreme irony of business management," he writes, is that "it is far easier for an inadequate CEO to keep his job" than for an inadequate subordinate to do so. Buffett cites in proof the fate of secretaries whose typing is too slow or salesmen who fail to sell. The CEO benefits from having a job that, unlike typing or selling, usually has no performance standards. Where they do exist, the standards for the CEO are "often fuzzy or they may be waived or explained away, even when the performance shortfalls are major and repeated. At too many companies, the boss shoots the arrow of managerial performance and then hastily paints the bullseye around the spot where it lands."

Buffett pinpoints another "important, but seldom recognized, distinction between the boss and the foot soldier." The CEO "has no immediate superior whose performance is itself getting measured." The board of directors ostensibly fulfills that role of superior, but "seldom measures itself and is infrequently held to account for substandard corporate performance. If the Board makes a mistake in hiring, and perpetuates that mistake, so what?"

"As a company with a major communications business, it would be inexcusable for us to apply lesser standards of accuracy... when reporting on ourselves than we would expect our news people to apply when reporting on others." *The Essays of Warren Buffett*

The excellent CEO

No doubt drawing on his own considerable boardroom experience, Buffett notes that "relations between the Board and the CEO are expected to be congenial. At board meetings, criticism of the CEO's performance is often viewed as the social equivalent of belching." He softens his

The supreme CEO

Buying seven percent of Coca-Cola gave Buffett an insider's view of the brilliant performance of its late CEO, Roberto Goizueta (left). His successor, Doug Ivester, found the going much harder.

criticism by observing that most CEOs and directors are "able and hard-working and a number are truly outstanding." But, in fact, rather few can pass his triple test: that they should "love their businesses... think like owners and... exude integrity and ability."

Why has it been not "all that difficult" for Buffett to find such people? The great majority of his managers came in with businesses that Buffett bought because of their outstanding record. On the face of it, if the record is outstanding, so is the manager. These people, moreover, think like owners because they have been owners. Buffett's management theory is akin to John Huston's approach to directing films: if you cast the right actors, the film will almost certainly look after itself.

As Buffett puts it, "They were managerial stars long before they knew us, and our main contribution has been to not get in their way." Because these are able managers of high character running businesses about which they are passionate, there is no need for demanding, intensive supervision: "You can have a dozen or more reporting to you and still have time for an afternoon nap."

Criticizing stock options

Buffett is just as frank (and heretical) about giving managers stock options. He says flatly that:

"When the result is equitable, it is accidental. Once granted, the option is blind to individual performance, and because it is irrevocable and unconditional (so long as a manager stays in the company), the sluggard receives rewards from his options precisely as does the star. A managerial Rip Van Winkle, ready to doze for 10 years, could not wish for a better 'incentive' system."

His criticism of stock options is based on the following:

- Stock options are inevitably tied to the overall performance of a corporation. Logically, therefore, they should be awarded only to those managers with overall responsibility. Managers with limited areas of responsibility should have incentives that pay off in relation to results under their control.
- Options should be priced at "true business value" and should not reward managers for plowing back the shareholders' own money.
- Incentive-compensation systems should reward key managers only "for meeting targets in their own bailiwicks." At Berkshire, this can mean incentive bonuses of five times base salary, if not more.

Despite this generous attitude toward his own executives, Buffett displays a puritanical strain in his attitude to managers and their remuneration, although he would prefer the description "rational" to puritanical. A remarkable passage in one of his annual reports sums up his views:

"At Berkshire, only Charlie and I have the managerial responsibility for the entire business. Therefore, we are the only parties who should logically be

"Except in highly unusual cases, owners are not well served by the sale of part of their business at a bargain price – whether the sale is to outsiders or insiders. The obvious conclusion: options should be priced at true business value."
The Essays of Warren Buffett

compensated on the basis of what the enterprise does as a whole. Even so, that is not a compensation arrangement we desire. We have carefully designed both the company and our jobs so that we do things we enjoy with people we like."

Work as pleasure

Buffett and Munger enjoy their work to the full. They cite Ronald Reagan's dictum: hard work never killed anybody, but why risk it? The pair, said Buffett, were "delighted" with their "cushy" jobs.

It is just as important to Buffett that "we are forced to do very few boring or unpleasant tasks." The pair also benefit from "the abundant array of material and psychic perks that flow to the heads of corporations." They do not "under such idyllic conditions... expect shareholders to ante up loads of compensation for which we have no possible need." That leads to an honest conclusion to which few other top managers would subscribe (not out loud, that is): "Indeed, if we were not paid at all, Charlie and I would be delighted with the cushy jobs we hold. At bottom, we subscribe to Ronald Reagan's creed: 'It's probably true that hard work never killed anyone, but I figure why take the chance.'"

Determined delegation

The "cushiness" results from Buffett's determined pursuit of delegation. In any case, the head office is too small to interfere across so large an empire. He once commented that he had expanded the office to 12.8 people: a new employee only worked a four-day week. He is by no means uncritical, however, saying that, "With almost every one of the companies Berkshire owns, I think I would do something different if I were running them – in some cases substantially different."

Yet he resists the temptation to interfere. Although he watches the figures for Berkshire's companies like the proverbial hawk, he usually waits for managers to contact him, rather than the other way around, telling his people:

"All of you do a first-class job in running your own operations with your own individual styles. We are going to keep it that way. You can talk to me about what is going on as little or as much as you wish with only one caveat. If there is significant bad news, let me know early."

The best measure of the strength of Buffett's ideas on managerial control, and of their application in practice, is that really bad news has been rare, and certainly much less common than in the majority of companies which are controlled in a far more bureaucratic and hierarchical manner. Buffett has a laconic way of describing his very different attitude: "I sort of accept things as they come." That is because his philosophies ensure that things come the right way and come out right.

Ideas into action

- Demonstrate higher-than-average ability by earning higher-than-average returns.
- Think of shareholders as owner-partners and yourself as a managing partner.
- Do not view the company as the owner of its assets.
- Try to further the long-term interest of shareholders at all times.
- Set clear performance standards for everybody, including the boss.
- Tie rewards only to results under a manager's own control.
- Let managers run their own operations in their own styles.

Transforming Berkshire Hathaway

Buffett began his move from obscurity in Omaha to world fame by abandoning success and inviting failure. After running the Buffett partnership with phenomenal success for some 13 years, he closed it down in 1969.

A few years earlier he had bought into a cheap textile company named Berkshire Hathaway. It was one of his biggest mistakes. "We went into a terrible business because it was cheap." The problems were plainly visible. Over nine years Berkshire had lost $10 million on sales of $530 million. Despite good management and a cooperative workforce, Buffett could not achieve success even after years of effort. After 1979 Berkshire "consumed major amounts of cash. By mid-1985, it became clear, even to me, that this condition was almost sure to continue."

The textile operation was at long last closed down. But success came out of failure. Very early on, in 1967, "cash generated by the textile operation was used to fund our entry into insurance." That proved to be the catalyst for Buffett's breakthrough. Insurance has been a powerful engine behind Berkshire's expansion – a prime explanation for a growth in book value per Berkshire share from $19.46 in 1964 to nearly $20,000 in 1997 – when the market valuation of the entire company passed $50 billion.

Insurance goldmines

Buffett's discovery of the joys of insurance long pre-dated his Berkshire purchase. As a student of Benjamin Graham, Buffett found that his hero was chairman of GEICO (Government Employees Insurance Company), "to me an unknown company in an unfamiliar industry." Buffett took a train to Washington, DC, to visit the company and got a four-hour lecture in insurance from a man who later became CEO, and who made Buffett "more excited about GEICO than I have ever been about a stock." He both bought and sold the shares – and much later, in 1976, started building a large position in the company. Berkshire's first third of GEICO cost $45.7 million; its final purchase of half cost the firm $2.3 billion. That is a measure of how richly the original investment had paid off.

With their funds invested in stocks chosen on the same principles as those for the old Buffett partnership, the insurance companies have been Buffett's goldmines. By 1999, the original buys had become the nucleus for an insurance group with revenues of $13.6 billion, and an operating profit of $1.24 billion.

If Berkshire had invested only in insurance, it would have been among America's most rewarding stocks. But Buffett learned to combine two apparently contradictory policies: vulnerability and spread of risk. Because he took huge positions (for example, in catastrophe insurance), Berkshire was vulnerable to bad performance in any of them. But he spread his risks by building the group on three separate foundations: insurance, publicly held stocks, and widely diversified, privately owned businesses. Berkshire was neither strictly a conglomerate (a holding company for various active interests), nor an investment trust, nor an insurance group. It was all three of those things at once.

"Should you find yourself in a chronically leaking boat, energy devoted to changing vessels is likely to be more productive than energy devoted to patching leaks." *The Essays of Warren Buffett*

Using reason

The person who always acts impetuously, illogically, unfairly, and obstinately is most unlikely to succeed in any activity. Assess how rational you are and take action to let your head rule your decisions and their implementation.

How rational are you?

The most important word in Buffett's vocabulary is "why." He always strives to discover the reason "why" things happen, "why" he should do some things, and not others, "why" one approach is better than another. Can you live up to his standards of rationality? Look at the following seven statements. Give yourself a score on a scale of zero to 10. You score zero for "I never think before acting," 5 for "I sometimes think," and 10 for "I always do."

- I think before acting.
- I have a logical justification for my actions and beliefs.
- I do not stop my inquiries until I am as certain as possible that I know the truth.
- I understand my emotions, but never allow them to determine my behavior.
- I strive to be fair in my dealings with others.
- I change my mind if other people, or new facts, show that I am wrong.
- I set out my arguments clearly and logically, so that others can follow them.

Using a checklist

Write down these seven statements on a card, and refer to them when working on anything to see if you are leaving the road of reason. Ask yourself every evening what you have done to harness the power of reason, and (using Buffett's metaphor) to get maximum output from your motor.

Analysis

- A score between 25 and 45 shows that you are a reasonable person but that some of the time you act unreasonably.
- Follow a rational course of action and improve on that unsatisfactory performance.
- Concentrate on the points of major weakness and find one simple way of correcting each fault.

1 Breaking the habit

Buffett believes that bad habits, such as irrational behavior, are not inborn but are developed at a young age, and become harder to dislodge with advancing years. Use the checklist on page 88 as a way of breaking poor intellectual habits that prevent rational behavior.

Stuck in their ways

Middle-aged managers are frequently guilty of stubbornly refusing to make changes that would provide great benefits, and even avert disaster. They become stuck in a mental habit or "mind-set." These fixed attitudes are often revealed in ritual phrases, such as:

- "That's not the way we do things around here."
- "If that is such a good idea, why isn't anybody else doing it?"
- "That's been tried before, and it didn't work."

Reject such statements as denials of rationality. They prevent serious, rational investigation that might lead to change for people who irrationally prefer an unsatisfactory status quo.

Develop your strengths

Whatever your age, welcome positive change and use Buffett's "role model" plan to align your performance to that of your hero. There is no reason why even old dogs cannot learn new tricks.

Role Model Plan
Choose the person you most admire.
Write down why you admire them.
Choose the person you most dislike.
Write down why you dislike them.
Imitate the qualities of the role model.
Never imitate the qualities of your anti-hero.

Role models are useful for everybody, but always remember that you have innate and unique strengths and weaknesses; only an identical twin has the same genes. Your genetic inheritance determines your personality as well as your physique. You can improve both with practice and techniques as long as you are honest with yourself about your qualities. Try to be objective and seek to build on your strengths and minimize your weaknesses.

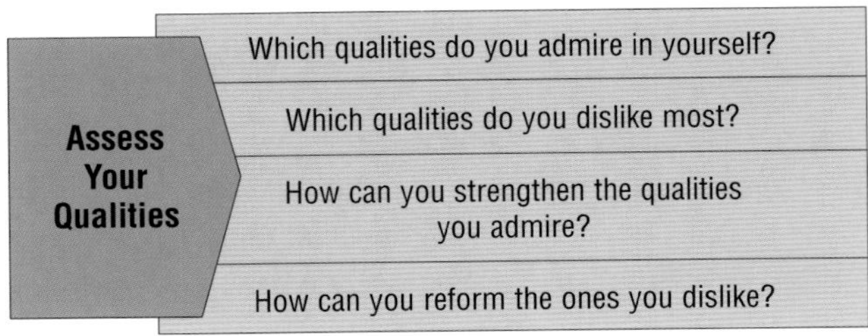

Be positive

Being completely honest about yourself is not always easy, especially when it comes to acknowledging your weaknesses. But do not turn inherited difficulties into impossibilities. It is all too tempting to allow what you consider a flaw in your personality or a weakness in your intellect to prevent you from achieving a desired goal. Remember that:

- The fact that you find learning foreign languages difficult does not mean that you cannot learn one.
- The fact that financial figuring comes hard does not mean that you cannot master accounts, budgets, and balance sheets.
- The fact that you often act impulsively and emotionally does not mean that you cannot learn to act rationally at all, or at least most, times.

Overcoming Your Weaknesses

Slow learners need more time, but, if allowed, they can learn well enough to excel. Taking your weak areas as opportunities can turn them into strengths.

The owner-manager of a company wanted to hand over management to his top-performing sales director who was "figure-blind." So, the boss made the director draw up budgets and management accounts, even though this resulted in lost sales revenue while the man wrestled with the figures. But he learned, and made a fortune for his old boss as a manager whose grasp of accounts became one of his key strengths.

2 Mastering emotions

You may feel that rationality cannot extend to the emotions. You cannot control your feelings: for example, you either like somebody or you do not; something either makes you angry or it does not. But you can learn to control the expression of that feeling.

Placing emotion under control

Buffett will work only with people he likes, but he makes sure that his liking does not prevent objective judgment of those people, or objective action if they let him down. No doubt, Buffett is sometimes angry. But does he allow anger to influence his decisions or his behavior? People often place their anger under control. For example, if another driver cuts you up in traffic, you will react angrily to a stranger, but very differently if the driver is your boss.

Dealing with anger

If you are angry, ask: "What purpose will my anger serve?" Usually, anger arises because somebody else is not behaving in the way that you want. Will your anger help to change their behavior? Probably not. You may think that "letting off steam" is good for you; but, in reality, it is an unpleasant condition that any rational person would try to avoid. Far better not to get angry in the first place, but if you do, subdue it swiftly by applying the four-point anger analysis plan:

Four-Point Anger Analysis Plan
1 What has caused my anger?
2 What is the objective I wish to achieve?
3 Is anger the best means to the end?
4 If not, what is the best alternative?

The cause of anger is often a *fait accompli*: a mistake has been made, say, and cannot be unmade. The uncontrolled emotion therefore serves no useful purpose. Equally, if you made the mistake yourself, the emotion of guilt is also useless, as it will neither correct the error nor help you to avoid making the same mistake in future.

3 Learning from mistakes

Buffett's attitude to error is among the most important aspects of his teaching. Expect to make mistakes sometimes and, if they occur, analyze the reason for them. Use the analysis to avoid the worse mistake: doing it again.

Accepting error

True rationality accepts that mistakes will happen, and it is deeply irrational to suppose that you have been, ever will be, or ever can be without fault. Every time you buy a stock, for example, you make a mistake; there is always another investment that will perform better than your choice. Buffett's avoidance of high-technology stocks, for instance, sounds reasonable because it is rational to invest only in businesses that you understand. But, ironically, Berkshire Hathaway's amazing record would actually have been better if Buffett had invested in Microsoft, and nothing else.

Analyzing your mistakes

The irrational response to error is to try to rewrite history; "if only I had..." is a familiar cry. Instead of being defeatist, analyze your mistakes. Once you have established the reasons why something has gone wrong, it is relatively easy to make sure you do not repeat the mistakes. Ask yourself the following seven questions:

- Did I lack adequate information about the present?
- Did I make an inaccurate prediction?
- Is this a mistake I have made before?
- Did I ignore logical lessons that I already knew?
- Does what happened teach me a new lesson?
- Did I do the wrong thing?
- Did I do the right thing in the wrong way?

Buffett's mistaken sale of shares in McDonald's in 1998, for example, was based on an inaccurate reading of the company's poor US sales figures, from which he predicted, possibly incorrectly, that its growth prospects had fallen below his requirements. Such mistakes have been rare in Berkshire's history because of Buffett's logical insistence on keeping stock indefinitely, knowing that bad short-term patches do not invalidate good long-term analysis.

Stick to your principles

In other words, Buffett ignored his own teaching. The advice given by Polonius to Laertes in *Hamlet* is particularly sound: "To thine own self be true." Many mistakes flow from aberrations that override this principle. The aberrations often stem from following conventional wisdom rather than your own (or, indeed, Buffett's). As an investor, have the courage to obey at all times the five rational principles expounded by Buffett:

Five Rational Principles
1 Focus on a few things, not many things.
2 Ignore short-term fluctuations, unless they invalidate your long-term expectations.
3 Do not believe that booms will continue forever, or that slumps will never end.
4 If you have done your homework thoroughly, have the courage of your convictions.
5 Be as ruthless when analyzing your success as you are when analyzing failure.

Analyzing your successes

You can learn from your successes as well as your failures. Subject them to the same scrutiny as your mistakes, and learn from them. People tend to pride themselves on their success and take it as proof of their brilliance. But success is often accompanied by serious mistakes that might have proved fatal. Ask yourself:

- Did you succeed in spite of your ignorance about the present and the future?
- Did success flow from repeating previous experience, or breaking into new ground?
- Did you do the right thing in the wrong way, but succeed because the thing was so right that your mistakes did not affect the outcome?

Reason is a hard master, but one whose lessons, like Buffett's, always repay intelligent obedience.

5

Applying the power of reason

How rationality determines the effectiveness of intelligence and talent • **Counting the cost of bad decisions, including errors of omission** • Using reason, not to predict, but to measure predictability • **"Margin of safety": the difference between price and value** • Ensuring that increases in earnings outstrip increases in capital employed • **Three rational ways to learn from failure and create success** • Limiting yourself to what you – and you alone – can do

Buffett believes that the secret of his business success lies not with higher intelligence but with the effective use of that intelligence, that is, the application of reason. To him, "the big thing" is always rationality, and the greater the rationality, the greater the effectiveness. As long as they follow the rational course, everybody "has the ability absolutely to do anything I do and much beyond." He looks at IQ and talent as representing the horsepower of the motor. The output, however, is "the efficiency with which that motor works" and that depends on rationality: "A lot of people start out with 400-horsepower motors but only get a hundred horsepower of output. It's way better to have a 200-horsepower motor and get it all into output."

Developing good habits

But this raises an important question: "Why do smart people do things that interfere with getting the output they're entitled to?" Buffett's explanation is that behaving irrationally gets embedded into the habits and character and temperament. So failure to achieve will arise "because you get in your own way, not because the world doesn't allow you." The bad habits are not inborn, in Buffett's view. Rather, they develop over time. This is an insidious process: the "chains of habit are too light to be felt until they are too heavy to be broken." So, he advises young people to work on their habits from the start:

> "Pick out the person you admire the most, and then write down why you admire them. Then put down the person that, frankly, you can stand the least, and write down the qualities that turn you off in that person. The qualities of the one you admire are traits that

you, with a little practice, can make your own, and that, if practiced, will become habit-forming. Look at... what you find really reprehensible in others and decide that those are things you are not going to do. If you do that, you'll find you convert all of your own horsepower into output."

The personalization of issues is a constant theme in Buffett's thinking and practice. In his mind, figures are much less important than people. As he points out: "I have turned down business deals that were otherwise decent because I didn't like the people I would have to work with." Such an attitude may appear overemotional, but Buffett regards his approach as highly rational. After all, he reasons, what is the point of working at things you dislike with people you dislike? Not only does he "get to do what I like to do every single day of the year" but he gets "to do it with people I like," in particular, his partner Charlie Munger. During his active years with Berkshire Hathaway, Munger seems to have have acted as Buffett's conscience, and a reminder that he is mortal and fallible: "You have to calibrate with Charlie, though, because Charlie says everything I do is dumb. If he says it's really dumb, I know it is, but if he just says it's dumb, I take that as an affirmative vote."

"We intend... working only with people we like and admire... working with people who cause your stomach to churn seems much like marrying for money – probably a bad idea under any circumstances, but absolute madness if you are already rich."
The Essays of Warren Buffett

Making the wrong decisions

Sometimes Buffett's decisions have indeed been dumb, including the very decision, the purchase of Berkshire Hathaway, that resulted in the most successful investment achievement in business history. "We went into a terrible business because it was cheap." Buffett refers to this as the "used cigar butt" approach to investing. "You see this cigar butt down there, it's soggy and terrible, but there's one puff left, and it's free." Buffett took the decision on rational grounds: Berkshire was selling below the value of its working capital, which was then Buffett's prime criterion, but buying it was still "a terrible, terrible mistake."

It was a mistake of commission. But Buffett's errors ("all kinds of bad decisions that have cost us billions of dollars") have mostly been mistakes of omission. In one case, he actually made a decision to buy, "and I just didn't execute. We would've made many billions of dollars. But we didn't do it." In other cases, he has failed to optimize his profit. As he says, conventional accounting does not record failures of this nature, but reason argues that the cost of lost opportunities, all the same, is no less real.

Following the rational course

Seizing opportunities must be more important than spotting the opening, whether it is specific (the availability of an excellent business at a fair price) or general (a trend, like the long postwar bull market). The best business decision Buffett ever made was to exploit that postwar trend, a general opportunity that was available to anybody, by becoming a professional investor. "It was just jumping in the pool, basically." But his jump was governed from the start by rationality. He worked out, for instance,

One-way street
The background to Buffett's success was the long, fabulous bull market in American stocks from 1965 to the present day. His own key decision, against that backdrop, was "just jumping in the pool."

that "you do not need a great many deals to succeed in the investment business." The rational course is to focus on a few things, not many things.

> "In fact, if... you got a punch card with 20 punches on it, and every time you made an investment decision you used up one punch, and that's all you were going to get, you would make 20 very good investment decisions. And you could get very rich, incidentally. You don't need 50 good ideas at all."

The vein of applied rationality runs through all Buffett's actions. For example, he has often been pressed to divide (or split) Berkshire's stock, so that it sells for a less intimidating price than $70,000 (or more) per share. But keeping the price high means that Berkshire attracts "a slightly more long-term oriented group of investors." Buffett thinks that entrepreneurs should prefer shareholders "very much like themselves, with the same time horizons and expectations."

This rational preference, in Berkshire's case, has the very sensible by-product, which is very important to Buffett, of saving time and trouble: "We don't talk about quarterly earnings, we don't have an investor relations department, and we don't have conference calls with Wall Street analysts, because we don't want people who are focusing on what's going to happen next quarter or even next year."

Measuring predictability

Buffett's own focus is famously long-term. Rationality says that you cannot predict the future, and the further out your forecasts stretch, the less accurate they are. But reason also says that you can measure predictability. For instance, Buffett is fully aware today that, "The technological revolution will change the world in dramatic ways, and quickly." Exactly how and when that change will come, though, is beyond Buffett and probably everybody else. That is why he avoids high technology stocks and heads for more "ordinary" businesses.

A reliable shave

Buffett gives Gillette as an example of a predictable company. Because men will still shave, the company is likely to look more or less the same two decades on. Buffett likes an "absence of change."

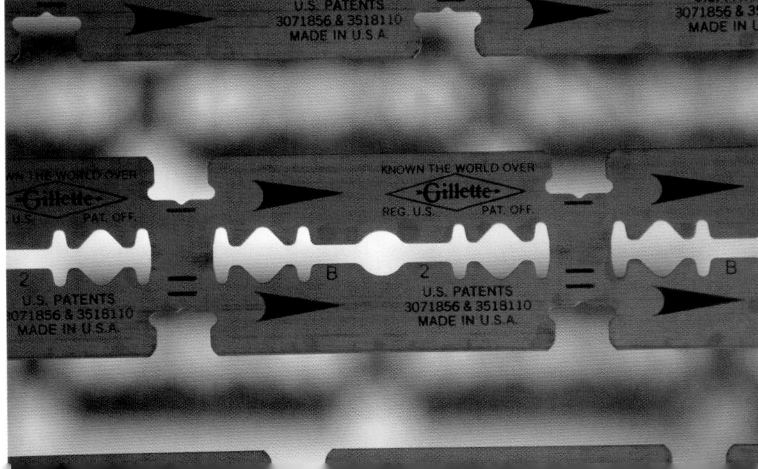

"I look for businesses in which I think I can predict what they're going to look like in 10 or 15 or 20 years. That means businesses that will look more or less as they do today, except that they'll be larger and doing more business internationally... So I focus on an absence of change."

He gives the example of Wrigley's chewing gum: "I don't think the Internet is going to change how people are going to chew gum." Nor does he believe that cyberspace will change the fact that Coke will be "the drink of preference" or affect its gains in global consumption per capita. Gillette is another example. Will the Internet change whether people shave or how they shave? Reason says "No." The event has very low probability and thus very high predictability, and "we are looking for the very predictable."

Reason is the only way to evaluate any financial market place or asset. For example, in 1998, Buffett noted that returns on equity in American business at large were much higher than they were in 1969 or 1974 (two previous highs), or at any other time in history. In valuing the overall market, therefore, the rational question is: "Do you crank in the present 20 percent returns on equity for American business in aggregate and say that's a realistic figure to stick on for this future that runs out until eternity?" Rationally, Buffett called this "a fairly reckless assumption" which does not leave much "margin of safety" and which therefore signals caution.

Searching for value

As noted earlier (see p. 26), Buffett learned about the "margin of safety" from Benjamin Graham at the Columbia Graduate Business School. Graham, another supreme rationalist, taught that price does not equate with value: price is what you pay, and value is what you get. Buffett found that picking stocks with value sounds trickier than it is. For instance, during his early days, leafing through a stock market manual page by page, Buffett found there were several stocks priced at one times earnings, that is, if $10, say, normally purchased $1 of earnings, these shares paid the same for only $1.

Reason told Buffett that this collection of stocks had to include tremendous bargains. "The truth is, you know them when you see them. They're so cheap." You do, however, require clear-sighted rational analysis to confirm your intuition and to establish the vital realities. For example, in 1985, Buffett was mulling over the lessons of three wholly owned businesses: Nebraska Furniture Mart, See's Candy Stores, and the *Buffalo Evening News*. The trio, he reported, had earned $72 million before tax in the previous year, compared to some $8 million 15 years earlier before Berkshire had purchased them. But Buffett still refused to rejoice unreservedly:

> "While an increase in earnings from $8 million to $72 million sounds terrific – and usually is – you should not automatically assume that to be the case. You must first make sure that earnings were not depressed in the base year. If they were instead substantial in relation to capital employed, an even more important point must be examined: how much additional capital was required to produce the additional earnings?"

"We simply attempt to be fearful when others are greedy, and greedy only when others are fearful." Berkshire Hathaway Annual Report, 1986

Testing performance

Berkshire's trio of businesses passed both rational tests with ease. Fifteen years before, all three had earned large amounts on capital. That capital had risen by some $40 million since then, well below the $64 million increase in profit. As Buffett pointed out, the average American business fell markedly short of this performance, requiring about $5 of extra capital to add $1 to its pre-tax earnings. This inspired the rationalist to acerbic comment: "When returns on capital are ordinary, an earn-more-by-putting-up-more record is no great managerial achievement. You can get the same result personally while operating from your rocking chair. Just quadruple the capital you commit to a savings bank and you will quadruple your earnings."

The rationalist seeks to apply meaningful tests to all issues and all achievements to ensure that success is real and reported as accurately as possible. The same is true of failure. Nothing marks out Buffett more distinctively than his honesty about his present and past follies. His letters to shareholders, his interviews, and the like, are peppered with admissions like, "Here I need to make a confession (ugh)... my decision to sell McDonald's was a very big mistake": or, more mildly, "Remember Wagner, whose music has been described as better than it sounds? Well, Berkshire's progress was not as good as it looks."

Buffett almost seems to revel in exposing his follies, not just when they first appear, but again and again. In 1983, for instance, he went right back to the start of his saga: "Charlie and I... controlled three companies, Berkshire Hathaway, Inc., Diversified Retailing Company, Inc., and Blue Chip Stamps, each a single business company, respectively in textiles, department stores, and trading stamps." They were not successful: "These cornerstone businesses (carefully chosen, it should be noted, by your Chairman and Vice Chairman) have, respectively, (1) survived but earned almost nothing, (2) shriveled in size while incurring large losses, and (3) shrunk in sales volume to about 5 percent its size at the time of entry. (Who says 'you can't lose 'em all'?)."

No dividends policy

There is always a rational point to these confessions, however. The passage above occurs in a discussion of dividends, which Buffett does not distribute. His reasoning is that historically Berkshire has obeyed his golden rule: more than $1 of market value has been created for every dollar of earnings reinvested in the business. Therefore, "any distribution would have been contrary to the financial interest of shareholders, large or small." Moreover, because of the poor performance listed above, "significant distributions in the early years might have been disastrous."

If the three companies had paid out in dividends all they earned, "we would almost certainly have no earnings at all now – and perhaps no capital either." Instead, the money was committed to "much better businesses," which was the "only way we were able to overcome those origins." Buffett goes on to comment that, "It's been like overcoming a misspent youth." In other words, Buffett drew three powerful rational conclusions from his triple failure:

- Invest money to earn more for shareholders than they can earn themselves.
- Diversify to spread risks by more than balancing failures with success elsewhere.
- Do not repeat mistakes, but use them as stepping stones to success.

Looking to the future
On Buffett's death, all his Berkshire Hathaway shares will go to his wife, Susan, who sits on the board of directors. If she does not outlive him, the shares will be given to a family foundation.

Berkshire after Buffett

Rational analysis and observation clearly show Buffett that his creation, for all the contribution made by Charlie Munger and others, including the managers of his operating companies, essentially hinges on one man (himself) who is mortal. He makes a point of telling people that he has faced this issue, as rationally, as ever: "I've already sent out a letter that tells what should be done, and I've got another letter that's addressed that will go out at the time, and it starts out 'Yesterday I died,' and then tells what the plans of the company are."

All his shares go to his wife, Susan, if she survives him, or to a foundation if she does not. Berkshire will then be "going forward with a vitally interested, but non-management owner and with a management that must perform for that owner." In theory, that should work well, provided that the "owner" takes the same eminently rational view as Buffett: that you succeed by limiting yourself to what you and you alone can do, and delegate everything else. His own retirement will consequently leave only two functions to be filled, one of which is to allocate capital, which is a straightforward intellectual exercise.

The overwhelmingly obvious fact, however, is that Buffett has allocated capital more successfully by far than any man in history. It is therefore unreasonable, and by no means rational, to suppose that somebody else will do as well. His second role is even more problematical: "to help 15 or 20 senior managers keep a group of people enthused about what they do when they have no financial need whatsoever to do it." He estimates that, "at least three-quarters of the managers that we have are rich beyond any possible financial need."

Fulfilling that second role depends not on the powers of reason alone but on those of empathy and personality. Buffett's unique character, with its combination of humanity and toughness, cold reason and personal warmth,

"Lest we end on a morbid note, I also want to assure you that I have never felt better. I love running Berkshire, and if enjoying life promotes longevity, Methuselah's record is in jeopardy."
The Essays of Warren Buffett

is what one business school professor has called "a five-sigma event," meaning a statistical aberration so rare it practically never happens. *Business Week* has commented that "just as no one other than Buffett could have created Berkshire Hathaway, it may well come to pass that no one other than Buffett can make it work."

Ideas into action

- Start as early as possible in your career to develop only good habits.
- Look at what you find really reprehensible, and avoid it.
- Try to do work that you like and only with people you like.
- Focus on a few good things, rather than making many investments.
- Look for businesses whose long-term futures are predictable.
- Confess your serious errors fully to yourself as well as to others.
- Invest money to earn more for shareholders than they can for themselves.

bill GATES

Biography

William Henry Gates III was born in 1955 to a well-to-do, well-connected Seattle family, which sent him to Harvard to study law (his father's profession). His story is not that of poor boy made good. The saga of Microsoft, however, is typical of the electronics industry – tiny, poor company made great and rich. Gates went to a private school, where he excelled at mathematics, and became fascinated from his early teens by personal computing, then in its formative stage.

With an equally enthusiastic Seattle friend, Paul Allen, Gates wrote a version of the BASIC computer language in 1975 for an early PC, the MITS Altair. Immediately following this success Gates and Allen formed Microsoft (initially Micro-Soft), and, in 1977, Gates abandoned college to concentrate on the new industry. The breakthrough for the pair came in 1980 when two IBM executives visited Microsoft to commission work on BASIC for their new PC – a rush program with unprecedentedly tight deadlines.

The IBM-ers found an engaging, bespectacled, highly intelligent and articulate man, physically restless and with great mental agility. Gates has not changed since. He reads voluminously, even in odd moments, specializes in "multi-tasking" (doing many things at once), and somehow contrives to give Microsoft his full attention, while also spending much time on public relations. He appears to have no outside interests other than his family, his Porsches and his magnificent, technology-crammed lakeside mansion in Medini, Washington. His investments outside Microsoft alone are worth $11.5 billion. His Microsoft shares are worth seven times that stupendous sum.

Creating the industry standard

All this wealth sprang, not from work on BASIC, but from IBM's other need, for operating software for their PC. Gates boldly bid for the contract. He then approached another software company – Seattle Computer Products – and bought an operating system called Q-DOS (nicknamed Quick and Dirty Operating System). Gates and Allen then modified it to suit IBM's needs, renamed it MS-DOS (Microsoft Disk Operating System) and delivered it to IBM for a relatively low price, undercutting rival software companies. Gates's purchase of Q-DOS for only $50,000 opened the doors to billions, largely because IBM, grossly underestimating the market for its PC, signed a contract allowing Microsoft to sell the software to any other PC manufacturer. When the PC took off, astounding IBM executives by its success, Microsoft's wealthy future was assured – to the rising annoyance of IBM.

The constant threat to Gates, even as his sales and profits grew astronomically with the rise of the IBM and IBM-compatible PCs, was that IBM would break the vital link with MS-DOS. Gates protected Microsoft as best he could by partnering IBM in the development of a new operating system, OS/2. When IBM executives sought to dissolve the OS/2 partnership, Gates won a reprieve at a June 1986 lunch with CEO John Akers.

Capturing the PC market

Little more than three years later, the war between IBM and Microsoft broke into the open. In 1990, Gates won hands down with the launch of Windows 3.0. Using the same technique – the "graphical user interface" – that had made the Apple Macintosh so popular, with its graphic icons and pull-down menus, the new product was selling a million copies a month by 1993. It gave users vastly improved access to applications, opening another door of opportunity for Gates. Now Microsoft could write and sell a whole new line of application programs for use with Windows.

Products like Word, the word processing program, and the Excel spreadsheet, are almost as dominant as MS-DOS and Windows, which hold 90 percent of the operating system market for PCs. Gates kept piling on the pressure. Windows NT, a more powerful product aimed at the corporate market, appeared in 1993. Like the first version of Windows, NT had serious defects. But Gates's approach has always been to launch first and improve later, radically if need be.

What worked so well with Windows 3.0 also triumphed with NT. Microsoft's sales and staff numbers soared, and up went the profits and the share price. Each advance in the stock made a new millionaire among the Microsoft ranks. But all the employee nesteggs were spectacularly outweighed by the fabulous fortune created for Gates himself. His reputation as a technological genius (undeserved) and as a superb businessman (definitely merited) was eclipsed by his unquestionable standing as The World's Richest Man.

The challenge of the Internet

Whether or not the adulation and success temporarily blunted Gates's vision, the company, having beaten IBM so decisively, nearly defeated itself by failing to react to the early, obvious challenge of the Internet. Since operating systems and applications could be loaded from cyberspace, Microsoft's hegemony could be undermined, like IBM's before it. By May 1995, Gates had become fully aware of the threat: one of the countless memos he regularly

Environmentally friendly futuristic house
Gates's Lake Washington estate was still under construction when the family moved in during 1998. Built from reclaimed Douglas fir timber, the 40,000 sq. ft. mansion is computer-controlled inside.

emails to "Microsofties" (as employees at Microsoft are known) was called "The Internet Tidal Wave." It gave the new technology "the highest level of importance."

Billions of dollars of development capital were switched to the assault on the new market – and especially on Netscape, the company whose Internet browsers, initially given away free, had taken it from an April 1994 start-up to $5 billion of market capitalization by December the next year. Gates had an immensely powerful weapon to deploy. The technique was to compel PC manufacturers to pre-load the Microsoft browser on to their machines as an allegedly integral part of Windows 95, the popular replacement for Windows 3.0.

Although commercially successful, the onslaught on Netscape made Microsoft vulnerable legally. In 1998 the US government's antitrust action went to trial, producing months of high embarrassment – and a hostile verdict – for Gates and the company. Now married to a former Microsoft employee – Melinda French – and with two children, Gates has arrived at a crossroads. Will the industry he has done more than anybody to create move away from his control? Can he reverse the growing tide of unfavorable opinion?

Unpopular figure

Public sentiment had run against Gates because of his very success. Some may have simply envied his enormous fortune, or resented that the multi-billionaire was not spreading his wealth as generously as he could afford. Within the computer industry, Microsoft's power to crush competitors, and to dominate its terms of trade with the PC manufacturers, aroused more than envy. Firms were anxious about their own profits and prospects as Microsoft extended the range of its products and its ambitions. As for the PC buyers, they typically accepted the Microsoft software bundled in with their purchases as a fact of life.

Many of the "techies," however, felt that Gates was a restrictive and too powerful force, whose hold over the technology prevented important advances and trapped users into costly upgrades to a system that was inherently old-fashioned. This mood led to an open hostility that expressed itself in many ways, ranging from Internet attacks to published books, such as *Barbarians Led by Bill Gates: Microsoft from the Inside*. A "cookbook" gave the recipe for "Breaking Bill Gates's Windows Monopoly (without Breaking Windows) with Linux CD Operating

System." This title referred to a new system, available either free over the Internet, or from intermediaries who charged vastly less than Microsoft did for its own system.

Fighting the antitrust action

Linux was seized upon by "techies" as the answer to their anti-Gates prayers. A significant number of corporate users also adopted Linux (which has important advantages over the Microsoft system). This gave Gates another weapon in his battle against the antitrust authorities. He argued that Microsoft cannot be described as a monopoly when competition is more intense than ever and when customers are gaining from falling prices and greater performance. Unfortunately, this defense was not helped by taped interviews with Gates. Along with other evidence (such as internal e-mails), the tapes showed Gates in an unflattering and sometimes apparently evasive light.

As a consequence of the antitrust trial, Gates had been forced into the public arena as never before. After a hesitant reaction, he responded with his usual determination. TV interviews showed a relaxed, smiling man, with no hint of defensiveness. Moreover, Gates and his wife decided to set up a gigantic charitable foundation to control and distribute the bulk of their wealth: they could hope (like the Rockefellers before them) to swing public opinion in their favor. Gates also pushed through a major reorganization of Microsoft to delegate more of his power, culminating in his switch from CEO to chief software architect, while continuing to direct its huge switch of strategy to the Internet. And on one issue he remains quite determined: to carry on doing the job he loves in an industry which, more than any other man, he has so long commanded.

1

IT changes absolutely everything

Creating a universal space for information sharing, collaboration, and commerce • **Interaction between the firm's "Web workstyle" and customers' "Web lifestyle"** • Why the Internet's universal connection produces a true customer-centric world • **How the Internet enables the vital "digital nervous system" (DNS)** • Management changes that flow from the economic impact of cyberspace • **Restructuring processes are more fundamental than any change since mass production**

Bill Gates's philosophy and success are inseparable from the Information Revolution. From the start he wanted to create "a tool for the Information Age that could magnify your brainpower instead of just your muscle power." He sees digital tools as the means of augmenting the unique powers of the human being: thinking, articulating thought, working together with other humans to act on thought. In management terms, his success has been built on the proposition that information technology must and will change everything – including the ways in which companies communicate, are managed, win competitive advantage, and do business.

After years devoted to advocating and enabling a revolution centering on the personal computer, his objective shifted in the mid-1990s to positioning Microsoft at the head of a new revolution founded on the Internet, which, he says, "is still at the beginning."

Underestimating the Internet

The Internet's central position in Gates's thought and action represents a great personal turnround. When the first Website appeared in 1993, to be followed shortly by Netscape's Internet browser, Gates could hardly fail to notice these events. But, as he has often admitted, he was slow to understand the fundamental significance of Internet developments. Appearing at a *Fortune* lecture in 1998 with the fabled investor Warren Buffett, Gates confessed that "when the Internet came along, we had it as fifth or sixth priority."

He told himself, "Yeah, I've got that on my list, so I'm okay." This was far from the truth. "There came a point when we realized it was happening faster and was a much deeper phenomenon than had been recognized in our strategy," he recalled. His realization was prompted, not by intellectual arousal, but by commercial necessity. Well before Gates woke up, many commentators had identified the Internet as a major threat to Microsoft's quasi-monopoly.

Entering the Web race

The time lag is especially astonishing in the light of Gates's own later views. By 1999, he saw the Internet as far more than a priority. It had become, in his mind and in actuality, a transcendent technology. "The Internet creates a new universal space for information sharing, collaboration, and commerce," wrote Gates in *Business @ the Speed of Thought* (1999). This "new medium" combines the functionalities of television and telephone with those of paper in a way that reshapes all relationships. As Gates observed, "the ability to find information and match people with common interests is completely new."

A clue to understanding Gates's initial failure to grasp the overwhelming importance of the Internet lies in an earlier lapse. In 1981 Gates affirmed, when forecasting the future of personal computers, that "640k ought to be enough for anybody." Today, when desktops routinely have 128MB of memory and six gigabytes of hard drive space, that prediction sounds ludicrous. But Gates's commercial

"We didn't see that the Internet, a network for academics and techies, would blossom into the global commercial network it is today."
Business @ the Speed of Thought

interests then seemed best served by stable development of PC power, rather than its headlong expansion. His erroneous thinking was wishful. His complacency regarding an Internet that threatened to bypass his quasi-monopoly of PC software was just as wishful.

By 1998 Gates saw clearly that the emerging hardware, software, and communication standards "will reshape business and consumer behavior." In fact, the "will" reads oddly, since that reshaping is already taking place on a broad front and a large scale. Most of the functions Gates offered as predictions were being widely applied even as he wrote. People "will regularly use PCs at work and at home," he asserted; they already do. They also already "use email routinely," and they are connected to the Internet by the millions. Many also carry digital devices containing their personal and business information.

Pocket-sized information

An enormous storage capacity coupled with a light, compact design make the digital personal organizer ideal for keeping track of appointments, addresses, and important dates.

Changing workstyle and lifestyle

It takes no great prophetic leap to see that these digital tools, already employed by many people, will spread to the great majority, even without the new consumer devices such as television set-top boxes that Gates confidently and rightly expects. Gates fits current and impending developments into two important constructs: "Web workstyle" and "Web lifestyle." Neither had been fully realized by 1999, but their shape was clear. "Web workstyle" springs from the use of digital methods to change business processes. "Web lifestyle" changes the nature of the relationship between consumers and the businesses that serve them.

Web workstyle and Web lifestyle obviously interact. Changed corporate processes are essential to meet the demands of customers who want to transact their business online. At present, corporations can still treat Web transactions as ancillary, since they represent only a tiny proportion of all trade; but Gates predicts that this will not always be the case. He believes strongly in a concept popularized by his friend Andy Grove, the CEO of Intel. The microprocessor leader stresses the importance of "inflection points," at which the technology generates "sudden and massive" change.

Gates predicts that this kind of change is what will happen when Internet connections leave the desktop and become portable, when "everyday devices such as water and electrical meters, security systems, and automobiles will be connected... reporting on their usage and status." The connection will be with the same portable devices that "will keep us constantly in touch with other systems and other people." The combined results will transform lifestyles and business styles alike.

Reshaping the way we live

Gates points out that earlier technologies entirely reshaped the way people lived. The convincing example that he cites is electricity. Until its infrastructure had become available, people had no idea of the powerful electrical devices, from telephones to television, that would change the world. The essence of the Internet is electronic applications. These have multiplied and are multiplying so fast that the "adoption of technology for the Web lifestyle is happening faster than the adoption of electricity, cars, television, and radio."

The practical results of this on-rushing technological revolution are clearly imminent. Even in 1998, only a tiny percentage of transactions in the US, let alone worldwide, were transacted on the Internet. Gates cites the fact that "only about one million of the 15 billion total bills in the United States were paid electronically." The growth rate, however, is so phenomenal – with Web use doubling every 100 days – that it is easy for him to predict a future in which digital transactions will not only be universal, but greatly enriched in functionality.

Each customer will have a personal banking page on the Web from which all transactions can be conducted and all financial information obtained. This is not a vision, but an extrapolation of irreversible trends. Gates is on the safest possible ground in predicting that one year into the millennium more than 60 percent of US households will have PCs and 85 percent of these will have Internet access. Drawing from his experience in the PC era, Gates believes in the unstoppable advance of the technology and the consequent profusion of popular applications.

The impact on lifestyle begins with television. "Over time the biggest impact of digital television will be the ability to integrate other digital data, providing interactivity, smart agents [software programs that act as pickers and choosers on your behalf], targeted advertising and sales offers, and access to the Web." Gates is fully conscious that technical obstacles still exist to ensuring "a simple and totally digital television experience for viewers." Difficulties include common standards and bandwidth, "the information carrying capacity of a digital communications system." But, as ever, he has confidence in technology's powers to remove the obstacles: "the advances on many fronts make it likely that the speed of improvement will surprise everyone in the next decade."

Bringing people together

Looking at the "enormous" social implications of the Web lifestyle and workstyle, Gates concludes that the Internet will bring people together rather than causing "society to fly apart." He sees its main product as universal communication, which broadens rather than narrows horizons. The "communities" that people began to build early in Internet history, in which groups with common interests joined together, are a new and powerful means of bonding. "The Web lets you join communities across the globe and provides the opportunity to strengthen connections in your own backyard," writes Gates.

People will win time for these new social interactions from the enhanced efficiency of Web transactions. Gates does not believe that the Web lifestyle will generate changes in human nature or fundamental ways of life, although he gives no evidence for this conclusion. Rather, he sees people following much the same interests, but "in a better way." For example, the Web brings shopping into the home, both in the selection of products and services and in their delivery, and offers infinite choice and variety. As Gates observes, this produces "a true customer-centric world."

Developing a DNS

Gates, however, devotes much more attention to the business transformation, the contours of which are clearly visible, than to the more opaque consumer world. The key digital applications for business include:

- Replacing paperwork with digital text
- Facilitating groupwork by enabling teams to use the same data simultaneously
- Providing up-to-the-minute information about sales and customers to improve responsiveness
- Facilitating relationships with business partners

Microsoft itself is used and cited as a test-bed for these applications. Gates makes large claims for the "new level of electronic intelligence" that has been infused into his company. His metaphor is the "biological nervous system that triggers your reflexes so that you can react quickly to danger or need." A "digital nervous system," or DNS, is the business equivalent. It consists of "the digital processes that enable a company to perceive and react to its environment, to sense competitor challenges and customer needs, and to organize timely responses."

Before his Internet conversion, Gates believed that the future lay with networking PCs, joining them together within organizations. He now describes this technology as "a mere network of computers" compared to a DNS, which combines hardware and software to provide "accuracy, immediacy, and richness" of information with "the insight and collaboration made possible by the information." The distinction is partly semantic, but it is correct that the sheer universality of the Internet, which is crucial to a DNS, is truly revolutionary in its consequences.

Changing how companies work

Companies are having to develop a digital nervous system in order to keep pace with markets in which "consumers are demanding faster service, stronger relationships, and personalization." Consequently, adopting the Web workstyle is not an option for management but a necessity. For businesses of all sizes, this certainly does mean fundamental changes in the way they are organized and how they work. In turn, these changes cannot take place without profound socioeconomic results, since people depend on businesses for their work, livelihoods, many relationships, and the supply of goods and services.

Gates accurately delineates the fundamental management changes engendered by the Internet's economic impact. The effects will be great and will spread far beyond companies. Many companies are already moving in the directions he describes:

- Focusing on their "core competencies" and outsourcing everything else to outside suppliers
- Maintaining a small central core of people, and employing others as and when required
- Expanding rapidly and even globally from small or medium-sized bases
- Escaping from geographic constraints by transferring work to where it is best and/or most economically done

- Refocusing all processes on the customer, and constantly mutating to meet changing markets and competition
- Increasing the pressure to shorten cycle time and increase the speed of all other processes

As for the consequences, they are already appearing. Secure full-time employment with companies is dropping away markedly and less secure, part-time, freelance employment is rising. Established companies have to counter increasing threats from many new competitors,

Working from home
The rise in the amount of work that is outsourced is bringing increased flexibility to the lives of many, making it easier to fulfill the demands of both work and family.

with size and geographical spread no longer the defensive bastions that they were in the past. Many jobs that have been available in the mature economies are being exported. Specialization is increasing markedly as the key beneficiaries of "outsourcing" concentrate and coalesce. Prices are falling as processes become faster and cheaper.

Gates observes that "almost all the time involved in producing an item is in the coordination of the work, not in the actual production.... Good information systems can remove most of that waiting time.... The speed of delivery and the interaction with the Internet effectively shifts products into services." It follows that the Internet turns each and every product company around by 180 degrees – from production first to customer first. The corporate cultures and infrastructures must "support fast research, analysis, collaboration, and execution" – which currently is far from reality.

Restructuring business processes

Perhaps influenced by Microsoft's own characteristics, which much more nearly reflect the needs of the digital revolution, Gates does not dwell on the upheavals (including the job losses) that will result as business leaders "streamline and modernize their processes and their organization" in the effort to "get the full benefit of technology." He argues strongly for these reforms, because giving people responsibility and authority without information leaves them "helpless." Moreover, a business loses a "huge advantage" by not moving into the Internet mode.

In this mode "information about production systems, product problems, customer crises and opportunities, sales shortfalls, and other important business news gets through the organization in a matter of minutes instead of days." The "right people," too, are "working on the issues within hours." Gates regards this restructuring of processes as "more fundamental than any other change since mass production." If this is correct, though, it surely invalidates his next statement: "every company can choose whether to lead or follow the emerging digital trends."

Embracing constant change

This option must have disappeared in what Gates describes as a time of "industry-wrenching change." He distinguishes the current era from previous economic epochs by stressing that industries used to be wrenched around for short periods, interspersed by long periods of stability. The evolutionary term for this is "punctuated equilibrium." The Age of the Internet, on the other hand, features an environment of constant change, or "punctuated chaos."

Gates uses financial crises – such as the one which raged in Asia in 1998 – as a metaphor for this condition. Already, all financial players are digitally connected, so "any downturn or upturn in a major market creates overnight reverberations in other markets." The wired world is a world in constant flux in which "digital interconnections will soon exist for all markets." The problem, though, is also the solution. "The digital world is both forcing companies to react to change and giving them the tools by which to stay ahead of it." IT provides the quick reflexes that connect business strategy with organizational response. Without IT, there will be no response – and presumably no company.

Gates puts this choice succinctly: "it's evolve rapidly or die." He sees no downside to the digital age. True, he sees that there are important political and social dimensions.

But the Internet issues he raises, which "include how we ensure access for everyone and how we protect children," are only subsets of the broader question: how to "ensure that the new digital age reflects the society" that citizens want to create. In his view, what they want is what they are getting. Gates sees only universal benefit: improved products and services, more responsiveness to complaints, lower costs and more choices, better government, and more economical social services.

Ideas into action

- Form teams able to use the same data simultaneously.
- Combine hardware and software for accuracy, immediacy, and richness of information.
- Meet customer demands for faster service, stronger relationships, and personalization.
- Focus on "core competencies" and outsource everything else to outsiders.
- Coordinate work to radically reduce time spent on production.
- Streamline and modernize to get the full benefit of technology.
- Choose right now to follow the emerging digital trends.

The opening of windows to the world

The early years and final triumph of Microsoft can only be understood in the context of the mighty IBM, with its massive market share, huge spending on technology, and stranglehold on large corporate customers.

Compared to IBM, for all its own success, Microsoft was a midget for its first decade. For that reason, Gates centered his strategy around IBM during this time. He needed to keep the corporation's business, because the colossus dominated the market.

But Gates also wanted to realize his vision of universal personal computing. That meant cheaper computers, widely distributed, and working to a common standard, enabling anybody to use any program on any computer. His vision was incompatible with IBM's strongest motivation, which was to sustain its sales of high-priced computers to high-spending corporates and to sell proprietary systems that could only be used by purchasers of IBM machines.

Its drive for exclusivity gave IBM a powerful motive for removing Microsoft from its path. This was impossible, however, as long as every PC sold by IBM used MS-DOS as its operating system. The strategy that evolved in 1984–87 was simple, although it required billions in investment: devise a new operating system, which would markedly improve on the "clunky" MS-DOS, and link the system to a new line of PCs that would blow the IBM "clones," all using Microsoft products, out of the water.

Dual strategy

Gates would have been destroyed in that explosion. To protect Microsoft, he pursued a dual strategy. First, hang in there with IBM at all costs, working with the company on the new system – OS/2. Second, build on MS-DOS to improve its performance and increase its attractions to software writers and customers, primarily by adding graphical capability.

If the "new" MS-DOS – which came to be called Windows – was sufficiently attractive, then IBM would be obliged to offer the system. Microsoft could retain its existing markets and build on the new technology base to broaden

"We'd lost the chance to make Windows and OS/2 compatible, and because we'd lost the struggle to make the OS/2 run on modest machines, it only made sense to continue to develop Windows."
The Road Ahead

and strengthen its own line of highly profitable applications.

The obvious drawback to this dual strategy was that Gates needed IBM more than IBM needed Microsoft. This was equally obvious to the IBMers, many of whom resented the fame and fortune that Gates had won through his brilliant contract with their company. While Gates resisted attempts to shut him out (even offering IBM up to 30 percent of Microsoft, and being turned down), co-operation on OS/2 went badly. "I felt that the OS/2 project would be a ticket to the future for both companies," he commented. "Instead, it eventually created an enormous rift between us."

Gates lists the failure among his greatest mistakes; but in truth the dual strategy worked fabulously to his advantage. As OS/2 failed in the marketplace, Windows took off to become the world's most successful software product. For Microsoft, Windows was not so much a ticket to the future as a golden passport.

2

Building a knowledge company

Mastering the five disciplines that make the learning organization work • **Why employee success depends more on good hiring than subsequent experience** • Developing a high corporate IQ by exchanging information widely • **The need to make sharing an integral part of work** • Using hands-on management to evangelize, recognize, reward, and review information usage • **Four ways in which bosses must raise the corporate IQ** • Bringing digital tools together to make solutions easier to build

Microsoft has been credited with being a genuine example of the "learning organization." This is not a phrase used by Bill Gates, perhaps because of its vagueness. As a hard-nosed businessman, Gates is only interested in concrete results. The key to the learning organization is "knowledge management." Even in the second edition of *The Road Ahead*, published in 1996, there is little sign of this theme. But his thinking has undergone a considerable change since then, and by 1999 knowledge management loomed very large in Gates's outlook. It is central to the philosophy he expressed in that year's book – *Business @ the Speed of Thought*.

Does Microsoft in fact practice what its master preaches? The company's principles and processes do embrace the five "learning disciplines" identified by Peter Senge – a professor at Massachusetts Institute of Technology and author of *The Fifth Discipline* (1990). These disciplines are described as the basis of "learning organization work." They are:

- *Personal Mastery*. Expecting people to develop their personal capacity to meet their own objectives, and thus those of the company, which in turn is organized to encourage that personal effort
- *Mental Models*. Developing the right "mind-set" to guide actions and decisions
- *Shared Vision*. Commitment of all members of the organization to its aims and its ways of achieving those objectives
- *Team Learning*. Exploiting the fact that group thinking is greater than the sum of its individual parts
- *Systems Thinking*. Acting on the understanding that actions and decisions cannot be isolated, but have ramifications throughout the organization

Increasing the "bandwidth"

These five disciplines also fit the picture which Randall E. Stross paints, in *The Microsoft Way* (1996), of Bill Gates as a "practical intellectual." In the software industry, this is not a contradiction in terms. It requires genuine intellect to write software, but the software is useless unless it works in practice. Narrow-minded technologists have never fitted Gates's broader ambitions. He is famous for using the word "bandwidth" to describe people's intellectual capacity: it is a metaphor drawn from the amount of information that a communications system can carry.

Gates believes that the greater the human "bandwidth" that he employs (in other words, the more collective intelligence Microsoft hires), the greater the strength of his company. He is less interested in the amorphous concept of a "learning organization" than in the harder notion of a "knowledge company," which stores and develops its intellectual resources, and augments them by its hiring policies. The knowledge company's raw material is brainpower. You hire the best and best-trained brains, create an environment in which they can create their best work, and build systems so that the knowledge that has been created is built into the fabric and operations of the business – where it can be shared and transmitted.

Hiring the super smart

The brightest and best of the new university graduates who approach the company (of whom only a small minority are hired) are invited to enter the Microsoft campus. The headquarters site in Redmond, Washington, has been described as "organized along the lines of a university." Gates seeks not just the smart, but the "super smart." According to Stross, the super smart have every one of the following attributes:

- Ability to grasp new knowledge very fast
- Ability to pose acute questions instantaneously
- Perception of connections between different areas of knowledge
- At-a-glance "linguistic" ability to interpret software code
- Obsessive concern with the problem on hand, even when away from work
- Great powers of concentration
- Photographic recall of their work

All of these attributes, including the amazing recall, are personal characteristics of Gates himself. He expects them to be accompanied by an emphasis on pragmatism, verbal agility, and swift response to challenge – qualities that also reflect Gates's own aptitudes. He believes that he was born, not made, and that the success of an employee at Microsoft

Campus environment
Microsoft headquarters in Redmond, Washington, has the appearance and atmosphere of a university campus, encouraging creativity and intellectual pursuits in the graduate employees.

depends more on the hiring than on the subsequent experience. That would explain why, to quote Stross:

> "... the best programmers are not marginally better than merely good ones. They are an order of magnitude better, measured by whatever standard: conceptual creativity, speed, ingenuity of design, or problem-solving ability. All else being equal, the company that recruits the largest number of... the alphas among alphas is most likely to win the biggest sweepstakes."

Deploying the best brains

This theory raises a practical problem. Although Gates has indeed won the biggest prizes, the company's history has been marred by conspicuous technical failures, such as the persistent clumsiness of MS/DOS, problems with the early versions of Windows, the almost fatal flop of Windows NT, and misfires with several applications. Clearly, hiring the best brains is not enough. How they are deployed and organized is decisive in the effectiveness of their output. This is where the knowledge company, as opposed to the learning organization, makes its mark.

Here, too, the hard head of Gates the businessman is at variance with the philosopher of mental bandwidth. For all the "campus" elements, Microsoft is no university but a hard-driving commercial enterprise, which, sometimes counterproductively, is only interested in hard results. In an effort to control costs, Microsoft has always deliberately sought to hire fewer people than it actually needs, following the formula "*n* minus one," where *n* equals the numbers required. While excessive headcount is to be deplored, inadequate numbers also exert a harmful effect: overwork and over-stretching carry obvious risks.

Sharing knowledge

Gates himself is clear that high individual intelligence is not enough "in today's dynamic markets." A company also needs a high corporate IQ, which hinges on the facility to share information widely and enable staff members "to build on each other's ideas." This is partly a matter of storing the past, partly of exchanging current knowledge. As individuals learn, their knowledge adds to the corporate store.

What matters most is quality, not quantity; how effectively that store is mobilized by collaborative working. "The ultimate goal is to have a team develop the best ideas from throughout an organization and then act with the same unity of purpose and focus that a single, well-motivated person would bring to bear on a situation," says Gates. That way, the super-smart, articulate person – the Bill Gates archetype – becomes the organization writ large. It is the boss's role to encourage collaboration and knowledge sharing, using not just exhortation but reward for the purpose.

Gates advocates setting up specific projects that share knowledge across the organization and making this sharing "an integral part of the work itself – not an add-on frill." Rejecting the old adage that "knowledge is power," Gates argues that "power comes not from knowledge kept, but from knowledge shared" – and managed.

"We read, ask questions, explore, go to lectures, compare notes and findings... consult experts, daydream, brainstorm, formulate and test hypotheses, build models and simulations, communicate what we're learning, and practice new skills." *The Road Ahead*

Managing knowledge effectively

On this reading, knowledge management must be of extreme importance. Yet Gates seems to downplay it when he writes: "Knowledge management is a fancy term for a simple idea. You're managing data, documents, and people's efforts." He goes on to explain at great length how these three processes can be deployed in the following four areas of any business:

- Planning
- Customer service
- Training
- Project collaboration

Some of the applications – for instance, in training and customer service – are not especially high-level, but they plainly serve essential purposes and answer important questions. What happens, for example, if Microsoft salespeople out in the field get queries from customers? The sales force cannot be expected to have the technical knowledge that resides in the product groups. By operating through a Website called the InfoDesk, Microsoft's product people can answer 90 percent of all questions within two days. Company-wide access to product knowledge is a crucial aspect of the corporate IQ.

Access to training is also critical and has an obvious relationship to the effectiveness of corporate brainpower. Again, the needs can be met with high efficiency online. Microsoft employees can find the course they want, get notified when it is available, and register through a single site. In addition, the Web can provide not only training information but the training itself (using multimedia and chat sites, for example). During 1998 online facilities at

Microsoft trained twice as many students as went on physical courses. Gates regards this as fundamental management of knowledge – which it clearly is.

Creating a collaborative culture

What excites him more, however, is creating a "collaborative culture, reinforced by information flow [which] makes it possible for smart people all over a company to be in touch with one another." The technology again plays a crucial role, helping to stimulate and energize the workplace. That happens as a "critical mass of high-IQ people," working in concert, share a vital experience, and

Stimulating atmosphere

By encouraging members of staff to work together and exchange ideas, Gates obtains a highly motivated and enthusiastic workforce happy to work long hours to achieve specified goals.

"the energy level shoots way up." Gates believes that cross-stimulation breeds new ideas, raises the contribution levels of the less experienced employees, and gets the whole company working "smarter."

That does not happen by itself. Effective knowledge management is both a means and an end. Every time an internal Microsoft consultant finishes an assignment, he or she is required to send technology solutions to a central Web location called InSite. But digital technology is not the whole answer by any means. Hands-on management is required to "evangelize," recognize, reward, and review the use of information. Gates himself regularly reviews customer information provided by the sales forces, and regards this review by superiors as possibly "the biggest incentive… to keep our customer base up-to-date."

Investing in intellectual capital

The expenditure of his own time in the day-to-day business of Microsoft is justified by Gates as an investment in "intellectual capital," which he defines as "the intrinsic value of the intellectual property of your company and the knowledge your people have." In the "information society," the argument that intellectual capital is the only kind that counts has become a cliché. Behind the cliché, however, lies the reality that Gates sees reshaping the world – above all, the world of business.

Thomas A. Stewart, author of *Intellectual Capital* (1997), has written of "the end of management as we know it." Gates's efforts at Microsoft exemplify how the old-style approach to management must be changed in order to nurture the three varieties of intellectual capital, as described by Stewart, which are:

- Human (individual powers and resources)
- Structural (accumulated knowledge and know-how of the organization)
- Customer knowledge (which in Stewart's view is "probably... the worst managed of all intangible assets")

The human aspect of intellectual capital is not only concerned with the obvious knowledge worker, such as the programmer or Gates himself, but with turning others into knowledge workers. "In the new organization, the worker is no longer a cog in the machine but is an intelligent part of the overall process," writes Stewart. Computers, for example, are largely limited to the one-dimensional, repetitive work at which they excel. The excellence of human beings is needed to manage processes, rather than merely to execute tasks. And that creates knowledge workers, who use good digital information to play unique roles.

Developing, investing in, and deploying all this intellectual capital – knowledge management – surely goes beyond Gates's dismissal of the latter as "a fancy term for a simple idea." In fact, what he goes on to describe is far from simple in execution. "Your aim should be to enhance the way people work together, share ideas, sometimes wrangle, and build on one another's ideas – and then act in concert for a common purpose." That goal sounds like a managerial Utopia, something seen in only rare and fleeting circumstances, the heartfelt and generally frustrated desire of the CEO.

Raising the corporate IQ

As the guiding genius of Microsoft, Gates has filled a specific role along the road to Utopia. The challenge, which continues, is "raising the corporate IQ" in four ways:

- Establishing an atmosphere that promotes knowledge sharing and collaboration
- Prioritizing the areas in which knowledge sharing is most valuable
- Providing the digital tools that make knowledge sharing possible
- Rewarding people for contributing to a full flow of knowledge

The third of these keys to knowledge management is a greater challenge to managers who lack Gates's technological background than he recognizes. He writes about "sophisticated" applications of knowledge management (so much for simplicity). Many managers are still unfamiliar with tools such as databases, email, workflow applications, electronic files, and Web technology – the "building blocks" of knowledge management, in Gates's phrase. These digital tools must be applied in various combinations, although, as Gates explains, the technology is bringing together the separate richness of all digital tools "to make solutions much easier to build."

The easier the solutions, the nearer Utopian management will come to being realized. Gates points out that scientists have been using the Internet for far longer than managers, and that exchange of knowledge between scientists in different countries, together with "critiquing one another's thinking via email," have become matters of routine. He believes that, used in business, the same collaborative, knowledge-managing tools can significantly cut down research and development costs, improve the quality of new product thinking, speed the progress of the new offering to market, and dramatically reduce the incidence of failure.

Learning from your mistakes

Microsoft's own failures have not been forgotten but stored as part of the intellectual capital. This has only come about because the company is prepared to learn from the unfortunate past. Gates used to publish and revise annually a memo under the title "The Ten Great Mistakes of Microsoft." The object was not to wallow in error, but to stimulate "Microsofties" into learning the lessons. Many of the mistakes, according to Gates, came from entering markets either late or not at all.

Outsiders, however, might be more inclined to dwell on the software releases that were inadequate or faulty. In these cases, Microsoft certainly does learn from its own errors, simply because it has to correct them or lose the customers. But however much the "library" of knowledge about past programs builds up, however strongly the tools for software writing are standardized, however much brilliance is hired, the knowledge demands simply get more intimidating. In 1999 armies of Microsoft people were struggling to get the latest version of Windows to market, writing millions of lines of code and confronting an endless procession of bugs.

Maintaining market control

As Gates well understands, the process of acquiring knowledge and applying it to new purposes never ends. Not only do the mountains to climb get progressively higher but the landscape is constantly being changed by the hosts of other brains, at other companies and universities, who are taking different lines of knowledge to different conclusions. The Gates monopoly is commercial, not technological. That is why he places so much stress on obtaining and managing knowledge about the customer.

But there is a central difficulty for Microsoft as a learning organization. It cannot know everything about all customers, nor about all information technologies.

Much of its knowledge management is dedicated to maintaining the company's proprietary position. This position is vulnerable to technological developments that are not conceived or controlled by Microsoft. In some cases the new knowledge can be bought, by acquiring the business involved, or shared via a partnership agreement. Gates uses both approaches to deal with external intellectual challenges. But he is defending a minority position in the market for ideas. The knowledge company can never afford to relax.

Ideas into action

- Expect people to develop their personal capacity to excel.
- Build up the intellectual resources of the organization.
- Deploy and organize people to get maximum effectiveness of output.
- Use Web sites to update knowledge and make it available.
- Hire smart people and keep them in touch with each other.
- Treat everybody as an intelligent part of the entire business.
- Obtain all the customer knowledge you can – and manage it.

Exploiting the info-revolution

Success in the future will depend very substantially on the Internet. That means understanding what Bill Gates calls the digital nervous system (DNS). At the same time, you must develop your ability to work in a "knowledge company" in which "knowledge management" is the key activity.

Understanding and using the DNS

The main benefits of the DNS are that it allows the same data to be used by teams simultaneously and provides up-to-the-minute information about customers and sales, thus enabling fast and appropriate response to customer needs and competitor challenges.

With the help of the DNS, Gates forced a massive shift in strategy at Microsoft, from sidelining the Internet to making it absolutely central to everything the company does and sells. Unquestionably, this is the kind of flexibility you will need in the years ahead.

Understanding the DNS and knowing how to apply its hardware and software to your management and business needs does not demand a high level of technical proficiency. If you can operate a typewriter keyboard and use a telephone, then you have the basic skills needed to exploit the DNS and manage knowledge.

Develop knowledge skills

There are four key skills that you will need, however, to become an efficient and effective knowledge manager. They are all concerned with the handling of information.

The Four Key Skills of the Knowledge Manager			
1 Understanding information	**2** Processing information	**3** Communicating information	**4** Correlating information

Think of yourself as a one-person company (Myself Inc.), and set out to become an effective practitioner of knowledge management. In other words, put into action on a personal scale the principles and practices of a knowledge company. Encourage everyone in the company to develop their full capacity. As individuals learn from each other – and the DNS – so the corporate intelligence increases.

1 Learning the disciplines

As the first step in your personal development toward becoming a knowledge manager, identify the demands of the five "learning disciplines" outlined by Peter Senge (see p. 30).

The disciplines and your role

The example of Microsoft demonstrates how understanding and applying these disciplines leads to higher levels of performance. Relate the disciplines to your own role as a manager.

The Five Learning Disciplines
1 Developing your personal abilities
2 Applying the right "mind-set" to guide your performance
3 Committing yourself to the company's vision
4 Improving your team-thinking abilities
5 Understanding how your actions affect the whole organization

Raising your skills level

See yourself as a person with valuable skills – what Gates calls a "skills set" – and the ability to raise your skills level. Give yourself measurable, stretching, and valuable objectives to focus your mind on improving your performance and position.

Developing a Powerful Skills Set
Analyze your "skills set".
Match your skills to the requirements of your present job – and the job you want next.
Update your existing skills where necessary.
Enhance and augment those skills that you need to achieve your current and future objectives.
Start now!

Your personal vision

You need a vision both for yourself and for your business. This is the overarching idea that embraces all your specific objectives. Gates had a very powerful vision: "A PC on every desk and in every home, using Microsoft software." Your vision can be just as powerful.

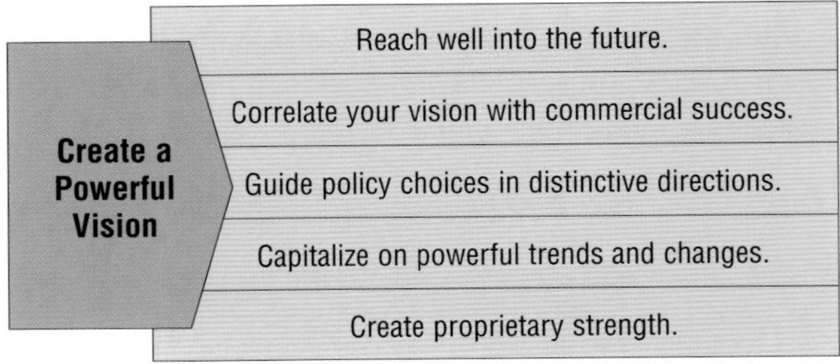

To reach your personal objectives – and realize your powerful vision – you also need the help of others.

Teamwork

Working in genuine teams (Senge's fourth discipline) is increasingly the norm. Team members need the same key skills, whether they are in a permanent or a temporary team. How good are your team skills? You should be able to answer "Yes" to these questions:

- Do you have one or more "partners" (people on whom you rely, and who rely on you, for complementary skills and advice)?
- Do you regard team leadership as "being the first among equals," rather than "being the boss"?
- Do you defer to colleagues, even of lower status, in the interests of achieving the team task?
- Do you align your personal objectives with those of the team?
- Do you ignore personalities and concentrate instead on people's actual contribution?

Looking at the whole picture

Systems thinking – Senge's fifth discipline – is another crucial managerial skill. It means thinking beyond the immediate: every action produces a reaction and every effect has side effects. Make sure you treat the root cause of any problem, not just the symptoms.

2 Using digital technology

The DNS is an excellent tool for two-way thinking. To make its advantages work for you, seize every opportunity to learn how to use the new technology to the full.

Exploit the DNS

Unlike other business technologies, the DNS is available to anyone – and at an economic price. It has four key uses that together keep you fully informed and up-to-date on a 24-hour basis.

Four Key Uses of the DNS
1 Producing, receiving, storing, accessing, and distributing documents and data of all kinds
2 Communicating and sharing information with other people anywhere in the world
3 Receiving "real-time", instant information about the operation and results of the business
4 Transacting business with customers and suppliers

While you can manage successfully without going near a screen, you will work more reliably and cheaply if you make use of the new technology. Find ways of replacing manual with digital means.

Conquer technophobia

If you are not an emailer, have not mastered spreadsheets, or cannot use groupware to connect with others, ask yourself whether technophobia is the cause. If so, eliminate it by:

- Confronting the fear head-on
- Finding out what hardware and software you need (both in the office and on the move)
- Obtaining all the equipment you require
- Mastering the machines and programs through training
- Using the technology intensively, until it becomes second nature

Do not leave the DNS to others, even the "experts." That will give them a great advantage – and put you at a great disadvantage.

3 Managing your knowledge

Your success and failure, like those of a corporation, depend on how much intellectual capital you have and how well you use it. Keep looking for ways of working "smarter." The DNS can help you exploit and augment your intellectual capital.

Analyze your knowledge

In order to improve your intellectual capital, first you need to analyze your capabilities. Take an objective view by answering the following questions:

- What individual powers and resources do you possess? Taken together, how high do these score when measured on a scale of 1 (minimal) to 5 (excellent)?
- What knowledge have you accumulated about the organization, its businesses, and the market sector? How does this knowledge rate on a scale of 1 (shallow) to 5 (deep)?
- What special skills have you acquired during your career that you can use in your work? How do these skills rate on a scale of 1 (of minimal use in your work) to 5 (highly effective)?
- What do you know about your customers, both internal and external? How does this knowledge measure up on a scale of 1 (shallow) to 5 (deep)?
- On a scale of 1 (poorly) to 5 (very well), how effectively do you apply your individual powers and resources, your knowledge and special skills, and your overall understanding of the customer?

Analysis

If you have answered the questions honestly, there is likely to be a significant gap between the maximum rating score (25) and your final judgment of yourself. Use the results in a positive way to assess what your next step should be. Ask yourself how you can improve by:

- undertaking further training
- seeking wider experience
- becoming more effective inside and outside the organization.

Reassess yourself regularly

Acquiring and applying knowledge is a never-ending process, so run through the questions above every six months. The knowledge company can never afford to relax – and nor should you.

Knowledge sharing

Managing your own knowledge is only part of the picture. To create the collaborative culture that Gates encourages at Microsoft, you need to have a two-way exchange of ideas by:

- Pooling your knowledge with that of others – both in your own team and outside
- Taking steps to have the knowledge of others readily available
- Learning from an objective analysis of past and present successes and failures (especially the failures)
- Continually looking at the outside world, through all available media and contacts, to receive the stimulation of new knowledge and new ideas
- Developing ways to turn new knowledge and new ideas into new products, processes, services, and methods

Learn to succeed

As you analyze your own performance, do not be dismayed if you fall short of the ideals recommended by Gates. Remember that there is no such thing as perfection in the management and mobilization of knowledge – and Gates and Microsoft do make mistakes. But as Gates demonstrated in his annual memo listing the company's great mistakes, you can always learn to do better. By constantly seeking knowledge and turning it into profitable reality, you too can achieve phenomenal results.

Using the DNS to Turn Failure into Success

Microsoft's belated conversion to the Internet as a top priority is a classic demonstration of sharing knowledge and new ideas to turn failure into success.

The Internet comeback started with a memo from one man, J. Allard, in January 1994. A week later, Steven Sinovsky made a report on booming Internet use at Cornell University. The two memos "set off a fire-storm" of emails. The development plan and action items were made visible to everybody. Teams were set up to develop the email-driven thinking and analysis; then "retreats" fleshed out the priorities and coordinated the response. The first major progress review in August 1994 saw "the newer employees running the show" as problems were solved on the run. By early 1995 every team's task was defined. Says Gates: "our DNS informed and propelled" the strategy unveiled that December.

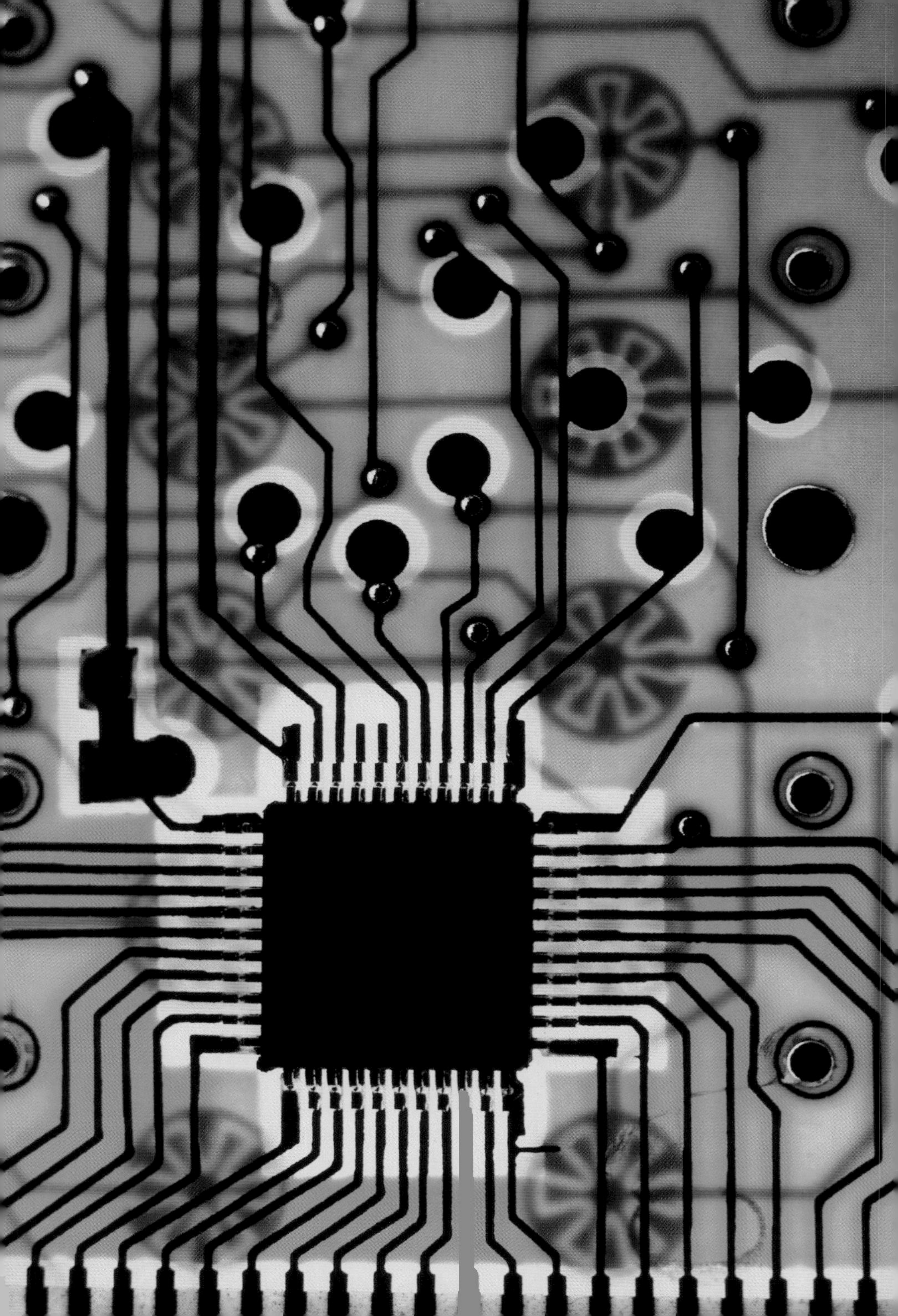

3

Developing software that sells

Organizing R & D around dedicated groups who concentrate on clear objectives • **Making many technological bets to improve the chances of success** • Why technology must be aimed at the highest possible targets • **Making your product the best, most useful, and cheapest** • Pursuing the continuous replacement of good products by something better • **Managing technology to attain and sustain a dominant proprietary position** • Translating great research into marketable products

Technology does not exist for its own sake, but for what it can do. At Microsoft, functionality is placed at the center of the research and development effort, which is organized around dedicated groups, who concentrate on clearly defined objectives. You do not seek breakthroughs, although you seize them with energy and enthusiasm if and when they arrive. You direct the effort at making major advances on your existing technological platforms – or other people's – to fulfill commercial aims. And you ensure that all necessary disciplines are available to you, preferably in-house.

This explains why, for example, Microsoft hired two husband-and-wife "statistical physicists" in 1997. *Fortune* magazine explained that they were seeking to "derive the observed behaviors of gases, liquids, solids, and other states of matter from the underlying microscopic worlds of molecules, atoms, and electrons." Their work involved the study of phenomena such as "independent percolation," which relates to "the distribution of oil in a porous medium to the distribution of matter in the galaxy."

Investing in research

Most research and development in the PC world is, in fact, development: basic research is rare, as it was at Microsoft until the late 1990s. Then Gates and his "chief technology officer," Nathan Myhrvold, began to build a chain of 645 researchers, placed at five centers around the world, including Microsoft headquarters in Redmond, Washington, and the famous university town of Cambridge in England.

Some of the brains assembled are very well known in microelectronics, including Gordon Bell, whose work on the VAX line of minicomputers for Digital Equipment

Creating the research lab
Gates meets Vice-Chancellor Professor Alec Broers and Professor Roger Needham of St. John's College, Cambridge, after investing $20 million in the computer research center at the university.

produced the world's first line of computers able to communicate easily with one another. Bell had, in fact, worked for Microsoft for some years before Gates decided to form "the next great research lab." He considered that $100 million a year was a relatively small investment in an enterprise that, one day, could pay off handsomely. Gates is mindful that the transistor sprang from research at Bell Laboratories, which was owned by the AT&T telecommunications giant.

Even more pertinent, today's PC, including the "graphical user interface," which made the Macintosh's operating system and Windows possible, was basically developed at the Palo Alto Research Center (PARC), founded and financed by Xerox Corporation. Obviously, such mighty breakthroughs are rare in the history of technology, let alone in that of any one company. But Gates believes in placing as many bets as possible, on the simple theory that this increases the chances of one bet winning colossally big. The bets, however, are carefully controlled – again on simple principles.

Directing research carefully

To determine an area of research you must first define a purpose on which to focus it. One of Microsoft's declared goals was to abolish the keyboard by enabling the PC to understand speech and to respond in speech. This led researchers into a number of disciplines: natural language processing, speech technology, user interface, and language-enabled applications. Because of its high value and wide scientific requirements, this project was assigned an especially large number of researchers in late 1997: 58, against a mere six trying to create better encryptions to make e-commerce more secure.

As it happens, Microsoft was beaten to the punch on the speech recognition project by other companies, including IBM, Dragon Systems, and Kurzweil, whose products were on sale while Microsoft was still researching. This is nothing new for Microsoft. Its research and development record has not been one of outstanding breakthroughs but of overhauling others by making more effective use of existing technology and then bringing more marketing muscle to bear. In 1992, Microsoft trailed Lotus in spreadsheets and WordPerfect in word processing. Microsoft's equivalent programs – Excel and Word – went on to surpass both by miles.

Joining research to commercial purpose is crucial, in Gates's view. He has fully learned the lesson of Xerox's astounding failure to market the PC developed at PARC. As Gates says, at PARC "the research was decoupled from product design": the PC technology could not find a commercial sponsor. At Microsoft Research, liaison with the product managers is a basic requirement. As an example, *Fortune* cites the independent researcher who, in 1995, developed a program that turned Internet chat into an interactive comic strip. A Microsoft product group heard of the idea, and took hold of both the research and the researcher to create Microsoft Chat 2.0.

A high degree of direction and organization (both of which come very naturally to Gates) is demanded by the sheer size of Microsoft's R & D operation. From the early days of Microsoft, Gates has practiced and preached the necessity of applying more than enough resources in manpower and money (which amount to the same thing) to solve the technological problems and supply the product needs. In late 1996, for example, he had 4,600 technologists working in the "platforms group," covering Windows, Explorer, and the other Internet applications. Another 1,800 were working on the desktop applications, which generated the highest profits.

Platforms cost Microsoft over $1 billion that year, desktop applications $400 million. Another $500 million went on

"... the tendency for successful companies to fail to innovate is just that: a tendency. If you're too focused on your current business, it's hard to look ahead...." *The Road Ahead*

projects, involving 2,000 technologists, that were not expected to contribute fully financially until the next millennium: these were interactive media, such as CD-ROM games and reference works, and online content. Then there was advanced technology and research, on which Microsoft spent a mere $25 million on 100 very expensive people, who were engaged in long-range research that might never pay off at all. Note the breakdown in the distribution of people: 75 percent on projects and products already generating vast profits, 24 percent on items expected to pay off in the near term, 1 percent on the bluer skies.

The disparity in money was equally striking: 20 times as much on interactive media as on speech synthesis and recognition and the other long-range research projects. The sheer quantity of the total effort is designed to be overwhelming. At the time when the Gates counterattack against Netscape had gathered full momentum, Microsoft's R & D staff numbered seven times more than the challenger's entire payroll, and the spending ran at nearly seven times Netscape's entire revenue.

Ambitious young partnership

Gates may not believe that success in managing technology is primarily a matter of massing men, women, and money, even though his actions certainly support that interpretation. His own experience would lead to a different conclusion: that quality counts for more than quantity. He and a friend from schooldays – Paul Allen – were in their early 20s and had just formed a partnership called Micro-Soft when Allen read about the first Intel microprocessor, the 4004. According to Gates, it was his partner who spotted the supreme importance of the invention – significantly, an unplanned by-product of Intel's unrelated work for a Japanese customer.

When Allen's belief, that the 4004 was only the beginning of major advances in microchip technology, proved true, the partners bought the greatly improved 8008 chip and used it for their first business project – Traf-O-Data – a program designed to help control Seattle's traffic. This project was unsuccessful. Moreover, it did not exploit the enormous potential of the microprocessor, which, Allen saw, promised far lower costs than conventional electronics. The partners concluded that their mistake had been to concentrate on "too narrow and challenging an area." They decided that in the future they would manage the new technology to hit the biggest possible targets. They then set their sights on nothing less than the whole market occupied by IBM and Digital Equipment.

Cofounder from school days

Like Bill Gates, Paul Allen was one of the group of computer geeks at Lakeside high school. In April 1975, he joined up with his old school friend to form a company called Micro-Soft.

Recognizing an opportunity

This might seem a breathtaking ambition. But even a small percentage of a vast market can mean huge income by start-up standards. Looking at the low cost and increasing power of microprocessors, "It seemed that [IBM and DEC] were screwed. We thought maybe they'd even be screwed tomorrow. We were saying, 'God, how come these guys aren't stunned? How come they're not just amazed and scared?'" Both those companies had access to the technology, better access than Gates and Allen by far, but the giants managed their technology toward a different destination: serving their existing corporate customers with their existing and constantly upgraded products.

Both companies had consequently missed the PC's precursors – the dedicated electronic word processors that made Wang rich. Wang in turn did not see (as Gates and Allen did) that general-purpose computers could process words and far more. But nobody at IBM or DEC, or Wang for that matter, had any great reason to take notice of the MITS Altair 8800: the "World's First Minicomputer Kit to Rival Commercial Models." That headline in *Popular Electronics* magazine in January 1975 inspired Gates and Allen to write a version of the well-known BASIC computer language for the machine to run on. They then persuaded MITS, a small Albuquerque company, to buy their version.

Later erroneous accounts describe Gates as having invented BASIC, which in fact he and Allen only adapted. This is the Gates pattern of technology management. Find an interesting technology and apply it to a new commercial purpose. Alternatively, find a new commercial purpose and look for the technology that will achieve it.

This second route became the dominant one for Microsoft. For example, the Japanese company Ricoh paid

Microsoft $180,000 to license every computer language the partners had – and then came back for more. Embarrassingly there wasn't any more. So Gates recalls asking, "What can we develop for you?" Ricoh responded with a list of software needs and Microsoft promised the company a package of products, including a word processor and a database. In reality the infant company could not deliver. They "had to go buy some of them from somebody else" – and even then the delivery was alarmingly late.

Competitive instinct

Sell now, make later became the established Microsoft pattern. It achieved its supreme moment with IBM, when two executives came to talk about buying Microsoft BASIC for the company's first PC (see p. 62). They took not only BASIC but two other languages. "It seemed just like Ricoh all over again," says Gates. "We had told IBM, 'Okay, you can have everything we make', even though we hadn't even made it yet." The two partners committed themselves to supplying IBM with an operating system two days before buying the necessary technology from another Seattle company.

At this point, another key element in Microsoft's successful business policy became critical: competitiveness. The Gates tenet is that being first is less important than being best, with best defined as providing the "biggest bang per buck" for the customer and for yourself.

"Getting in on the first stages of the PC revolution looked like the opportunity of a lifetime, and we seized it."
The Road Ahead

Setting the industry standard

Few people know that two other operating systems were created for the IBM PC: one by Digital Research – then the leading producer of microcomputer software – and the UCSD Pascal P-System. Gates overcame this opposition with a three-point plan, which is an extraordinarily simple, decisively strong blueprint for success:

- Make your product the best.
- Make your product the most useful.
- Make your product the cheapest.

The greater utility was achieved by helping other software companies to write applications that would work on the MS-DOS platform. The cheapness came from charging IBM a mere $80,000 for a perpetual, royalty-free right to use MS-DOS. This meant that IBM could charge customers only $60 or so for MS-DOS, compared to $450 for the UCSD Pascal P-System and some $175 for the Digital product. It was no contest. As the number of PCs and MS-DOS applications rose, the Microsoft partners achieved their commercial objective. The IBM PC, using their operating system, became the industry standard.

If your technology becomes the standard, you are by definition the industry leader. When Gates sees another company's product in a leadership position, his immediate reaction is to seek to usurp that role. The approach has not always succeeded. Gates went after the network market, led by Novell, with Microsoft Network – and failed. When the same thing happened in personal finance software, where Microsoft Money came nowhere near Intuit, Gates sought (and failed) to buy the latter. His competitive urge remains a huge driving force. He seldom gives up. It took all of five years before Microsoft Exchange became a real competitor to Lotus Notes in groupware.

When survival is at stake, Gates shows at its most powerful the force of technology focus. The most recent and striking example was the launch of Explorer as an Internet browser in competition with the deeply entrenched and threatening Netscape. In less than a year from December 7 1995 to the autumn of 1996, Gates forced through the development of a product at least as good as Netscape's. He then gave the browser away. Just as with the IBM PC, Gates managed the price of the product to create market penetration, reasoning that if you possess the market, you eventually possess the profits.

Extending the power base

The operating system base gives Gates an inestimable advantage over his competitors. By bundling Microsoft applications with the operating software, Microsoft can in effect lock rivals out of the market. Gates cannot do this without the cooperation of the PC makers. But a circle develops (benevolent for Gates, vicious for the competition): the more popular Gates's software becomes, the greater the incentive for PC manufacturers to include the application programs in their package.

The temptation to reinforce this incentive by unfair commercial pressure is evident. The antitrust (monopoly) charges brought against Microsoft in 1998 were largely concerned with whether or not that temptation had been sufficiently resisted. As an exercise in managing technology, however, the use of the operating system as foundation has been a model. Gates has reinforced that model by his exploitation of technological improvement.

No other industry has possessed the technological engine that drives profit in microelectronics: that engine is the continuous replacement of a perfectly good product by something that is better. The American car manufacturers in the 1960s tried to achieve the same result of "planned obsolescence" with styling. But the PC hardware and software industries apply the same principle with the far more powerful means of higher functionality. From microprocessors via PCs to software, customers are driven to upgrade their purchases in a process that seems without end.

Safeguarding a position

This upgrading entered a new dimension when Gates decided, with the launch of Windows in 1985, to add a graphical interface to IBM-compatible PCs. Once again, the technology did not originate with Microsoft. As noted, the graphical user interface was developed at PARC by Xerox and first exploited by Apple in 1984, with the Macintosh. What became two enormously lucrative Microsoft applications – Word and Excel – were also originally developed for the Mac. Microsoft's work with Apple on applications helped Gates to find a wonderful escape route from a joint product with IBM – OS/2, the operating system that was intended to replace MS-DOS.

While Microsoft has been and is involved in innumerable partnerships, its technology has always been managed to sustain its proprietary position – what it sells, it owns. That sovereign principle would not have applied with OS/2, a new system intended to protect and enhance the proprietary strength of IBM. Gates claims that all along the strategy of outflanking IBM never entered his mind. But the Windows strategy, in hindsight, has been even more beneficial to

Gates than his original IBM alliance. Again, tenacity was required: "The success of Windows was a long time coming," Gates acknowledges.

The delay was as much with applications providers as with customers. But as Windows won acceptance, the Microsoft applications, such as Word and Excel, after being developed to work with Windows, overtook products that did not. Reflecting upon this and other experiences, Gates has observed, accurately enough, that "translating great research into products that sell is still a big problem for many companies." In his case, it is the translation, rather than the greatness of the research, that has been decisive.

Ideas into action

- Assemble the best brains you can find for product development.
- Concentrate people and money on the most promising R & D objectives.
- Try to find interesting technologies and apply them to new purposes.
- Try to find new purposes and look for appropriate technology to fulfill them.
- Aim to give the customer the "biggest bang per buck."
- Seek ways to make your product indispensable to the buyers.
- Persevere tenaciously with new products until you get them right.

Making MS-DOS central to the IBM PC

Among all the sagas of start-up triumph, that of Bill Gates and Microsoft trumps them all. The pivotal moment came in 1980 when two IBM emissaries arrived in Seattle to quiz the infant firm about its software.

They initially talked about buying the Microsoft version of the BASIC language for the still-secret PC project. But when the IBMers went on to discuss two other languages, Gates told them, "okay, you can have everything we make." The major issue for the partners was whether to offer IBM an operating system as well. Although Gates was a little reticent, "we decided, why not?"

They had been talking to a local firm, Seattle Computer Products, about its Q-DOS (Quick and Dirty Operating System), which they thought could "probably" be adapted for IBM's purposes. To hold Seattle Computer Products' price for Q-DOS down to as little as $50,000, they kept IBM's interest secret from the vendor (they also poached its chief engineer, Tim Patterson). The partners then offered IBM a perpetual license to use the operating system, with no royalties, for only $80,000.

With both deals done, the partners started working day and night, not just on the software, which they renamed MS-DOS (Microsoft Disk Operating System), but also on the design of the PC. According to Gates, although working with IBM engineers, "by the end Paul [Allen] and I decided every stupid little thing about the PC: the keyboard layout, how the cassette port worked, how the sound port worked, how the graphics port worked."

They also successfully (and critically – leapfrogging the competition from Apple) encouraged IBM to use a more powerful, 16-bit chip. Although the pair got $186,000 for their contribution, they were not even invited to the official launch of what (to IBM's surprise, but not that of Gates) was the biggest instant hit in computing history.

Central force

Gates had a far stronger perspective on that history than IBM. To the latter, the PC was an "entry-level" product that would justify itself by leading on to sales of larger computers. To Gates, it

"... we practically gave the software to IBM. Giving software away to create strategic value has since become a well-established marketing technique in the industry, but it was uncommon at the time."
The Road Ahead

was the birth of a whole new world. "We could see that, with its reputation and its decision to employ an open design that other companies could copy, IBM had a real chance to create a new, broad standard in personal computing." Without that standard, the coming of Gates's vision – a computer on every desk and in every home – would be long delayed. With that standard, all his ambitions for Microsoft and the PC revolution could be realized.

It took only a year for Microsoft to oust the two other operating systems initially offered on the IBM PC (see p. 58). Gates today refutes the widely held view that Microsoft "somehow got the better of IBM," and that the latter should have taken full ownership of MS-DOS. Gates argues that the deal, which left Microsoft free to supply all IBM's rivals, enabled IBM to become "the central force in the PC industry." He is being disingenuous. That central force proved to be Microsoft.

Mastering the business

Bill Gates's career teaches unbeatable lessons in business management. Although he built his fortune on highly technical products, his business mastery is even more important than his technical skills. By using his basic strategy, you can emulate Microsoft's success in your company – and yourself.

Compete for success

Whatever business you are in, the principles for achieving market dominance are the same. Master your own market, using the six-part competitive strategy:

The Six-Part Strategy
1 Concentrate your effort on a market with large potential but few competitors.
2 Get in early and big.
3 Establish a proprietary position.
4 Protect that position in every way possible.
5 Aim for high gross margins.
6 Make the customers offers they cannot refuse.

The early success of Gates and his partner, Paul Allen – the result of supreme ambition grounded in reality – was founded on this strategy. It can be applied to anything from high-tech products to sausages – as long as they are a new, inimitable kind of sausage. Use technological advances to achieve non-technical commercial aims.

Plan strategically

The best strategies aim to give you a position of clear "competitive advantage" such as that that Gates enjoys. Use the matrix on the right to analyze your own strategy. Which of your products fits into which square? "Different and better" is by far the best.

Different and better	Different and worse
The Same and worse	The Same and better

Go for the best

For Gates, being the best is more important than being the first. Customers want "the biggest bang per buck" and will usually pay more for something that they perceive as better. Gates believes that you should continually invest resources in research and development to get the right products, and develop your products and services to find ways in which they can be constantly improved.

While not all Microsoft's products have achieved market leadership, in general they have been seen as sufficiently different – and effective – to support the quasi-monopoly that the company obtained through its connection with IBM.

Following the principles

Note the way in which Gates and Allen won that contract. These two absurdly young and confident entrepreneurs perfectly applied the six-part strategy outlined opposite:

- They pursued a potentially huge market (built on IBM's PC sales), in which they faced only two competitors.
- They got in first, even though they originally had no product.
- They kept the proprietary right to sell to anybody and everybody.
- They protected their IBM position by charging the lowest price for their product.
- They earned a high gross margin on sales to third parties.
- They made IBM an offer it could not refuse – a perpetual license to use MS-DOS, with no royalties.

Outwitting IBM

Gates and Allen gained a tremendous advantage from riding on the coattails of IBM, which made it much easier to pursue the six-point strategy.

Early on, Gates and Allen realized that the microcomputer would become powerful enough to challenge IBM. They dedicated themselves to ensuring success for IBM's PCs, knowing full well that "there were going to be clones." They "structured that original contract to allow them. It was a key point in the negotiations."

When IBM sought to attack the clones with new PCs and software, since Gates had to carry on working with IBM, he "sunk hundreds of millions of dollars" and countless worker-hours into the OS/2 joint venture. That folded in 1992, but Gates had won time to develop Windows. As a bonus, one OS/2 product became Windows NT.

1 Applying the strategy

At the outset, Microsoft's position was exceptionally favorable. The company entered on the ground floor of an industry of inexhaustible growth, and worked with a giant that depended entirely on outsiders such as Gates and Allen to make its PC project succeed.

Launching a business

You may not be able to make your fortune as easily as Gates and Allen did, but you can save yourself from losing one by asking yourself the same questions that Microsoft answered. Will you:

- Have a large enough market – now and in the probable future?
- Win a big enough share of the market to make a major impact on your business?
- Get in early enough?
- Be able to sustain a big enough effort?
- Establish a proprietary position that is based on being different and better?
- Be able to protect that position from challenge?
- Earn high gross margins at economical prices?
- Offer the customers a unique deal?

Many businesses launch ventures without posing these questions, let alone answering them. You need to be able to answer "Yes" to all eight questions. This may not be possible immediately – at first, Gates and Allen did not know whether their purchased product would work well enough for IBM's purposes. But going through the questions and changing your plans where necessary is an invaluable exercise. Approach it in a realistic but optimistic spirit: you are not trying to kill your idea but working to make it succeed.

Staying ahead

Keep asking the questions again and again as markets change and new technologies and new competitors arrive. Gates offers textbook examples of how to reposition your strategy as circumstances change; for example, breaking the umbilical cord with IBM, or reversing his stand on the Internet. Never allow past successes to lull you into a sense of security. The lesson is a hard one to master, but simple to remember: "If at first you *do* succeed, try, try again."

2 Building the brand

Every business is a "brand": the sum total of the perceptions of all its customers, employees, suppliers, etc. Work on achieving brand excellence for your company, and also for your personal "brand."

Focus on performance

To achieve brand excellence, performance is far more important than publicity. Gates won with the Windows brand by spotting an idea (from Apple) and acting on it. You can follow in his footsteps.

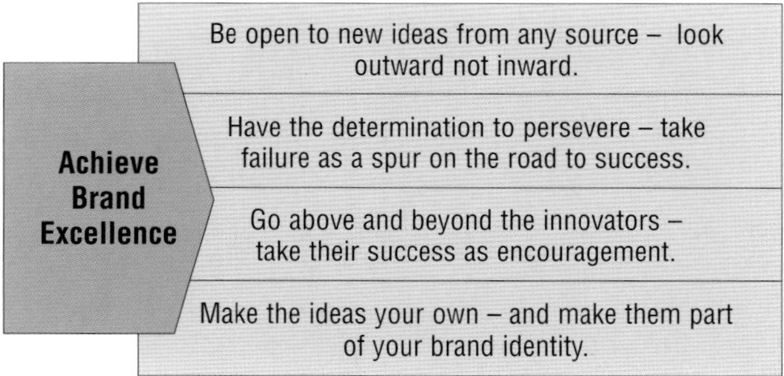

As a manager, you clearly need to achieve, support, and strengthen brand excellence in every way you can. But remember this applies not only to your business, but to your own "brand": the perceptions that others have of you and your performance. Think of yourself as "Myself Inc.," and apply to yourself the same brand-building strategy. Apply the four strategic aspects to your own personal career: they are highly effective.

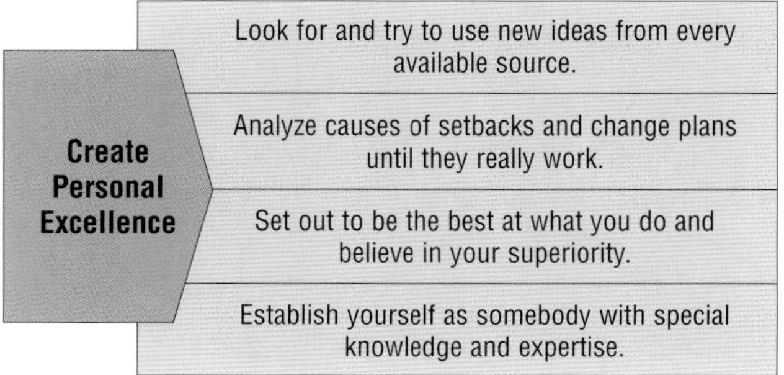

3 Leading decisively

Business success depends ultimately on leadership. But as a manager you have to grasp two apparently contradictory principles. Give clear command from the top, but harness as much collective effort as you can from all ranks of the organization.

Involving people

It is particularly important to get everyone involved if yours is a high-tech business, because you cannot possibly master all the technical knowledge – or do all the work – on your own. The key is to practice both "soft" and "hard" management.

The "soft" management approach

The soft style of management, which has influenced the open culture in Microsoft, focuses on collective effort. You should:

- Encourage a free-and-easy atmosphere.
- Create a flat structure with few levels of hierarchy.
- Split the company into small groups.
- Give groups well-defined tasks for which they are completely responsible.
- Encourage discussion and debate (especially by using email).
- Recognize and reward individual and team successes.

If your company does not have such an atmosphere, resist its rigidities as best you can.

The "hard" management approach

A proper exercise of control from the top is fundamental to effective management. Everyone in the company needs to know who exercises authority in each area of the organization.

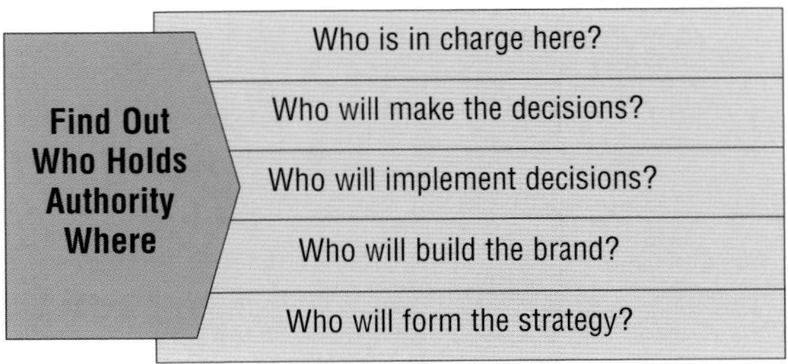

Delegating leadership

In Microsoft's case, the clear answer to every question, before the 1999 restructuring, was Bill Gates. Somebody, to use a Gates phrase, must be capable of an "act of leadership." But many other people can and must contribute before any final decision is made. The issue is how widely and deeply the leader delegates, and how big a part he or she plays before having the last word.

Giving autonomy

In the Microsoft restructuring, eight autonomous divisions were established under separate managers. Giving them the authority to lead was partly designed to stop Gates continuing to take on too much himself, which had the effect of slowing down the decision-making process at Microsoft to an alarming degree.

To stop that happening to you, make sure that you apply the five Es that are basic to Microsoft. It will create an atmosphere in which everybody can contribute to success, and which motivates and stretches everybody, including you.

Applying The Five Es
1 EMPOWER people to undertake tasks for which they are competent and to see those tasks through from start to finish.
2 Adopt an EGALITARIAN attitude toward everybody, and insist that they do likewise.
3 Place an extraordinary EMPHASIS on performance, first making clear precisely what is expected.
4 Use ELECTRONIC means to send and receive messages to and from anybody, and maintain continuous, open, constructive debate on issues of interest or importance.
5 ENRICH people with rewards for success, using not only financial rewards but also praise and recognition.

If you are not already working in a five-E company, reconsider your position. Decide whether you – and your staff – are able to give of your best, and whether your effort is recognized. If not, think seriously about moving Myself Inc. to a new home.

4

Dividing, delegating, and leading

Why even the most successful companies must reinvent themselves • **How managing with the force of facts requires information technology** • Five people e-policies: enrichment, egalitarianism, emphasis on performance, email, empowerment • **Using email to get simultaneous debate of issues at many levels** • Achieving a small-company culture by dividing to keep units small • **Why Microsoft is always two years away from crisis** • Exploiting opportunities and leading decisively

In the spring of 1999, Bill Gates's approach to management underwent a crucial change. The company was split into eight new divisons, each run by executives who, in theory, had all the autonomy required to manage their empires. The reorganization was required to implement "Vision Version 2" ("VV2"), which reorients Microsoft from personal computers to all forms of information software and hardware, and focuses the company around the needs of customers. As Gates explained, "Even the most successful companies must constantly reinvent themselves."

Until VV2, though, the Microsoft management style had not been invented, in the sense of deliberate planning. It inevitably reflected the personality of its founders, Gates in particular. He first established a working relationship with Paul Allen, and then went on to surround himself with people and systems who suited his personal style.

Learning to manage

In the early days of Microsoft, the style was "a little loose," in Allen's words. The partners shared every decision and alternated tasks so often that who did what remained unclear. Allen, however, tended toward the new technology and new products, and Gates toward "negotiations and contracts and business deals." The division of labor is interesting in view of Gates's later reputation as the supreme nerd, the man to whom technology is all.

At Microsoft, the technology is managed toward well-defined business ends, acquiring and retaining customers, and creating and defending profit streams. The systems, largely digital, on which the organization runs, have evolved according to need and are not based on any theory.

That's understandable when you consider that, as managers, the pair were largely self-taught, with experience their main teacher. Gates recalls their approach: "Okay, we have to hire people; so what do we do? Okay, we're going to rent space; how do we do that? Okay, we're going to do contracts with people now; I'd get advice from my dad." William Henry Gates II was a leading corporate lawyer in Seattle, so the advice was undoubtedly sound.

Founding management style

Gates and Allen were very bright, "super-smart" computer geeks, people who could take a computer apart, write software, and understand new technology. As they developed management skills on top of their technical expertise, they sought other technical experts, some of whom, over time, would likewise evolve into managers. Hiring managers is not Microsoft's way. Even today the company hires people for their ability as marketers, programmers, content providers. Microsoft management is highly professional, but it is inseparable from other professional skills – much as in the early days.

Two other lasting features of Microsoft management style also developed during the early days. Decisions were made in very long discussions – known as "marathons" – that lasted for six to eight hours. They are still a regular occurrence today. And the pair expected others to copy their habit of working extremely hard and long. Gates has never lost the habit. One awesome description of his progress on a world tour in 1997 reveals an extraordinary ability to cram a host of activities into the day, with no time wasted, and with the main objective – selling more Microsoft software – never escaping from sight.

Sloan as role model

Hard work and long hours, however, do not explain how to manage a company doubling every 18 months and employing (at the end of 1998) 30,000 people. Gates is evidently a highly competent manager who employs competent subordinates and deploys them effectively. But "management" does not figure in the index of either of his books. Nor is Gates featured as a role model in management studies. That is probably because Gates does not subscribe to any particular management theories or follow any role model himself – with the exception of the long-dead Alfred P. Sloan, the man who made General Motors great.

What impressed Gates about Sloan (as gleaned from the latter's *My Years at General Motors*, 1963) was his "positive, rational, information-focused leadership." Gates is especially interested in the personal attention that Sloan paid to the dealer network, and his use of a standardized accounting system that gave every dealer and every employee "categorized numbers in precisely the same way." Sloan's personal visits to dealers (imitated by Gates in his world tours) appealed to Gates's constant urge to sell software. As for the reporting, that feeds his business, too. "To manage with the force of facts...," writes Gates, "requires information technology."

Until 1999, Gates had never publicly shown any interest in the structural principles that Sloan famously applied to

"It's inspiring to see in Sloan's account of his career how positive, rational, information-focused leadership can lead to extraordinary success."
Business @ the Speed of Thought

turn a sprawling bunch of car companies into an organized and highly effective corporation. The VV2 reorganization, however, follows Sloan's principles to the letter, dividing the company into separate business groups and, says Gates, "holding the leaders of our new business divisions accountable to think and act as if they are independent businesses." The crucial issue here is whether Gates and his recently named president, Steve Ballmer, can stand aside enough to allow their managers genuine independence of thought and action.

According to *Business Week* (August 1999), before VV2, with "decisions large and small being funneled to the top, the pair became a bottleneck." This contributed to Microsoft's "snail's pace for decision making." Compared to the hectic pace of the Internet world, Microsoft had begun to look "sluggish, even bureaucratic." The reorganization aimed "to free Microsoft from its bureaucratic morass" and to free executives from a constant top-down scrutiny that "undermined the confidence of managers below."

Management involvement

The reality of the pre-VV2 Microsoft is expressed by a former top officer at Microsoft, Mike Maples: if Gates or other senior managers "want to review where the teams are, [they] can ask to do so." They not only could, they did. Maples noted that the teams "never have to wait until they've been reviewed... they just go from start to finish by themselves." But that only happened if the senior managers did not get involved: mostly they did, and some considerable top involvement will surely remain basic to Microsoft management. On his own estimate, before VV2 Gates was spending 70 percent of his time on reviewing teams, holding two or three such meetings a day, keeping numbers low, and running the discussions in an informal, non-hierarchical, but highly penetrating, business-oriented style.

Gates inadvertently reveals how much he and other top people have been accustomed to intervene – or interfere – in passages from *Business @ the Speed of Thought* that are designed to show Microsoft management at its best. In these accounts, Gates tells how he met with headquarters colleagues to look closely at the "numbers" of all the overseas subsidiaries; how he got involved in a change to the way these "financials" were reported to give him a faster, clearer picture; and how he conducted executive reviews to consider, for example, the detail of a project to identify the best US cities for a new marketing campaign.

Until a customer CEO advised him to stop, Gates even passed top people's expense accounts, including Ballmer's. He knew all about the system for hiring, managing, and paying temporary staff – and so on. All this immersion in operating detail, however, is now supposed to belong to the past. The leaders of the eight divisions are enfranchised to exercise autonomous authority over operations, reporting to Ballmer.

Microsoft people policies

This new empowerment adds a fifth E to the four that are well-established aspects of Microsoft's basic people policies. The five Es are:

- Enrichment
- Egalitarianism
- Emphasis on performance
- Email
- Empowerment

Enrichment recruits, motivates, and retains people, not through high salaries but by the prospect of large capital gains. When employees are rewarded with the stock of the century, this wealth must be a potent means of binding them to the company and binding the company together. Egalitarianism treats all employees as equal and largely ignores all behaviors except for performance, which is (in both senses) highly stressed. In his book, *Company Man* (1995), Anthony Sampson quotes an employee's description of the egalitarian approach: "They're not interested in your clothes, your style, or when and how you work: you can work at home all the time. But they're sure interested in what you produce. They review your progress twice a year, with marks from one to five. Four means exceptional; one means you're out."

What Sampson calls "a casual, egalitarian style" fits Gates like a glove. The glove, as the above quote indicates, conceals an iron fist; that is, the emphasis on performance. You do not work for Microsoft unless you are prepared to work a 60-hour week at times, and in exceptional times, 100 hours or more. Nor do you live high: when the chairman and CEO travels economy class (business class only on international flights), you do not fly higher than the billionaire – even if you are a millionaire yourself. The millions used not to affect employee retention, either: the possessors could all retire, and now some choose to.

Using email purposefully

The former high loyalty survived Gates's abrasive style and very open intolerance of what he calls "stupid" thinking. His fierce criticism is expressed both verbally and through the fourth distinguishing factor of Microsoft management: electronic mail. The use of email, according to Mike Maples, helps to accomplish several of Gates's management polices, which are:

- Eliminate politics, by giving everybody the same message.
- Keep a flat organization in which all issues are discussed openly.
- Insist on clear and direct communication.
- Prevent competing missions or objectives.
- Eliminate rivalry between different parts of the organization.
- "Empower" teams to do their own thing.

Maples adds that email "encourages people at multiple levels to enter the debate simultaneously, so you don't have to have a workgroup debate an issue, take it to the manager, debate the issue again, take it to another manager, for more debate, and filter it up the chain of command. Instead, decision making happens in real time with people at all levels in the organization." That organization is dedicated, according to its founder, to the quest for an "atmosphere in which creative thinking thrives and employees develop to the fullest potential."

Small-company dynamic

Gates achieves this culture, he writes, by the "way Microsoft is set up... you have all the incredible resources of a large company yet you still have that dynamic small-group, small-company feeling where you can really make a difference." He envisages this set-up as a form of dialogue. The individuals produce ideas, and Microsoft responds by making it possible for those ideas to become reality. "Our strategy has always been to hire strong, creative employees, and delegate responsibility and resources to them so they can get the job done," adds Maples.

To achieve the small-company culture, Gates keeps units small. As soon as a team gets beyond a comfortable size (say, 30 people), it is divided. Gates is a believer in controllable size and in "project management," in which you place tasks under leaders who in turn subdivide the task among subordinates who work in a coordinated program to achieve the desired result. Gates then encourages constructive controversy between the divided parts of the corporation, and cements the latter with a central vision as well as personal enrichment – rewarding success but swiftly penalizing failure.

Managing change

The constant formation of new units is one means of gearing up for change. Gates sees Microsoft as an agent of transformation in a society that has reached an "inflection point." He says that "the human experience is about to change." "The transition will be exciting and historic, empowering to individuals and brutal to some companies and institutions that don't keep pace." According to Gates, if you do not practice the change management that looks after the future, the future will not look after you. And you dare not miss the moment: "Once certain thresholds are crossed, the way we work and live will change – forever," he warns.

Gates has said that Microsoft is always two years away from crisis; that is, failure to react to discontinuous change. The experience of nearly missing the explosive take-off of the Internet (see p. 106) has not been forgotten: "That kind of crisis is going to come up every three or four years," he acknowledges. His recipe for dealing with discontinuous change is to "try and make sure today's not the day we miss the turn in the road. Let's find out what's going on in speech recognition or in artificial intelligence. Let's make sure we're hiring the kinds of people who can pull those things together, and let's make sure we don't get surprised."

The new preface of the second edition of his first book, *The Road Ahead* (1996), gives Gates's views on change: "I work in the software industry, where change is the norm. A popular software title, whether it's an electronic encyclopedia, a word processor, or an online banking system, gets upgraded every year or two with major new features and continuous refinements. We listen to customer feedback and study new technology opportunities to determine the improvements to make." But this, of course, is not discontinuity: it is the continuous improvement that the Japanese call *kaizen*.

What forced Gates's about turn on the Internet was what the Japanese call *kaikaku*, or radical change, or "sea changes," as they are known at Microsoft. Gates told Geoffrey James, author of *Giant Killers* (1997), that the "most important and exciting part of my work as chairman is recognizing [sea changes] and articulating the opportunities they present to each person in the company.

"One thing is clear: we don't have the option of turning away from the future.... No one can stop productive change in the long run because the marketplace inexorably embraces it." *The Road Ahead*

We then empower employees with as much information and as many productivity tools as possible, so they can achieve results within the framework of that vision."

Decisive leadership

That key element of Gates's role as CEO – taking all the big strategic decisions – will surely continue. *The Wall Street Journal* pieced together a full account of how Gates handled the discussion on a crucial issue: should Microsoft continue with Windows, using that as an entry point for the Internet, or should it launch a "cross-platform" replacement, using Java software, that would run on all computers – as many corporate customers wanted? For months the opposing camps wrangled over email, exemplifying Gates's principle of letting people fight issues out.

Then, in March 1997, a meeting of top managers heard Gates deliver his verdict. He did not "discuss" the Java idea: he shot it down in flames. "In no uncertain terms, Mr. Gates had decided to protect Windows at all costs," the article concluded. The 2,000 employees in the Internet group were "reassigned," and two key teams were returned to the Windows group. This vital decision was implemented with a massive drive to take the Web browser market from Netscape by bundling Microsoft's rival Explorer with Windows – a strategy that backfired in the antitrust action of 1998 (see p. 59).

Important Microsofties were badly bruised by the decision: the losing senior executive in this struggle had previously masterminded the enormously profitable launch of Windows 3.0. The strategy could also still backfire in the marketplace, if rival attempts to launch a cross-platform attack on Windows should succeed. But the episode demonstrates five central principles in Gates's theory and practice of management. They are:

- The boss is the boss.
- As boss, he listens to all opposing arguments, and then makes a clear, unarguable decision.
- He makes sure that the decision is followed through.
- The boss concentrates on solutions that will best protect and profit the company's proprietary position.
- He takes the decision that embodies the best trade-off between risk and return.

Keeping the wheel turning

Gates's role is not so much "recognizing sea changes and articulating the opportunities they present" as exerting leadership. Spotting major trends is part of leadership, but only part. Gates will speak of an "act of leadership," meaning that he takes charge and wills what he wants to happen. But "leadership," like "management," does not figure in Gates's writings. That is because he is not interested in the theory of leadership, only in its practice. Without this particular leader, however, the Microsoft wheel would lack its vital hub. Would it keep turning?

The system easily surmounted the early retirement of Paul Allen. Gates says: "my best business decisions have had to do with picking people. Deciding to go into business with Paul Allen is probably at the top of the list, and subsequently, hiring a friend – Steve Ballmer – who has been my primary business partner ever since." This partnership with somebody totally trusted and totally committed, with the same vision, but some difference in skills, is the only balance to the total decision power of the chief executive.

Gates sums up the partner's role: "Some of the ideas you run past him, you know he's going to say, 'Hey, wait a minute, have you thought about this and that?'" While the point is true and valuable, Gates's words do not suggest that he gets tremendous opposition, even from this source. He argues that he and his top managers spend time talking about succession issues, and the importance of growth in making Microsoft "able to spawn off very, very big jobs for people." But the question must be whether the biggest job of all isn't too big – even after the implementation of Vision Version 2 – for anybody except Bill Gates.

Ideas into action

- Hire the brightest people with the greatest specific "skills sets."
- Improve management information to get exactly what you need – fast.
- Treat everybody as a close colleague from whom you expect plenty.
- Keep the organization flat, using email to debate issues openly.
- Watch out for radical change, and change radically to meet it.
- Keep teams small and delegate responsibility and resources to make them effective.
- When it's time to lead, make sure you lead decisively.

Making a success of Windows NT

The story of Windows NT shows the Gates philosophy working at its best. This operating system, designed to take sophisticated (corporate) users into the 21st century, came out in 1993 and was an instant flop.

Windows NT missed its targets and market so badly that wags called it "Windows Not There." Any conventional management would have given up then and there, and withdrawn the product. But one of Gates's major principles is that you never give up without a fight, and, if you fight well enough, you won't need to give up at all.

Three years on, Microsoft had established Windows NT as one of its key products and major growth areas: a billion-dollar business whose sales doubled in 1996 and have soared ever since. The winning approach exemplifies another pillar of Gates's philosophy. Give the problem to the best person you can find and tell the appointee to fix it in their own way. A key Microsoft executive, Jim Allchin, NT's chosen savior, has observed: "some other companies would have said, 'I give up'." Instead, the NT team used failure as the springboard for recovery.

This attitude accords perfectly with the view of a previous king of computing, Thomas Watson of IBM, who remarked: "That's where success is. On the far side of failure." Allchin systematically established connections with the engineers and customers who had been woefully neglected during the $500 million development program for NT. He reacted to every criticism, including those in the trade press, not with denial, but with immediate action. As the software improved, corporate buyers were won over – and NT's subsequent triumph has been founded on the booming market for servers.

Taking decisive action

The difficulty of getting acceptable technical performance was very considerable: for example, 16 programmers had to be hired just to quicken little pieces of the NT code. Gates has a false reputation as a technological genius. He is not. It was the non-technical triple whammy of

knowing what to do, knowing how to do it, and actually doing it that produced the NT bonanza. Without that, Gates would have been far worse positioned for his Internet strategy (see p. 106). NT has 38.3 percent of the market in operating systems for corporate networks and Web servers. The penetration is far below Microsoft's 90 percent of the PC operating systems and applications market. But without NT and its overdue successor, the Windows 2000 application, Gates could not hope to master the market for large Websites and corporate computing centers. And Windows 2000 has been another model of persistence – five years in the making.

"Once you embrace unpleasant news not as a negative but as evidence of a need for change, you aren't defeated by it. You're learning from it." *Business @ the Speed of Thought*

Similar benefit is available to any manager in any industry who is prepared to recognize harsh reality, take criticism on the chin, and act on the corollary to Murphy's Law. The law states that "whatever can go wrong, will." The Gates corollary says that "whatever goes wrong can be made right." Don't deny, bite the bullet, and even abject failure can be turned into success.

Making the future happen

A "vision" is a call to action. The original Bill Gates vision – "a PC on every desk and in every home, using Microsoft software" – was specific, highly ambitious, and clearly linked to the company. It contrasts strongly with the vague visions drawn up by many large companies. Follow Microsoft's example and invent your own future.

Get ahead of the game

The purpose of a vision is to train your sights on achieving a future that is better than your present – not by small degrees but by orders of magnitude. With this mind-set you (like Gates) win an enormous advantage over other people who are not purposeful and progressive. Draw up your own vision:

- Take a piece of paper.
- Write across the top where you want yourself (and/or your business) to be in no less than five years' time.
- Write across the bottom – with merciless accuracy – where you are right now.
- Fill the space in-between with the steps you need to take in order to move from the bottom of the page to the top.

The whole exercise should take no more than an hour, though you may well find that the most difficult part of the task is starting.

Make things happen

A lot of managers are reluctant to take part in this exercise. If this includes you, ask yourself why:

- Are you just unambitious?
- Do you find it hard to think ahead?
- Are you reluctant to confront hard truths about the present?
- Are you put off by the major tasks and hard work that may be needed to create your future?
- Do you just prefer simply to wait on events?

If Gates and Allen had answered "yes" to any of these questions, the Microsoft phenomenon would never have been born. Be ambitious about your goals, think about the future, learn to face realities, and be prepared to work hard to make things happen.

1 Setting your goals

Do you set evolutionary or revolutionary goals? In fact, to be successful, you must do both. Improve your products or services on a continuous basis to remain competitive, and launch totally new products or services to seize the chance of winning big.

Go for mega-aims

Most R&D at Microsoft has involved evolutionary improvement. You also need to look for better ways of doing what you are doing already. But mega-prizes are only possible with mega-aims: what have been called "big, hairy audacious goals."

Recognizing Big, Hairy Audacious Goals
They make a very large difference to future success.
They stretch you well beyond the present levels of achievement.
They involve a considerable degree of risk.
They include major tasks that you have never previously accomplished.
They appear "impossible" in the eyes of others, including competitors.

Revolutionize your thinking

Typical examples of audacious goals at Microsoft were the offer of MS-DOS for the IBM PC, and the investment in Windows and Internet Explorer. Each of these developments set the organization in a new direction and radically changed its prospects.

Big, hairy, audacious goals may look frightening at first sight. But sometimes investing in them is the only way you can reach your revolutionary destination. Act without fear:

- Exploit the exceptional motivation of the big prize.
- Grab opportunities that you might otherwise have missed.
- Approach new tasks with new ideas.

Remember that you can often achieve far more than you actually expect of yourself. In addition, the perceived "impossibility" of your audacious goals will deter many other companies from competing effectively against you.

2 Managing by fear

To make the future happen, you need confidence: but fear is also valuable. It is a vital element in Gates's approach to business. He regards Microsoft as an underdog. Emulate his attitude: fear the competition, and you will be unlikely to fall into complacency.

Believe in the opposition

Many managers are all too eager to write off the competition. That leads them either to delay response or, still worse, not to respond at all. It is very dangerous to underestimate competitors. On the contrary, you should always believe that the opposition is capable of:

- Doing the impossible
- Defeating you
- Destroying your success

When Microsoft attacked the browser market, which was totally occupied by Netscape, the latter believed that the attack could never succeed. But with Netscape charging for Navigator, Microsoft offered Explorer for free. Had Netscape responded to the challenge by immediately abandoning its prices, Microsoft Explorer would have faced a far harder task.

Stay ahead of the game

Even more damaging, Netscape did not maintain a clear product lead over Explorer: it failed to make evolutionary improvements. Failure to keep updating and improving your product runs unacceptable risks. It may make recovery difficult, if not impossible. To avoid this situation in your own business, keep asking your customers (not yourself) how well or badly they rate the products or services you offer – in detail.

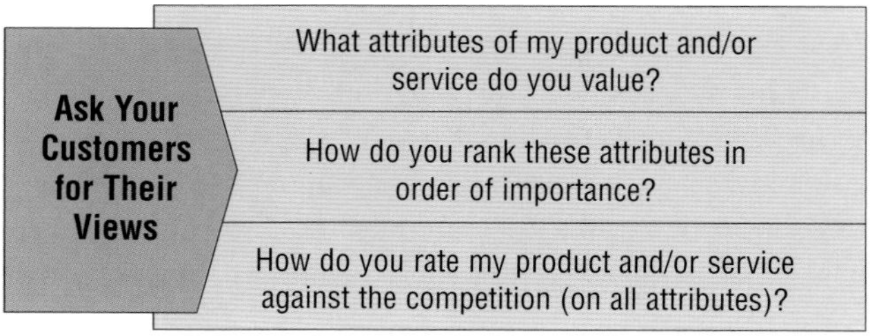

Ask Your Customers for Their Views

- What attributes of my product and/or service do you value?
- How do you rank these attributes in order of importance?
- How do you rate my product and/or service against the competition (on all attributes)?

Keeping ahead

This analysis will immediately show where you have an advantage over the competition. But you can only keep one step ahead of the competition by deciding how to add value for your customers.

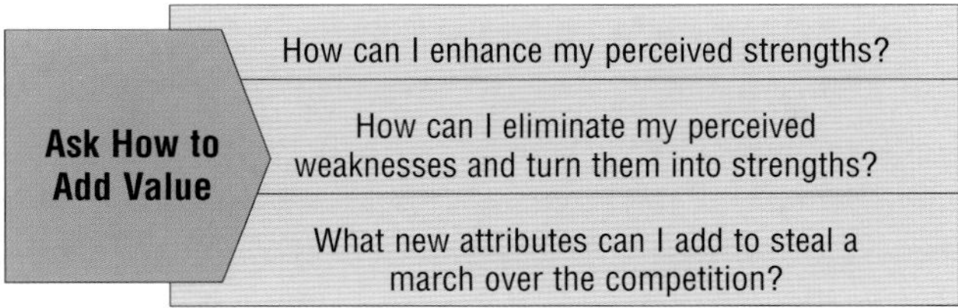

Paranoia helps you to tackle your task with real vigor. It did not avert Gates's near-fatal reluctance to see the overwhelming importance of the Internet. Gates had huge financial and technological resources to help him recover. You do not. Leaving well enough alone, although tempting, may not be good enough at all. It is a far riskier policy than making intelligent changes.

Taking risks

One of the greatest fears is of taking risks. Logically, there is only one risk: that of being wrong. You can make mistakes in:

- Calculating the value of an idea
- Planning how to exploit the idea
- Implementing the plans

These risks can never be eliminated. But you must be sure that fear of risk is not a cover for lack of confidence in your own abilities. Use the fear of competition to overcome the fear of risks, keeping in mind Gates's words: "If you decline to take risks early, you'll decline in the market later."

Healthy paranoia

The principles that apply to corporations are just as important for Myself Inc. You need a healthy paranoia that does not impair confidence, but keeps you on your toes. See any competition you face as potentially formidable and use the threat to motivate you to improve. Take very seriously the perceptions of your customers – and work relentlessly to shift those perceptions in your favor.

3 Owning the customer

Gates ensured that IBM PCs came only with the Microsoft operating system, which meant that all IBM-compatible PCs also had to use MS-DOS. The PC customer had no choice but to "buy" Microsoft's product. Like Gates, strive to bind the customer to you as closely as possible to establish unique market strength and secure your future.

Set the standard

It is unlikely that you have or could create a built-in position of such power as Microsoft's. Still seek to ensure that your product is so good that customers can see no reason to buy anyone else's. Gates would never have succeeded if Microsoft's products had been markedly inferior to those of the competition. MS-DOS was good enough to deter purchasers from demanding something else.

You need to give the customer reasons to buy only from you even when there are plenty of options. Gates's object was to make Microsoft the industry leader by:

- Offering the best products
- Making its products the most useful
- Keeping prices below the competition.

Do not take "best," "most useful," and "below the competition" for granted. You can be very wrong on all three counts unless you regularly complete the "ask your customers" exercise on page 88 and, most important, then act on any competitive weaknesses.

Creating Captive Customers

Getting your "business model" right is vital. That means not only the right relationship between costs and prices but the right route to retaining customers.

King C. Gillette had dozens of rivals for the safety razor market. Although safety razors had advantages over the cutthroat, they cost $5 – five times a day's wage. The Gillette product was more expensive to make than others, but no better. All the same, Gillette swept the market. He sold the razor far below cost, but designed it so that only his patented blades could be used. He sold these at a 400 percent mark-up. But customers happily paid five cents a blade because, with six or seven uses, each shave cost only a cent, which compared well with the 10 cents charged by barbers. Gillette had created captive customers by pricing shaves, not razors.

Analyze the market

You cannot sustain a dominant position in the marketplace with your product or service without having first analyzed carefully your customers and competitors. Find out more about customers – their perceptions and demands – by asking four more questions:

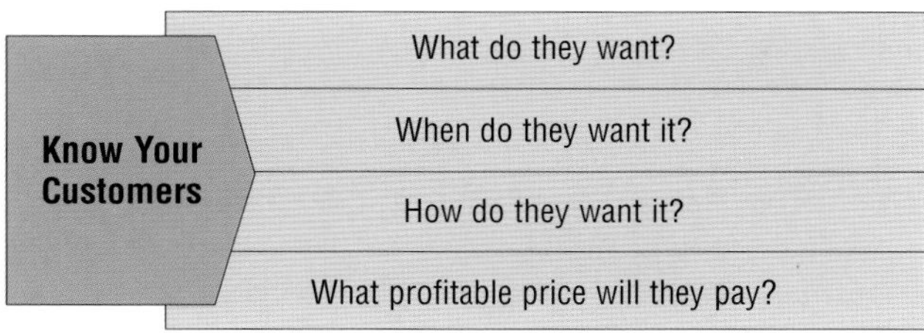

Provide value

Keep checking that you are meeting the demands of your customers. Microsoft overcomes the last hurdle – giving customers an acceptable yet profitable price – by "bundling" much of its software into the PC package. Customers are therefore unaware of the price.

In most cases, that is an impossible ideal. But it is in your interest to keep price out of the decision to buy. If customers have strong enough reasons for buying your products, they will be relatively indifferent to price – so making your life much easier.

Build on your assets

Think of the customer as your greatest asset – then think how to build on that asset. Gates did so by adding hugely profitable applications (such as Word and Powerpoint) to MS-DOS. To see where you can build, draw a square and complete the following customer/product matrix:

- Enter existing customers along the top line.
- Put existing products down the left side.
- Mark off which customers take which products.

How can you fill in the blanks? Your first aim is to sell more existing products to existing customers. New products and new customers are vital, but harder to win, and they take longer to make a profit. Learn from Microsoft, which sometimes failed existing customers but made golden profits by correcting that failure.

1.0 μF
63-B
WIMA
0.47
63-B
WIMA
B3
0.47
B3

5

Turning vision into value

Focusing vision on what you know and understand for maximum effectiveness • **How Gates got the Internet wrong – and then got it right** • Chasing "big, hairy audacious goals" to achieve market leadership • **Backing up vision with the necessary resources, capability, and energy to succeed** • Learning from making mistakes – and admitting that you made them • **Developing the right subordinate visions by turning to the customer** • Viewing Microsoft as "always kind of an underdog thing"

Gates regards vision as opportunity. His intuitive belief that personal computing was the future was certainly visionary. But, as he points out, "vision is free. And it's therefore not a competitive advantage in any way, shape, or form." Unless your vision translates into a marketable product or service, it has no value. If your central vision is tightly focused on what you know and understand, you can develop enough momentum to correct your inevitable misreadings of a fast-moving future.

The core of Bill Gates's thought is an intense belief that the future is progress. In his philosophy, the meaning of human life, society, the economy, technology, and business lies in sustained, vigorous, forward movement. He applies this credo strongly to his business. He expects the technology to become obsolete and to be replaced. He expects the business to mutate as it grows. He believes that change is inherent in all organisms, and that the great manager and the great business proactively turn change to their advantage.

Poor predictive powers

Vision is not prediction. Gates is a prime proof of the dictum of Alan Kay, one of the great intellectual fathers of the PC, that "the best way to predict the future is to invent it." Gates made the future happen by the commercial acumen and drive he brought to the technology solutions that suited his interests. His predictive powers, however, have often failed him, most notably over the all-encompassing future of the Internet.

Gates received criticism amounting to ridicule for the omission of the Internet from the first edition of *The Road Ahead.* He was apparently blind to the fact that the information highway led through the Internet. The book was published in 1995. In the previous spring, according to Gates, Microsoft was betting that the Internet would be "important some day.... But we didn't expect that within two years the Internet would captivate the whole industry and the public's imagination.... Seemingly overnight people by the millions went on to the Internet."

By 1996, when the second edition of the book was published, it was "no exaggeration to say that virtually everything Microsoft does these days is focused in one way or another on the Internet." This astonishing turnabout explains much about "vision" (one of the most used and over-used words in modern management) and much about Gates himself. In *Business the Bill Gates Way* (1999), Des Dearlove writes that Gates regards himself as "an expert in unraveling the technological past from the technological future." His "talent is for understanding what's just around the corner."

That description is wholly contradicted by the Internet story, when the technological future and what was actually happening, let alone just around the corner, eluded Gates for a significant time. The same episode also contradicts Gates's own philosophy of risk-taking: "You can't look at just the past or current state of the market. You have to also look at where it's likely to go, and where it might go under certain circumstances, and then navigate your company based on your best predictions. To win big, sometimes you have to take big risks."

"The Internet had burst into the public's awareness, and the perception was that Microsoft hadn't been invited to the party.... The Internet signified our doom."
Business @ the Speed of Thought

Focusing on the drawbacks

In putting the Internet on the back burner, Gates was influenced by the drawbacks then prevailing. The technology could not support "video conferencing and high-bandwidth applications such as video-on-demand – to say nothing of the needs for security, privacy, reliability, and convenience." Gates also looked too long at the past: "the years of waiting for online services to catch on had made us conservative in our estimate of how soon significant numbers of people would be using interactive networks."

There were also "irritating deficiencies," which caused complaint. The Internet needed faster modems, cheaper communications switches, more powerful PCs in more places, and "richer content." A true visionary, however, would have ignored these quibbles and concentrated on what the Internet really represented: a universal network. As the prime advocate of networking, Gates should have been better placed to spot this future (and to make it happen). The true visionary would also have been encouraged by precedent.

Looking for patterns in the past

The world had seen a previous example of a promising technology with serious limitations that seemed to restrict its value and market. But the deficiencies did not prevent rapid take-off and, as they were remedied, the market exploded. Gates knew all about this precedent. It was the IBM and IBM-compatible PC market, the expansion of which had made him and Microsoft so rich (see p. 26). Extrapolation of the past into the future can be highly misleading, but looking for patterns in the past can be highly illuminating.

A fresh face for computing
The graphical user interface developed at PARC transformed the early PCs, which were not very user-friendly, requiring skills that were counterintuitive and hard to learn for most people.

As Gates has written: "Ironically, when a technology reaches critical mass its weaknesses and limitations almost become strengths as numerous companies, each trying to stake a claim in what quickly turns into a gold rush, step forward to fix the deficiencies." That analysis is perfectly correct. It follows that the task of the visionary is to spot the build-up to critical mass before it occurs, in order to stake the first claim and mine the richest seam of gold.

Taking big risks

When Gates writes about risk, he implies that Microsoft is just such a visionary organization. He states in *Business @ the Speed of Thought*: "To be a market leader, you have to have what business writer and consultant Jim Collins calls 'big, hairy audacious goals'." Gates counts the foundation of Microsoft as just such a venture – a "big bet." Only in hindsight, he argues, does Microsoft's success look preordained. At the time, "most people scoffed." But any company starting at any time in any industry is embarking on a "hairy audacious" venture. It is only in hindsight, if the venture succeeds, that its founders appear to have had vision.

The real problems arise when success has come, and when the successful market leader is confronted with a new, disruptive technology. "Many industry leaders hesitated to move to new technologies for fear of undercutting the success of their existing technologies," explains Gates. This was the case with IBM. That fear explains why it so underestimated the PC market and thus blinded itself to the consequences of its naïve deal with Bill Gates (see p. 63). As he says, the hesitant leaders "learned a hard lesson." The hardest part of the lesson is that they learned it too late.

Hedging your bets

Gates says, very rightly, "If you decline to take risks early, you'll decline in the market later." His policy, however, is not so audacious as he suggests. He likes to hedge his bets, covering as wide a range as possible (see p. 53). This is not quite what he says: "If you bet big...only a few of these risks have to succeed to provide for your future." In fact, the initial bet on the Internet was very small, even though by the spring of 1991 "Microsoft was betting that the Internet would be important someday."

Microsoft was ensuring that its software could support the Internet: $100 million was being spent annually on "interactive networks of various kinds," although only part of that was expended on the Net. The figure soared to billions once Gates realized that critical mass had arrived before he was ready for it. "The Internet," he now says, "is in an even stronger position than the PC was 15 years ago." Microsoft's position, however, is not as strong as it was then for a variety of reasons, which include a transient failure of vision.

Turning vision into reality

Vision does not start on the far horizon, or even the middle distance. It begins right under your nose, in the proper understanding of what is going on in the here and now. To repeat, vision to Gates is "not a competitive advantage in any way, shape, or form." It has to be accompanied by the action that will turn the vision into reality. That action, in turn, is impossible unless the company has in place, or can acquire, the necessary resources, capability, and energy. For example, when the PC market started to take off, IBM had resources and capability in abundance, but its understanding was erroneous, its vision defective, and its energy misplaced.

In the Gates philosophy, the concentration of organizational energy on the object at hand is inseparable from vision. What you can do, and actually do, has to match what you must do. Necessity does not extend to blue-sky or far-fetched ventures that will "bet the company": that is, risk total failure in the event of error – even though Gates approvingly quotes Boeing's CEO of 1969–86, Thornton "T." Wilson, who said: "If you want to look at it that you're betting the company, I hope we keep doing it."

Boeing is also one of Gates's chosen examples of excellence in the use of the digital nervous system. The

"You can't just look at the past or current state of the market. You also have to look at where it's likely to go, and where it might go under certain circumstances, and then navigate your company based on your best predictions."
Business @ the Speed of Thought

company was a bad example to pick, however, because of Boeing's record of periodic blundering, not in its bets, but in the execution of its choices. In 1998, the aircraft company plunged into losses after taking orders that could not be met with the extant organization of its production machine. Heads rolled, and massive reforms were put in hand. That does not fit Gates's idea of vision.

Evolution rather than revolution

Whatever his strategic and tactical failures, Gates has always ensured that Microsoft is able to execute the vision. That is partly because the vision is deliberately limited to what can be achieved from the existing base – to evolution, rather than revolution. In 1999 the "current audacious goals" were:

- Make the PC "scale in performance" beyond all existing systems.
- Develop computers that "see, listen, and learn."
- Create software to power the new personal companion devices.

These are quite plainly normal evolutions from Microsoft's existing products and capabilities, in no way representing great, daring jumps into the unknown. It would be strange to the point of absurdity if Gates were not pursuing these avenues, which are not so much "initiatives" (his word) but developments, and far from revolutionary. In fact, products already on the market perform the "see, listen, and learn" functions, while software for handheld computers is well-established: although here Gates faces serious opposition from rivals to his own Windows CE product.

On this evidence, "Microsoft's response to digital convergence, in which all devices will use digital technology to work with one another" is singularly tame. It certainly does not justify Gates's claim that "one fact is clear: we have to take these risks in order to have a long-term future." What risks? The risk of inertia, especially for a company with $19 billion of cash available, would have been far greater. It almost seems as though Gates wants to be seen as possessing precisely the type of vision – far-sighted, imaginative, bold, and quite possibly wrong – which he rejects in both word and practice.

Pragmatic visionary

The pragmatic way in which Gates regards vision is amply illustrated by his admissions of mistakes: "believe me, we know a lot about failures at Microsoft." These failures are product failures, rather than consequences of defective vision. The first Microsoft spreadsheet flopped. So did the first database. So did the OS/2 operating system. Other failures included an office machine product and TV-style Internet shows. But Gates claims that the lessons of much of this failure paid off in later products that were smash hits for Microsoft.

The actual vision exemplified by Gates is a vision of Microsoft and what its place should be in the world of information technology. Gates expressed this vision very simply and very clearly in the early days of Microsoft in his original mission statement: "a computer on every desk and in every home, running Microsoft software." Compared to nearly every other mission statement (including his own revised Vision Version 2), this one has every advantage: short, sharp, to the point, and distinctive. Although Gates later dropped the last three words of his statement, getting a computer in every home and on every desk would, of course, have been meaningless to him unless Microsoft provided the software.

Subordinate visions, or strategies, flow from the overall idea. It followed that, as the profit moved downstream, to the software applications that rested on the operating system, Microsoft had to join the movement. Gates took a *cosa nostra* approach to the industry. The customers were "our thing": Microsoft should achieve the largest possible share of the applications market, emulating its achievement in operating systems. As every customer for an IBM or IBM-compatible PC was *de facto* a Microsoft customer, the vision demanded that Microsoft should seek to supply each and every software need, too.

To find the right direction for these subordinate visions, Microsoft turned to the customer. "In software customers always want more," says Gates. "Our customers are always upping the ante, as they should." The difficulty about following the customer, though, is that the customer often has to be led. Indeed, the great breakthroughs come, not from responding to customer demands, but from anticipating them. You could argue that Gates did exactly that with Windows. Before it appeared, only Apple Mac users could have envisioned it. But too often Microsoft has waited for the

"You have to study what customers say about their problems with your products and stay tuned in to what they want, extrapolating from leading-edge buyers to predict future requirements."
Business @ the Speed of Thought

Surviving through paranoia
Andy Grove, CEO of the microchip company Intel, concurs with Gates that fear of the competition is a major driving force behind the long-term commercial success of any business activity.

message from outside, and the wait has sometimes been too long, enabling others to steal valuable leads.

Nothing in Gates's or Microsoft's history resonates with the same visionary importance as Moore's Law. In 1965, Gordon Moore, the cofounder of Intel, foresaw that the trend line for the improvement in chip performance relative to price would continue. In 1975, having been proved right, Moore pronounced what became his law: that chip capacity would double every 18 months with no increase in cost. This had profound implications for Intel, but Gates and Allen were quick to understand the equal impact on Microsoft.

The greater the power and speed of the computer, the more and more potent the applications that it could use. To exploit this explosive potential, Gates formed a pragmatic vision around factors that included the importance of software as opposed to hardware, the role of compatibility (so that machines and programs could work together), and the need to initiate rather than follow trends.

Driven by fear

The presence of the last is ironic in view of the trend-following habits that Microsoft has usually demonstrated. Those habits in turn are curious, given a fundamental characteristic that Gates shares with his partner in the Wintel (Windows and Intel) quasi-monopoly, Andy Grove, the CEO of Intel. The latter called his 1996 book *Only the Paranoid Survive*. In his view, fear contributes powerfully to vision, just as its opposite, complacency, dulls the sight.

Gates expressed this attitude strikingly in a 1995 *Fortune* joint interview with his cofounder, Paul Allen: "The outside perception and inside perception of Microsoft are so different. The view of Microsoft inside Microsoft is always kind of an underdog thing.... In the early days that underdog, almost paranoid, view was a matter of survivial.... Even though if you look back and see that our sales and profits grew by basically 50 percent a year for all these years, what I really remember is worrying all the time."

Allen endorses this recollection, saying that the partners could always see the "downside," even while working away to explore an upside that still dazzles Gates. "We've been climbing a steep mountain here, and you know there's still lots ahead of us," he says. The balance is all-important. In

Gates's idea of vision, you head for the highest peaks, but in the expectation that you may fall off the mountain at any time. Like any expert climber, therefore, you take every precaution to ensure that you stay firmly on the upward slope. The dangers and threats are immediate: the mountain top is in the distance.

Ideas into action

- Make the future happen by driving the business forward vigorously.
- Concentrate on the potential of new developments, not the drawbacks.
- Never impede progress for fear of undercutting the current business.
- Base vision on proper understanding of what is happening now.
- Take all necessary action to protect the long-term future.
- Keep your vision statement short, sharp, to the point, and distinctive.
- Run scared – always bear in mind the risks and threats.

Making a U-turn and invading the Internet

Bill Gates has tried to play down the full extent of his failure of vision over the Internet. The fact remains, however, that Gates subconsciously wished away the full significance of the Net because it is fully "open."

Anybody can enter the Internet and use any of its services with any computer. You do not need the Windows gateway. Worse still, Microsoft's hold on the applications market, and even the systems market, is threatened by the ability to download other people's software from the Net at low prices – or, in many cases, at no cost at all.

By Gates's own account, Microsoft spent very little money or time between 1991, when it hired an "internetworking specialist," and April 1994. Then Gates took key staff away on a "retreat" to discuss the Net; he also devoted his own "Think Week" to the subject (this is his twice-yearly break "to concentrate on the most difficult technical and business problems facing the company"); and he emailed a strategic U-turn to his staff in which he stated, "we're going to make a major bet on the Internet." As a result, within a year, "every team at Microsoft had defined its Internet charter and begun development."

In May 1995, another Gates email, titled "The Internet Tidal Wave," "summarized our strategic directions and decisions, and announced a corporate reorganization" to fit his new analysis of the Net. "The Internet is the most important single development to come along since the IBM PC was launched in 1981," he now stated. That product had created the Microsoft fortunes: now Gates diverted a massive share of $1.4 billion in research and development spending to defend that wealth. By the end of August 1996, a million users had downloaded free copies of Explorer 3.0, Microsoft's massive riposte to Netscape.

Successful launch

Unlike other Microsoft products, Explorer was a wholly credible alternative to the competition from the start. Its launch was a great example of Gates's tenacity and the responsiveness of the organization. He stresses how employees began his awakening

"To get a big company moving fast, especially on a many-headed opportunity like the Internet, you have to have hundreds of people participating and coming up with ideas." *Business @ the Speed of Thought*

with emails. ("Do people all over my company feel free to send me email because we believe in a flat organization?", he asks, "Or do we have a flat organization because people have always been able to send email to me?") The trickle of emails developed into a flood ("just fantastic") after the Microsoft fightback got under way.

As late as March 1997, however, for all Explorer's huge success in seizing market share from Netscape, the Microsoft camp was still sharply divided on whether Windows could be saved. Gates ended the debate decisively: Microsoft would continue to support and upgrade Windows as the interface between the PC user and the Internet (see p. 81). The final decision will be made by a market which, thanks to the Internet, Microsoft no longer owns outright and cannot control. Thanks to Gates's definitive U-turn, though, Microsoft has won breathing space and a battling chance.

peter DRUCKER

Biography

Peter Drucker was born in 1909 in Vienna. Even though he has lived in America for over 60 years, the influences and memories of middle Europe in general, and Vienna in particular, are still strong. Despite his heavy German accent, Drucker is an English speaker of astonishing clarity and fluency, whose logic is remorseless, and who has seemingly perfect recall of the facts, figures, and anecdotes that he uses in profusion to illustrate his ideas.

His writings have been more widely read, and have embodied more breakthroughs, than those of any other management thinker. But it is Drucker's appearances as a teacher, both in universities and in all manner of management forums, that have indelibly impressed two generations of practicing managers. He represents in the US today the mid-European intellectual tradition into which he was born, combining academic distinction with practical application.

Multi-disciplined intellectual

Drucker's lawyer father was the top civil servant in the Ministry of Economics in the Austro-Hungarian Empire. His mother, unusually for the time, had been a medical student. His intellectal family (they knew Freud and many other Viennese luminaries) were in very comfortable circumstances. Living in such a cultured family played a major part in Drucker's education. The cultured ease, however, was harshly interrupted by the horrors of World War I, which broke out when Drucker was five: its end brought near-famine to Austria.

After finishing his schooling at the Gymnasium in Vienna, Drucker left for a clerk's desk in a Hamburg exporting company. To please his parents, he studied law in Hamburg: he also read voluminously in three languages and published his first article. Then he moved to Frankfurt to work for a Wall Street firm as a trainee analyst, carrying on with his law studies, and studying statistics as well. His familiarity and ease with numerical facts and their meaning has been a major factor in his accurate, often uncannily prescient, reading of today and tomorrow.

His interest in current events, and in numbers, makes it seem natural that he became a financial journalist after the collapse of his employer in the Wall Street crash of 1929. He won rapid promotion on Frankfurt's largest paper, and also got a doctorate at the university, where he met Doris Schmitz, a successful technologist, who would later become his wife. While Drucker worked as a newspaper correspondent abroad, German society was disintegrating: the triumph of fascism was the spur for his first book, *The End of Economic Man: The Origins of Totalitarianism* (1939). Not surprisingly, it was published after 1933, when Drucker left Hitler's Germany for good.

Humanitarian thinker

The book, a hostile examination of the deep irrationality of fascism, established one of the main strands in Drucker's philosophy. He is a humanitarian thinker, who approaches business, management, and economics as aspects of social and political history, not as ends in themselves. His profound understanding of 20th-century tides has conditioned his management thought. So has his experience of practical matters, including a spell in London, where he

General Motors in wartime
Alfred P. Sloan (left) dominated the management of General Motors during the period of Drucker's detailed analysis of the corporation, when it was manufacturing only defense equipment.

worked in insurance, again as an analyst. During this time Drucker became reacquainted with Doris after a chance meeting on the escalators at Piccadilly Circus.

Drucker spent four years at a small London merchant bank, got disillusioned with economics after listening to John Maynard Keynes, and contributed freelance articles to American publications. In 1937 he married Doris and, sponsored by London financial papers, emigrated to the US, where he has lived and worked ever since, as journalist, author, speaker, consultant, and teacher (of both management and Oriental art). These occupations have a common link: writing. Drucker considers himself first and foremost as a writer, and least of all as an entrepreneur, for which he claims to have no talent whatsoever.

Lucid writer, fluent speaker

As a writer Drucker has set new standards for lucidity and strength of argument, publishing many articles throughout his long career. As he approached 90, Drucker was still contributing to the Wall Street Journal and Harvard Business Review. The latter, in the March-April 1999 issue, published "Managing Oneself," an excerpt from Drucker's latest book, Management Challenges for the 21st Century. The excerpt is typical in its clarity and in the way in which Drucker astonishes his readers with an idea that, once studied, appears irrefutable. Witness this sentence: "There is one prerequisite for managing the second half of your life: you must begin doing so long before you enter it."

He has managed his own life with extraordinary skill and great mental agility. Every year or two, Drucker sets himself to master a new subject. He devours books and magazines, and has a memory so capacious that it appears inexhaustible. Its feats extend from remembering not only all his innumerable friends and their families but also volumes of historical and personal anecdote and the entire content of his lectures. Sitting on a chair or the edge of a table, he delivers lectures without notes or audio-visual aids, with total fluency, at a steady pace: he holds a watch, does not seem to look at it, but finishes dead on time.

Key corporate study

Drucker's speaking skills were obviously developed by his long career as a college lecturer, starting in America in 1939 and continuing all his life. During World War II, he worked part-time for the Board of Economic Warfare and published his second book, *The Future of Industrial Man*, in 1942. It made a considerable impact, and a year later, Drucker was invited by the vice-chairman of General Motors to make a study of the world's largest industrial corporation. As he wrote in his autobiography, *Adventures of a Bystander*, "It was literally for me the finger of providence."

The book resulting from his study of General Motors, titled *Concept of the Corporation* and published in 1946, remains the only corporate study of lasting intellectual merit. It inevitably played a crucial role in developing Drucker's knowledge of management. Alfred P. Sloan Jr., then the head of GM, was a brilliant and wise practitioner from whom Drucker learned a great deal. There were very few other sources of management wisdom at that time, certainly few in writing, and Drucker was able to combine his social ideas with the practical observation of what actually happens inside a profit-driven organization.

Discovering management

Despite the success of *Concept of the Corporation*, Drucker went through a fallow period as a book writer until 1950. *The New Society* was published that year, one of three works on social and political topics produced in the Fifties. But his discovery of management as a discipline in its own right, and as a major force in society, was germinating throughout the post-GM years. His thinking culminated in the publication in 1954 of *The Practice of Management*, which drew on a variety of sources: not only the GM experience, but his teaching of management at New York University, and his work as a consultant for major companies.

Drucker seldom refers directly to his consultancy work, which is individual (he has no organization), top-level, and highly prized. The two-way traffic between his ideas and his clients has been important, however, in shaping his thought. *The Practice of Management* was originally conceived as a guide for client managers, filling a huge gap. Since then management books have flooded forth, and he has contributed heavily to the flow: seven more books, ranging from the highly practical (*The Effective Executive*, 1966) to the wide-ranging, with the latest, *Management Challenges for the 21st Century*, published in 1999.

Lifestyle preferences

Even though he has spent so many decades advising friends who run wealthy corporations, Drucker has adopted none of their lifestyle habits. He lives simply, does not have a secretary, and bangs out his own letters on a typewriter. In practical (though not literary) terms, the Information Revolution has passed him by. His globe-trotting, though, has always included as much cultural tourism as time allows, mostly organized around appearances that range from whole-day seminars to keynote speeches.

His schedule used to include annual trips to Europe and Japan. Drucker was among the first Western observers to spot the huge importance of the upsurge in Japanese competition and management expertise. In return, the Japanese were among the first to spot and adopt Drucker's most important teachings. In later years Drucker has preferred to stay at home in Claremont, near Los Angeles. When conference organizers have wanted him (and they do, all the time), the new technology has come in handy, presenting him on screen via satellite. His hearing has worsened with advancing age, but his brilliance at understanding and interpretation is unimpaired. He remains the supreme master of his craft – which he did, after all, invent.

1

Organizing for success in business

How decentralization contributed to the success of General Motors • **Why the "self-governing community" is the ideal management system** • The importance giving workers a say in decisions • **How people want to identify themselves wit product and company, and to be held responsible for quality and performanc** • Understanding the importance of the "theory of the business" in winning success • **The need to challenge every product, service, policy, and distributic channel every three years** rucker's reputation as a management expert got enormous impetus from his study of General Motors commissioned by the directors in 1942 and most erfully influenced by GM's creator, Alfred P. Sloan. The ear-old consultant and writer was given complete lom during the 18 months that he spent studying the d's first manufacturing mega-corporation. Nor did GM any control over what he wrote afterward about its iods and nature. The book Drucker produced, *Concep ie Corporation* (1946), made him the first, as well as the insightful, writer to explore and explain the evolution ie business corporation as a key institution of society.

rucker wished to generalize from the GM study, but the pany was especially particular because of Sloan. An ic man, Sloan not only lived for the company, he lived , mostly sleeping in a little bedroom in the Detroit es. His apartment on Fifth Avenue, New York, and the e on Long Island were largely unused trappings for this lless, dedicated executive. He was atypical, not only of top corporate managers of his time, but of all their essors. The company over which he reigned cannot be rated from Sloan's personality or his methods.

onsequently, GM was not the best possible source eneralizations. Drucker is no believer in the Great theory of history. Like Tolstoy, he is far more rested in the historical tides that carry away all and women, great or small. But many of the key ns that Drucker learned from GM were taught by n personally, rather than by the organization – for nple, the sovereign importance of personnel decisions. we didn't spend four hours on placing a man and ng him right," taught Sloan, "we'd spend 400 hours ning up after our mistakes."

Decentralized structure

Above all, Sloan taught Drucker about decentralization. Drucker argues that, at GM, this principle had been taken far beyond its normal usage. "In over 20 years of work... Mr. Alfred P. Sloan Jr. has developed the concept of decentralization into a philosophy of industrial management and into a system of local self-government." Drucker was not, however, content to leave Sloan's principle as just a better way of organizing management within a major institution. "It is not a mere technique of management but an outline of a social order," he claimed.

By the standards of the day, Sloan gave his divisions (nearly 50 of them) great independence. Drucker estimated that all but 5 percent of decisions came within the ambit of the individual divisions. This relative autonomy, however, was considerably limited by the powers retained by the center, which made the 5 percent very telling. The divisional managers had no control over prices, the cost of labor, the capital they employed, or the financial function. Moreover, the managers of these "profit centers" (a Drucker-invented term not then in use) were held highly accountable for their results.

That was one sterner aspect of the decentralization that Drucker described: the balance of delegation was tilted heavily toward the center. Drucker observed that headquarters "refrains as much as possible from telling a division how to do its job; it only lays down what to do." However, by dictating what divisional managers at GM should be doing, central managers at GM paid little more than lip service to the freedom given to their subordinates under the decentralized regime; in reality, they were kept on a tight leash. You could look at Sloan's GM as the power structure of a control freak, or as a liberating mechanism.

Corporation as human effort

Drucker leaned toward the second alternative. GM, he wrote, had "realized its concept of decentralization sufficiently to obtain from it an overall pattern of behavior and a basis for the successful solution of the most difficult concrete problems of economic life." He was particularly impressed by the impact of the decentralized structure on GM executives, whose placement was so important in Sloan's plan. They were placed in jobs where, as relative youngsters, they could take responsibility without endangering the whole corporation, and, as they rose, so they broadened and applied their skills.

The very title of the book's section on decentralization gives away the author's main concern: "the corporation as human effort." Drucker was far less concerned with issues of efficiency or profitability (although he regarded profit as "the basis of all economic activity") than with the social and economic themes that dominate two-thirds of *Concept of the Corporation*. GM loomed large in these discussions, but only as evidence for the case: that such organizations were now America's "representative institution," that "the large mass-production plant is our social reality."

Drucker says that "only now have we realized" this truth, which is a modest way of saying that it was his discovery. He felt that the corporation was an engine with huge potential for good, which "has to carry the burden of our dreams." It was still, however, far from achieving the ideals enshrined in Drucker's dreams. GM's idea of employment was to achieve the highest production for the lowest possible cost. The role of the workers was to do as they were told, without complaint or individual contribution, as they served the monotonous, mindless machines of the assembly line in just as mindless a fashion.

Helping hand

Established in 1908 by William C. Durant, General Motors had become the largest car manufacturer in the US long before 1953, when this young apprentice was being taught his trade.

Self-governing plant community

This attitude to employees was anathema to Drucker who, even at this extremely early date, was preaching "empowerment." He thought GM could and should create "the self-governing plant community," whose members would contribute to improving their work and would take pride in what they were doing. Such an approach would inevitably mean scrapping the assembly line, which Drucker criticized on both economic and human grounds. The line moved at the pace of the slowest worker, nobody produced a finished product, and – in his view – the monotony was literally counterproductive. Needless to say, the argument fell on deaf ears at GM, over whom Drucker believed he had no influence whatsoever.

But any other major corporation would have reacted similarly. This was the age of economies of scale. Giants like General Motors built huge plants to milk these economies. Profitability hinged on using these industrial mammoths to the highest possible capacity, reducing operations to repetitive tasks, and relying as little as possible on variable human skills, as opposed to machinelike consistency. Drucker clearly recognized this fact of economic life: "... we know today that in modern industrial production, particularly in modern mass production, the small unit is not only inefficient, it cannot produce at all."

Not surprisingly, this made the author sound like an advocate of the large corporation, even though he believed the "small unit" was far better placed to give the worker economic dignity. But smallness was incompatible, not only with productivity, but with the heroic status Drucker wished the corporation to assume. Unfortunately, neither GM nor any other giant wanted to assume the mantle of leading the US into a new industrial order, especially given the forms of leadership Drucker had in mind.

Drucker wanted to humanize the treatment of workers, and to give them a say in workplace decisions. He wanted the long-term workers to have a guaranteed annual wage. This meant that their livelihoods would not be destroyed

"Management is about human beings. Its task is to make people capable of joint performance, to make their strengths effective and their weaknesses irrelevant. This is what organization is all about, and it is the reason that management is the... determining factor." *The New Realities*

by downturns in the market. In fact, this was a brilliant perception, both for the company and society. As Drucker argued, guaranteed pay would maintain the purchasing power of workers during a recession. It would also retain and motivate the workers, no longer treated as expendable by the management.

Unfortunately, GM's labor troubles at the end of World War II made it impossible for its management (including Sloan) to listen sympathetically to a case for better treatment of the employees. In nature, Drucker's arguments were perilously close to those of Walter Reuther, the forceful head of the United Auto Workers Union, and GM's sworn enemy. As so often, Drucker was ahead of his time, both in preaching empowerment and in his ideas on wages: a long time later the guaranteed wage was adopted by the corporation. In fact, under "Engine" Charlie Wilson, Sloan's successor, Drucker was used as a consultant on labor matters.

Corporation as pillar of society

Wilson was the source of a famous misquotation: "What's good for General Motors is good for America." He actually said, "What's good for America is good for General Motors, and vice versa" (1953), which is not the same thing at all. The accurate quote plainly, if clumsily, reflects Drucker's view of the corporation as a pillar of the wider society. Presumably under Drucker's influence, Wilson also sought employees' opinions, which turned out to include a desire to help improve their jobs. Neither union boss Reuther nor other GM managers thought much of this concept. "Managers should manage and workers work", maintained Reuther.

That didn't square at all with Wilson's findings, which, according to Drucker, showed that employees truly wanted "to identify themselves with product and company and to be held responsible for quality and performance." This was the desire that became the seed for the postwar rebirth of Japanese management (see p. 24) and its much later Western versions. But at GM, Drucker's study, which enormously influenced the behavior of other corporations worldwide, led only to Sloan's book, *My Years at General Motors* (1963). Intended as a response, to set the record straight, Sloan's book neither mentions Drucker nor pays any great attention to the period of his study: a war in which GM made only defense equipment.

Organizational genius
General Motors owed much of its enormous success to Alfred P. Sloan (1875–1966), who restructured the corporation in the early 1920s. He became president in 1924 and chairman in 1937.

Drucker, on the other hand, enormously values Sloan's achievement, both as a manager who ruled by moral authority and as a superb organizer. As Drucker wrote in 1994, "GM had an even more powerful, and successful, theory of the business than IBM.... The company did not have one setback in 70 years – a record unmatched in business history. GM's theory combined, in one seamless web, assumptions about markets and customers with assumptions about core competencies and organizational structure." And that was predominantly Sloan's work.

Theory of the business

According to Drucker, every organization, "whether a business or not," has a "theory of the business." Sounding very close to "concept of the corporation," "theory of the business" sums up the "assumptions on which the organization has been built and is being run." The conventional view is that these assumptions, especially in large corporations, ossify, and management then becomes "bureaucratic, sluggish, or arrogant." The trio of adjectives certainly seemed to explain what happened to GM in the early 1980s, years "in which GM's main business, passenger automobiles, seemed almost paralyzed." Yet GM in the same period had two great successes with expensive acquisitions, Hughes Aircraft and EDS, which hardly fits the adjectives.

"What can explain," asks Drucker, "the fact that... the policies, practices, and behaviors that worked for decades – and in the case of GM are still working well when applied to something new and different – no longer work for the organization in which and for which they were developed?" His answer is that the car market had changed, so that GM's basic plan, to have massively long runs of unchanged models aimed at each income segment, ceased to fit. As a result Sloan's entire divisional structure and production system were undermined: "GM knew all this but simply could not believe it.... Instead, the company tried to patch things over... [which] only confused the customer, the dealer, and the employees and management of GM itself."

Drucker explains that every "theory of the business" has three parts. "First, there are assumptions about the environment of the organization.... Second, there are assumptions about the specific mission of the organization.... Third, there are assumptions about the core competencies needed to accomplish the organization's mission." A company does not arrive at a theory overnight. "It usually takes years of hard work, thinking, and experimenting to a reach a clear, consistent, and valid theory of the business."

But what makes this theory valid? Drucker lays down four conditions:

- The assumptions about the environment, mission, and core competencies must fit reality.
- The assumptions in all three areas have to fit one another.
- The theory of the business must be known and understood throughout the organization.
- The theory of the business has to be tested constantly and altered if necessary.

Drucker points out in *Managing in a Time of Great Change* (1995) that GM was especially strong on the second point. "Its assumptions about the market and about the optimum manufacturing process were a perfect fit. GM decided in the mid-1920s that it also required new and as-yet-unheard-of core competencies: financial control of the manufacturing process and a theory of capital allocations. As a result, GM invented modern cost-accounting and the first rational capital-allocation process."

Maintaining a valid theory

If any of the assumptions, let alone all of them, become falsified, the theory of the business must collapse. How does an organization stop that happening? "There are only two preventive measures," asserts Drucker. The first he calls "abandonment," by which he means that: "Every three years, an organization should challenge every product, every service, every policy, every distribution channel with the question, 'If we were not in it already, would we be going into it now?'"

This approach forces the company to ask the following crucial questions: "Why didn't this work, even though it looked so promising when we went into it five years ago? Is it because we made a mistake? Is it because we did the wrong things? Or is it because the right things didn't work?"

The second preventive measure "is to study what goes on outside the business, and especially to study non-customers." Drucker points out that, although "knowing as much as possible about one's customers" is important, "the first signs of fundamental change rarely appear within one's own organization or among one's own customers." The people who are *not* buying from you "almost always" reveal those first signs, to which, Drucker emphasizes, managers must pay acute attention. They should also bear in mind that a "theory of the business always becomes obsolete when an organization attains its original objectives."

Another "sure sign of crisis" for any company is rapid growth. "Any organization that doubles or triples its size within a fairly short period of time has necessarily outgrown its theory," he observes. In these circumstances, to "continue in health, let alone grow, the organization has to ask itself again the questions about its environment, mission, and core competencies." Rapid growth at least was rarely GM's problem. The corporation did, however, ignore "two more clear signals that an organization's theory of the business is no longer valid."

Unexpected success and failure

One of these signals is "unexpected success – whether one's own or a competitor's. The other is unexpected failure – again, whether one's own or a competitor's." GM provides a model, or rather a warning, on both counts. Drucker maintains, for example, that "had it paid attention to the success [in minivans] of its weaker competitor, Chrysler, GM might have realized much earlier that its assumptions about both its market and its core competencies were no longer valid." In fact, light trucks, and therefore potentially minivans, were an area in which GM might have expected to dominate.

As for unexpected failure, none was more unexpected or more devastating than the collapse of GM's market share before the postwar onslaughts of the Japanese – who had adopted Drucker's ideas concerning empowerment, set out in *Concept of the Corporation*, and ignored by GM, with great enthusiasm. "My popularity in Japan," wrote Drucker, "where I am credited with substantial responsibility for the emergence of the country as a major economic power and for the performance and productivity of its industry, goes back to *Concept of the Corporation*, which was almost immediately translated into Japanese, eagerly read and applied."

The irony is unmistakable. A book extolling the virtues of GM at its peak became the text for many Japanese manufacturers, above all Toyota, whose managers did much to topple Sloan's creation from its eminence. This achievement testifies less to GM's weaknesses than to the abiding strength of Drucker's ideas about corporate organization.

Ideas into action

- Spend all the time you need on making decisions that affect people.
- Make sure that everybody understands what your business is really about.
- Study what is going on outside the business, and among customers and non-customers.
- If the business is growing fast, question your assumptions all over again.
- Look out for and learn from unexpected success – your own and others'.
- Do exactly the same with unexpected failure, especially your own.

The meeting with General Motors

Drucker's epochal work, *Concept of the Corporation*, was an opportunity waiting to happen. He had made several unsuccessful attempts to get inside a major organization when the call from GM came "out of the blue" in 1942.

Drucker had a guinea pig, the biggest in the world, for establishing and exploring the theory of organizations. The only catch was GM itself: a business making profits, run by corporate managers, about whose work Drucker was ignorant.

Drucker found that there was almost no literature on the management and structure of large businesses and set out to repair the omission. GM originally wanted a study for internal eyes only, but Drucker held that employees would not trust or confide in him unless he was seen as impartial and independent from top management. It was agreed that Drucker should instead write an independent book, which GM would correct only for factual error.

A free hand

The key to the analysis of GM was Alfred P. Sloan, the man who had assembled GM from separate automobile manufacturers, and who dominated its management with a style that was by no means domineering. For example, although he objected to the Drucker project, he let himself be outvoted. He then told Drucker, "I shall not tell you what to write, what to study, or what conclusions to come to.... My only instruction to you is to put down what you think is right.... Don't you worry about our reactions."

Unacceptable views

As it happened, the management's reactions were decidedly unfavorable. The book came out in 1946 when GM was experiencing severe labor troubles, which helped to make Drucker's conclusions unacceptable. For example, he proposed paying a guaranteed annual wage, which was also sought by the union, and argued for more worker involvement in decision making (see p. 58). Sloan had originally told Drucker not to concern himself "with the compromises that might be needed" to make his recommendations acceptable. Now he repudiated the book, and

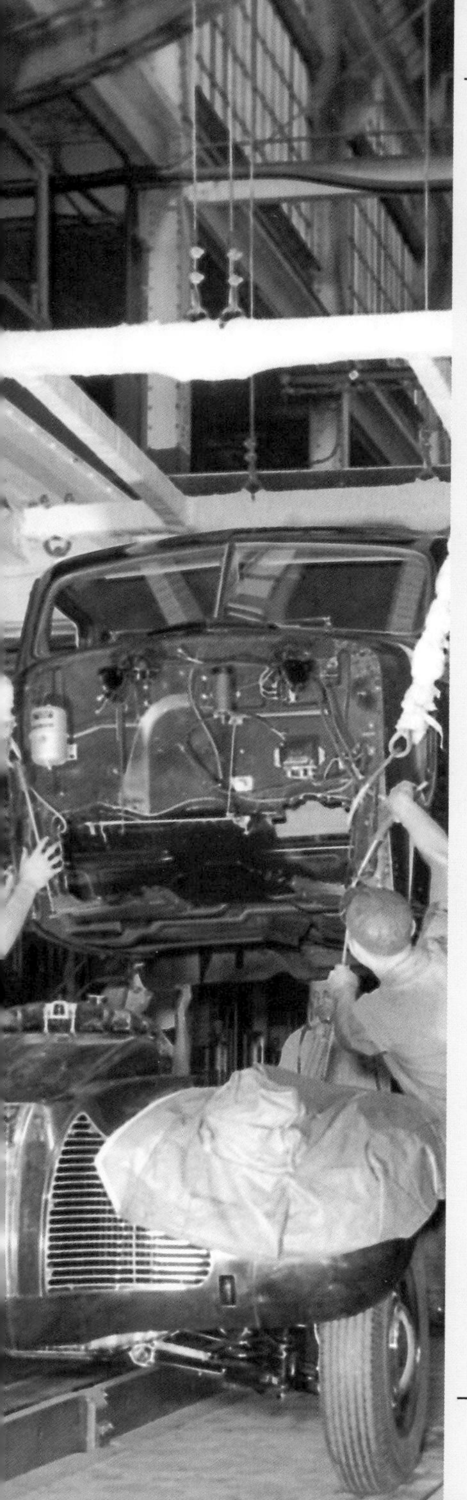

"Sloan has developed the concept of decentralization into a philosophy of industrial management and into a system of local self-government. It is... an outline of a social order."
Concept of the Corporation

wrote his own, *My Years with General Motors*, itself a management classic, almost as a rebuttal.

The circumstances for Drucker's 18 months of research were not ideal. As it was wartime, GM was making no cars, only defense equipment, such as tanks, aircraft, and machine guns. The operation of the company as a marketing machine or as a producer of consumer goods was therefore outside his scan. Also, war workers tend to have high morale, making GM's unsympathetic and counterproductive management of its workforce hard to uncover. His vision of GM's postwar leadership of industrial society was not founded in reality, nor shared by the corporation's leaders.

For all that, Drucker stayed in close contact with GM, and some of the credit he won for developing the concept of a benevolent, socially responsible capitalist organization, rubbed off on the corporation. And the day came when its workers did receive a guaranteed annual wage.

OUTPUT GRAPHS FOR 16 PIN DEVICES
PELLET SORT
PVC
MOUNT
BOND
BOND CHECK

2

The art of management in practice

Why 90 percent of management concerns are shared by all organizations • **Making the strengths and knowledge of each individual more productive** • Founding the business on customer values and customer decisions • **The five basic elements in the work of the manager** • The three key questions that govern true delegation • **Using the Feedback Analysis to compare expectation with results and improve performance** • How to use new measurements to achieve improved performance from everyone

Drucker is a humanist who upholds the traditional liberal values of the European intelligentsia. That he should also be the leading exponent of management theory is no paradox. He stresses that, without management, organizations cannot meet the social purposes that transcend them. He calls management a "liberal art," not a science. Here there is a paradox, since many of the writers and teachers who spread the concept of "scientific management" were following in Drucker's footsteps. That is because his footsteps are unavoidable.

Starting in 1954 with *The Practice of Management* (still considered his greatest contribution by some experts), Drucker on his own account invented his subject. He observes that hardly anything on management, as opposed to subjects like selling, advertising, and manufacturing, existed before the book appeared. He reckoned that even people in business "often do not know what their management does and what it is supposed to be doing, how it acts and why, whether it does a good job or not," so Drucker set out to fill this enormous gap, combining theory with eminently practical advice.

His approach has set him at odds with the vast majority of business management academics (although he has long been such an academic himself). He criticizes their excessive focus on academic respectability. Because they were long scorned by other university faculties, the business schools have been eager to prove their true, rigorous academic credentials. That focus ignores Drucker's proposition that management is art rather than science. To Drucker, management is "an integrating discipline of human values and conduct, of social order and intellectual inquiry." It is an art that "feeds off economics, psychology, mathematics, political theory, history, and philosophy."

The scope of management

Most managers would be amazed, if flattered, to learn that this description defines their daily activity. The false scientists in the business schools are equally far from practicing what Drucker preaches. Most of the curricula lay heavy stress on financial analysis and other mathematical disciplines. He regards this approach as another excess, which confuses management with "quantification." Not surprisingly, given his early statistical background, Drucker's own teaching does emphasize the importance of establishing the numerical and financial facts. But that is a foundation of managing, not the whole of management.

Few managers would make as great claims for their discipline as Drucker does on their behalf. They think of their art (Drucker has also called it a "social science") as specifically *business* management. Drucker finds this definition far too narrow. He recognizes that there are differences between managing "a chain of retail stores and managing a Catholic diocese (although amazingly fewer than either chain stores or bishops believe)." He does not regard these differences as significant.

The "greatest differences" are in the terms that individual organizations use. "Otherwise the differences are mainly in application rather than in principles," Drucker asserts. He goes on to argue that all executives in all organizations spend about the same amount of time on people problems: "and the people problems are nearly always the same." He puts the "generic" element of management at a huge 90 percent of the whole. That leaves very little that "has to be fitted to the organization's specific mission, its specific culture, its specific history, and its specific vocabulary." The argument is sweeping, probably too sweeping, but it sets the stage for the following large claim: "management is the specific and distinguishing organ of any and all organizations."

This is the latest statement (taken from *Management Challenges for the 21st Century*, 1999) of a position Drucker has held since the 1950s. At that time, he applied the word "organ" in a quasi-medical sense: "management is an organ, and organs can only be defined through their function." This "specific organ of the business enterprise," in author Jack Beatty's summary, has three functions: to manage a business, to manage managers, and to manage worker and work. Today, however, Drucker argues that "one does not 'manage' people. The task is to lead people. And the goal is to make productive the specific strengths and knowledge of each individual." That is a high internal ambition.

Importance of the customer

As an "organ of society" the "business enterprise" has an ultimate purpose outside itself. Drucker maintains, "There is only one valid definition of business purpose: to create a customer." He regards this definition as one of his crucial ideas. It has had an incalculable influence on the preaching and practice of management, culminating in today's pursuit of "customer focus" (or putting the customer first), and in the contemporary ideal of the "customer-centric" business, organized from beginning to end around customer satisfaction.

In one way or another, the customer theme runs through all Drucker's work, from *Concept of the Corporation* right up to the present day. "The foundations have to be customer values and customer decisions," he argues. "It is with those that management policy and management strategy increasingly will have to start." It follows logically from this that the customer must also be the starting point for the actual practice of management.

What management does

Drucker has explored the practice of management with unfailing vigor and insight since the 1950s. In 1973, he produced *Management: Tasks, Responsibilities, Practices*, which became a bestselling must for aspiring Masters of Business Administration. It summarizes the three decades of theorizing and practical observation that began when he entered the gates of General Motors. In the book Drucker identifies five basic functions of a manager.

"A manager, in the first place, sets objectives. He determines what the objectives should be. He determines what the goals in each area of objectives should be. He decides what has to be done to reach these objectives. He makes the objectives effective by communicating them to the people whose performance is needed to attain them.

"Second, a manager organizes. He analyzes the activities, decisions, and relations needed. He classifies the work. He divides it into manageable activities and further divides the activities into manageable jobs. He groups these units and jobs into an organization structure. He selects people for the management of these units and for the jobs to be done.

"Next, a manager motivates and communicates. He makes a team out of the people that are responsible for various jobs. He does that through the practices with which he works. He does it in his own relations to the men with whom he works. He does it through his

Communicating with individual units
A manager should provide team members with the information they require to do a good job, communicating with them frequently, and giving them clear guidelines on the results that are expected.

'people decisions' on pay, placement, and promotion. And he does it through constant communication, to and from his subordinates, to and from his superior, and to and from his colleagues.

"The fourth basic element in the work of the manager is measurement. The manager establishes yardsticks – and few factors are as important to the performance of the organization and every man in it. He sees to it that each man has measurements available to him which are focused on the performance of the whole organization and which, at the same time, focus on the work of the individual and help him do it. He analyzes, appraises, and interprets performance. As in all other areas of his work, he communicates the meaning of the measurements and their findings to his subordinates, to his superiors, and to colleagues.

"Finally, a manager develops people, including himself."

Hero chief executives

Of all those self-developers, the most important is the person at the top. Carrying out all of the first four duties for a major corporation is an heroic task, and articles in the media suggest that top management heroes duly abound. But Drucker believes that the hero chief executive (a type whose hype recurs through thick and thin, boom and bust) exceeds the normal limits of human capacity. Four quite different types of person are required to fulfill the role of chief executive successfully: thought person, action person, people person, and front person.

According to Drucker, "those four temperaments are almost never found in one person. The one-man top management job is a major reason why businesses fail to grow." One of the exceptions to his rule was the very man who led General Motors, the company whose study opened the doors to Drucker's thoughts on the practice of management – Alfred P. Sloan. Sloan, however, was a practicing manager who reduced management to two simple ideas: incentive compensation and "decentralization with coordinated control." The latter provided opportunity, the former produced motivation.

"I have held from the beginning that management has to be a discipline, an organized body of knowledge that can be learned..." *The Frontiers of Management*

Effective self-management

Sloan was also extremely efficient at a critical aspect of every manager's job: managing oneself. Drucker has always paid close attention to the individual manager's work. His most famous formulation in this regard forms the basis of the delegation without which decentralization cannot work. He suggests that every manager should periodically ask themselves the following three key questions:

- What am I doing that does not need to be done at all?
- What am I doing that can be done by somebody else?
- What am I doing that only I can do?

This simple and elegant set of questions goes to the heart of the use of time and the employment of talents – your own and other people's. Drucker has developed his thinking about self-management to keep in step with the rise of the knowledge worker (see p. 93), which imposes "drastically new demands" on individuals. They have to ask:

- Who am I?
- What are my strengths?
- How do I work?
- Where do I belong?
- What is my contribution?

There is only one way to answer the first three of these five questions: the Feedback Analysis. "Whenever one makes a key decision, and whenever one does a key action, one writes down what one expects to happen. And nine months or 12 months later one then feeds back from results to expectations. And every time I do it I am surprised. And so is everybody who has ever done this." Using the results of the Feedback Analysis, managers concentrate on using and improving their revealed strengths.

Managers must also take "relationship responsibility," which Drucker calls an "absolute necessity. It is a duty." He points out that "organizations are no longer built on force. They are built on trust." Personality conflicts arise mostly because "one person does not know what the other person does," or how that is done, or its contribution, or the expected results. The manager "owes relationship responsibility to everyone with whom one works, on whose work one depends, and who in turn depends on one's work."

Measuring performance

In this new world of the knowledge worker, Drucker argues, new measures are also required. The old methods of accountancy, for example, were geared to an economy that is fast vanishing. You cannot measure a knowledge company by the same criteria as one producing nuts and bolts. He has said that "performance will have to be defined non-financially so as to be meaningful to knowledge workers and to generate commitment from them."

He calls traditional measures "an X-ray of the enterprise's skeleton," but points out that "the diseases we most commonly die from… do not show up in a skeletal X-ray." In the same way: "… a loss of market standing or a failure to innovate does not register in the accountant's figures until the damage has been done. We need new measurements – call them 'a business audit' – to give us effective business control."

Increasingly, "result control" is obtained from "activity-based costing" which recognizes that the "cost that matters for competitiveness and profitability is the cost of the total process," and includes the costs of "not doing" (such as machine downtime). Going further, a company has to know the costs of its "entire economic chain," going outside the company to determine the final cost to the customer. Drucker strongly advocates "price-led costing," in which companies work back from what the customer is prepared to pay.

Customer focus

Creating a customer, says Drucker, is the only "valid definition of business purpose": therefore customer values and decisions are the starting points for policy and strategy.

The diagnostic toolkit

He adds, however, that "enterprises are paid to create wealth." That requires four sets of diagnostic tools which together "constitute the executive's toolkit for managing the current business." They are:

- Foundation information
- Productivity information
- Competence information
- Resource-allocation information

Foundation information refers to familiar measures like cashflow, sales, and various ratios, which conventional businesses have long used. If they are normal, fine; abnormality indicates "a problem that needs to be identified and treated." Productivity information looks at the productivity of key resources, including labor – with manual labor currently much easier to measure than knowledge and service work. Drucker stresses that you also need measures like "economic value-added analysis" to demonstrate that a business is earning more than its capital costs, together with "benchmarking" to show that its performance is as good as or better than the best competition.

With competence information, Drucker ventures on less well-trodden ground. How do you measure "core competencies" like the Japanese genius at miniaturizing electronic components? "Every organization... needs one core competence: innovation," he asserts. How, again, do you measure performance in this critical area? Unusually, Drucker has no answers, only questions such as: "How many of the truly important innovation opportunities did we miss? Why? Because we did not see them? Or because we saw them but dismissed them?" Much of this, he admits, "is assessment rather than measurement" – an omission that he would plainly like to rectify.

With resource-allocation information, Drucker is on home ground. He long ago spotted that none of the traditional measures of capital employment – return on investment, payback period, cashflow, or discounted present value – was enough on its own. "To understand a proposed investment, a company needs to look at all four," and to ask two key questions that do not figure in most capital appropriation processes:

- What will happen if the investment fails to produce the promised results? Would it seriously hurt the company?
- If the investment is successful, especially more so than we expect, what will it commit us to?

Drucker adds that "there is no better way to improve an organization's performance than to measure the results of capital spending against the promises and expectations that led to its authorizations." Capital, however, is only one key resource of the organization. "The scarcest resources are performing people." He calls for "placement" of people with specific expectations as to what the appointee should achieve and with systematic appraisal of the outcome. Again, although Drucker is certain about the end (to allocate human resources "as purposefully and thoughtfully" as capital), he is less sure about the means.

In any case, businesses need to measure the future as well as the present. "Strategy has to be based on information about markets, customers, and non-customers" and about technology, finance, and the "changing world" outside. "Inside an organization there are only cost centers. The only profit center is a customer whose check has not bounced." Drucker notes the first efforts to organize "business intelligence," information about actual and potential competitors worldwide. But here, as elsewhere, he perceives a serious lag and challenge. "The majority of enterprises have yet to start the job," he observes.

Once managers know what information they need for their work and what information they owe to others, they can develop methods to turn "the chaos of data" into "organized and focused information." With that in hand, they can begin to exploit the "most valuable assets of a 21st-century institution: its knowledge workers and their productivity."

Ideas into action

- Make sure you communicate clearly and often with colleagues, superiors, and subordinates.
- Do the Feedback Analysis as a matter of course to build on your strengths.
- Gain really effective control by conducting a comprehensive "business audit."
- Work back to costs from what customers are prepared to pay.
- Look at several measures of capital employment – not just one.
- Have specific expectations for people's performance and appraise it systematically.
- Develop "business intelligence" about actual and potential competitors worldwide.

The invention of management

Jack Beatty, in *The World According to Drucker* (1998), dates Peter Drucker's defining moment as a management author precisely: "On or about November 6, 1954, Peter Drucker invented management."

The date refers to the publication of *The Practice of Management*, and the author has no doubts about its importance. "When I published *The Practice of Management*, that book made it possible for people to learn how to manage, something that up until then only a few geniuses seemed able to do, and nobody could replicate it."

Drucker has no doubt that "management" was his brainchild. An interview with Warren Bennis in May 1982, titled "The Invention of Management," includes an account of a visit to one Harry Hopf, who was supposed to have "the biggest management library in the world. The only one." Among the "thousands and thousands of volumes," however, there were only six about management. Of these Drucker found that half "weren't quite management. So practically nothing existed." As his host explained: "The rest are all about insurance, selling, advertising, and manufacturing." None of these activities can be conducted without "managing." They all need recruitment, remuneration policies, decision making, planning, strategies, and many other activities that plainly come under the heading of management. So what exactly had Drucker "invented"?

Key book

For all intents and purposes Drucker invented the management book. There were business books and books on various techniques available at the time. Before Drucker even visited General Motors, for instance, the great entrepreneur Forrest Mars was using the performance measurement techniques presented in *Higher Control in Management* by a little-known Briton, T. G. Rose.

There were plenty of other experts and expert authors – including management consultants. None of these contributed more than James O. McKinsey, who was a pioneer of scientific management 29 years before Drucker's "invention." Three

"You can't do carpentry, you know, if you only have a saw, or only a hammer, or you never heard of a pair of pliers. It's when you put all those tools into one kit that you invent." *The Frontiers of Management*

years before that, the *Harvard Business Review* published its first issue. So management journalism also existed, as did the academic faculties from which the *Harvard Business Review* sprang. Its founder, the dean of the Harvard Business School, specifically wanted the journal to help "improve the practice of management." Drucker brought together all these strands.

In *The Practice of Management* Drucker took on board the pioneering of the consultants, who mostly developed their ideas from financial accounting; the organizational feats of men like Sloan; the gradual build-up of academic knowledge and teaching; the body of expertise on subjects ranging from marketing to mass production; and the experience of numberless managers in myriad firms. He embraced all this in an intellectual framework that explained to managers what they were doing and why – and, even more important, told them what they should do.

Managing effectively

Several decades of practical observation led Drucker to conclude that there are five essential functions that combine to form the basis of every manager's job. Aim to improve your skills in each of these five areas, and assess your progress throughout the learning process.

The Five Functions of a Manager				
1 Setting objectives	**2** Organizing the group	**3** Motivating and communicating	**4** Measuring performance	**5** Developing people

Effectiveness versus efficiency

Drucker stresses the vital distinction between effectiveness (doing the right thing) and efficiency (doing things right). For each of the five functions of a manager, ask yourself these two key questions:

- Am I truly effective?
- Or am I merely efficient?

To quantify the results, do a simple exercise. Set out two columns headed "Effective" and "Efficient" on a piece of paper, and write the five functions down the side. Against each function list the activities involved. For each function mark yourself out of 10 for effectiveness (doing the right thing) and for efficiency (doing things right).

Assessing your performance

Add up your score and compare it with the analysis below. A perfect total of 100 is unlikely. There is always a gap between actual performance and perfection – your score will show how far you have to go. Next, look at the balance between the effectiveness and efficiency scores. This is as important as your total; doing the right things badly and the wrong things well are both ineffective. Now concentrate on developing all five skills in the sections that follow.

Analysis

- 35 or below: your performance is inadequate. Act fast to improve your efficiency and effectiveness.
- 35–70: your performance is average to good, but requires improvement.
- 75 or above: you are efficient and effective, but cannot afford to relax.

1 Setting objectives

Setting objectives involves a continuous process of research and decision-making. Ensure that your personal objectives and those of your job (at the unit and organizational levels) are the same.

Self-knowledge

Knowledge of yourself and your unit is a vital starting point in setting objectives. To discover how your strengths contribute to the organization's objectives, Drucker advocates asking five questions. Ask them, not only about yourself, but about your unit. The answers will identify what changes must be made in order to get the results you expect. The next step is to undertake a feedback analysis to compare actual results with expectations.

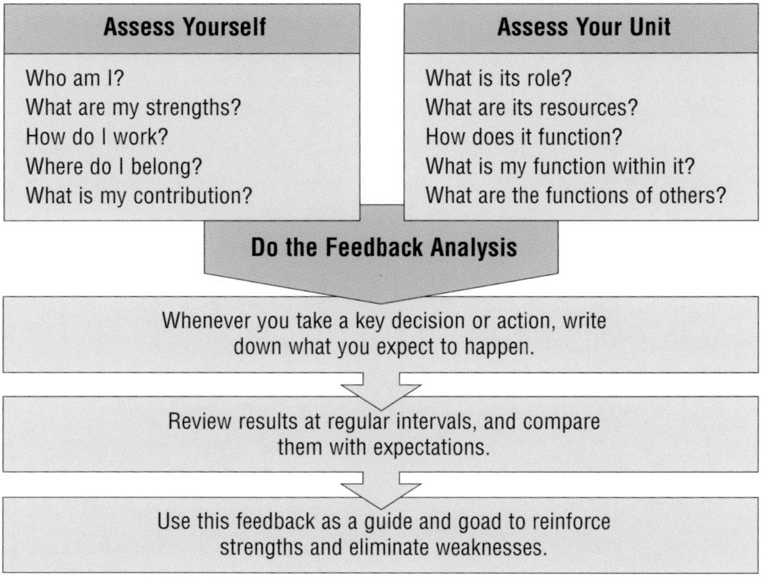

Assess Yourself

Who am I?
What are my strengths?
How do I work?
Where do I belong?
What is my contribution?

Assess Your Unit

What is its role?
What are its resources?
How does it function?
What is my function within it?
What are the functions of others?

Do the Feedback Analysis

Whenever you take a key decision or action, write down what you expect to happen.

Review results at regular intervals, and compare them with expectations.

Use this feedback as a guide and goad to reinforce strengths and eliminate weaknesses.

Applying the Feedback Analysis

Carry out the Feedback Analysis as often as you feel necessary, and ask the people who work for you to do likewise. The results of each analysis will provide a strong foundation for the next round of setting objectives, both for you and your unit.

2 Organizing the group

Unless the way in which your unit, or group, is organized is suitable for its purposes and the people in it, failure will result. Once you have set the objectives (see p. 45), provide the human resources needed to meet them, and ensure that they are effectively deployed.

Defining work

In the well-organized group, nobody does anything superfluous, and the leader only does the tasks that nobody else can do. To help you define and allot tasks, including your own, ask yourself three of Drucker's most penetrating questions:

- What am I doing that does not need to be done at all?
- What am I doing that can be done by somebody else?
- What am I doing that only I can do?

Delegating tasks

Always drop unnecessary work altogether. Necessary tasks that you do not need to do should be delegated. Delegation itself – finding the right person and giving them the right work – is the one task that you cannot delegate. Resist the temptation to keep tasks to yourself as a means of control or, worse, a demonstration of power. You should be interested in authority, but only in the authority of expertise – that is, your delegates (and your peers) follow your lead because you are good at your job. Resist, too, delegating in a haphazard fashion. Always ensure that your choice of delegate is based on a fair and objective assesment of his or her skills and abilities in relation to the requirements of the task.

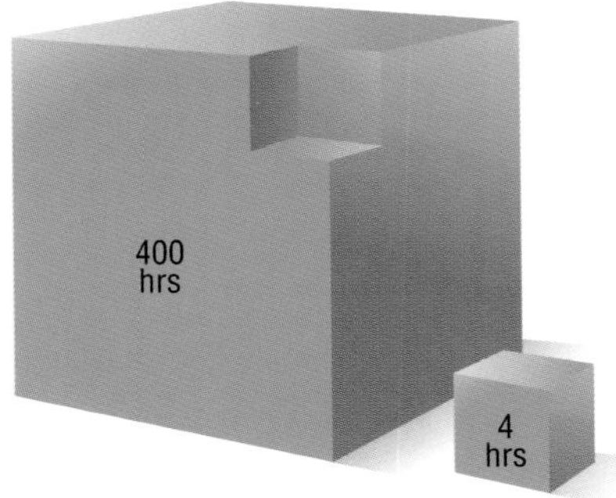

Saving time

Alfred P. Sloan, the GM executive who gave Drucker masterclasses in management, said of selection: "If we didn't spend four hours on placing a man and placing him right, we'd spend 400 hours cleaning up after our mistakes."

3 Motivating and communicating

The good motivator motivates people to motivate themselves. Rather than relying on your powers (exhortation, reward, or punishment, for example) to provide a spur, use the powers within people.

Sharing motivation

Ideally, those who work for you share your motivation. To find out if they do, both as individuals and as a group, ask yourself:

- Do they identify themselves with the organization and their own group?
- Do they identify themselves with its products and/or services?
- Do they accept individual and group responsibility for the quality and performance of their work?

The more positive the answers, the stronger the foundations for teamwork and for leadership, which is about your personal example, how you conduct your relationships with your people, and the decisions you make on the all-important Three Ps.

The Three Ps		
1 Pay	2 Placement	3 Promotion

A two-way relationship

Have clear reasons for your decisions on the Three Ps, and always communicate these reasons to everybody concerned. Ask yourself:

- What information do I owe to the people with whom I work and on whom I depend?
- In what form?
- And in what time frame?

Make sure that you use the answers to these questions as the basis for your communications. Do not think of communication as a separate and periodic task. Use every means available to let everyone working with you know your plans and your reasons. Remember that communication is two-way, so ensure that the channels are fully open to others so that they can give you the information you need. That includes, as a vital matter, feedback to make certain that communication has become understanding and consensus.

4 Measuring performance

In most companies, the measuring of performance is dominated by financial numbers – sales figures, cash flow, and profit – giving a limited, one-dimensional picture of progress. To obtain a clear and wide-ranging view of performance levels, always use the greatest variety of indicators possible.

The whole picture

Write down a list of the things you need to know and the issues you need to manage in order to perform your job effectively. Then write beside them the indicators that will measure that effectiveness. The following are likely to appear as entries on your list:

- Market share
- Quality
- Innovation
- Competitiveness
- Customer satisfaction
- Employee morale
- Cost of waste
- Use of capital
- Productivity

Although all of these contribute to the outcome in cashflow and profits, none can be measured by either figure. Think very carefully about each indicator you choose. Take market share: the crude division of total cash sales will be misleading, for example, if your unit sales are disproportionately low (you may be over-pricing) or high (you may be buying market share). You need to look at both unit sales and cash share to get a comprehensive and accurate picture of your overall performance. Ensure that all members of a team are involved in measuring performance to keep everyone focused on raising standards across the board.

Measuring in the Round

The use of capital is a classic Drucker example of measuring performance in the round. Do not take the usual one-dimensional view of profits as a percentage of capital employed. To measure a potential investment, answer six questions. Once the investment has been made, ask how the outcome compared with expectations.

- How long will it take for profits to pay back the investment?
- When will the cash stop flowing out and start returning?
- Do we really have to make this investment?
- What is the return on investment?
- Is that return comfortably above the true cost of the capital invested?
- Looking ahead, and allowing for interest rates, what is the future pay-off worth in today's values?

5 Developing yourself and others

You have a responsibility, what Drucker calls a "relationship responsibility," for those with whom you work. Trust and know your colleagues. This is a moral responsibility that you owe to everybody, for you depend on their work as they depend on yours.

Test your knowledge

Carrying out this responsibility develops the abilities of manager and managed alike. Consider these questions:

- Do I know what everybody else does?
- Do I know how they perform?
- Do I know what they contribute and what results are expected?
- Do I trust the people I work with?
- Do I treat each of them as individuals?
- Do I know their strengths?

Work toward a positive answer to each of them.

Focus on strengths

Developing people starts with the self. Do the Feedback Analysis (see p. 45) to show you where your strengths and weaknesses lie. Based on this information, form a six-step action plan:

Six-Step Action Plan
1 Identify your strengths
2 Improve your strengths
3 Increase your knowledge
4 Eliminate bad habits
5 Practice good manners
6 Avoid weak areas

Drucker advises that you should concentrate on your strengths and waste as little effort as possible on improving areas of low competence. Ask everyone who works for you to adopt an action plan. With your help, it will take them forward – and you with them.

3

Managing by objectives & self-control

The eight key areas where managers must pursue clear objectives • **Why managers must master five basic functions to be effective** • Producing results on the outside – in the market and the economy • **Creating strategy that is customer-focused, entrepreneurial, market-leading, innovative, and tied to decisive opportunities** • The essential principles of empowerment • **Getting the right music from the managerial orchestra** • How to make the right decisions about people – including yourself

Unlike other management writers, Drucker has rarely been identified with particular cure-all remedies. In the hands of others, the panacea approach has been used as a Unique Selling Proposition, the weapon with which to establish an academic reputation, or a rich consultancy practice, or (not infrequently) both. Drucker's skeptical mind subjects cults and bogus claims to withering analysis. Yet he himself has been closely identified with one of the longest-lasting and most widely accepted wonder techniques of all: Management by Objectives (MBO).

Jack Beatty, in *The World According to Drucker* (1997), calls MBO "Drucker's signature management concept." In *The Witch Doctors* (1996), John Micklethwait and Adrian Wooldridge of *The Economist* say that "Drucker invented" MBO, which they call "one of the rational school of management's most successful products." They do not, however, define the product, and seem to confuse Drucker's prime and unarguable insight – that management must set and have clear objectives – with what MBO became, a highly arguable system of command and control. While the setting of objectives is essential for an effective company, management by objectives is not.

Integrated management system

The MBO technique is only one way of seeking to control, coordinate, and motivate managers – and it is not necessarily the best. Starting from the top of a company, the six stages of MBO are:

- Define corporate objectives at board level.
- Analyze management tasks and devise formal job

specifications, which allocate responsibilities and decisions to individual managers.

- Set performance standards.
- Agree and set specific objectives.
- Align individual targets with corporate objectives.
- Establish a management information system to monitor achievements against objectives.

Support for all six elements – sometimes strong support – can be found in Drucker's writings. The trouble comes when the six elements are combined to comprise a system of management. The complete MBO system is supposed to get managers off and running, busily acting to implement and achieve their plans, which automatically achieve those of the organization. The review mechanism enables bosses to make sure that their managers are performing as they should – especially in the "key result areas" that are a strong feature of MBO.

Determining company objectives

For MBO to be effective, individual managers must understand the specific objectives of their job and how those objectives fit in with the overall company objectives set by the board of directors.

Performing in key result areas

In his book *The Practice of Management* (1954), Drucker names eight of the key result areas where managers need, above all, to pursue clear objectives:

- Marketing
- Innovation
- Human organization
- Financial resources
- Physical resources
- Productivity
- Social responsibility
- Profit requirements

In reality MBO, as applied in hundreds of companies, has concentrated far more on achieving objectives in the last of these key areas – profit – than in any other area. The bottom line figures largely in salary review, which is important in the MBO system, along with matters such as management development and career progression. Obviously, these activities take place in companies that have no MBO system or anything like it. Obviously, too, you cannot run a proper budget system without setting objectives, and you cannot run MBO without proper budgeting.

However, in recent years opinion has moved away from the idea of packing everybody into a formal, rigid system of objectives. Today, when maximum flexibility is essential, achieving that rightly seems more important.

"A manager's job should be based on a task to be performed in order to attain the company's objectives... the manager should be directed and controlled by the objectives of performance rather than by his boss." *The Practice of Management*

Achieving a balance

Flexibility has always had great importance for Drucker. As Micklethwait and Wooldridge argue, the fading of MBO has been linked with a rising "fashion for that other great Drucker theme, handing decisions back to workers through delayering and empowerment." They ask: "Why did the prophet of empowerment turn to such a rigid approach to management?" The answer is that he did not: other students of management theory did so, in their development of his ideas. But the two writers are correct to observe that Drucker "was trying – as he has done ever since – to create a balance between what was best in both the humanist and rationalist" schools of management.

That balance has to be struck, not by thinkers, but by practicing managers. Turning their aims into successful actions, says Drucker, forces managers to master five basic operations: setting objectives, organizing the group, motivating and communicating, measuring performance, and developing people, including yourself (see p. 33). These MBO operations are all compatible with empowerment, if you truly follow Alfred P. Sloan's principle of decentralization: telling people what you want done, but letting them achieve it their own way. To make the principle work well, people need to be able to develop personally, which Drucker viewed as the most important part of the five operations.

In addition, for the quintet to succeed, you have to forget a fallacy that, according to Drucker, underlies almost everything ever written about people management: "There is one right way to manage people – or at least there should be." Drucker himself once believed in the fallacy but unusually, on this issue he radically changed his mind. In *The Practice of Management* he more or less accepted that

Douglas McGregor's "Theory Y," which maintains that the natural instinct of everyone is to work willingly and well, was the only sound approach to managing people. But eight years later Abraham Maslow proved Drucker "dead wrong," showing "conclusively that different people have to be managed differently" if they are to perform well and achieve their potential.

This is the antithesis of a rigid MBO system. Fascinatingly, there is not a single mention of "objectives" in the index to Drucker's 1999 book, *Management Challenges for the 21st Century*. The single aspect of his thought with which Drucker has been most identified no longer looms large – or indeed even looms at all. However, he does suggest a new starting point for management theory and practice that is not too far removed: a "definition of results" and then "managing for performance" to achieve those results.

Managing for results

In 1964, a decade after publication of the definitive *The Practice of Management*, Drucker published a "how-to" book entitled *Managing for Results* (1986). It expands the theory of MBO into the only place where meaningful results can be won: the outside world. The theory of how to "produce results on the outside, in the market and the economy" rests on eight perceptions, neatly summarized by Jack Beatty in *The World According to Drucker*:

- Resources and results exist outside, not inside, the business.
- Results come from exploiting opportunities, not solving problems.

- For results, resources must go to opportunities, not to problems.
- "Economic results" do not go to minor players in a given market, but to leaders.
- Leadership, however, is not likely to last.
- What exists is getting old.
- What exists is likely to be misallocated (i.e., the first 10 percent of effort produces 90 percent of the results).
- To achieve economic results, concentrate.

This list is plainly aimed at top management, and is concerned with strategy (a word Drucker used to spurn, but to which he has become reconciled). A solid, sound strategy is customer-focused, entrepreneurial, aimed at market leadership, based on innovation, and tightly focused on "decisive opportunities."

Individual responsibility

The crucial argument for MBO was that it created a link between top management's strategic thinking and the strategy's implementation lower down. But the required nature of the link has changed profoundly since 1964.

The critical difference is that responsibility for objectives has been passed, as Drucker shows, from the organization to its individual members: "in the knowledge-based organization all members have to be able to control their own work by feeding back from their results to their objectives." Writing 40 years after *The Practice of Management*, Drucker says that this is what he called "Management by Objectives" and "Self-Control" (see p. 61). The underlining is his. Today the worker is a self-manager, whose decisions are of decisive importance for results.

Drucker cites as a current example the mini-mill that makes steel with under 100 workers, one-tenth the number of a conventional plant with similar output. Each worker, he points out, "makes decisions all the time that have a greater impact on the results of the entire mini-mill than even middle managers ever had in the conventional mill". In such an organization, management has to ask each employee three questions:

- What should we hold you accountable for?
- What information do you need?
- What information do you owe the rest of us?

Each worker, under this arrangement, participates in the key decisions on equipment, scheduling, and "indeed what the basic business policy of the entire mill should be." Drucker asserts that people managed in this way – people who know more about the job than anybody else – react to being held responsible by acting responsibly. This is an essential principle of "empowerment," the movement that gathered so much inspiration from Drucker's work. His commitment to the principle has never wavered, although he dislikes the term.

Empowerment recognizes "the demise" of the command-and-control system, but remains a term of power and rank. True, people are still subordinates in the sense that they can be "hired or fired, promoted, appraised, and so on." But the "superior" is increasingly dependent on the subordinates for getting results in their areas of responsibility, where they (and not the boss) have the requisite knowledge. "In turn these 'subordinates' depend on the superior for direction. They depend on the superior to tell them what the 'score' is."

Conducting knowledge workers

A manager should view members of his or her team much as a conductor regards the players in the orchestra, as individuals whose particular skills contribute to the success of the enterprise.

The management orchestra

The word "score" is carefully chosen. Drucker's favorite metaphor for modern management is musical. In his opinion, the superior-subordinate relationship "is far more like that between the conductor of an orchestra and the instrumentalist" than the traditional organizational norm. "In the knowledge-based company, the superior cannot as a rule do the work of the supposed subordinate any more than the conductor... can play the tuba," states Drucker. However, everybody knows what piece the orchestra is playing, what results everybody wishes to achieve, and what specific part each of them has to play. All the members of the orchestra work together using the same score, as a band of skilled individualists.

There is nothing the conductor, however able or autocratic, can achieve without the willing support and contribution of the players. Increasingly, full-time employees have to be managed "as if they were volunteers." Because they receive no pay, volunteers tend to require greater job satisfaction than paid workers. Drucker thinks, however, that non-volunteer needs are just the same:

- Challenge, above all
- "To know the organization's mission and to believe in it"
- Continuous training
- The "need to see results"

Thus, the development of the knowledge society has finally brought about that elusive "balance between what was best in both the humanist and rationalist" schools of management. The organization and its senior management are as intently focused on results as ever. But the other people in the organization fulfill its needs and their own, not in response to top-down dictation, but by effectively exercising their own abilities and motivation.

"… the knowledge worker is dependent on the superior to give direction and, above all, to define what the 'score' is for the entire organization, that is, what are standards and values, performance and results." *Management Challenges for the 21st Century*

Intelligent self-management

The issue of personal effectiveness has long occupied Drucker, whose 1966 book, *The Effective Executive*, reads like the individual's companion volume to the organization's *Managing for Results*. Drucker had been very impressed by his observations of "self-control" at General Electric. He liked the fact that GE's unit managers, and not their superiors, received the results of the annual audit. He believed that a GE atmosphere of "confidence and trust in the company" could be traced to "using information for self-control rather than control from above."

Self-control is the tool of effectiveness. Drucker distinguishes powerfully between "efficient" (doing something well) and "effective" (doing the right thing well). The effective executive knows what to do, knows how to do it, and (above all) gets it done. In all three phases, the effective executive exercises intelligent self-management, starting with the management of their own time. They use that time systematically for work that only they can do, and they establish priorities by putting first things first – and putting second things nowhere. They also make decisions effectively – or some of them do.

Know yourself

Despite his belief in people and their potential, Drucker sometimes writes as if innate qualities cannot be altered. He poses as a "crucial question" for managers, whether "I produce results as a decision-maker or an adviser," and adds: "The person who has learned that he or she is not a decision-maker should have learned to say 'No' when offered a decision-making assignment." The distinction is impractical, however, as managers at every

Freedom to manage yourself
The laptop computer frees managers to work wherever and whenever they choose. It is the perfect tool for knowledge workers, who rely chiefly on themselves for motivation and direction.

level have to make decisions whether they want to or not, for example, on people issues. Here Drucker offers useful advice, which any manager would be wise to follow. He suggests managers ask themselves the following four questions, regarding an employee:

- What has he or she done well?
- What is the person likely to do well?
- What do they have to learn to be able to get the full benefit from their strength?
- If I had a son or daughter, would I be willing to have them work under this person?

He has similarly thought through the process of decision-making in general, and gives equally shrewd advice about the practicalities. For example, he suggests separating the recurrent issues (which are handled by the system) from the unique (which are dealt with independently); and he advises on how to determine which decisions to delegate and which to retain. It is hard to think of any manager who would not benefit from learning to ask the right questions to obtain the right information. But when Drucker also insists that "people way down the line" have to "learn how to… make effective decisions," he again throws doubt on his distinction between the innate decision-maker and the innate adviser.

Drucker also believes that there are two distinctive ways of absorbing information – through the written or the spoken language – and that everyone tends to have a leaning toward being either a 'reader' or a 'listener'. He argues that knowing your style is the "first thing to know about how one performs," lamenting the fact that very few people indeed know "which of the two they are," even though this ignorance is "damaging." Once you understand which is your naturally dominant learning style you are in a position to improve the way you perform. Drucker advises: "… do not try to change yourself – it is unlikely to be successful. But work, and hard, to improve the way you perform. And try not to do work of any kind in a way you do not perform or perform badly."

This sage advice has to be squared with the statement that "more and more people in the workforce will have to manage themselves. They will have to place themselves where they can make the greatest contribution; they will have to develop themselves." Drucker believes that there are "many" areas where the individual lacks "the minimum endowment needed," so the energy, resources, and time should go, not into making "an incompetent person into a low mediocrity," but into making "a competent person into a star performer."

Know where you belong

Drucker stresses that "how a person performs" is just as much a "given" as their strengths and weaknesses. "A few common personality traits" (such as the difference between readers and listeners) "usually determine how one achieves results." You plan your objectives, therefore, to fit the givens, but "to be able to manage oneself," you finally have to know the answer to the question: "What are my values?" The answer indicates what organization you should join: its values and your own must be "close enough so that they can coexist."

When you know your strengths of ability and performance and your values, you can find where you "belong." Then the self-manager must ask not the MBO question "What am I told to contribute?" but the post-MBO question "What should I contribute?" Drucker regards this as "a new question in human history" because "until very recently, it was taken for granted that most people were subordinates who did as they were told." This is generally still the case, so Drucker is being somewhat Utopian in his latest formula for effectiveness, in which the manager asks him or herself:

- What does the situation require?
- How could I make my greatest contribution with my strengths, my way of performing, my values, to what needs to be done?
- What results have to be achieved to make a difference?

This leads to action conclusions: what to do, where to start, how to start, what goals and deadlines to set. The formula differs hardly at all from the definition of effectiveness Drucker has always used: knowing what to do and how to do it, and getting it done. The difference lies, however, in transferring all the responsibility to the individual, not to "do one's own thing," but to set and achieve one's own objectives – one's unique contribution.

Ideas into action

- Understand that there is no one right way to manage people.
- For best results, give resources to opportunities, not to problems.
- Get to know the organization's mission and to believe in it.
- Find out what you should do, and how – then go ahead and do it.
- Ask yourself whether you produce results as a decision-maker or an adviser.
- Help yourself and others to learn how to manage yourselves.
- Ask yourself what you should do, rather than simply doing what you are told to do.

Managing by objectives

The essential message taught by Drucker through Management by Objectives is that managers need to identify and set objectives both for themselves, their units, and their organizations. Ensure that you set the right objectives if you want to achieve the right results.

What is MBO?

The principle behind MBO is to make sure that everybody within the organization has a clear understanding of the aims, or objectives, of that organization, as well as an awareness of their own roles and responsibilities in achieving those aims.

MBO and the individual

Start with yourself by reading the following six questions and answering them as best you can. The responsibility on all six counts rests with you as an individual. None of the answers depends entirely on other people, and some do not depend on them at all.

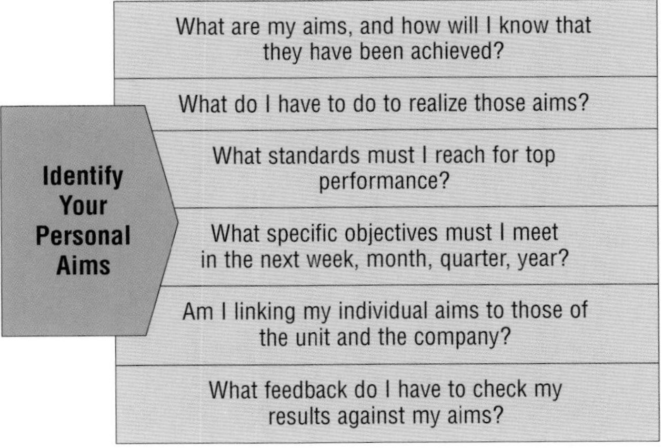

If you can answer some of the questions only partially, try to find out what you need to know in order to answer them fully. Keep returning to your answers to check that you are still working along the right lines, and review them as necessary – you will find that many of your answers change over time.

MBO and the organization

There are too many managers who think and act as if the higher strategy of their organization is no business of theirs – in fact, it is everybody's vital business. Never forget that your organization's objectives affect you directly and personally. Refer back to the questions on the opposite page – it only takes small changes in the wording of the questions to make them apply to your company and to your unit. Repeat the exercise, writing down the answers, first as if you are the boss of your unit (whatever your actual position), and then as if you are the chief executive. If you do not know some of the answers, try to obtain them.

Personal empowerment

If you find that you cannot identify your or your company's aims satisfactorily, remember what Drucker advocates: you need four powers to do an excellent job. These four powers are a combination of the personal qualities that an individual brings to the job, and the powers made available to everyone by the organization. The powers are not only essential to perform an excellent job, but also to produce job satisfaction, the prime motivator.

The Four Powers
1 Freedom to challenge everything and anything
2 Continuous training and development on the job
3 Knowledge of, and faith in, the organization's mission
4 The ability to achieve and see results

The right organization

If your company or unit does not have an overall objective that you can identify, or you are unable to challenge their strategy, your ability to grow on the job will be hamstrung, and your efforts to achieve real results will become frustrated. Some organizations may place a lower priority than you might like on allowing staff to exercise the four powers. In either case, find somewhere else where you can really make a contribution – and go there!

1 Making a contribution

Be aware of what is expected of you and why – this is one of the most valuable lessons of Drucker's teachings. That awareness will determine your ability to contribute to your organization.

Asking the right questions

The question "What is MY contribution?" needs to be properly understood within the context of the organization. Which of the following three questions is the most apt?

- What do I WANT to contribute?
- What am I TOLD to contribute?
- What SHOULD I contribute?

The last question is the most appropriate one to ask. It means "What does the situation require?" Once you have succeeded in identifying what is required, you can start to consider how you can use your own unique powers to contribute to what needs to be done.

Your Unique Powers		
Your strengths	Your way of performing	Your values

Identifying strengths

To understand how you can best match your unique powers to your required contribution, carry out a SWOT analysis on yourself. Draw a box with four compartments. Set down your Strengths in one, your Weaknesses in another, then list your Opportunities and the Threats to your success in the third and fourth compartments. The required contribution should rely on your strengths and not depend on areas in which you are weak. It should give you opportunities to shine, but should not involve threats to your personal fulfillment. Ask:

- Will my contribution involve doing what I really want to do?
- Will it be rewarding and stimulating?

If you would really rather be doing something else, and if the rewards and interest you need are lacking, it is foolish to continue. Your contribution will inevitably fall short in the area that should dominate everything: results. Drucker's advice is paramount. Always ask: "Where and how can I have results that make a difference?"

2 Setting standards

The temptation for all managers is to find something at which they excel, and which comes quite easily, and to continue doing it for as long as possible. If you want to improve as a manager, however, adapt your contribution to change, and see each level of achievement as a stepping stone to something higher and better.

Improving performance

In searching to identify where your results can really make a difference, follow these guidelines:

- Choose target results that "stretch" your abilities above and beyond your present limits.
- Pick a target that is achievable, but at the same time one which enlarges the bounds of possibility.
- Make sure the results will be meaningful and clearly visible.
- Unless it is absolutely impossible (which is rarely the case), find a way of measuring your results.

Never be satisfied by present standards of performance, whether other people's or your own. If you can find superior performance elsewhere, in your own company or outside, make bettering that level your benchmark. Make a personal habit, too, of selecting key aspects of your work which you can measurably improve, such as answering your phone within five rings or arriving at meetings five minutes early, and ask colleagues to help keep you up to scratch.

Exceeding Targets

What actually is achievable can exceed your wildest dreams, as illustrated by the following case study. You should never set your staff unachievable targets – it is a pointless exercise and will be demoralizing for them.

James Adamson saved NCR's factory in Dundee from extinction by turning it into the world's prime source of automatic teller machines (ATMs) for banks. Yet Dundee started from far behind the leaders in the field – ninth in the world. NCR's first two ATMs, moreover, were so terrible that the customers returned them. Adamson called in his engineers and asked them not just to match competitors' reliability, but to do twice as well. He was laughed at, but he refused to give up – and the engineers found out how to improve reliability, not twice, but threefold.

3 Making it happen

"What 'impossible' things can I accomplish?" Base your answer on three key elements: your individual talent, having a true "stretch target," and achieving your chosen contribution. You will achieve this last, all-important element if you are successful in execution.

What, how, where, and when?

Drucker breaks down execution into making four decisions. Make it your practice to plan systematically, never failing to address these four decisions, and always work to a realistic deadline.

The Four Decisions of Execution			
1 What to do	**2** How to start	**3** Where to start	**4** What goals and deadlines to set

James Adamson's thinking at Dundee (see p. 69) is an excellent example of four-stage execution. The "What" was to improve reliability. The starting point was re-engineering the product. The "Where" was in the engineering department. The goal was doubled reliability – and he set a deadline for its achievement. The director of engineering went through exactly the same process in going beyond his boss's request to achieve the "impossible." In addition to exceeding the goal originally set by Adamson, an invaluable consequence of this success was to improve the overall efficiency and effectiveness of the whole operation.

Unlocking the Key

Successful achievement of an objective may depend on finding the "key" to a specific aspect of the operation. Learn from a case study cited by Drucker in which the "key" unlocked the full potential of a stagnating enterprise.

A hospital administrator needed to revitalize a large hospital, and found the "unlocking key" in the emergency room, which was "big, visible, and sloppy." What to do? How to start? Where to start? The administrator gave the ER staff an extremely stretching target: every patient had to be seen by a qualified nurse within one minute of arrival. The deadline for achievement was two years. In the event, the target was met in half that time. Two years later, the whole hospital had been transformed.

4 Managing yourself

The skills, qualities, and values you bring to your job are of crucial importance in achieving your objectives. Aim to be the kind of manager who gets the best from staff, and who does the best for them.

Assessing yourself

Drucker's advice on hiring people can be turned inside out to provide a searching test of how good a manager you are. Drucker tells recruiters to look for evidence of past success, potential for further achievement, the ability to learn more, and the qualities of a good manager. Assess yourself on these four points to identify areas in which you should improve. Analyze your answers very carefully, making sure that they are totally honest.

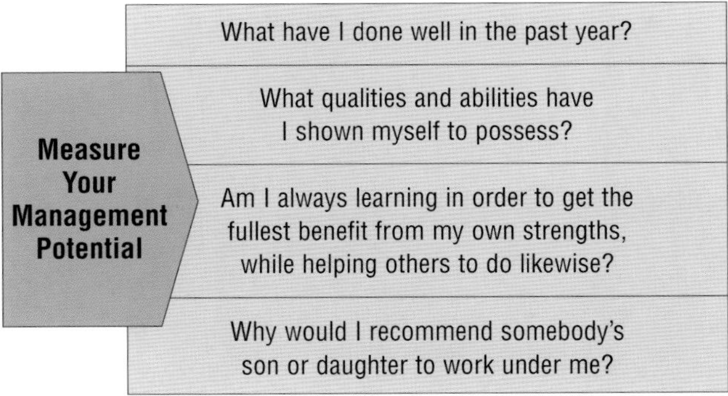

Consider your values

Drucker is insistent that playing your part, which he refers to as "managing oneself," depends on your values as well as on your strengths, weaknesses, and personality. One of the essential values is honesty. If you are honest with yourself, you will treat other people honestly, too. Never work in an organization whose values are unacceptable to you. Ignore this principle and you will condemn yourself to frustration and non-performance. "In respect to ethics," writes Drucker, "the rules are the same for everybody." There is only one test – "the mirror test" – and you must make sure you pass it. It consists of one question: "What kind of person do I want to see when I shave myself, or put on my lipstick, in the morning?"

4

Harnessing the power of innovation

How to seek out, respond to, and exploit change as opportunity • **Watching out for significant changes in population, perception, and knowledge** • Why bright ideas are important, but purposeful innovation matters more • **Mastering the five do's and the three don'ts of successful innovation** • Why entrepreneurs seek to define and confine risks • **Keeping new ventures well apart from the company's established business** • Using the "business X-ray" to discover how much innovation you need

Drucker calls innovation "the specific tool of entrepreneurs." Doing new things, or doing old things in new ways, is how entrepreneurs "exploit change as an opportunity for a different business or a different service." They "see change as the norm and as healthy." Usually they do not bring about the change themselves. But... "the entrepreneur always searches for change, responds to it, and exploits it as an opportunity."

This process of exploitation, Drucker says, had a profound influence on the American economy as the 20th century approached its end. In the period between 1974 and 1984, the total number of jobs in the US economy grew by a record 24 percent, while Western Europe's job losses totalled between three and four million. Nor was the American growth solely, or even mainly, high-tech. Although the high-tech explosion was special, "of immeasurable qualitative importance," the new jobs came "from anywhere and nowhere" as "new applications of management" made possible "the emergence of the entrepreneurial economy."

These observations inspired Drucker to write *Innovation and Entrepreneurship* (1984), which was then, and remains, the best manual on the practice and principles of its subject. As with management 30 years before, Drucker tackled innovation as a discipline that can be taught and learned, the sources, nature, and symptoms of which can all be studied. By studying innovation, the entrepreneur and the entrepreneurial manager learn where and how to succeed. Turning innovative ideas into profitable action is the essence of the entrepreneur. Typically, Drucker tore away the mystique surrounding his theme. "Entrepreneurship is risky," he snorted, "mainly because so few of the so-called entrepreneurs know what they are doing."

Searching for changes

The book set out to remedy that defect. Drucker is convinced that innovation can be approached methodically, by a "purposeful and organized search for changes" and by identifying the opportunities that such changes might offer. Within the established company or industry, he isolated four sources for these entrepreneurial opportunities:

- The unexpected – the unexpected success, the unexpected failure, the unexpected outside event.
- The incongruity – between reality as it actually is and reality as it is assumed to be or as it "ought to be."
- Innovation based on process need.
- Changes in industry structure or market structure that catch everyone unawares.

As always, Drucker has vivid, wide-ranging examples to support each source of entrepreneurial opportunitiy. For the unexpected success, he cites the unexpected demand for TVs from "poor" Japanese farmers, which was exploited by Matsushita, but by nobody else. For the unexpected failure, he gives the example of the surprise flop of the Edsel, a large, "gas-guzzling" sedan, which opened Ford's eyes to fundamental market changes. The company then exploited this change with the launch of the sporty, smaller Thunderbird. In his discussion of incongruities, Drucker cites the rise of the mini-mill at the expense of large integrated steel mills, and loading containers on land instead of loading freighters on the water. To illustrate process need, he quotes an innovation in eye surgery, while structural change brings mention of the shift in US physicians from single to group practice.

External sources of changes

This quartet of sources visible within the enterprise or its industry are only part of the story. Drucker also identifies three external sources:

- Demographics (population changes)
- Changes in perception, mood, and meaning
- New knowledge, both scientific and non-scientific

Dead certainty can always be found in the first of these sources. One example of demographic certainty is a "forecast" that Drucker made in 1957. By combining the increase in births (which had already happened) with another established trend, the rise in the proportion of young adults going to college, Drucker estimated that there would be 10 to 12 million students by the 1970s – a huge increase. Nearly all the large US universities regarded this as preposterous but the new entrepreneurial universities exploited this dead-cert prediction to their great profit.

As an example of a change in perception, Drucker mentions the spread of "dining," as opposed to merely "eating," from the well-to-do to the less privileged. As for new knowledge, innovators who want to exploit it, he stresses, need only apply "a careful analysis of the knowledge available and the knowledge needed." He cites his own success in the field of management as an example:

"Entrepreneurs need to search purposefully for the sources of innovation, the changes and their symptoms that indicate opportunities for successful innovation." *Innovation & Entrepreneurship*

> "Many of the required pieces of knowledge were already available: organization theory, for instance, but also quite a bit of knowledge about managing work and worker. My analysis also showed, however, that these pieces were scattered and lodged in half a dozen different disciplines. Then it found which key knowledges were missing: purpose of a business; and knowledge of the work and structure of top management; what we now term 'business policy' and 'strategy'; objectives; and so on."

His response was to provide the missing pieces and combine them with the others to form a coherent whole.

Innovative bright ideas

Despite this personal example, the classification of sources does not altogether work. It is too schematic. As Drucker himself admits, these "seven source areas of innovative opportunities are blurred, and there is considerable overlap between them." Innovation cannot be tied down as easily as Drucker suggests – which in effect he admits when he says that "innovations based on a bright idea probably outnumber all other categories put together."

The untidiness of bright ideas bothers him. They are the "riskiest and least successful" source, and no one knows which ideas "have a chance to succeed and which ones are likely to fail." Attempts have been made to reduce this unpredictability, but have not been "particularly successful." Bright ideas are also "vague and elusive." For all that, Drucker states that "an entrepreneurial economy cannot dismiss cavalierly the innovation based on a bright idea." He cannot escape from the fact that the genesis and fate of innovation, ultimately, follow no rules.

Principles of innovation

Drucker still sticks to his schematic guns: "The purposeful innovation resulting from analysis, system, and hard work… surely covers at least 90 percent of all effective innovations." It is unlike Drucker to put forward a statistic with no hard supporting evidence. He is on firmer ground when arguing that general principles do exist, which he labels "do's," "don'ts," and "conditions." The "do's" are:

- Analyze the opportunities.
- Go out to look, to ask, to listen.
- Keep it simple, keep it focused.
- Start small – try to do one specific thing.
- Aim at market leadership.

The fifth principle – thinking big – seems to contrast illogically with the fourth. But, as Drucker says, "Innovations had better be capable of being started small, requiring at first little money, few people, and only a small and limited market." That gives the innovator more time (and space) within which to correct the inevitable errors. All the time, however, you "aim at dominance in an industry or market." Don't undershoot, or you "will simply create an opportunity for the competition" – which could be taken as another "don't" to add to the following list:

- Don't try to be clever.
- Don't diversify, don't splinter, don't try to do too many things at once.
- Don't try to innovate for the future.

The first and last "don'ts" are counterintuitive but their sense quickly becomes apparent. "Innovations have to be handled by ordinary human beings [whose] incompetence is...in abundant and never-failing supply. Anything too clever is almost bound to fail." As for the future, Drucker advises "innovate for the present!" in the sense that the innovation, if it could be successful this instant, will be just as successful in the future. It may take ten years of development to bring a new drug to market, but the medical condition that it will cure is prevalent right now.

These pragmatic recommendations are hardly consistent with the romantic image of risk-taking entrepreneurs. But Drucker dismisses this icon. He observes that entrepreneurs mostly cut "unromantic figures, and are much more likely

Master of innovation

An inventive genius, who took out more than 1,000 patents, Thomas Alva Edison (1847–1931) found it impossible to manage any of the companies he formed once they reached medium size.

to spend hours on a cashflow projection than to dash off looking for 'risks'." Most innovators, in his experience, "are successful to the extent to which they define risks and confine them." What governs their success is the way in which they "systematically analyze the sources of innovative opportunity, then pinpoint the opportunity and exploit it." They are conservative people, focused not on risk, but on opportunity.

Managing innovation separately

Unlike most writers on entrepreneurship, Drucker goes beyond this point to the crucial matter of management. How does entrepreneurial management differ from the usual variety? Both have to be "systematic, organized, purposeful." But if an entrepreneurial business is placed inside an established management system, it is more than likely to fail.

Drucker maintains that the established company will load insupportable burdens on the new venture: burdensome examples include highly structured reward programs, return-on-investment targets, and lack of clear accountability for the venture. So should companies abandon all efforts to govern new ventures? What about the policies and practices which Drucker recommends? He himelf asks: "Don't they interfere with the entrepreneurial spirit and stifle creativity? Cannot a business be entrepreneurial without such policies and practices?" His answer is that you might get away with it, but "neither very successfully, nor for very long."

Drucker is deeply aware of the fundamental difficulty in converting a large organization, which has built up policies, people, and practices along set lines, into the anarchic modes of the entrepreneur. He is full of warnings: "the most important caveat is not to mix managerial units and entrepreneurial ones" in any way. Also, steer clear of diversification, which, whatever its other benefits, "does not mix with entrepreneurship and innovation." Finally, don't try to solve the problem by "buying in" – acquiring small entrepreneurial ventures. He observes that "I myself know of no case where 'buying in' has worked."

Forming the business X-ray

Not only must the "entrepreneurial, the new" be organized completely separately from "the old and existing," but "there has to be a special locus for the new venture within the organization, and it has to be pretty high up." However small the new venture may be in relation to its parent, "somebody in top management must have the specific assignment to work on tomorrow as an entrepreneur and innovator."

Among other needs, this manager is responsible for "the business X-ray," which "furnishes the information needed to define how much innovation a given business requires, in what areas, and within what time frame." To discover this information Drucker suggests asking four questions, which are based on the work of management consultant Michael J. Kami. They are:

- How much longer will this product still grow?
- How much longer will it maintain itself in the marketplace?
- How soon can it be expected to age and decline – and how fast?
- When will it become obsolescent?

The answers establish the gap between what already exists and what is required to achieve the corporate ambitions: "the gap has to be filled or the company will soon start to die." But Drucker maintains that the company needs to aim beyond the measured gap because of the high probability of failure and (even higher) delay. "A company therefore should have under way at least three times the innovative efforts which, if successful, would fill the gap." In Drucker's experience, most executives find this threefold demand too high. In fact, the logic is irrefutable.

Managing new ventures

The issues of managing an entrepreneurial venture are at least as acute outside established businesses, in brand-new operations. Drucker puts it neatly: "In the existing business, it is the existing that is the main obstacle to entrepreneurship." In the new venture, it is its absence. Every one of the great Thomas Edison's companies "collapsed ignominiously once it got to middle size, and was saved only by booting Edison himself out and replacing him with professional management." Wonderful as an inventor, Edison never mastered all four requirements for managing the development of a new venture:

- A focus on the market.
- Financial foresight, especially in planning for cashflow and capital needs ahead.
- Building a top management team long before the new venture actually needs one and long before it can actually afford one.
- A decision by the founding entrepreneur with respect to his or her own role, area of work, and relationships.

An example would be the foundation of Compaq Computer, whose successful attack on the portable computer market was based on this quartet of principles. But none of these four requirements is cut and dried. "When a new venture does succeed, more often than not it is in a market other than the one it was originally intended to serve, with products or services not quite those with which it had set out, bought in large part by customers it did not even think of when it started, and used for a host of purposes besides the ones for which the products were first designed." "Market focus" in these circumstances means flexibility: spotting what has gone wrong, and moving quickly to turn error into advantage.

Financial focus, too, requires entrepreneurs to change their minds: "Entrepreneurs starting new ventures... tend to be greedy. They therefore focus on profits. But this is the wrong focus for a new venture, or rather, it comes last rather than first." Cashflow, capital, and controls come much earlier in the new venture's development. Without them "the profit figures are fiction – good for 12 or 18 months, after which they evaporate." Drucker stresses that financial foresight demands more thought than time.

Even if the new enterprise gets its market focus and financial foresight right, "serious crisis" threatens unless a common ailment, "lack of top management," is cured. Drucker pinpoints the catch-22 difficulty. If you cannot afford top management, how can you obtain it? His answer is to build the team from within, by dividing roles among the founding group and developing their management skills. All this, however, is plainly easier said than done, partly because the founder or founders have to evolve – and to devolve authority. Few find it easy either to articulate their proper role or to step back (let alone step down).

Entrepreneurial strategies

Forming strategy comes much easier than forming management structure, in the sense that every entrepreneur has some kind of plan. Drucker has isolated four strategies that he thinks specifically entrepreneurial:

- Being "Fustest with the Mostest" – the "greatest gamble," aiming from the beginning at permanent leadership
- "Hitting Them Where They Ain't" – either by "creative imitation," which surpasses the original innovation; or by "entrepreneurial judo," a concept highly developed by the Japanese, which enables newcomers "to catapult themselves into a leadership position... against the entrenched, established companies."
- Finding and occupying a specialized "ecological niche" – "obtaining a practical monopoly in a small area."
- Changing the economic characteristics of a product, a market, or an industry – by "creating utility," or pricing, or adaptation to the customer's social and economic reality, or delivering what represents true value to the customer.

He gives examples for each method of achieving the fourth strategy. For utility he cites Rowland Hill's penny post; for pricing he cites Gillette's cheap razors with expensive blades; for adaptation to the customer's reality, he provides the example of Cyrus McCormick's leasing of harvesters to farmers; and for delivering true value, he cites Herman Miller's move from selling individual items of furniture to offering whole office systems. Drucker recognizes the difficulty of all this diversity: "it is far less easy to be specific about entrepreneurial strategies than it is about purposeful innovation and entrepreneurial management."

He nevertheless makes a formidable effort to systematize an activity that makes up its own rules as it goes along. Inevitably the effort falls short of the aim. But there's not one innovator or entrepreneur who cannot benefit from Drucker's analytical approach – and that goes double, if not triple, for managers.

Ideas into action

- Maintain a purposeful and organized search for new opportunities.
- Look for incongruity between reality and what it is assumed to be or "ought" to be.
- Innovate for a present need, not for a future possibility.
- Give a new venture a senior "godfather" or "godmother" to whom it reports.
- Keep flexible – spot what goes wrong and turn error to advantage.
- Focus on cashflow, capital, and controls – not profit.
- Build your team from within, developing its own management skills.

Recognizing the sea change

Drucker's emergence as a profound thinker on society, the economy, and politics predates his discovery of management. His thinking was years ahead of his time, although founded on close observation of the present.

His first two books, *The End of Economic Man* (1939) and *The Future of Industrial Man* (1942) established him as an insightful political scientist. *The Age of Discontinuity*, published in 1969, was decades in advance of conventional thinking – and his insights were proved right.

Drucker spotted three discontinuities: in technology and industry, the world economy, and government. Of the three, it was the first that proved crucial. He saw four techno-industrial changes, including new materials, exploitation of the oceans, working from home, and the rise of the information industry. The first three visions all had substance; only the fourth was an inspired reading of the present, and thus of the future.

In a later book, Drucker expressed his discovery in suitably apocalyptic terms: "With the advent of the computer, information became the organizing principle of production. With this a new basic civilization came into being." Writing 13 years before the IBM PC changed the world of computing, and 24 years before the World Wide Web opened for business, in *The Age of Discontinuity* Drucker compared the future abundance of information with electricity.

Knowledge workers

He saw that the determining power in the economy and in society would be knowledge, which he defined as "systematic, purposeful, organized knowledge." A new army of "knowledge workers" was coming to the fore, and its soldiers would impose new norms on organizations and society as a whole.

They would be first among the millions of telecommuters; they would be the leaders in rewriting the rules of employment – by changing employers and careers more readily. They would be a major force in creating new demands for goods and services as the world moved from national economies to a world economy. *The Age of Discontinuity* set the intellectual

"Certainly young people, a few years hence, will use information systems as their normal tools, much as they now use the typewriters and the telephone." *The World According to Peter Drucker* by Jack Beatty

agenda for the upheavals that were to come – which Drucker continued to monitor and explain with uncanny precision. Books like *The New Realities* (1989), *Managing for the Future* (1992), and *Post-Capitalist Society* (1993) described a society that could not have been predicted by extrapolation from the past.

Drucker forced recognition that the discontinuities changed everything. "A great deal these days", he wrote, "is being said about the impact of the new information technologies on material civilization, on goods, services, and businesses. The social impacts are however as important – they may be more important." One was an entrepreneurial surge: Drucker saw innovations in politics, government, education, economics, the nation-state, the city.

The Age of Discontinuity did not create this sea-change. But it marked out the new seascape, named its features, and irreversibly changed perceptions to take account of the new realities.

5

Responsible knowledge management

Making the service economy and knowledge workers more productive • **Predicting the future by fully understanding the present** • Why knowledge continually makes itself obsolete • **The need to shift from inside information to external information** • Employing people as outside contractors rather than internal staff • **How the nonprofit organizations can teach management lessons to businesses** • The emergence of knowledge as the "absolutely decisive factor of production"

How does the manager exploit the great trends in society and the economy? Broad historical changes have been Drucker's dominant themes from the beginning of his writing career. He was the first to define the "great divide" of the 20th century, a seismic split that produced and is producing major social change: the knowledge revolution. As manual work has become fabulously more productive, thanks in recent decades partly to the new technology of information, the manual labor force has become a minority – following in the footsteps of farm workers. According to Drucker, the challenge for management today is to make the service economy and knowledge workers (see p. 93) far more productive, again using the new electronic armory.

Since the 1980s, if not earlier, Drucker has been looking beyond the millennium. Yet he disclaims any intention of posing as a prophet. In 1986, he characteristically argued that the millennium was already here, that "we are well advanced" past that landmark, and emphasized that he had never written about the "next century." He has now. In 1999 he published *Management Challenges for the 21st Century*. It represents a typical balance between Drucker's views of eternal verities and his acute analysis of changing forces in management.

"For the next twenty or thirty years demographics will dominate the politics of all developed countries. And they will inevitably be politics of *great turbulence*. No country is prepared for the issues." *Management Challenges for the 21st Century*

Identifying future developments

An especially cogent statement of Drucker's overall vision was published considerably earlier, in the September/October 1997 edition of the *Harvard Business Review*, which marked the 75th anniversary of the journal. Drucker has long been one of its most distinguished contributors. With typical assurance, he called the piece "The Future that has Already Happened." Predicting the future at all, let alone for the next 75 years, is pointless, he asserted. "But it is possible – and fruitful – to identify major events that have already happened, irrevocably, and that will have predictable effects in the next decade or two."

Drucker singled out demography as the first of these ineluctable forces. "The developed world is in the process of committing collective suicide. Its citizens are not having enough babies to reproduce themselves." Although you can definitely dispute his explanation (that younger people are cutting down on babies to offset the cost of looking after the aged), you cannot argue with the first two conclusions he draws from this depopulation of the West and of Japan (where a 56 percent fall is predicted for the 21st century).

- Retirement age will rise (Drucker expects this to be 75 well before 2010).
- Economic growth can come only from a very sharp and continuing increase in the productivity of knowledge work and knowledge workers.

Drucker's third conclusion that "there will be no single dominant world economic power" is more difficult to agree with. Given the US domination of the new technologies it hardly convinces – especially as the US population is stable while other populations in the developed world are falling.

Raising knowledge productivity

The overriding concern for Drucker is that all the developed countries, including the US, have a critical need for "continual systematic work on the productivity of knowledge and knowledge workers, which is abysmally low." Raising that productivity is the way to convert the developed world's quantitative lead in sheer numbers of knowledge workers into a qualitative one. Only thus will these states be enabled "to maintain their competitive position in the world economy." Knowledge productivity will not be the only competitive factor, but it is "likely to become decisive," at least for most industries in the developed countries.

Knowledge differs from all other resources in that it "constantly makes itself obsolete, with the result that today's advanced knowledge is tomorrow's ignorance," Drucker goes on to observe that "the knowledge that matters is subject to repeated and abrupt shifts," giving as examples the sudden impacts of pharmacology and applied genetics in health care, PCs and the Internet in computing. In fact, all four technologies have continued to develop – and, indeed, to interact. What Drucker is really saying is that new, disruptive technologies have been appearing at shorter and shorter intervals.

This phenomenon supports his "overarching" view "that the world economy will continue to be highly turbulent and highly competitive, prone to abrupt shifts." It is hard to imagine anybody, even someone far less perceptive than Drucker, believing otherwise. In this fast-moving and ever-shifting context, the information needs of business are also changing. Drucker writes with apparent approval of practices such as "activity-based costing," the "balanced scorecard," and "economic value analysis." But even these innovations fall short in the drive to increase productivity because they aim only "at providing better information about events inside the company."

According to Drucker, "approximately 90 percent or more of the information any organization collects is about inside events." The phrase "approximately 90 percent or more" is one that, if uttered by a student, Drucker would certainly have shot down in flames for lack of precision and hard evidence – but it makes his point. His assertion is that "increasingly, a winning strategy will require information about events and conditions outside the institution: non-customers, technologies other than those that are currently used by the company and present competitors, markets not currently served, and so on."

Managing knowledge workers

Developing rigorous methods for "garnering and analyzing outside information" is a "major challenge." Even if a business rises to the challenge, the revolutionary impact of the shift to the knowledge economy will remain inescapable. Knowledge workers, differing from their manual equivalents, "carry their knowledge in their heads, and therefore can take it with them." You cannot manage such people in the traditional manner. "In many cases they will not even be employees of the organization for which they work." Instead, contractors, experts, consultants, part-timers, joint-venture partners, and so on "will identify themselves by their own knowledge rather than by the organizations that pay them."

The whole meaning of organization, Drucker concludes, must change in consequence. He talks about the age-old search for the one "right" organization, up to and including "the present infatuation with teams." He states bluntly that "there can no longer be any such thing" as the one "right" organization. There never was, of course. Drucker has set up a straw man, which he conclusively knocks down. "Every organization in the developed countries (and not only businesses) will have to be designed for a specific task, time, and place (or culture)," he asserts.

Extending the manager's role

In putting forward this argument Drucker is setting the stage for his *Harvard Business Review* peroration. "Management will increasingly extend beyond business enterprises, where it originated...as an attempt to organize the production of things." Now the emphasis has switched to the management of society's knowledge resources – "specifically, education and health care, both of which are today over-administered and undermanaged."

Two long-running Drucker themes flow together in his wide-ranging article. First, management's importance as a social institution is not synonymous with its economic importance. Management outside the business corporation – in nonprofit organizations and in social institutions – is equally important in establishing the manager's claim to legitimacy and power. Second, the task facing management cannot be described in economic terms alone. Knowledge is not the exclusive property of the business class but a universal possession, the uses of which extend to all of society.

Behind Drucker's beliefs in the far-reaching role of management in society lies a third assumption, which is: what is, will be. Drucker ends the *Harvard Business Review* article by saying: "Predictions? Not at all. Those are solely

Stock market "shareholder value"
Amid a climate of economic greed, in which shareholders acquire large profits, Drucker champions the nonprofit sector and calls for a more responsible, longer-term perspective.

the reasonable implications for a future that has already happened." But if education and health care are over-administered and undermanaged (as he rightly says) that statement cannot be true: their reform has hardly begun to take place. At bottom, Drucker is not simply a recording angel. He would otherwise have been a less potent and influential thinker. He has positive views about the directions society should take. So his hopes and wishes become "reasonable implications."

Moral responsibility

A strong sense of moral purpose is one of the characteristics that sets Drucker apart from and above other writers on management. Even though he is recognized as the prophet of privatization (*The Age of Discontinuity*, 1969), Drucker has always had strictly limited faith in the powers of free enterprise, which in his opinion is only as good as its contribution to society. As the second half of the century – and his own thought – evolved, Drucker's definition of the society served by managers turned into a powerful critique. He argued in 1989 that society was "post-capitalist," "post-business," that even "in business proper, the values of business are no longer held with conviction and commitment."

That was plainly true of Drucker's own feelings. But since those words were written "business proper" has been indulging itself in some highly improper ways – and to Drucker's disapproval. At a time when the greatest stock-market boom in history was still creating and expanding gigantic fortunes, Drucker mentally turned his back on the profit-making sector. In May 1999 he told *The* [London] *Observer*'s Simon Caulkin "I don't pretend to understand the current US economy." He pronounced himself "appalled and rather scared by the greed of today's executives."

Drucker cited as "both obscene and socially destructive" awards of $20 million bonuses "for firing 100,000 workers." Nor did he accept that management wonders justified the huge wealth currently being awarded to corporate executives. "I am not impressed by the way many businesses... are being managed," he stated. Where other commentators saw the end-of-century outpouring of Western riches as the beginning of a new growth economy, Drucker seemed to see the phenomenon as an ending. To quote Caulkin, he thinks that "nonprofit organizations – particularly in education, health, and religion – are the growth sector of the 21st century."

This emphasis on "nonprofits" has featured in Drucker's writings for some time. He has a personal interest in some nonprofits, as participant and adviser, and feels that, not only can they benefit from better management, but that they can teach its principles to commercial organizations. As so often, Drucker is turning the conventional management wisdom on its head.

Corporate governance

Led by Thatcherite Britain, the theory and practice of the public sector have been dominated by the view that private-sector, profit-minded management would automatically yield far better results. But Drucker has no truck with the self-serving mysticism that surrounds the prevailing cult of "shareholder value," which tells boards of directors to maximize the share price (used to justify enormous rewards for those same directors). He regards "shareholder value" as entirely preoccupied with short-term results and calls for a balance between these and "the long-range prosperity and survival of the enterprise."

So what happens if directors show no interest in achieving this balance? That raises the whole issue of "corporate governance," already the subject of much debate. Drucker thinks the debate has only scratched the surface of what is going to be a major issue. He points out that knowledge workers, using their intellects as the tools of their trade, have opposed interests: as employees, shareholders, and future pensioners. The tensions aroused by these conflicts, he says, will have to be resolved.

Who will resolve the tensions? It cannot be "capitalists," according to Drucker, who argued in 1992 that they had been replaced by professional managers. "Instead of the old-line capitalist," moreover, "in developed countries pension funds increasingly control the supply and allocation of money." These funds in 1992 owned half the share capital of large US corporations and almost as much of their debt. "The beneficiary owners" are "the country's employees." Just as Karl Marx wanted, the employees own the means of production. Paradoxically, "the United States has become the most 'socialist' country around, while still being the most 'capitalist' one."

Toward the knowledge society

Drucker asserts that "the real and controlling resource and the absolutely decisive 'factor of production' is now neither capital, nor land, nor labor. It is knowledge." He states in *Managing for the Future* (1992): "From now on the key is knowledge. The world is becoming not labor intensive, not materials intensive, not energy intensive, but knowledge intensive." A "new and very different" form of society is in consequence rapidly superseding capitalism. "The same forces" that destroyed Marxism and Communism are also "making capitalism obsolescent." The new post-capitalist society "will use the free market as the one proven source of economic integration." But the period is really one of "transition" to the "knowledge society" that "some of us dare hope for." This society is one that is built around the exchange of knowledge, and away from physical production and rampant capitalism.

Drucker saw this transition period as "a time to *make the future* – precisely because everything is in flux. This is a time for action." Despite this clarion call (addressed to everybody, right down to individuals), Drucker does not offer a plan of action. He instead issues directives. Pension funds, for example, "*have to make sure that the business is being managed*" (presumably, well-managed). He predicts, rather than prescribes, the "business audit," which will track "the performance of a company and of its management against a strategic plan and against specific objectives." Whether this will happen according to his predicted time (by 2013) is still debatable.

During his career as an observer of management, Drucker's prescriptions have been less readily accepted than his insights, such as his devastating critique of the evolution of political organization from nation-state to megastate and then beyond to today's "transnationalism, regionalism, and tribalism." In his view, the trio "are rapidly creating a new polity, a new and complex political structure, and one without precedent." The question is how, with only the tools of the nation-state and its government at hand, the "performance capacity" of government is to be restored. Drucker comes down decisively against using "the fiscal state" to redistribute income: that, he asserts, merely produces "the pork barrel state," with its "legalized looting" of the commonwealth.

"That knowledge has become *the* resource, rather than *a* resource is what makes our society 'post-capitalist.' It changes... the structure of society. It creates new social dynamics. It creates new economic dynamics. It creates new politics." *Post-Capitalist Society*

Forming the social sector

The state should rather focus on creating the "right climate" for economic well-being. Drucker contrasts this with trying to control the economic "weather," which he disparages. The proper aim of fiscal policy, he says, has to be encouragement of a benevolent climate, by "investment in knowledge and in the human resources, in productive facilities in business, and in infrastructure."

But this in itself will not solve the social problems that so far have been tackled mainly by government. Drucker accuses "the nanny state" of having had "very few results." So he offers an alternative: "...where we have had non-governmental action by autonomous community organizations, we have achieved a great deal. The post-capitalist society and the post-capitalist polity require a new, a social sector – both to satisfy social needs and to restore meaningful citizenship and community."

Drucker admits that "citizenship in and through the social sector," through nonprofit organizations, communities, and voluntary work, is no panacea. "But it may be a prerequisite for tackling" the post-capitalist ills. For Drucker "community has to become commitment." The last is a word which also rings out loud and clear when Drucker discusses education: the school "will have to commit itself to results." This is among the "major changes" that (he foresaw in 1989) "are ahead" in schools and education. The knowledge society will demand the changes, "and the new learning theories and learning technologies will trigger them off."

There is no ignoring the aspirational tone. Drucker deeply wants to see a greater society, better attuned to the needs of knowledge – and its managers. "We do not have an economic theory of the productivity of knowledge investment – we may never have one. But… we know, above all, that making knowledge productive is a management responsibility," he states. The manager thus returns to center stage: government cannot run the knowledge society, and neither can market forces. "It requires systematic, organized application of knowledge to knowledge." Management could hardly ask for a nobler role.

Ideas into action

- Use new measures, such as the balanced scorecard and activity-based costing.
- Develop rigorous methods for gathering information from outside the company.
- Employ people for their knowledge and manage them accordingly.
- Don't search for the "right model" – design your own organization.
- Concentrate on getting good long-term results while summarizing specific objectives.
- Track the company's performance against a strategic plan and specific objectives.
- Make managing knowledge a prime concern in managing the business.

Managing innovation

Are you an entrepreneur? Are you an innovator? Entrepreneurship and management "are only two different dimensions of the same task" according to Peter Drucker. To be a successful entrepreneur, learn how to manage; to be a successful manager, learn how to innovate.

Winning by ideas

In the knowledge economy, ideas win. Everybody has ideas all the time, but few exploit them to the full. The key is to build continuous innovation into your work. The greater emphasis you place on generating ideas, Drucker argues, the more they will flow.

Drucker urges you to encourage entrepreneurial thinking inside your unit or organization to achieve success outside. Even more important, you need to be purposefully searching the outside world for entrepreneurial opportunities. Assess your own management of opportunities using the questions and analysis below. Are you:

- Constantly looking outside the business, to the customers and the marketplace?
- Getting all the market information you can from customers and suppliers?
- Creatively using the information that comes back from the outside world?
- Watching out for changes that will signal opportunities (as they always do)?
- Organizing the business to take opportunities when they occur?

Analysis

If you answered "Yes" to three or more questions, you are performing well, but you must strive to improve in the weak areas you have identified. If you answered "No" to more than three questions you need to take action now – you are wasting vital opportunities.

Encouraging innovation

If these questions do not seem relevant to you in your current role, remember that, in time, your ability to conceive, sponsor, and execute entrepreneurial initiatives will be decisive. Start practicing now.
In today's competitive world, a reputation for enterprising ideas can only benefit your career.

1 Innovating for the present

Forget the many myths about entrepreneurship – and never rule yourself out because you do not fit the traditional image of an innovator. Innovation is not about taking risks or predicting the future – focus rather on the opportunities of the present.

Identifying the future

Nobody can predict the future, but you can unlock the secrets of the present, which will be more revealing than any crystal ball. Drucker describes the shape of things to come as "the future that has already happened." To identify that future, ask these questions in sequence:

Where Are We Now?
What is the current situation of the business?
How is the situation changing?
How will the changes affect the business?
How will the changes affect its competitors?
How can the changes be turned to advantage?

Understanding the present is relevant even to product innovation. Although people cannot buy something that does not exist, remember Drucker's advice: "Innovate for the present." When Edwin Land invented instant photography, he was not anticipating the desires of generations still unborn. He just thought that his contemporaries, like himself, would want to see their photographs immediately. The test of an innovation is that it creates value. So ask:

- If this product or service were available now, would people want it?
- Is the idea better than, and different from, anything currently available?
- If it were on sale, would people pay for it – and pay at a profitable level?

Do not confuse innovation with novelty. Novelty, says Drucker, "only creates amusement," and will not last into the future.

2 Exploiting opportunities

Do not confuse innovations with new products. New processes and methods can be more powerful than new inventions. Use innovative products and processes to win lasting competitive advantage.

Do things differently

Everything you do as a manager, and every operation you direct, can be improved. Improvements can always be made in small steps, and often in large strides. But equally, your competitors can also improve. To stay ahead, you must keep:

- Challenging every assumption in your own operations – ask: "What can be done differently and better?"
- Analyzing and improving on your competitors – ask: "What are they doing differently and better?"

The entrepreneur is always seeking changes and the opportunities that such changes offer. Find creative ways of using change by:

- Looking outside the competition – are there analogies you can draw with other industries to turn into innovative opportunities?
- Studying your own successful changes – where else can you apply these innovations?

Thinking Creatively

The Japanese success in world markets was founded less on product innovation than on innovative productivity and marketing. Creative thinking led to simple, but highly powerful, improvements.

Taiichi Ohno was a production expert at Toyoda (later renamed Toyota), a company making textile machinery. To prevent costly breakdowns, he used sensors that were able to detect any irregularities and stop manufacture before the trouble became serious. He then drew an analogy between the machines and the employees. Why not let the employees act like the sensors, allowed to stop and start the production line when faults appeared? This simple innovation became the basis of the production system with which the company and its cars led a worldwide manufacturing revolution.

Changing the rules

Seek ways of doing things so differently that you change the rules of competition to your advantage. Toyota made its cars more quickly and cheaply. Gillette's first safety razors may not have shaved better than its rivals, but selling cheap razors with expensive blades gave the customer a much lower cost per shave. Learn from these examples: establish economic advantage by being radically different.

Look outside to the customer. Analyze what you are supplying or proposing to supply and break it down feature by feature. Rank each attribute by its value in the customer's eyes. Then rank your major competitors in the same way. Compare the results by asking:

- Where do your competitors excel, and where do you excel, on the attributes most valued by customers?
- What can you do to enhance your strengths and exploit your competitors' weaknesses?

Selecting opportunities

Such a systematic approach will yield more opportunities than you can easily handle. Bear in mind Drucker's general principles of innovation to sort out the great ideas from the not-so-good:

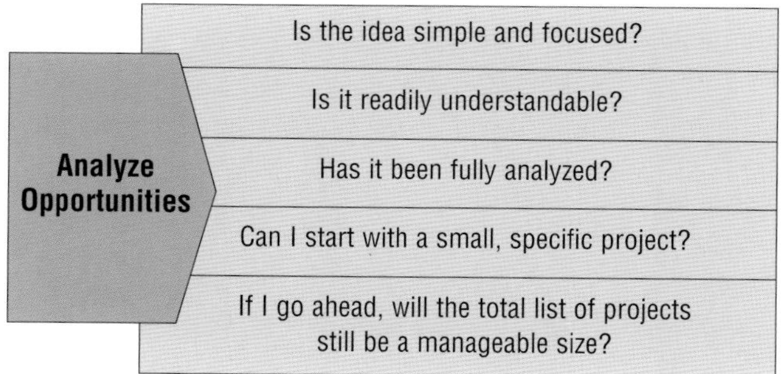

Minimizing risk

Drucker does not include taking excessive risks in his warnings, because he equates risk not with unpredictability but with ignorance. The more you know about what you are doing, the less risk you run. You can define risks and seek to limit them, but you are really interested in opportunities. The biggest risk is missing them. Look back on any missed opportunities in your own career. Why did you miss them? Use your past mistakes to learn how to recognize opportunities and embrace change in the future.

Exploiting the unexpected

At any time things can happen that were neither predicted nor expected. Drucker maintains that unexpected, challenging developments are major sources of opportunities. They provide chances to break the mold. Most people either ignore unexpected successes, failures, or events, or they ignore their significance.

Managers are often expected to do the impossible – make accurate predictions, for example. Every budget and business plan is an exercise in futurology. Drucker insists instead on focusing on what is known and turning that knowledge into future opportunities. Look, for instance, at the sales of one product and ask:

- Why did this unexpected success or failure occur?
- What do those reasons teach me?
- How can I exploit what I have learned?

Assessing opportunities

Selecting the right opportunity is crucial. Drucker recommends four different strategies that can turn opportunities into profitable action. Decide which of these strategies can be applied to your opportunity:

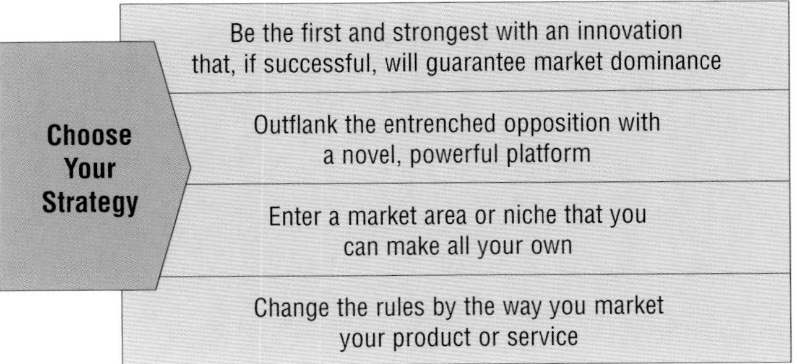

Unless you pursue one of these strategies, or have another, clearly defined and effective strategy of your own, you should not proceed. Your ultimate test is not the amount of entrepreneurial and innovatory zeal you can display, but how successful you are in creating new enterprises and effective advances. As a Japanese sage once taught: "Never let an opportunity pass by, but always think twice before acting."

3 Starting new ventures

A new product or service may be launched either from within an established management system or from a brand-new operation. Either way, see autonomy as a precondition of success.

Acting independently

While independent companies may have no greater entrepreneurial ability, at least they do not have to argue with superiors or put up with interference. They can more readily fulfill their potential.

The Advantages of Independence
Analyzing all the available opportunities
Selecting the best opportunity
Exploiting the chance to create a new, profitable business

In contrast, the in-company venture enjoys the benefits of the company's greater resources and reputation. But, Drucker warns, established business is also "the main obstacle to entrepreneurship."

Developing new ventures

Drucker argues that there are five fundamental requirements for the successful management of a new venture:

The Five Critical Success Factors for New Ventures
1 Focusing on the market
2 Planning and re-planning cashflow and capital needs
3 Building stronger management systems than you need now
4 Deciding clearly on your own personal role
5 In an established business, insulating the new venture

Getting autonomy for a new in-company venture may help it operate more like an independent. Whatever the circumstances, take a professional, managed approach to bring about successful innovation.

tom PETERS

Biography

Tom Peters has an unusual background for a management guru. Born in 1942, he worked in the Pentagon for two years before studying civil engineering at Cornell. He served in Vietnam, got an MBA at Stanford, and then returned to Washington for a spell at the Office of Management and Budget. He thus brought an unusual breadth of experience and education to McKinsey, the leading management consultancy, which he joined as a consultant in 1974, at a crucial juncture in its history.

At this time, a rival and much younger consultancy, Boston Consulting Group, had seized intellectual leadership in the profession by developing and publicizing its "matrix," which assessed products and businesses by plotting their share of a market against the growth rate in that market. While simplistic, and now long out of favor, the Boston matrix caught the interest of top managers, who saw it as a clear and quick guide to strategic decisions on the best way to invest corporate funds. McKinsey needed a rival product that would steal back its thunder.

The "excellent company" project

In 1977, Peters was assigned to what became known as the "excellent company" project; his brief, to discover what characteristics distinguished the company that excelled in performance from any other firm. The project was joined by two other McKinsey consultants, one of them Robert Waterman, and by two academics: Anthony Athos, an expert on corporate cultures, and Richard Pascale, a student of American and Japanese companies.

The first result of the research was the "Seven-S" formula for analyzing a company (see p. 14). Although "Seven-S" never matched the Boston matrix for popular appeal, Waterman, in talking to one chief executive, was struck by the idea that managing excellent companies produced identifiable, transferrable common practices. Could the essence of excellence be distilled and then instilled into other managements? Using the "Seven-S" formula, he and Peters began their analysis of 43 large US companies whose financial records indicated excellence.

The discovery of eight common characteristics, or attributes, attracted publishing interest, and Peters and Waterman set to work on what proved a highly taxing project for both men – and for their firm, which provided a small army of helpers. Neither had written a book before. Working from home, Peters produced enormous numbers of words, which had to be heavily edited into shape. Nobody had any idea that the result would be much of a success when it was published as *In Search of Excellence* in 1982.

The launch of a writing career

Sales started to advance into the millions as company after company bought the book in volume to give to their executives. The success generated great sums in royalties. Under the consultancy's contracts, any such income belonged not to individual consultants but to the firm. Luckily for him, Peters had left the consultancy a year before publication so was entitled to receive his share of the royalties personally. These royalties and the fame resulting from the enormous success of the book helped him to build an independent and richly successful career as author, consultant (with his own organization, the Tom Peters

Group), and, above all, crusader for his revolutionary, vehement management ideas.

These ideas are not the same ones as those that *In Search of Excellence* promulgated so successfully. In many respects, Peters performed a U-turn after leaving McKinsey and ending his collaboration with Waterman. The latter, altogether a less driven man, stayed on as a McKinsey partner until 1986 and also for some time kept his faith in the large companies, led by IBM, which were the role-models for *In Search of Excellence*. This was despite the evidence – which started to appear soon after publication – that many of the selected companies were deeply flawed.

Over time, three-quarters of the companies featured in the book failed either relatively or absolutely (some very soon). But long before the final failure, Peters was already well launched on his new career as writer, highly paid and much sought-after speaker, and peripatetic consultant. He declared in 1987 that there were no excellent companies; his heroes now were not large businesses, but small ones. He became the leading voice of management counter-culture – a fiery, theatrical, fiercely critical, inspirational preacher who exhorts his audiences to forget what they (and he) were taught at business school and embrace "revolution."

An evangelical approach

Peters' huge display of nervous energy as he marches around his audience is not assumed. He drives himself ferociously, sometimes over the brink of exhaustion. He has complete command of his material and his audience, developed by years of practice. His skills as a speaker were one reason why *In Search of Excellence* achieved its astonishing breakthrough. He is said to have given "excellence" seminars to 100,000–200,000 people in the three years after publication, and he must have reached far larger numbers through TV appearances. By his marketing efforts, Peters brought the management book down the corporate hierarchy to the ranks of aspiring managers.

The evangelical approach had begun to appear when Peters was still preaching the big company message. He started the "Skunk Camp" in 1984, an annual event the name of which was drawn from "skunkworks," meaning an innovative group established well away from the main corporation (see p. 41). Peters described the delegates as: "Forty brave souls who have been going their own way [and] met in California and swapped tales about the battles fought, the scars accumulated, and the personal and soul-satisfying experiences that have come from watching their people become winners."

Liberating managers

By 1992, when Liberation Management *was published, Peters was urging companies to abandon hierarchy and adopt flexible, free-flowing structures with large, efficient networks.*

In praise of leadership

Peters was moving away from the boardroom and on to his new battleground, in which "skunks" lower down the management structure rebelled against the corporate norms in order to care for customers, innovate, and manage people by exerting individual leadership. The key element here is MBWA: "Management by Wandering Around." With a new coauthor, Nancy Austin, Peters published *A Passion for Excellence* in 1989. The subtitle was "The Leadership Difference", and the admired leaders were no longer just corporate chieftains of companies such as IBM, but also people like Frank Perdue of Perdue Farms. The essence of Peters' new enthusiasms was entrepreneurialism.

He has also practiced what he preached. The Tom Peters Group, located in Palo Alto in Silicon Valley, is a very active training organization, offering a variety of courses. They range from the Leadership Challenge Workshop ("how to get extraordinary things done in organizations") via Corporate Cultures ("aligning action with values throughout the organization") to Customer Service ("providing distinctive service that Wows the customer"). Peters has nine associates in the firm, which also offers "skillful facilitation" and "strategic consulting." He and his wife, Kate Abbe, whom he describes as "spouse, poet, publisher, pal," live in Palo Alto when not on their farm in Vermont.

The TPG is obviously Tom Peters writ large. As a one-man industry he has reeled off not only books but audio and video programs galore. There are 20 videos extant, starting with *Excellence: the Film*, which came out in 1985. Although he has so decisively rejected the large companies that were the original models of excellence, Peters is well aware of the continuing brand value of his first book: witness a 1999 audio project, with accompanying paperback, titled *Excellence Aerobics*. However, the book that launched Peters' career was a suit-and-tie affair; his later work is jeans and open-neck shirt.

Revolutionary message

The flavor of his later work is well communicated by the video title, *Ten Rules for Giving Incredible Speeches and Why They're Irrelevant*, which came out in 1990. He loves to shock and startle with paradox and slangy prose. The editing that pared down *In Search of Excellence* was nowhere visible in *Thriving on Chaos*, published in 1987, which runs to over 500 pages and contains no less than 45 main precepts for managers to follow. It set out the agenda for Peters' future career and for the revolutionary course on which he wished to launch American companies.

From his own point of view, *Thriving on Chaos* and its later variations have worked excellently, even though he has become more and more extreme in presentation and language. In the Nineties *The Pursuit of Wow!* (1994) was "every person's guide to topsy-turvy times," while *The Tom Peters Seminar* (1994) announced that "crazy times call for crazy organizations." It has been said that Peters was lucky in his timing: *In Search of Excellence* brought reassurance to US managements feeling threatened by Japanese incursions; *Thriving on Chaos* offered a new faith to replace the certainties demolished by the 1987 stock market crash.

But the Peters phenomenon is more than good timing. While his work is fallible, and open to critical attack on all sides, he has pounded home the truths derived from the new wave of entrepreneurs. They have shown that what Peters teaches is true: that there is a different, better, and perhaps essential way in which to manage.

THIS NOTE IS LEGAL
FOR ALL DEBTS, PUBLIC AND
SERIES 1996
Treasurer of the United States.
100
SERIES 1996
50
5
20

1

The discovery of excellence

Imitating the eight key attributes that lead to excellent financial performance • **How the 43 "excellent" companies failed to live up to their billing** • The appearance of listening to customers as key management practice • **Getting out of the office and walking the plant floors** • Challenging the corporate world to adopt better ways of managing • **Getting improvements in productivity by going beyond incentive payments** • Rejecting the model of rational, highly organized, "scientific" management

The purpose of Peters and Waterman's *In Search of Excellence* – to restore intellectual preeminence to McKinsey among its corporate clientele – was amply achieved, even though academic and other critics found no difficulty in demolishing the book. In fact, the technique used by Peters and Waterman, basing conclusions on studies of actual corporations, was, and still is, the backbone of academic "research" into management.

The first result of McKinsey's research, the "Seven-S" formula, was as respectable as any academic treatise, although it had been carefully plotted to appeal to a lay audience through its catchy, alliterative title. Its seven categories – structure, strategy, systems, style of management, skills, staff, and shared values – provided a reasonably comprehensive guide to analyzing the culture and behavior of corporations, using non-financial criteria. However, the selection of corporate subjects for the "excellence study," which was started in 1977, was based on financial performance and on the clear implication that imitating those subjects would, in turn, produce a similar performance by the imitators.

The 43 companies chosen for the study, which included such big names as IBM, Johnson & Johnson, Exxon, Procter & Gamble, and General Electric, had for two decades led other businesses in *Fortune* magazine's list of America's 500 largest corporations on six factors:

- Growth in assets
- Growth in equity value
- Ratio of market value to book value
- Return on capital
- Return on equity
- Return on sales

The eight attributes of success

In developing the excellence concept, Peters and Waterman identified eight attributes that they deemed were shared by the selected 43 companies. As with the Seven-S formula, these attributes were all non-financial:

- Bias towards action
- Simple form, lean staff
- Continued contact with customers
- Productivity improvement via people
- Operational autonomy to encourage entrepreneurs
- Stress on one key business value
- Emphasis on doing what they know best ("sticking to the knitting")
- Loose-tight controls

There is an obvious difficulty in proving the existence of these attributes (and in explaining what is meant by "loose-tight"). It may be possible to show that 43 financially successful companies, with high returns on capital, equity, and sales, do indeed share a common characteristic, such as a "bias towards action." But that does not establish any connection between the bias and the return. You can conclude more justifiably from studying Olympic gold medalists in the 100 meters that being black is a common feature. But that doesn't establish African ancestry as a necessary condition, or even an explanation.

"Our fixation with financial measures leads us to downplay or ignore less tangible non-financial measures."
Thriving on Chaos

Unlike the criteria for selecting the 43, none of the eight has the one essential quality for solid comparisons: measurability. How can you calibrate "stress on one key business value" or prove that Company A emphasizes doing what they know best more than Company B? Equally, how can you demonstrate that this difference (which you cannot measure) has any impact (which you also cannot measure) on Company A's superiority of any kind – let alone its financial characteristics? You can measure productivity improvement, true; but how do you separate the improvement achieved by investment, or by higher sales volume, from that supplied by better people management?

Anecdotal evidence

The "evidence" supplied in support of the thesis was mainly anecdotal. The conclusions were only as good as the anecdotes, and, as evidence of corporate excellence, the stories were not very good. They were examples of fine management, possibly; but were they isolated examples rather than proofs of some general excellence?

If Peters and Waterman had any doubts on this score, they were swept aside in the tide of anecdotal reporting. This is one of Peters' great strengths. He writes and talks vividly about companies and their managers, and the anecdotes in *In Search of Excellence* bear his stamp. For example, Digital Equipment, the computer manufacturer, would have bands of only five to 25 people testing out ideas on a customer, often using cheap prototypes. That took just a few weeks, while the typical company might have had 250 people working on a new product in isolation for 15 months. However, no conclusions could safely be drawn from Digital; it was dominated by one eccentric entrepreneur,

Ken Olsen, who bent the company to his will in often painful manner. His greatest mistake – to disparage and ignore the personal computer – spelt Digital's doom. It became one of the celebrated failures among *Excellence*'s heroes.

In fact, *Excellence* did point out one drawback of the methods employed by Olsen: "At Digital the chaos is so rampant that, one executive noted, damn few people know

Digital's downfall

Ken Olsen founded Digital Equipment in 1957. His eccentric style of management created huge success, but ultimately led to the company's decline. In 1998, it was bought by Compaq Computer.

Mine's a Big Mac
McDonald's, which started life in 1948 as a hamburger stand in San Bernardino, California, was one of the 43 "excellent" companies that has maintained its performance and reputation for years.

who they work for." This chaos, however, was presented by Peters and Waterman as a saving grace, part of the eighth attribute: "loose-tight controls." The looseness, on this reading, was offset by tightness, by the alleged fact that "Digital's fetish for reliability is more rigidly adhered to than any outsider could imagine." The authors were themselves outsiders, of course. But as usual in all anecdotal business studies of this kind, their theory about Digital was not derived from observation from the outside. The observations were selected to support the theory. If you have selected 43 companies as examples of "excellence," you are not looking for evidence of their fallibility. Had they investigated more closely, they would have found their chosen companies lacking, not just on the eight non-financial attributes, but on the very financial criteria that had led to their selection.

From the 43, the authors picked 14 companies as particular examples: Bechtel, Boeing, Caterpillar Tractor, Dana, Delta Airlines, Digital Equipment, Emerson Electric, Fluor, Hewlett-Packard, IBM, Johnson & Johnson, McDonald's, Procter & Gamble, and 3M. Taking ten of these companies, their average position out of *Fortune*'s top 500 companies, over the decade 1971–81, was 243rd for total return to investors and 167th for growth in earnings per share. The 1981 figures for net return on shareholders' equity and net return on sales, while not wonderful, were better (especially the sales number). But long-term performance, rather than that of a single year, was supposed to be the distinction of the chosen few. With the criteria and the conclusions both dubious, *Excellence* was on flimsy ground.

Themes of excellence

For all that, the study laid several foundations for Peters' later thought, even though the ideas he went on to develop seemed far from those advocated in *Excellence*. It was here that the theme of customer service first surfaced. The authors approvingly quote an IBM marketing supremo (and adulator), Frank (Buck) Rogers: "It's a shame that, in so many companies, whenever you get good service, it's an exception. At such companies, managers know that the best product ideas can come from customers – if you listen intently and regularly." Did it matter that IBM actually failed to practice what Rogers preached? Those virtues *should* have existed, after all.

It was a short step from describing virtue to prescribing it, to laying down (as Peters did in the post-*Excellence* years) the "right" ways to run companies. One of those ways, marking another Peters theme, also surfaced at this early point: MBWA "Management by Wandering Around" (see pp. 37–8). The authors praised bosses who were known for walking the plant floors, men such as Ray Kroc, the chairman of McDonald's, who rightly and regularly visited outlets and assessed them on the factors he held dear: QSC&V (Quality, Service, Cleanliness, and Value).

Innovation is another theme running through all Peters' work. He and Waterman were impressed (as were many others) by 3M, which won fulsome appreciation for being "so intent on innovation that its essential atmosphere seems not like that of a large corporation, but rather a loose network of laboratories and cubbyholes populated by feverish inventors and dauntless entrepreneurs who let their imaginations fly in all directions." The description reads like the unreal nonsense it was. There was greater

"A lot of companies are spending jillions on innovation but all they're producing is the 64th variety of spaghetti sauce. I don't think you get innovation for free. But a lot of it has to do with the spirit of the enterprise."
The Pursuit of Wow!

apparent sense in the fourth Peters theme: that the way to learn better management is to study what other managers actually do and adapt or adopt their methods.

An imaginary reality

The eight attributes were valuable qualities for businesses to have, and far superior to the prevailing norms. Peters and Waterman were, after all, writing for a corporate world that was biased toward inaction rather than action. Far from having simple structures, corporations had convoluted bureaucracies, stuffed with too many staff. They were production-led, inbred, and paid too little attention to what customers wanted in terms of product or service. Their productivity lagged largely because they treated front-line people as mindless cannon fodder. Any stirrings of entrepreneurship or initiative were stifled by a culture of interference and lack of autonomy. The values and strategy were unclear and cluttered by contradictions.

Far from "sticking to the knitting," that is, staying with what they knew best, typical large companies diversified into areas they knew nothing of. Far from coupling "loose" management with tight controls over finance and reporting, they turned control systems into straitjackets that imprisoned every manager. That was the truth. But *Excellence* succeeded because it blazoned forth an imaginary reality, a nonexistent world in which virtue – American virtue – was triumphant:

> "The findings from the excellent companies amount to an upbeat message. There is good news from America. Good management practice today is not resident only in Japan. But, more important, the good news comes from treating people decently and asking them to

Knowledge workers
Technology has given people the freedom to work away from their desks, encouraging innovation and creativity. According to Peters, the suited, office-bound executive has become outmoded.

shine, and from producing things that work. Scale efficiencies give way to small units with turned-on people. Precisely planned R&D efforts aimed at big-bang projects are replaced by armies of dedicated champions. A numbing focus on cost gives way to an enhancing focus on quality. Hierarchy and three-piece suits give way to first names, shirtsleeves, hoop-la, and project-based flexibility. Working according to fat rule books is replaced by everyone's contributing."

This was the stuff of dreams. But it conveyed enormous reassurance to the American chief executive. Not only was he now convinced that his company was doing a good job – rather, an excellent one – but it was all his own work. All of the eight attributes were his to command. He could give operational autonomy, ordain contact with customers, "stick to the knitting" by rejecting diversification and concentrating on the company's real strengths, promulgate the core values he had chosen, and so on. As for Japanese competition (barely mentioned in the book), that was irrelevant. Not only could America win: its major companies really were winning, even if the facts of Japanese market penetration showed otherwise.

Faltering giants

The publication of *Excellence* was timely in that it appeared when American business was anxious for comfort. But that was also the point when the mighty were about to fall. Hence, the infamous record of decline and disappointment of the companies featured in the book. The awful setbacks that lay in store for Caterpillar Tractor, Boeing, Digital Equipment, Fluor, McDonald's, and IBM (the star of the book) were general as well as specific. As the US economy faltered, so did its giants. Which came first, the chicken or the egg, was actually irrelevant. It is very likely that any random selection of big US companies would have fared as badly as the heroes of *Excellence*.

Peters and Waterman's thesis about US excellence may have contributed to the complacency. But behind the cheerleading for American management lay a serious examination of profound changes that truly were being forced on all major companies. The old strategy taught management to eliminate overlaps, duplication, and waste by concentrating on massive production runs. Provided that everything was carefully and formally coordinated, big would always be better. Scale economies took companies a massive stride toward being the low-cost producer, and thus the surefire winner.

What mattered most to customers in this old business model was cost. The authors argued, however, that economies of scale were losing their sovereign power, diminishing in importance as customers sought variety, and as quality (or value) became decisive. They were right. Quality, moreover, was no longer just a matter of inspection, discipline, control, and exhortation. As taught by the new quality gurus (almost all of them Americans, as it happened) and actually practiced by the Japanese, quality was a new way of corporate life.

This style of corporate life sprang from the intelligent management of people and from obtaining their collaboration in the work of continuous improvement. The authors turned their back on the traditional idea that if you got the incentives right, productivity would inevitably follow, and that income was everything. In this theory, the right payment programs, giving top rewards to top performers, and weeding out the 30 to 40 percent of deadwood (that is, those

"It doesn't matter whether… you are section head or chairman of the board. If you knowingly ignore a tiny act of lousy service or poor quality, you have destroyed your credibility and any possibility of moral leadership on this issue." *Thriving on Chaos*

who did not want to work anyway), would encourage people to do things right and work intelligently. Here, too, the conventional ideas were being displaced as the knowledge workers moved to the fore; that is, professionals who "identify themselves by their own knowledge rather than by the organizations that pay them" (Drucker – *Management Challenges for the 21st Century*, 1999).

Rejecting rational management

The changes under way in the business world were incompatible with the traditional view of the corporation as a machine. Peters and Waterman rejected the idea that analysis was all, and that "scientific," rational management was always the answer. This rational approach held that good market research helped to avoid big foolish decisions, and that financial analysis could be usefully applied to risky investments such as research and development. In addition, budgeting was an obvious model for long-range planning, and forecasts were plainly important. It seemed only sensible to set hard numerical targets on the basis of those forecasts.

The rationalists saw the top manager's job as making decisions, getting them right, balancing the corporate portfolio of investments, and buying into the attractive industries. He used his subordinates as controllers whose job was to keep things orderly and avoid surprises; they worked within a detailed organizational structure, wrote clear job descriptions, ensured that every possible contingency was accounted for, issued orders, resolved issues in black and white terms, and regarded people as factors of production. Effective planning went hand-in-hand with a massive commitment of resources to the chosen projects.

In Search of Excellence rejected this model, even though Peters and Waterman, as management consultants, belonged to a breed of professionals whose bread-and-butter (and plenty of honey) derived from applying the rational approach indiscriminately to all their clients. But the authors' critical attitude was straight common sense. Economies are not the only things that matter in business, and, what's more, all really good companies have excellent policies that analysis would certainly rule out as uneconomic. The pair cited the over-commitment to reliability by Caterpillar Tractor ("48 hours parts service anywhere in the world, or CAT pays").

Allowing for mistakes

Peters thus began his conversion to "crazy" management by underlining the problems of being too rigidly rational, arguing that rigidity rules out experimentation and does not allow for mistakes. The authors pointed out that the IBM 360 was a vast success of American business history, yet its development was sloppy. IBM's response was to design a product-development system that would prevent such a problem recurring. However, as IBM chairman Frank Cary said, "Unfortunately, it will also ensure that we don't ever invent another product like the 360." The system was duly scrapped, to Peters' approval, but IBM never did "invent another product like the 360." It did have a massive big hit with the Personal Computer, true; but that was originally developed outside the IBM system altogether, in a separate organization in Boca Raton, Florida.

This anecdote illustrates the central difficulty on which the *Excellence* thesis foundered. In management, there is an undeniable conflict between the need for control (which is real) and the need for freedom (which is essential for creativity). In *Excellence*, the authors tried to balance these two opposites but did not quite succeed. Waterman, in his later books, continued with this difficult exercise. Peters, on the other hand, lost patience and proceeded to tilt the balance decisively toward freedom.

Ideas into action

- Study what other managers do and adapt or adopt whatever works.
- Tear down cultures of bureaucracy, interference, and lack of autonomy.
- Dedicate "champions" to leading the drive for innovation in products and processes.
- Break the business down into small units with "turned-on people".
- Ensure staff collaborate to achieve continuous improvement in performance.
- Put customer satisfaction ahead of numerical targets and financial goals.
- Avoid rigid management that rules out experiment and trial and error.

Filling a gap in the market

The astonishing success of *In Search of Excellence* in 1982 turned Peters from a management consultant into a superstar, although he shared the limelight and glory with his coauthor, Robert Waterman.

The flamboyant drive that Peters brought to everything was a major factor in the mounting millions of sales. On his own account, the sales were no accident, but the result of "an unsystematic (but in retrospect thorough) word-of-mouth campaign" that began two years before publication.

Peters turned the book's long gestation period into an advantage. In 1980, a 125-page presentation of "what became the book's principal findings" was bound and "circulated surreptitiously among business executives." In all, the authors printed 15,000 copies to satisfy what Peters (with a touch of bombast) calls "underground demand." He adds that at least an equal number of photocopies swelled "the network."

The pair also "assiduously courted opinion leaders in the media over several years." According to Peters, this paid off within days of the book's launch. He says that "supportive reviews" appeared, and the network "hurried to buy the real thing, often in bulk for their subordinates." Other, differing accounts record that *Excellence* came out to largely hostile reviews and achieved only modest sales – until suddenly, apparently spurred by one company's large purchases, the book took off.

Effective marketing

Peters claims the book could not have been better marketed than if the whole process had been planned meticulously. But the success owed less to Peters' word-of-mouth campaign than to lucky timing – its publication coincided with mounting anxiety about the US economy – and to the simple appeal of the book's basic idea. This theme was first exposed in a *Business Week* article that summarized the eight attributes of excellence, but more important was the notion that excellence was transferrable by example: study how top performers performed, and you, too, could have a top company.

"When Aunt Mary has to give that nephew of hers a high school graduation present and she gives him *In Search of Excellence*, you know that management has become part of the general culture." Peter Drucker

This has been the foundation of Peters' preaching and practice ever since, and its critics fastened on the simplistic weakness of the approach. The management expert Peter Drucker commented on how easy *Excellence* made management seem: "All you had to do was put the book under your pillow and it will get done." But, of course, that was the book's secret. It not only made a difficult subject seem easy, but promised easy results. All the same, selling five million copies in three years indicated a huge, yawning gap in the market, a demand not so much for the book's content as for its talismanic effect.

That must be true if Peters is right in estimating that over half the purchasers did not even turn the pages of *Excellence*. Half-a-million, he thought, had read five chapters. A mere 100,000 had read the whole book. In other words, the market had been defined, but not yet fully exploited. Making good that defect became the engine of Peters' future career.

2

Managing with passion

How Peters turned against some old heroes and found new ones • **Abandoning the "vaunted American management mystique" and going "back to basics"** • The two ways of getting "superior performance over the long haul" • **Why winners succeed, not through cleverness, but attention to detail** • Managing by wandering around • **Why only one perceived reality counts – the customer's view** • Championing "skunks," the rule-breakers and individualists, to promote innovation

Peters' rejection of the large company models for *Excellence* was eminently justifed by their performance after the book's publication in 1982. The relative or absolute failure of heroes like IBM became a running joke. It led both Peters and Waterman to query and analyze what had gone wrong. Waterman still believed in big companies, especially IBM, long after Peters had turned against the old heroes. But Peters' total conversion was by no means immediate.

For his next book, *A Passion for Excellence*, co-written with Nancy Austin and published in 1985, he still stuck to "old friends," including IBM, Hewlett-Packard, and 3M. He praised a Ford plant, too, and (in contrast to the all-American *Excellence*) found European heroes like Marks & Spencer and the Scandinavian airline, SAS. But brand-new US names also joined the pantheon, some of them plucked from obscurity, like Stew Leonard's, a one-store Connecticut operation selling milk, cheese, rolls, and eggs, or Sunset Scavengers in the San Francisco Bay area ("most say the best-run garbage company in America").

Other newcomers to Peters' admiration, however, were far bigger. They included the manufacturer of Goretex, the "breathing" synthetic fiber, Milliken & Company, the privately owned textile giant, and Domino's Pizza, created by a self-help fanatic named Tom Monaghan. Some of the new heroes were propelled into lasting management fame by Peters' blessing. However, the kiss of death that disfigured *In Search of Excellence* was still present. The airline People Express, which ranked, in some respects, as the fastest-growing business in the history of the US, was heading for a final crash. And then there was Apple Computer, whose "free-form organization and unbridled enthusiasm may well be the company's most lasting contribution to the US business scene." Apple, unlike People Express, survived, but its disorganization and lack of bridles almost killed the computer pioneer.

With such high-profile examples, Peters was still adding to what he called the "vaunted American management mystique," even though "it had quickly turned out to be largely just that – mystique."

Back to basics

Peters concluded that the "battering" taken by American business during the 1981–83 recession (which bridged the publication of *In Search of Excellence*) had "humbled every American manager." There was no trace of humility in *Passion*, however, save for a rhetorical warning: "Is there anyone who thinks the recovery means we're permanently out of the woods?"

But Peters believed that a path led through the trees and to the high upland beyond. For the first time, he preached "revolution." The upheaval involved, though, was far from cataclysmic. He sounded the familiar call of "back to basics." Companies had departed from these basics as they adopted the "management systems, schemes, devices, and structures" promoted during the past quarter of a century:

"The average employee can deliver far more than his or her current job demands and far more than the terms 'employee empowerment,' 'participative management,' and 'multiple job skills' imply."
The Tom Peters Seminar

"Each such scheme seemed to make sense at the time. Each seemed an appropriate answer to growing complexity. But the result was that the basics got lost in a blur of well-meaning gibberish that took us further and further from excellent performance in any sphere. We got so tied up in our techniques, devices, and programs that we forgot about people – the people who produce the product or service and the people who consume it."

In most companies, there was too great a distance between top management and these two vital groups of people: staff and customers. Peters stressed the importance of labor relations, listening to what the workforce has to say, acting on what one hears, and treating them as full partners (although he rather spoiled his case by naming IBM, which did nothing of the sort, as a star example). He emphasized that going "back to basics" did not mean going back but going forward – even if some companies had, in fact, been practicing the basics for decades.

What were these basics? How should companies achieve sustainable growth and equity? Peters could not even find "pride in one's organization and enthusiasm for its works" indexed in 25 leading textbooks on management. Nor could he find much about other key concepts, even leadership, which he felt was "crucial to the revolution now under way – so crucial that we believe the words 'managing' and 'management' should be discarded." In contrast to the images of management – "controlling and arranging and demeaning and reducing" – leadership connoted "unleashing energy, building, freeing, and growing."

Peters was very conscious that this sounded uncomfortably like a change from "tough-mindedness" to "tenderness." Concepts like value, vision, and integrity look "soft" to managers who want to produce "hard" results where it counts and is counted: on balance sheets and on bottom lines. So Peters went far, probably too far, to emphasize that his new heroes, such as Perdue Farms, relentlessly applied "the pressure to perform," and, indeed, that the pressure was "nothing short of brutal." These were "no excuses" environments "where extraordinary results are... routinely expected because the barriers to them have been cleared away."

Creating a paradox

The subordinates could be forgiven for thinking they had jumped out of the frying pan of management control into the fire of "radical decentralization," from "obey – or else" to "succeed – or else." Peters was aware of the paradox, which he said was epitomized by the businesses that served as his new models. He maintained that, "All are tough as nails and uncompromising about their value systems, but at the same time they care deeply about and respect their people; their very respect leads them to *demand* (in the best sense of the word) that each person be an innovative contributor."

Here Peters fell into two traps. First, he repeated the error of hero-worship exhibited in *In Search of Excellence*: misplaced confidence that "superb" chiefs could be identified and that their principles and behavior were transferable. Second, he tried to reconcile the irreconcilable – a hard-driving boss with people who are supposed to drive themselves. The first error would be revealed by events like the total failure of People Express and the slump of IBM into heavy losses. The second error was simply accepted. The paradox could not be avoided:

"We must confront the paradox, own it, live it, celebrate it if we are to make much headway in achieving excellence."

Living a paradox sounds complex, but Peters was adamant about the essential simplicity of his new model. "Many accused *In Search of Excellence* of over-simplifying... we have reached the opposite conclusion. *In Search of Excellence* didn't simplify enough!" He and Austin had reduced the creation and sustaining of "superior performance over the long haul" to "only two ways." They were, first, to "take exceptional care of your customers... via superior service and superior quality," and, second, to "constantly innovate." As the authors wrote, "That's it."

Even Peters realized this was too extreme. Firms also needed sound financial controls and sound planning, which he viewed not as a luxury but as a necessity. And "turned-on people" were essential to success. He recognized, too, that businesses can suffer from external forces, such as an overvalued currency: "but one sustains performance by adding enough value to the product so that it is profitably saleable despite international monetary variability." These were significant corrections to the simple two-way model, but they did not address its main weaknesses.

What did "exceptional care," "superior service," and "superior quality" actually mean? More important, how were they to be obtained? True, innovation was important – but surely not as important as the nature of the innovation? Which products, services, or markets did you choose? Peters resembled a parent who tells children to be good, to which they all naturally agree. But the specifics are crucial. Peters thought that the good lay in the detail. He observed, "The winners stun us not by their cleverness, but by the fact that every tiny aspect of the business is just a touch better than the norm." However, the devil is in the detail, too.

Managing by wandering around

According to Peters, the main managerial productivity problem in America was that managers were remote from the detail – by which he meant that they were out of touch with their people and their customers. Peters' answer to the problem was "the technology of the obvious." The way in which leadership became effective in any well-run organization, be it a school, hospital, bank, single-store operation, or industrial enterprise, was MBWA – "Management by Wandering Around." In *A Passion for Excellence*, Peters gave several examples of MBWA, applied in "bugging [that is, bothering] customers," "naive listening" (that is, with a completely open mind), treating the supplier as a customer, and so on.

Peters reeled off lists of questions, all of them pertinent, such as: "What is the frequency of 'all-hands' meetings? Why? Could you do more?" This hardly adds up to "technology of the obvious" or anything else for that matter. Peters was really urging the case for hyperactive, out-of-the-office, interventionist top management. The

Communicating face to face
Management by Wandering Around – irregular, informal meetings with staff, customers, and suppliers in their places of work – is how, according to Peters, managers become effective leaders.

flavor (he referred to it as the "smell") is clear from the following seven injunctions:

- Publicize the fact that you are out wandering 50 percent of the time, and that your colleagues are as well (if you and they are).
- Be meticulous in having meetings in others' offices/spaces rather than yours.
- Evaluate managers in part – and directly – on the basis of their people's assessment of how well/how frequently they are in touch.
- Fire a supervisor who doesn't know all his people's first and last names.
- Hold meetings and reviews in the field.
- Start randomly popping into offices and asking the inhabitants why they aren't out.
- If you are a manufacturing, or an R&D, boss, etc., make sure you have a second office in the workplace.

The MBWA prescription suffered from the same authoritarian, top-down bias ("Fire a supervisor"...) as the formula put forward in *In Search of Excellence*. And although there was an eighth injunction that suggested that the boss should hold back from bossing, Peters and Austin significantly found this "an especially tough one. When you're harried and need some information badly, and only Mrs. X has it, and you discover upon calling that she's out on a field visit – don't call her in the field and tell her to rush back and get the answer. *Wait!*" Nevertheless, the hands-on top management implicit in MBWA was greatly preferable to the desk-bound, out-of-touch alternative, even though the better mode could hardly support a full-length book, and particularly one that ran to more than 400 pages.

Applying integrity

Peters and Austin went on to develop a theory of business that they claimed was permeated by MBWA, but which, in reality, was largely independent of that panacea. They were aware of the danger that managers would pay only lip-service to their teachings, and chose to describe this as lack of "integrity." They observed that "virtually every device we suggest is doomed to be useless unless applied with integrity." Despite Peters' insistence on the simplicity of this approach, their ideas added up to an incredibly complex and heavy burden: "Ah yes, that's it. A million devices, each important – *and* integrity."

Starting with the customer, managers were urged to use "common courtesy" as "the ultimate barrier to competitor entry." As for what the customer was sold, Peters said flatly that there was no such thing as a commodity. The job of the manager was to observe the "evidence favoring differentiation and higher-value-added products and service," which was "close to overwhelming." Acting as if cost and price were the only variables that could be manipulated was wrong. Peters agreed that "market dominance combined with lowest industry cost is nice if you can achieve it." However, he stressed that quality should always be the driving force and come first.

Quality, moreover, is in the eye of the beholder, the customer. Peters was one of the first management thinkers to emphasize that "*perception* is all there is.... There is only one perceived reality, the way each of us chooses to perceive a communication, the value of a service, the value of a particular product feature, the quality of a product." Coming to grips with these perceptions is the essence of "managing and marketing. And leading." Quality is not a technique, but a product of managers who "live the quality message with passion, persistence, and, above all, consistency," who judge and measure their success by customer perceptions, and who follow no less than 22 "aspects of a true customers-first orientation." The authors admitted, though, that this was an "idealized portrait," and they knew of no company that managed to follow all 22 precepts with equal intensity.

Encouraging innovation

An "idealized portrait" is a description that can also be applied to the whole of *A Passion for Excellence*: Peters and Austin repeat their disclaimer when listing the ways (23 this time) to know when your company "smells" of innovation. This inability of companies to live up to the innovatory ideal is inevitable, provided you accept the book's portrayal of innovation as essentially contrarian. The great innovators behave illogically. They succeed by ignoring five "popular myths" (see below) and following "counterpoint" approaches.

- Myth One: Substantial strategic or technological planning greatly increases the probability of a "no surprises" outcome.
- Myth Two: Complete technical specifications and a thoroughly researched market plan are invariant first steps to success.
- Myth Three: Time for reflection and thought built into the process are essential to creative results.
- Myth Four: Big teams are necessary to blitz a project rapidly, especially a complex one.
- Myth Five: Customers invariably only tell you about yesterday's needs.

Skunk-free zone
The large, sprawling offices and rigid systems typical of most big businesses do little to encourage innovation. Peters believes that skunkworks are far superior for development of new ideas.

Peters had been impressed in his research by the "inherent sloppiness" of innovation. Its "given precondition" is a "messy world." The necessary solution had three parts, each one leading on to the next: "experimentation: champions: decentralized bands." The authors gave these stages nicknames: "tries, skunks, and skunkworks." Skunks are the iconoclasts, the rule-breakers, the individualists who strive to accomplish new things and mostly suffer for it, either failing or being fired. They are safer in skunkworks, separate units, preferably set apart from the main company, possibly in rural seclusion, and given a specific, innovatory remit. Management's task is to generate the right climate for experimentation, creativity, and individualism. This climate requires managers to take advantage of that "inherent sloppiness" of innovation – swimming upstream against the myths.

Peters and Austin did not turn these mythical propositions upside down, but their "counterpoints" offered a different mindset. True innovators based their work on uncertainty and ambiguity, experimented, lived by the one dictum "try it now," used small teams, and drew their inspiration from "forward-looking customers," who are "usually years ahead of the rest, and are the best source of leading-edge innovation." The authors ignored the fact that the great innovations of their time, including the mainframe computer, the PC, and the jetliner, were generated internally, often without any customers in sight.

Rejecting bigness

That is also true of many lesser innovations, including the 3M Post-It pads which *A Passion for Excellence* selects as a prize example. The book cites 3M as one of its key sources in learning about the basics of "constant innovation." Yet Peters does not mention the company's almost lethal opposition to the Post-It idea during most of its development. This emphasizes the point that his anecdotes are highly selective. He rejoices in the time he and Austin spent "with today's great entrepreneurs," stars who could do no wrong: or, rather, Peters concentrated on what they appeared to do right. Yet he denied they were the most important people who had shaped his thinking:

> "Most important are those whose names are absent from these pages. Tens of thousands have attended our seminars. They're often enmeshed in stodgy, bureaucratic organizations. Yet they've had the guts to try again, after years of depression and suppression of their ideas. They're out wandering, and proud of it. Out nurturing skunks. Out celebrating their people's successes."

Peters was thus beginning to sing a different tune, asserting that he and Austin were not fans of the executives of the Fortune 500 companies, but "special fans of those, most often in the mid-sized or smaller companies, who are making the American economy grow." In talking to and writing for the dominant companies, Peters had come to believe that he was preaching, not to the converted, but to the unconvertible. It was a short step from that conclusion to his next phase – that of the corporate revolutionary.

Ideas into action

- Be "soft" in managing people, "hard" in expecting good performance.
- Take exceptional care of customers through exceptional quality and service.
- Stay away from your desk as much as you possibly can, and keep in touch with your staff.
- Remember that price and cost are not the only variables in business.
- Live the quality message with "passion, persistence, and, above all, consistency."
- Generate a climate that encourages iconoclasts, rule-breakers, and individualists.
- Ignore the myths of innovation, and rely on forward-looking customers.

Achieving Excellence

Tom Peters' and Robert Waterman's concept of imitating excellence is one you can try out yourself. Find an excellent role model, either an individual or a company, analyze what makes them successful, and relate their methods to you and your organization's needs.

Imitating excellence

You can learn some valuable lessons in the pursuit of excellence from observing other managers from a distance – so long as you bear the following four principles in mind:

The Four Principles of Excellence
1 Excellent financial results cannot be equated with excellence: results may not last, and may not spring from superior management.
2 Your observations should relate to your needs and circumstances: avoid following courses of action that add no value to your business.
3 Shun lip-service. Methods or approaches that suit you and your business should be sought out, adopted, and adapted.
4 Any remedy is only good for as long as it works: do not become slavishly committed to a modus operandi forever.

The eight attributes of success

In addition to observing the four principles listed above, use the eight attributes of success described by Peters and Waterman (see p. 15) to provide a valuable checklist and a spur to striving for excellence. These attributes translate into the following highly penetrating personal questions to ask yourself:

- What is the time-lag between your confronting an issue and reaching a decision, and between having made the decision and taking action?
- Do you use the fewest possible people for the highest possible output in the most effective possible setup?
- Are you in regular, personal contact with customers, and do you use the contact constructively to increase their satisfaction?

- Do you manage people policies in order to achieve rising productivity and employee satisfaction?
- Do you delegate fully and effectively, allowing your staff the freedom to do their best?
- Do you have one strong guiding principle?
- Do you concentrate on what you are really good at?
- Do you keep tight control over the "housekeeping," while allowing plenty of latitude in creative work?

You will probably find yourself unable to answer "Yes" to all eight questions. It is extremely unlikely that you, your company, or your unit, are perfect on all eight counts. Go back and look at the questions to which you answered "No," work out what you need to do, then take steps to change the negatives to positives.

Financial indicators

It is significant that none of the eight attributes refers to financial results. This is because the attributes are concerned with your performance as a manager, and financial results are a product of your performance, not the performance itself. All the same, in addition to the eight key attributes, there are five financial questions that will give you vital indicators of how you are performing:

The Five Financial Questions
1 Are you creating wealth?
2 How highly do investors rate your company?
3 How efficiently are you investing capital?
4 How well are you using the shareholders' money?
5 How effectively are you managing costs and revenues and thus the all-important gap between them?

Balance is everything: you can have excellent results on all five counts while managing poorly in key aspects, but you are not managing well if your answers to the five questions are negative. Remember, the proof of excellence is excellent results – financial or non-financial.

1 Confronting problems

Once you have identified any problems in your performance, or in the performance of your unit or organization, set about solving them. Do not be afraid to challenge the status quo.

Reasons for failure

The lessons of failure are invaluable, but only if you learn from them – and act. The way to deal with failures is to ask why they have occurred.

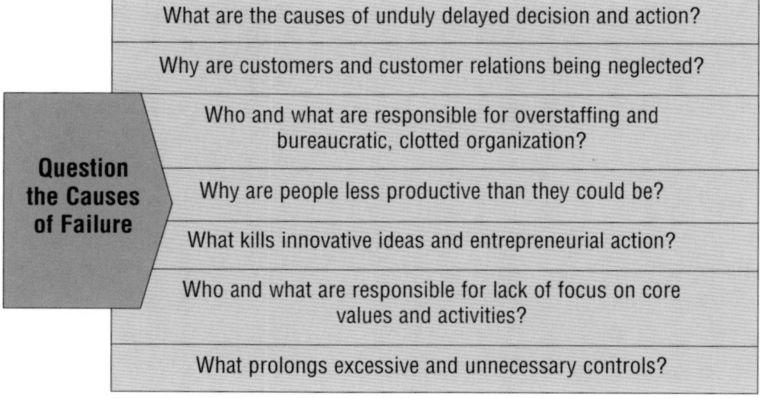

Identifying root causes

Try to identify the root causes of failure. Your instinct will probably be to blame the management. You are part of the management. Delve into the specifics. Some of your explanations may be:

- Too many committees/levels of management.
- Insistence on "the way we do things around here" and therefore resistance to change and reform.
- Rewards/bonuses and staff appraisals do not take customer satisfaction into account.
- Nobody acts on employees' ideas for improving their work.
- A climate of fear penalizes failure and discourages initiative.
- Staff do not share in the shaping of the vision or the plans.
- Rule books and financial controls dominate and therefore hinder management processes.

Overcoming failures

You may feel that all the root causes of failure are outside your control. Peters will have none of that – and he is plainly right. If you are not a "skunk," a rule-breaker, innovator, and individualist, why not? You can always learn how to become one.

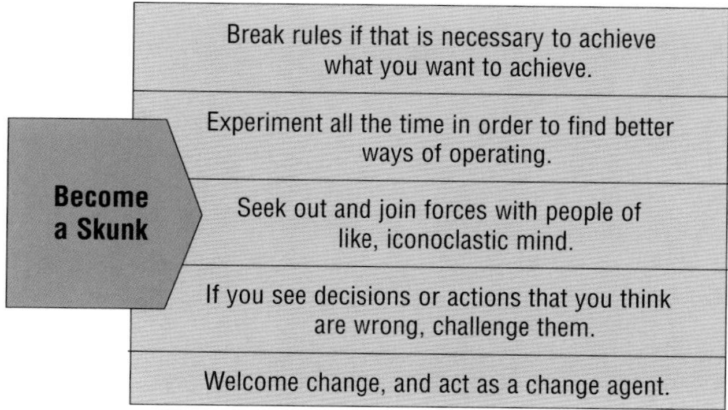

If you do not strive to become a skunk, then you are not really entitled to complain about your "stodgy bureaucratic organization." If you wait for the people at the top to act, the company (and your job) may be in crisis before anything happens.

Unleashing creativity

The opposite of bureaucracy is innovation, another *Excellence* theme. Accept some disorganization. Try to find assignments in what Peters calls "decentralized bands" in which you can apply freedom rather than control to win success. He is certain that innovators function best when set free (in a separate department, or "skunkworks") to follow anarchic non-rule rules:

- Cherish untidiness, uncertainty, and ambiguity.
- Experiment, experiment, experiment.
- Try it now.
- Appoint champions to head small teams.
- Have "lead customers" with whom you work on innovations hand-in-glove.

Be brave: you have been born in fortunate times. Today skunks are more likely to win – and less likely to be fired.

2 Leading from the front

Peters stresses the importance of leadership, rather than mere management, in the pursuit of excellence. There are four functions in the practice of management that differentiate between leaders and administrators. Strive to fulfill the role of leader.

The Four Differentiating Functions			
1 Controlling others	**2** Organizing work	**3** Facilitating success	**4** Building the business

Leader or administrator?

If you spend most of your time on functions 3 and 4, you are a leader. If 1 and 2 dominate, you are more of an administrator. "Admin" matters a great deal, but leadership is what makes the vital difference to corporate achievement and personal careers.

Balancing needs

One of the leader's key roles is to decide when to sacrifice one good in part for the sake of another. For example, you have to balance the "hard" need to press people to achieve the best results with the "soft" need to encourage self-motivation and individual initiative. Learn to apply pressure in a way that achieves a successful balance.

Leading by example

The impact of an enthusiastic, deeply interested, friendly leader is bound to have a positive effect on others.

- Always show your pride in the company and in your people.
- Be enthusiastic about what you or others are thinking/doing.
- Delegate authority to people and encourage them face-to-face.
- Visit colleagues and customers in their own "space."
- Make impromptu visits, not to check up on people, but to inform yourself about their work and share their enthusiasm.
- When you are in your office, operate an "open-door" policy.
- Hold frequent meetings with everybody present and involved.

Leadership is not a solo activity. Your success as a leader depends on your team's success, and your respect for each other must be mutual.

3 Aiming for perfection

Tom Peters and Nancy Austin admitted proudly to simplifying the business of succeeding in business. Their basic principles number only three and need only six words. Live up to those principles – though you will find it is by no means simple.

The Three Principles of Successful Business		
1 Superior quality	**2** Superior service	**3** Constant innovation

Customer care

The aim of excellence is to combine quality, service, and innovation so as to add exceptional value in the eyes of the customer. You are aiming for perfection, though in the knowledge that in "customer care" perfection can rarely be achieved. Use the following eight rules of customer care as a guide to working toward perfection:

- Continually assess levels of service quality by both quantitative and qualitative methods.
- Aim for continuous improvement in the quality of the product and the service.
- Pay close attention to detail, and make sure others do likewise.
- Manage by wandering around your business.
- Manage by wandering around your customers.
- Be incredibly polite and helpful to your customers, and ensure that everybody else in your team is, too.
- Listen to what your customers tell you, and act on it.
- Understand that perception is reality: what the customer thinks is right, even if you think it is wrong.

Placing value before price

The last two rules also apply to innovation – customers are excellent sources of product ideas, and their perceptions will determine whether the innovation succeeds or fails. Peters strongly advises companies to pursue differentiated products and services with higher added value, because value is more important than cost or price. Studies confirm that Peters is right. Customers will happily spend more for higher value. That is the payoff for true excellence.

3

Practicing the theory of chaos

Realizing there are no "excellent" companies • **Four mega-problems: unpredictability, technological advance, demanding customers, outdated assumptions** • The five guides for management in "a world turned upside down" • **"Loving change, tumult, even chaos" as a prerequisite for survival** • Specializing to create niche markets and differentiate your products and services • **Ask, how is the business positioned in the customer's mind?** • How to make managers feel involved

By the mid-Eighties, Peters had concluded that nothing in the status quo was defensible, including large companies in general. Irresistible economic, social, and technological forces had changed the world completely and made the model identified in *In Search of Excellence* obsolete. The need was for highly adaptable companies and leaders capable of *Thriving on Chaos*, the title of Peters' next book.

The myth of excellence

In *Thriving on Chaos*, Peters discovered the "upside-down world." He had talked about "revolution" in the previous book, and now he built *Thriving on Chaos* entirely around that concept. This was the "handbook for a management revolution." In *In Search of Excellence*, Peters and Waterman had looked at American industry and pronounced its leaders "excellent." Now Peters, speaking alone, said tersely: "Excellence Isn't". Looking at his very own broken idols, Peters drew a drastic conclusion:

> "There are no excellent companies. The old saw, 'If it ain't broke, don't fix it', needs revision. I propose: 'If it ain't broke, you just haven't looked hard enough.' Fix it anyway. No company is safe. IBM is declared dead in 1979, the best of the best in 1982 [by Peters and Waterman, in fact], and dead again in 1986. People Express [Peters' own selection] is the model 'new look' firm, then flops 24 months later."

Peters did not blame these sad events on any bad judgment of his own. An era of "sustainable excellence" had ended. Nobody had a solid "or even substantial" competitive lead any more. The "champ to chump" cycles were getting shorter. Peters noted that some companies were responding by buying and selling businesses "in the brave hope of staying out in front of the growth industry curve." But *Thriving on Chaos* paraded facts that demonstrated "accelerating American decline" in both manufacturing and services. Merging and demerging had little relevance in that context: Peters' damning verdict was that this buying and selling of businesses was "shuffle for shuffle's sake" and "just part of the madness."

Merger-crazy managers were taking an unreal route to solve four mega-problems. First, predictability was a thing of the past. Second, technological advance was changing everything. Third, customers were more demanding, with more fragmented tastes. Fourth, as these forces interacted, old assumptions went "askew." One by one, Peters demolished the pillars of conventional thought, starting with "bigger is better, and biggest is best" and "labor... is to be ever more narrowly specialized, or eliminated if possible." He concluded that big firms had *never* been more innovative than smaller ones, or even more efficient.

The Japanese example

Where *Excellence* and its successor had ignored the Japanese, *Thriving on Chaos* recognized the far faster growth in Japanese productivity and embraced "the Japanese passion whose time has come." By that Peters meant smallness. In a curious passage, he dwells on "folding fans, miniature gardening, the tea ceremony" and argues that a "deep-seated Japanese trait" gave Japan an innate advantage in the age of miniaturized electronic products. There is no mention of superior Japanese management. In discussing superior attitudes to labor, Peters couples "long-standing Japanese traditions" with those of Europe. Both

European and Japanese business cultures, he asserted, were "less dependent on big scale, more dependent on broadly skilled labor" and more "conducive to economic success."

In fact, Japanese industry was (and is) dominated by large-scale firms. But in most respects, the Japanese world-class company did provide an excellent model for Peters' painting of the successful firm of the future, described as:

- Flatter (with fewer layers of organization structure)
- Populated by more autonomous units (with fewer central staff second-guessers, more local authority to introduce and price products)
- Oriented toward differentiation, producing high value-added goods and services, creating niche markets
- Quality conscious
- Service conscious
- More responsive
- Much faster at innovation
- A user of highly trained, flexible people as the principal means of adding value

Looking to Japan
In Thriving on Chaos, *Peters acknowledged the rise of Japan's top firms. But the great bulk of his examples were still Americans, whose practice, however, was being influenced by Japan.*

Animating the workforce

The list of model attributes is an oddly restrained ideal for a "handbook for a management revolution." Any management, however conservative, would find this recipe highly acceptable, in theory, if not in practice. Peters had remained more wedded to the conventional corporate lifestyle than he acknowledged. To him, at this stage, the organizational structure was not the problem, which lay rather in the spirit that animated people within the structure. The ideal spirit was enshrined in no less than 45 precepts, which sought to turn the traditional company upside down to match the inverted environment. These precepts fell into five groups, or general injunctions:

- Create total customer responsiveness.
- Pursue fast-paced innovation in all areas of the company.
- Achieve flexibility by empowering all people connected with the organization.
- Learn to love change (instead of fighting it) to instill and share an inspiring vision.
- Control by building simple support systems for a world turned upside down.

At first sight, these divisions seem little different from those that Peters had used in *A Passion for Excellence*: common sense, customers, innovation, "people, people, people," leadership. There were major differences, however. Startlingly, "Management by Wandering Around," the cornerstone and essence of the earlier book (see pp. 37–8), had almost vanished from sight. Peters devoted just two pages to MBWA – and that was only to rebut an influential critic who had nominated MBWA as the "most ridiculous recent management fad." But the critic was right in one respect: "wandering" was an ill-chosen word, with its overtones of aimlessness. Now Peters was preaching "visible management."

Peters' five injunctions were not radical in the light of current preaching, but only in the light of current practice, with its "inflexible factories, inflexible systems, inflexible front-line people – and, worst of all, inflexible managers." Peters demanded flexibility. He devoted much of the book to "exploring what it means to succeed by loving change." That was crucial: "Today, loving change, tumult, even chaos is a prerequisite for survival, let alone success." Again, however, the trumpet call is not matched by revolutionary concepts in the actual recommendations.

For example, under the heading "Financial Management and Control," Peters wrote about the past and present situation (which he described as "Was/Is"): in this case, that meant "centralized, finance staff as cop." The future need (he called this "Must Become") was defined as "decentralized, most finance people in the field as 'business team' members, high spending authority down the line." In the real world, by 1987, that change in deploying and employing financial staff was not revolutionary, but was becoming standard "best practice."

Some of the "Must Become" imperatives are purely aspirational, even optimistic, and not practical guides with measurable dimensions. Thus, sales and service people are no longer to be viewed by other managers as second-class citizens, dominated by moving the product. They are to become "heroes, relationship managers (with every customer, even in retail), [a] major source of value added, [a] prime source of new product ideas." The creation of sales heroes was one of ten prescriptions under a heading dear to Peters' heart: "creating total customer responsiveness."

Customer strategies

The guiding premise of Peters' customer theories is that mass markets have fragmented and are continuing to fragment. The supplier has no viable alternative but to specialize, to create niche markets, and to differentiate his offering from the competition. That premise leads directly to "five basic value-adding strategies":

- The company has to supply top quality, as perceived by the customer.
- Its service also has to be superior, and to emphasize the "intangibles." The motto here is "little things mean a lot," such as calling customers 30 days after delivery to see if they are happy.
- The company has to achieve extraordinary responsiveness to customers.
- It is necessary to be internationalist because of "the true globalization of the economy," in which opportunities are available to smaller firms as well as large.
- Be unique – how a firm (or a division) is positioned in the customer's mind is the key determinant of "long-term success in a chaotic marketplace."

To realize all five strategies, "capability building blocks" are required, one of which is the conversion of salespeople into the heroes mentioned above. Likewise, manufacturing has to be turned into a marketing weapon. A company obsessed with listening, especially to its customers, can "launch a customer revolution," and become "customer obsessed." Peters asserts:

> "Opportunity now lies, not with perfecting routines, but with taking advantage of instability – that is, creating opportunities from the daily discontinuities of

the turbulent marketplace. To do this, the customer, in spirit and in flesh, must pervade the organization – every system in every department, every procedure, every measure, every meeting, every decision."

"Fast-paced innovation," to which Peters devoted a whole section of *Thriving on Chaos*, is also required for customer responsiveness. He argued that innovation is "a numbers game" – the more avenues you try, the greater the chances of finding one that leads to the pot of gold. So he advocated customer-oriented small starts, rather than "over-emphasizing giant technological leaps." The right methodology is "team-based product development," involving all key functions and key outsiders, such as suppliers, distributors, and customers.

The innovative ideas, too, can come from outside. Peters nicknamed this "creative swiping": you steal and adapt ideas from anywhere, including competitors. In pursuing these ideas, the teams are not to get "bogged down writing long proposals unsupported by hard data." Instead, Peters called for many pilots – "rapid and practical tests in the field." His final piece of advice on the subject was to sell the new product or service by systematic word-of-mouth marketing campaigns. But none of these strategies, he stressed, can be decisive without an innovatory climate brought about by deliberate, pervasive management tactics.

The innovator-in-chief finds and supports "persistent and passionate champions." Without these, he or she cannot hope to sustain innovation "in the face of low odds and corporate rebuffs." Peters called for any "silly" rules that impeded fast action-taking to be defied. Rather, the manager has to run his or her daily affairs to defend and back innovatory efforts. That means supporting "thoughtful failures" and learning from them. If this all sounded "soft," Peters was not being "soft"; he demanded "hard" number targets, properly measured and used purposefully in reward systems.

As the prescriptions in *Thriving on Chaos* unfolded, so did Peters' new vision of a "newly flexible, responsive, and adaptive organization." More and more, he saw the typical organization as the enemy of progress. His theme had become people. Peters asserted that there was no limit to what the average person could achieve if thoroughly involved. To tap people power most effectively, though, "human-scale groupings" were needed, by which he meant teams, and specifically self-managing ones.

Getting involvement

To promote a greater degree of employee involvement in the company, Peters instructed management to introduce, and apply at all times, what he called the "Five Supports":

- Create "an atmosphere marked by constant opportunities (both formal and informal) for everyone to be listened to – and then recognized for their smallest accomplishments."
- Focus recruitment explicitly on desired values and qualities, such as the ability to work in teams.
- Make training and retraining mandatory to constantly upgrade skills.
- Offer incentive pay, based upon contribution and performance, to everyone.
- Offer "some form of employment guarantee [that is, job security] for a major part of the workforce," if people do perform acceptably.

Although this five-part platform was quite extreme (should one really recognize people "for their smallest accomplishments"?), it was not enough. The enemies of progress had to be attacked directly by removing the "Three Inhibitors." This involved managers in:

- Abolishing complex structures with too many layers and traditional first-line supervision; stopping the use of the middle manager as "cop and guardian of functional fiefdoms"
- Turning middle managers from bureaucrats into agents of "true autonomy and speed action-taking at the front line"
- Eliminating "silly bureaucratic procedures and, worse still, demeaning regulations and dispiriting work conditions"

All this – installing the supports and sweeping away the inhibitors – had to be done "all at once," which Peters admitted was "a tall order." But this is true of the whole *Thriving on Chaos* "handbook." The program is intimidating, even though Peters had constructed the book as helpfully as possible. It is organized clearly into sections, with summaries at all key points, simple charts, innumerable instructive anecdotes, and many checklists and questions – such as these, on delegation:

- Have you first transmitted the overarching vision with clarity? That is, does the delegate, through demonstrated behavior, clearly "buy in"?
- Have you set high standards in the past that make it clear what level of performance you demand?
- Have you demonstrated in the past, in small ways, that you trust the delegate's judgement?

Teacher training
Peters believes that training and retraining should be mandatory, and that staff who are encouraged to upgrade their skills are better motivated and, as a result, greater assets for their company.

Impossible demands

The list of checklists relating to delegation goes on for a dozen questions in all. As this tiny, partial glimpse of the whole shows, *Thriving on Chaos* is truly indigestible – a collection of homilies and prescriptions, which, while mostly excellent and consistent, would swamp any manager who sought to live by the book. Peters was making enormous, impossible demands on leaders. How could anybody with a job to do juggle his 45 principal prescriptions, let alone the hundreds of subordinate recipes? He side-stepped this key issue by presenting the management of impossiblity as the central leadership task: "The core paradox… that all leaders at all levels must contend with is fostering (creating) internal stability in order to encourage the pursuit of continual change."

Peters presented no less than 18 paradoxes (and even they were only "a small sample") which, he wrote, turned conventional assumptions upside down. In fact, many of these paradoxes were fast becoming conventions – such as "more competition requires more cooperation," "more productivity comes from having fewer suppliers," "tighter control can be achieved through more decentralization." The real difficulty is that he was still expecting existing organizations and their leaders to adapt to a new order that challenged every principle of their beings.

Yet his formula for the new leadership was commonplace: leaders had to "develop an inspiring vision," "manage by example," and "practice visible management." Teachers of "leadership" had always offered the same prescription. Peters' recipe for empowerment was equally familiar: "Pay attention," "defer to the front line," "delegate," "pursue 'horizontal' management by bashing bureaucracy."

Within the tried and true formulas, however, the radical prescriptions kept mounting up: for instance, the section headed "40 Factors that, Reinforcing One Another, Induce Flexibility." Peters wanted his leaders to become obsessive about change. He demanded that they make "What, exactly, have you changed?" the most common question in the organization, to be asked at least a dozen times a day. Everyone was to be evaluated on "his or her love of change" – another new, heavy, and ill-defined burden.

At times, Peters seemed to realize that he was asking too much. By page 388, the "all at once" demand of page 282 had been sensibly moderated: "While you can't do 'everything at once,' no one prescription makes much sense in a vacuum." Yet Peters ultimately never let reality deflect him from his ideals. He saw *Thriving on Chaos* as the "awesome but minimum acceptable agenda." The only solution was to apply enormous energy: "Every managerial act must be seen as an unequivocal support for urgency in pursuit of constant testing, change, and improvement."

Reaching into the book, managers could pull out many valuable plums that would benefit themselves and their companies. But in teaching how to thrive on chaos, Peters had produced a diet that, swallowed whole, could only have created chaos. That, he was soon to conclude, was not his fault, but that of the large corporate consumer.

Ideas into action

- Create "total customer responsiveness" with superior quality, superior service, and fast reaction.
- Create opportunities from "the daily discontinuities of the turbulent marketplace."
- Have many pilot programs going – rapid and practical field tests.
- Realize that there is no limit to what involved people can achieve.
- Instigate the five supports of involvement, starting with listening and recognition.
- Eliminate silly bureaucratic procedures, demeaning regulations, and dispiriting working conditions.
- Ask people, "What, exactly, have you changed?", several times a day.

Setting up the Skunk Camp

In Search of Excellence created Peters' reputation and launched him as an independent consultant and guru. It also inspired his flowering as the scourge of big business and the proponent of revolutionary organizational reform.

On leaving both McKinsey and Waterman, Peters took another look at his idols of *Excellence*, and concluded they had failed to change in a world that had altered radically, and that radical change required a radical new management model.

His second book, *A Passion for Excellence*, stopped short (though not very short) of this revolutionary creed. But the creed's inspiration, according to Peters, was one of the heroes of the book: Kelly Johnson. Johnson had created and named the first "Skunkworks" at Lockheed – a "modest-sized band" that, over 44 years, had created 41 new military aircraft, including the renowned U-2, together with working prototypes and production models. According to Peters, Johnson delivered advanced and reliable products "in a tenth the expected time at a tenth the expected cost." Johnson, the "corpocracy beater," became the symbol Peters was seeking for *Thriving on Chaos*.

Seminars for activists

Peters decided that his first book had not been imperative enough. Its recommendations were "nice-to-do" in 1979, when the excellence research began. In the late 1980s, the nice-to-dos had become "must-dos." Writing and speaking were not enough, either. Peters launched what he called a "modest effort of my colleagues and myself to focus on applications of the principles for success we had described." This was "spearheaded" by a five-day executive seminar, titled "Implementing *In Search of Excellence*", unofficially called the "Skunk Camp."

The first session in September 1984 attracted mostly Peters' "heroes," such as the quality-crazy chicken tycoon Frank Perdue. But Peters was surprised and inspired at how the attendance developed: "The regular meetings were dominated by (1) people who headed mid-sized companies and (2) action takers, such as plant or division managers, from giant firms."

"To meet the demands of the fast-changing competitive scene, we must simply learn to love change as much as we hated it in the past."
Thriving on Chaos

These people were "activists, not theorists" with a practical question: "What in the heck are we supposed to do?" Faced, too, by overwhelming evidence that "America wasn't cutting it in any industry," Peters moved from descriptive to prescriptive. "So a nice-to-do 'reduce product development cycle time' became hard-edged", with a 75-percent target and a two-to-three year time-scale. "An innocuous 'reduce the layers' became a sharp 'no more than five layers'... and 'get rid of all first-line supervisors'."

Peters had found his revolutionary cause. To be excellent was no longer enough, "because 'to be' implies stasis." The only excellent firms were those "that are rapidly evolving" in a new direction: companies that got "everyone involved in almost everything," that "trained like the dickens," and introduced "major pay-for-knowledge and profit-distribution plans." The radical formula was completed by urgency. The new breed of excellent firms did it all "NOW."

Working flexibly

Are you and your organization well equipped for rapidly changing and challenging times? "Chaos" is more than likely to prevail in your own workplace. Make flexibility a priority, both in the systems you establish and in your behavior and that of the people who work for you.

How flexible is your company?

The flexibility of a company depends on its ability to meet seven requirements. Assess the flexibility of your own organization by answering the questions below relating to these seven needs. Answer on a scale from 1 to 5 where number 5 represents "always," 4 "often," 3 "sometimes," 2 "rarely," and 1 "never." Compare your results with the analysis that follows.

- Does the company respond fast and well to the customer?
- Does it innovate in all areas?
- Is the innovation fast-paced?
- Is everybody treated in a flexible, empowering way?
- Do the organization and its staff welcome change?
- Does management communicate and share an inspiring vision?
- Are support systems and controls simple and effective?

Analysis

A maximum score of 35 is very unlikely, while a score below 28 is unacceptable and indicates that there are improvements to be made. Look at the questions for which you scored between 1 and 4, and work toward converting them to a 5.

Size matters

You will probably find, as Peters suggests, that the larger your organization, the less likely it is to meet the seven requirements for flexibility. But small companies are not without fault, either. Mistreating customers, innovating seldom and slowly, disempowering people, resisting change, functioning without any vision of the future, and operating by strict, oppressive, and often ridiculous controls are common to all types of organization.

If your ideal is to work in a flexible environment (as it should be), do not be inflexible yourself. Be open to innovation, commit to change, respond to customer needs, and build on small but firm foundations.

1 Setting the agenda

Whatever the size of your organization, set the agenda for yourself as well as others. If you work for an inflexible organization, you will surely be impeded in managing in the way you think best. All the same, go as far as you can along the Peters road.

Start with yourself

You do not need to have a rebellious nature to adopt your own program. Valuing innovation and adapting to change should be encouraged by sensible seniors, even if only by lip-service. Refuse to work ineffectively, unless you have absolutely no other option.

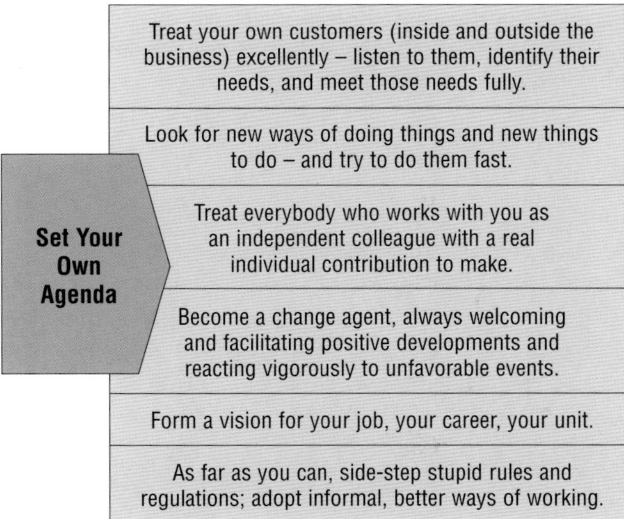

Broaden your range

A lot depends on your colleagues: seek out those who feel the same way as you do, and make them your allies. If it is within your power, divide your staff into the smallest possible groups consistent with getting the task done efficiently and properly. If one person can see a particular task through from start to finish, then that is the best plan to follow. Such people will belong to a larger grouping, but allow them, too, to set their own agenda.

2 Involving others in change

"Get everyone involved in almost everything," says Peters. Start by listening to your staff. People respond well to being asked for their informed opinions, and you will benefit from their inside knowledge. But you need to do more than just listen. You must act, and doing that will lead to changing accepted polices and practices.

Going beyond limitations

Unfortunately, lip-service is especially common when managers talk about involving or empowering people, and you may well find yourself working "against the organization." Check how many of the following features characterize your company:

- Complex structure
- Too many layers
- Traditional front-line supervision
- Functional separatism
- Bureaucratic procedures
- Demeaning regulations
- Dispiriting work conditions

If any of these apply, ask yourself if you are at all responsible for perpetuating such corporate vices. Ask your staff what improvements they would like to see, and adopt the most useful suggestions. This not only raises morale but may also save expenditure.

Involving people is a two-way process. The following questions will enable you to focus on achieving objectives and to mobilize other, truly involved people to do the same. If your answers are not all "Yes," change your ways. Help others to answer positively, too. The results will be rewarding both psychologically and financially.

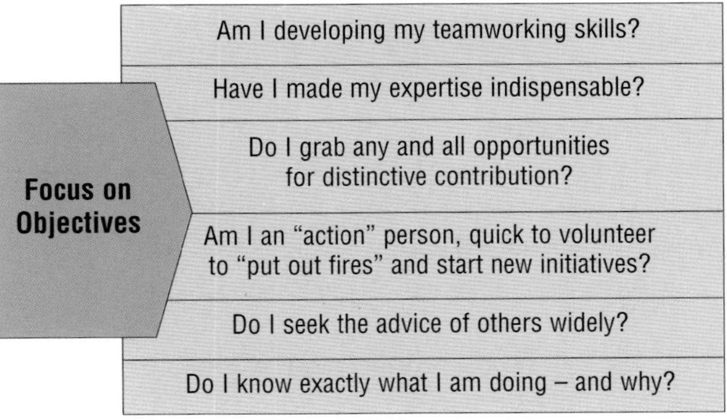

3 Responding to the customer

According to Peters, "total customer responsiveness" is essential. Make it your prime objective. To achieve this, you must be flexible and ready to handle every situation. You cannot respond totally to customers by "perfecting routines" – the exceptional will inevitably occur for which a standard response will be inappropriate. Contact customers as often as you can and find out what you need to do to improve the relationship. Act on what they tell you.

Dealing with customers

Check your customer responsiveness by completing these statements:

- I last spoke to a customer ___ days ago.
- I target myself to talk to ___ customers every month.
- I reply to customers' letters within 24 hours/3 days/a week.
- I call customers back within 24 hours/3 days/a week.
- I always/sometimes/never ask customers if they have any complaints or criticisms.
- I always/sometimes/never set targets for improving quality and meet them.
- I always/sometimes/never look out for "little things" that please customers and supply those benefits.

This should help you to understand more about responding to customers. But you can go further than this: step into the shoes of your customers to determine how they view you and your organization. Remember that most customers who have cause to complain say nothing, but may well take their business elsewhere.

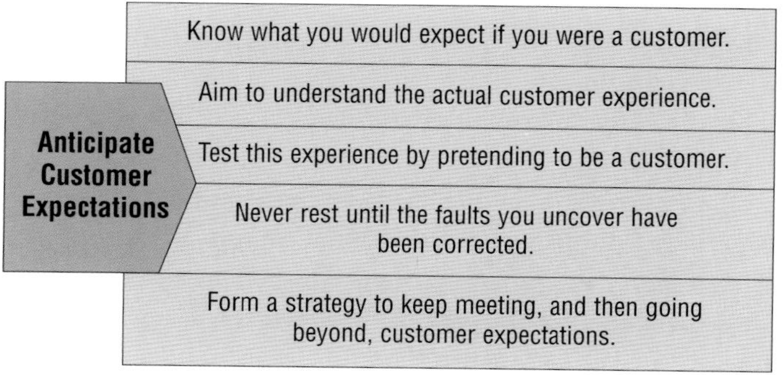

Keeping it small

Most managers work in large organizations that, by virtue of their size, tend to be very inflexible. Whatever the size of your firm, follow the model that Peters recommends – the small one.

Subdividing into small groups

Peters reverses the long-held view that large companies have superior management practices. In "a world turned upside down" by social, economic, and technological forces, the large company needs what comes second nature to the small. That should be easier than it is, because large companies naturally subdivide into myriads of smaller groups, and even the biggest of these subdivisions will not have many people. The issue is not one of size, but whether the group can exploit the advantages of smallness.

The Advantages of Smallness
Everybody knows everybody else, which makes teamwork easier.
Action is taken faster because there is no chain of command.
Communications and sharing of information are much easier.
People identify more readily with the group and its purposes.
Everyone can share in decision-making and other so-called "management" processes.

Applying effort

None of these advantages, though, comes about by itself. They all require positive effort, and there is no reason why that effort cannot be widely applied across the organization.

- Make friends and acquaintances. This is vital, not just for use in your present organization, but also when you move on. Peters lays great stress on having a filing system of useful names, which is a vital part of your personal capital.
- Take responsibility when action is delayed or does not take place. Do not sit back and let it happen. Try to hurry things along to a positive conclusion.

- Keep talking to your colleagues, and listen to what they have to say. If you do not have the information you need, do not feel you should continue without it. Ask for it.
- Be an enthusiast for the group, its task, and its future.
- Do not be a one-man band or an isolationist. Be sure to involve others in your decisions and work, and take a close interest in what they decide and do.
- Finally... AIM BIG – BUT THINK SMALL.

Creating skunkworks

You can, to a certain extent, create the atmosphere of one of Peters' beloved skunkworks (see pp. 41 and 64–5). Skunkworks are usually set up away from the main operation and peopled by teams of creative and innovative staff who tackle a specific project from start to finish with total responsibility for its achievement.

To create an effective skunkworks that follows Peters' principles, adhere to the following guidelines:

- Recruit new staff with care. Be convinced that they will get on well with the existing members of the team and that they are experts in specific areas.
- Create heroes by giving people clear opportunities to succeed and applauding their success.
- Offer members of the team exceptional rewards that are linked mainly to the exceptional achievements of the group.
- Create a "can-do" culture based on rapid response and continuous training and development.
- Inside the skunkworks have full and genuine, informal consultations and discussions of all issues.
- Focus on a clearly defined, shared purpose.

Have great ambitions

Taking a flexible approach to your business makes it easier to achieve your ambitions. Start in a small way and build from there. Peters advises that these "small starts for small markets" should aim at practical applications. His advice applies in equal measure to small firms and large. It is a new version of the famous acronym KISS (Keep It Simple, Stupid!)... KEEP IT SMALL, STUPID!.

4

Small is very beautiful

Teaching the lessons of excellent small businesses to large companies • **How new management theories ignore the issues of creativity and zest** • Erasing "change" from your vocabulary and substituting "abandonment" and "revolution" • **Why an accelerated pace of change demands crazy management for crazy times** • The eight-point program for generating "a whirlpool of incessant, exciting activity" • **Learning about the "new corporate metabolism"** • Why employees should be loyal only to their own list of contacts

Management gurus have generally sought to offer smaller companies lessons drawn from large ones. Peters has reversed this flow, learning from small companies, such as a Midwest plumber, and offering these parables to management at large. Even in *In Search of Excellence*, Peters hymned the virtues of staying small; he and Waterman thought then that those virtues could be practiced within large corporations. They maintained:

> "The message from the excellent companies we reviewed was invariably the same. Small, independent new venture teams at 3M (by the hundred); small divisions at Johnson & Johnson (over 150 in a $5 billion firm); 90 PCCs at TI; the product champion-led teams at IBM; 'bootlegging teams' at GE; small, ever-changing segments at Digital; new boutiques monthly at Bloomingdale's... Small is beautiful."

That message was part of the reassurance that *Excellence* offered to large companies, who were, of course, also McKinsey's clients. They could have all the benefits of being small, while continuing to luxuriate in the strengths, prestige, and rewards of the big corporation. But new venture teams, small divisions, and "champions" could only make their contribution within the overall corporate context. The device itself accomplishes little; it's how the big company uses smallness that makes the difference, and Peters became increasingly and sharply critical of their inability to have their large cake and eat it in small slices.

Freeing management

Condemning all big companies as "crap" came much easier to a man who had left behind the large corporate world and large fees of McKinsey. The switch to smaller companies even had a virtue, since in every economy they far outnumber the large. Peters greatly widened his potential market by turning against giants in favor of pygmies – and the switch by no means removed the giants from his potential audience. When Peters offered the lessons of smaller companies not only to their owners and managers but to large corporates, the latter proved highly amenable to the idea that they could learn from plumbers. Most did not apply the lessons, of course, but that was hardly the teacher's (or preacher's) fault.

As Peters moved further and further away from the big company world, so the advice he gave and the language he used diverged more and more radically from anything a McKinsey consultant might have offered. His book *Liberation Management*, published in 1992, advises managers to "get fired," "take off your shoes," and "race yaks." The title aptly summed up Peters' feelings about the imprisoned manager. But the book did not approach the spectacular success of *Thriving on Chaos*, which was on the *New York Times* bestseller list for 60 weeks. Maybe managers did not want to be liberated.

That, at any rate, appeared to be the author's conclusion. "What has kept me awake at night since writing *Liberation Management* is the growing realization of how stale, dull, and boring most organizations are," he stated. Peters looked at the "new theories of management" and found them painfully wanting. He felt that they steadfastly ignored "the issues of creativity and zest," and actually implied strangling the former and suppressing the latter, even though the pair had become "the prime creators of economic value." Having defined the gap, Peters headed straight for it. He decided that he needed a new clarion call and a new banner.

Going beyond change

The new banner – "crazy times call for crazy organizations" – appeared beneath an oddly bland main title: *The Tom Peters Seminar*, Peters' next book, published in 1994. "Change management" had become a major theme at other gurus' seminars and inside companies. Peters noted that a "relentless refrain" preached the need to learn how to "deal with change, thrive on it" – and he shot the message down in flames: "Astoundingly, we must move beyond change and embrace nothing less than the literal abandonment of the conventions that brought us to this point. Eradicate 'change' from your vocabulary. Substitute 'abandonment' or 'revolution' instead."

This came from the man who, only half-a-dozen years before, had ordered leaders to become "obsessive about change" and to evaluate everyone on "his or her love of change." The apparent inconsistency did not bother Peters at all. It was not only change that he had left behind. His new gospel preached the need to go beyond change, and decentralization, and empowerment, and loyalty, and disintegration, and reengineering, and learning, as well as TQM (Total Quality Management, see p. 93).

Given that most organizations had not embraced many of these concepts (if any), Peters was making the most extraordinary demands. He was asking managements to leapfrog the very latest ideas in order to enter uncharted areas. His thinking was now dominated by an accelerated pace of change that made seven years seem like several lifetimes. The essence of craziness was acceleration. He noted that a laptop launched in February 1993 and bought by him in June had been discontinued by the December of the same year – and that, by the standards of the later Nineties, was a long PC life cycle.

The crazy life cycle

Against this background, Peters constructed a life cycle for crazy management. First, managers had to recognize that crazy times called for more intellect and imagination. This, in turn, demanded a succession of radical developments that turned the manager into a business entrepreneur and the company into a whirlpool of incessant, exciting activity:

- "Deconstruct" the company, eliminating bureaucratic structure and sub-dividing into "spunky units."
- Make every person a businessperson.
- Develop in all employees "the mindset of an independent contractor."
- Create an organizational network ("the corporation as Rolodex").
- Leverage knowledge by "creating a corporate talk show."
- Change the bland organization into a "curious corporation."
- Go beyond looking at "Things Gone Wrong" (TGW) and "Things Gone Right" (TGR) to the creation of excitement – Wow!.
- Do it all over again, accepting the need for perpetual revolution.

Peters presented his program as an evolution. As companies moved from stage to stage they built on the demolition work already completed as they knocked down yet another fortress of the old management. Once again, however, Peters was less radical than he appeared (or boasted). The language was often racy and gimmicky: a "gotta unit" was one of modest size which "routinely does the impossible.... Without that effort, it goes out of business. Kaput… they do it 'cause they gotta'." But much of the writing was standard business book prose, just as the argument relied for support on Peters' old standards of cases, quotes, anecdotes, and data.

The new prescriptions reflected, sometimes well ahead of their general acceptance, developments in the real world: most companies actually were being broken down into more autonomous units freed from day-to-day central control; the Japanese had long insisted that all managers be trained and deployed as business people; more and more employees were being hived off (or hiving themselves off) as independent contractors to their previous employer; networking was becoming general as corporations were forced by the pressure of technology and markets to form alliances; the needs to change radically and continuously, and to adopt "knowledge management," were becoming clichés of gurudom.

The missing ingredient that Peters injected was excitement: not only excitement, but the wholesale rejection of the status quo. He had become an avid collector of eccentricities and an advocate of their cultivation, saying to seminar participants: "Forget your detailed note-taking today. Instead take a single piece of paper and simply write on it, 'every', 'abandon' and 'everything'. That's it. Then, when you get back to work, slip the page beneath the glass on your desktop. Refer to it hourly."

Using "abandonment" (a Peter Drucker word) instead of change was only part of the self-indoctrination. Among other "crazy" questions, Peters asked readers if they routinely used "hot" words like revolution, zany, weird, freaky, nuts, and crazy itself. They were to learn about the "new corporate metabolism (voom, varoom)" and to do that learning "on the fly, forever." Referring to the book's epigraph, "Only the paranoid survive," a phrase taken from Andrew Grove, chief executive of microprocessor king Intel, Peters mused, "How about the Paranoid Corporation?". He found it "not a bad idea, and perhaps a good one."

Realizing the vision

But was anybody in the real world actually realizing Peters' vision? Oticon, a hearing-aid manufacturer, caught his eye. Significantly, it is Danish. Since *In Search of Excellence*, with its almost exclusive use of American models, Peters had been adding more and more foreign companies, primarily European ones, to his hero roster. Under the direction of Lars Kolind, Oticon had become a self-styled "spaghetti organization," getting rid of the entire formal apparatuses (departments, managers' titles,

Coining paranoia

Andrew Grove, chief executive of the giant microprocessor organization Intel, coined the phrase "only the paranoid survive." Peters approved of it and borrowed it for his book's epigraph.

secretaries, red tape, and so on) "to create a 100 percent project-directed entity in which employees invent the tasks that need to be done, then physically arrange themselves as they see fit to get them done."

Like Oticon, companies were advised to "self-DESTRUCT (and live anew)." Peters could not shake free from his habit of compiling exhaustive checklists. But they were now full of labels ("The Age of Pygmies?") rather than instructions. Peters saw the mood of the organization as critical. He wanted it to be, not decentralized, but "atomized" into "spirited, often pint-size, subunits with their own personalities, and headed by disrespectful chiefs." The latter would be "entrepreneurized, along with every job in the business." Peters even had a recipe for "businessing" a job, detailed as follows:

- Cross-training – training in nearly all the skills required to perform the job from start to finish
- Budgeting – responsibility for the formulation, tracking, and amendment of budgets
- Quality control – quality measurement, quality monitoring, and quality improvement processes
- Autonomy – a place of one's own within a delayered, reengineered organization, as well as the authority to make decisions, including committing substantial resources (including money) without recourse to higher-ups

"... businesses, to compete, have to be not just decentralized but deorganized. The logical limit of deorganization is the entrepreneur – the business unit of one."
The Tom Peters Seminar

- Access to expertise, from instantly available staff specialists (who in effect – "no, make that in reality" – work at the beck and call of the front line) and from outside consultants as required
- Having one's own real live customers, whether they are internal or external, who enhance the businessperson's sense of ownership
- A (limitless) travel budget

The last item embodies four key points. First, you want and need people to travel. Second, if they are empowered in large matters, how can you remove that power in small ones? Third, by removing travel controls, you remove a chunk of bureaucracy. Fourth, "trust or go bust": "if the trust is missing (genuine, unstinting respect) heaven help you, your career, your firm in the changing 90s." But there was a catch to all this atomization and independence. What would happen to loyalty, the traditional cement of the organization? Peters' solution was: forget it.

Liberating individuals

The employee should try being loyal only to his or her Rolodex, to the network of contacts, inside and outside the company. Thinking like an "independent contractor" would paradoxically "up the odds" on retaining "today's big-company job (should you wish to do so)." Note the words in brackets. As Peters' thought developed, he was becoming less interested in the organization and more obsessed with liberating the intellect, imagination, and energies of the individual. He suggested that managers should frequently ask themselves the questions that a job-seeking resumé should answer:

- What the hell do I do?
- What have I actually done?
- Who among my customers will testify to it?
- What evidence is there that my skills are state of the art?
- Who new do I know, far beyond the company's walls, who will help me deal with an ever-colder world?
- Will my year-end resumé look different from last year's?

To Peters, it was a sad fact that the average middle manager or professional staffer was unable to answer any of these questions effectively. But the resumé routine was not meant to assist a standard vertical ascent. Rather, managers were told: "Tack. Jibe. Twist. Turn. The whole (big) idea of moving 'horizontally' is critical.... 'Careers' today involve jumping around, up sideways – and occasionally down." In a "futzed-up" marketplace, nothing sat still for "more than a few nano-seconds." Peters saw that this was not a comforting message: "The bottom line is equal parts terrifying and liberating." Coping with discomfort was all up to you – up to a point.

You needed other people, and they needed you, to complete the network. Peters described this as "the process of putting the demolished companies and the independent spirits back together." The new, reassembled organization would not be a "vertical monolith": the jobs would not be the same, year after year; and employees would not be "around for the duration." For each project, employers would collect the talents they required, in much the same way as a Hollywood producer hires the cast, crew, and production staff for a movie. Peters warmly endorsed the growing practice of "outsourcing," whose most avid users farm out to suppliers everything save their own few essential core activities.

Rolodex loyalty

Peters uses the Rolodex as a symbol to expound his views on employee loyalty. He advocates being loyal to one's network of contacts, as filed in the Rolodex, rather than to the organization.

"How many people in your unit," asked Peters, "work at home at least one day a week?" The implication in the question is very clear: the more the better. You are hiring, not people's presence, but their intelligence and knowledge. But you need to do more: "We either get used to thinking about the subtle processes of learning and sharing knowledge in dispersed, transient networks. Or we perish." Peters was absolutely sure that this kind of progress was being made toward "bringing corporations into the post-industrial, knowledge-sharing information age." But the new theories of "knowledge management" were still hard for him to pin down – and hard for others, too.

Unanswered questions

Peters wrote that "the geniuses of leveraging knowledge are the first to admit that they still have many more questions than answers." So did he. But Peters was happy as long as he had agitated minds and got people to at least ask, "What if he's even half right?" He confessed to being unsure if he was right even to that degree. The cocksure dealer in certainties of *In Search of Excellence* was now dealing tentatively with uncertainties. "The curious corporation" was still a long way away, "in this book and in business," but what was it? He could only come up apologetically with a "not that great" list of its possible policies:

- Hire curious people.
- Hire a few genuine off-the-wall types.
- Weed out the dullards, nurture the nuts.
- Go for youth.
- Insist that everyone take vacations.
- Support generous sabbaticals.
- Foster new interaction patterns.
- Establish clubs, bring in outsiders, support off-beat education.
- Measure curiosity.
- Seek out odd work.
- Look in the mirror.
- Teach curiosity.
- Make it fun.
- Change places.

Just as the author says, the list is not that great. *The Tom Peters Seminar* was a work in progress, peddling ideas that were semi-formed, and perhaps could never be completed. Peters concluded that "in a crazy world stable, sensible organizations make no sense." His problem is obvious: how could a preacher of "no sense" management convince managers that his own preaching made sense?

Ideas into action

- Recognize that crazy times call for more intellect and imagination.
- Leverage and spread knowledge by participating in "a corporate talk show."
- Develop small units with their own personalities and disrespectful chiefs.
- Seek the autonomy required for making decisions and committing substantial resources.
- Think like an independent contractor, even if you are not one.
- Look for horizontal career opportunities, not the standard vertical ascent.
- Get used to thinking about sharing knowledge in transient networks.

5

Management through provocation

Provocation as a technique for galvanizing managers into radical improvement • **Delighting the customer, not by systems, but by spontaneous Wow!** • Developing an emotional link between customer and product or service • **Greater efficiency as the hard-nosed way to win customer loyalty** • How to stand out from "the growing crowd of look-alikes" • **Why revolution has ousted change and continuous improvement** • Moving forward through constant action and bold embrace of failure

As his thinking about management evolved, from financially oriented rationalism to people-oriented, semi-controlled anarchy, so Peters moved from cool consultant to fiery, wildly unorthodox, evangelical preacher. He now urges managers to go for "Wow!", and encourages advanced eccentricity: "crazy" management. But behind the show-biz approach there lies a sane idea: that managers need provocation, however wild it may appear, to jerk them out of established, ineffective ways, and to galvanize their businesses.

Not only is the idea rational; it can and does work. Thus, a Maltese businessman traveled all the way to Scotland to attend a Peters seminar and was inspired by the guru's provocation to tackle the problems of his beer enterprise in a radically different way. On his return to Malta, he split the brewery into units, none larger than 100 people, each headed by a general manager who was made responsible for meeting financial targets and rewarded accordingly. Sales and profits both shot up dramatically.

This solution did not result directly from Peters' teaching, however, and by no means amounts to "crazy" management. The master's contribution was to persuade the businessman to go "outside the box," to stop trying to improve his business within the confines of the established system and philosophy. When you are told to be crazy, in other words, you stop being crazy enough to run your business in an unproductive way. That is what makes sense of a paradox posed in *The Tom Peters Seminar*: "This is the craziest chapter in the book. This is the most sober chapter in the book." Its theme could have been posed by the most buttoned-up McKinsey consultant: how to "meet customers' needs in ways that will stand out in an incredibly crowded and kinetic marketplace."

Preacher teacher

Tom Peters now bears little resemblance to the McKinsey consultant he once was. Casual dress and unorthodox teaching have replaced the sober suit and conventional theories of management.

New and different

Even German managers, who are renowned for their conservatism, needed no teaching in the next proposition: quality is not enough. "New competitors from around the globe, quality-conscious all, are joining us in flooding the market with flawless products." To stand out from the crowd, new marketing strategies are needed – not just new products. They are not enough, either. They have to be new and *different*.

Peters pointed out that researchers in 1993 gave "a grade of D or F" to half the new products they tested, including entries from great companies like Procter & Gamble. The Japanese, Peters noted, had learned the lesson. He quoted a cosmetics boss who warned that until that time Japan had relied on its technological advances and high quality to sell its products, but that would no longer be enough. Their products must now have "spirit," too.

There is a long distance between this sober truth in *The Tom Peters Seminar* and Peters' ideas in *The Pursuit of Wow!*, the title of another book published in 1994 and based substantially on his syndicated newspaper columns. Here, Peters took to extremes the new orthodoxy about the need for customer delight and excellent service, and with justification. The customer notices exceptions, good or bad, so "exceptional" service is unorthodox, "crazy" if you like. Peters cites an Auckland restaurant that has on its walls framed letters – not of praise, but of complaint. His attention is constantly caught by such details. But, then, so is that of customers.

Peters no longer tried, as in *In Search of Excellence*, to systematize his concept, because by definition customer delight is not a matter of system, but of spontaneity. Instead of prescriptions, he offered questions, such as:

"… if employees are inundated with practical customer information rather than vague exhortations, they won't be able to keep their distance. They'll begin to 'think customer' – and, maybe, even start to dream about customers."
The Pursuit of Wow!

- Is your company's average product offering ho-hum?
- Does the very act of defining [quality] precisely dessicate the product and obscure the more important elements of quality?
- Does "have fun" apply to the experience of customers dealing with your company? Should it? Could it?
- Love. Love. Love. Use that word in business?
- Are you snuggling up – boldly, proactively, lovingly – to your customers?
- Are you spending 20 percent of your marketing budget on acquiring information about customers?

Relationship marketing

The last question came from two other consultants, Don Peppers and Martha Rogers, who wrote a book, very influential in the mid-Nineties, advocating "relationship marketing." In *The One-to-One Future* (1995), they claimed that, thanks to new technology, even the mass marketer could "assume the role of small proprietor, doing business again with individuals." The result, as mass marketers responded with enthusiasm to the thesis, was to unleash a flood of junk mail that often only dissatisfied customers, the very opposite of Peters' intentions. He was aware that relationship marketing was not the whole answer. This lay more in "adding 'Wow' to your basic products and services."

Peters conceded that putting the product second to customers, as Peppers and Rogers proposed, "is hardly a guarantee of success." But it is a condition of success. In *In Search of Excellence*, Peters and Waterman had mentioned the customer only once in their eight attributes. Managers were urged to maintain "constant contact with customers," which in itself said nothing about the latter's treatment. Now Peters regarded this treatment as fundamental. He quoted another guru, Robert Peterson, who had found "that there is a large 'affective' component to service – from the customer's view." To win repeat business (an acid test), firms had to develop "an emotional link" between the customer and the product or service.

That message resonated for an emotional man like Peters. He made a film on the subject, which was produced by Video Arts, and called it *Service with Soul.* Built around a live seminar, the film sang the praises of new heroes who went to extraordinary, deeply committed, and caring lengths to gratify the customer. Yet, even in Peters' vehement presentation, these hero managements do not really seem "crazy," or to be operating in a crazy environment. They include, for instance, plumbers and suppliers of plastic moldings – what might be called "ho-hum" businesses which for the most part have been barely touched by the digital revolution, the upheavals in consumer markets, and the acceleration of change.

Supplier partnerships

Peters' emphasis on the revolutionary environment and the threat of change, though, is part of the provocation process. With the plastics firm, Nypro, which had adopted a common sense but radical strategy, Peters' purpose was to provoke others into showing similar readiness to adopt new ideas and abandon old ones. Nypro had become a prime exponent of "supplier partnership," a rapidly spreading trend in which the two sides of a business relationship cooperate on all aspects of the product or service. Vistakon, the Johnson & Johnson subsidiary that makes disposable contact lenses, links with this supplier "to assess production processes, product quality, and productivity" in meetings that last for two days every six weeks. The computer links between the two enable Vistakon in Florida to check on Nypro's "real-time performance" in Massachusetts: "how many units are being produced, the amount of waste, even the on-line statistical process control numbers." For their part, Nypro managers can use the computers to get equally detailed information from Vistakon. By acting on the pooled, once private, information the partners get extraordinary results, such as a billion molds delivered to Vistakon without a single late shipment or quality defect, and cuts in the customer's annual costs that have run from 5 percent to 20 percent.

This operation would win the total approval of experts in TQM (Total Quality Management), a hard-nosed business discipline, focusing the entire organization on achieving higher quality of all products and processes, that does not work in terms of the undisciplined pursuit of "Wow!". Peters was equating the pursuit of operating efficiency with the achievement of an "intimate relationship" with the customer. In fact, the intimacy in this case was the only way to optimize the efficiency; the two attributes, like the Vistakon and Nypro technical teams, are Siamese twins. Likewise, a California plumbing firm called De-Mar used greater efficiency as its prime weapon in winning customer loyalty. According to the *Service with Soul* video, De-Mar's basic offering is simple:

- Standardize prices and list them.
- Provide service round the clock, seven days a week, on the day of the inquiry.
- Guarantee all work for one year.

Customer service

Peters was attracted by the methods that De-Mar's proprietor, Larry Harmon, used to achieve these aims, such as 6-a.m. training sessions (part of a sustained training program) that start with Harmon shouting, "Can I get an amen!" at the "Service Advisers," that is, plumbers. Their pay depends on a points system that measures six aspects of customer service. Good phone calls about the advisers, good letters, and customer requests for a named adviser earn respectively 1,000, 2,000, and 1,000 points. Bad phone calls, bad letters, and "does not want adviser back" rate subtractions of 1,000, 2,000, and 2,000 points.

Harmon is not much good at hiring (in one year half his hires were fired), but he is plainly a highly effective manager and good at motivating his employees. The familiar doubt arises, however. Will what works for one company or one manager in one business transfer to another company, manager, or business? Peters' own answer, strangely, is "No." On the contrary, companies need, above all, to be different from one another, "standing out from the growing crowd of look-alikes." The hero companies, on this reading, can no longer act as role models to other companies. They are provocations, stimuli for "generating yeasty responses – personal and corporate – to these very yeasty and frequently frightening times."

"In the age of e-mail, supercomputer power on the desktop, the Internet, and the raucous global village, attentiveness – a token of human kindness – is the greatest gift we can give someone."
The Pursuit of Wow!

Yet the books published by Peters in 1994 belied his own thesis. If management is not a generic subject, how could Peters theorize on its conduct? If customer-supplier partnerships, as applied by the businesses Nypro and Vistakon (see pp. 92–3), achieved superior results for both parties, would not the same be true for other businesses with different products? If companies aiming, like De-Mar, to achieve excellence in customer service successfully linked reward to that excellence, why would that not work generally? Having founded his career on the creation of management templates, Peters now argued that they were impossible, while, at the same time, perversely continuing to endorse transferrable, imitable procedures.

Disorganized and disjointed

Peters gave up trying to resolve the paradox in *The Pursuit of Wow!*. This book tackles all the problems posed by a disorganized, disjointed world by being disorganized and disjointed itself. It makes almost no attempt at coherence, unlike *The Tom Peters Seminar*, which is tightly organized, each chapter leading on to the next, and the whole forming an integrated theory of management. In *The Pursuit of Wow!*, Peters lets his long experience of business "lead my mind where it will." The result is a hodgepodge of 210 homilies and quotations, brief case histories and anecdotes, management theory and maxims. It all leads up to a pained lament: "My average seminar participant comes dressed in a drab suit, uses drab language – and noticeably quivers when I suggest that the most likely path to career salvation is to get fired. Do you know how depressing it is to look out at a sea of cookie-cutter clean-cut faces?"

The lavish income Peters earned from the seminars did little to ease the pain: "Even at my obscene rates, it's discouraging," he complained. He often had "to fight an urge to… scream" at this unpromising audience: "Ye gads, wake up! Breathe! Go down swinging. Try something. Try *anything*. Be A-L-I-V-E, for heaven's sake!" The *agent provocateur* had a clientele that refused to be provoked. But you could hardly blame them. In the real world, people still

Small is beautiful

Richard Branson of the Virgin Group is seen by Peters as a "small-unit, split-'em-when-they-grow-big guy" who says that, above 50 or 60, people "get lost in the corridors of power."

want careers. Managers are still responsible for seeing that their businesses are competently and honestly administered. Schedules must still be drawn up and adhered to. Middle managers are still required for all kinds of non-crazy purposes.

How crazy, in reality, can a company become? In *The Witch Doctors*, the co-authors John Mickelthwait and Adrian Wooldridge, who both write for *The Economist*, criticize Peters' extreme "anti-rationalist stand." They disparage his approach: "The world has gone bonkers, he rants, and to cope with it we must go bonkers too." They accuse him of arguing mistakenly that managers must abandon their attempts to manage scientifically and turn themselves from careerists into entrepreneurs. They criticize the idea that cutting down on bureaucracy and hierarchy is old hat, and that companies should rather abandon any attempt at central control in order to set free the energies and initiatives of the people they employ – who can themselves be as crazy as they like – in fact, the crazier the better.

The critique is fair. But Peters, as so often, is making an extreme statement of a rational and, indeed, generally accepted thesis. In calmer tones, he himself writes: "Change and constant improvement (*kaizen* per the Japanese), the watchword of the Eighties, are no longer enough. Not even close." In going on from that observation and calling for "revolution, and perpetual revolution at that," Peters was singing much the same song as most gurus. Nor was there anything "crazy" about a statement like this: "only a bias for constant action [echoing, curiously enough, one of the eight attributes featured in *Excellence*] and a bold embrace of failure, big as well as small, will move companies forward."

Constant disequilibrium

Peters approvingly quotes "management grandee Peter Drucker", who is the arch-apostle of sanity: "The most probable assumption is that no currently working 'business theory' will be valid ten years hence." Managers, concluded Peters, had to thrive "amid constant disequilibrium." The finishing line in the corporate race kept changing, even for companies that successfully practised "The Five Virtues." These were presented with supporting examples, quoted from specific "transformation leaders":

- *"Pedal to the metal"* – i.e., put your foot right down on the accelerator and keep it there. ("Organizations are capable of taking on more than their leaders give them credit for")
- *Action* ("put our heads down [and] engineer like mad")
- *Embrace failure* ("he [Branson] doesn't give a f...")
- *No tepid responses* ("make something great")
- *Focus amid mayhem* ("you've got 12 minutes")

The evocation of individual leaders, such as Richard Branson of Virgin, Ed McCracken of Silicon Graphics, and textile tycoon Roger Milliken, emphasizes the overweening importance of the dynamic boss in transformation. Even if some of the business idols develop clay feet, Peters never loses his faith in the superstar CEO, who is always, "Pushing the needle all the way over, unabashedly championing revolution, and getting the company anarchists to the barricades." This "great man" theory of management sits uncomfortably with Peters' cult of the self-managing, self-realizing individual ("reinventing civilization begins with reinventing thee and me"). But it is the unifying theory of all his thought, from *Excellence* onward.

It is not possible to achieve extraordinary results without extraordinary people at the top, and you know they are extraordinary because of their extraordinary results. The tautology is basic to Peters' research and teaching. Like any good hot gospeller, he preaches in parables. The faith is more important than the logic, and the passion outweighs the intellect. Yet logic and intelligence do underlie Peters' thought, and they provide its enduring value. The idea that organizations can confine and suffocate the talents and ambitions of individuals is not new. But Peters the prophet is needed to provoke managers into recognizing this stupidity for what it is, and to strive to be both different and better.

Ideas into action

- Think "outside the box" to fundamentally improve the business system.
- Keep on questioning every aspect of the business, especially service.
- Found your "crazy" initiatives on solid, common sense ways of serving customers.
- Link up with suppliers and customers to share improved efficiency.
- To achieve superior service, link rewards to measured customer satisfaction.
- Try radically new and different ideas whenever you get the chance.
- Know that your organization can do more than you expect.

Replacing rationality with anarchy

In *The Tom Peters Seminar*, Peters pronounced that "The one mistake I'm not making with this book that I've made in some (all) of the others is to think that I've arrived at THE ONE ANSWER FOR ALL TIME."

That would no doubt surprise the people who paid up to $1,000 apiece to attend the seminars from which the book was derived, for Peters exudes conviction as he expounds his doctrines. He truly believes in what he is saying, but only while he is saying it. In the early Nineties, he concluded that successful businesses had to follow much the same line: nothing is forever, or even for long. He approvingly quoted a consultant named Roger Martin: "Whatever you've built, the best thing you can do… is to burn it down every few years…. Don't change it, but b-u-r-n i-t d-o-w-n."

In a world where the outrageous has become the norm, Peters made outrage his norm, too, appearing on the cover of *Seminar* in multicolored boxer shorts. He became ever more fervent in his attack on traditional forms. The doctrines he started to preach through every medium, from seminars to CD-ROMs, drummed home the theme "Crazy Times Call for Crazy Organizations" and won him vast fees and an enthusiastic following.

Charismatic entertainer

Peters had become the nearest thing yet to a management Messiah. His seminars resembled revivalist meetings rather than management lectures. He had learned to match his physical energy to the vehemence of his message. Marching among his audience with a microphone, backed up by dramatic visual aids, Peters harangued people, who applauded enthusiastically, but who mostly did not put his precepts, or anything like them, into practice. Peters was now a successful entertainer, but that was weakening his reputation as a serious management thinker.

Now living in Silicon Valley, he had unrivalled opportunities to observe the management of its successful firms. They practiced the free-wheeling, responsive, and highly entrepreneurial style he favored, starting small and subdividing all the time to avoid

"We're flattening our organizations, shedding our bureaucratic excesses. That's good – and long overdue. But as to entering the Age of Imagination, we're just barely sniffing at the doorway." *The Tom Peters Seminar*

the blight of bigness. Yet his two 1994 books made scant reference to the Valley or to its micro-electronic multi-millionaires and billionaires, such as Bill Gates.

The likes of Gates responded to change and challenge with all the speed and flexibility that Peters had been demanding. But they were not anarchists; they were highly disciplined empire-building businessmen, ruled by logic, not by WOW!.

In *Excellence*, Peters had promoted large corporate businesses, to which he remained faithful, though increasingly critical, for some years. Then he transferred his allegiance to medium and smaller enterprises, with a sprinkling of large-scale corporate heroes. But neither of these audiences came along for the whole of his revolutionary ride. His abandonment of rationality had left Peters without a constituency. To change the metaphor, the followers still came to worship, but there was no church, just a fiery preacher of easily ignored sermons.

Finding method in madness

The Peters mantra, "crazy times call for crazy organizations," sounds crazy itself. But the author is perfectly sane. Separate out the hype and exaggeration and the underlying message is one that all managers should heed: prepare to reinvent yourself and embrace change.

The new orthodoxy

According to Peters, nothing is forever. Orthodoxy itself is changing. To succeed in management, you need to move toward the new orthodoxy – or the orthodoxy of the moment. Already managers are having to learn how to work in organizations that have moved decisively from traditional vertical structures toward horizontal ones. In these more flexible companies autonomous units, or even temporary ones, are the key building blocks.

Developing skills

The new orthodoxy requires managers with all-around business skills. You need to be as knowledgable as an independent contractor, which is what many people have become. Already, your dependence on people networks, both inside and outside the organization, is far greater than that of previous generations. Increasingly your day-to-day work, and what you ultimately produce and sell, involves more knowledge (or "software") and relatively less "hardware."

The certainty of change

This intellect-dominated output is what is required by today's market, which places a large premium on what is new. It demands that you must be intellectually inquisitive and productive. Managing efficiently is important, but it is no longer enough. The only certainty in today's environment is that it is continually changing. To meet this challenge, strive to reach ever higher levels of effectiveness and adaptability.

Revolutionary management

Peters calls this process the "perpetual revolution." To deal with this new state of affairs, aim to be an eminently sound and successful business manager as well as the revolutionary that Peters describes.

1 Meaning business

Mastering the principles of business is anything but crazy. Peters stressed that all managers must "know the business." Work to understand fully not just your own function but business generally.

Understand business

Knowing the business means knowing the economic and financial consequences of your own actions, as well as the economics of the entire company. To do this, you need the following skills.

The Essential Business Skills
Understanding and being able to write a business plan
Understanding and being able to write a budget
Distinguishing between direct and indirect costs
Distinguishing between profit and contribution
Analyzing marginal costs
Appreciating the concept of "opportunity cost"
Defining and applying standard financial measures such as return on capital, return on equity, cash flow, and gross margins
Knowing how to use Pareto's Law

The amount of information available to you is endless, but unless you have and use the basic tools listed above your business knowledge, or equipment, will be seriously deficient.

Applying knowledge

By using these skills you are better placed to put Peters' ideas into action. For instance, Pareto's Law separates the "insignificant many" from the "significant few." This is the 20/80 rule. So 20 percent of your customers contribute 80 percent of sales or profits. To be an effective manager, concentrate the bulk of your efforts on the significant fifth of customers and find low-cost ways of serving the rest. Ineffective managers treat all customers equally.

Adding value

The financial skills are essential tools for ensuring that you make a real profit and optimize your financial return. Take, for example, indirect costs, or overheads. The higher the overheads in relation to sales revenue, the harder it is harder to earn a profit. The ideal is to charge the best possible price but also keep a tight control on costs.

However, Peters emphasized that cost reduction is not the only priority. Some expenditure is vital, for instance on innovation, quality, and customer service. Anything that damages a customer's perception of your business will damage the business. The pursuit of excellence means striving always to enhance the value of the business.

Taking control

Managers are often told to run their section of a company like their own business. Ask yourself how you might act if the business really was your own, and you could organize it as you wished:

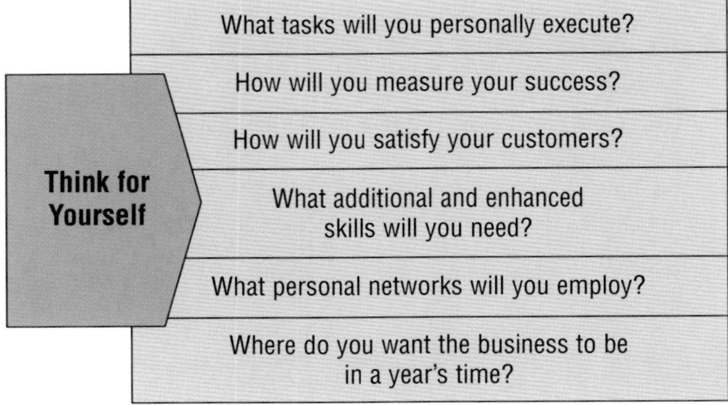

Knowledge is strength

You will certainly need to answer these questions if you do become an independent contractor – an increasingly likely option today. Keep asking the questions until the answers become instinctive. At the same time, take every opportunity to increase your knowledge – and do not stop with yourself. The "open-book" style of management allows everyone to know key numbers, results, and plans. The stronger everyone's knowledge of the business, and the more they can put that knowledge into action, the stronger the whole operation.

2 Living with change

You are living in an unsettled, dynamic world, where change is the only constant. Take a moment to write a list of your latest significant purchases and your current interests. How many of them would have been on the same list a decade ago? Five years back? Last year? Even if the purchases and interests are similar, the way you buy and pursue them will almost certainly have changed.

Think differently

These changes also affect your customers. They are constantly seeking novelty and differentiation. Peters stresses the need for new and different thinking. He urges you to develop a new mentality:

- List the products and/or services your company offers and ask "Are they scintillating? Dazzling?"
- Ensure that you and your colleagues appreciate the shift toward services and intellectual components, and adjust your priorities to reflect the importance of these "soft products."
- Be seriously imaginative.
- Subject processes and products to continuous, impersonal scrutiny, and drop those that are outdated.

Act differently

You cannot respond to changing market needs unless you are open to change yourself. Adopt new practices to meet new conditions.

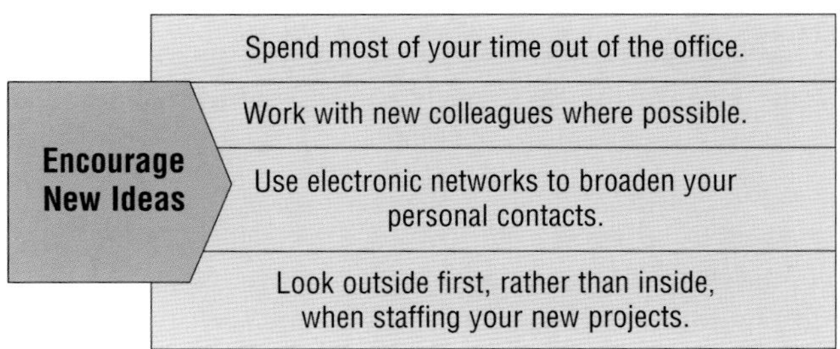

Above all, create excitement for your colleagues and your customers. Peters tells you to ask "On a scale of 1 to 10, how dull is your unit, your company, your closest competitor? How dull are you?" Be honest with your answers – and make a commitment to banish dullness.

3 Managing your career

Whether you choose to stay in the corporate world or not, take responsibility for developing your own career – do not leave it up to your company. Peters' advice is to "think independent".

Manage yourself

Be prepared to move jobs and companies. Keep updating your resumé every six months. Follow Peters' recommendations for taking control of your own destiny:

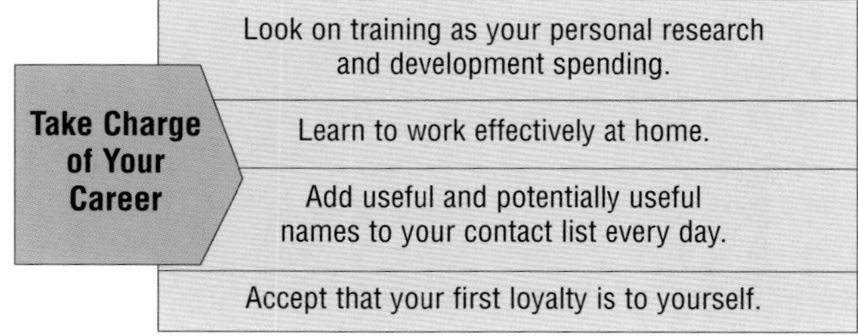

As the security of a job for life fades into the past, you need to be able to survive in today's chaotic marketplace. Equip yourself as well as you can for a "non-linear, opportunistic" career.

Competence is the key

Peters poses a key question: "What do you want to be famous for?". The answer should be "Towering competence." Your obligation to yourself demands nothing less. Achieving and applying that competence also justifies your employment by others, since that is how you meet your obligation to them. Take every opportunity to develop your competence.

- Draw up and follow a learning plan that you review every three months.
- Design your own job (as far as you can).
- Act on your own initiative wherever possible.
- Learn from colleagues the secrets of their success.

Above all, keep looking for career moves, not necessarily promotions, that will teach you "something new and special," associate you with talented people, and confront you with a tough challenge.

4 Managing by provocation

There is a very sane reason for Peters' extroverted, show-biz approach. Shock tactics are needed to provoke action. To thrive in chaos, think and act in completely new ways.

Provoking a response

Much of Peters' teaching seems to have little to do with management and more to do with paradox. Take these maxims:

- Success begets failure.
- Fiction beats nonfiction.
- Unintended consequences outnumber intended consequences.
- Reject simple explanations.

In contrast, conventional management teaching uses hard statistics. For example, Forum Corporation's research tellingly revealed that 70 percent of customers deserted major manufacturers not because of price or quality problems, but because they did not like "the human side" of doing business with the supplier. The aim of both approaches is to provoke you into action.

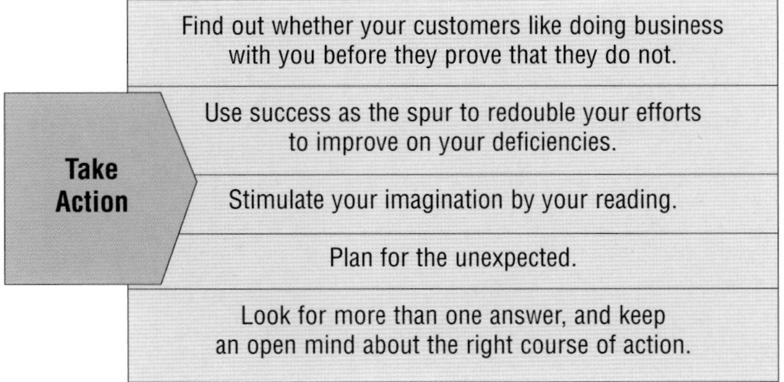

Searching for excellence

Provocation jerks you out of your rut and into new and more effective ways of acting. "One-minute excellence" is one of the most useful Peters provocations of all. It means deciding to act now: "You do it and it's done.... As of this second, quit doing less-than-excellent work." This is the language of the seminar guru and the showman. But why not take up the challenge?

stephen COVEY

Biography

Stephen R. Covey was born of Mormon stock in Utah in 1932. His career was originally academic. Armed with an MBA from Harvard and a doctorate from Brigham Young University (BYU), he taught organizational behavior as a professor in the latter institution. The MBA not only brought a solid business background to his teaching, but it also developed valuable skills. In the businesslike but theocratic setting of BYU he showed considerable organizational talent, acting as director of university relations and assistant to the president. The current BYU president, Merrill J. Bateman, exemplifies the same Mormon dualism; he was previously, among many other things, a Mars, Inc. executive and Presiding Bishop of the Mormon Church.

Inspired by Mormon belief

The Mormon Church of Jesus Christ of Latter-day Saints has had a huge influence on both Covey's career and his thinking. For a start, it is not difficult to see a strong connection between the "13 fundamental beliefs" set out by the Church and the "seven habits" explained in his blockbuster, *The Seven Habits of Highly Effective People* (1989). Mormonism must be the source of Covey's belief that there are fundamental, unarguable principles, which have a defined number. Some of the beliefs, such as the thirteenth, "We believe in being honest, true, chaste, benevolent, virtuous, and in doing good to all men," have direct relevance to Covey's own gospel of personal, interpersonal, and organizational effectiveness.

Covey can claim to be one of the most successful educators in history: by his own account, his student body is numbered in the millions. He very often quotes the Chinese philosopher Lao Tzu, and his "timeless adage": "Give a man a fish and you feed him for a day; teach him how to fish and you feed him for a lifetime." The knowledge he gained through teaching persuaded Covey that people could improve themselves radically if only they understood how to make those improvements happen.

Voice of enlightenment

But Covey's rider to Lao Tzu's wise words has been just as important in his career: "Develop teachers of fishermen, and you lift all society." Like his evangelical predecessors, Covey seeks to lift individuals into enlightenment so that their families, their organizations, their whole society will follow them along the paths of righteousness. Just like St. Ignatius Loyola with his Jesuits, Covey has created disciples and an organization that can spread the word far more widely than a lone individual, even one as amazingly industrious as himself.

Here his business abilities and his Harvard MBA have proved highly effective. Covey left BYU to found Stephen R. Covey and Associates and fulfill his ambition of having a major influence on American management. With a handful of associates, Covey rapidly developed the firm to the point where major worldwide expansion was feasible. In 1984, he took his commercial activities into a new management training organization, named the Covey Leadership Center. Thirteen years later this merged with Franklin Quest, famous for its time-managing Planner, to become Franklin Covey Company, of which he is cochairman today.

His chairman partner is Hyrum W. Smith. Theirs is a thriving public company, traded on the New York Stock Exchange since 1997, with over 4,000 staff or "members." There are 128 Franklin Covey Seven Habits retail stores, mostly selling the company's products in North America, but also found in over 30 other countries. Translated into 28 languages, the Covey products have carried the message of this latter-day evangelist around the world. Each year the members train more than 750,000 people, and help to sell over 1.5 million books. The huge sales (over 10 million copies of *Seven Habits* alone) contribute heavily to a turnover in excess of $550 million.

Spreading the word

In total, Franklin Covey has 15 million books in print, with all other titles dwarfed by the blockbuster *The Seven Habits of Highly Effective People*. Published in 1989, when Covey was in his mid-fifties, *Seven Habits* has spawned dozens of offshoots in both book and electronic form. But the company's activities have reached far beyond training and books. Its facilities in the Rocky Mountains of Utah, where Covey and his wife live, "empower" trainees to spread the Covey doctrine around the world – together with the products that apply the ideas to individuals, organizations, and families.

Covey has actually written more about the family than business; *The Seven Habits of Highly Effective Families* (1998), like its model, has spawned many derivatives, from *The Seven Habits Family Journal* to *Balancing Work and Family* (both 1998). A deep belief in the family and its values is fundamental to Mormonism. In Covey's work, it appears not only in his writings on the family, but also in his philosophy at large. Yet, despite their very substantial personal and ethical content, Covey has no doubt that his major nonfamily works are definitely "business books."

The evangelism, in fact, is thoroughly businesslike. That commercial emphasis explains why Franklin Covey's clients include all but 18 of the 100 biggest American companies by sales, and two-thirds of the top 500. The corporate clients, including many organizations operating on a much smaller scale, are offered consulting, personal coaching, and on-site training; or they can send people to the workshops that the company conducts in over 300 cities – again, outside as well as inside North America. There are also more than 7,000 "licensed client facilitators" whose mission is to teach the Franklin Covey curriculum.

Family man
Drawing much of the inspiration of his books from experiences within his family and marriage, Stephen Covey has found an avid readership in the international business community.

The interest that Covey has evoked in management is essentially pragmatic. As he says in his book, *The Seven Habits of Highly Effective People*, "helping individuals, organizations, and families become more effective" meets the desire of companies to attain higher productivity from self-motivating employees. Management Covey-style seeks to align individual and corporate aims, not only through agreed plans and targets, but also through personal development. Covey is unique among management gurus in treating personal and public virtue as one and the same.

Other gurus have tended to concentrate on either improving the individual or improving the organization. Covey presents them as inseparable – and his own business success supports his argument. Just as Franklin Covey qualifies its founder as a teacher of corporate executives, so his family life supports his authority on matters of family management. Covey and his wife Sandra have nine children, and he proudly describes himself, above all other distinctions, as "husband, father, and grandfather."

Philosophy of achievement

Child-bearing and rearing aside, the principles that Covey has espoused so successfully are normally associated with otherworldly, spiritual lives. But Covey's pride and pleasure over the progress of a previously disappointing son (see p. 26) are based on the same material achievements that would lead any pushy, over-identifying, purely secular parent to boastfulness. Thus, after Covey changed his parental tactics and strategy to what developed into the Seven Habits philosophy, the underachieving boy "was elected to several student leadership positions, developed into an all-state athlete, and started bringing home straight A report cards." Covey concluded that the change of philosophy that worked so well with Covey Jr. offered the same hope to everybody: you can be true to yourself and still achieve what you want.

Better still, goodness and success fed off each other. The other abiding element that emerged from this experience with his son was the idea that the family is a source of more widely applicable wisdom. Covey's books make liberal use of other anecdotes from his children's upbringing and his relationship with his wife – and relatively little use of anecdotes culled from identified businesses.

Drawing income from wisdom

The identification of family truths with performance factors in larger organizations is at the core of Covey's thought and practice. His writing and commercial activities have promulgated these ideas in a purely secular context – and with excellent commercial results for Covey himself. The Mormon readiness to serve God and also make money suits him well, for Mormons truly see no conflict: serve God well, and your business will also succeed.

Covey's own career, while inspired by religion, has been marked by many secular distinctions; in 1996 he was named by *Time* magazine as one of the top 25 Most Influential Americans. That same year he was cited by the magazine *Sales and Marketing Management* as among the top 25 Powerbrokers. As a successful businessman, Covey has very few peers among the ranks of the management gurus: nor can many match his success as a preacher. Practicing what he preaches has worked well enough for Covey in person to serve as evidence that, at least for some people, the Seven Habits actually work – highly effectively.

1

Building basic effectiveness

The importance of ensuring the long-term production of golden eggs • Why integrating basic, enduring principles into your character leads to true personal and business success • **Exploiting the freedom to choose how you will respond to stimulus** • The Seven Habits that make people highly effective • **Developing the Seven Habits from dependence to independence and then interdependence** • How to achieve the correct P/PC balance between Production and Production Capability

Stephen Covey's fundamental thought is simple but powerful. He believes that "there are basic principles of effective living... people can only experience true success and enduring happiness as they learn and integrate these principles into their basic character."

Covey calls this teaching "the Character Ethic," basing it on "natural laws in the human dimension that are just as real, just as unchanging, as unarguably 'there' as laws such as gravity are in the physical dimension." Covey regards this statement as an "objective reality." The natural laws "are woven into the fabric of every civilized society throughout history." They "comprise the roots of every family and institution that has endured and prospered."

Character versus Personality

Covey distinguishes the Character Ethic from what he calls "the Personality Ethic" – a more complex idea, for which he has no such clear and simple definition. In contrast to the Character Ethic's "principle-centered" philosophy, the Personality Ethic is concerned only with practicalities. It embraces all efforts to "change outward attitudes and behavior," with emphasis on the "outward." Covey does not suggest that such efforts are invariably futile. On the contrary, some of the Personality Ethic's elements – "personality growth, communication skill training, and education in the field of influence strategies and positive thinking" – are beneficial, "in fact sometimes essential for success." But Covey regards even the essentials contained within this ethic as secondary, and "secondary traits alone have no permanent worth in long-term relationships."

Moreover, the search for short-term fixes is eventually self-defeating. He argues: "If there isn't deep integrity and fundamental character strength, the challenge of life will cause true motives to surface and human relationship failure will replace short-term success." To Covey, the contrasting value of obedience to the natural laws is not open to argument:

> "Principles are guidelines for human conduct that are *proven* [my italics] to have enduring, permanent value.... They are essentially unarguable because they are self-evident."

Covey's Character Ethic is a close fit with Christian ideals. He denies that his ideas are "esoteric, mysterious, or 'religious'," asserting that, while not one of them is "unique to any specific faith or religion, including my own," they all play "a part in most every major enduring religion, as well as enduring social philosophies and ethical systems."

Changing character

Covey opposes most psychologists by arguing that changing one's character is just as feasible as changing behavior. There is an evident problem here. Clearly, being faithful, temperate, just, or industrious are behaviors. The extent to which people behave in these worthy ways is governed by their personalities, which, scientists would say,

"The essence of principle-centered living is making the commitment to listen to and live by conscience. Why? Because of all the factors that influence us in the moment of choice, this is the factor that will always point true north."
First Things First (1994)

Hollywood insight
Cecil B. DeMille commented during the making of his epic film The Ten Commandments: *"It is impossible for us to break the law. We can only break ourselves against the law."*

are created by heredity and experience, nature and nurture. Covey rejects the concept that, like the dogs famously researched by the Russian physiologist Ivan Pavlov (1849–1936), men and women are conditioned to "respond in a particular way to a particular stimulus." Rather, mankind has a unique ability: "*Between stimulus and response, man has the freedom to choose.*" The italics are Covey's. This gap between stimulus and response is key to Covey's thinking. By the exercise of independent will, people can act on their self-awareness, "free of all other influences." They can exploit imagination and obey the promptings of conscience, which Covey defines as "a deep inner awareness of right and wrong, of the principles that govern our behavior." This philosophy will have none of the view (which is, however, perfectly tenable) that the qualities exalted by Covey are also conditioned by heredity and experience. That view is what he calls a paradigm, "the way we 'see' the world... in terms of perceiving, understanding, interpreting." Covey says that "we have many, many maps in our head," divided mostly between maps of "the way things are, or realities, and the way things should be, or values." These maps are indeed conditioned. But, argues Covey, shift the paradigm, change the map, and you alter attitudes, behaviors, and relationships.

Shifting the paradigms

This is the essence of Covey's teaching, and of his appeal. Human beings, whether as individuals or when gathered together, have problems, which they naturally wish to solve. They want to be better spouses, parents, employees, employers, and so on. Covey teaches that "the way we see the problem is the problem." In a marriage that has gone flat, for example, the husband might hope that "some new book, some seminar" will improve the wife's understanding. "Or maybe... it's useless, and only a new relationship will provide the love I need." Covey urges a fresh look:

> "But is it possible that my spouse isn't the real problem? Could I be empowering my spouse's weaknesses and making my life a function of the way I'm treated? Do I have some basic paradigm about my spouse, about marriage, about what love really is, that is feeding the problem?"

What does this questioning, valid or otherwise, have to do with business management? Covey bills *Seven Habits* as a "business book," so how does he make the connection? His answer is that an "inside-out" approach to personal and interpersonal effectiveness – from the inner mind and spirit to external relationships – applies in both public and private aspects of life. Indeed, "private victories precede public victories." Covey postulates a Win/Win trade-off: if you want to have more freedom, more latitude in your job, you win them by a private victory – "be a more responsible, more helpful, and more contributing employee."

The Seven Habits have a crucial role in forming the bridge between private victory and public victory: or between the Character Ethic and effectiveness. They are:

- Be Proactive
- Begin with the End in Mind
- Put First Things First
- Think Win/Win
- Seek First to Understand… Then to be Understood
- Synergize
- Sharpen the Saw

Virtually every self-help writer, whether selling the Character Ethic or the Personality Ethic, has offered some, if not all, of these precepts. People have long been urged to

"If you want to improve in major ways – I mean dramatic, revolutionary, transforming ways – if you want to make quantum improvements, either as an individual or as an organization, change your frame of reference."
Principle-centered Leadership (1990)

take control of their destinies, to form objectives, to prioritize, to seek mutual benefits, to learn by listening, to make the whole worth more than its parts, and to exercise their talents and faculties ("sharpen the saw"). But why does Covey call these precepts "habits"?

He defines "habit" along the lines of a well-known management formula: knowing what to do, knowing how to do it, and (the difficult part) actually doing it. As Covey rewords the formula: "Knowledge is the theoretical paradigm, the *what to do* and the *why*. Skill is the *how to do*. And desire is the motivation, the *want to do*." In Covey's view, the Seven Habits accompany an all-important personal development mirroring that of the human being from a dependent infancy to independence and finally, as "we continue to grow and mature," to increasing awareness that "all of nature is *interdependent*," including human life – and business management.

Maturity continuum

Along this developmental route, the first three habits, developed in sequence, thus achieve a private victory that takes the individual from dependence to independence. Public victory comes about through adopting, one by one, the next four habits, which take the individual into interdependence and continued self-improvement. Covey describes this as a Maturity Continuum, for which he makes the largest possible claims:

> "The Seven Habits are not a set of separate or piecemeal formulas. In harmony with the natural laws of growth, they provide an incremental, sequential, highly integrated approach to the development of personal and interpersonal effectiveness."

The large claims do not stop with that amazingly confident statement. Because the Seven Habits are based on enduring and universal principles, writes Covey, "*they bring the maximum long-term beneficial results possible*" [my italics]. If that generalization sounds implausible, Covey breaks it down into subordinate claims, more specific but no less sweeping, that present the habits as high roads to effectiveness. They create "an empowering center of correct maps" that show you how to solve problems and maximize opportunities. Moreover, you can "continually learn and integrate other principles in an upward spiral of growth."

Character-forming habits

These enormous benefits follow, Covey maintains, as the Seven Habits "become the basis of a person's character." In other words, prioritizing your time is not merely an example of effective behavior, like keeping your car in good condition, but a foundation of your ethical being. He thus reverses the normal concept of character, which is that good character reveals itself in good behavior. In Covey's view, good behavior creates good character.

The seven particular elements of good (or rather effective) behavior that he selects are all you need, he believes, to achieve wonderful results in practical affairs. Behave better, and you will do better. Employers thus learn to treat their employees better, in order to be met half-way by employees who want to do better work. The teaching radiates optimism. Covey firmly believes in people's ability to improve, to work together for their mutual advantage, and to sweep away the many impediments that stop organizations and those who work in them from realizing their full potential.

The P/PC balance

Covey is by no means blind to these obstacles or to their importance. But in *Seven Habits* he elevates one barrier above all others – an imbalance between Production (P) and Production Capability (PC). Here he switches his emphasis from family and self to organization and organizer. Where he normally argues from the personal to the organizational (as from parental relationships to business), in this passage he argues from business to persons.

The P/PC Balance is a well-understood, rock-solid concept that is basic to all effective management. The determining force is not ethical but economic. If you run a machine flat out, it will eventually break down and production will stop. Run the machine with time allowed for preventative maintenance, however, and you will optimize the machine's life and thus its output. The principle, like so much of management, is plain commonsense, and *Seven Habits* illustrates this eternal truth with a story from Aesop, the great Greek master of the commonsensical.

Aesop famously tells about the farmer who, blessed with a goose that lays golden eggs, kills it to get at them more quickly – and thus loses the supply forever. Whether the assets are physical, financial, or human, Covey shows that such results-obsessed greed neglects the P/PC balance and leads to ineffectiveness – often total failure. The physical asset, the machine, may become irreparable. The financial asset, the capital with which you bought the machine, will disappear unless the machine's production earns more than the cost of that capital. Drive the human assets to achieve the highest possible output at the lowest possible employment costs, and demoralized people will frustrate your aims.

Covey's clear conclusion is that managers are wrong to measure effectiveness by results alone – by the production of golden eggs. True effectiveness, he says, is "a function of two things: what is produced and the producing asset or capacity to produce." Concentration on results can be deeply counterproductive: awful examples crop up in the financial pages every day. Companies that fall from grace often appear to have suffered some sudden calamity. In reality, they have been steadily killing the golden goose for years, by neglecting staff, or customers, or investment, or innovation – perhaps all four – while continuing to report apparently excellent profits.

Short-term success

Pressure placed on subordinate managers to produce short-term results often accompanies this debilitating process and has the same counterproductive effect. Covey illustrates the consequences well by describing a manager who is eager to make a good impression on his superiors and ramps up production, with no downtime and no maintenance. "He runs the machine day and night. The production is phenomenal, costs are down, and profits skyrocket. Within a short time, he's promoted."

The manager's successor, though, has to invest heavily to compensate for the neglected downtime and maintenance. "Costs rocket; profits nose-dive." The new person, of course, gets blamed for the loss of golden eggs: but the departed manager is the true villain who, says Covey, "liquidated the asset." The accounting system was also guilty: it "only reported unit production, costs, and profit." Without information on PC, management can look far better than it is, but only for a time. Eventually, reality asserts itself.

Covey echoes well-established research that confirms the commonsense expectation that declines in quality relative to price will result in loss of customers. The customers' regard for the value that they receive is the marketing equivalent of a machine's capacity to produce. Lower the value – Covey cites a new owner who watered

Optimizing production
Production Capability (PC) is enlarged in auto manufacturing by the use of robots. But the robots themselves must be maintained to prevent gradual erosion of the optimum Production/PC balance.

down a restaurant's famous clam chowder – and you reduce your sales capability. The conduct of the cheating restaurateur is thus bad business as well as bad ethics. Covey has made the necessary connection between character and effectiveness.

The argument is just as strong when it comes to employees. They, Covey argues, are a vital part of the marketing equation, because they deal with the customers and therefore relate directly to sales capability. "*The PC principle is always to treat your employees exactly as you want them to treat your best customers.*"

Profit in the long term

Covey does not dwell on the paradox that sacrificing profit (by spending money on employee training and welfare, say) increases profit (by raising employee and customer satisfaction and thus sales). He simply observes that immediate profit – "a short-term bottom line" – is important, "but it isn't all-important." That raises the obvious question of how and where the balance is drawn. Covey admits that there is no easy answer. Rather...

> "To maintain the P/PC Balance, the balance between the golden egg (production) and the health and welfare of the goose (production capability) is often a difficult judgment call."

His argument is that, if you constantly keep the principle of balance in mind, it serves as a "lighthouse," guiding you toward the destination of optimum effectiveness. In *The Seven Habits of Highly Effective People*, Covey calls it "the very essence of effectiveness" and declares that "We can work with it or against it, but it's there.... It's the definition and paradigm upon which the Seven Habits... are based."

Universal profits

According to Covey, anybody can become highly effective by changing their lives and lifestyles through the adoption of a few easily presented and understood principles of conduct. No matter what your genetic inheritance, no matter what your life circumstances, you can become a much better person and (by no coincidence) a much better employee and manager. He stresses that this is no quick fix, but a continuous program of self-improvement, easy to follow, whose benefits never cease, but only increase. The input is spiritual, but the benefits are also material and, above all, universal.

Ideas into action

- Do unto others as you would have others do unto you.
- Accept full responsibility for your own character and behavior.
- Understand that very often the way you see the problem is the problem.
- Use the "inside-out" approach to effectiveness, advancing from private victories to public success.
- Remember that effectiveness is a function of both what is produced and the capacity to produce.
- Do not apply pressure for short-term results at the expense of long-term capability.
- Replace quick fixes with continuous self-improvement.

Finding the Character Ethic

Stephen Covey is precise about the moment when his key idea, the difference between the Personality and Character Ethics, "clicked into place." He described it as "one of those 'Aha!' experiences in human life."

Typically for Covey, the moment was rooted in a family situation. One of his sons was doing badly at school, academically, socially, and in athletics, especially baseball. Covey and his wife tried as hard as they could to encourage the boy to improve.

The example Covey gives as evidence of their encouragement is baseball, not schoolwork. "We attempted to psych him up using positive mental attitude techniques." Their overanxious coaching failed. "Our son would cry and insist that he'd never be any good and that he didn't like baseball anyway." The parental struggle ("Nothing we did seemed to help, and we were really worried") happened to coincide with bimonthly presentations in which Covey was teaching communication and participation to IBM executives as part of their development program.

The teaching taught him about perceptions. His work on expectancy theory and self-fulfilling prophecies led to "a realization of how deeply embedded our perceptions are." Embedded perceptions, the Coveys came to see, had influenced their attitude toward their son. "When we honestly examined our deepest feelings, we realized that our perception was that he was basically inadequate, somehow 'behind'." At this point, a third factor coincidentally came into play.

Principled ways

Covey had been engaged in an "in-depth study of the success literature published in the United States since 1776." For the first 150 years, he observed, this literature had concentrated on principles as the foundations of success – "things like integrity, humility, fidelity, temperance, courage, justice, patience, industry, simplicity, modesty, and the Golden Rule [do unto others as you would have others do unto you]." These were the qualities he was to enshrine in his Character Ethic.

For the last 50 years, though, success literature had changed radically, and not, in Covey's opinion, for the better. Much of the writing was superficial, leading to what Covey describes as the Personality Ethic: "Success became more a function of personality, of public image, of attitudes and behavior, skills and techniques, that lubricate the processes of human interaction."

In their efforts with their son, the Coveys had been following "the basic thrust" of the latter: "quick-fix influence techniques, power strategies, communication skills, and positive attitudes." Their son's problems, in other words, lay as much with his parents as himself. The Coveys decided to adopt a basically sensible attitude: "We decided to relax and get out of his way and let his own personality emerge." Left to carry on "at his own pace and speed," the boy blossomed in all the areas – academic performance, social relations, and athletics – where he had previously been found lacking. For the father, this was a moment of epiphany.

"... we began to see our son in terms of his own uniqueness. We saw within him layers and layers of potential that would be realized at his own pace."
The Seven Habits of Highly Effective People

2

Winning private victories

Racing to your goals via self-affirmation and visualization of success • Using "self-awareness, imagination, conscience, and independent will" to be proactive • **How reactive language becomes a self-fulfilling prophecy** • Enlarging the Circle of Influence that contains what is within your control • **The importance of making and keeping commitments and promises** • How the "first creation" (the plan) relates to the "second creation" (the execution) • **Writing your personal "mission statement"**

The idea of the "private victory" is indispensable to Covey's whole body of thought. His philosophy stands or falls on the proposition that man is the master of his soul and the captain of his fate. The issue is not what befalls you, but how you respond to the event – the "stimulus." In the deterministic model that Covey scorns, the response is conditioned by nature and nurture, and the individual reacts accordingly. In Covey's model, "Freedom to Choose" is the governing force.

Even when trapped physically in a Nazi concentration camp, the prisoner could "*decide within himself how all of this was going to affect him*" [Covey's italics]. The guards could humiliate and destroy the body, but they could not control the mind. By exercising that control, the victim can win a private victory that cannot be taken away. If freedom of choice can be exercised in such extreme circumstances, how much easier it is, Covey implies, to deal with the challenges of normal life. The key word in his freedom model is "proactive," defined by one dictionary as:

> "... tending actively to instigate changes in anticipation of future developments, as opposed to merely reacting to events as they occur; ready to take the initiative, acting without being prompted by others."

Choosing your response

The definition contains the essence of Covey's doctrine – especially the contrast between "mere" reaction and acting on one's own initiative. In this philosophy, the individual who chooses to adopt Covey's Habit One – "Be Proactive" – brings four powerful weapons to bear: self-awareness, imagination, conscience, and independent will. All four weapons are available to everybody. The difference between the highly effective person and others is that the former consciously uses the weapons. That demonstrates responsibility, or rather "response-ability," which Covey defines as "the ability to choose your response." Highly proactive people, he argues:

> "recognize that responsibility; they do not blame circumstances, conditions, or conditioning for their behavior. Their behavior is a product of their own conscious choice, based on values, rather than a product of their conditions, based on feeling... if our lives are a function of conditioning and conditions, it is because we have, by conscious decision or by default, chosen to empower those things to control us."

This extreme individualism comes somewhat oddly from an adherent of a rigorously prescriptive fundamentalist religion. Neither Covey nor his children chose to be born into the Mormon Church, and religions naturally do not encourage those visited by the accident of birth to make a different choice. Proactive decisions and eternal verities are contrasts, not complements. But Covey squares this circle by the three words "based on values." So, if Mormon children were able to exercise total freedom of choice, their decision would surely be to live by the Mormon faith they have been taught – consequently, no conflict arises.

"Because of our unique human endowments, we can write new programs for ourselves totally apart from our instincts and training. This is why an animal's capacity is relatively limited and man's is unlimited." *The Seven Habits of Highly Effective People*

Being proactive, not reactive

Covey takes the argument for proactive behavior to extremes. By arguing that people are essentially proactive, he comes near to criticizing reactive behavior – even though it is completely natural. "When people treat [reactive people] well, they feel well," he notes, with apparent disapproval. Does enjoying others' approval really merit the criticism that reactive people "build their emotional lives around the behavior of others, empowering the weaknesses of other people to control them"? True, becoming "defensive or protective" when criticized may justify that assertion, but the "fight or flight" reaction to attack is as basic to human nature as "smile and the world smiles with you."

Negative responses

Covey insists that "It is our willing permission, our consent to what happens to us, that hurts us, more than what happens to us in the first place." But even he admits that "this is very hard to accept emotionally." It is hard because he is asking people, not to suppress their emotional reactions, which at least is a possibility, but to stop the emotions arising in the first place.

"If we have a deep understanding of our center and our purpose we can review and recommit to it frequently. In our daily spiritual renewal, we can visualize and 'live out' the events of the day in harmony with those values." *The Seven Habits of Highly Effective People*

The negative response to stimulus, however, may well be more powerful than the positive incentives to overcome the negatives. Covey knows this very well from experience. You can take the horse to water, but you cannot make him drink. The reaction to what Covey calls "solution selling," and describes as "a key paradigm in business success," is typical of many consultants' experience:

> "Over the years I have frequently counselled people who wanted better jobs to show more initiative... to study the industry, even the specific problems the organizations they are interested in are facing, and then to develop an effective presentation showing how their abilities can solve the organization's problems.... The response is usually agreement – most people can see how powerfully such an approach would affect their opportunities for employment or advancement. But many of them fail to take the necessary steps, the initiative, to make it happen."

Taking proactive initiatives

The difference in effectiveness between those who take initiatives and those who do not is not 25–50 percent, says Covey, but "a 5,000-plus percent difference, particularly if they are smart, aware, and sensitive to others." The figuring may well be exaggerated – 5,000 percent is 50 times more effective – but Covey is plainly right. If you do not take the initative, things will happen to you, but you will not make things happen (except permissively).

Proactive initiatives are taken at the personal level. For example, anyone can see the illogic of the statement "He makes me so angry." As behavioral psychologists have long taught, nobody makes you angry: you choose to react angrily to somebody's provocation. The logic is as obvious as the illogic. You, not the other person, are responsible for your anger, which you can prevent or eliminate. You know how to respond differently. You need simply to escape from reaction to proaction, as exemplified by the other changes of language given below:

Reactive Language	Proactive Language
He makes me so angry	I control my own feelings
There's nothing I can do	Let's look at alternatives
That's just the way I am, I can't change	I can choose a different approach
I can't	I choose
I must	I prefer

As Covey points out, "a serious problem with reactive language is that it becomes a self-fulfilling prophecy." If you assume that somebody will not agree to your request and do not make it, you guarantee that you will receive a refusal – you say "No" on their behalf when they might, with or without suitable persuasion, say "Yes." However, you have to accept that, even when you do take a proactive course in such circumstances, you may still not be able to control, or even influence, the final decision.

"Businesses... organizations of every kind – including families – can be proactive. They can combine the creativity and resourcefulness of proactive individuals to create a proactive culture within the organization." *The Seven Habits of Highly Effective People*

Seeking to influence

Covey observes that everybody has a "Circle of Concern," containing everything that matters to them. But "there are some things over which we have no real control and others that we can do something about." The latter can be circumscribed within a smaller "Circle of Influence." Proactive people focus their efforts in this circle and seek to enlarge it. Reactive people focus on the entire Circle of Concern and focus on the weakness of other people, the problems in the environment, and other circumstances over which they have no control.

The result is that their Circle of Influence contracts, and they become less effective. Theirs is the mirror image of another aberration in which "because of position, wealth, role, or relationships... a person's Circle of Influence is larger than his or her Circle of Concern." The autocratic boss who treats his or her people as "gofers," subject to every whim or command, is a case in point. Covey regards this "self-inflicted emotional myopia" as ineffective because it makes people purely reactive.

Covey provides an example of an underling who rose above a reactive crowd of executive "gofers" by proactively anticipating his autocratic boss's needs and exceeding his expectations. The case reads uneasily like currying favor, and Covey does say that some of the man's colleagues reacted vindictively. They were probably wrong, however, to place their boss's tyranny in the third of Covey's three categories of human problems:

- Direct control (involving our own behavior)
- Indirect control (involving other people's behavior)
- No control (problems that we can do nothing about, such as our past or present situational realities).

The colleagues' Circle of Concern contained the following statement: "*If only I had* a boss who wasn't such a dictator." The italics are Covey's. He observes that the Circle of Concern is filled with "have's." The Circle of Influence, however, is filled with "be's": thus, "I can be a more effective executive who isn't pushed around." The hero of his anecdote, to improve his situation, worked not on his boss's weaknesses but on himself.

Covey is by no means naive, and recognizes that people can neither control all the consequences of their actions, nor avoid making mistakes – the two obviously being linked. "The proactive approach to a mistake," he writes, "is to acknowledge it instantly, correct and learn from it. This literally turns a failure into a success." Failing to observe this principle "usually puts a person on a self-deceiving, self-justifying path, often involving rationalization (rational lies) to self and others."

The proactive course of action is not to lie, but "to make and keep commitments and promises." Covey teaches as a crucial part of the Character Ethic that "As we make and keep commitments, even small commitments, we begin to establish an inner integrity that gives us the awareness of self-control and the courage and strength to accept more of the responsibility for our own lives." Reaching an objective is delivering on a commitment. The proactive person learns "to set a goal – and work to achieve it," which brings Covey to the second of his habits for private victory.

Defining the objective

Covey's Habit Two is "Begin with the End in Mind." Behavioral psychologists sometimes invite people to compose their own epitaphs or obituaries as a means of focusing on their objectives in life. Covey goes further by inviting readers to their own funerals. At that ceremony, what would you want a family member, a friend, a colleague, or a church or community member to say about you and your life? "What contributions, what achievements would you want them to remember?"

The funeral is a strong metaphor for how to "begin with the end in mind." Another Covey metaphor is the business plan, which must start with a clear definition of what you are trying to accomplish. "The extent to which you begin with the end in mind determines whether or not you are able to create a successful enterprise." Most business failures, he observes, begin when this stage of mental or "first" creation leads to problems "such as under-capitalization, misunderstanding of the market" or simply having no plan. The correct process is as follows:

> "You carefully think through the product or service you want to provide in terms of your market target, then you organize all the elements – financial, research and development, operations, marketing, personnel, physical facilities, and so on – to meet that objective."

Personal mission statements

The business plan, or "first creation" in Covey's terms, is followed by the "second creation," which is putting the plan into practice. Covey makes the telling point that "there is a first creation to every part of our lives." The issue is whether people work to their "own proactive design," or "are the second creation of other people's agendas, of circumstances, or of past habits." To become your own first creator, according to Covey, requires considerable imagination and conscience. Combining these with self-awareness "empowers us to write our own script" – in other words, to write our own "personal mission statement."

The concept is familiar to the corporate world, where vision and mission statements try, usually with some difficulty, to follow Covey's recipe. The statement "focuses on what you want to be... and to do... and on the values or principles upon which being and doing are based." The difficulty for corporations is that their statements end up sounding much alike. Individuals, too, are likely to subscribe to similar values – that, after all, is one of Covey's basic tenets: thus few people would disagree with one of Covey's friends who recommends "Keep a sense of humor" or "Be orderly in person and in work."

It follows that preparing your personal mission statement must be taken very seriously. Covey expects "deep introspection, careful analysis, thoughtful expression, and often many rewrites." As with the corporate equivalent, "the process is as important as the product." Writing a statement or reviewing it (which Covey personally does "fairly regularly") changes you "because it forces you to think through your priorities deeply, carefully, and to align your behavior with your beliefs."

Visualizing and affirming

Making the statement brings into play the right side of the brain, where intuition and creativity are primarily located. Covey observes that ours is "a primarily left-brain dominated world, where words and logic are enthroned." He is apparently not an expert in brain function, since he seems unaware that women are much less likely to be dominated by the left hemisphere. But that does not affect his main point, which is that imagination or visualization (both right-brain functions) are important ways of changing and improving how you perform.

"Before a performance, a sales presentation, a difficult confrontation, or the daily challenge of meeting a goal, see it clearly, vividly, relentlessly, over and over again. Create an internal 'comfort zone.' Then, when you get into the situation, it isn't foreign. It doesn't scare you."

Visualization is accompanied in Covey's philosophy by "*affirmation*." By that he means a personal statement that keeps your vision and values before you and aligns your life to be "congruent with those most important things." A good affirmation has five basic ingredients: it is personal; it is positive; it is present tense; it is visual; and it is emotional.

Drawing an illustration of visualization from carefully considered domestic life, Covey cites a parental statement that "It is deeply satisfying that I respond with wisdom, love, firmness, and self-control when my children misbehave." Having made the statement, you visualize the situation – a child misbehaving badly in this case – and visualize your proactive response. Repeating this process day after day will, he teaches, change your behavior until you are "living out of the script" that you have written from your own "self-selected value system."

"You will find that there is enormous power in the principle of keeping promises and honoring commitments. It leads to strong self-esteem and personal integrity, the foundation of all true success." *Principle-centered Leadership*

Committing to goals

Covey often talks of life management in stage terms (such as "script"). He also recommends that you break down your mission statement into the "specific role areas of your life" (maybe acting as salesperson, manager, or product developer in your business role). You then decide on "the goals you want to accomplish in each area." Goal-setting is again a right-brain function, which "uses imagination, creativity, conscience, and inspiration," and which focuses "primarily on results rather than activity." Covey argues that simply identifying the various areas of your life and the two or three important results you wish to achieve "gives you an overall perspective of your life and a sense of direction."

Covey believes that mission statements should not only be drawn up by organizations, but also by families (his own puts the statement on a wall and reviews it frequently). In both these cases, involvement of everybody is crucial. In fact, Covey gives this principle extraordinary emphasis: "Without involvement there is no commitment. Mark it down, asterix it, circle it, underline it. *No involvement, no commitment* [his italics]."

Managing yourself

Achieving "personal victory," by which you turn your vision into reality by proactive, purposeful self-control, and thus escape from dependence into independence, requires a third Habit. Habit Three – "Put First Things First" – is the "fulfillment, the actualization, the natural emergence of Habits One and Two" [to wit, "Be Proactive" and "Begin with the End in Mind"]. Those who acquire the Third Habit become "principle-centered day-in and day-out" by living the habit and "practicing effective self-management." This habit is not theoretical: it is a practical program. The Franklin Day Planner, a bestselling time organizer that today brings in large profits for Covey's company, was inspired by Habit Three.

Covey's approach (see also Masterclass 3, on p. 88), is based around a Time Management Matrix, which divides activities into the four "quadrants" outlined below. Covey emphasizes that "Time Management" is "really a misnomer – the challenge is not to manage time, but to manage ourselves... Rather than focusing on things and time... focus on preserving and enhancing relationships and on accomplishing results – in short, on maintaining the P/PC Balance [see p. 21]."

TIME-MANAGEMENT MATRIX

	Urgent	Not Urgent
Important	I Crises Pressing problems Deadline-driven projects	II Prevention, PC activities Relationship building Recognizing new opportunities Planning, recreation
Not Important	III Interruptions, calls Some mail, reports Some meetings Proximate, pressing matters Popular activities	IV Trivia, busy work Some mail Some phone calls Time wasters Pleasant activities

People who focus on the problems in Quadrant I can look forward, says Covey, to stress and burnout as they forever put out fires and practice "crisis management." Those locked in Quadrant III, focusing on "things that are urgent, assuming that they are also important," also suffer the pains of crisis management, along with short-termism, shallow or broken relationships, and a reputation for having a "chameleon character." Quadrant III inhabitants see goals and plans as worthless, and feel victimized, out of control. As for those "who spend time almost exclusively in Quadrants III and IV," they "basically lead irresponsible lives," asserts Covey, being dependent on others or on institutions for basic support. They are in total contrast to the Quadrant II dwellers, who, spending most of their time on important but not urgent matters, show vision and perspective, balance, discipline and control, and suffer few crises.

Managing through delegation

But effective personal management paradoxically involves others. "We accomplish all that we do", writes Covey, "through delegation – either to time or to other people. If we delegate to time [allocating it to the purpose concerned], we think efficiency. If we delegate to other people, we think effectiveness."

Covey argues that effective delegation, which he calls "stewardship," gives people a choice of method and makes them, and not the delegator, responsible for results. The key is to secure "clear, up-front, mutual understanding and commitment regarding expectations in five areas":

- Desired results: agree on what needs to be accomplished, focusing on what, not how.

- Guidelines: identify the parameters within which the delegate should operate – as few as possible.
- Resources: identify the human, technical, financial, or organizational resources available.
- Accountability: establish the standards that will be applied, and when reporting and evaluation will take place.
- Consequences: specify what will happen, both good and bad, as a result of the evaluation.

The formula is basic to Covey's theories of business management. It is the bridge between the personal victory and the public achievement that springs from that success.

Ideas into action

- Demonstrate "response-ability," or the ability to choose your response.
- Do not wait for something to happen or someone to take care of you.
- Combat bad times by adopting practical, do-able countermeasures.
- Do not waste time over matters you can do nothing about.
- Acknowledge mistakes instantly, correct them, and learn from them.
- Always start new ventures with a clear vision of your goal in mind.
- Think through your priorities carefully and align your behavior with your beliefs.

Choosing the response to stimulus

One year, Stephen Covey took a writing sabbatical from his university job, living near a college in Laie (right) on the Hawaiian island of Oahu. A passage in a book (which he does not identify) caught his attention.

Covey writes: "My eyes fell upon a single paragraph that powerfully influenced the rest of my life." It contained a short phrase that "hit me with fresh, almost unbelievable force." The words seem quite ordinary – "a gap between stimulus and response." But they immediately suggested a simple idea of great appeal to Covey: that the key to human growth and happiness is how people choose to use that space between stimulus and response.

He "can hardly describe the effect that idea had on my mind." Since he had been "nurtured in the philosophy of self-determination," the force of this revelation is perhaps surprising. The impact lay less in the novelty of the idea than in that very force. It jolted Covey outside his existing paradigm:

> "It was as if I had become an observer of my own participation. I began to stand in that gap and to look outside at the stimuli. I reveled in the inward sense of freedom to choose my response – even to become the stimulus, or at least to influence it, even to reverse it."

Covey followed up his revelation by beginning a prolonged practice of "deep communication" with his wife, Sandra. He called for her just before noon every day, and they cycled out to a secluded beach with their two preschool children, picnicked, and talked, going deeper and deeper into their "internal worlds… our upbringing, our scripting, our feelings, and self-doubts."

Inner exploration

The couple "began to use that space between stimulus and response… to think about how we were programmed and how these programs shaped how we saw the world." The experience involved some pain as we "unfolded the inner layers of vulnerability" – though the example Covey gives is certainly odd. Sandra "seemed to have an

obsession about Frigidaire appliances that I was at an absolute loss to understand."

The obsession is no odder than the fact that it became "a matter of considerable agitation to me." Both slightly manic afflictions were cured when the probing revealed that Sandra's obsession sprang from her deep relationship with her father, whose business had been saved when the Frigidaire company financed his inventory.

What Covey and his wife had discovered in that "wonderful year" of mutual psychological exploration was that the "outside-in" approach was ultimately ineffective. When the couple began to "work from the inside out, we were able… to resolve dysfunctional differences in a deep and lasting way."

Covey had defined the underpinning idea of his multi-million bestseller: that working on their essential paradigms, people have the ability to center their lives on correct principles "and become empowered in the task of creating effective, useful, and peaceful lives."

"It takes courage to realize that you are greater than your moods, greater than your thoughts, and that you can control your moods and thoughts."
First Things First

Exercising self-leadership

Leading and influencing other people require first that you take control of yourself, in the positive sense of making the most of your abilities and opportunities. To achieve this, you must learn to think proactively and to take the initiative whenever possible. You must also set your own short- and long-term goals and develop your capability to achieve them.

Use self-awareness

Stephen Covey regards self-awareness, the ability to think about your own thought processes, as a unique human ability and the secret of human success. It is the first of four keys to freedom of choice between reactive behavior (being controlled by others) and proactive behavior (taking control of yourself).

Start to take control of your life by practicing active self-awareness. Do the following self-awareness assessment. Can you answer "Yes" to the first five questions and "No" to the last?

- Can you view yourself as though you were someone else?
- Can you identify your present mood?
- Can you name what you are feeling?
- Can you describe your present mental state?
- Is your mind working quickly and alertly?
- Are you torn between doing this exercise and evaluating the point to be made from it? The point is, if you answer "No" to the questions, practice until you can answer "Yes."

The proactive course

According to Covey, the other three keys to proactive behavior are: conscience (a sense of right and wrong); independent will (the readiness to act on your own, as your self-awareness dictates); and imagination (the use of the creative, right-hand side of the brain).

By exercising and developing all four abilities, you can become a more effective human being, gaining the power to be and do what *you* want, not just what others want from you. By winning this freedom of choice you empower yourself to take control of your own destiny and fulfill your potential. This masterclass shows you ways of improving all four of Covey's key abilities.

1 Watching your words

The language you use is a strong indicator of whether you are merely reacting to events or proactively influencing them. Adopt proactive language to bring a positive transformation in how you view yourself and in how others respond to you.

Self-limiting language

The principle is simple. If you do not enter a race, you cannot win. Covey's argument, a very true one, is that people underperform because they consciously or unconsciously limit their ambitions. They show this self-limitation by their language. Analyze your own language to see how much you hold yourself back in the way you express yourself. For every self-limiting, or reactive, phrase there is a proactive equivalent that puts you in the driver's seat.

Reactive and Proactive Language

Reactive Language	Proactive Language
There's no point in asking my boss, he'll only say "No."	I'll make him an offer he won't be able to refuse.
I couldn't do that, it's not my kind of thing.	I've never done that before, but I'd love to try.
I've got no head for numbers and making mental calculations.	I'm going to work hard to improve my math abilities.

Use positive language

Concentrate for a full day, advises Covey, on listening to your own language and that of others. Ask yourself, how often do I use and hear reactive phrases such as "If only," "I must," or "I have to"? You will almost certainly be surprised at the frequency.

From then on, whenever you find a reactive phrase coming to your lips, turn it around to the proactive opposite. For example, replace "If only" with "I will," "I must" with "I prefer," and "I have to" with "I will choose." The shift will work to reverse any unconscious passivity in your attitude and can dramatically change your behavior and raise your effectiveness.

2 Taking the initiative

You can take control of your destiny. That most people do not, says Covey, is contrary to proactive human nature. Do not empower conditions and conditioning to run your life. Empower yourself by your behavior and by widening your influence over events.

Develop proactive behavior

Covey suggests that you check how proactive you are by using a program that demonstrates your responsibility for your own effectiveness. For a period of 30 days, try to adhere to the following seven instructions in all your activities, at work and in the home:

- Make small commitments and keep them.
- Be part of the solution, not part of the problem.
- Be a model, not a critic.
- When you make a mistake, admit it, correct it, and learn from it – immediately.
- Do not blame and accuse.
- If you start to think the problem is "out there," and not your responsibility, stop yourself.

At the end of each day, write down how you have performed on each of the seven instructions. Keep the instructions in the forefront of your mind and aim to improve every day.

Use your imagination

Encourage yourself to take the initiative by using visual "affirmations," which might be called purposeful daydreaming. A successful afffirmation contains five distinctive elements.

The Five Elements of Visual Affirmation
It is personal.
It is positive.
It is present tense.
It is emotional.
It is visual.

For example, faced with a senseless decision from your superior that you do not wish to carry out, use a visual affirmation to help you take the proactive course – persuading your boss to change his or her mind. Your affirmation might be: "I get a real high (emotional) because I (personal) respond (present tense) with honesty, courage, and self-control (positive) to stop mistakes from being made." Then visualize yourself entering your boss's office and convincing him or her. Next, do it – and do not be surprised when it works.

Widen your circle of influence

There are some matters over which you have control, and others that concern you, but where you can do nothing. They all belong in what Covey calls the Circle of Concern. Those you can affect are directly in the core, the Circle of Influence.

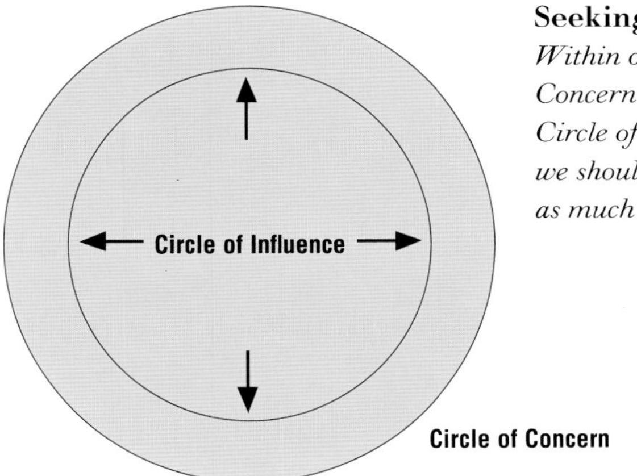

Seeking to influence

Within our Circle of Concern is the smaller Circle of Influence, which we should work to enlarge as much as possible.

Use your initiative to widen your Circle of Influence, and use your self-control to concentrate your time and energy on issues you can affect. When you face a problem, always ask:

- Is this something over which I have no control?
- Is this something over which I have direct control?
- Is this something over which I have indirect control?

If the answer is (1), learn to live with the difficulty. If the answer is (2), use your powers to resolve the issue. If the answer is (3), use your powers to influence people in the direction you want.

3 Setting your goals

Identify where you want to go and how you are going to get there. Doing so is fundamental to taking control of yourself. Without a clear objective, you will miss the signposts that show you the way. As Louis Pasteur observed, "Fortune favors the prepared mind."

Decide your mission

Write down your chief ambition in a mission statement. Make it short and to the point. For example, "To be chief executive of a major publicly traded company by the age of 40." Just deciding on that prime objective is a major step toward achieving it.

You can now focus all your other activities and lesser objectives toward that end. You will then start to notice events, opportunities, material, and contacts (the signposts) that will help you attain your prime objective. Putting a time to the target is very important in disciplining and directing your efforts – and you may well find that the objective is reached earlier than you thought possible.

Plan strategically

Naming your prime objective is only the start. You are engaged in personal strategic planning, and need to follow the same procedure as a corporate planner. That involves answering these questions:

- Where am I now (position A)?
- Where do I want to be, and when (position B)?
- What resources are required to get from A to B?
- Which do I possess now?
- What development do those resources need?
- What other required resources must I find?
- How can I find them?
- What stages must I pass before reaching the final objective – and when?
- What help will I need, and from whom?

Covey describes this process as mental creation. Begin by applying it to a project that you will be undertaking in the near future. Write down the results you desire and the steps that will lead to those results. Success in smaller projects will build your confidence in the planning of your long-term personal mission.

4 Optimizing your capability

Effectiveness does not operate in the single dimension of the work you get through and how well it is done. You must also nurture and enhance your capacity to perform, your Production Capability (PC), if you are to make the most of your abilities.

Develop capability

The more knowledge you have, the greater your ambition, and the more and better the components of your skills set, the more effective you will be. The Seven Habits all provide critical elements of PC, which needs to be developed in just the same way as athletes build body power (their form of PC) – by training and exercise.

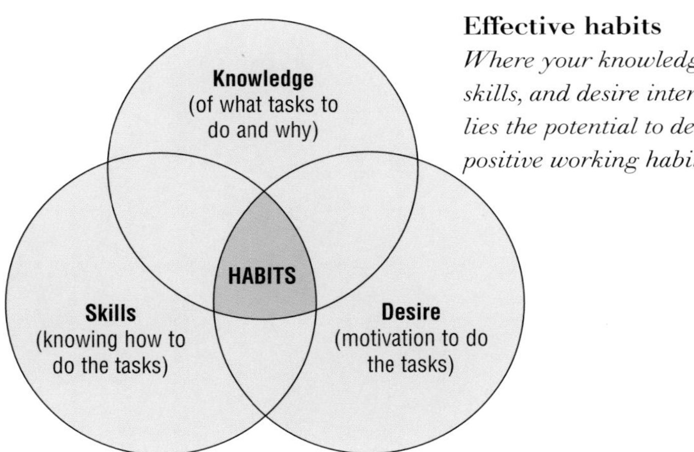

Effective habits

Where your knowledge, skills, and desire intersect lies the potential to develop positive working habits.

Conduct regular audits of your personal PC development and that of your organization to identify weak spots where more could be done to improve capability and thus performance. Are you acting to:

- Exert control over your destiny?
- Form valuable objectives?
- Prioritize the use of your time?
- Work with others for your mutual benefit?
- Learn by listening?
- Coordinate your work with that of others?
- Improve your physical, human, and financial resources?

3

From private to public victories

How abundance thinkers believe that "the pie is big enough for everyone to have a slice" • Five key areas for achieving effectiveness by delegating to others • **The four-steps that achieve "Win/Win" solutions** • Empathetic listening as the key to making deposits in the "Emotional Bank Account" • **Gaining influence over others by letting yourself be influenced** • Why synergistic cooperation is essential to deal with the ambiguity of creativity • **The four dimensions of personal renewal**

The first step from independence to interdependence, and thus toward Public Victory, is Habit Four: "Think Win/Win." Delegation (related to Habit Three: "Put First Things First") leads to the happy outcome sought through adopting Habit Four. Successful delegation means that the delegator wins, because he or she has accomplished more than could have been achieved unaided: while the delegate wins the psychic and material rewards of that success. Covey describes Win/Win as a total philosophy of human interaction. It is one of six possible paradigms:

- Win/Lose: the authoritarian ("I get my way, you don't get yours.") and competitive approach ("Life is a zero sum game where some win and some lose."). This is the dominant mode, encouraged by childhood rivalry, athletics, adversarial trials in law, etc.
- Lose/Win: giving in or giving up. In leadership, "it's permissiveness or indulgence. Lose/Win means being a nice guy, even if 'nice guys finish last.'"
- Lose/Lose: becoming centered on an enemy, wanting them to lose at any price. This is also the philosophy of the highly dependent person.
- Win: what matters is that you get what you want, irrespective of the effect on others.
- Win/Win or No Deal: if you cannot agree on a mutually beneficial solution, you agree to disagree and go your separate ways.
- Win/Win: all parties feel good about the decision and committed to the action plan.

Covey's overwhelming preference for the last course does not exclude him from recognizing that other paradigms may at certain times be the most effective. Win/Lose has to be the correct approach in sports. Lose/Win is appropriate if "the expense of time and effort to achieve a win... just isn't worth it." But Covey argues that: "Most of life is an interdependent, not an independent, reality. Most results you want depend on cooperation between you and others." In that context, Win/Lose is dysfunctional – as many executives, managers, and parents find out.

They consequently "swing back and forth, as if on a pendulum, from Win/Lose inconsideration to Lose/Win indulgence" – and then back again. Win/Lose is also inappropriate when "two determined, stubborn, ego-invested individuals interact... both will lose." Even if a Win/Lose approach appears to win – if a supplier exacts an onerous deal from a customer, say – it may prove to be a long-term Lose if repeat business is jettisoned. His analysis leads Covey to a highly predictable conclusion: "Most situations... are part of an interdependent reality, and then Win/Win is really the only viable alternative."

Character and Win/Win

Win/Win has five dimensions, according to Covey:

> "It begins with character and moves toward relationships, out of which flow agreements. It is nurtured in an environment where structure and systems are based on Win/Win. And it involves process; we cannot achieve Win/Win ends with Win/Lose or Lose/Win means."

Character, "the foundation of Win/Win," has three essential traits: integrity, maturity, and "abundance mentality." Covey defines integrity as "the value we place on ourselves" and maturity as "the balance between courage and consideration" (equating with the "I'm OK, you're OK" attitude of the psychological theory known as transactional analysis). "If I'm high on courage, and low on consideration," asks Covey, "how will I think? Win/Lose." Those who are low on courage and high on consideration, on the other hand, are trapped in Lose/Win. But with the high-high balance, you can listen and empathetically understand, but you can also "courageously confront."

The abundance mentality (see p. 80 for its key role in leadership) contrasts with the scarcity mentality, which sees life as "having only so much, as though there were only one pie out there," so that a bigger slice for one person means less for another. Abundance thinkers hold that there is "plenty out there and enough to spare for anybody." They are therefore in a much stronger position to reach the agreements that flow from good relationships and good communication.

The Win/Win environment

Covey is emphatic that Win/Win agreements will not work "in an environment of competition and contests." All an organization's systems have to support Win/Win; training, planning, communication, budgeting, information – and compensation. Many reward systems, notably for salespeople, are highly competitive, with winners taking home very big bonuses and losers sometimes even losing their jobs. Covey reports a case where a company switched from Win/Lose, with only five percent of the sales force getting the management's awards for top performance, to self-selected individual and team objectives. After the change, four-fifths received awards – and almost all of the 800 "winners" matched the individual performances of the previous year's top 40 high-achievers.

Win/Win in four steps

You can only gain such Win/Win solutions, says Covey, with Win/Win processes – "the ends and the means are the same." He suggests a universal four-step process:

- See the problem from the other point of view.
- Identify the key issues and concerns involved.
- Determine what results would constitute a fully acceptable solution.
- Identify possible new options to achieve those results.

This process leads straight into the next two habits, Five and Six, with which it overlaps: "Seek First to Understand... Then to be Understood" and "Synergize." Covey calls Habit Five "empathetic communication." As so often with his work, the lesson is not new. People who want to improve their communication skills have always been urged to become better listeners. But he argues that comparatively few people have actually had any training in how to listen, let alone how to "really, deeply understand another human being from that individual's own frame of reference."

Most people, as he notes, "do not listen with the intent to understand; they listen with the intent to reply. They're either speaking or preparing to speak. They're filtering

"Synergy is exciting.... It's phenomenal what openness and communication can produce. The possibilities of truly significant gain, of significant improvement are so real that it's worth the risk such openness entails." *The Seven Habits of Highly Effective People*

everything through their own paradigms." People who say they are listening may be ignoring, pretending to listen by nodding, etc, listening selectively, or being attentive, all of which fall far short of listening empathetically. Empathy is not sympathy, or even understanding the words used. "You listen for feeling, for meaning. You listen for behavior. You use your right brain as well as your left."

Empathetic listening

Covey regards empathetic listening as "the key to making deposits in Emotional Bank Accounts." The latter are among his key concepts. They are "a metaphor that describes the amount of trust that's been built up in a relationship.... If I make deposits into an Emotional Bank Account with you through courtesy, kindness, honesty, and keeping my commitments to you, I build up a reserve." That trust can be built higher by six suggested steps:

- Understand the individual.
- Attend to the little things.
- Keep commitments.
- Clarify expectations.
- Show personal integrity.
- Apologize when you make a "withdrawal."

The apologies must be sincere: "repeated apologies interpreted as insincere make withdrawals." While the reserve is there to be drawn upon, there is a limit to the amount that can be taken out; "if I have a habit of showing discourtesy, disrespect, cutting you off, overreacting, ignoring you, becoming arbitrary, betraying your trust, threatening you, or playing little tin god in your life, eventually my Emotional Bank Account is overdrawn." But empathetic listening is, in and of itself, says Covey, "a tremendous deposit in the Emotional Bank Account."

It is also a great help in reaching the right solutions. But in contrast to the "selfless," impersonal listening of a trained doctor, most people listen "autobiographically," relating what they hear to their own experience and filtering it through that experience. According to Covey, people tend to respond in one of four ways:

Listening without prejudice
Doctors are trained to listen impersonally to information from their patients before making a diagnosis. Managers benefit enormously when they apply the same technique in their work.

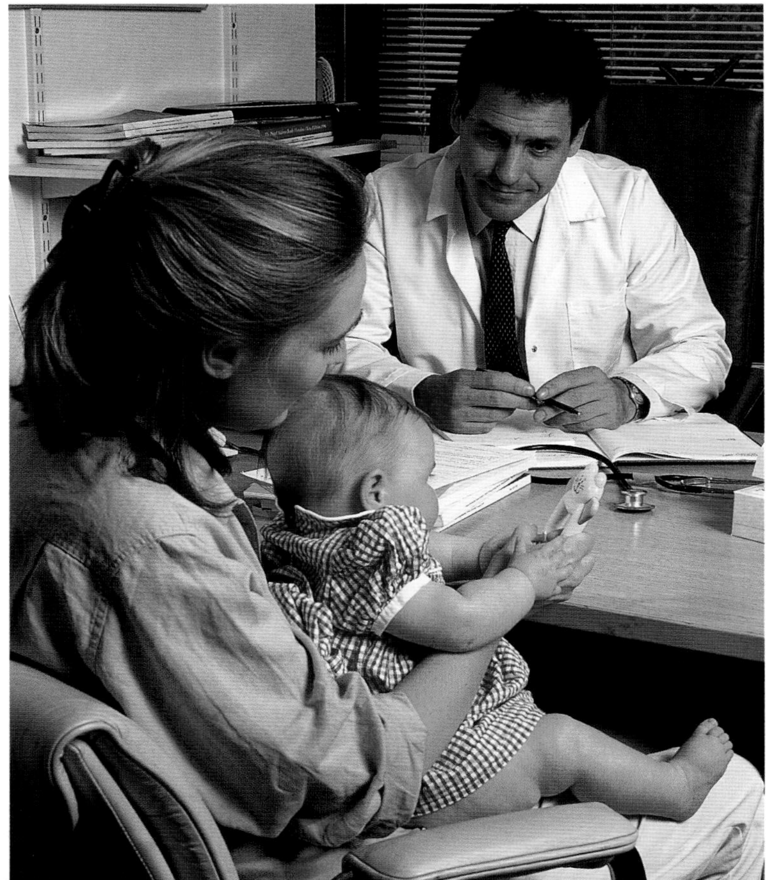

- They evaluate – either agreeing or disagreeing.
- They probe – asking questions that come from their own frame of reference.
- They advise – giving counsel based on their own experience.
- They interpret – trying to "figure out" people, to explain their motives and behavior, based on their own motives and behavior.

Covey's generalizations here are too sweeping. People commonly question, advise, and interpret with open minds as well as closed ones, and they also refer to others' experience as well as their own.

Developing empathy

Covey takes listening through four developmental stages. You mimic content by simply repeating what the other person has said. It is slightly more effective to rephrase what you have heard ("School is for the birds!" – "You don't want to go to school any more"). You go further when you reflect feeling ("You're feeling really frustrated"). Covey claims that the fourth stage, when you both rephrase and reflect feeling ("You're feeling really frustrated about

"Empathetic listening gets inside another person's frame of reference. You look out through it, you see the way they see the world, you understand their paradigm, you understand how they feel." *The Seven Habits of Highly Effective People*

school"), has "really incredible" results – "the barrier between what's going on inside him and what's actually being communicated to you disappears".

In reaching that Win/Win solution, though, the other half of Habit Five, knowing how to be understood, is equally critical. Covey uses early Greek philosophy to construct a sequential three-word model: ethos (your personal credibility), pathos (empathy, your alignment with another's emotional thrust), and logos (reasoning). "Most people go straight to the logos, the left-brain logic of their ideas." You will convince others more effectively, Covey suggests, if you first put ethos, and next pathos, into consideration – and then present your logical argument.

Influencing others

He points out that many factors in interdependent situations are in your "Circle of Concern" – problems, disagreements, circumstances, and the behavior of other people (see p. 35). These factors are outside your control. Understanding, however, is within your "Circle of Influence," or control. Moreover, because "you really listen, you become influenceable. And being influenceable is the key to influencing others." Covey therefore rightly advises setting up one-to-one time with employees, together with systems that generate "honest, accurate feedback at every level: from customers, suppliers, and employees."

Deep mutual understanding, he says, means that differences, instead of being stumbling blocks to communication and progress, become the stepping stones to winning synergy – Habit Six. Covey does not use "synergy" in any special sense. He defines it simply as meaning that the whole is worth more than the sum of its parts. The relationship between the parts, however, is itself a part, and one that rouses Covey to extreme enthusiasm: "the most catalytic, the most empowering, the most unifying, and the most exciting part."

The synergy that so arouses him is that between people, especially when they collaborate to achieve creative results. Although much of Covey's teaching could be said to encourage new ideas, creativity as such is not featured in the Seven Habits. But he regards synergistic cooperation as essential for dealing with the sheer untidiness of creation.

> "Most all creative endeavors are somewhat unpredictable. They often seem ambiguous, hit-or-miss, trial and error. And unless people have a high tolerance for ambiguity and get their security from integrity to principles and inner values they find it unnerving and unpleasant to be involved in highly creative enterprises. Their need for structure, certainty, and predictability is too high."

Synergistic interaction

The linkage Covey establishes between this accurate diagnosis and synergy is, by his own standards, vague and short on usable content. He says, somewhat loosely, that: "As I think back on many consultative and executive education experiences, I can say that the highlights were almost always synergistic." As such experiences by definition involve several people, that is not surprising. Whether, as people interact synergistically, "whole new worlds of insights… are opened up and thought about" is much less certain. So, it may be argued, is Covey's statement that these new ideas "usually come to some kind of closure that is practical and useful."

Covey does quote one business example that is close to his heart. He uses words like "empathetic... courageous... exciting" to describe the "synergistic process" that led to the creation of his own company's mission statement – a process that "engraved it in the hearts and minds of everyone there." This is the result:

> "Our mission is to empower people and organizations to significantly increase their performance capability in order to achieve worthwhile purposes through understanding and living principle-centered leadership."

Despite Covey's pride in its creation, that statement reads as if it were written by a committee, which perhaps it was. There are times, as every manager knows, when two and two make three, not five. Covey is so enthusiastic about the enormous potential of synergy ("the crowning achievement of all the previous habits") that he glosses over the fact that it may not come naturally, and forgets, too, that generating successful alternatives need not be synergistic. He is, however, correct in saying that there are nearly always alternatives – and it is also true that two or more heads are generally better than one.

Regular self-renewal

Habit Seven, "Sharpen the Saw," surrounds "Synergize" and all the other habits "because it is the habit that makes all the others possible." The phrase comes from the man who takes an inordinately long time to saw a log because he is too busy sawing to sharpen the saw. It makes Covey's point that "balanced self-renewal" is essential for "preserving and enhancing the greatest asset you have – you." Self-renewal has four dimensions:

- Physical: eating the right kinds of foods, getting sufficient rest and relaxation, and taking adequate exercise on a regular basis.
- Spiritual: clarifying values and commitment, studying and meditating, to provide "leadership for your life."
- Mental: reading, visualizing, planning, and writing (and watching relatively little television).
- Social/emotional: centering on the principles of interpersonal leadership, empathetic communication, and creative cooperation.

Daily private victories

Covey warns that to "neglect any one area negatively impacts the rest," both for organizations and individuals. "Things you do in any one dimension have positive impact in other dimensions because they are so highly interrelated." As the key to the integrated development of the Seven Habits, he advocates the Daily Private Victory – "a minimum of one hour a day in renewal of the physical, spiritual, and mental dimensions." Covey asserts that renewal is "the principle – and the process – that empowers us to move on an upward spiral of growth and change, of continuous improvement."

"Your economic security does not lie in your job; it lies in your own power to produce – to think, to learn, to create, to adapt. That's true financial independence. It's not having wealth; it's having the power to produce wealth." *The Seven Habits of Highly Effective People*

"Growth," "change," and "continuous improvement," of course, are vital parts of modern management language, essential to the ambitions of any progressive organization. Covey's teaching suggests that the *Seven Habits* philosophy, applied to themselves by members of an organization, will transform its performance. That, however, will not happen without leadership – the theme that, developed in later writings, has generated Covey's most significant contributions to management theory and practice.

Ideas into action

- Focus your attention first of all on relationships, rather than things or time.
- Make delegates fully responsible for achieving their results in their own way.
- Ensure that everybody knows the plan and feels good about it.
- Always strive to see a situation from the other person's point of view.
- If you need to apologize to anybody, do so immediately and sincerely.
- Get people on your side emotionally before presenting your logical case.
- Set aside time for regular activities that contribute to your personal improvement.

Working with other people

Interpersonal relationships are the defining medium of management. How you relate to superiors, colleagues, and subordinates governs your ability to succeed – and often theirs as well. The desire to serve mutual interests, good communication techniques, and the appreciation of opposing views result in increased trust and synergistic teamwork.

Establish good relations

Internal relationships need to be fostered just as carefully as the decisive connections outside the firm. Treat everyone you relate to – suppliers, bosses, peers, and other employees – in the same way you treat external customers; as people with specific (if unexpressed) demands, which they expect you to serve. Some companies identify the internal customers of departments and carry out customer satisfaction surveys, on the same lines as those conducted externally, to help appraise a particular department's effectiveness. It can then correct any faults that have been identified.

Satisfy all parties

The most desirable outcome with any customer – inside or outside the company – is benefit to both parties. Your objective with an external customer is to give perceived value. Pursue that aim just as vigorously inside the organization. Adopt the six-stage cycle of customer satisfaction with each relevant individual or group.

The Six-Stage Cycle of Customer Satisfaction
1 Discover customer wants by asking the customers.
2 Find out how well you are currently supplying the wants.
3 Take decisive action to eliminate deficiencies.
4 Identify and install added customer value.
5 Re-check customer satisfaction.
6 Repeat stages 2–5 and continue the cycle.

1 Serving mutual interests

The barriers to finding mutually acceptable and beneficial solutions are very often emotional. Hold both yourself and the other party in high esteem, act accordingly, and you greatly improve your prospect of achieving a mutually satisfactory result in any negotiation.

Encourage emotional security

Covey describes a satisfactory result for both parties as Win/Win, which equates to the top level of emotional security ("I'm OK, You're OK") described by the school of psychology called transactional analysis (TA). He identifies three other common outcomes to any negotiation. You must be high on both personal courage and consideration for others to effect a Win/Win outcome.

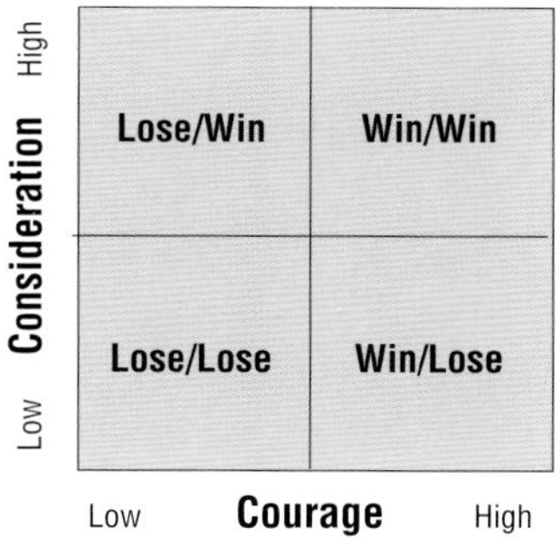

Achieving Win/Win

As this matrix shows, both sides in a negotiation must display a high level of courage and consideration to achieve a Win/Win outcome.

Performance agreements

Win/Win is essential to the success of any performance agreements created by manager and subordinate (see p. 54). To form a Win/Win agreement, follow Covey's four-step action plan.

The Four-Step Action Plan to Win/Win
1 Establish what the other person's interests really are.
2 Identify the key issues and concerns involved.
3 Determine what results both sides would accept.
4 Find possible new options to achieve those results.

2 Mastering communications

Effective communications depend mainly on trust. Learn how to establish and sustain trust by avoiding hidden agendas and ill-considered actions. Focus also on developing your ability to handle disagreement, listen empathetically, and be understood yourself.

The importance of trust

Covey makes the important point that trust must be built over time, and that its level will rise and fall as different experiences have different effects. The greater the trust between two parties, the greater the degree of cooperation.

Trust \ Cooperation	Low		High
High			**Synergistic** (Win/Win)
		Respectful (Compromise)	
Low	**Defensive** (Win/Lose or Lose/Win)		

Toward synergy
This matrix demonstrates how synergy occurs when all parties show high trust and cooperation.

Establish trust

Full trust is never easily achieved. But it can be earned. To make effective the time and effort spent on creating, enhancing, and restoring trust, you must abide by the golden rule: "Do unto others as you would have others do unto you." Therefore:

- Do not "give a dog a bad name." If you treat individuals as incompetent, you will get incompetence. Treat them as competent, encourage what they do well, and they will excel.
- Do not make a promise that you cannot keep. If you are forced to dash an individual's hopes, apologize and make amends at the first opportunity. Their trust will be hard to recapture.
- Do not disappoint expectations. Remember that expectations can only be fulfilled by actions. To quote Covey: "Honesty is telling the truth…conforming our words to reality." Integrity is "conforming reality to our words."

Face up to disagreement

At times your message will be met by disagreement or even outright confrontation. Sometimes a subordinate will say that they agree when in fact they do not, resulting in only half-hearted cooperation, if that. To deal with such situations you need to master four essential communication skills.

The Four Essential Communication Skills
1 The ability to put yourself in the other person's shoes.
2 The ability to communicate your understanding of the opposing view.
3 The ability to listen carefully.
4 The ability to interpret the meaning of body and facial language.

Use empathy

The first two skills are different aspects of empathy. Ask yourself why the other person is thinking and acting in a contrary manner. By understanding their reasoning, and the underlying emotions, you can rescue communication from failure, and even strengthen it.

To demonstrate your understanding, play back to the other party their own view in an empathetic way, putting their case as strongly and accurately as you can. Then present your case from their point of view. Now ask the other party to explain your position as best *they* can. This will lead to better understanding on both sides and to a greater chance of reaching agreement.

Seek the full meaning

Be very sure to listen carefully. People commonly start thinking about their reply well before the other party has finished speaking. Hear the other person out. Watch them intently, too. Facial gestures and body language often contradict the words. If so, it will be the accompanying words that are misleading.

Try watching somebody talking on television with the sound turned off, while you record the program. What do the person's gestures communicate? Now rerun the program with the sound on, and check your analysis. How misleading are the words?

3 Winning synergy's rewards

The most effective solutions to issues are often achieved by group effort. Organize brainstorming sessions to promote the discussion of ideas, the interchange of views, and the exploration of alternatives so as to achieve synergistic agreement on the best way forward.

Using the dialectic

To bring about synergy, use the dialectic of philosophy – ensure that opposing views are aired, and that individuals are committed to finding a satisfactory solution for the group.

Dialectical Synergy		
I put forward a thesis.	You propose the antithesis.	We agree on a combined synthesis.

Debating in a force field

The conflict between positive and negative forces is as natural and as essential to synergy as the opposition of views. When you are debating an issue, you will find yourself in a force field, in which driving forces are opposed to restraining forces.

Opposing Forces in Debate

Driving Forces	Restraining Forces
Positive Thought	Negative Thought
Reason	Emotion
Logic	Illogic
Consciousness	Unconsciousness
Economics	Social Factors

You will find that trying to strengthen the driving forces is not enough. So long as the restraining forces are there, they will push back, and the harder you drive, the harder they will push. But take a Win/Win attitude; try to understand the opposing point of view, and make sure you are understood yourself. Then a constructive interaction will take place – and synergy will be achieved.

Two-brained thinking

Synergy sessions require the use of both sides of your brain. The division is similar to the opposition of driving and restraining forces (see p. 70). The analytical, logical, verbal left brain – which is full of driving forces – does not generate the creative, contrarian, exciting ideas. You generate these in the emotional right brain, which is intuitive, creative, and visual.

Your left brain provides the framework and the facts. The right brain provides the insight and inspiration. As Covey points out, getting the two sides of the brain to work together is synergy in itself – psychic synergy.

Group synergy sessions

To achieve two-brained working in a group, first ask: "Is everybody with a potential contribution involved?" Actively seek out people with different points of view. When you have the right group together, the leadership defines the issues. Get the group to debate and agree the agenda items – all of them – then review the agenda.

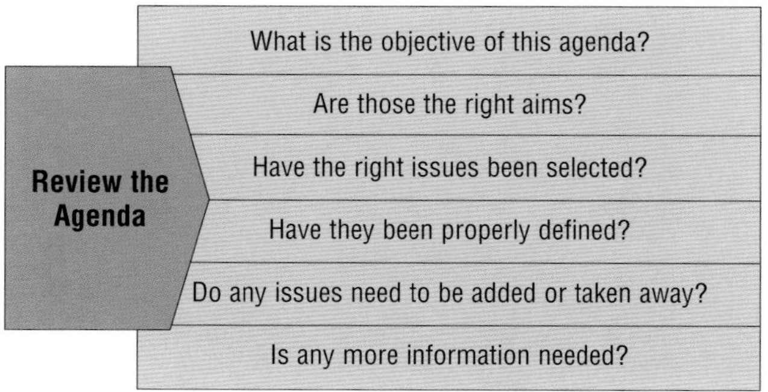

With these matters settled, you can start to generate alternatives and choices. Encourage everyone to speak. Aim to achieve an atmosphere in which no one feels threatened – use humor but outlaw ridicule. Ask people to speak in rotation. When each participant has made his or her point, questions are allowed, but do not have an adversarial debate. Use agreed time limits and checkpoints to refocus the group on the main objective of the meeting. Then restart the discussions – and work together to achieve that objective.

4

The principles of leadership

How all workers (including the members of an orchestra) need leadership before management • How principle-centered leadership confers "legitimate power" • **10 ways to increase a leader's honor and power with others** • Mastering the three "attitudes" and the three "behaviors" of effective communication • **Why "abundance thinkers" have a great advantage over the "scarcity mentality"** • Maximizing people's contribution by automation, participation in decision-making, and self-management

Stephen Covey's theories on leadership first appear in *Seven Habits* when he is discussing the second Habit ("Begin with the End in Mind"). Covey regards Habit Two as based on principles of personal leadership, of developing self-awareness and becoming responsible for the mental or "first creation." He describes leadership as a first creation that deals with the top-line question, "What are the things that I want to accomplish?" Leadership operates through the physical execution, or "second creation," which is management. Management answers the bottom-line question, "How can I best accomplish certain things?"

Covey is not, of course, alone in distinguishing between leadership and management. He cites both management guru Peter Drucker and leadership guru Warren Bennis: "Management is doing things right; leadership is doing the right things." However, times of rapid change, Covey argues, make "effective leadership more critical than it has ever been... the metamorphosis taking place in most every industry and profession demands leadership first and management second."

Not managers but leaders

He has in mind "environmental change," including market shifts so rapid "that many products and services that successfully met consumer tastes and needs a few years ago are obsolete today." So industries must "monitor the environment, including their own work teams, and exercise the creative leadership to keep headed in the right direction." Otherwise, "no amount of management expertise can keep them from failing."

This diagnosis is obviously accurate, and so is Covey's further observation: "But leadership is hard because we're

Thinker of influence

In distinguishing between leadership and management, Covey is consciously following in the footsteps of Peter Drucker. Another link between the two is time management – a Drucker speciality.

often caught in a management paradigm." To illustrate, he quotes the case of a company president who, during a year's executive development program with Covey, realized that he "was deep into management, buried by pressing challenges and the details of day-to-day logistics." He had never "been into leadership." The man decided to withdraw from management, at the price of suffering withdrawal pains as he stopped handling detail and "started wrestling with the direction issues, the culture building issues, the deep analysis of problems, the seizing of new opportunities." His colleagues shared the pain of his withdrawal, but he reported: "I persisted.... Today our whole business is different.... We have doubled our revenues and quadrupled our profits."

Like most of Covey's discussions on business management, his distinction between managing and leading is cogent. Executives do commonly get bogged down in the day-to-day and consequently fail to pay adequate attention to the year-to-year, let alone the decade-to-decade. But *Seven Habits* does not devote significant space to organizational leadership – that is dealt with at length in *Principle-centered Leadership* (1990).

This book, derived from a Covey newsletter entitled *Executive Excellence*, is in many ways a companion volume to his great bestseller. In fact, the second chapter is actually titled "Seven Habits Revisited," and the first half of the book also includes chapters entitled "Eight Ways to Enrich Marriage and Family Relationships," and "Making Champions of Your Children." Covey sees nothing strange in this content. He criticizes people who "see no correlation between the quality of their personal lives at home and the quality of their products and services at work."

Reactive executives

Unless business people adopt the Seven Habits, they may "use a variety of ill-advised approaches in sincere attempts to improve their relationships and achieve desired results". They may well end up by turning the Seven Habits upside down, with consequences that provide not an amusing and unrealistic caricature but a painfully accurate description of all too many executives:

- They are reactive: they doubt themselves and blame others.
- They work without any clear end in mind.
- They do the urgent thing first.
- They think Win/Lose.
- They seek first to be understood.
- If they can't win, they compromise.
- They fear change and put off improvement.

In no way is this a model of good leadership, certainly not the "principle-centered leadership" that Covey preaches. His central point is that "Real leadership power comes from an honorable character and from the exercise of certain power tools and principles"; it does not come from genetic "great man" theories, personality "trait" theories, or behavioral "style" theories. To make his point, Covey intriguingly illuminates the different modes of leadership by looking at followers and asking: "Why do they allow themselves to be led?"

Sometimes followers have no option; they are made offers they dare not refuse. They are responding to what Covey calls coercive power. More commonly, followers follow voluntarily to earn benefits: this "may be called utility power because the power in the relationship is based on the useful exchange of goods and services." Finally, following

"To value oneself and, at the same time, subordinate oneself to higher purposes and principles is the paradoxical essence of highest humanity and the foundation of effective leadership."
Principle-centered Leadership

can be "based on the power some people have with others because others tend to believe in them and what they are trying to accomplish." This is legitimate power.

Clearly, power in organizations may well carry elements of all three of the above types. Someone with legitimate power must still satisfy his people's utility need for a good standard of living, and will probably also possess the coercive power of dismissal. Covey is disdainful of coercive power, but he accepts that utility power "is based on a sense of equity and fairness" and that, in key ways, it works well:

> "Leaders are followed because it is functional for the followers. It gives them access to what the leader controls, through position or expertness or charisma. The nature of followership when based on utility power is still reactive, but the reaction tends to be positive rather than negative."

Legitimate power

For all that, utility power has limitations: "It is being increasingly acknowledged that relationships based on utility power often lead to individualism rather than teamwork and group effectiveness." Individuals are locked into a kind of perpetual bargaining as they decide what is best and right and fair. Covey contrasts this "situational ethics" with legitimate power, where "ethical behavior is encouraged because loyalty is based on principles as they are manifested in persons."

The leader is free to make a personal choice between the three types of power. But Covey's preference for legitimate power is overwhelming: "The more a leader is honored, respected, and generally regarded by others," he writes, "the more legitimate power he will have with others." He makes 10 suggestions "for processes and principles that will increase a leader's honor and power with others":

- Be persuasive: commit to stay in the communication process until mutually beneficial and satisfying outcomes are reached.
- Be patient: maintain a long-term perspective and stay committed to your goals in the face of short-term obstacles and resistance.
- Be gentle when dealing with vulnerabilities, disclosures, and feelings that followers might express.
- Be teachable: appreciate the different points of view, judgments, and experiences that followers may have.
- Show acceptance: withhold judgment, giving the benefit of the doubt.
- Be kind: remember the little things (which are the big things) in relationships.
- Be open: give full consideration to followers' intentions, desires, values, and goals, rather than focusing exclusively on their behavior.
- Be compassionate: in confrontation, acknowledge errors and mistakes in a context of genuine care, concern, and warmth, making it easier for people to take risks.
- Be consistent: do not use your leadership style as a manipulative technique in order to get your own way.
- Show integrity: honestly match words and feelings with thoughts and actions.

Legitimate power also rests on effective communication. Covey states that "perception or credibility problems" are at the root of most communication difficulties. For "clearing the communication lines," he advocates adoption of six "essential" attitudes and behaviors:

- I assume good faith; I do not question your sincerity or your sanity.
- I care about our relationship and want to resolve differences.
- I am open to influence and I am prepared to change.
- I listen to understand.
- I speak to be understood.
- I start dialogue from a common point of reference or point of agreement, and move slowly into areas of disagreement.

Cynics might object that all the above add up to no more than saying that goodness is good. But Covey is a pragmatist in material things. He gives unstinting admiration to businessmen such as J. R. Simplot (1909–), who founded his wealth on selling vast quantities of potatoes to McDonald's. He links their success to one of his most prized abilities: an "abundance mentality" (see p. 56) – they share "a bone-deep belief" that natural and human resources abound to realize their dreams, and a conviction that consequently their success need not mean failure for others.

Covey contrasts this with the scarcity mentality (see p. 56), which holds that resources are limited and that success has to be won at other people's expense. "If you see

"The more principle-centered we become, the more we develop an abundance mentality, the more we love to share power and profit and recognition, and the more we are genuinely happy for the success… and good fortune of others." *Principle-centered Leadership*

life as a 'zero sum' game," he comments, "you tend to think in adversarial or competitive ways, since anyone else's 'win' implies your loss." That is an insecure person's position. The abundance mentality, however, "springs from an internal security" that Covey attributes to being "principle-centred," a quality that he attaches to "abundance thinkers." He writes that thinkers such as Simplot, the potato king, share seven characteristics:

- They return often to the right sources.
- They seek solitude and enjoy nature.
- They "sharpen the saw" regularly.
- They serve others anonymously.
- They maintain a long-term intimate relationship with another person.
- They forgive themselves and others.
- They are problem solvers.

Goodness and success

It might well be objected that some highly competitive businessmen could pass all or most of these seven tests, and that Covey's heroes (he includes Ray Kroc, the forceful creator of McDonald's, and J. Willard Marriott, who built his family's hotel chain) were definitely tough in their business lives. But Covey says that there is a fundamental link between goodness and commercial success:

> "In *The Seven Habits of Highly Effective People*, I suggest that the most fundamental source, and the root of all the rest, is the principle source. If our lives are centered on other sources – spouse, work, money, possession, pleasure, leader, friend, enemy, self – distortions and dependencies develop."

Hamburger hero
The late Ray Kroc, founder of McDonald's, won Covey's approval as a principle-centered entrepreneur whose "abundance thinking" is rooted in a balanced adherence to God and free enterprise.

Covey's "distortions and dependencies" create chronic problems for both individuals and organizations. Covey lists seven chronic problems that might well be called the Seven Habits of Highly Ineffective Organizations:

- "Poor alignment between structure and shared values, between vision and systems: the structure and systems poorly serve and reinforce the strategic paths."

- "No strategic path: either the strategy is not well developed or it ineffectively expresses the mission statement and/or fails to meet the wants and needs and realities of the stream [the environment]."
- "No shared vision and values: either the organization has no mission statement or there is no deep understanding of and commitment to the mission at all levels of the organization."
- "Wrong style: the management philosophy is either incongruent with shared vision and values or the style inconsistently embodies the vision and values of the mission statement."
- "Poor skills: style does not match skills, or managers lack the skills they need to use an appropriate vision."
- "Low trust: staff has low trust, a depleted Emotional Bank Account, and that low trust results in closed communication, little problem-solving, and poor cooperation and teamwork."
- "No self-integrity: values do not equal habits; there is no correlation between what I value and believe and what I do."

Curing the problems

When Covey sees that "the senior executives want to blame everybody and everything else for those problems," they are told to look in the mirror "to identify one of the primary sources." His cure for the seven problems is to share vision and values, build all corporate activities on those solid principles, and both the organization and its people will fall into step behind one common cause, pursued with high effectiveness.

Covey backs up this argument for principle-based leadership with four basic management paradigms.

FOUR MANAGEMENT PARADIGMS

Need	Metaphor	Paradigm	Principle
Physical/economic	Stomach	Scientific authoritarian	Fairness
Social/emotional	Heart	Human relations (benevolent authoritarian)	Kindness
Psychological	Mind	Human resource	Use and development of talent
Spiritual	Spirit (whole person)	Principle-centered leadership	Meaning

Covey argues, first, that people are not motivated primarily by their quest for economic security. Second, recognizing their social needs as well "still leaves management in charge, still making the decisions and giving the commands." The third paradigm comes very near, however, to winning his outright approval:

> "When people are seen as economic, social, and psychological beings... managers try to create an environment in which people can contribute their full range of talents to the accomplishment of organizational goals."

The key word is "try." In Covey's view, managers will not fully succeed without principle-centered leadership. The fourth paradigm recognizes that people are also "spiritual beings" who "want meaning, a sense of doing something that matters." They want to "contribute to the accomplishment of worthwhile objectives." So, "Pay me well," certainly. "Treat me well," of course. "Use me well," absolutely. But above all: "Let's talk about vision and mission, roles and goals. I want to make a meaningful contribution." To that end, principle-centered leaders:

- Automate routine, boring, repetitive tasks.
- Give people a chance to take pride in their jobs.
- Encourage participation in important matters, including decision making.
- Encourage self-direction and self-control.

Covey has a "PS Paradigm." The P stands for People. The S stands variously for Self, Style, Skills, Shared vision and principles, Structure and systems, Strategy, and Streams [operational environments]. Business management, he stresses, will underperform and often fail unless it embraces all the S-aspects in a consistent, dynamic framework.

Ideas into action

- Concentrate first on "What are the things that I want to accomplish?"
- Delegate "management" responsibilities to leave yourself free to lead.
- Help others to believe in you and what you want to achieve.
- Look for credibility problems and make resolution of them a high priority.
- Build trust between you and those you work with on the basis of your trustworthiness, not politics.
- Ensure that you are seen as fully competent in your area of professional expertise.
- Get people to work with you on vision, mission, roles, and goals.

Managing your time

Time is the main asset of the manager. How you allocate time and how well you use it are the keys to effectiveness. But time management is far more than drawing up and keeping to schedules; you must also identify core priorities, build in time to address nonurgent but important issues, and learn when and how best to delegate tasks.

Opportunity cost

A vitally important question in time management is: "What am I doing that can only be done by me?" People rarely ask, however, what they *should* be doing and are not: "What am I *not* doing that can only be done by me?" Every use of time precludes, during that use, doing something else. The concept resembles what is known in accounting as "opportunity cost" – the return on your money that you lose by spending the funds on something else.

Question your approach

Covey suggests that you ask yourself two questions that force you to think about what you do and to identify the gaps:

- What one thing could I do (and am not doing now) that, if done regularly, would make a tremendous positive difference in my personal life?
- What one thing in my business life would bring similar results?

Now use the rest of this masterclass to help you prioritize tasks, delegate effectively, and plan your time efficiently.

Benefiting from a Radical Rethink

Whatever your working role, it is likely that a radical rethink of how you allocate your time could produce far greater personal effectiveness.

Al Zeien, the former Chief Executive Officer of Gillette, had never thought of conducting appraisals of his executives. His Human Resources advisors persuaded him – not without some difficulty – to do so. Carrying out 300 appraisals a year took up a great deal of Zeien's time, but the time spent with his staff gave him unparalleled knowledge of his people and the business. The partial reallocation of the CEO's work week to staff appraisals made a powerful contribution to the impressive worldwide performance of the company during his tenancy.

1 Picking your priorities

Covey has boiled down the principles of time management to just five words: *organize and execute around priorities.* But "Putting first things first" (Covey's Habit Three) does not mean concentrating on doing first what seems to be most urgent. You must focus on "preserving relationships and accomplishing results."

Prioritize by urgency

Some important things need not be done immediately. But this does not mean postponing them indefinitely or not doing them at all. Time management programs, with their emphasis on efficient scheduling and control of time, often do not help in this respect. Their daily planning processes "rarely get past prioritizing the urgent, the pressing, and crisis management."

Are you addicted to urgency?

When priorities are set by urgency, responding in kind can become addictive. In fact, most managers are addicted to urgency to some degree. Has this happened to you? Find out by seeing how the following 10 statements apply. If your answer to a statement is "Never," score 0; if your answer is "Sometimes," score 2 points; if your answer is "Always," score 4.

- I do my best work under pressure.
- I am too busy to do certain things I know are important.
- I hate to wait or stand in a line.
- I feel guilty when I take time off work.
- I seem to be rushing between places and events.
- I push people away to get on with a project.
- I feel anxious when I'm out of touch with the office.
- I am preoccupied with one thing when doing another.
- I'm at my best in a crisis.
- I think that some day I will do what I really want to.

Analysis

- 12 or below: you are probably immune from addiction to urgency.
- 13 to 24: you are vulnerable to addiction and should assess your priorities.
- 25 or above: you are addicted to urgency and should find a cure.

Analyze your use of time

Covey's Time Management Matrix (see p. 41) shows that the pattern of activities is more complex than a simple division between "urgent" and "not urgent," or "important" and "not important."

Study the matrix and then estimate what percentage of your time you spend in each of the four quadrants. Next, for three days, log how you actually spend your time, divided into 15-minute slots. Check how accurately your log compares with your estimate; the greater the discrepancy, the less your control of your time. Are you fully satisfied with the result?

Urgent and important

If you are an urgency addict, you are probably spending nearly all your time in Quadrant I – engaged in "urgent and important tasks." This inevitably means that you will not be doing enough of the "important and not urgent" tasks belonging to Quadrant II.

According to Covey, this quadrant includes seven requirements that are fundamental to good performance. Ask yourself: "Am I spending enough time on these seven important activities?"

- Improving communications with other people
- Preparing my activities more effectively
- Improving my planning and organization
- Looking after my personal business
- Taking new opportunities
- Developing my skills and knowledge
- Empowering other people

If you are not paying enough attention to these activities, you need to change. These activities can probably be done only by you, which makes it doubly important to focus on them.

To gain time for Quadrant II activities you must take strong action in Quadrants III and IV, where activities are either unimportant or not urgent, or both. Look at the amount of time you spend in these two quadrants and ask yourself: "What tasks am I doing that need not be done at all?" Now ask yourself: "What am I doing that could be done by someone else?" You will find that many of the activities in Quadrants I, III, and IV can be undertaken just as effectively by others, lightening your own load considerably.

2 Delegating tasks

Delegating tasks appropriately is one of the most effective time savers. It enables you to concentrate on Quadrant II activities, which include empowering other people. Select tasks to delegate with care, and always plan your delegation thoroughly.

Win/Win delegation

Covey advises you to make a list of your responsibilities and then select those that can be delegated. For each task, choose people who can either do the job already or who can be trained for the purpose. Carry out the delegation of each task as soon as possible.

An effective delegation is one that results in the forging of a Win/Win agreement for both sides. Plan the delegation interview: make sure that nothing is left to chance and that both you and the delegate fully understand what is involved. Give clear guidelines on the results you expect and the time available for completion. Encourage the delegate to ask questions. Good communication between the delegate and yourself is the key to ensuring success.

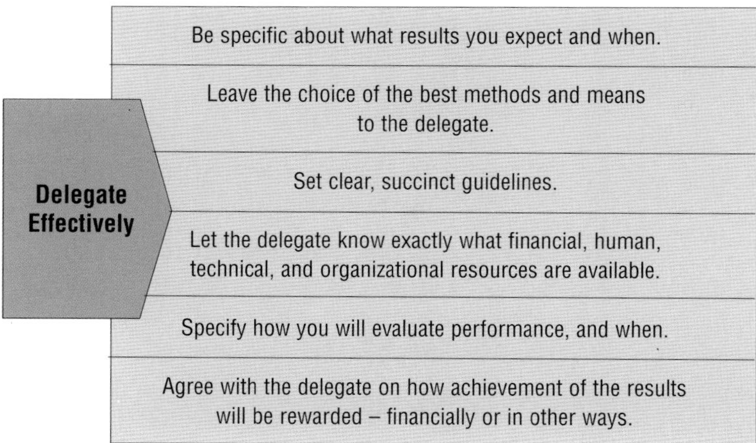

Effective delegation allows you to eliminate wasted time and exploit major opportunities as they occur. You can then give a rounded management performance that includes the important things and not just those that are – or seem to be – urgent.

3 Planning each week

Every manager plays many parts, or roles, in his or her week. To ensure that you use your time effectively you must perform all the roles properly, and set goals for each of them week by week.

Identify your roles

The parts you play will vary from time to time. Study your week and write down the roles you are currently filling, both personally and professionally. The list may look something like this:

- Individual
- Spouse/parent
- Manager, global marketing
- Leader, Project Alpha
- Manager, staff development
- Manager, administration
- Chair, charity fund

Schedule your roles

Your personal life should not be squeezed into the space left after work is scheduled. Use the four-step weekly planner to ensure that you allocate plenty of time for the whole person.

The Four-Step Weekly Planner			
1 Identify roles.	**2** Set goals.	**3** Allocate time.	**4** Schedule week.

For each role you have written down, identify two or three significant goals that can be achieved in the week. Make sure that some fit into the critical "important but not urgent" category. How much time will you need to spend on achieving each goal? Now schedule that time into the week.

Covey's trademarked system is the Weekly Worksheet, which lists all the roles with their goals next to them. All goals are numbered and allocated slots in a straightforward seven-day, hour-by-hour, 8.00 a.m. to 9.00 p.m. daybook. It turns out that even with as many as 17 weekday goals, seven of them allotted two hours each, you still have 41 hours of unscheduled time. Do the exercise yourself.

Review the workload

However well you plan the week, daily pressures are likely to upset the plans. Crises do occur, tasks take longer than expected, people cause unforeseen problems. You need to adapt. Take a little time at the start of each day to review the week's schedule. See what needs altering and check to ensure that you are not losing sight of your goals. You may well find that what confronts you as a particular day begins will take longer than the hours available.

Apply discipline

Covey gives the example of an executive with at least 11–12 hours of work looming ahead. How do you fit a dozen hours into eight? If you do not delegate, the usual response is to prioritize the tasks, nearly all of which will seem urgent, do as much as you can, and push the rest forward into the future. By taking a disciplined approach, however, you can control your time much better.

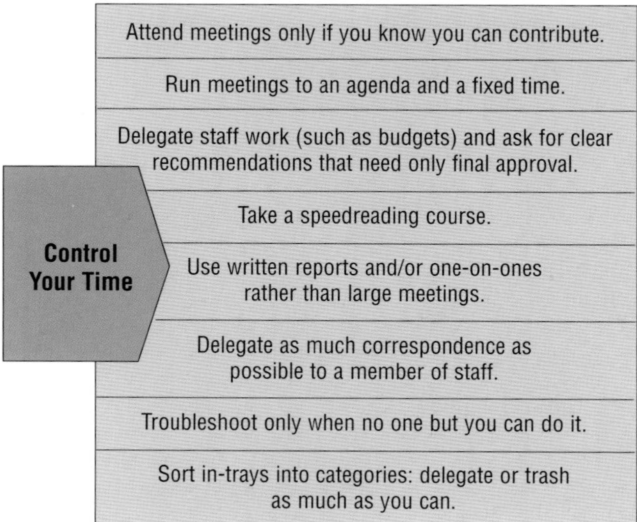

Above all, organize and execute around priorities, that is:

- Eliminate tasks that do not need to be done at all.
- Identify tasks that could be delegated.
- Focus on tasks that only you can do.

5

Making leadership work

Team-building: how every "cog and wheel" must work efficiently within the organization for business success • Using the five-stage technique of "completed staff work" to tackle problems • **The four indispensable conditions for achieving true empowerment** • W. Edwards Deming's 14 points of quality management • **Why "Win/Win" performance agreements are far more than job descriptions** • Why leaders of organizations need a transformational style

However strongly Stephen Covey encourages business managers to develop lasting principles, and to use these as the engines of leadership, management comes down to making and implementing practical decisions and winning practical results – in the short, medium, and long terms. In nearly all cases, managers find that the organization, not the competition, is their main opponent, as they strive to get the right performance and the right outcomes. As Covey himself explains in *Principle-centered Leadership*:

> "... the question becomes one of implementation. How can a top executive act on the 'whole person' assumption? How can the organization reflect this enlarged view of people? How can managers uproot a deeply imbedded authoritarian or benevolent authoritarian style? How can they rid the company of excess psychic and structural 'baggage' and give people the freedom and flexibility to think and act in ways consistent with this enlarged view of man?"

The second half of *Principle-centered Leadership*, dealing with "Managerial and Organizational Development," sets out to answer these questions.

Enabling staff workers

Some of the advice is eminently practical and seems self-contained; one example is the chapter on "completed staff work." The warmly endorsed principle is to have staff "think through the whole problem area, analyze the issue in depth," identify several alternatives and their consequences, and finally (and firmly) recommend one of the alternatives. Covey suggests a five-step process of enablement for these staff workers:

- Provide a clear understanding of the desired results.
- Give people a clear sense of their level of initiative.
- Clarify assumptions.
- Provide the people involved with as much time, as many resources, and as much access to other executives and departments as possible.
- Set a time and place for presenting and reviewing the completed staff work.

The chapter is less self-contained than it seems. All Covey's practical thoughts on leadership come back to the same sensible foundation: that, to "motivate people to peak performance," you should find where "organizational needs and goals overlap individual needs, goals, and capabilities." That done, Win/Win (see p. 56) agreements can be made, allowing people to "govern or supervise themselves in terms of that agreement."

Ideal empowerment

The leader/manager then serves as a "source of help," backed up by "helpful organizational systems within which self-directing, self-controlling individuals... work toward fulfilling the terms of the agreement." The

"Management must empower its people in the deepest sense and remove the barriers and obstacles that crush and defeat the inherent commitment, creativity, and quality service that people are otherwise prepared to offer."
Principle-centered Leadership

individuals also become accountable as they "evaluate themselves against the criteria specified" in that agreement. Overall, the picture is an attractive, if Utopian, portrayal of ideal "empowerment." The word means allowing people to take responsibility for their own work, which, says Covey, starts with the four indispensable conditions mentioned above:

- Win/Win agreements
- Self-supervision
- Helpful structure and systems
- Accountability

Foundations of Win/Win

The pivotal condition is the first, the Win/Win agreement. The five foundations upon which any Win/Win agreement rests are, importantly, those that also underpin any delegation that is effective (see p. 43). True empowerment follows from true delegation, and vice versa, and the five steps are all essential:

- *Specify desired results.* Discuss what results you expect. Be specific about the quantity and quality. Set budget and schedule. Commit people to getting the results, but then let them determine the best methods and means to achieve them. Set target dates or timelines for the accomplishment of your objectives.
- *Set guidelines.* Communicate whatever principles, policies, and procedures are considered essential to getting desired results. Impose as few procedures as possible to allow freedom and flexibility. Keep policy and procedure manuals brief. Guidelines should also identify

"no-nos" or failure paths that experience has identified as inimical to organizational goals or values.

- *Identify available resources.* Identify the financial, human, technical, and organizational resources available to assist in getting desired results.
- *Define accountability.* Specify how you will evaluate performance. Also, specify when and how progress reports are to be made and accountability sessions held. Note that when the trust level is high, people will be much tougher on themselves than an outside evaluator or manager would ever dare be.
- *Determine the consequences.* Reach an understanding of what follows when the desired results are achieved – or not achieved. Financial and psychic rewards include recognition, appreciation, advancement, new assignments, training, flexible schedules, leaves of absence, enlarged responsibilities, perks, or promotions. Negative results lead to consequences ranging from reprimand to retraining to dismissal.

Conflicts of expectations

Performance agreements on this model are Covey's answer to all "conflicts of expectations," not only within the company but outside, with customers. If people agree on the expectations surrounding roles and goals, he argues, "management has solved many of its problems." Team building is one internal problem. Covey likes to solve it by getting different groups together – salespeople with manufacturing or purchasing people, say – to share role-and-goal expectations in an "atmosphere that isn't emotionally charged." Get everybody's agendas on the table, he urges, and the negotiation process can begin.

The resulting Win/Win performance agreement "is much more than a job description." The latter merely lays down what the job is, and what is expected of the incumbent. Most job descriptions "have very little sense" of what constitutes a "win" for the employee, and most usually focus on external control. In contrast, the Win/Win agreement looks for internal control, to a situation where people can say "I understand, and I am committed because it is a win for me, too."

The empowered person can then practice self-supervision, which Covey presents as the antithesis of organizational control. As he says, many people see "a conflict between the need for operational integrity and the benefits of greater self-supervision." This conflict, repeated again and again, "precludes building either value, creating a downward spiral of trust that leads to cynicism, 'snoopervision,' tightening control, and constant tension." Resolving the conflict can only stem from recognizing that both values are sound – in fact, they are "vital to an effective organization."

The resolution comes back to the Win/Win agreement. As people realize such an agreement, no need arises to have "some people controlling others." The organization itself – the sum of all the people – is in control, because the parts

"There's a difference between expectation and reality. An expectation is an imaginary map, a "should" map rather than an "is" map. But a lot of people think their maps are accurate, that 'This is the way it is – your map is wrong.'" *Principle-centered Leadership*

"work together responsibly to create the desired results." Both the organization and its people are accountable: the organization must produce the overall results that its members desire, and they in turn must account to the organization for their self-supervised performance.

Organizational backing

Covey is aware that managers cannot go far along the route to self-supervision without organizational backing. But he has no convincing remedy for the common situation in which the manager wants to adopt these eminently sound policies, but the organization does not. Nor does Covey specify in detail how systems and structures (the fourth "condition" of empowerment) are supposed to be "helpful." It is no particular use to be told sweepingly that "All the systems within an organization must be totally integrated with and supportive of the Win/Win agreement." He does list six systems that "are common to most organizations," but mostly the listing is more aspirational than instructive:

- Information, which must be "accurate, balanced, and unbiased."
- Compensation, which should generate both financial and self-developmental rewards, encourage synergistic cooperation, and create team spirit.
- Training and development, with the learner "responsible for the learning" and with close correlation between the training goals and individual career plans.
- Recruitment and selection, which are done carefully, matching each candidate's abilities, aptitudes, and interests with the requirements of the job.

- Job design that gives people "a clear sense of what the job is about, how it relates to the overall mission of the company, and what their personal contribution could be."
- Communication, organized around a shared vision and mission. For this, there is a longer and more specific agenda, including one-on-one visits; staff meetings with action-oriented agendas and minutes; employee suggestion programs; open-door and due-process policies; annual interviews with the level above your immediate superior; anonymous opinion surveys; and *ad hoc* committee brainstorming.

Total Quality Management

Covey, as a highly experienced consultant, is likely to be aware that his Utopian ideals of empowerment are seldom, if ever, realized in practice because of organizational obstacles (including unhelpful systems and structures) which, in turn, are both created by and reinforce individual prejudices. If you have managers who have not mastered the Seven Habits, the organization will not have principle-centered leadership – unless you can find a system that automatically enshrines the Seven Habits.

One of Covey's enthusiasms, in his view, promises to do precisely that: Total Quality Management (TQM). He says that "certain universal principles and purposes must be observed in order to obtain total quality of services and products." Moreover, this pursuit makes people care "about the quality of our lives and our relationships." Total Quality Management also enshrines the same principle of continuous improvement that Covey enjoins on individuals. It is "an expression of the need for continuous improvement in four areas":

- Personal and professional development
- Interpersonal relations
- Managerial effectiveness
- Organizational productivity

Covey's enthusiasm for TQM gives heroic status to the late US statistician W. Edwards Deming (1900–93). Covey calls Deming "the economic Isaiah of our time," and Deming's "14 points" are as famous in quality management as Covey's Seven Habits are in self-improvement. Deming's 14 points are as follows:

- Create constancy of purpose for the improvement of product and service.
- Adopt the new philosophy.
- Cease dependence on inspection to achieve quality.
- End the practice of awarding business on price alone.
- Improve constantly and forever the system of production and service.
- Institute training on the job.
- Institute leadership to help people and machines and gadgets to do a better job.

"Profound, sustainable, cultural change can take place within an organization… only when the individuals within the organization first change themselves from the inside out. Not only must personal change precede organizational change, but personal quality must precede organizational quality."
Principle-centered Leadership

A taste for quality
The 14 points set out by W. Edwards Deming are cited by Covey in support of his Seven Habits. Deming's writing provides a wealth of solid, down-to-earth, practical advice for management.

- Break down barriers between departments.
- Drive out fear, so that everyone may work effectively.
- Eliminate slogans, exhortations, and targets for the work force asking for zero defects and new levels of productivity.
- Eliminate work standards (quotas) on the factory floor and management by numerical goals. Substitute leadership.

- Remove barriers that rob the hourly worker of his right to pride of workmanship.
- Institute a vigorous program of education and self-improvement.
- Put everybody to work to accomplish the transformation.

In appraising the 14 points, Covey seeks to emphasize the sovereign importance of the Seven Habits if you want to "transform the paradigms of people and organizations from reactive, control-oriented management to proactive and empowerment-oriented leadership." He clearly felt a need to link his moral philosophy with Deming's drive to raise American quality and productivity to meet the Japanese challenge in the 1970s and 1980s. That need for a linkage reflects the fact that Covey's basic program, directed at the individual, is less easily applied to organizations.

Covey argues that his philosophy is the the "missing key" to TQM. But, if properly operated (which rarely happens), TQM is complete in itself, truly an "integrated, interdependent, and holistic" system of organizational management and corporate leadership. The adjectives are Covey's, who claims them for the Seven Habits, too.

Vast changes ahead

Covey's principles, he asserts, "when applied consistently in countless specific practices, become behaviors enabling fundamental transformations of individuals, relationships, and organizations." Transformation is required, not just to correct internal underperformance, but to respond to revolutionary external changes in virtually every industry and profession – changes so vast that, in

Covey's view, they will "alter forever the way many companies operate." The changes include the shifts:

- From "brawnpower" to "brainpower."
- From mechanical to electronic technology.
- From growing birth rates to declining ones.
- From stable male workers to women, minorities, baby boomers.
- From acceptance of authoritarian, hierarchical roles to rising expectation of employee involvement.
- From externally driven/material values to internally driven/quality-of-life values.
- From a corporate drift away from dominant social/economic values in business to the reaffirmation of those values.

Transforming management

Covey writes, "The scope and scale of these changes require leaders of organizations to adopt a transformational style." He defines this as meaning that "we change the realities of our particular world to more nearly conform to our values and ideals," and he contrasts it with "transactional leadership." The latter is concerned with "an efficient interaction with the changing realities, focusing on the "bottom-line" and centered on events. In contrast, only transformational leadership, focused on the "top line," merits the title "principle-centered."

Covey has thus quickly moved the emphasis away from real-world transformations in technologies, markets, industries, and economics and transferred it to the moral transformations that are at the heart of his doctrine. He does not explain how "building on man's need for meaning" [a transformational contribution] produces a more effective adoption of new developments – e-commerce, say – than the contrasting transactional equivalent, which might be expressed as "building on man's need to get a job done and to make a living."

In truth, transforming management to meet transformed times is one of the supreme challenges of the 21st century. But Covey has not provided a text for meeting that challenge. His concern is always with what he holds to be eternal verities, in the firm belief that they will guide leaders through any upheaval to the green pastures – and the promise of Golden Eggs – beyond.

Ideas into action

- Allow people to govern or supervise themselves within Win/Win agreements.
- Seek mutual understanding on expectations surrounding roles and goals.
- Organize communication around a shared vision and mission.
- Have subordinates write you a "manager's letter" outlining their responsibilities.
- Organize systems for processing work that enable people to maximize their productivity.
- Use random sampling to discover the perceptions of all customers, workers, and investors.
- Make total quality a prime concern and objective for the business.

Exchanging teaching for business

Stephen Covey's decision to leave Brigham Young University, after 20 years as a professor, changed the direction of his career – but not of his philosophy. By that time, it was formed and ready for a wider audience.

As a colleague, Blaine Lee, recalls it, Covey had "plans for affecting management in America" by applying the principles that were to be enshrined in *The Seven Habits of Highly Effective People*. Initially, Lee was contracted to spend a year training and coaching Covey's "handful of professionals." The year went so well that Lee promptly joined Covey as one of the owners who, in 1984, turned Stephen Covey and Associates into the Covey Leadership Center.

Even before the publication of *Seven Habits* in 1989, the new company gave Covey an indispensable vehicle. On his own, he could never have spread his ideas, or earned income from corporate customers, anything like so widely. He simultaneously created a valuable business asset: the center was named as one of America's fastest-growing private companies in1994. While a few other gurus have followed similar strategies, none has played the corporate game more successfully than Covey, whose pathfinding included rapid expansion into overseas markets. In1994, Covey was International Entrepreneur of the Year.

The center, led by like-minded associates such as Lee, several of them authors or part-authors of books themselves, institutionalized Covey's evangelism. He focused this on "teaching the transforming power of principles or natural laws that govern human and organizational effectiveness." The center was basically a people business on both sides of the equation: people teaching people, rather than people selling products.

Commercial gains

Franklin Quest, however, had achieved an equal reputation as a purveyor of products, led by the Franklin Day Planner, a bestselling time-management tool. When *Seven Habits* spent five consecutive years (1991–95) as America's top nonfiction bestseller, the door opened to

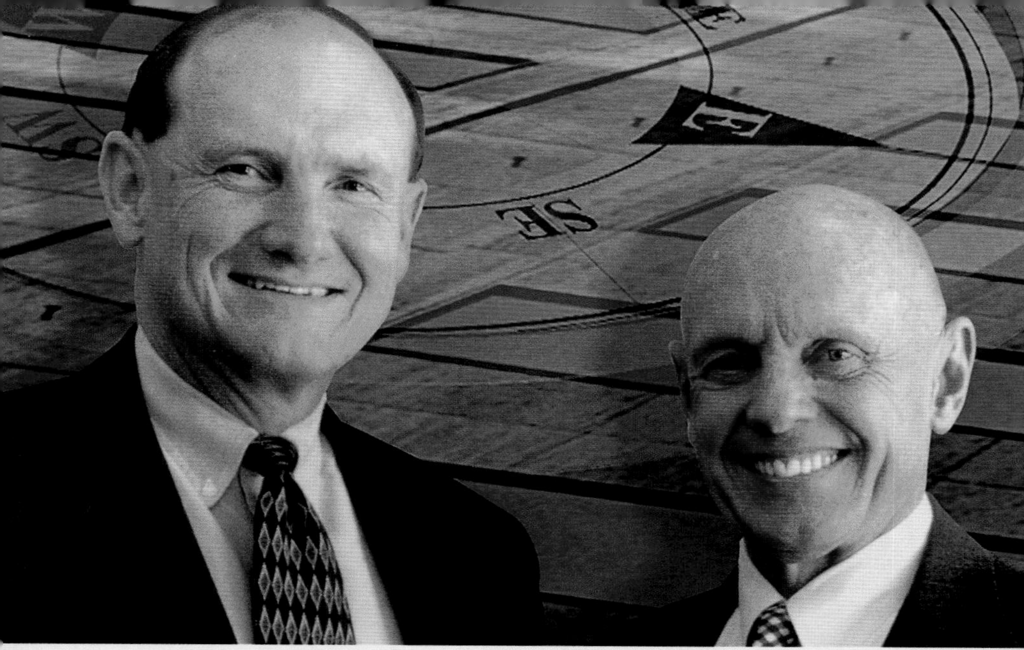

massive brand exploitation, from *The Seven Habits Family Collection* to *Loving Reminders for Couples* (not to mention *for Kids*). The complementary nature of the two businesses seemed to create a natural fit, and they were duly merged in June 1997. The combined company is far more than Stephen Covey writ large – although its chairman, Hyrum Smith (above, at left), formerly boss of Franklin Quest, is another man after Covey's heart, author of *The 10 Natural Laws of Successful Time and Life Management.*

Since the company was already publicly traded, the merger gave Covey an automatic path to stock market wealth. The path has not been smooth, however. In 1999 the share price fell by over half; a Utah commentator explained that the "management continues to battle to integrate the operations of the two companies." Since Habit Seven is "Synergize," that integration should have proved simple enough for a Covey company. Practice and preaching do not always move in step, but Covey's crucial gain is already accomplished – the message has new, multimillion dollar muscle.

"Once people have experienced real synergy, they are never quite the same again. They know the possibility of having other such mind-expanding adventures in the future."
The Seven Habits of Highly Effective People

jack WELCH

Biography

John Francis Welch, Jr., was born in 1936 in Massachusetts. His father, a railroad conductor, and mother were both in their forties at the time, and had no other children. The young Jack was devoted above all to his mother, Grace, who taught him the importance of controlling one's own destiny and of bluntly confronting reality. Blessed with Irish blood, charm, and high intelligence, Welch was the first member of his family to go to college. He studied chemical engineering at the University of Massachusetts, going on to earn a Ph.D. at the University of Illinois.

Neither university was fashionable: despite his intellect, Welch had failed to win an Ivy League scholarship. This failure, and his relative poverty, only reinforced his drive to succeed. This driving ambition was obvious from the moment he arrived in Pittsfield, Massachusetts in 1960 to take his first job, working in General Electric's plastics business. It was not a typical GE company: dominated by electrical products ranging from vast turbogenerators to domestic appliances and light bulbs, GE had strayed unprofitably into plastics via research into industrial resins.

Outstanding performance

After being dissuaded from leaving by his boss and mentor, Reuben Gutoff, Welch found this small and far from lucrative operation of 300 employees ideal for developing and displaying the "turnaround" talents that were later applied so successfully to the entire giant company. Rising rapidly, he became general manager in

1968, taking sales to $2 billion. Wherever he went, and whatever he did, Welch proved himself highly competent – and highly ambitious. In 1973 he had risen to divisional vice-president, looking after the consumer products and services businesses. There his performance won this glowing tribute from Gutoff:

> "Overall Jack's 1972 performance was outstanding [underlined]. He managed a portfolio of diverse businesses to achieve exceptional short-term profit results while simultaneously investing aggressively for future growth... technically very strong, has entrepreneurial drive, is bright & quick. Sets high standards for himself and demands same of people who work for him. Extremely imaginative and creative. Likes to operate 'outside the dots,' but at the same time is very 'maze bright.' Jack is profit & results oriented – disdains diversions that detract from business accomplishments. Has great marketing skills. Strong leader."

Nor was that all. The boss discerned "Another key result: Clearly developed a runner-up for his job in event of promotion." The divisional vice-president himself had no doubt where that possible promotion should lead. That 1973 Evaluation and Development Summary states firmly that his "longer-range" intention was to be "Chief Executive Officer of General Electric Company." Eight years later, aged 45, he had the job, and proceeded to turn the company upside down – even though GE had just been voted the best-managed company among the *Fortune* 500 (the biggest US industrial and commercial groups).

For good measure, Welch's predecessor, Reg Jones, had been hailed as the best CEO among the 500. The new appointee would dismantle much of Jones' legacy; but the most important part of that inheritance was GE's tradition of periodically branching out in new directions under a new, internally appointed CEO. Jones did not (like all too many departing CEOs) want a successor who would preserve the status quo. On the contrary, Jones felt that the culture had become constipated and that bureaucracy was rampant. According to an article in *Fortune* magazine by Thomas F. O'Boyle, "Welch's tendency to rattle cages and shake things up was exactly what Jones wanted."

The cage-rattler's appointment was a triumph of succession planning, which had long been a GE strength. There was plenty of competition for the top job, although Welch, despite (or because of) those maverick ways, was plainly a very strong candidate. In 1977 he moved (against his will, but at Jones's insistence) to Fairfield, Connecticut, where GE has its headquarters, becoming vice-chairman and executive officer in 1979. He had added to his plastics laurels by recording successes in medical diagnostics (another turnaround) and in GE's financial business. This grew out of supplying credit for purchases of GE equipment and, as GE Capital, was to be a sustaining, superb engine of growth during Welch's reign.

Blitzkrieg aggressiveness

Achieving that growth has been the dominant theme of Welch's career since he won the crown – a promotion announced in December 1980. For all the successes of Welch and other GE managers over the previous decade, the company's performance was far worse than the *Fortune* 500 accolades indicated. Adjusted for inflation, the share price had halved. Welch made it his mission to reverse this decline in value, and to do so in spectacular fashion: he wanted to make GE the world's most valuable company – in the late 1990s, it vied with Microsoft for that distinction. That meant removing all the obstacles to profitable growth, and doing so forcibly.

When *Fortune* named Welch as "Manager of the Century" in 1999, the citation noted that the new CEO had "proposed to blow up [GE's] portfolio of businesses, its bureaucracy, many of its practices and traditions, its very culture." True to form, Welch not only proposed – he disposed, acting "with what seemed at the time like blitzkrieg aggressiveness." But in retrospect, Welch believed he had moved too slowly.

He founded his blitzkrieg on a simple proposition. GE's businesses had to be first or second in their market, or they would be radically reformed, sold – or closed. Scores were shut. GE's workforce came down by 100,000 in a ruthless clear-out that earned Welch the nickname of "Neutron Jack," after the bomb that kills people but leaves buildings intact. The "slain" included 400 corporate planners who

Laughing with intent
Training of GE executives at Crotonville is galvanized by the searching, take-no-prisoners style of Jack Welch (right), who uses the sessions to promulgate his values companywide.

had been Jones' pride and joy: they went, along with the much-praised process they had created.

Welch preferred to run strategy through meetings, ranging from 500 top executives gathered in Florida in January (preceded by a preparatory meeting of 140) to quarterly gatherings of the 30 topmost people at the company's own business school at Croton-on-Hudson, NY. Leaders of each division got full days with the boss to review three-year strategic plans, annual budgets, and development of the managers (GE had 3,000) who were within their division.

A relentless tide of profits

As that generous allocation of his time indicates, Welch is a hands-on, confrontational, face-to-face manager who talks and talks (despite a slight stammer) and believes that "The idea flow from the human spirit is absolutely unlimited," and that "All you have to do is tap into that well." His two decades at GE have been marked by major new companywide initiatives – recently, for example, a high-powered drive for fault-free quality – which have created and been reinforced by a relentless tide of profits. Net income rose from $1.5 billion in 1981 to $8.2 billion in 1997 on a tripling of sales.

Two-fifths of those sales are accounted for by GE Capital. The tremendous success of Welch's "baby" has disguised the fact that, had GE been confined only to its industrial interests, its growth would have been far from outstanding. The gains have also been boosted by acquisitions: in Welch's first two years, GE got into 118 new businesses, joint ventures, or buys, while selling 71 old ones. The big buys since then include an unhappy venture into Wall Street and the purchase of RCA, whose NBC television channel became highly successful under GE management.

Welch's GE salaries, bonuses, and stock options have made him a billionaire. But he is by no means all work and no play. Always big on sports, he has become an avid golfer who plays with the best, such as the great golfing professional Greg Norman. Divorced and remarried, he has two children. His family has had to accommodate to a hectic schedule as Welch whirls (often literally, in a helicopter) around the GE empire. His packed schedule as both leader and educator of GE's managers means that he moves fast – sometimes too fast.

He can make judgments too quickly and on too little knowledge. He is, however, equally quick to correct his errors. He does not intellectualize about management. Rather, he has taught by example and proved theories in practice. His personal style has translated admirably into an organizationwide culture that has transcended the infamous disadvantages of size.

The question of succession

Welch has continued, as in his early career, "to achieve exceptional short-term profit results while simultaneously investing aggressively for future growth," and to insist that his executives do likewise. Other early strengths, like his farsightedness in developing his own replacement, became vital in the 1990s. In 1991, with a decade to spare, Welch said that "From now on, choosing my successor is the most important decision I'll make. It occupies a considerable amount of thought every day." That succession, and its achievements, will be the final test of a performance that has already left an indelible legacy.

1

Making managers lead

Getting into the saddle and leading fr[illegible] the front • How Welch distinguishes leadership from management and turn[illegible] managers into leaders • **Mastering the seven basics for business success** • Fighting the battle to beat bureaucra[illegible] by cutting out layers and eliminating r[illegible] tape • **Using meetings to galvanize an[illegible] integrate management** • Spreading bes[illegible] practice between managers and betwee[illegible] companies • **How to balance hands-off management and delegation with hands-on, personal leadership**

he distinction between leaders and managers, and the driving necessity to transform the latter into the former, is at the core of Jack Welch's preaching anc ice. His seven-point program for management by ership was clearly articulated, not just by his words but ctions, as he led one of the world's largest business iizations into unprecedented success:

evelop a vision for the business.
iange the culture to achieve the vision.
atten the organization.
iminate bureaucracy.
npower individuals.
aise quality.
iminate boundaries.

one of these stages could occur without leadership, to h management plays a secondary, supporting role. As h sees it, the difference between a leader and a ager is that between a general and an officer down the The leader's job is to allocate the available resources of le and money rigorously so as to generate optimum ts. Those results will, however, be won under the nagement" of the officers.

elch awards his generals a directive, strategic role, for h he demands exceptional qualities. "It takes courage tough-mindedness," he says, "to pick the bets, put the irces behind them, articulate the vision to the loyees, and explain why you said yes to this one and no at one." The tactical work is left to others – and that is without interference. Even the language used is ortant. "Call people managers," he says, "and they are g to start managing things, getting in the way."

In the light of that forceful view, it is a supreme irony that in November 1999, *Fortune* magazine named Welch "The Greatest Manager" of the century just ended. He is, however, deliberately overstating his case. GE's managers are expected to lead at every level, not just at the top. Welch wants the people all the way down to be, like himself, hands-on executives engaged in the restless pursuit of better and better performance. He simply wants to emphasize that the job of a manager is to make dynamic choices, not to spread resources out evenly, "like butter on bread." In Welch's view, that is bureaucracy, on which he has waged unrelenting war for decades.

Controlling bureaucracy

Large corporations breed structure upon structure, layer upon layer, bureaucracy upon bureaucracy, rules upon rules. Welch, however, believes in minimalist form. As he cut layers, he doubled (if not more) the "span of control" (the number of managers reporting to a single superior). Having to handle, say, a dozen sub-managers imposed a major extra workload on business leaders. Their psychological burdens also intensified after Welch abolished the highest layer of all, the "sector heads" who shared responsibility for groups of businesses, but whose real role was vague – and harmful.

Most large organizations have these superfluous levels, which in nearly all cases slow decision-making, blur responsibility, and create undoable jobs. Welch will not tolerate any of these three defects. He decreed that heads of the businesses (themselves reorganized into coherent entities) would report directly to him. Welch's own span of control thus became a dozen on that count alone. But the burden weighed lightly on his shoulders, because the business chieftains were left (in fact, forced) to make their own decisions: in a word, to lead.

Before Welch, some 300 managers had enjoyed "P&L [profit and loss] responsibility." They had profit and revenue targets to meet and were judged on their financial results. By the time Welch finished, the numbers had been decimated: just 30 leaders were P&L-responsible. Before Welch, GE had actually pioneered the idea of dividing a company into "strategic business units," or SBUs, each with its own accounts and a responsible manager in charge.

In theory, creation of SBUs makes the unwieldy manageable, while teaching and testing many executives in exercising full business responsibility. The system's virtues, however, are offset by vices: managers often will not cooperate with other businesses and will do all they can (sensibly or not) to protect their short-term profits – which, of course, have to be examined continually by central financial monitors. At General Electric, control had become the be-all and end-all under the reign of the company's bureaucracy.

Sharing information

Welch showed that the systems beloved by bureaucrats can be turned into dynamic forces by dynamic leadership. As a supreme example, Welch uses meetings and committees, not as controls, but as his most powerful management tool. The critical sessions are those of the Corporate Executive Council. The CEC meets once a quarter at the company's in-house business school, Crotonville, at Croton-on-Hudson, NY. Attended by 30 of the leading executives of the corporation, these sessions are described as "food fights." Welch uses them to check on progress, to display leadership (his own) and encourage it in others, and to exchange ideas and information:

> "The enormous benefit we get from our meetings is that we end up being smarter than anybody else. It's not that we have a higher I.Q. But after two days with the CEC, having to talk about everything from TV networks to the Indonesian economy just to understand our own businesses, we can walk out and talk to anybody at a cocktail party, and be the smartest guys in town. And we may not be as smart as most of the other people there – it's just that we're exposed to so much more information."

The CEC sessions also subject the organization's leaders to challenges and tests; share the lessons of success and failure; and transfer new ideas, derived from different businesses, from one to the others. Sharing is also vital to the Boca Raton meeting in January, when 500 executives troop down to Florida to discuss the year ahead. The lucky ones get the chance to present their achievements in front of their peers. That meant 29 of the 500 in 1998. Welch takes notes (a constant habit) as they talk, in part preparing for a final wind-up speech that pulls no punches.

Welch does not believe that leaders should peddle comfort. Their role is to rock the boat, to urge people forward by forcible, even excessive language. The magazine *Business Week* reported this wind-up in 1998:

> "The one unacceptable comment from a GE leader in '98 will be 'Prices are lower than we thought, and we couldn't get costs out fast enough to make our commitments'. Unacceptable! Unacceptable behavior, because prices will be lower than you're planning, so you better start taking action this week."

The whole Welch message is recorded on video and sent immediately to the 500 executives' desks, complete with instructions on its use with their own people. In 1998 that meant 750 videos in eight languages, including Mandarin and Hungarian. By the end of January, some two-thirds of GE's workforce had seen the tape.

Pursuing best practice

The CEC and Boca Raton meetings are weapons in the war for "best practice," which plays a key part in Welch's management philosophy. If every part of an organization uses the best ideas and methods discovered anywhere else, the whole group's performance will be optimized. For example, a stellar performance in industrial diamonds (in four years, a fourfold rise in return on investment, and a halving in costs) attracted hundreds of other GE managers. They were understandably eager to discover how the diamond plant had raised efficiency so much that no investment in plant and machinery would be required for another 10 years.

Welch uses the regular meetings to publicize such achievements and the methodology behind them. But the decision to adopt a given best practice is left (following Welch's basic principle) to the individual businesses and

"We are out to get a feeling and a spirit of total openness. That's alien to a manager of 25 or 30 years ago who got ahead by knowing a little more than the employee who works for him [or her]."
Jack Welch Speaks **(1998)**

their leaders. Welch loves new ideas, and insists that they get a full airing. He will act as hot gospeler for the ideas he likes. But he does not believe in telling general managers how to run their companies. That is their job alone.

Delegating responsibility

Welch's leadership theory obviously depends heavily on the power of delegation. That is needed in all organizations and depends in turn on the excellence of selection. "People say people are important in every business," he notes. But their importance and that of delegation are magnified by the very nature of GE. In a multibusiness company, the CEO's knowledge of those businesses is far less than that of somebody running a concentrated company like Coca-Cola. Welch has to have "real experts and real good people" to run his businesses: "If I don't have them, the game's over."

But the leader cannot simply hand over all power to good people and then abdicate his authority. Welch neatly balances hands-off management – giving his business heads full autonomy and the power of decision – with hands-on leadership. In addition to his major corporate activities, Welch directly intervenes in lesser matters, such as:

- The launch of a joint venture cable TV program by the NBC broadcasting company and its partner, Dow Jones.
- The decision to enter pet insurance in the UK.
- The flat rejection of an advertising campaign. ("I like advertising. I like promotion. I'm the advertising manager of our company. I love it.")
- The upgrading of the comparatively poor performance of tubes used in GE's X-ray and CT-scan machines.

The unpredictability of Welch's interventions itself acts as a powerful stimulus to the managers on whom he might pounce. Welch can afford the time for this detailed intervention because the quarterly and annual results seldom bring any surprises. He monitors performance against exact and exacting performance targets. His "direct reports," and especially the dozen operating heads of GE businesses, exercise the same control over their subordinates. Welch's personal forays, however, add ginger to what might otherwise degenerate into an arid, figure-bound system. "Gingering up" is the essence of his leadership style, which is fundamentally confrontational.

Exceeding commitments

Intense internal competition makes such confrontation a fundamental aspect of life at GE. Welch's style guarantees that his managers go into his one-to-one meetings "psyched up," or, as one of them puts it, "ready for combat." Pulling punches is not allowed here, either: so, says the same man, "You'd better have a thick skin, or when you come out you will be a hurting person." The hurt is also felt in larger gatherings, especially by anybody running a low-performing business. According to a former GE executive, "When somebody is floundering, there is a little bit of... shunning; the guy's not so popular at the coffee breaks."

Those who flounder cannot complain: they know what is expected. Welch leads by having goals for all important measures – productivity, inventory turns, quality, working capital, customer satisfaction, and so on. The goals are clearly set out and treated as rock-solid "commitments." At the quarterly meetings, the competition sets in as every combatant seeks to come out top in exceeding commitments. This law of the jungle suits Welch well. He believes in the survival of the fittest and applies that law to all businesses within GE, to GE itself, and to all executives, not just those at the top.

Winning hearts and minds

At a time when middle managers were widely seen as a desperately endangered species, Welch saw their liberation and empowerment as the key to productivity gains, without which GE could not achieve his goal of significantly outgrowing the US economy. Getting the 2,000 top executives to share his ideas was not even half the battle, even though that fight alone took eight years and massive removals, replacements, and reshuffles. Another 100,000 lower managers still had to be reached. Welch's recipe for winning their hearts and minds – and, of course, their effort – had four parts:

- Free managers to manage – and to rise.
- Defeat bureaucracy and rigidity.
- Generate and use new ideas.
- Empower workers to flourish and grow.

It is not enough to preach these principles. How you practice them is vital. Welch believes that leadership must be personalized. So nobody at GE, even the topmost executives, gets a formal letter from the CEO. His message may well be blunt, but it comes in his own neat handwriting. Nor are salaries, bonus payments, and stock options dished out automatically to the two dozen people who report to him directly. Rewards are always accompanied by frank, face-to-face evaluation.

Rewards for these top executives, like those all the way down, are large, depending on the achievement: bonus payments can quadruple from one year to the next, and reach as much as 70 percent of base pay. Within an overall target of, say, 4 percent more on the salary bill, somebody exceptional may pocket a 25 percent raise without promotion. Welch also spreads stock options far more widely than in the past; a third of his professional employees have become eligible. Options have created over 1,200 GE millionaires; the CEO himself is a billionaire.

As run by Welch, the rewards and options differentiate sharply between one manager and another, one year and the next, one business and another. "I can't stand non-differentiated stuff," he has said. "We live in differentiation. You can't run these 12 businesses as if they were one institution." It is like working for a hard-nosed, demanding, but generous entrepreneur – a description that fits Welch to a T, and which he thinks should describe the behavior of all leaders.

Knowing the people

Welch believes in appointing business heads whose approach is compatible with his entrepreneurial thrust, and who can be trusted to run their operations without interference from above. His greatest pride lies in his ability to find and nurture highly able managers. This is not a matter of hunch, but of hard, organized work. On his reckoning, half of his time goes on people issues – and on getting to know people. A cardinal Welch principle is that the leader should really know the top people in the organization – their faces, their names, what they do, their key abilities, and how they manage.

One writer found that Welch personally knew at least a thousand of his managerial subordinates. When a job needs filling, Welch already knows the candidates, and will pick or endorse the person he considers best for the job, regardless of seniority or rank – or how many others are leapfrogged in the process. The main mechanisms involved, again, are meetings. So-called "Session C" reviews run from April through May and cover all the businesses and 3,000 executives, with special emphasis on the top 500.

A team of four led by Welch may work from 8.00 a.m. to 1.00 p.m. at the headquarters of the business with its CEO and his human resources head. Welch comes armed with a full briefing on every person to be discussed. He knows how they themselves assess their strengths and weaknesses, what development they are thought to require, what their goals are, and what their bosses think about these same issues. Even lunch on these packed days is concentrated work. Welch makes a point of lunching with women and minority managers as part of his effort to increase their presence in GE's senior ranks. (They are still not strongly represented, but Welch does at least try.)

Session C meetings are typically confrontational. Throughout the day, Welch challenges the business leaders to defend their plans for promotions, succession, and postings. In the end, the leaders get who they want, but they have to convince Welch that they, like him, are on the hunt for people who clearly possess what he describes as "E to the fourth power." "E" stands for:

- Energy
- Energizing others
- competitive Edge
- Execution

The subordinate bosses are put through a stiff test of their own leadership qualities at the C sessions. Stiff testing is a key characteristic of Welch's leadership style; but are the tests, as some critics have argued, too stiff?

Toughing it

In his early years, Welch became the unwilling exemplar for a mode of management that was quite contrary to his true ideal. In 1984, *Fortune* magazine named him as the toughest of America's tough bosses, a man who made people tremble by his aggression in meetings; who attacked others, "criticizing, demeaning, ridiculing, humiliating"; who you contradicted at your intellectual peril. Welch hated this "toughest boss" accolade and has never received it again. He is certainly tough, and, as noted, is nothing if not confrontational. But he can be outargued, and he is both human and humane. As one executive told Noel M. Tichy (the academic and consultant who revitalized GE's Crotonville academy for Welch):

> "...if you're confident about what you're doing, and willing to stand up for what you believe, you're probably going to be OK...If he ever catches you 'winging it' [improvising on inadequate preparation] you're in trouble. Real trouble. You have to go in with in-depth information."

That toughness is an essential element in the leadership that Welch practices and admires. It is applied without fear and favor to both insiders and to executives imported as a result of GE's innumerable takeovers. When RCA was acquired, for a then-record $6.5 billion, Welch examined the management of its best-known business, the NBC broadcasting network, the largest in the land, and found it wanting. Managers were mired in the past and had to change. If not, Welch told 100 of them, "I'll guarantee you, there's somebody else out there who will want to do it."

None of them was selected for the top spot. Robert C. Wright, head of GE's financial operations, was eventually appointed – somebody Welch could trust to carry out his leadership philosophy, and who did so with consummate success. No taken-over executive can claim, however, that

New broom
Robert C. Wright left GE's financial services to become head of NBC television, acquired as part of RCA in 1986, vaulting over the heads of the NBC managerial hierarchy then in place.

Welch as leader is any more demanding with them than with insiders – including himself. The demands include the stipulation that senior executives should strive to develop their own excellent replacements.

Looking to the future

Welch's approach to his own succession bears some similarity to the often criticized four-year process that took him to the top of the company. The method is "to put lots of people in lots of different jobs... and have the board and the senior management team look at them and see how they perform under all kinds of different circumstances." Managers who perform well in some circumstances may not do so in others.

"Some people can do just fine as long as the growth curve's growing," says Welch, "but when all hell breaks loose, you see them change their whole personality. Some can adapt to any situation." Even when you have observed people over time, however, selection is not scientific. In the end, you have to "take a guess and pray you're right."

When Welch succeeded Reg Jones, the latter deliberately sought a leader possessing very different qualities to his own. The excellence of his choice of Welch is an exception to the general rule that CEOs should never choose their own successor; without meaning to, they usually pick somebody whose record will not outshine theirs. Welch's ideas about his own successor, however, sound like a self-portrait. Among the characteristics he seeks are:

- Incredible energy
- Ability to excite others
- Ability to define a vision

- Finding change fun and not paralyzing
- Feeling comfortable in Delhi or Denver
- Ability to talk to all kinds of people

Such leaders are not easily found. Welch's own sensational performance as leader was based on his diagnosis of the grave faults that, if left unhealed, would have laid GE low. It seems unlikely that his successor will find similarly easy targets, equally severe faults, to correct. However, as Welch fully knows, the ultimate test of a leader is not what happens during his or her leadership – but what follows after he or she has departed.

Ideas into action

- Develop a vision for the business, and change the culture to achieve the vision.
- Insist that managers share their ideas, information, and experiences with their colleagues.
- Let people manage their delegated business as they see fit.
- "Ginger up" management by making unexpected visits and engaging in confrontational argument.
- Fix goals for all important measures, and treat them as solid commitments that management must keep.
- Brief yourself fully on everybody who works for you and make sure you recognize them.
- Be tough, but do not be hard, with everyone with whom you have dealings.

Taking the helm at General Electric

Jack Welch's advent in 1981 was not warmly welcomed. Executives assembled at the training HQ at Croton-on-Hudson, NY, showed little sympathy for his strategy of reducing the workforce and restructuring the portfolio.

Welch recalls the occasion: "I went there when 60 percent of the audience would sneer at me. Most of them wondered, 'Is this guy a nut? Should he be arrested?' It was difficult."

His path through the difficulties, however, was dead straight. Welch took into his management philosophy ideas that he had learned, more or less literally, at his mother's knee. As his tenure as CEO drew toward its end in 2000, these were still his governing principles:

- Face reality as it is, not as you wish it were.
- Be candid with everyone.
- Don't manage, lead.
- Change before you have to.
- If you don't have a competitive advantage, don't compete.
- Control your own destiny, or someone else will.

None of these six principles was compatible with the bureaucracy that Welch had experienced in his rise through GE's ranks. Welch made clear his feelings about his legacy, which the company's fine but aging skyscraper in New York (see right) could be seen to symbolize:

> "The cramping artifacts that pile up in the dusty attics of century-old companies: reports, meetings, rituals, approvals, and forests of paper that seem necessary until they are removed."

Welch set out to remove them – even though many had been added by the former CEO, Reginald Jones, who picked Welch as his successor. Under Jones's regime, one GE business alone generated seven daily reports, each of them 12 ft (3.6 m) high.

Forcing the pace

The new man cut a wide swath, not only through the paper, but the whole organization of long-service people: they averaged 13 years of service with a company that they did not want to see change. But their CEO calculated that GE needed to

"Incremental change doesn't work very well in the type of transformation GE has gone through. If your change isn't big enough, revolutionary enough, the bureaucracy can beat you." *Jack Welch Speaks*

increase profits by 4.5 to 6 percent annually – up to double the probable growth of the US economy – to meet his ambitions for the company. This was far higher than GE's own planners thought feasible, and in 1982 revenues in fact fell slightly. All this only confirmed Welch's view that radical restructuring was essential to cut costs, obtain regular quarterly rises in earnings, create a dynamic future for the company, and enrich the investors.

His major weapon was to become a famous one – the rule of "number one or number two." Unless a company either led its market or was a good second, or could rise to that position, and also had the financial results that should accompany such strength, Welch would close or sell the business. Wielding this bludgeon, whatever the internal opposition, achieved the rapid transformation that the CEO wanted – and placed him firmly and permanently in command.

Exercising leadership

Leaders set the direction for the people and the organizations they lead, integrating new-style management skills with traditional demands. Assess and build on your leadership qualities, and master the art of running a team and optimizing individual performance to get collective success.

Managing and leading

The pressures on managers are changing dramatically. Managers today are expected to have mastered all the traditional techniques of management – of implementation, maintenance, and watching the bottom line – but also to have mastered the new-style management skills that make them leaders, people who think for themselves.

Management Techniques	
Old-style management skills	**New-style management skills**
Planning	Counseling groups
Organizing	Providing resources
Implementing	Encouraging ideas
Measuring	Thinking for yourself

Using all the skills

Mastery of all the old-style management skills was crucial to Jack Welch in bringing dramatic change to GE. Welch:

- Planned: "Be number 1 or 2 in your global market or else" is strategic planning at its best – short, sharp, and to the point.
- Organized: Welch restructured GE into a dozen businesses with no supervisory layer between him and the business leaders.
- Implemented: Welch put his "big, big ideas," such as Work-Out and Six Sigma, into operation within months.
- Measured: Welch put measures on everything by which he wanted to judge performance.

However, the new-style techniques he now restlessly encourages in his managers are indispensable in a fast-moving business world and are far better suited to developing the full strengths of an organization.

Personal attributes

New-style ideals, like old-style managing, are only as valuable as the energy with which you pursue them. Welch is a superlative example of how greatly leadership revolves around personal attributes. Excellent ideas, of course, are indispensable, but you will not translate them into excellent action without the qualities that Welch admires in leaders. Test your own attributes. Do you have:

- Enormous energy and passion for the job?
- An ability to excite, energize, and mobilize an organization?
- The understanding that the customer is the arbiter of performance and the source of profit?
- Technical grasp backed by strong financial understanding?
- A desire to achieve better profits through better products, services, and processes?

Developing your leadership skills

If you do not possess all of the above attributes, do not despair. Some people are natural-born leaders, but you can develop any of the five attributes if you have the desire to lead and are willing to work at it.

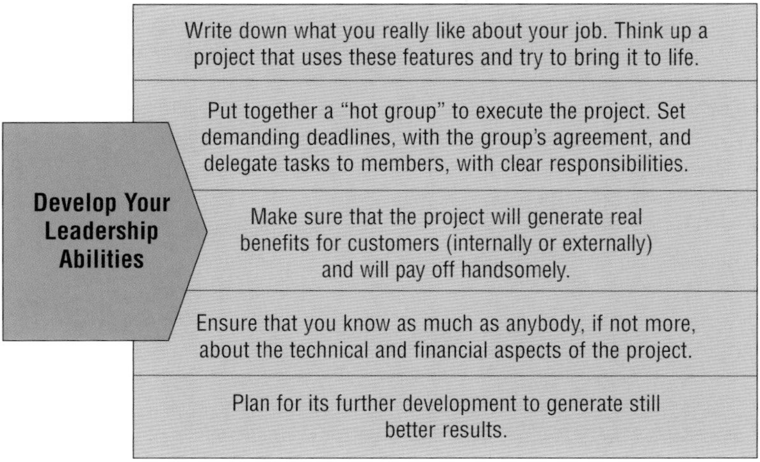

Develop Your Leadership Abilities

- Write down what you really like about your job. Think up a project that uses these features and try to bring it to life.
- Put together a "hot group" to execute the project. Set demanding deadlines, with the group's agreement, and delegate tasks to members, with clear responsibilities.
- Make sure that the project will generate real benefits for customers (internally or externally) and will pay off handsomely.
- Ensure that you know as much as anybody, if not more, about the technical and financial aspects of the project.
- Plan for its further development to generate still better results.

It is true that you risk failure when you take an initiative like this. But you cannot become an effective leader unless you are prepared sometimes to fail on the way to overall success.

1 Leading a team

Every leader has both a task to complete and a team to lead. To live up to the expectations of a Jack Welch, you must not only produce your personal best: you must also work as the team member who gets top results from the whole team.

Practicing leadership

As team leader, your two prime, linked jobs are to decide what needs to happen and to make it happen. Both jobs operate through six highly practical channels: meetings, communications, delegation, approvals, ideas, and relationships. When operating in any of these channels of leadership, always proceed by using six key steps.

The Six Key Steps
Pick the right people.
Have a clear purpose.
Put it in writing.
Work to a strict timetable.
Plan action.
Act on the plan.

Leading meetings

The first channel – meetings – are often led ineffectually. Make sure with every meeting that you follow the six key steps. Ensure that:

- all those present have a reason for being there and a role to play – which they actually do play.
- there is a clear purpose and a written agenda, distributed beforehand with full supporting papers.
- meetings start and finish on time.
- you end up with an action plan, with deadlines and designated responsibilities.
- you set up feedback to ensure that actions are taken – or modified if necessary.

Achieving positive results

Taking the right steps will not of itself make you a successful team leader. The world is full of leaders who run meetings well, communicate effectively, give or withhold approvals rapidly, have plenty of good ideas, and get along well with everybody – but who have failed or are failing. You must get good outcomes.

To get positive results from your team you must behave positively. If your behavior is negative you will achieve only mediocre results. How positive is your behavior? Study the two columns below and score yourself separately on each count. For each negative or positive conduct, score 0 for Never, 1 for Sometimes, and 2 for Always.

Negative behavior

- Ignoring values
- Being a bureaucrat
- Underachieving
- Starting slowly
- Changing reluctantly
- Words, not action
- Lacking focus
- Not acting on the facts
- Blaming others
- Mismanaging time

Positive behavior

- Living the values
- Being an entrepreneur
- Hitting high targets
- Starting decisively
- Embracing change
- Doing what you say
- Concentrating focus
- Managing on the facts
- Forgiving honest error
- Organizing yourself

Total each column, then subtract your Negative behavior total from your Positive total. If your score is below 20, start making improvements to advance toward the highest standards of leadership.

The Impact of Positive Behaviour

When Carl Schlemmer made a huge error of judgment, Welch supported him and Schlemmer went on to turn failure into success.

Schlemmer led the team running GE's locomotive business. In 1979, with Welch's approval, they embarked on a $300 million investment built around the "Dash 8" model, predicting a doubled market. In fact, by 1986, the market had fallen by three-quarters.

Welch forgave this honest error and, instead of giving up, Schlemmer focused the team's energies on drastic restructuring. They cut expenses even faster than the fall in sales. By 1987, profits were almost as high as they were before the fall.

2 Picking winners

Leaders are ultimately only as good as the people who follow their lead – and who succeed them. Concentrate a great deal of your time and attention on selecting and developing leaders and potential leaders. You and your organization cannot afford to do otherwise.

Objective assessments

To select potential leaders from your team, make an objective assessment of each candidate's current performance according to specific "hard" and "soft" criteria.

It is not always easy to be objective about people's performance, even on hard, objective measures, such as financial results or market share. Soft, subjective criteria are at least as important but even more difficult to judge. Is it possible to put a number on how open somebody is or how directly people face reality? Welch told his staff: "You're going to have to. Come up with the best numbers you can, and then we'll argue about them."

Rating potential leaders

Go through the same exercise, because objective company results flow from the subjective behaviors of employees. Write down the qualities you want from an appointee to a leadership position, then rate each candidate according to the qualities that they have displayed in their current job.

Your criteria might be covered by the following eight questions. Award points for each on a scale of 0 for "not at all" to 5 for "wholly."

1 Are they power-oriented?
2 Are they fair?
3 Do they protect their territory?
4 Are they self-confident?
5 Are they mean-spirited?
6 Are they open?
7 Do they believe in keeping up barriers?
8 Do they see reality as it really is?

Analysis

Subtract the scores for odd-numbered questions from those for even numbers.

- 15 to 20: an excellent candidate with good leadership abilities.
- 6 to 14: a candidate with potential but probably not yet ready for promotion.
- 0 to 5: a candidate without leadership potential.

Thorough investigation

If you are unable to rate a candidate, investigate further. Welch teaches that you can never devote too much time to getting the right people in the right positions. That is why he holds exhaustive Session C reviews (see p. 23) of all top-echelon managers.

To match Welch's thoroughness, subject the members of your own team to the same painstaking analysis of their accomplishments.

Accomplishment Analysis

Produce a full, fair report on people's strengths and weaknesses, including your assessment of their development needs.

Give them the report and discuss its findings.

Get them to appraise themselves – and read and discuss that document, too.

Demanding high standards

As part of your thorough assessment of candidates, you should adhere rigidly to the Can Do, Will Do guide. Welch makes no exceptions on this matter and neither should you.

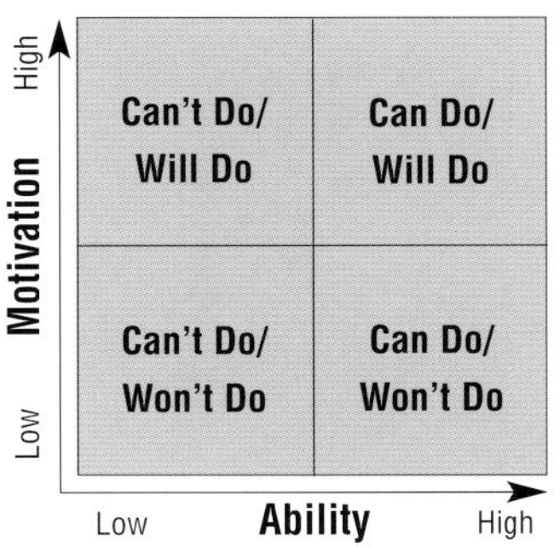

Evaluation guide

This simple matrix will resolve most of your people decisions. How do employees rate on ability and motivation? Let that rating guide your actions.

- Value employees who Can Do and Will Do, and reward them with training, promotion, and stock options.
- Train those who Will Do but Can't Do.
- Motivate or fire all those who Can Do but Won't Do.
- Let go those who Can't Do and Won't Do.

YORK

2

Mobilizing the workforce

Hitting the home run for your company • Creating competitive strength by making the company leaner and fitter – and keeping it that way • **How to target the limitless potential for higher productivity** • Taking out the boss element and removing the "whips and chains" • **How to make it compulsory to share people-based values** • The Work-Out method for improving performance and mobilizing participation • **Learning and applying lessons from other companies** • How quality can be a unifying force

If gratifying the shareholders is the only test of a chief executive, Jack Welch's management ideas, and their execution, must be pronounced a triumph. To delight shareholders, however, a CEO need only preside over exceptional rises in the share price. Welch made this increase in shareholder wealth, or the value of the company, his great ultimate objective. He would be quick to say, however, that other interests have to be satisfied in other ways first – especially those of the workforce.

How to mobilize and satisfy employees (200,000 to 300,000 over the course of his tenure) is an area in which Welch has made some of his most cogent contributions to management thought and practice. Yet in his early years, Welch's reputation for good management was at best uncertain, largely because of his treatment of labor.

Cutting out corporate fat

As "Neutron Jack" Welch sold, closed, and "restructured" businesses (or cut back their employment), the job cuts were not the only cause for bitter complaint. The unions were pressured to agree to wage and benefit cuts and reformed working practices. Such actions are guaranteed to produce unrest, but as Welch told *Business Week*, he refused to accept that morale was suffering as a result: "I don't sense that. I sense a rapidly escalating appreciation for the world competitive market, and for what we have to do to work smarter together."

The quotation, if optimistic at the time, sums up Welch's philosophy. His attitude to fellow employees is the same from top executive right through to the shop floor. The corporate staff, in fact, were cut by two-fifths to 1,000 immediately as Welch took over – proportionately a far larger cut than the 100,000 cuts (25 percent) on the shop floor between 1981 and 1987. To Welch, competitive strength is all. Excessive numbers make costs uncompetitive, and bad working practices hamstring productivity. Whatever the passing pain, he believes that people who find themselves working more effectively in a leaner and fitter business will eventually respond positively. Welch expressed himself thus: "You want to open up the place so people can flower and grow, expand, hit the home run. When you're tight-bound, controlled, checked, nitpicked, you kill it."

Improving employee value

For all that, many years after the Neutron Jack days the same criticisms more than lingered on. In mid-1998, an important union organizer told *Business Week* that: "No matter how many records are broken in productivity or profits, it's always 'What have you done for me lately?' The workers are considered lemons, and they are squeezed really dry." To that, Welch would reply in two halves. He would reject the squeezed lemon analogy; and he would argue strenuously that it truly doesn't matter how many records are broken in productivity or profits – it is always possible, indeed essential, to do better still.

On this argument, the alternative to Welch's vision of a highly competitive, aggressive, driven hyperperformer is not a benevolent, collaborative, harmonious, all-around center of excellence: the alternative is failure. The workforce plays a crucial part in following the only winning way. That is not only because labor costs loom large in the corporate budget (they averaged 40 percent of costs in GE when Welch took over, although in some businesses labor represents a tiny percentage of total spending). Even more important, the way in which employees work has a profound impact on performance – and on its potential for unbounded improvement:

> "The facts are, it's limitless. Our productivity is at the beginning stages. There's so much waste. There's so much more to get, it's unbelievable. And somehow or other, people think all these things are finite."

That quotation does not refer to Welch's early, pre-reform days, but to much later. There are two approaches to workforce productivity. The first, or Neutron Jack, phase is about cutting, making a company leaner and fitter by obvious, sweeping actions that involve major losses of jobs. Once management has "taken out the fat" (Welch's words), that route has reached a dead end. At that point, management must change gear to travel a new road.

Banishing traditional bosses

Following that route places heavy demands on management as well as labor. In 1991 Welch declared that "We've got to take out the boss element. We're going to win on our ideas, not by whips and chains" – one of his most pregnant remarks. Without that massive cultural shift, he did not believe that GE could arrive at his three ideals of "speed, simplicity, and self-confidence." While not

"For a lean organization, the only route to productivity is to build an energized, involved, participative, turned-on workforce, where everyone plays a role, where every idea counts." *Control Your Destiny or Someone Else Will* **(1993)**

sacrificing any of his emphasis on profit to those three virtues, Welch clearly saw that concentrating mainly on the delivery of short-term results – even excellent ones – was inimical to his new ideas. Only changed managers could lead a changed workforce.

Managers and other employees, he argues, must act boldly outside functional boxes and traditional lines of authority in a climate of learning and sharing. Otherwise, the long-term interests of a company will suffer, and the people-based management that Welch considers vital for productivity cannot become a reality. This is not an issue of motivating and empowering alone. Management determines productivity, not only by these "soft" processes, but also by the "hard" production and other systems that it establishes and supervises.

Studying GE practices

In 1988–89, an internal GE "Best Practices" study showed, for example, that GE's new product development had been counterproductive. The developers had looked for great leaps forward, but the study report pointed to a superior strategy – that is, to plan ahead in stages, with each version of the product making controlled advances on its predecessor. That way, products get to market faster, and sudden technological crashes are avoided. It turned out, too, that GE's celebrated habit of rotating executives fast from job to job was also counterproductive. Among other things, it slowed new product development. Both defects had a serious impact on the performance figures attributed to employees; unless the system under which they work is changed, however, they are powerless to improve their contribution.

Handling executives

Effective people management does not end with installing the most effective and economic system, or with meeting targets. Delivering on commitments – financial or otherwise – is not enough. Managers, however good at delivery, must show that they share the company's people-based values.

High-achievers at GE who act counter to the values can expect short shrift. They typically breach the behavior on which Welch insists: they force performance out of people rather than inspire it. Welch describes them with the words "autocrat, big shot, tyrant," and finds the titles intolerable. In his 1995 annual report, he duly pronounced sentence on all managers who would not or could not accept GE's people-based values. As one former GE executive commented: "The Welch theory is that those who do, get; those who don't, go."

Cultural revolution

The company did not want bosses who won results "without regard to values, and in fact often diminish them by grinding people down, squeezing them, stifling them." Some of the tyrants learned to change. Those who

"Every organization needs values, but a lean organization needs them even more. When you strip away the support systems of staffs and layers, people have to change their habits and expectations, or else the stress will just overwhelm them." *Jack Welch Speaks*

did not were dismissed: "it had to be done if we wanted GE people to be open, to speak up, to share." Welch was mounting a cultural revolution, and resistance was not acceptable. In 1991, Welch explained to *Fortune* that:

> "The only ideas that count are the A ideas. There is no second place. That means we have to get everybody in the organization involved. If you do that right, the best ideas will rise to the top."

With that greater involvement in mind, he launched new initiatives to accomplish three purposes:

- Involve employees in decision-making.
- Transfer ideas quickly between different businesses and different departments.
- Simplify production and other processes.

Working with Work-Outs

Company efficiency was to benefit from three initiatives: Work-Outs, Best Practices, and Process Mapping, in which a process is followed diagrammatically from start to finish, and then replanned and redrawn to simplify and speed up the operation. The last two contribute powerfully to the first. Work-Outs, started in March 1989, were designed for a purpose that goes beyond their immediate achievements. They produce short-term improvements in efficiency and costs, while serving a long-term educational aim. Their methodology is easily imitated, dear to Welch's heart and mind, and basic to the cultural revolution he is imposing on GE.

Basically, the unit boss takes some 40–100 staff from all levels to spend three days in informal session off-site, at a conference center or hotel. The boss sets the agenda, which might deal broadly with cutting down on meetings and paperwork, or with more technical matters to do with product and production. After a "town meeting" in which everybody considers the agenda, the group splits into teams, which for two days work on their part of the agenda with a facilitator – and with the boss conspicuously absent.

On the third day the boss returns to hear the proposals – which can number over a hundred. The great majority of these team proposals will be accepted, and very quickly. A key principle in Work-Out, important psychologically as well as practically, is that the manager, listening to his subordinates' proposals at the front of the room, can only say "Yes" or "No" – or request a specified delay, of a month or less, for gathering more information. This insistence reflects Welch's own attitude to decision-making. As one management consultant told *Business Week* in 1998: "Welch will say 'Yes.' Welch will say 'No.' But he never says 'Maybe.'"

From trivial to fundamental

The CEO, of course, will be deciding on greater matters than, for example, new protective shields for grinding machines. That was the biggest saver ($80,000) in the 1991 proposals from one unit's Work-Outs, which cut costs in total by $200,000.

The individual sums saved by Work-Out sessions are not huge, although they get multiplied by many Work-Outs all over GE. The main benefit to the company is psychological and cultural. Welch uses Work-Outs to recreate the same no-holds-barred atmosphere that he famously enjoys so wholeheartedly in his confrontations with GE executives in "The Pit," a large amphitheater at the Croton-on-Hudson Management Development Institute, or Crotonville.

Work-Outs start as highly artificial activities, unfamiliar and unsettling to both boss and bossed. Until trust has been built, the impact of the process is limited. But dealing with what Welch calls "administrivia" (like unwanted forms) is more important than it seems. It produces quick victories and prepares people for the tougher stuff: "If you jump right into complicated issues," says Welch, "no one speaks up, because these ideas are more dangerous." The Work-Out process crosses functional boundaries in what can be a threatening manner, and inevitably involves implied and explicit criticism of current management.

Extending Work-Out benefits

In a more advanced phase, teams are drawn, not from different parts of the unit, but from co-workers or people employed along the same "value chain" of linked, sequential processes. Customers and suppliers can be added to the team for mutual benefit. Nor do the teams rest content with generating ideas internally. The business development staff, whose major activity is studying other companies as acquisition targets, has also sought to identify those companies' "best practices" – approaches that could be emulated by GE on an exchange basis.

"[We] like to say 'Work-Out blew up the building.' Consider a building: It has walls and floors; the walls divide the functions, the floors separate the levels. Work-Out took out the floors and walls, leaving all the bodies in one big room."
Jack Welch Speaks

Exchanging practices

Best practice exchanges can take place both externally and internally. For example, a GE appliance plant in Canada successfully adopted the operating ideas of a small New Zealand manufacturer. What happened next graphically illustrates the changes Welch wants and the processes that satisfy his wishes. A senior vice-president visiting the Canadian site saw that the new working methods offered huge potential for GE's giant (and then troubled) Appliance Park in Louisville, Kentucky. He set in motion a program that covered ways to:

- Cut the time from order to production by 90 percent.
- Get the key and most costly 5 percent of components delivered as needed – "just in time."
- Design models to share components.
- Stock parts on the line, not in stores.
- Speed up "changeovers," when the line switches from one model to another.

The changes at Louisville were accomplished through Work-Out "town meetings," plus study trips to Canada for managers and employees (including union shop stewards). The gains at Louisville returned the $3 million cost of the so-called "Quick Response" program a hundred-fold. But to Welch, the results mean far more than that. The progress at Appliance Park, as at many other GE sites, is yet another step toward developing "people whose real income is secure because they're winning, and whose psychic income is rising because every person is participating."

Although Work-Out has such importance in Welch's plans for mobilizing and motivating everybody in the company, its ambitions were transcended by the Six Sigma quality crusade that he launched in 1998 (see p. 50). By commanding every GE business to pursue the Six Sigma goal of no more than 3.4 defects per million parts or operations, Welch aimed to kill several birds with one stone. Major cost savings would flow from huge gains in productivity (for defective output has to be remedied or replaced); and the resulting profit increases would be enhanced by higher customer satisfaction.

Moreover, the detailed training for Six Sigma projects, followed by their execution, would indoctrinate and enthuse employees as they learned how much they could do, as individuals and in teams, to transform performance. When Welch picks 29 managers to sing their Six Sigma successes before 471 peers gathered at Boca Raton, he is not only encouraging the propagation and sharing of quality ideas. He is sustaining the top-down pressure for greater efficiencies and wider effectiveness – and encouraging others to spread the message in turn.

Unifying to achieve quality

As Janet C. Lowe reported in her 1998 book, *Jack Welch Speaks*, Welch told her: "It's the job of the leader, the job of the manager, the job of the employee – everyone's job is quality." This would hardly have come as news to Welch's Japanese peers, or to any of the millions of Americans who in 1970 watched a TV documentary that shook corporate America with its revelations about Japan's vast superiority in quality. It remains a mystery why Welch, with his enthusiasm for borrowing "best practice" ideas from elsewhere, took so long to imitate Japanese quality methods, which had actually been inspired in the early post-war years by an American, W. Edwards Deming.

Japanese wake-up call
Welch's drive to involve everyone at GE in the Six Sigma quality-improvement program was spurred by the knowledge that Japan had far outstripped the US in delivering top quality.

Welch, however, expropriated Six Sigma almost as a proprietary product for GE. As he explained in Robert Slater's book, *Jack Welch and the GE Way*, it started as a quality program; then "we turned it into an internal productivity program, saving waste and all that, then we turned it to our customers." Thus, in 2000 GE started measuring Six Sigma success by monitoring customer satisfaction, and not just monetary savings. But Six Sigma transcends even the cause of customer satisfaction: "It's the most important management training thing we've ever had. It's better than going to Harvard Business School. It's better than Crotonville. It teaches you how to think differently." He believes that this is "changing the fundamental DNA of the company."

Welch puts forward the achievements of GE as undeniable evidence that making changes in attitudes and environment is both possible and highly effective. He believes that Neutron Jack has been left far behind, that he has "proved that productivity is not a matter of cut and burn." Motivating the workforce to achieve "has nothing to do with whips and chains. It's a never-ending process that's based on empowerment. It's what happens when you get people excited about finding solutions to their problems."

Ideas into action

- Go for the three-S ideals of speed, simplicity, and self-confidence.
- Outlaw autocracy and tyranny to help people to be open, to speak up, and to share.
- Insist that managers (including yourself) make their decisions clearly and quickly.
- Start off improvement teams on quick fixes, including elimination of "administrivia."
- Adopt total quality methods to save costs, raise productivity, and delight customers.
- Never relent in the insistent pursuit of better personal and company performance.
- Use quality programs as the key means of management development.

Finding the Six Sigma quality principle

Jack Welch was actually absent on the day that Six Sigma came to GE and changed it forever. When the 30-strong Corporate Executive Council was meeting in June 1995, he was recovering from a heart operation.

The hit speaker at Crotonville was a close friend, Lawrence A. Bossidy, a former vice-chairman of GE. Bossidy, now CEO of Allied-Signal, sang the praises of the radical quality program he had introduced there: Six Sigma. As he explained, any activity that generates fewer than 3.4 defects per million manufactured parts (or the equivalent in services) merits the technical description, Six Sigma.

In August, when the returned Welch heard about Bossidy's reception, he responded with enthusiasm. In fact, GE was surprisingly (and very) late in joining the quality movement. Motorola, as the leading example, had already been pursuing Six Sigma for a whole decade. But Welch showed his typical drive. Before the year ended, GE had 200 projects under way.

The projects were to be backed by intensive training. Employees have to master statistical and other techniques, and the effort must be led by highly trained people: using judo terms, GE called the latter "master black belts, black belts, and green belts." In 1996, the first full year, the project total soared to 3,000, and in 1997 it doubled. The payoff was estimated at $320 million in higher productivity and profits. While this figure was double Welch's original target, it was still far short of the total deficit between Six Sigma and actual performance: a gap somewhere between $8 billion and $12 billion annually.

Six Sigma successes

The achievements that GE can attribute to the Six Sigma program so far include:

- A 98 percent cut in defects on a billing system used in transactions with the Wal-Mart store chain (see right).
- A cut in preparation time for one jet engine from two days to some 10 hours.
- A cut in chest-scan time from three minutes to 17 seconds.

Welch, however, wanted intangibles as much as the tangibles. He seized on Six Sigma as a way of uniting management and workforce in the practical, continuous pursuit of lower costs and higher efficiencies – the ideal killer combination that he had been advocating since taking over. His vehemence on the issue can be ferocious. After one diatribe in 1999, Welch explained that "the only way I can get attention around here is not to be rational."

Still, the sight of senior managers vying with each other to boast about their Six Sigma gains was balm to Welch's heart and more than justified his efforts in support of the program. "Six Sigma has spread like wildfire across the company," he announced in *Fortune* magazine, "and it is transforming everything we do."

"We want to make our quality so special, so valuable to our customers, so important to their success, that our products become their only real value choice." *Jack Welch Speaks*

West
Mobil

3

Winning competitive advantage

How the team with diverse, combined strengths always takes the trophy • Being number one or number two in the market – and exiting if you are not • **The necessities of battling with giants** • Why worker empowerment and liberation are competitive essentials • **Why cutting costs, and then cutting them again, is crucially important** • Setting out to triple the annual rate of increase in productivity • **Running a multibillion conglomerate with a "grocery store" mentality**

Jack Welch is a fierce believer in competition, but only in competition that he can win. He sees no advantage in fighting what are doomed to be losing battles. His directive, "be number one or number two in your market, or else," expressed a strongly held philosophy that sprang from his earlier experiences at General Electric. Unlike many executives in the company, he had run high-growth businesses like plastics, and seen "opportunities in wonderful things like GE Capital." Rapid growth and great opportunities excited him personally – and they were plainly the way to create corporate success.

On the other hand, as a corporate vice-president, Welch also had big, bureaucratic businesses a century old reporting to him: "I saw businesses that ... we were holding on to as a shrine to our past." GE had trained Welch in good businesses, as well as bad, while other managers never saw a good one, and Welch felt sorry for them.

Simplifying the strategy

These bad businesses were only compared with their direct competitors. If their returns were 9 percent on capital and their competitor in the same industry earned 7 percent, they thought they were doing well. "The fact that they should be getting 15 percent was difficult to comprehend." Welch could not abide this satisfaction with inadequate returns. Hence his fourfold thrust to:

- Ensure that GE only operated in the right, good sectors.
- Move into growth businesses with competitive advantage.
- Organize the company to respond rapidly to change.
- Use the three far-reaching reforms above to earn greater returns on capital.

The sky was the limit for those returns. Welch wanted to make "as much out of the capital employed as we could." This simplistic financial strategy was not based on the kind of intellectual analysis for which GE's army of corporate planners (nearly all now axed) had been famed. Complex concepts like Economic Value Added and Market Value Added have since formalized the need for companies to earn more than their cost of capital. But "We didn't understand EVA and MVA or any of these things," says Welch.

Playing to win

What he did understand to the core of his being was that companies got into trouble by investing a lot of capital, and getting little from it. At GE, using capital efficiently became a driving force. Losses are not efficient uses of capital. However, Welch's competitive drive has sometimes taken him into areas where loss is possible. Here he would rather play than give up: "I like to fight like hell before I lose." He would always prefer to pick something else, though. The exceptions prove the important rule cited earlier: "Don't play with businesses that can't win."

Winning the competitive fights does not mean picking on somebody smaller than yourself. Few companies in the world are bigger than GE. Its opposition, however, can muster great strengths: "We compete with giants. So we have an enemy, if you will. We compete with companies and governments." He is far from being afraid of government-backed competition, however. Welch believes that the free enterprise system in America is freer than any other and a potential source of great competitive advantage.

There is a threat to this strength: "If we put bureaucracy and rigidity into our system, we play into our competitors' hands in global markets." He sees US companies as lacking the benefits of protected markets, government support, and political favors. This is a view that non-US competitors would certainly not share, to put it mildly. But it reinforces Welch's argument for his own policies: "if we let our people flourish and grow, if we use the best ideas they come up with, then we have the chance to win."

Winning worldwide

His drive to liberate and empower the workforce (see p. 38) is therefore not enlightened management for enlightenment's sake: "it's a competitive necessity. When you look at the global arena, that's what our competitive advantage is. We have got to unleash it." Welch had seized on the fact that in the global economy, no corporation can be an island unto itself.

Accordingly, early on in his reign, he modified the famous "number one or number two" rule. Originally, GE businesses had to seek this ranking in their domestic markets. Welch changed the stipulation to the whole world market. This was not just a matter of semantics. Welch's globalism dates back to 1985, when revenues outside the US were only a fifth of the corporate total. The proportion was

"There will only be one standard for corporate success: international market share.... The winning corporations – those which can dictate their destiny – will win by finding markets all over the world." *Control Your Destiny or Someone Else Will*

little higher two years later. By 1998, however, global sales came to $42.8 billion, more than total revenues in 1987, and representing over two-fifths of the total.

To put that another way, GE's sales rose by $60.1 billion between 1987 and 1998. Over half that increase came from abroad, with Europe supplying the lion's share of the sales. The principles were strong, direct, and simple:

- Move into global markets fast and powerfully.
- Build a solid, domestic base before launching the attack.
- Use acquisitions to create or enlarge a bridgehead.
- Strengthen underperforming businesses by acquisition and pooling assets.
- Concentrate on major businesses where you can win (in GE's case, that meant seven global activities ranging from jet engines to medical systems).
- Develop local management, and bring expatriates home as soon as possible.

The key to the global takeoff was a 1987 swap deal for which Welch was widely criticized. The French company Thomson ceded ownership of its medical imaging business, which greatly strengthened GE's position in the European market. In return, Thomson took over TV manufacture from GE. This provoked protests from many about surrender of key US businesses to foreign competition. But Welch knew exactly what he was doing when he made the deal. A primarily domestic, low-growth business suffering from intense competition is not his idea of a strong strategic asset. A global business specializing in a high-growth, high-profit field meets his prescription exactly.

Welch regards globalization as a three-stage process. First, "we started out going after markets and expanding our horizons.... Then we took globalization to the next step, which was globalizing components, products... sourcing around the world." The third step is "globalizing the intellect." Speaking in Robert Slater's *Jack Welch and the GE Way*, he mentioned Indian research laboratories, Russian scientists and materials, and various "medical centers of excellence" – the emphasis is "local, local."

Cutting the costs

Welch puts his businesses through a tough catechism that gives a clear picture of his nakedly competitive thrust. The questions asked are not comfortable. Nor are they asked – though they should be – by all CEOs:

- What does your global competitive environment look like?
- In the last three years, what have your competitors done to you?
- In the same period, what have you done to them?
- How might they attack you in the future?
- What are your plans to leapfrog them?

As the catechism shows, Welch's strategy is founded on a refusal to let his company join the usual procession of competitors, marching abreast with much the same product offers, winning some contracts and losing others. He wants to differentiate and to win. To that end, Welch preaches (and tries very hard to practice) both high performance and low cost, but with the final emphasis on the latter. If you want to sell turbines to developing countries, for example, you very probably have to operate from a low cost base.

It follows logically that the businesses have to be more productive, not just compared to their own past records, but compared to the best competitors. To Welch, cost is a driver that you have to keep benchmarking – making comparisons with the best you can, and cutting costs to the best levels anywhere, whatever the impact in human terms.

After the purchase in 1985 of RCA (when six major businesses were sold or closed, affecting 41,000 employees), Welch's people found 700 job cuts even at RCA's broadcasting arm – and NBC was supposed to have the lowest costs in the business. Welch does not reshuffle GE's businesses simply to save costs, however: the real purpose is to sharpen their competitive edge.

Welch pointed out in 1995 that a refrigerator cost about the same price as when he was appointed CEO. In contrast, the price of an automobile had risen something like two-and-a-half times since 1981. In many industries marked by severe competition, US companies have conspicuously failed to meet the challenge of increasing margins and returns on capital. Not so at GE. Welch reckons that the price index for GE's product range in 1989–95 was probably negative; yet its profits grew at double-digit rates. "That comes from using capital more efficiently, using people more efficiently, from systems behavior."

Welch's overarching goal went much further, however. It was nothing less than to become "the most competitive enterprise on this earth." In a sense, the goal is more important than its attainment. That is because the goalposts are always being moved, sometimes by the actions of

"In the end, you could have performance, you can have quality, but you'd better have cost." *Control Your Destiny or Someone Else Will*

competitors, sometimes by changes in technology, sometimes by developments in markets. Welch thus committed GE to a relentless pursuit of unachievable perfection. He drove the company to:

- Achieve the industry's lowest costs.
- Increase sales by creating new markets.
- Lead the world in customer service, with sophisticated fulfillment and distribution systems.
- Lead in product quality.
- Raise productivity.

Productivity power

From early on, Welch aimed to triple GE's annual rate of productivity increase – a huge ambition. The link between productivity and competitiveness is obvious to any manager, but to Welch productivity goes deeper still: "When a business becomes productive, it gains control of its destiny." That is the justification for putting a company through the pain of restructuring:

> "... you go through trauma, you bottom out – and then you start to see results. Once you get back to being productive, the jobs come back, you succeed in the marketplace, your profit margins rise. You were hurting for awhile, but now you feel great."

The task of management is to create systems, within a sensibly structured business, that enable people to achieve higher productivity and greater competitive advantage. In their book, *Control Your Destiny or Someone Else Will*, Noel M. Tichy and Stratford Sherman cite the case of a plant that makes wire, another that wraps the wire into coils, and a third that assembles the coils into lamps. If these are organized as three separate businesses, each optimizing its own performance, the totality may well not be optimized. Organized as a single unit, however, those three plants can seek the optimum balance of opportunities: for instance, making a costlier wire may help to produce a cheaper lamp.

Lessons of success

Half-way through Welch's period in office, however, it became apparent that GE's productive systems were defective in key respects. The best practices that GE discovered in other companies in 1988–89 were less technical than managerial. What made some companies successful where others failed? The answers were quite disturbing for GE, which found that it compared badly on eight basic points. It noted that successful companies:

- Managed processes, not people.
- Used techniques (like "process mapping" and "benchmarking") to achieve continuous improvement.
- Valued incremental gains.
- Measured performance by customer satisfaction.
- Introduced new products faster than the competition.
- Designed new products for efficient manufacture.
- Treated suppliers as partners.
- Managed inventory in superior fashion.

The first of these secrets of success was crucial. Learning its lessons, GE shifted from *what* it was doing to *how* it was being done: in other words, it focused on how people produced, not how much. Instead of keeping score and relating results to targets, with a wholly financial staff checking the numbers, the audit staff was changed until half the auditors were operational experts who knew ways to improve the how. But Welch does not rely on staffwork to regulate and raise competitive prowess. That is a job for committed line managers – for leaders.

The CEO himself must be as deeply committed as anybody else, if not more so. Welch believes in trying to know every employee and every customer, just like a village grocer. Welch even nicknames GE "the grocery store":

> "What's important at the grocery store is just as important in engines or medical systems. If the customer isn't satisfied, if the stuff is getting stale, if the shelf isn't right, or if the offerings aren't right, it's the same thing. You manage it like a small organization. You don't get hung up on zeros."

The informal approach

Nor do you allow formalities to get in the way. "Jack" to everybody, Welch acts in informal ways and inevitably sets an informal style for others. Welch regards his emphasis on informality as a "big thought." He says: "I don't think people have ever figured out that being informal is a big deal." Informality means a set of key actions by the CEO, all of which heighten competitiveness:

- Breaking the chain of command
- Communicating freely, up and down
- Paying for performance as an entrepreneurial boss would pay
- Achieving wide personal contact
- Making surprise visits
- Ignoring hierarchical layers
- Sending reams of handwritten notes

An excellent example of the CEO's informal but powerful role in pursuing the competition is that of the tubes used for X-rays and CT-scans. In 1993 Welch heard in one of his customer conversations (which take 15–20 percent of his time) that competitive products offered a tube life more than double GE's. Highly displeased, and bypassing two levels in the hierarchy, Welch found the right manager, called him into HQ, and demanded a quadrupling of tube life. According to James A. Byrne, writing in *Business Week* in 1998, the exact words were, "Fix it. I want 100,000 scans out of my tubes!" (note the "my").

Honing the competitive edge

It was much easier said than done. Over four years Welch received weekly reports on progress, to which he replied regularly with handwritten notes alternating praise with impatience. The campaign paid off: tubes finally appeared that lasted for 150,000 and 200,000 scans. The new methods created productivity gains worth some $14 million. You have to wonder at the long gestation, and at the mismanagement that allowed so large a competitive gap to emerge. But you also have to marvel at the persistence with which the CEO pursued improvement at a relatively small operation. That illustrates one of four key aspects of Welch's intensely competitive approach:

- Persistence: you never give up the thrust to achieve a better product, superior marketing, greater internal efficiency, better customer relations, and so on.
- Detail: the leader creates the broad competitive strategy, but uses detailed intervention when necessary to help maintain its integrity.

- Customer responsiveness: the arbiter of the company's competitive success is the external purchaser, not the internal management.
- Culture: the persistent, detailed, customer-facing approach of the leader establishes a role model for the whole organization.

That competitive culture is Welch's ultimate weapon in the global wars. His whole time at the top can be seen as a massive effort to prove that big corporations – even one with a quarter of a million employees – can be as pugnacious and responsive as small ones: "We are trying to get the soul and energy of a start-up into the body of a $60 billion, 114-year-old company." Welch's own career had taken off with his transformation of GE's tiny plastics business. He wanted to turn GE into plastics writ large – very large. Not only were major initiatives like Work-Out and Six Sigma, and course after course at Crotonville, enlisted in the cause: Welch doggedly pursued "vision and values" at every opportunity.

Soft values, hard results

These "soft" issues, embedded in carefully crafted "shared statements," are not easily associated with the "hard" management for which Welch has come to be famous. But the values promote what he wants: a company that is lean and agile, that pursues high excellence and high quality, where entrepreneurship is encouraged and practiced, where reality and candor dominate exchanges of all kinds. In this vision, managers are stewards of the owners' assets. They have to deal with paradox as a way of life, to accept that change is continual and nothing is sacred. There are to be no secrets, but "constructive conflict" has to flourish in the pursuit of customer satisfaction.

In his final decade, Welch began preaching other values, too: respect for others, openness, and "ownership" of jobs, in an atmosphere where every contribution counts. Here Welch is reflecting a critical change of strategic direction. The hard facts of competition remain crucial: but living the softer values that unite the components of a diversified business creates the indispensable difference between big winners and large losers. Welch wants to build a company that, like its leader, competes hard, hates to lose, and is only interested in winning big.

Ideas into action

- Make the return on capital employed as high as you can.
- Do not play with businesses that cannot win the competitive wars.
- Differentiate your business from competitors to make it easier to beat them.
- Commit management to the relentless pursuit of unattainable perfection.
- Seek to optimize the totality of the business rather than the profits of its components.
- Focus on how people are producing, not on how much they produce.
- Establish and share values and practical ideas that will boost competitiveness.

Changing company culture

Transforming an organization may be vital to improving performance. This cannot be accomplished without changing its culture – the values and attitudes shared by its members. To do this, you establish key company values, change the behavior of individuals, and abolish bureaucracy in favor of a creative, enterprising climate of "best practice."

Establishing a new culture

To Jack Welch, reality, candor, and integrity are not ideals but essential weapons in the battle for competitive success and profitable growth. They are fundamental to the culture he established at GE. Do you face reality, tell the truth to everybody (including yourself), and display honesty in all your dealings? If this is not the case, you will not cope well with business needs or earn the trust on which performance ultimately depends.

The role of a values statement

Welch spent years and involved 5,000 people in producing a values statement for GE that made it clear what attitudes and behavior he expected from employees. As more and more of his staff tried to live by these values, they changed the culture of GE. Today every GE manager has a card that reminds them of the values. It states that GE leaders ("always with unyielding integrity"):

- have a passion for excellence and hate bureaucracy.
- are open to ideas from anywhere.
- live quality... and drive cost and speed for competitive advantage.
- have the self-confidence to involve everyone and behave in a boundaryless fashion.
- create a clear, simple, reality-based vision... and communicate it to all constituencies.
- have enormous energy and the ability to energize others.
- stretch... set aggressive goals... reward progress... yet understand accountability and commitment.
- see change as opportunity... not threat.
- have global brains... and build diverse and global teams.

1 Establishing values

Adapt GE's values for your own purposes. Ensure that they are lived by your team or department by producing a workable values statement, and enforce those values by using the three Rs technique (below).

Drawing up a values statement

Before you expect people to live by a values statement, you must make sure it meets six key criteria.

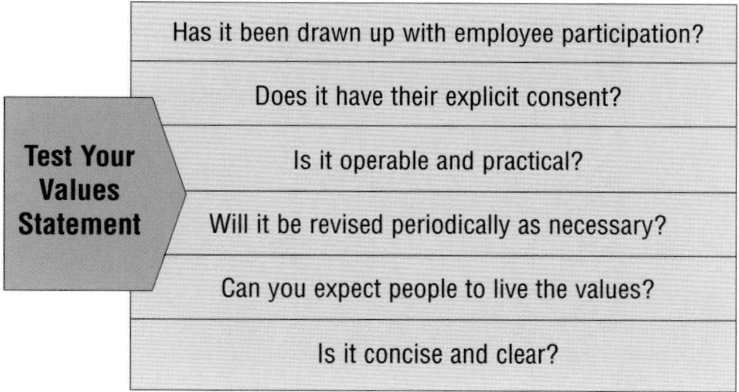

Enforcing values

Maintain commitment to the company values statement by using the Three Rs – Reward, Repetition, and Removal. At GE, Welch fits managers into one of four categories or types. Type I delivers on performance commitments and shares the company's people-based values; Type II does not meet commitments and does not share the values; Type III misses commitments, but shares the values; Type IV delivers on commitments but does not share the values. Each Type requires different treatment. Follow these principles:

- Type I: keep by progressing and promoting (Reward).
- Type II: do not keep in the organization (Removal).
- Type III: give a second chance, preferably in a different environment (Repetition).
- Type IV: provide an opportunity to change their ways (usually very difficult for them) or fire (Repetition or Removal).

Above all, remember the importance of personal example from the leader at all times. This is the fourth R: Role Model.

2 Changing behavior

Fundamental to changing the culture of an organization is altering people's behavior. Welch achieved great success with the introduction of Work-Outs and Six Sigma – and so could you.

Practicing Work-Outs

The Work-Out program (see p. 43) that Jack Welch launched in 1988 was designed to make the behavior of both bosses and bossed more positive, while bringing substantial benefits to the bottom line.

The Purposes of Work-Outs
To develop a climate of trust.
To empower people to improve their own performance.
To cut out wasted work, time, and cost.
To establish a new corporate culture of collaboration and sharing.

These results can be won in any company. Take members of your unit off-site for up to three days and present them with a list of problem areas for discussion. Ask them to recommend reforms, ranking them according to the criteria of payoff and effort.

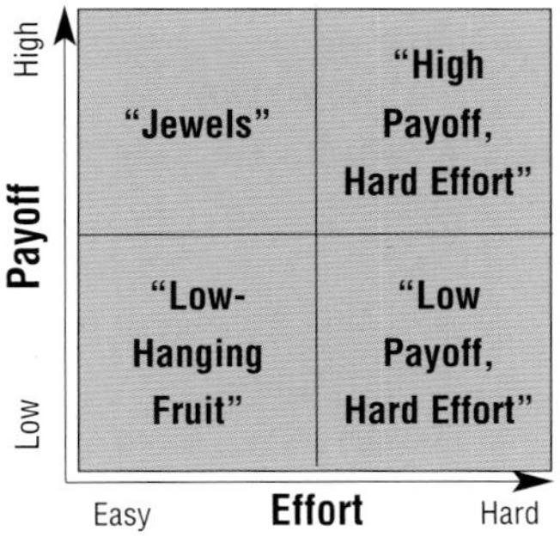

Payoff \ Effort	Easy	Hard
High	"Jewels"	"High Payoff, Hard Effort"
Low	"Low-Hanging Fruit"	"Low Payoff, Hard Effort"

Choosing issues

Place at the top of your list high payoff, easy reforms, known as "jewels." Follow with low payoff, easy reforms, known as "low-hanging fruit."

When delegates make their proposals, reply at once with one of three responses: "Yes," "No," or "Come back with more information inside a month." Implement the accepted proposals.

Achieving Six Sigma

The Six Sigma program (see p. 50) that Jack Welch launched in 1995 comes from the perfectionist world of Total Quality Management. Six Sigma means that 99.999997 percent of what is produced meets specification and is free from defects. Welch regards it as highly educational and a huge force for cultural change. The objectives are common (or should be) to all companies.

The Objectives of Six Sigma
To satisfy the customer.
To reduce the costs.
To improve the quality of purchased supplies.
To lift internal performance.
To enable better performance by better design.

Practicing Six Sigma

To benefit from the Six Sigma approach, you must first insist on measurement of what is being done at present (for example, the percentage of rejects). Next, analyze how performance can be improved, and set new targets that will, when achieved, prove that performance has become markedly better. Then install controls to ensure the operation keeps up the good work. Finally, never give up or let up – there will always be massive improvements possible.

Six Sigma in Action

The application of Six Sigma was crucial to ending the dissatisfaction of GE Lighting's biggest customer – Wal-Mart.

The billing system between GE and the retail giant Wal-Mart was malfunctioning. Faced with disputes, payment delays, and a dissatisfied customer, GE realized that its system required adapting to Wal-Mart's system and needs. Six Sigma was put to work, backed by some IT improvements and $30,000 in investment. Within four months defects came down by 98 percent. Wal-Mart became much happier, and GE Lighting earned back its investment many times over.

2 Beating bureaucracy

All too often minor rules and regulations (and fussy people) that make no sense but seem almost impossible to circumvent can swamp and clog an organization. Learn to identify the classic signs of bureaucracy, and act to eliminate them before the damage is done.

Identifying the disease

How much of your energy is expended on purely internal activities? How much is directed toward exernal customers? If you spend less than 20 percent of your energy on external customers, then bureaucracy has taken hold. Are the classic signs present?

Classic Signs of Bureaucracy
Detailed monthly budget approvals
Centrally-driven strategic planning only
Powerful staff members with no line responsibility
Many-layered approval procedures
Many-layered, strictly observed payment bands
Rigid status symbols
Hefty corporate manuals and "bibles"

Tackling the problems

Bureaucracy makes work and creates a climate in which the customer comes third – well after the management and the company's other employees. Eliminate it as follows:

- Move financial reporting from monthly to quarterly.
- Make senior managers responsible for their own strategies.
- Eliminate all staff jobs unless proved to be essential.
- Push approval levels right down the line.
- Broaden and reduce the payment bands.
- Scrap the status symbols and "burn the bibles."
- Identify nonsenses and eradicate them.

3 Becoming the best

Ideas for managing better are one thing you can safely beg, borrow, or steal. If a successful organization anywhere uses practices that you do not, their example may help you reach the same high standards. Adopt their good practices wherever you can.

Using best practice

Many GE businesses employ a tool called the Trotter Matrix to check on their use of best practice. The idea came from Lloyd Trotter, who ran the Electrical Distribution and Controls side of GE. He listed a number of desirable attributes for each of his plants, and then scored each attribute.

The Trotter Scorecard	
0 points	Aware of best practice: no plans to adopt
1 point	Plans to adopt: no current activity
2 points	Current activity on best practice
3 points	Best practice implemented on some product lines
4 points	Best practice implemented on all product lines
5 points	Model site for best practice

Score your own activities on a similar basis. Sadly, most companies earn a zero on everything they do, because they are either unaware of the best practice or else believe they have nothing to learn.

Learning from others

It is only realistic to assume that somebody has found, and is using, better ways for all that you do. Learn from them: most firms are surprisingly generous about letting other managers study their methods. For example, Japanese car makers were perfectly happy to let their Western rivals into their secrets – they knew that by the time the West had followed suit, they would be far ahead, thanks to newer and even better ideas. Avoid the car trap: act fast.

Recreating the role of Crotonville

Before becoming CEO, Jack Welch had never personally attended a course at GE's Management Development Institute in Croton-on-Hudson, NY, the training establishment known as Crotonville.

Welch originally shared his company colleagues' somewhat jaundiced view of Crotonville (see right) as something of a consolation prize for people who had been passed over. But as CEO he realized that he could use the institute as the mainspring of the management system and style he wanted. Crotonville offered a unique and valuable opportunity to indoctrinate the entire GE management corps with his ideas on how a business should be run.

GE's training institute has consequently occupied a major part of his time. In 17 years, the chief executive attended Crotonville 250 times, exposing some 15,000 managers to his ideas – and listening to theirs – in four-hour sessions at which no holds are barred. Welch held that Crotonville would have high academic standards, but its work would not be abstract. The academy would work on GE's strategic issues and would help executives to tackle their own problems directly.

The 70-odd managers who attend the top three-week development program at Crotonville, repeated many times over, are both beneficiaries and missionaries for Welch's ideas – which he delivers in person, usually at the end of the course. Speaking without notes, he expects and welcomes critical, penetrating questions from the students. Spending time socializing with them after business hours, he is there as both boss and professor.

Taking the pulse

The institute also employs the services of numerous academic lecturers, many of them distinguished. It has a large catalog of courses, from entry-level to the above-mentioned, top-level development programs. Welch loves addressing these. He talks with great vigor, but also listens hard because, as he told *Fortune* magazine, the monthly visits are "a great way to take the pulse of the organization."

The revolution sponsored by Welch at Crotonville gave new vigor to GE's reputation as a management pioneer. Welch had scrapped the "Blue Books," five heavy volumes that had been compiled by leading experts, such as Peter Drucker, to guide all GE managers through their work. To Welch, that approach put the cart before the horse. Rather than following the thoughts of others, managers should learn to think for themselves as they tackled their tasks – and should then pass on their thinking. Crotonville made GE the world's supreme example of on-the-job "action learning."

More than symbolically, Crotonville is also the meeting-place for the 30-strong Corporate Executive Council, created in 1986 as a quarterly summit forum. The council does not make decisions and has no clear authority to impose its collective will on the GE organization. But this is where Welch and his senior colleagues thrash out the issues, sharing and generating the ideas and policies that will guide GE's future.

"I like it [Crotonville] more and more. I think of it as the most important thing in the transformation. We put money in when we were downsizing the company. We're expanding it." *The GE Way Fieldbook* (2000)

4

Pursuing shareholder value

Raising the company's stock market valuation to create wealth • Making General Electric the world's richest corporation by outgrowing the economy • **How to restructure a company around core businesses and eliminate noncore ones** • The concept of the "business engine" as the driver of diversified growth • **The pursuit of integrated diversity by keeping businesses separate but sharing their strengths** • Raising the corporate profile by celebrating real achievement

The elevation of "shareholder value" to pole position in the management race became a cliché by the end of the 20th century. The concept did not exist in 1981, when Jack Welch set out to enrich his shareholders beyond their wildest dreams by making General Electric the world's most highly valued company. The market capitalization rose nearly 30 times, adding an astounding, unique $385 billion of shareholder value as Welch dynamically and doggedly pursued the policies that, he believed, would turn his ultimate objective into reality.

Naming the targets

That meant achieving two subordinate targets of equally intimidating size. GE had to outgrow the US and global economies, and its growth rate had to outstrip inflation. Welch wanted no repetition of the previous decade, when growth had narrowly exceeded that of the Gross Domestic Product, but market capitalization had shown no increase at all. He pays informed and incisive attention to the national and world economies and drives GE to adapt dynamically to this environment.

Three elements in his thought thus emerged clearly from the very start of his career as CEO. First, businesses (and managers) must set their own targets. Second, those targets must be "stretch targets," demanding that managers outperform the past and their own expectations. Third, decisions and actions must be directed towards enhancing the real, underlying value of the business in ways that will, in turn, create a richer investment for shareholders (who Welch meaningfully calls "shareowners").

Welch's paradigm of the wealth-creating company has an essentially simple, four-point basis. You should:

Hub of technology
Making jet engines (above) is an activity in which General Electric enjoys definite competitive advantage. Welch led GE away from operations where it could not lead the market.

- Lead the market from a position of number one or number two.
- Achieve "well above average real (that is, after inflation) returns" on investment.
- Have a unique selling proposition based on giving customers value that competitors cannot equal or surpass.
- Build on what the company does best.

In implementing these policies, Welch acts much like an aggressive fund manager who handles a portfolio of shares by deciding which sectors merit investment and buying or selling stocks to meet his financial objectives. In one of Welch's first and most telling analyses, applied a year after taking charge, he divided the company into sharply defined groups. First, he took clearly worthwhile activities and drew three circles round the related businesses. The circles covered, respectively, technology, services, and core manufacturing.

Under technology came medical systems, aircraft engines, and materials. Services included construction and engineering and nuclear services. The core operations were activities such as lighting and transportation (including locomotives). All businesses inside the circles were long-term holdings, which Welch did not expect to sell unless circumstances changed. Any other businesses went outside the circles; Welch put them in three categories: "support," "ventures," and simply "outside." All were candidates for disposal – even the businesses that were supposed to support the core activities.

Balancing the portfolio

High on the list of outside operations was "housewares," the small appliance business whose toasters, kettles, and irons had played the foremost role in spreading the GE trademark around America's homes. That impressed Welch not at all. Housewares in total had the number one position in the US market: but that was not true product by product. The operation came nowhere near Welch's financial requirements and, despite vehement internal opposition, out it went.

Noel M. Tichy and Stratford Sherman comment in their book, *Control Your Destiny or Someone Else Will*, that:

> "The sale of Housewares was the first of many assaults on GEers' sentimentality that made enemies among the very people Welch meant to lead. The corporate equivalent of blasphemy became a trademark of his regime. *Although the moves were financially sound* (my italics), they hurt his public reputation."

But the idea of financial soundness was inescapable for Welch. You cannot create value for shareholders by destroying value. You dare not invest capital in businesses that do not pay. Anybody can invest unprofitably, but the task of the manager is to invest the owners' funds more wisely and successfully than they can themselves. Less exciting performers, however, have a place in achieving this goal. The rapid growth of a business like plastics might well be erratic. The dependable businesses, though, give a company "enormous staying power," in Welch's words, and underpin a balanced portfolio.

Mutual protection

Thus, Welch can approve plans for the dependables "to go from A to B," knowing how the businesses are going to make the journey, and knowing in consequence that the group as a whole will reach its planned destination. You can never be sure that a collection of businesses (or products, for that matter) will get from A to B exactly as planned. You can be certain that you have the power to complete the voyage from A to B, however much plans have to be altered:

> "If one of the businesses is going to be weak, and it's a great business, but it's in a difficult moment, I can support it. If I'm a single-product guy in a weak business like that, in a business that cycles dramatically, I get whacked. So the staying power that our businesses have allows us to stay for the long haul."

"The businesses I eliminated were not simply in the red for two or three years; they had been depressed for 30 or 50 years in the long history of GE. And their employees had consciously become underdogs."
Jack Welch Speaks

Welch systematized this approach in 1988 as the "business engine." He used the term to make it clear that, despite its diversity, GE was not a holding company whose investments operated independently. The components were parts of a larger whole, the pistons of an engine whose driver sat in the Corporate Executive Office, fueling the forward progress with human, financial, and technical resources. The businesses had to optimize their own market and financial performance by increasing productivity, allocating their resources effectively, improving their turnover of assets, and selling disposable businesses: but the earnings they generated were used for the common good.

Restructuring GE

An allied strength in a diversified business – if management is properly entrepreneurial – is the ability to pick winners that stock markets cannot see. Winners may lurk in industries that are not perceived as growth industries, but do contain growth elements. As an example, Welch cites the growth of his favorite, plastics: "We are on every PC that's being sold today, with a high-margin product. So plastics is growing." In retail lighting, the strategy was to go with the winners in distribution, like Wal-Mart, the world's largest retailer.

Portfolio structure, in Welch's philosophy, is concerned with the "hardware" of business management, which he

"The point is that you can take what seemingly look like mature industries and tie your horse to winning elements."
Control Your Destiny or Someone Else Will

distinguishes from the "software." Hardware is what you make and sell, and where you locate those operations. Software is broadly culture. The hardware inevitably comes first: operating wrong and wrongly structured businesses with improved management leads nowhere. Between 1981 and 1989 Welch took 350 product lines and business units and placed them into 13 major businesses, while many operations were eliminated in one way or another.

The $9 billion of disposals in that first decade was small in comparison to the $18 billion of acquisitions. Under Welch, GE has been a hyperactive investor. By 1998 the company had completed no fewer than 600 acquisitions. They have been swiftly and successfully integrated along the same tough lines as the original hardware restructuring of GE's existing businesses. Nobody is spared from these disciplines. In 1981–89 most of the nine layers of GE's hierarchy were removed, with 29 pay levels reduced to just five bands – and, as the total workforce fell by 100,000, profits and market value soared.

Focusing on the software

Welch was moving fast towards his goal of making GE the richest corporation, but that by no means satisfied him. Cutbacks do not create shareholder value: they reverse its waste, but creation requires positive strategies. He acted in the 1980s on concepts that were to be articulated by thinkers in the next decade, when, in a belated reaction against "downsizing" – reduction in employment by closures, sell-offs, and layoffs – observers began to notice that downsized businesses had difficulty in growing.

Cutbacks produce relatively easy, short-term payoffs. But they do not help, and may positively hinder, the generation of new business growth. Without that, Welch could not meet his targets. He saw very clearly that this was a matter of software, of the effectiveness of managers, systems, and the workforce as a whole. Creating a balanced portfolio and managing it as one entity had been achieved. "The hardware was basically in place by mid-1988," he told Tichy and Sherman in 1991. "We liked our businesses." But you also have to like the way that they are managed – and here Welch was much less happy.

Managing the agenda

Inevitably, software ideals take time to turn into reality. And Welch's next bid to raise shareholder value – "integrated diversity" – was certainly idealistic. The phrase means that businesses are run independently, but pool ideas, people, experience, best practices – everything that can improve their performance and that of the whole corporation. Work-Outs and Six Sigma (see p. 43) are essential to this very great ambition. They lead on toward a fluid, flexible, and innovative organization that can seize opportunities for long-term growth and profit.

This long-term emphasis is underpinned by a hard and unremitting emphasis on meeting short-term commitments and exercising strict cost control. A fundamental tenet of Welch's is the need to combine future results with present achievement, long-range shareholder value with immediate management results. "You can't grow long-term if you can't eat short-term," he has said. "Anybody can manage short. Anybody can manage long. Balancing these two things is what management is." His highly effective short-term action agenda is calculated to avoid anything that damages long-term performance:

- Do not add any costs.
- Speed up turnover of inventory.
- Consolidate acquisitions.
- Use intellectual capital to replace investment in plant and equipment.
- Campaign against price concessions.

The program presupposes that organizational fat has already been carved away, which was certainly true at GE. Throughout his first decade, Welch only once failed to report a quarterly rise in earnings – and that failure was down to a technical change in accounting rules. Operational earnings continued to march upward, quarter after quarter, in the next decade as well. Even though there is no evidence to show that short-term gains in earnings equate with long-term creation of shareholder value, Wall Street analysts are notoriously fixated on quarterly results.

Investor perceptions

Short-term performance therefore has a powerful effect on investor perceptions. Those have been of enormous importance in the creation of GE's corporate wealth. A string of short-term earnings, of course, translates into consistent year-by-year increases: but that is not the sole explanation for the Welch bonanza. From 1988 to 1998, earnings per share rose by 11.2 percent annually: bettered by only 87 of the 500 largest US companies. But total return to investors (meaning mostly the rise in the share price) advanced two and a half times as fast.

Part of the difference is explained by the general sustained boom on Wall Street, which had been especially marked in big corporate stocks like GE: a substantial part, however, arose from perceptions – the Welch effect. Welch made sure, via contacts with academics and the media, that the ways in which his excellent results were produced received as much publicity as the results themselves. In 1987, though, the jury was still out: "How good a manager is he?" asked one business magazine. But subsequent titles of magazine articles speak for themselves:

- "Inside the mind of Jack Welch: GE's chairman is pushing ideas that could transform the art of management" (*Fortune*, March 27, 1989).
- "How Jack Welch keeps the ideas coming at GE" (*Fortune*, August 12, 1991).
- "CHAMPS! When it comes to creating shareholder wealth, these guys (Welch and the late Roberto Goizueta of Coca-Cola) are in a league of their own" (*Fortune*, December 11, 1995).
- "How Jack Welch runs GE: a close-up look at America's No.1 manager" (*Business Week*, June 8, 1998).

Welch understands very clearly that perception is reality and has a profound effect on shareholder value. That explains some of his sensitivity to corporate wrongdoing, where GE's record is by no means free of accusations and embarrassments. That is an occupational risk of pressing hard for performance – and sometimes pressing too hard.

Adding economic value

Pressure for performance is one way in which the concept of creating wealth for the shareholders is translated into the life of the manager down the line. It is not the most important method, however. If managers can be persuaded to think like owners, their work is much more likely to benefit the latter. Welch strives to achieve this identification. Much of his approach is in tune with the idea of Economic Value Added (or EVA). The basic, simple notion is that the company should earn more on its capital than the capital employed actually costs – which means that individual managers must do the same.

What lent wings to this age-old principle in the 1990s was the redefinition of capital to include equity. If you look at the cost of the dividend alone, equity is usually much cheaper than debt. But equity shareholders expect a higher total return on their investments than debtholders: with that premium expectation added in, equity capital is more expensive than debt. The return that must be achieved on capital, once the latter has been defined in this way, is also substantially higher. The targets are stretched – as Welch insists that they must be.

Less outlay, more return

Reducing total capital employed while increasing its productivity sums up the basic thrust of Welch's wealth creation. Meeting his targets demands that managers cut down the total capital they need (by reducing inventories, for example) while increasing the efficiency with which it is used (for instance, by getting more productivity from the machines). If the individual managers meet their targets, so must the company. The emphasis shifts heavily to the efficient management of resources and getting a bigger bang per buck.

Although Welch did not specifically use EVA, the results of following this general philosophy were just what its advocates would predict. In 1995, GE's cost of capital was calculated by *Fortune* magazine at 12.9 percent. Its return on that capital was 14.8 percent. That added up to an excess of $863 million, which the stock market multiplied an amazing number of times. Market Value Added, or MVA, basically calculates all the capital that a company has accumulated over time and compares that sum with the current stock market value of the equity and debt.

The ultimate endorsement

For 1994, that calculation gave GE an MVA of $52 billion, nearly all of it added during Welch's reign. The MVA went on increasing over the rest of a decade in which GE's and Welch's reputations continued to soar. There were still dissenting voices, however. In 1997, the German magazine *Der Spiegel* called Welch "The Brutal Manager" and pointed out, in an interview with the GE boss, that: "As the number of employees was halved, the share price increased almost twentyfold." Then it asked Welch whether shareholder value was more important to him than the families of his former employees. His answer was "No":

> "In a global economy, you cannot manage a company in a paternalistic way just because it feels better. If you don't sort things out in good time they will eventually explode in your face. Then you have to become brutal and cruel."

Welch's approach, at any rate, has received the highest possible endorsement at home. In February 2000, *Fortune* magazine reported that Welch's peers among America's 500 top executives had voted GE the country's most admired company for the third year running. It won by its all-around achievement on the list of eight attributes of admirable performance; they included innovativeness, employee talent, financial soundness, use of corporate assets, long-term investment value, social responsibility, and quality of products and/or services.

The rating vindicates Welch's simple-sounding theory that you create the right value by taking the right actions, right across the organization and all its activities. The great manager enriches the owners (and thus himself) by investing in the right businesses, exiting from the wrong ones, pressing and incentivizing business leaders for optimum performance, and launching powerful initiatives to sustain momentum and exploit the forces of change. And in these tasks, the leader never rests.

Ideas into action

- Make managers set their own stretch targets and ensure that these are met.
- Balance fast-growth, higher-risk businesses with dependable and steady ones.
- Eat short-term if you want to grow long-term – concentrate on the present as well as the future.
- Educate managers to think like owners, and give them sound incentives to do so.
- Make sure that you like both your businesses and how they are managed.
- Reduce total capital employed while raising its productivity.
- See that employees are enriched along with the outside investors.

5

Exploiting the forces of change

How the internet creates immense new business opportunities • Why reaching the top is a beginning, not a culmination • **How Welch discovered a potential crisis behind GE's bulging order books** • The way to force through change in a company that is apparently successful • **Reaching down into the organization to inspire everybody** • The way to govern strategy by latching onto a single strong idea • **Boundarylessness** • Living by the three themes of reality, quality/excellence, and the human element

Jack Welch's entire career at the summit of General Electric is testimony to a truth in which he strongly believes. He argues that becoming Chief Executive Officer is not, as many CEOs have thought, the culmination of a career: it is a beginning. His own predecessors at GE acted in the same belief. The tradition is that each incoming CEO takes a fresh look at the corporation's position, external and internal, and ordains the changes that changing times make mandatory.

Welch saw clearly that he had taken command at a watershed. The hyperinflation of the 1970s had coincided with threats from the East, primarily from Japan, where poor quality and low price had been succeeded by a deadly combination of high quality and low price. GE was in the firing line in many of its businesses. There was no option: GE's plants, quality, and discipline had to change to achieve the level reached by competitors overseas.

Facing the competition

Welch has never hesitated to express the truth as he sees it. In October 1981, 120 leading executives were given a blunt ultimatum. The issue for his audience, the new CEO told them, was having to face reality about troubled situations. That was not a difficulty for Welch and his top team at the Fairfield, Connecticut, headquarters:

> "We can take good news and we can take bad news. We're big people and we've been paid well, all of us. You own these damn businesses. The idea of coming into Fairfield, and Fairfield yells, and Big Daddy gets you – it's an insane system we've built. No, you are the owners of your businesses. For God's sake, take them and run with them. Get us out of the act."

Welch wanted the business leaders to examine their situation in 1981, then look at the likely position in 1985 and ("probably more important") 1990. Could they participate in those arenas as the number one or number two player? This meant tremendous change along three dimensions. Welch wanted to establish a wholly new contract between Fairfield and the businesses. He wanted their leaders to take full responsibility, not just for their financial results, but for the totality of their management. And any businesses that could not pass the one-or-two test would be axed or radically changed, one way or another.

The problem Welch faced was one that defeated a contemporary CEO at IBM, John Akers, who once told a similar group of senior managers that "everyone is too comfortable when the business is in crisis!" In IBM's case, the crisis (which went uncured) was already apparent in falling market shares. But GE's problems were hidden by a gigantic backlog of orders. Welch is brilliant at looking behind the figures. He could see that the $28 billion orderbook that he had inherited was a snare and a delusion.

Losing battler

While GE was steered clear of the competitive threat by Welch, IBM, then headed by John Akers (below), never succeeded in reclaiming its former dominant position in computer hardware.

As GE went on delivering power stations, turbines, and locomotives – all products with long lead-times, ordered in the previous decade – the revenues and profits would roll in during the 1980s, however badly current sales were doing. To the managers he was trying to change, however, the backlog was a comfortable cushion. All they could see was the corporation's good overall performance: they could not relate Welch's diatribe to a financial year in which profits had risen 9 percent to some $1.7 billion.

The challenge of change

Change (the biggest challenge, according to Welch) is always easier to propose than to achieve, even for an exceptionally vigorous manager. Welch was accused of going too far, too fast. He has often said, though, that his mistake was not in moving too fast, but too slowly. He makes a distinction between evolutionary change and revolution. Welch is widely perceived by outsiders (and no doubt insiders also) as revolutionary. Yet he thinks that: "We didn't get at these things fast enough. It took us a decade to do a lot of the things we had to do."

In presenting the challenge of change to his people, Welch does not pretend to be a prophet. He works on general feelings about the dominant trends of the times. His reading of the trends is based on observation and personal experience. For example, he reckoned in the late 1990s that "my job is three times as fast as it was." Compared to 1980, in his view, the activity and pace in the CEO's role make it hardly even the same game.

One crucial factor in this continuing acceleration is that "information's going to be everywhere." Typically, Welch reacted more rapidly than most leaders of established companies to the advent of the internet. GE led the way in setting up a corporationwide website through which the purchase of goods and services could be centralized, with potential savings in the billions. As a supplier, you either tendered via the website, or you waved goodbye to GE.

But Welch realizes that the internet is a sea change. Its threat and opportunity go far deeper than improvement, however rewarding, in existing processes. What about the brand new? Long before the dot.com companies were born, established competitors had almost universally shown themselves incapable of resisting the challenge of new disruptive technologies – of which the net is an extreme example. Any GE business, Welch reckoned, might be disrupted by someone who had a new way of serving customers that left GE behind. His reaction was pure Welch: disrupt yourself rather than be disrupted.

Destroyyourbusiness.com

In 1999, he ordered every division to select an e-commerce leader: they were to launch "destroyyourbusiness.com," an operation that would seek to pre-empt disruptive moves by outsiders. The e-leaders placed in charge of the dot.com attackers had to be well versed in the internet and possess disruptive temperaments. Welch was determined to see GE win a large share of the e-commerce pie, and he used "e-briefs" on the internet to make his intentions clear.

"I don't know what the world's going to be; all I know is it's going to be nothing like it is today. It's going to be faster."
Control Your Destiny or Someone Else Will

For all his awareness of the internet problem, Welch declared that the destroyers would not be rewarded with separate equity linked to their dot.com ventures. This meant that GE risked losing the brightest and best to start-ups that could make them multimillionaires overnight. Having succeeded so long (and so greatly) with integrated diversity, Welch was deeply unwilling to disintegrate his creation. He was prepared to reward people for performance, but the team came first: in Welch's GE even the top 30 Corporate Executive Council members would not last long "if they're not team players."

The ultimate resolution of this particular dilemma, however, must rest with his successor. In 2000, his last year, Welch simply lacked the time to demonstrate that GE, unlike many past giants, could win the competitive wars with a new, disruptive technology or marketing approach. To some extent, GE could learn to win by acquisition. For instance, in 1999 the company bought xoom.com, a direct marketing website of phenomenal growth (616 percent in a single year) that was fed into NBC and without question brought with it a wholly different culture.

No central strategy

How would such injections affect the immensely strong culture of GE? The enormous impact of the world wide web, with the first website opened as late as 1993, amply confirms two of Welch's main tenets. First, change is not predictable. Second, it cannot be controlled. These two governing ideas, which reflect Welch's lifetime in a highly diversified corporation, have led him to take a wholly pragmatic approach to cultural change and corporate strategy – which must go hand in hand.

As early as December 1981, he told a business audience that "We have all learned... that it is impossible to forecast with any precision," and that "It just doesn't make sense for neatness' sake to shoehorn these initiatives into an all-inclusive, all-GE central strategy." Rather, Welch put his faith in "a central idea – a simple core concept that will guide General Electric... and govern our diverse plans and strategies." He thought that in the slow-growth environment of the 1980s, the winners would insist on being "the number one or number two leanest, lowest cost, worldwide producers of quality and services or those who have a clear technological edge, a clear advantage in a market niche." He cited business guru Peter Drucker's famous "very tough question:"

> "'If you weren't already in the business, would you enter it today?' And if the answer is no... (there is) a second difficult question: 'What are you going to do about it?'"

United responses to change

Welch has enormous respect for Drucker, whom he has often consulted: but his favorite management writer, significantly enough, is a soldier – Helmuth von Moltke, once military adviser to the Ottoman Empire. Von Moltke argued that "strategy was not a lengthy action plan, but rather the evolution of a central idea through continually changing circumstances." Being number one or number two was a tangible central idea: but Welch surrounded it with intangible central values, "unifying dominant themes that, because of GE's common culture, will become second nature in the organization." In the face of change, Welch proposed that GE should embrace three specific themes:

- Reality: getting the organization and the groups of people within it to see the world the way it is, and not as they would wish or hope to see it.
- Quality/excellence: creating an atmosphere where every individual in the organization strives to be proud of every product and service that it provides.
- The human element: creating an innovative atmosphere where people are confident that how far and how fast they move is constrained only by the limits of their creativity and drive and by their standards of personal excellence.

But there is a fourth, equally important theme: Welch's belief that these "soft values" truly can become "second nature in the organization." To him, it is feasible to "permeate every mind in this company." He talks elsewhere (see p. 49) of "changing the fundamental DNA of the company." In fact, GE's own experience under this most enthusiastic of management hot gospelers – who has often expressed disappointment with the limited degree to which minds in GE have been permeated – demonstrates that cultural change has important limits.

Educating the organization

Limits to cultural change are established by differences in individual makeup and by different interactions among individuals in groups. This kaleidoscopic pattern changes over time, but usually the change is slow. The pattern was severely and sharply disturbed by Welch:

> "For a long time our actions muddied communications. We were taking out lots of people. We were taking out layers of management. We were selling off businesses. We were impacting people's lives."

As that passage indicates, Welch may be a hyperactive leader but he is not a hyperactive change manager. Rather, he recognizes that one of the greatest mistakes in change management is to pursue too many initiatives for too short a time – initiatives that are very often abandoned well before the objectives are achieved. "If you have an idea *du jour*," he says, "you're dead."

The role of leaders is to drive home the themes that matter, to expand the reach of their communication, refine it, get better at it. In GE's case, says Welch:

> "... it began to snowball. If you have a simple, consistent message, and you keep on repeating it, eventually that's what happens. Simplicity, consistency, and repetition – that's how you get through. It's a steady continuum that finally reaches a critical mass."

Boundarylessness

The final theme of Welch's reign, a preoccupation that grew more and more insistent over the 1990s, was "boundarylessness" – a "big, big idea." Hard to describe, and harder still to put into action, the boundaryless ideal arises when somebody "knows where I stand. I know where he stands. We don't always agree – but we trust each other." Welch hammers home the need for an open, trusting sharing of ideas, a willingness to listen and debate, and a determination to take the best ideas and act on them. As Noel M. Tichy and Stratford Sherman reported in *Control Your Destiny or Someone Else Will*, Welch said in 1992: "If this company is to achieve its goals, we've all got to become boundaryless. Boundaries are crazy."

He regards trades unions, with whom his relations, often uneasy, have nevertheless been productive, as just another boundary. Managers have to reach across that boundary, just as they need to reach across the boundaries separating them from customers and suppliers, and from colleagues overseas and at home. With boundarylessness, as with his other key ideas, Welch embarked on a long road of indoctrination:

> "... we've got to keep repeating it, reinforcing it, rewarding it, living it, letting everybody know all the time that when they're doing things right, it's because their behavior is boundaryless."

It is unlikely that the ideal of boundarylessness became second nature inside GE by the end of 2000. The difficulty is that drawing bounds, and refusing to cross them, is also natural. Top management thus has an additional educational role – and, in fact, Welch's GE has often been praised as a true "learning company," an organization that builds collective and individual knowledge.

The thinking company

Welch places equal emphasis, though, on the "thinking company," whose capital is ideas and which exploits these intellectual assets by debate and by change. He seeks "the antithesis of blind obedience." Within a context of strong financial and other disciplines, people must develop enough self-confidence to express opposing views, get all

"Companies need overarching themes to create change. If it's just somebody pushing a gimmick or a program, without an overarching theme, you can't get through the wall."
Control Your Destiny or Someone Else Will

the facts on the table, and respect differing opinions. "It is our preferred mode of learning; it's how we form balanced judgements. We value the participation, involvement, and conviction this approach breeds."

The acme of the thinking, changing company is seen at the sessions in "The Pit," the large amphitheater at Crotonville. Welch thinks that people feel comfortable in this setting: "Everyone's close together. The people asking questions are looking down at the speaker. Somehow that opens up the questioning." That helps to establish the facts. Welch believes that bright people, when confronted with the same facts, in an atmosphere of openness and candor, will come up with the same answers:

> "This may not be true in religion and philosophy and a lot of other things, but in business you're dealing with a fairly quantitative process. It's concrete. It's simple. This is not rocket scientist work. If we all have the same information, we'll all come to roughly the same conclusions."

Faster responses

As the 1980s ended, however, Welch was feeling increasingly frustrated. No matter how hard he pressed the case for openness, candor, and change, they were not being achieved in the businesses. He needed these and other attributes to achieve his growth targets. Flying back by helicopter from GE's Crotonville management center in September 1988, Welch discussed this software issue with its then director, James Baughman. How could the open exchange of ideas at Crotonville be transferred into the businesses? A week later Baughman came up with an answer: Work-Out (see p. 43). In January 1989 – four

Architect of Work-Out
James Baughman, as director of Crotonville, designed the Work-Out procedure for Welch, providing a means by which employees could suggest ways to improve working processes and practices.

months after the chopper trip – the 500 top operating managers learned that the plan was already being enacted.

Fast responses are critical to Welch's philosophy. He notes that many businesses wait to act and tolerate long lead-times – not just for product development, but for corporate change. Managements often allow trading to deteriorate for years before trying to institute reform. They may pay lip service to change, but in reality they fear and distrust a process that by definition threatens the status quo and their managerial control. Welch has this to say:

> "The old organization was built on control, but the world has changed. The world is moving at such a pace that control has become a limitation. It slows you down. You've got to balance freedom with some control, but you've got to have more freedom than you ever dreamed of."

His genius lies not only in recognizing this truth, but in forcing through radical changes when GE was riding high, when the case for change was in his mind, rather than in the marketplace or in the minds of his managers.

Ideas into action

- Make business managers lead by taking total responsibility for their units.
- To change people's mind-sets, first seek to change their results.
- See the internet challenge through the eyes of a hungry competitor.
- Ask, "If I was not in the business already, would I enter it today?" If not, leave.
- Introduce the soft values that you want and make them become second nature in the organization.
- Never fall into the trap of having a constantly changing "idea *du jour.*"
- Press for a faster speed of response as the key to competitive advantage.

Breaking bounds

Welch's bid to make GE a boundaryless organization itself has no frontiers. Whether a boundary is inside or outside the company, it limits performance. Individuals unwittingly set their own bounds, limiting what they achieve. Challenge all barriers and seek to tear them down. And set stretch targets for your company and for yourself.

Examining the boundaries

When Welch took over GE, the company structure included nine layers of management, from the CEO to the shop floor, each forming a boundary. Welch took out whole layers, but delayering affects only vertical boundaries: there are two other types.

The Three Types of Boundary		
1 Vertical The hierarchical steps that separate different layers of management.	**2 Horizontal** The barriers between different functions, departments, country units, operating units.	**3 External** The frontiers between the business and its suppliers, customers, and competitors.

Breaking down internal barriers

The fewer internal borders there are to cross, the better for the overall efficiency of your company. Tackle vertical and horizontal barriers by implementing the following practices:

- Scrap inhibitions about crossing a layer – encourage managers to talk to the subordinates of other managers, and *vice versa.*
- Use development programs and task forces to mix different vertical levels in a nonhierarchical setting.
- Use cross-functional, interdepartmental teams to break down horizontal boundaries.
- Ask people who interrelate with other areas of the company to provide assessments of the service they receive; link rewards to the ratings given.
- Mingle purposefully, positively, and often.
- Encourage people to visit others from whom they can learn.

Breaking down external barriers

The most dramatic moves towards boundarylessness are external, and not confined to the inner workings of a company. To optimize your business you must optimize the whole business system by bringing in the key outsiders: suppliers and customers.

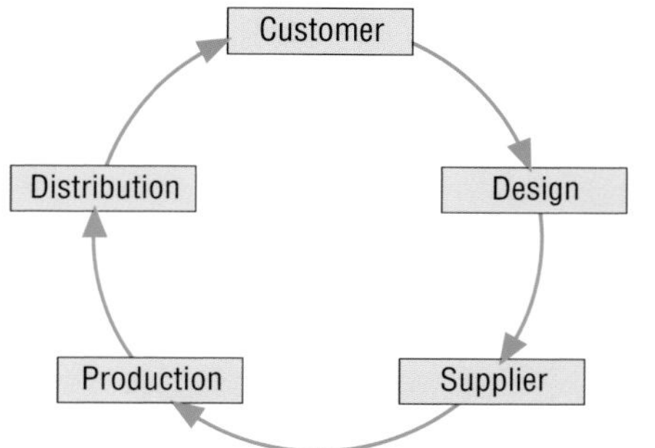

The business system

Remove barriers and strengthen links between each element in the business system to achieve improved company performance and greater satisfaction.

Strengthening links

Encourage the fall of barriers between the company and the outside world. Go to see customers and find out what improvements you can make for their benefit, and implement findings wherever possible. Work with suppliers to reform the business system to achieve shared gains. Form alliances, even with competitors, to take advantage of any complementary strengths. Then take the following systematic steps with your new "allies":

- Customers: involve in product development, encourage self-service, and obtain and act on feedback.
- Distributors: integrate with supply, and turn into inventory holder – even subcontractor.
- Producers: link production to outside suppliers, distributors, and customers; make to order.
- Suppliers (external): link to production/distribution, supplying daily, just in time.
- Design staff: involve suppliers and customers, to build in value, quality, and superior performance.

Ask yourself: "Am I helping my colleagues, customers, and suppliers to get the best from me?" and "Am I working to get the best from them?" Make sure you get the right answers.

1 Stretching other people

What you measure in management generally governs what you get. So if you set goals below the capability of a person or an organization, underperformance is likely to result. Transcend the aims that people believe feasible, and the opposite may well happen.

Establishing realistic targets

Jack Welch's concept of stretch starts with producing realistic targets – for profitability, for instance, or new product introductions. Such targets must pass the following three criteria:

- They are "do-able."
- They are reasonable.
- They are within the organization's or individual's capabilities.

Set your own targets for your part of the business, making sure they fulfill these three criteria. These realistic targets are indispensable since they enable you to set a baseline, to authorize expenditure, and to apply comparisons that help to monitor trends and spotlight problem areas.

Setting stretch targets

Now take your realistic targets and attach a much higher goal – a stretch target – to each one. These goals may "at the outset seem to require superhuman efforts to achieve," says Welch, but "by reaching for what appears to be impossible, we often actually do the impossible; and even when we don't quite make it, we inevitably wind up doing much better than we would have done."

Achieving the Impossible

Welch imposed on one of his managers a daunting stretch target to improve productivity: the impossible-seeming goal was achieved in four years.

When Jack Welch found that rival makers of CT-scanners and X-ray machines were getting 50,000 scans per tube, against GE's 25,000, he demanded a quadrupling of tube life. Confronted with this "impossible" target, the division eventually accomplished the superhuman. Tubes finally appeared that lasted for 150,000–200,000 scans. The new methods required also provided other very valuable benefits.

Work out your stretch targets every bit as carefully as your realistic targets. If, for example, your stretch target is to double the budgeted level of sales, ask yourself:

- What does that imply for revenue per salesperson, per customer, and per product?
- What are the consequences for production and distribution – can the commitment be met?

Searching out sin

Without high aims, you will not achieve extraordinary results. Most companies are all too satisfied with run-of-the-mill performance, complacent in the assumption that their achievement is superior. One of Welch's greatest lessons is that success always conceals failure. However good the organization is, it is certain to be guilty of many sins – of omission and commission.

Left unconfessed and uncured, these sins can undermine the strongest companies. The only safe course is to be your own Grand Inquisitor, constantly probing for points of weakness and setting new stretch targets. If you can cut costs, raise productivity, and sharpen competitive edge when business is good, the payoff is far greater than if you wait for bad results to stimulate action.

Do not make the inquisition negative. Challenge your company with six key questions that will raise everyone's sights and encourage people to become positive inquisitors themselves.

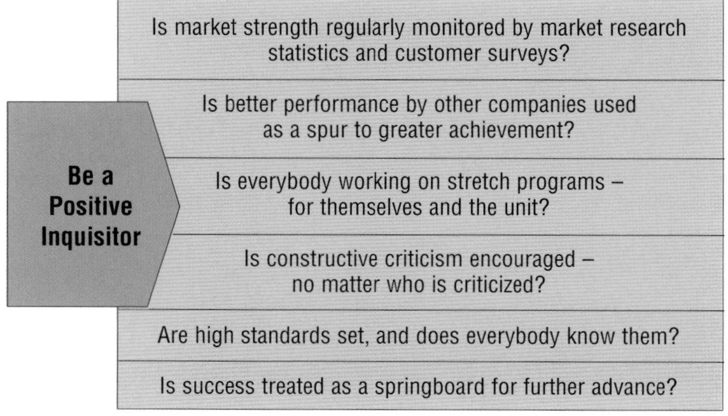

2 Stretching yourself

Apply the concept of stretch to your own career and you will find that, as with company stretch targets, the higher you aim, the more you are likely to achieve. Back up your lofty aims with ambitious self-development to ensure complete success.

Reaching the summit

When Jack Welch named his personal objective – to be Chief Executive of GE – eight years of effort lay ahead before he reached the top. He was still the youngest CEO in the company's history. Study the steps of his 21-year climb listed below and write down your own hoped-for progression. How high do you want to go? What time must you allow? What preparations must you make?

Jack Welch's Road to the Top	
Years with firm	**Progress to the summit**
+21	Chief executive (run whole organization)
+19	Challenge for top (named vice-chairman)
+17	Head several businesses (run business sector)
+13	Get corporate position (run business group)
+8	General manager (run plastics business)
+3	Take charge (head chemical development)
+0	Use expertise (develop plastics)
0	Learn expertise (chemical engineering)

Developing motivation

You may not share Welch's level of ambition. Few people do. But most people operate with a view of their potential that significantly limits that potential.

Every manager knows cases of failed and fired employees who, transferred to another business, have far exceeded their previous performance. The explanation is not only that they moved from a demotivating environment to one where their talent was given a real chance. Their personal motivation was also spurred by the impact of dismissal and the need to make good in a new job. Develop that motivation in yourself by reaching for the skies.

Aiming high

Do not be satisfied with the best you can do now and the best you think you can do. Be bold, like Welch, and strike out for the highest promotions and achievements that may be within your reach. Appoint yourself as your own career manager, and approach the task as you would an important project for the organization.

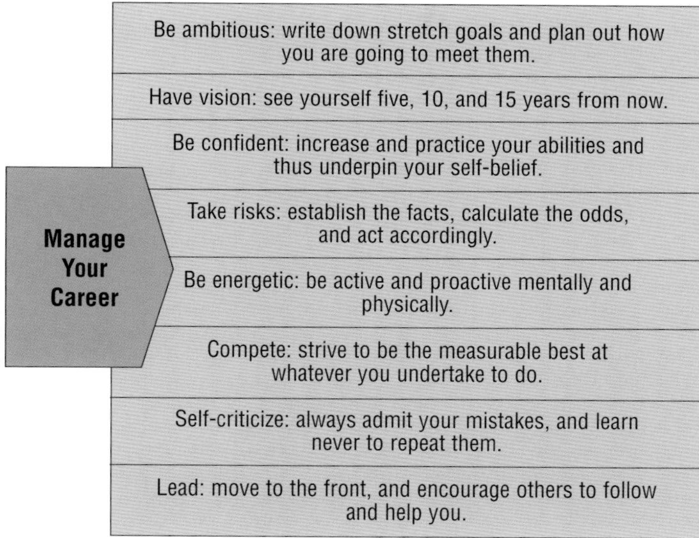

Looking ahead

Taking the long view in your career will concentrate your mind on what you need to do in preparation for the next promotion. It is a test of your self-confidence. Nobody will have confidence in you unless you have confidence in yourself.

As a relative junior, Welch would introduce his requests for capital with an account of his successful use of previous allocations. That is not bragging. It is being objective about what you can do or have done. The young Welch also took the initiative energetically, taking the lead in seizing his plastics opportunities.

You will not always win the competition, or always be the best. But if you do not try, losing will become a self-fulfilling prophecy. Welch made his own and his company's luck. You can do the same.

charles HANDY

Biography

Charles Handy was born in 1932 in Kildare, Ireland, to an ecclesiastical family: his father was the local archdeacon. Although his career has largely revolved around business management, Handy has also been influenced by his religious upbringing and beliefs. There is a discernible and important moral vein in his writings on management and organizations.

The works that won him an international reputation were founded on a not especially successful career in business. After leaving Oriel College, Oxford, with a first-class honors degree in "Greats," Handy crossed the Atlantic to Boston, to study at the Massachusetts Institute of Technology's Sloan School of Management. On his return from the US, Handy worked for two mighty multinationals: Royal Dutch Shell (in the marketing and personnel divisions) and the Anglo-American Corporation, the mining conglomerate (as an economist). He was drawn toward the academic world, however, joining the brand-new London Business School in 1967. He become a professor in 1972 and held his chair until 1994.

Even though, by his own account, he found his career at Shell stultifying, Handy stayed for the best part of a decade, working as a marketing executive at home and abroad. The experiences at the oil company, however disappointing, provided plenty of material for his later writings. His stint with the Anglo-American Corporation was much briefer – a year or so – and generated less grist for what was to become a highly productive mill. Starting with *Understanding Organizations*, published in 1976, Handy had written 10 books by 1995, when *Beyond Certainty* appeared.

His first book, while mainly descriptive, contained some original ideas, which were then fully developed in *Gods of Management*, published in 1978. This was a characteristic Handy title, ambiguous and allusive. The titles of *The Empty Raincoat* (1994) and *Waiting for the Mountain to Move* (1995) likewise force the browser to guess at what lies within. The content, however, is never ambiguous, even though it typically mixes management theory, real-life anecdotes, sociological insights, moral observations, and ethical conclusions. The mix has been very attractive to readers on both sides of the Atlantic, and most of Handy's books are still in print.

Because of his combined interest in business management and religion, Handy was a natural choice for the post of warden of St. George's House at Windsor Castle in England. The purpose of this private study and conference center, where Handy served as warden from 1977 to 1981, is to bridge the gap between God and mammon by concentrating on social ethics and values. Handy also broadcasts regularly on *Thought for the Day*, BBC Radio 4's religious and philosophical spot on the *Today* program, and he has published a collection of those thoughts.

His views on management are always firmly rooted in reason, experience (his own and that of others), and study. In 1987, Handy was asked to conduct a comprehensive examination of management development in the US, Japan, Britain, and Europe. This added still more to the profound store of knowledge that was especially evident in *Understanding Organizations*. His work as an executive and academic has also been influenced by a considerable amount of consulting work for a wide range of organizations. Many of these are nonprofit operations – in education, health, government, and the voluntary sector.

As Handy developed his ideas on the nature and behavior of organizations, all these various influences came into play, together with original ideas on human life and needs. Unlike many management writers, he shows real concern for the health of society and the individual. This concern runs at least as deep as his interest in improving the effectiveness of business. Not surprisingly, he is himself a dedicated individualist; he likes to be described as an "independent" writer, teacher, and broadcaster.

Practicing what he preaches

Handy does not just generate ideas: he lives them. He has used his own life as a test bed for his prophetic ideas on the new ways of organizing a satisfying balance of work and recreation, with his wife Elizabeth acting as a full partner in the enterprise. They married in 1962 and have a son and daughter. Moving between three homes, in London, Norfolk in England, and Chianti in Italy, they lead a highly organized life in which both can pursue their work: Liz Handy is a portrait photographer, and Handy takes pains to ensure that her work is allotted adequate time.

His own work fits the pattern of the "portfolio career," a growing phenomenon, which he was the first to describe. Treating his various occupations as you might stocks in a portfolio, Handy seeks to optimize the return, not only in financial rewards, but in personal satisfaction and contribution to society. In this, Handy is only practicing what he preaches, which is not always true of prophets – and almost became untrue of him. "I was writing books saying people should get the hell out of organizations at the age of 50," he told *The New York Times*, "and I realized I was 49 and in an organization."

So Handy left St. George's House and started filling his self-employed portfolio. From 1986 to 1988 that included chairing Britain's Royal Society for the Encouragement of Arts, Manufacture, and Commerce. But otherwise he has avoided institutions as his life follows the S-shaped "Sigmoid Curve" (see p. 73), which he thinks is basic to all human life, including that of organizations. Even his marriage has tested this theory. Handy believes that marriages break down because couples wait until "point B" on the downward swing of the Curve before acting:

Working partnership
Charles and Elizabeth Handy live what Handy has termed "a portfolio life," balancing their skills and their time to make the most of their independent careers.

"Too often, couples cling on to their old habits and contracts for too long.... They find other partners. On the other hand, I sometimes like to say, teasingly, that I am on my second marriage – but with the same partner, which makes it less expensive.... I would not deny, however, that [it] was difficult as we struggled to keep what was best in our past while we experimented with the new."

The result of their experiments is a most remarkable lifestyle. "We divided our work roles together," he says, "and then we divided up our time in a very organized way." As his son Scott describes it: "My parents spend 100 days a year working, 100 writing, 100 for charity and 65 on vacation. Six months of the year, my mother decides where they are going to be, and six months of the year, he decides – I think they've been apart for nine days of their marriage."

Handy adds that "having divided up our work roles, our time, and our places, we also have different categories of work that we devote specific time to" – that is, Handy will only accept public engagements that take place during the winter months, while his wife takes on photographic jobs only from March to October. *The New York Times* commented that Handy sounds as if he is talking about "a new management project, not a marriage." But the marriage is very much a working arrangement. Liz Handy "accompanies her husband on trips, handles his calendar, fields his calls, negotiates his contracts, and decides whom it is worthwhile for him to see."

Handy is convinced that other people will have to learn the art of self-management. "We'll all leave organizations earlier, and we're all likely to have 30 years on our own now. So I believe that from the age of 50 onward, every man and woman will have to learn to manage their own life."

As it happens, Handy's own self-management skills do not include making money. When his wife took charge of that aspect, their financial situation improved markedly, although in 1997 Handy was happy to limit himself to an annual income of $75,000 for the rest of his life. That equals only two or three lecture fees for gurus of no greater international standing than Handy. But earning less money gives Handy more time for his nonworking interests: he likes to go to the theater, to cook, and to travel. He stresses that his lifestyle "is a deal for your 50s and older," which has to be planned for and treated as seriously as employment.

Social philosopher

But however much Handy talks about a portfolio career, he really has only one central job: as a social philosopher who takes an exceptionally broad view of society, embracing business management as well as religion, corporate man as well as the private citizen. He philosophizes in books, lectures, broadcasts, articles, and so on, but his ideas and his life form a seamless whole. Both the philosophy and the lifestyle, moreover, stem not just from Handy's reasoning, but his personality.

His antiauthoritarian positions, for example, reflect the fact that he is no authoritarian himself. As Scott Handy explains: "My mother allowed my father to be the philosopher king by being the rigorous chief of staff... there's something naughty about my father, who allows himself the freedom to be so unauthoritarian." Scott adds, however, that this refusal to be a male authority figure meant that "I had to decide for myself." That must be greatly to Handy's satisfaction, for freedom of choice, and acting on that freedom, are the backbone of his teachings.

The understanding of management

In the mid-1970s, half a dozen years into his career as a management teacher, Charles Handy sat down to write his first book, titled *Understanding Organizations*. It immediately filled a real gap in the market.

In Handy's own words: "there were few books published on management or organizations, and almost none in Britain." Moreover, his book was written, not for academics, but for practicing managers – people who at that time tended to think that their jobs revolved around nothing but commonsense and natural ability.

The gap was defined by Handy's own famous saying that only three occupations in Britain required no qualifications or training. Sadly, they were of the greatest importance: parent, politician, and manager. "Society suffered much," he later remarked, "when the school of hard knocks was the only school for its managers." Handy did not want to preach or teach "scientific management," with its study of strategy, structures, and systems. He wanted to encourage leaders to "understand the needs and motivations" of those they led, not in inanimate organizations, but in living, animated human communities.

In the new millennium, Handy's original criticism hardly applies. As he records: "There were two MBA programs in Britain when I started to write the book; there are now over 200." For that educational explosion, Handy can claim significant credit. His book systematically went through the various concepts of organization and management that other writers had developed, examined the application of the concepts, and told readers where they could continue their studies. His own ideas naturally permeated the book, but it was primarily a textbook, although written with unusual lucidity, flow, and charm. It was certainly not Handy's own manifesto.

Nonetheless, *Understanding Organizations*, which was published in 1976, laid the foundations for the highly original works that were to follow. These are in a sense rebuttals of most of the writings that appeared during the long boom in management lore.

"If we could understand... the ways in which individuals were motivated we could influence them by changing the components of that motivation process."
Understanding Organizations

Handy found the bookstores "crammed with volumes of varying size and quality, directed at the practicing executive, full of the latest nostrums or gimmicks." He contends that witch-doctoring is no good substitute for "old-fashioned commonsense." Whatever managers are taught much can only be learned in the school of experience.

Handy confidently asserted in 1998 that this explained why his book was still "essential reading for anyone interested in organizations and how to make them work better." His "guidebook," as he called it, was "larded... with anecdotes and examples from my own and others' experience." The larding (embellishing) emphasized that useful theory must be grounded in reality. But Handy also wanted to make his book pleasurable to read, "even fun at times." In that way, the book defined not only Handy's area of contribution, but his distinctive, accessible, and diverting style.

1

Sorting out the cultures

How most of the world's large organizations are structured like an ancient Greek temple • Understanding the way organizations work • **The four remedies that combat role stress** • Eight ways in which management groups can go wrong • **Matching the organization's structure to its culture** • Distinguishing the four types of culture – power, role, task, and individual • **Why the chosen responses of most organizations will not work in future** • The changing patterns of work and organizations

Charles Handy's iconoclastic and pathfinding theories all developed out of his first book, *Understanding Organizations*, which was published in 1976. Neither challenging nor heretical, it is a work of scholarship, a *tour de force*, but not recognizably the work of the free-thinking radical that Handy was to become only a couple of years after that first publication. It is as if he needed to immerse himself in the conventions of organizations and in the writings of other management gurus before reaching the conclusion that both organizations and their existing theorists were inadequate.

This almost encyclopedic exercise was to reach its climax in the development of a powerful, unscientific theory about the role of organizational cultures and the clash between the different varieties. But the book began very differently, with Handy hoping to find "laws governing the behavior of people and of organizations as sure and as immutable as the laws of physical sciences." He discovered, to his initial "dismay and disillusionment," that his subject had nothing to do with predictive certainty.

Too many variables, he discovered, hinge on any one organizational situation. And then there is "the inherent ability of the human being to override many of the influences on his behavior." Understanding organizations is still feasible, though, because:

- Most of the variables remain constant most of the time.
- Most individuals do not override the influencing factors most of the time.
- Most interpretations will be valid for the future as well as the past.
- Prediction tends to improve as the study turns from individuals to collections of individuals.

In the book, Handy describes no less than seven main schools of organizational thought, starting with "scientific management," fathered by the Quaker engineer Frederick Winslow Taylor (1856–1915). Then there was the school that looked at organizations in terms of human relations, and five others that concentrated respectively on bureaucracy, power, technology, systems, and institutions. None of them "proved to be wholly wrong" in their thinking, but none proved to be wholly right, either. So Handy set out to compile a "sort of personal anthology," which he intended to be of practical use to practicing managers.

Frederick Taylor
Taylor was the inspiration behind the 1880s' school of "scientific management." Radical for the time, it prescribed how businesses should be run, and advocated such procedures as planning ahead.

Looking at motivation

Achieving such a practical anthology was harder than it sounds. For instance, when Handy starts off looking at motivation, the book becomes rather dense without meeting Handy's hope "that motivation theories would reveal to me the true purpose of my life and my *raison d'être*." Instead, the theorists treated man as a semi-conscious mechanism, responding to a variety of impulses in a partly predictable way. The description, Handy admitted, was apt for many of his colleagues at work, but as for himself: "This wasn't me, I cried."

Motivation, true, was useful in understanding "how most individuals behaved, *given who they were*" [his italics]. But how does that "who" get created? Handy came to the conclusion that no single factor will do as an answer. Several factors are involved:

- The self-concept of the individual
- One's role in the organization
- The psychological contract between the individual and others in the organization
- One's perceptions of the situation

Handy found this motivational analysis inadequate. Unimpressed, he concluded: "We need to go much further to understand the behavior of people in organizations." But looking at the roles that people played inside organizations, and the interaction between those roles, proved a more fertile field. As he moves meticulously through the literature dealing with this subject, Handy shows how role problems, such as ambiguity, conflict, overload, and underload, produce individual tension, low morale, and poor communications.

Role stress is inherent in organizations, and can be either unhealthy or healthy. Role theory, Handy felt, provides one way of looking at stress, at individuals under stress, and at the situations that cause it. He suggested four remedies:

- Compartmentalize roles appropriately, particularly between work and family (that is, do not involve the wife in her husband's work, or, presumably, vice versa).
- Prepare for role transition (pay more attention to ways of learning a new role).
- Encourage a second career as a way out of the role underload of the sideways-shunted executive.
- Remember that many of the problems that exist in organizations have arisen from role strain, misconceptions about role, role underload, or bad communications because of false role expectations.

The leading role

Presumably the least underloaded and the most important of all the roles is "leader." In Handy's later work, leadership achieves (properly enough) a leading role in both senses. But, in the 1970s, he was ambivalent: "Leadership as a topic has rather a dated air about it." Two decades later, the topic is right back in fashion, but thinkers are no nearer to a satisfactory definition than Handy was in *Understanding Organizations*. There he wrote that "the role of a leader is a complex one, riddled with ambiguity, incompatibility, and conflict."

That sounds most unpromising. Handy devoted a section to the requirements of leadership, but its content is a good deal less than dynamic: for example, the leader should "be prepared to set moderately high standards for himself and his coworkers and to give and receive feedback on performance." Following on from that lame thought, Handy came perilously near to concluding that leadership was for all intents and purposes innate and unteachable, although the "individual and the organization can... build on what is already there."

This is plainly true of all human development, not just leadership. His tentative approach to this issue meant that Handy did not discuss to any great extent the role, often crucial, of the dominant individual in exercising power and influence. Charisma, he thought, resides not so much in the person as in the position. Handy saw that power, too, rested with position, and thus, to an extent, swung the balance of influence toward authoritarianism.

"Participative management," he observed, "implies expert power sources, influence by persuasion, and response by internalization. Great if it works." But generally it did not work: the likelihood of it happening amid "the hustle and bustle of organizational life" was low. Giving more control to subordinates, moreover, was a source of power that was "not obviously compatible with the emerging forms of the giant corporation, [nor] with the task requirements of most managerial roles in the organizations of today, or of tomorrow."

In view of Handy's later writing, that "or of tomorrow" seems inordinately pessimistic. He was at least equally unhappy about the prospects for management groups. With these, all too many things can go all too wrong:

- The task is inappropriate.
- The constraints are impossible.
- The group is badly led.
- It has inefficient procedures.

- It has the wrong people.
- It has too many people.
- It has too little power.
- It meets too infrequently.

If any one part is badly out of line, Handy concludes, the result will be either "an activation of negative power or a badly attended, noneffective group, wasting people, time, and space." Worse, "the chances of this happening are, in fact, very high. If 50 percent of managerial time is spent in groups, the cost of wasted time begins to look colossal, let alone the damage done by the use of negative power."

In the light of the latter, and still current, enthusiasm for group working, which Handy shares, this passage reads rather oddly. But Handy's pessimistic view of how organizations actually worked had not yet been succeeded by greater optimism about how they *might* work. Handy began to cross this line when he turned to the question of company culture. He concluded that the cultures of organizations rightly differ from each other, and that they are affected by a variety of factors, which in turn affect the diversity of structures and systems.

He argues that many organizational ills stem from the mismatches that exist between structures and cultures. This insight led Handy, more than in any other section of *Understanding Organizations*, to become what he termed "prescriptive." He tackled two crucial issues, those of differentiation and integration. Each organization needs to contain different cultures to cope with different types of activity: steady state (routine), innovation, crisis (the unexpected), and policy. "One culture," said Handy, "should not be allowed to swamp the organization." But the cultures have to work together.

Four types of culture

Handy concludes that for differentiation to succeed "there must be integration." He sets out seven "integrative devices," ranging from direct managerial supervision to "clustering" all the differences into one unit. But these issues proved less important in Handy's thought than he believed them to be at the time. In moving on, and moving far, his later books picked up on other themes, some of which had appeared almost incidentally in *Understanding Organizations*. One short section above all proved especially pregnant. It covers less than a dozen pages, the most original in the whole, long book, and defines four different types of organizational culture:

- The power culture
- The role culture
- The task culture
- The individual culture

The power culture "is frequently found in small entrepreneurial organizations, traditionally in the robber-baron companies of 19th-century America, occasionally in today's trade unions, and in some property, trading, and finance companies." The culture usually revolves around one dominant person.

The role culture is often stereotyped as bureaucracy. The structure for such a culture can be pictured as a Greek temple, with the pillars of the temple representing its functions or specialities. These pillars, which are strong in their own right, are the finance department, the purchasing department, the production facility, and so on. Their work, and the interaction between each of the pillars, is controlled by the following devices:

- Procedures for roles, such as job descriptions and authority definitions
- Procedures for communications, such as required sets of copies of memoranda
- Rules for settlement of disputes

As for the task culture, it could be seen not as a temple but as a net. The whole emphasis of this culture rests on getting the job done. It "seeks to bring together the appropriate resources, the right people at the right level of the organization, and to let them get on with it." The chosen members of the task force may include individuals who come from the fourth culture, that of idiosyncratic individualists. If there is a separate structure or organization for this last group, Handy noted, it can "exist only to serve and assist the individuals within it."

With these four cultures, Handy had found the germs of his first, great, original theme. Fully developed, it asserts that the cultures of organizations are crucial to their performance and that the dominant culture of traditional organizations is in the process of changing radically, not before time, in the face of irresistible pressures. By "culture," Handy meant that, like tribes and families, organizations have "their own ways of doing things, things that work for them and things that don't work."

Handy described four basic cultural patterns in these ways of working, and tentatively identified them with the Greek gods: Zeus (power), Apollo (role), Athena (task), and Dionysus (individual). For his next book, published in 1978, this metaphor took center stage and provided the title *Gods of Management*. Like his later, equally whimsical and obscure titles, this one had a strong point. In fact, the meaning is fundamental.

After completing *Understanding Organizations*, Handy became convinced that such understanding was impossible without the full comprehension of these four differing cultures. Moreover, culture was not the product of deliberate "scientific" management. Rather, organizational management was "more of a creative and political process, owing much to the prevailing culture and tradition in that place at that time." Enter the gods.

The dominance of Apollo

In *Gods of Management*, Handy expanded his definitions of four basic cultural patterns. An organization that follows Zeus, the all-powerful, capricious father of the gods, has a power culture and, accordingly, has its own father figure, the leader from whom all authority flows.

The culture is very different from that of Apollo, the god of reason, "for this culture works by logic and by rationality." The Apollonians, bowing to the deity of order, roles, and rules, vest authority in the system. Handy saw that their model – the role culture – had come to dominate nearly all the world's large organizations.

Athena, the warrior goddess, is best suited to preside over the task role. The people inside Athena's organizations, built around tasks, rather than roles, are problem solvers. They come together for a specific task, make up the rules as they go along, and disperse, proceeding to the next problem when the task is either completed or abandoned.

So far so good. It is easy to identify Handy's account of the gods with actual organizations: a multinational oil giant like Shell (Handy's former employer) with Apollo; any number of firms dominated by founding entrepreneurs with Zeus; advertising agencies with Athena.

Dionysus, "the god of the self-oriented individual, the first existentialist" is a more difficult case. His specialities – wine and song – at first sight have little to do with any organizations, except for cabarets, which are often, as it happens, in the thrall of a Zeus. Handy recognized this difficulty; in a book about organizations, he had identified a form of organizational culture that did not exist and could not exist, at least not in the same way as the others.

Zeus, Apollo, and Athena, in their very different styles, preside over organizations that in turn preside over their members. In Handy's Dionysian vision, the organization is dominated by individuals who are members only because they choose to be. This culture, Handy observes, "is something which causes shudders in any more usual organization or managers – precisely because of the lack of mandated control." However, managers will seldom need to shudder. Where will they ever meet Dionysus?:

> "One would not expect to find many such organizations around, certainly not in the business or industrial scene, where organizations, by their charters, have objectives that outlive and outgrow their employees."

The inclusion of the Dionysian nonorganization is, however, of vital importance to Handy's theory of organizations, which he calls "a Theory of Cultural

"The best way to run an efficient chocolate factory will not be the right way to run an architects' partnership, a primary school, or a construction site. Different cultures, and gods, are needed for different tasks."
Gods of Management

Propriety." This holds that what matters is getting the right culture in the right place for the right purpose, which all sounds quite bland and neutral; Handy even calls it a "low definition" theory, which "suggests rather then prescribes." In fact, Handy proceeded to develop the four gods idea toward a distinctly prescriptive end. The predominant form of organization, he plainly feels, is producing the wrong culture in the wrong place for the wrong purpose.

Organizations can only be righted, Handy argues, by admitting the cult of Dionysus into their office blocks and other places of work – like it or not. Handy is explicit about the topsy-turvy consequences. In "this fourth existential culture, the organization exists to help the individual achieve his purpose," not, as in the usual dispensation, the other way around. Handy is not thinking just of the need to allow a relatively few talented individuals their freedom: "the cult of Dionysus is growing and is no longer related to individual talent."

In some way, management needs to create a contradiction in terms: a Dionysian establishment, a disorganized organization. Handy is careful to avoid identifying himself as a prophet of this vision, but *Gods of Management* really does plead a cause. Like Luther railing at the Roman Catholic Church, Handy is protesting against what he sees as the mounting failure of the traditional organization:

> "... the chosen route to efficiency via concentration and specialization which resulted in the multilayered and multistructured organization has reached a dead end."

"No culture, or mix of cultures, is bad or wrong in itself, only inappropriate to its circumstances." *Gods of Management*

Diseconomies of scale

One of Handy's explanations for the failure of the traditional organization is familiar: scale means largeness, and "scale creates costs as well as economies," although, in normal circumstances, the economies outweigh the costs. Large organizations, as everybody knows, are less flexible, which offsets the strengths of their wider scope, although by no means entirely. But Handy does not rely on organizational economics to make his case against bigness: "more importantly, it runs counter to the cultural preferences of most of the people it needs to make it work."

What were these truly widespread ("most of the people") cultural longings? Handy was apparently contending that "most" people are Athenians or Dionysians by preference, yet he writes: "An Apollonian structure staffed by Athenians and Dionysians would be an expensive disaster." Whether or not that is true, the argument hinges on Handy's unsupported and unprovable view of human preferences. Those preferences explain why, in his calm but almost apocalyptic prophecy, "the chosen responses of most organizations are not going to work because they all seek to find ways of perpetuating the Apollonian dominance."

Do most people truly prefer either to work in dedicated, fluid groups, or as footloose, self-motivating individuals? Handy is here articulating the familiar refusal of the intellectual, whose work is almost always Athenian or Dionysian, to believe that mass-production workers, clerks, shop assistants, even middle managers, can enjoy their work. As thinking has become more important in relation to doing – brains conquering brawn – this intellectual revulsion has acquired greater relevance. But rules, roles, and order – the Apollonian characteristics – are by no means inimical to the human spirit or to human progress.

Changing work patterns

However, that does not stop Handy from arguing that Apollo's day is done, and adding a polite good riddance. His chapters "suggest," or rather forecast, that "the employment organization, centered around the works or the office," will give way to "a more contractual, dispersed, and federal organization." The potential consequences are greatly to Handy's liking:

- More small businesses, particularly in services
- More part-time work in all institutions
- More opportunity for more people to combine jobs with other interests in life
- More work located near to where people live

Handy thought that communities would perhaps become more complete when they ceased to be mere dormitories. Flexible working lives, built around several jobs rather than one, might become the norm rather than the exception. In other words, everybody's life in the future could be like Handy's own in the present. He might think that desirable, but the possible alternative is not. Handy feared that the old split between labor and owners or management might be replaced by a new split between "professionals and key staff, with job security and fringe benefits, and the secondary fringe of temporary labor, part-time help, and self-employment – free maybe, but often poor."

All of the above cautious predictions, the welcome and the unwelcome, have come to pass in varying degrees. But the hard fact remains that the world and national economies remain dominated by very large, structured organizations of the type Handy condemns to slow death. Many of these organizations have grown vastly larger (in everything except numbers employed). Unlike the dinosaurs, they have adapted to changing conditions. But Handy gives no timescale for their disappearance. What he does is make a full and fair case for abandoning Apollo, which was to be the next stage of his great theme.

Ideas into action

- Organize your business to fit its real-life circumstances, not some ideal model.
- Remember that many organizational problems stem from people's difficulties with their roles.
- Make sure you get the right culture in the right place for the right purpose.
- Do not let the "Apollonians," with their specified rules and roles, dominate the organization.
- Rely increasingly on "Athenians," task-force members who tackle specific projects.
- Make room for the "Dionysians," talented individuals who "do their own thing."
- Provide more opportunities for people to work part-time and near to their homes.

2

Balancing the organization

The growth of Dionysian individualism in organizations • How and when people revert to their favorite culture • **The three critical areas of management – thinking and learning, influencing and changing, motivating and rewarding** • Letting each part of the organization develop its own methods of coordination and control • **The waning of the employment society** • The danger of sabotage by the "organizational hijack" • **Why megacorporations are unmanageable and have to change**

The plural title of Handy's second book, *Gods of Management,* is slightly misleading; a single god of management would have given a sharper picture. Zeus organizations rise and fall with the founder/father's physical life cycle, and have to become more Apollonian to survive. Purely Athenian organizations are few and far between (and task forces can work perfectly well inside large, bureaucratic organizations, anyway). Dionysian organizations (or dis-organizations) can hardly be found anywhere. Apollo is the true god of management.

Handy's account of the supergod's creations is full of insight and deep understanding. His criticism, however, is heavily influenced by his experience of what he believes to be a Dionysian culture: the university. Its professionals possess several advantages over managers:

- Job security
- Agreed pay scales
- "Allocated territories or spheres of influence"
- Guarantees of independence
- Selection or promotion (usually) by groups of equals
- Uninterrupted power in their particular workplace
- Freedom from normal industrial disciplines

Dismissal, money, perks, and punishment are not in the hands of the academics' nominal leader, either. In this environment, command can operate only by consent, and not by delegated authority. This culture, says Handy, "causes shudders" in any more usual organization or manager "precisely because of the lack of mandated control." Here, however, he surely exaggerates both the freedom enjoyed by academics and the authoritarian power of business managers.

Large sets of jobs

Academics are subject to (and generally resent) all manner of constraints, while managers ultimately cannot manage effectively without the consent of the managed. The degree of freedom, of managers or managed, depends on highly variable circumstances and relationships. By Handy's own admission, his Greek gods never reign entirely alone. He asks: "Why would these three very different gods be required in the same organization?," and answers that organizations "are just large sets of jobs to be done." He divides these tasks into three types: steady state, development, and "asterisk."

The first type of task is programmable and predictable, and ideal for systems, routines, rules, and procedures. This is Apollo country and may represent 80 percent of all work. The second type requires the development of solutions to situations or problems: enter Athena and the Athenians. The third type, the "asterisk," is the realm of "personal intervention" and thus of both Zeus and Dionysus. Asterisks are "the exceptions, the occasions where the rulebook has failed, the emergencies where instinct, and speed, are likely to be better than logical analysis or creative problem-solving." Handy's prognosis is puzzling. Why cannot "creative problem-solving" be accomplished instinctively and fast? His conclusion is equally problematic:

> "Management happens when these activities are linked together in an appropriate fashion and given some common purpose or direction... The manager therefore has to embrace within himself all four cultures."

If that is the case, the separate significance of the cultures becomes unclear. If organizations have to possess all four cultures (otherwise they have no "management"), the four gods metaphor comes under strain. Handy meets this difficulty by saying that "the simultaneous call of four gods is too much for most people." So they revert to their favorite culture, "particularly when tired or stressed" (which seems a strange qualification). Thus, instead of organizations constraining the natural instincts of the people within – the generally accepted view – it is the people who constrain the organization.

In addition, Handy states that while organizations need more than one god, individuals are monotheists. To each his own god, which means his own different approach to the three "critical areas" of management:

- Thinking and learning
- Influencing and changing
- Motivating and rewarding

The individual preferences, Handy suggests, explain why organizations are the way they are. So, if Apollo dominates most organizations, it follows that their inhabitants must be predominantly Apollonians – not by force, but by nature. This is a contradiction that he never resolves.

Left-brained Apollonians

Apollonians are left-brain thinkers: logical, sequential, and analytical. They learn by acquiring more knowledge and skills through training, and they influence by exercising the authority that has been granted to them by the system. In this culture, change can come about only by altering roles and responsibilities, or changing the whole network of rules and procedures.

When it comes to motivation and reward, Apollonians are, once again, organization people to the core. They want the security of long-term organized employment, fringe benefits – especially pensions – and status. Handy does not actually mention graduated pay scales and bonuses, but these are presumably part of the picture, too. Plainly, such preferences determine a whole set of approved behaviors – ones that members of Handy's two other predominant organizational cultures find objectionable. Thus, "a Zeus will chafe under an Apollonian regime and forget to trust his intuition or his network." Then, "Apollonians will be seen as useful but boring" by Athenians. The Dionysians live, of course, on a different planet: "They like to be individuals, exceptions to all generalizations," but presumably not to this generalization itself.

In fact, Handy admits that it is difficult, and perhaps even mistaken, to describe Dionysus as a class at all. But he also points out that: "... the growth of individualism in organizations is becoming one of the central dilemmas of society... so the difficult must be attempted." This attempt is essential to support Handy's central idea, that "the healthy, happy organization is one that uses the appropriate methods and assumptions of influence in a particular culture." For the purposes of Handy's argument, that must certainly include Dionysians.

"Differences are necessary and good for organizational health. Monotheism, the pursuit of a single god, must be wrong for most organizations. But the choice and blend of gods cannot be haphazard. The wrong god in the wrong place means pain and inefficiency."
Gods of Management

Cultural coexistence

In this theory, the four cultures can coexist, and must, to create a wholly successful organization. In practice, the conflicts are deep-seated, and the dominant culture will use its dominance to resolve the issue to suit itself. Apollonian techniques and rules, writes Handy, "get ignored by Zeus figures unless it suits their proposers to use them." That is only one example of what happens if the mix of culture is "wrong, or badly balanced, or is not changed when change is needed." The result is "slack" or ineffectiveness – "the lurking cancer of organizations."

The chances of avoiding, or curing, the cancer by reaching an effective mix will be influenced by the size, life cycles, work patterns, and people in the organization. The larger the company, the more Apollo thrives. "The higher the rate of change, the larger the influence of Athena." The more that work flows and needs to be replicated, the stronger the Apollonian influence again. Handy's generalizations, however, need a great deal of qualification. People, he confesses, do not fit neatly into the above plan: "The tendencies of the 'people forces' are too varied to be summarized."

Whatever balance is achieved, anyway, will not last. "Organizations must respond continually to the environment" and their circumstances. Here, Handy cites the familiar cycle of growth. Once a business reaches a certain size, its founder (Zeus) must bring in professional managers (Apollonians). Then Athenians are required to develop the business further. So "management," as noted earlier, comes to mean the coordination of all three, and sometimes four, gods in one whole.

If there is "a mismatch between the demands of the work and the ways of managing it, success has bred inefficiency through cultural imbalance." The obvious answer is to change the balance. The catch is that "cultural change of the order needed in these situations is hard to bring about deliberately." Handy notes that organizations usually need to be frightened into major change by "imminent bankruptcy, a slump in sales, major strikes," and so on. Then new people, new directions, and new groupings alter the corporate constellation.

For that to be effective, "linkage between the cultures is essential," involving cultural tolerance, bridges, and a common language. If these fail, mixed-up management, and thus Handy's dreaded "slack," will occur. But, sadly, the different gods have different ways of coordination:

> "The first step, then, to effective linkage is to allow each part of the organization to develop its own appropriate methods of coordination and control and to tolerate differences between the cultures. Otherwise, one enters the 'spiral of distrust,' when what seems sensible coordination to you appears intrusive control to the other."

Building bridges

Handy stresses that cultural tolerance is not enough. The bridges that are also required take various forms. The first question is: "How many bridges and where?," to which Handy answers, the fewer the better. The second question is the method of bridging. Do you proceed by grouping, that is "putting all the functions... into one group with one objective," central information, or liaison ("the most tenuous form of bridge")? Handy obviously regards bridging as a messy affair; and his own account is appropriately messy itself. He finally boils it down to the swing of the pendulum between centralization and decentralization, and arrives at a gloomy conclusion:

> "The search for balance is never-ending. The swinging is inevitable, but, if done with cultural understanding, the pain is less."

Handy is similarly doubtful about efforts to create a common language: "Language… can be a barrier as much as a bridge." He points out that the vocabulary of organizations includes buzzwords and statistics, and that this vocabulary governs how people act: "The choice of what you count, what you compare with what, what you show to whom, has a clear effect on behavior." A Zeus culture's internal memo "will often read like a family letter"; Apollonian memos, however, bristle with initials. All these codes, writes Handy, are baffling to the outsider and may even be misunderstood inside the organization.

In sum, efforts to resolve the clash of cultures cannot rescue Apollo from a crucial dilemma. "The pressures to become more Apollonian, to make organizations tidier and more formal, are pressing and convincing, but so are the opposing pressures to recognize the individuals who make up these organizations and the need to give them more scope, more rights, and more independence."

According to Handy, these more individualistic pressures are inexorable outcomes of a richer and freer society. The end result will be "new kinds of organizations, new structures, and new ways of relating individuals to organizations" – in short, "an organizational revolution" that will affect not only the way that institutions are managed, but also the way in which people plan and live their lives. The prophet even dated his prophecy, suggesting that "the year 2000 will see the waning of the employment society as we have known it."

The root cause of this is the Apollonian paradox, which embodies "the tendency for Apollo to self-destruct. For just as size creates an internal need for Apollonian methods, so the very increase in that culture tends to make the total organization less responsive to its environment, less capable of changing, more dinosaurlike than ever – impressive but out of touch, and often out of control."

The symptoms of Apollonian breakdown are familiar, such as unfinished tasks, or nobody knowing how or by whom decisions are made. These organizations can be seen as "inevitably alienating places," which cannot tolerate much discretion, because it would violate their consistency.

> "One can redesign jobs to allow marginally greater discretion, introduce flexitime or autonomous groups, create work councils, but these all remain placebos..., to relieve the pain and alleviate the inherent incompatibility between man and this kind of work."

In Apollonian organizations, the individual is a *role* more than a *person*; initiative comes from above, not from within; and creativity is too often counted as disruption. This flies in the face not only of creativity but also of social and educational changes. "We are bringing up the young in a Dionysian tradition – individuality and personal expression – with Athenian overtones – groups, projects, and shared values. It is not surprising that they then reject the Apollonian culture when they begin to meet it at work."

Organizational hijack

This growing clash in Western society between organizational logic and the feelings of the individual leads to what Handy calls "the organizational hijack." This occurs when a "cog, or work group, a subassembly unit, a department" brings the overtightly designed organization to a halt by withholding labor, skill, or talent. Handy for some reason bleakly exaggerates this negative power:

"The monolithic overtight design of our organizations is an invitation to hijack and a major contributory cause to wage inflation. We have given what is called *negative power* in huge amounts to those people most likely to use it. Apollonian cultures come equipped with this time bomb, which will destroy the whole temple if it is not defused."

The megacorporations, Handy firmly concludes, have reached a crossroads. "The truth is that they have become, literally, unmanageable." He sees great consequences following as organizations structure and rebalance in the sheer need to stay alive:

"In 30 years' time, it may be as odd to talk of an employee as it already is to talk of servants." The new technologies need Dionysians and Athenians before Apollonians, and that means looser organizations whose key workers earn fees rather than wages. Even for the professional core, "employment will be only a phase of life," not much longer than the educational phase. Early retirement will become the norm for expensive top managers and specialists.

The displaced middle-aged will at best enter a world of small-time employment, of small Zeus figures, private Dionysians, and illicit (black market) Athenians. "Whether we like it or not, more and more of us are going to have to follow Zeus and Dionysus for more and more of our lives." Tightly regulated but loosely structured, the remaining organizations will be smaller and less dominating, "with less room in them and more selection about both entry and exit. Even the people in these smaller temples may no longer think of themselves as employees."

Sharing ownership

Handy argues that sheer size, and the consequences of it – complexity, inflexibility, and slack – are not the only causes of the flight from Apollo; another is the "reluctance to be owned by another, even if the pay is good." More and more requests for a share in the fruits of ownership will follow, notably through stock options. "It is an obvious way in which to marry labor and capital, with the result that top managers do not, in those firms, usually think of themselves as employees but as co-owners, partners, or as members of the organization."

Much of the above is highly debatable, including the last statement. Handy also foresaw a spread of ownership lower down the organization, and more cooperatives. The first has come to pass, thanks more to politicians than to internal pressures in corporations. The second has not happened. Nor has employee ownership (any more than employee representation, Euro-style) had much impact on the realities of management.

Handy concluded that if Dionysians could not get more ownership to replace their dependence on the Apollonian structure, "then the right to be consulted, personally, will become more pressing; in other words, organizations will have to get smaller until the individual, not his or her representative, can be heard at the top." Handy's thinking here is certainly wishful, as organizations have, in fact, been getting much larger, mostly through merger and acquisition, and through globalization.

His forecast that women will have a "proper influence" on organizations as these become more Athenian or Dionysian may also be a little wishful. Women will, true, fit easily into a more flexible world, in which credentials matter most, in which fewer people can define themselves, Apollo-style, as an ICI man or a Shell woman. Many people will have "flexilives," with multiple-job portfolios of work, as opposed to a single occupation; this, too, will suit many women well.

Problems of change

Flexilives also greatly suit Handy's philosophy. But he foresaw problems. What would people live on? How would they educate themselves? And how would they protect themselves? "Put rather starkly," Handy writes, "if we are working half the hours we used to and if we can look forward to twice as many years after employment, we ought to be putting aside, as a nation or as individuals, four times as much money for our retirement." But nothing like that is happening.

As for education, organizations now need to think of themselves as schools, encouraging their people to acquire the means of freedom, even if "they sometimes set themselves free before the organization would have wanted it." Protection for all will have to come from broader-based unions, otherwise, the latter will effectively signal their own decline. (Unions have indeed declined, but not for the reason Handy gives.)

Handy's predictions are a mixed bunch, both in their depth and in their accuracy. Their general thrust has certainly proved correct. But it is impossible to avoid the evidence of wishful thinking. Looking into his crystal ball, Handy too often saw what he wanted to happen, rather than what was truly likely to come about. In particular, organizations have proved much more resilient than he expected. He saw, it is true, one escape route, one way in which firms could cheat fate:

"Unusually, however, and fortunately, their destiny is in their own hands. Organizations may usually wither and decay instead of changing, but it does not have to be that way. This book is written in the hope that if more managers understand what is happening and what possibilities are open to them, then more will experiment with the future, instead of ignoring it."

The level of corporate experimentation, right into the 21st century, has remained low, however. Handy could be right in arguing that "our society may well decay as its organizations wither." But the day of withering seems to have been indefinitely postponed.

Ideas into action

- Adopt the academic work-style, where command operates only by consent.
- Prepare for the exceptions and emergencies where the rulebook will fail you.
- Combine the four basic types of culture to obtain lasting success.
- Continually review the organization and adjust it to the changing environment.
- Give individuals as much scope, as many rights, and as much independence as you can.
- Keep the organizational design flexible and loose to reduce vulnerability.
- Spread the fruits of ownership as widely in the organization as possible.

Organizing the culture

The culture of an organization – the way it works and what people believe about it – has a major effect on performance and overall results. Identify the dominant culture of your organization using the Handy-based questionnaires set out in this masterclass. Then seek to balance the cultural mix to obtain maximum effectiveness from everyone.

Understanding the cultures

Handy identified four cultural patterns, each characterized by a different Greek god. Most organizations are dominated by one of the three cultural patterns below. The fourth culture, ruled by Dionysus, is that of the individual, and its followers are not interested in organization or in organized cultures.

The Three Types of Organizational Culture		
1 Power ruled by Zeus	**2 Role** ruled by Apollo	**3 Task** ruled by Athena

Each Handy culture has its particular strengths. The personal power of Zeus dominance can work wonderfully well even in large companies – given the right father figure. But larger companies also require the order and control that Apollo's role culture embodies, with its emphasis on systems, routines, and predictability. In today's fast-moving environment both Zeus and Apollo find the Athenian task-oriented approach increasingly essential.

Finding the right balance

Achieving the right balance between Handy's gods involves countering the excesses that all three cultures can easily develop – respectively, autocracy, bureaucracy, and disintegration. A successful mix will also embrace individualistic Dionysus.

The combination of all four gods satisfies Handy's definition of good management. For this you must use Zeus to provide purpose and direction, Apollo to look after the steady-state needs, Athena to keep the organization moving forward, and Dionysus to supply the vital spark of creativity.

1 Identifying power

Handy compares the Zeus culture to a spider's web. All authority radiates outward from the center, and the closer managers are to that center, the more important they are.

Following Zeus

To discover if your organization is ruled by Zeus, answer Yes or No to the following propositions. Do they describe the organization's typical values, beliefs, and forms of behavior?

- A good boss is strong, decisive, firm but fair.
- A good subordinate is hardworking, loyal, resourceful, and trustworthy.
- A good member gives first priority to the personal demands of the boss.
- People who do well here are politically aware risk-takers.
- The organization treats individuals as people at the disposal of the bosses.
- People are controlled and influenced by rewards, punishments, or charisma.
- It is legitimate to control others if you have more power.
- Tasks are assigned here on the personal say-so of the bosses.
- Competition is for personal power and advantage.

Analysis

- Nine "Yes" answers: a pure power culture, dominated by a Zeus figure or figures.
- Nine "Nos": the culture is remarkably free of bossism.
- Three or fewer "Yes" answers: the culture is not generally autocratic.
- Three or fewer "Nos": the culture is generally autocratic.

Countering autocracy

If your organization is dominated by the power culture it will need to resist autocracy. To do this, increase the number of Athenalike autonomous task forces. Task forces are mini-Zeus cultures, with a boss, a web, and a mission. Autocrats can understand their value and the way they work, and can therefore accept them in the organization. Such groups do not threaten the autocrat's power, but they do make it less easy for him or her to exert centralized control.

2 Defining the roles

Handy represents the highly organized, systematic Apollonian role culture as a Greek temple with each pillar representing a function or division, and control resting with the senior executives at the top. Is this your organizational picture?

Organization man

To discover if your organization is ruled by Apollo, answer Yes or No to the following set of propositions. Are they or are they not the organization's typical values, beliefs, and forms of behavior?

- A good boss is impersonal and correct.
- A good subordinate is responsible and reliable.
- A good member gives first priority to duties, responsibilities, and customary standards.
- People who do well here are conscientious, responsible, and loyal.
- The organization treats individuals as if they are under contract.
- People are controlled and influenced impersonally by enforcing procedures and standards.
- It is legitimate to control others if you have formal responsibility.
- Tasks are assigned here on functions and responsibility.
- Competition is for high formal status.

Analysis

- Nine "Yes" answers: a classic "organization man" culture, dominated by Apollo and the Apollonians.
- Nine "Nos": the culture is remarkably free from systems and controls.
- Three or fewer "Yes" answers: the culture is not generally bureaucratic.
- Three or fewer "Nos": a definite inclination toward bureaucracy.

Countering the excesses

The potential excesses of an Apollonian role culture are dehumanized behaviors and the creation of a powerful bureaucracy. Countering these excesses requires finding ways of injecting individualism into what is essentially a collective culture.

One way of forcing a general cultural change is to alter the reward system. Apollonians love rigid pay scales tied to rigid hierarchies, under peculiar rules, such as "nobody can be promoted more than two grades at a time" or "lower grades cannot be placed over higher grades." Do not reward people simply for coming to work. Give exceptional rewards for exceptional performance, and make the rewards psychic (celebrations, congratulations, etc.) as well as real (money and promotion).

Another way of reducing the impersonal nature of the role culture, in which people are treated not as human beings but as cogs in a well-oiled machine, is to apply the Golden Rule: "Do unto others as you would have them do unto you." Until a Golden Rule culture is established, dehumanized behavior will be the norm.

Changing specific behaviors

You can change the culture of an organization only by changing the behavior of its individual members. There are eight specific Apollonian behaviors that together lead to a dehumanized and bureaucratic organization. Each one has an antidote, which, if routinely employed, will decrease these unhelpful tendencies.

Ways to Change Apollonian Behaviors

Bad behavior	Antidote
1 Refusing to entertain contradictory/unorthodox views.	Empower people to oppose the consensus.
2 Ignoring evidence that argues against chosen policies.	Require proposers to provide a full list of pros and cons.
3 Making decisions that are unethical or inhumane.	Publish a code of ethics and appoint an ombudsman.
4 Seeing opponents and colleagues as stereotypes rather than individuals.	Arrange face-to-face meetings supervised by an impartial facilitator.
5 Pressuring people to conform to group opinions.	Reward individual initiatives and demand new ideas.
6 Forming cliques that keep to themselves.	Send outsiders into groups as co-opted members.
7 Leaving people in groups no option but unanimity.	Solicit everybody's opinion in rotation.
8 Continuing with policies that have been proved false.	Make admitting and correcting mistakes imperative.

3 Tackling the tasks

More and more managers are working in temporary groups that cut across departmental boundaries, mingle disciplines, and exist to complete a common task. The Athenian task-force mode is changing most Apollonian cultures. How far has it affected your culture?

The task-force mode

To discover how much influence Athena exerts in your organization, answer Yes or No to the following propositions. Are they or are they not the organization's typical values, beliefs, and forms of behavior?

- A good boss is egalitarian and can be influenced.
- A good subordinate is self-motivated and open to ideas.
- A good member gives first priority to the requirements of the task.
- People who do well here are technically competent, effective, and committed.
- The organization treats individuals as committed coworkers.
- People are controlled and influenced by personal commitment to achieving goals.
- It is legitimate to control others if you know more about the task.
- Tasks are assigned here on ability to execute.
- Competition is for excellence of contribution.

Analysis

- Nine "Yes" answers: an organization that puts performance ahead of personalities and gives people many opportunities to succeed.
- Nine "Nos": the culture is either authoritarian or bureaucratic, or both.
- Three or fewer "Yes" answers: the culture is not an open one.
- Three or fewer Nos: the culture is open – most of the time.

Improving the network

The task-oriented culture is essentially a network. It may well extend outside the borders of the company to suppliers and customers. To optimize the effectiveness of this kind of culture and to ensure its continued dominance in your organization, use the latest information technology to connect yourself to the network, and think of yourself as an essential node.

4 Injecting creativity

Any culture, despite its defects, can succeed with just one great idea – one so powerful that it transcends those defects. Creative self-oriented Dionysian individuals can provide such ideas. Does your organization contain enough of these people?

Creative Dionysus

Dionysus has nothing to do with organization, but he has a lot to do with culture. God of the nonorganization, his disciples are primarily individual and creative thinkers who find it very difficult to work in large, highly structured, Apollo-ruled organizations.

No organization can do without this type, however, if it is to deal successfully with the exceptional situations where the normal responses have failed to provide a result. In these circumstances only the quick, individualistic thinking of Dionysian types is likely to provide a solution. Are you such a Dionysian individual? Do you:

- Give your subordinates stimulating work?
- Respect the needs and values of others?
- Give priority to individuals and their needs?
- Excel in personal relationships?
- Treat colleagues as interesting and valuable people?
- Get deeply interested in and excited by your work?
- Manage with the full consent of others?
- Make all appointments strictly on merit?
- Compete primarily to beat your own best standards?

Working within an organization

The attributes and behaviors of a Dionysian individual would be applauded by all of Handy's three organizational cultures: the autocrat, the bureaucrat, and the taskmaster would all say that they want managers to fit this excellent pattern.

But saying and doing are not the same thing. In organizations of every culture, you will find lip service to the Dionysian ideal, coupled with actions, procedures, and interactions that make Dionysian behavior difficult in practice. Do not despair. Bear in mind that, while cultures are collective, the collective is made up of individuals. Live up to your best Dionysian ideals at all times.

3

Working in the new society

The principles of "the Shamrock Organization" • Treating the three leaves of the shamrock in separate ways • **The evolving world of the flexible labor force** • Getting the core of the shamrock right, and managing it right • **The rise of the "federal" company and the role of its center** • How "subsidiarity" will become a self-fulfilling prophecy • **Using a fast-track Japanese approach to promoting young people** • The Triple I organization with intelligence, information, and ideas

Charles Handy began his questioning march into the future in his 1989 book, *The Age of Unreason*. Here, he unveiled "the Shamrock Organization," a new coinage that was his response to the changes in the world of work. These had been created by changes in organizations that were themselves adapting to that same changing world of work. He wastes no time on which came first here, the chicken or the egg, but leaps straight into the heart of the matter: the increased pressure for results.

The new thinking on organizations, Handy wrote, is visible in several ways, including a shake-up in the careers and lives of managers, and the emergence of the shamrock: "the new alliance of different types of work and workers."

The structure of the shamrock

Handy uses the Irish national emblem to symbolize this division of today's organizations into "three very different groups of people, groups with different expectations, managed differently, paid differently, organized differently":

1 The professional core of qualified professionals, technicans, and managers.
2 People outside the organization, but who work for it as subcontractors.
3 The flexible labor force of part-time workers and temporary workers.

Between them, the essential people in the core own the knowledge that distinguishes one organization from another. Organizations cannot afford to lose them, so go to great lengths to bind them with "hoops of gold, with high salaries, fringe benefits, and German cars." In return, the core members have to work hard and long, with total commitment and flexibility.

The huge expense of these people means that companies cut down on their numbers as much as possible. "Every successful organization," Handy says, "will tell you that they have at least quadrupled their turnover in the last 10 years, but have halved their professional core." Contracting out, of course, reduces the core need. Handy calls the work involved "nonessential," but he is wrong: some firms even contract out the assembly of their key products. But the principle is clear: work that could be done by others is given to specialists who can, in theory, do it better for less cost.

The third leaf, the flexible labor force, now the fastest growing part of the employment scene, has existed for a long time. So, in embryo, has the three-leaved workforce. "What is different today is the scale," writes Handy. "Each of the leaves is now significant."

Managing the leaves

Each leaf also demands separate treatment, starting with the professional core of key people, including managers. Their lives are going to resemble those of independent consultants, working in flat structures, rarely promoted, but often rewarded in ways other than salaries and benefits:

"Economic necessity... will force more organizations to rethink the way they reward their senior core people, turning them... into partners rather than employees, colleagues rather than bosses and subordinates, names not roles."

"The contractual fringe" has always earned its rewards differently, being paid for results, not time, and in fees, not wages. This "means that the central organization can exercise control only by specifying the results, not by overseeing the methods." Handy calls this revolutionary for managers who are used to the maxim: "Control the means and the methods, and the results will be as they should be." In fact, many outsourcing companies do oversee methods intently, and Handy underplays the crucial role of trust in these relationships. Nevertheless, he approves in general: "The contract [between "employer" and "worker"] is now more explicit and in many respects more healthy for that."

The more worrying leaf is the third, the flexible workers. "In crude terms, these people are the labor market... into which employers dip as they like, and when they need, for as little money as they have to pay." Handy condemns this as shortsighted philosophy and calls for changed attitudes:

> "If the flexible labor force is seen to be a valuable part of the organization [the latter] will be prepared to invest in them, to provide training, even training leading to qualifications, to give them some status and some privileges (including paid holidays and sick leave entitlement).... Then and only then will the organization get the temporary or part-time help that it needs to the standards it requires."

This is more pious hope than confident prediction. But Handy draws a clear picture of an evolving world in which customers do more and more work for their suppliers (making their own reservations over the internet, for example); in which more and more people are based at home, as networked employees or as "telecommuters"; in which more and more head offices, small and often half-empty, function as a "working club"; in which "homework," once just another means of exploiting female labor, may become an efficient and rewarding way of tapping the pool of educated women with small children.

In his last words on the shamrock, Handy says: "The core is the critical hub of an organizational network. It is essential to get it right and to manage it right." The network will have important features other than the three parts of the shamrock. Alongside the latter, Handy sees "the federal organization" developing. He means the alliance of a variety of individual groups under a common flag with some shared identity. It is the answer to the paradox that businesses need to be big and small simultaneously.

The federal organization

According to Handy, "big" provides marketplace and financial clout, and possibly economies of scale, while "small" gives flexibility, "as well as the sense of community for which individuals [and Handy] increasingly hanker." Federalism differs from decentralization, in which the center delegates, initiates, directs, and ultimately controls. Federalism features "reverse thrust organizations," in which "the initiative, the drive, and the energy come mostly from the parts, with the center an influencing force, relatively low in profile."

Handy sees the rise of federalism as another involuntary piece of discontinuity. Organizations have cut down their cores, and have fewer people to interpret the information transmitted by the new technology, who can then act on that information to control decentralized operations. The consequences for managements are inevitable:

> "It is better in the end that they do not even try, but concentrate instead on the things they can control and the decisions which they alone can take. Small cores make federalism ultimately inevitable, and large cores make decentralization ultimately too expensive."

What, then, does the federal center do? Handy says that it must be more than a banker. It must manage the future. It must "think in terms of global strategies which may link one or more of the autonomous parts." It must "cling to its key functions of [recruiting] new people and [finding] new money." But fuller control is not on the menu, even if control is reduced to making the long-term decisions and leaving implementation to the parts. That reduction still "reeks of the old engineering language of management." The new language requires a new image of the corporation.

The center is now genuinely the center, and not the top. It makes its decisions in consultation with the chiefs of the parts. "It has to be a place of persuasion, of argument leading to consensus." Leadership of ideas takes over from leadership by personality. The leadership may even be shared by two or three people, backed by "a staff whose concerns will largely be with the future, with plans and possibilities, scenarios, and options."

Independence and unity

Today, most large organizations reflect this new image, if only in part. Handy's comment remains true: "Because organizations evolve there are, as yet, few federal corporations in pure form." Perhaps that will always be true, given the difficulty of balancing independence with a meaningful unity. "Too much independence... can lead to breakaway or to a random collection of disparate parts." Misunderstood federalism becomes inefficient decentralization. True understanding, though, involves new concepts, like "subsidiarity."

By this Handy means giving away power: "the federal organization will not work unless those in the center not only *have* to let go of some of their power but actually *want* to do so." Only then will the new decision-makers be trusted to reach and implement the right decisions. Handy accepts that Catch-22 applies: you want to give responsibility only to people who are capable, but you do not know if they are capable until they have been given responsibility. To resolve the catch, Handy turns to hope. The best subsidiarity will attract the best people: so "ultimately subsidiarity is a self-fulfilling prophecy."

He puts forward as an alternative analogy the "inside-out doughnut" (see pp. 89–101). The job consists of a core, which is clearly defined, and a surrounding space where you have discretion. Federal organizations "require large doughnuts, whether they are group ones or individual ones." The organization has to be managed by specifying the results that are required from each doughnut. This is Management by Results – "a major change in our ways of managing," and one that requires "a new language to describe them."

Much of that language ("of federations and networks, of alliances and influences... shamrocks and doughnuts") has been popularized or invented by Handy. He thinks that it must be recognized as the *right* language. "No one, after all, has ever liked being managed, for anyone who has tried to run an organization has always known that it was more like running a small country than a machine." Handy has no room for so-called scientific management, saying that only theorists have tried to "apply the hard rules of number and logic and mechanics to an essentially soft system."

Anyone who tries to manage without those hard numbers, though, is certainly courting early and severe failure. The hard-soft conflict is another basic paradox of management, which Handy glosses over in his enthusiasm for the new language. As he notes, the shift away from hard concepts is general: "Leadership is now fashionable and the language of leadership increasingly important."

Principles for leaders

Handy believes that leadership has to be endemic in organizations, whose people, if they have pretensions to be anybody, "must begin to think and act like a leader." What does that mean? Handy recognizes that leadership is "mysterious" and hard to define, but settles for this statement: "A leader shapes and shares a vision which gives point to the work of others."

Creating and sharing a vision, however, is much easier said than done, as Handy recognizes. But he isolates five principles for leaders to live by:

1 The vision must be different: "A plan or a strategy which is a projection of the present or a replica of what everybody else is doing is not a vision."
2 The vision must make sense to others: "It must stretch people's imaginations but still be within the bounds of possibility." It must be related to people's work and not to some grand design.
3 The vision must be understandable: "No one can communicate a vision that takes two pages… or is too full of numbers and jargon." It has to stick in the mind.
4 The leader must live the vision: "He, or she, must not only believe in it but must be seen to believe in it…. The total pragmatist cannot be a transforming leader."
5 The leader must remember that the vision will be the work of others: Otherwise, the vision will stay just a dream. "A leader with no followers is a voice in the wilderness."

Thinking like leaders

There is nothing new or radical about this quintet. The five points deserve Handy's own judgment: "simple, obvious even." The difficulty, which is considerable, lies in the delivery. Like many other gurus, Handy wants managers to think like leaders, and believes that they can: "If it happens, and in places it is happening, it will mark yet one more important discontinuity turned to advantage."

If Handy is right, organizations are going to need a great many thinking leaders: "lots of them, all over the place and not only in the center." He sees the federal organization as flat, with no more than four or five levels at the cores of their parts, which, wherever possible, will never exceed 500 people in all. That has profound consequences for managers, who will no longer progress simply by climbing the promotion ladder, gaining a rung every two or three years.

Handy recommends instead a Japanese-style route for young people. The Japanese "have a fast-track route for them, but instead of it being a vertical fast-track up through the organization, it is a horizontal fast-track, a succession of different jobs, real jobs with tough standards to be met, but all at the same level." The same system, writes Handy, can work for all ages everywhere as the flatter organization allows people to discover new abilities and new interests.

This is another example of Handy's "upside-down thinking," horizontal careers as a good thing. Not only do corporations need an inverted approach to employment,

"If the new organizations are going to succeed, and they must succeed, our managers must think like leaders."
The Age of Unreason

On the fast track at Toyota
Handy recommends organizations adopt the Japanese method of horizontal promotion, where employees have the opportunity of testing and improving their skills in a wide variety of roles.

they also require a new formula for success and for effectiveness: $I^3 = AV$, "where I stands for intelligence, information, and ideas, and AV means added value in cash or in kind." His formula gave Handy yet another phrase: "The Triple I Organization." This would most resemble a university, and not the traditional corporation, as it obsessively pursued quality:

"To that end the wise organization increasingly uses smart machines, with smart people to work with them. It is interesting to note how often, already, organizations talk of their 'intellectual property.' Once again, words signal the way things are going."

Quality, affirms Handy, is not another gimmick. It is the opposite of the old "money-is-all" objectives of business: the fast buck, or the short-term bottom line of residual profit, or the medium-term earnings per share. The world has become much more competitive, and "organizations will only survive if they can guarantee quality in their goods or their services. Short-term profit at the expense of quality will lead to short-term lives."

Quality, however, does not come easily. "It needs," says Handy, "the right equipment, the right people, and the right environment" (to which one might well reply, what doesn't?). The Triple I Organization fits the bill: "Everyone is paid to think *and* to do, including the machines." The myth is that automation deskills workers. Smart organizations, however, "see the computers and their machines as aides to clever people." In a dumb organization, Handy notes, smart machines are merely attended by "sometimes very dumb people." But the hard facts of economic life, he says, will compel organizations:

- To invest in smart machines to achieve effectiveness.
- To use skilled and thinking people to get the most out of the machines.
- To pay these people more and, if possible, employ fewer of them.

More of these smart people will be women, not for egalitarian reasons, but because the smart supply will be inadequate if half the population is excluded. The most important difference, however, is that "everyone in the core will have to be a manager while at the same time no one can afford to be only a manager." Professional or technical experts will also "rapidly acquire responsibility for money, people, or projects, or all three." In the newer, higher technology firms in the US, Handy notes, the language is already reflecting this: people are called, not managers, but "team-leaders," "project heads," or "coordinators."

In this new society, "Management ceases to be a definition of a status, of a class within an organization, but [becomes] an *activity*... which can be defined, and its skills taught, learned, and developed." That process, though, cannot stop with business education and early qualifications:

> "... everyone in the core will increasingly be expected to have not only the expertise appropriate to his or her particular role but will also be required to know and understand business, to have the technical skills of analysis *and* the human skills *and* the conceptual skills, and to keep them up to date."

The culture of consent

With their new careers, their new knowledge, and their new organizations, people entering Handy's new world of business seem to have bright prospects. They become brighter still when you consider "the Culture of Consent." As Handy says, "you cannot run this sort of organization or these sort of people by command... Intelligent organizations have to be run by persuasion and by consent." This is hard work, and can be frustrating; Handy emphasizes that "the cultures of consent are not easy to run, or to work in." This is partly because the culture "puts a premium on competence – there are few hiding places in these organizations."

Handy may well exaggerate the difficulties and underestimate the human potential for overcoming them. But he is setting the stage for a message close to his heart:

that people have to be "educated and prepared" for the culture of consent. "There lies the challenge for our society."

Can that challenge be met – and will it be? Handy ends *The Age of Unreason* with six hopes, involving "work done for others," religion, "village living," early success, and "the nature of man himself and particularly of woman." In all these areas, improvement could flow: original sin exists, but so does original goodness. Handy still saw many dangers in the world of looser organizations, but thought that the looseness could encourage truly adult behavior earlier in life. "If that is so then the Age of Unreason may become an Age of Greatness." The important words are "if" and "may."

Ideas into action

- Contract out anything that can be done better and/or cheaper by others.
- Exercise control by specifying the results, not by overseeing the methods.
- Ensure that decisions are made with the advice of key subordinates and by consensus.
- Make your vision different, sensible, understandable: then live it as transforming leader.
- Use flatter organizations to allow people to discover new abilities and interests.
- Employ skilled and thinking people to get the best from investment in smart machines.
- Run the organization by persuasion and by consent, putting a premium on competence.

The discovery of paradox

Handy dates to his boyhood the discovery that paradox is a necessity in life. A motto with a golfing metaphor hung in his bedroom: "Life goes, you see, to golf's own ditty: Without the rough there'd be no pretty."

In later years, Handy recognized this as his first, if subliminal, introduction to the importance of paradox. The religious upbringing inevitable for an archdeacon's son did the rest.

Handy was taught that God's great gift to mankind is choice. That, he eventually saw, was itself a paradox, "because the freedom to choose implies the freedom to choose wrongly, to sin." You could not have one without the other. He came to realize that paradox was what made life interesting. "If everything was an unmixed blessing… there would be no need for change or movement. Offer me a heaven without paradox and I will opt for hell."

That line of thought culminated in a revelation for Handy: "Life will never be easy, nor perfectible, nor completely predictable." The trail of paradox led from religion to practical affairs, as Handy discovered when he was a young executive working for Shell in South Malaysia. "Young, enthusiastic and, I suppose, naive," he was negotiating an agency agreement with a Chinese dealer. They shook hands on the deal, "drank the ritual cups of tea," and then Handy took out the official company agreement and filled the form with the relevant figures, ready for signature.

The somewhat alarmed dealer asked why a form was necessary, and protested: "If you think that I am going to sign that you are very much mistaken." If they had agreed the figures, why did Handy want a legal contract? It made the dealer suspicious. Had Shell got more than him from the agreement? In the 1990s, Handy still recalled the Chinese man's words:

> "In my culture a good agreement is self-enforcing because both parties go away smiling and are happy to see that each of us is smiling. If one smiles and the other scowls, the agreement will not stick, lawyers or no lawyers."

Handy found that the Chinese contract embodies a crucial principle. "It was about the importance of compromise as a prerequisite of progress." It rested on a basic paradox: "Both sides have to concede for both to win." Just as the possibility of sin is necessary for the pursuit of virtue, so accepting some loss led to optimum profit. "We have no chance of managing the paradoxes," wrote Handy, "if we are not prepared to give up something, if we are not willing to bet on the future and if we cannot find it in ourselves to take a risk with people."

"Living with paradox is not comfortable nor easy. It can be like walking in a dark wood on a moonless night. It is an eerie and, at times, a frightening experience."
The Empty Raincoat

That thought and its infinite number of variations led him away from dogmatism and toward his basic attitude: to challenge all dogma, but to recognize whatever value exists, even in ideas and practices that are plainly contradictory.

4

Managing the paradoxes

Why human beings are not designed to be "empty raincoats, nameless numbers on a payroll" • Employing half the people at twice the pay and three times the productivity • **The pressures of the Nine Paradoxes** • Averting disaster by adopting change before the "Sigmoid Curve" reaches its peak • **Winning the equal benefits of the "Chinese Contract"** • The "Trinitarian" thinking of Liberty, Equality, and Fraternity • **Using "inside-out" or "upside-down" thought to challenge the conventional wisdom**

Handy has had the rare satisfaction of seeing many of his prophecies come true, but not to his comfort. The predicted changes in the world of work have created "much more fundamental, confusing, and distressing" results than he expected. He has diagnosed the main cause:

"Part of the confusion stems from our pursuit of efficiency and economic growth... In the pursuit of these goals we can be tempted to forget that it is we, as individual men and women, who should be the measure of all things...."

Here, Handy is expressing the distaste of the intellectual puritan for the ethic of the mass-market economy. The passage is from *The Empty Raincoat*, published in 1994. Why the odd title? It comes from part of a sculpture that Handy saw in Minneapolis: a bronze raincoat, standing upright but with no one wearing it. Human beings, Handy concludes, "were not designed to be empty raincoats, nameless numbers on a payroll...."

His central thrust remains unchanged. Organizations will become "smaller and bigger simultaneously, flatter, and more flexible." People will have to make things happen, rather than wait for them to happen. But Handy is left with the paradox that "the new freedoms... often mean less equality and more misery."

Handy states that many jobs have been priced out of existence in the industrialized world. Only people from poorer backgrounds will take these jobs (as many Latinos have in the US). But even good jobs have their drawbacks. Large corporations are pursuing the policy: "$\frac{1}{2}$ x 2 x 3 = P." For profit, they employ half the people at twice the pay and three times the productivity. So half the staff lose their jobs, and the other half work so hard that they can neither enjoy their families nor avoid burnout in a mere 30 years.

Handy is convinced that there has to be "more to life than winning or we should nearly all be losers." Looking around, he saw that management and control were breaking down, and that "The new world order looks very likely to end in disorder." He no longer believed in "a Theory of Everything," or in "the possibility of perfection." Such a belief was always odd for a rational observer of human affairs. But Handy now saw that scientists themselves had undermined "the myth of science, the idea that everything could be understood, predicted, and therefore managed." On the contrary, society was evolving through the pressures of nine paradoxes.

The nine paradoxes

Handy's first paradox is intelligence. He observes, rightly enough, that brainpower has taken over from fixed assets and mobile muscle as the prime means of production. Intelligence is thus "the new form of property." But this form behaves paradoxically, like no other property.

You cannot redistribute or bequeath intelligence: you cannot own somebody else's. Handy also cites management pioneer Peter Drucker: "The means of production can no longer be owned by the people who think they own the business." Intelligence, moreover, is also extraordinarily difficult to tax. Handy's insight seems to promise a more open society, with low-cost entry. Yet it also carries a threat: that society will be divided into a new set of haves and have-nots, separated by intelligence.

The second paradox is that of work. Handy says that "enforced idleness seems to be the price we are paying for improved efficiency." The paradox is that "organizations want the most work for the least money while individuals typically want the most money for the least work." Handy points to the irony that "the more you price work, the less paid work gets done, because so much of it [like small home repairs] is not now worth the cost." That is the inevitable result of the pursuit of higher productivity, which is Handy's third paradox.

"Productivity means ever more and ever better work from ever fewer people." Handy recognizes that the age-old process of improving efficiency ultimately benefited the workers, so long as jobs were available. "This time, however, the new growth structure for work is the do-it-yourself economy." People displaced from organizations do their own thing: their output is invisible, but increasing all the time. Managements have encouraged specialization and efficiency, but have in consequence "priced some of that new work out of existence." Handy admits that the resulting joblessness is "a fallout from progress," but calls it one of the most uncomfortable modern paradoxes.

Time – the fourth paradox – is familiar to everybody: "we never seem to have enough time, yet there has never been so much time available to us." Despite longer lives, automation, part-time work, flexitime, and so on, the average American now works the equivalent of an extra month per year compared to two decades ago. "Time turns out to be a confusing commodity," writes Handy. "Some people will spend money to save their time, others will spend their time to save money." As for organizations, they want fewer people working longer to save money, while individuals agree to work longer because they want money: "The paradox is that they seem to know it is stupid."

The fifth paradox – riches – is that economic growth depends on increasing numbers buying increasing quantities of goods and services. But the rich populations, which can afford to buy, are declining in numbers, while the poor nations cannot take their place until they have the know-how and capital needed to export to the rich. "Ultimately, therefore, we will have to invest in our potential competitors in order to fuel our own growth." Handy, back to his puritan vein, offers another, weaker paradox: the growth that society needs depends more and more on "a climate of envy," which increases social divisiveness.

With the sixth paradox – organizations – Handy is on stronger ground, and ground that he has made his own. Organizations are beset by the need to reconcile opposites, where they once could choose between them. Handy cites global yet local, small yet big, centralized yet decentralized, planned yet flexible, differentiated yet integrated, and so on. He argues: "The organizations of the future may not be recognizable as such.... The challenge for tomorrow's leaders is to manage an organization that is not there in any sense which we are used to." It will be an organizing organization, not an employing one.

Age, the seventh paradox, is "that every generation perceives itself as justifiably different from its predecessor, but plans as if its successor generation will be the same as them." This assumption has been thrown out of the window, according to Handy. Conventional jobs and careers will be scarcer, working lives will begin later and end earlier; "education will have to be more prolonged, if not indefinite"; women will be in paid work for most of their lives; child rearing and learning will involve both sexes; and values and principles will change as the roles of the sexes change.

The eighth paradox, that of the individual, is that people are being encouraged as never before to express their individuality, but "Looking up... at these office blocks in every city... one has to wonder how much room there is for

‘I’ amid the filing cabinets and the terminals.” Handy is expressing another paradox of the organization. It requires teamwork, which means working together for the common good, while simultaneously expecting team members to be self-managing and motivating individuals. Handy has wider worries about the future of belonging: “Who will be the ‘We’ to whom we would want to belong?”

The ninth paradox is that of justice. People expect society to treat them fairly, to give them what they deserve, and to be impartial. Handy becomes apocalyptic about the prospects for a society that is perceived to be unjust: “… there will be no good reason for anything other than selfishness. Such a society is doomed, in the end, to destroy itself.” Thus the debatable view of the prophet, but the paradox is firmly based. Capitalism thrives on the principle that those who achieve most should get most:

> “But it will not long be credible or tolerated if it ignores its opponent. To put it another way, capitalism depends on the fundamental principle of inequality – some may do better than others – but will only be acceptable in the long term in a democracy if most people have an equal chance to aspire to that inequality. It is a paradox which we cannot afford to ignore.”

Handy develops strong ideas for ways of resolving his paradoxes, although his prophecies are not watertight. He writes: “Governments seem surprised when each recovery soaks up fewer of the unemployed.” But, as the millennium ended, this phenomenon was no longer relevant in the US, and less relevant in Britain. That, however, does not remove the need to live with contradictions and simultaneous opposites. Handy offers three methods of doing so: the Sigmoid Curve, the Doughnut Principle (see pp. 89–101), which is the most famous, and the Chinese Contract.

Explaining the Sigmoid Curve
Charles Handy explains to managers that the secret of continued growth is to take a new course at point A, before reaching a peak of success, and well before disaster looms at point B.

The Sigmoid Curve

The Sigmoid Curve is S-shaped (see also p. 85). It describes a familiar pattern, that of life itself. "We start slowly, experimentally, and falteringly, we wax and then we wane." Progress along the curve has increased. "What used to take decades, even generations, now takes years, even months." The secret of constant growth, Handy says, is to start a new curve just before the crest of the old. But that is when everything seems fine: "It would be folly to change when the current recipes are working so well."

The true folly is exposed when the curve continues around the bend and below the crest, where "you are looking disaster in the face." Now, huge effort is required to remedy the situation and get back on an upward trend – a second growth curve – because resources, energies, morale, and credibility are all low. Upheaval follows. At this point:

> "... institutions invariably start the changing process... by bringing in new people, because only people who are new to the situation will have the credibility and the different vision to lift the place back onto the second curve."

The tough question is: "How do we know where we are on the first curve?" Handy advises organizations to assume that their present strategies will need to be replaced within two to three years, and that product life cycles are shorter than they were. Even if this assumption proves to be wrong, no harm has been done. The organization has merely explored the new possibilities without making major commitments, and the "discipline of the second curve" is useful in itself, keeping one skeptical, curious, and inventive.

In fact, Handy is contradicted by many examples of companies that have changed winning strategies fatally and unnecessarily. Moreover, major commitments are often required earlier than he suggests. But it remains true that "nothing lasts forever or was there forever," although many managers act as if it does. He cites the MIT professor Peter

"It is one of the paradoxes of success that the things and the ways which got you where you are, are seldom the things to keep you there."
The Empty Raincoat

Senge for pointing out the importance of "mental maps," the fixed ideas that everybody carries around. "We need to check that these assumptions are still valid, because they lock us into our existing curve."

Second-curve thinking, Handy insists, comes most naturally from the second generation. Elders should entrust "curvilinear thinking" to younger people who "can see more clearly where the first curve is heading and what the next curve might look like." The danger is that their visionary thinking will be obstructed by the powerful elders.

> "The thinking, however, is only part of it. There needs to be the commitment to carry it through, to endure the early dip before the curve climbs upward, to live with the first curve while the second one develops. These things cannot be done by outsiders. To manage a paradox, you need to live with it as well as analyze it."

The Chinese Contract

A further way to handle paradox is covered by another of Handy's mysterious titles: the "Chinese Contract." Agreements made in Asia are supposed to rest, not on the letter of a legal contract, but on reaching a compromise that suits the interests of both parties. He notes that "the morality of compromise" sounds contradictory. Compromise, especially on "principles," is usually seen as weakness. Handy argues that strong people always know when to compromise and that "all principles can be compromised to serve a greater principle."

If this sounds odd coming from a religious man, Handy has a convincing explanation. Most dilemmas are not a choice between right and wrong, but between two conflicting rights: "I want to spend more time on my work, *and* with my family." Similarly, managers want to give their employees freedom and keep control over their activities. Businesses are always confronting the paradox of conflicting rights. Investment, for example, "involves taking something from today to improve tomorrow." So how far should you short-change or compromise the present to benefit the future?

Third-angle thinking

Handy urges that you should seek the answers to such questions through "Trinitarian," or third-angle thinking. The name is another of his potent analogies. The trinity is that of the French Revolution: liberty, equality, and fraternity. The first two are in conflict, but adding fraternity reconciles them; likewise, you should always be on the lookout for another approach to resolving conflict – the third angle. The idea brings Handy's social ethics to the fore: "if money is so divisive, why not de-monetarize society" by making more of the good necessities of life free to all?

He does not answer his own question, which raises far weightier economic issues than the divisiveness of money. But he does make a strong case for challenging Western cultural traditions along the lines of the "Chinese Contract":

- Reject the idea that winning necessarily means that someone loses.
- Regard compromise as a sign of strength.
- Seek a good agreement, not a good lawyer.
- Reject the idea that if you look after the present, the future will look after itself.

The four pieces of advice are excellent. But neither the Chinese Contract nor the Sigmoid Curve is as powerful as the Doughnut Principle. The doughnut Handy refers to is an inverted ring doughnut, with the "middle" representing a core of essential activities surrounded by discretionary space. It is another example of the "inside-out" or "upside-down" thinking, central to Handy's later writings, that leads him, always alert for paradox, to challenge so much conventional business wisdom.

He quotes John Akers, who just before leaving the IBM leadership complained that: "The average IBM-er has lost sight of the reasons for his company's existence. IBM exists to provide a basic return on invested capital to the shareholders." Handy is baffled by the persistence of this wrong premise and its false assumptions, which are denied by his own experience in business and by logic. His view on the purpose of business is utterly different:

> "The principal purpose of a company... is to make a profit in order to continue to do things or make things, and to do so ever better and more abundantly."

Saying that profit is a means to an end, not an end in itself, makes a serious moral point; the opposite view, according to St. Augustine, "is one of the worst of sins." Yet Handy's own words on the subject are surprising. If the principal purpose of a company is to make a profit, why undertake one activity rather than another? Profit is neither an end nor a means, but an end result, the reward that flows from doing or making, better and more abundantly, what you want to do or make – as the favorite jargon of the year 2000 would say, by optimizing customer satisfaction.

Handy does recognize this truth later on in *The Empty Raincoat*, when he says: "A company will only be allowed to survive as long as it is doing something useful, at a cost which people can afford, and it must generate enough funds for... continued growth and development." This “existential” company combines selfishness with public contribution (another resolved paradox) within the “hexagon contract.” This is a form of Chinese Contract, implicitly agreed by a company’s six different stakeholders: the financiers, employees, and suppliers most obviously, but also the customers, the environment, and society as a whole.

Most of these stakeholders, says Handy, are likely to have “a vested interest in immortality,” seeking perpetuity for a business that will continue only for as long as it is good. The conflict between satisfying the interests of investors (who want the highest financial returns) and employees (who want the highest possible reward) is tackled by the existential company that lives for its own virtuous purpose: for example, growing “better not bigger.” That, Handy writes, is one definition of a purpose, one way to grow, “one recipe for immortality.”

Institutional immortality

Handy is forced to concede, however, that few corporations are following his recipe. “In a business, quarterly reports and an average lifespan of 40 years for big companies tend to put immortality on the back burner.” Handy says that boardrooms do not trust numbers more than four or five years ahead. Such numbers, anyway, are bound to be deeply untrustworthy. But Handy thinks this short-sightedness ill-founded; institutions, he declares, can be immortal.

“The Mitsui Corporation and my old Oxford college are both over 600 years old, both still going strong and thinking far,” according to Handy, who adds, rather mystifyingly: “You only look ahead as far as you can look back.” His “fragile” hopes are that job-hopping will become more perilous, and shareholders less powerful, and that the “virtues of membership” will be rediscovered. Then “the corporate world may see a desire for permanence creep in again" – a hope that reads unconvincingly against the millennial background of megamergers and demergers.

The recipe for immortality, though, has to be read in the context of the point where *The Empty Raincoat* begins: "that there is no perfect solution to anything, and that no one can predict the ultimate effect of any action." There is neither certainty nor sure authority – the paradoxes are too complicated for that. Yet Handy offers a certain and authoritative conclusion: "We have to put these principles into practice, in our work and in our lives." Offering a solution when there is no solution is Handy's own paradox.

Ideas into action

- Assume that your present strategies will need replacing in two to three years' time.
- Entrust planning radical "second-curve" strategy to the younger generation.
- Be prepared to compromise in the interests of reaching a better solution.
- Always look out for another approach to resolving conflict – the third angle.
- Be alert for paradox, and use its contradictions as a springboard for success.
- Satisfy all six stakeholders: financiers, employees, suppliers, customers, the environment, and society.
- Build a company with a recipe for immortality – like being better, not bigger.

Organizing the organization

There is no one perfect way of organizing a business. Whatever method you choose, it must combine control with flexibility to be successful. Structure groups for optimum communication and balance of roles, and for maximum efficiency avoid creating too many hierarchical levels. Above all, renew the organization regularly to avert decline and fall.

Designing the setup

Always take time and care to plan your organization, whether you are setting up a small unit or a whole business. An effective setup greatly increases the chances of success.

Follow the Goldilocks principle – "not too little, not too much, but just right." That means having no more people than the task requires, but also building in plenty of flexibility. To help you plan the structure of the group and its personnel, make sure you know the answers to the following questions:

- What is the prime purpose of this organization?
- What are the subobjectives?
- What tasks must be performed to meet the aims?
- What skills do the tasks require?
- How many people are needed to deliver the skills?
- What are the natural groupings of people?
- What are the desired/required results?
- What is the optimum size – that is, the minimum number consistent with obtaining the desired results?

Once you have planned the setup according to your answers, you must ensure that everybody knows what their responsibilities are, to whom they are responsible, and who makes the final decisions.

How an organization grows

Organizations tend to grow from simple forms to complex ones. They must mutate to cope with changing demands. As an organization matures and grows larger, it passes through four distinct evolutionary phases, each ended by a revolutionary or crisis stage, which enables it to move on to the next evolutionary phase. Your organization will pass – or will have passed – through the same stages of evolution.

The Four Phases of Growth
1 Growth through creativity, ending in crisis of leadership.
2 Growth through direction, ending in crisis of autonomy.
3 Growth through delegation, ending in crisis of control.
4 Growth through coordination, ending in crisis of red tape.

Preventing stasis

During phase four, more and more processes are put into place to exercise control (over everything from spending to planning), to find out what's happening, and to keep efficient records. These good intentions rapidly develop into bad practices: filling in forms, following written procedures, getting authorizations, endless meetings. The organization becomes a static bureaucracy.

To break the stranglehold of red tape and to prevent it from recurring, always remember KISS (Keep It Simple Stupid), and follow antibureaucratic practices at all times.

Counter Bureaucracy

- Have an annual spring cleaning, using the principles of zero-based budgeting: every administrative procedure and expenditure is unnecessary unless proved otherwise.
- Wherever possible, use trust instead of controls.
- Authorize people to miss meetings where they cannot make a contribution and to challenge the value of any forms and reports.
- Reward administrative departments for task-force successes in streamlining and eliminating procedures.
- Reward good ideas that cut red tape and administrative costs.
- Be radical and courageous in seeking reforms.

The rule book of retailer Nordstrom begins on a single page saying "Use your best judgment at all times." The second page says "There are no other rules." Both rules are excellent.

1 Making groups work

How well your organization works depends on the effectiveness of its groups – both internally and in their interactions with other groups. Make sure any group you set up communicates well and is composed of members who together provide a good balance of roles.

Communicating with others

Handy lists three basic patterns for intergroup relationships. In the first you communicate primarily with the person in the center; in the second you communicate with each other in sequence; and in the third you link up with whomever you want whenever you need.

The Three Group Communication Patterns		
1 Wheel center-led	**2 Circle** sequential	**3 Web** participative

Using the web pattern

The web is the most effective communication pattern you can use. It is participative, involving, and improves quality, although, warns Handy, it tends to disintegrate into a wheel under time pressure. "In complex open-ended problems," Handy reports, "the web is the most likely to reach the best solution." In business today, complex open-ended problems abound. So making the web work is the acid test of a good group, and of your effectiveness as a manager.

Use the wheel only when speedy results matter even more than quality, bearing in mind that much depends on the peerless leader at the hub. Avoid using the circular pattern at all times. It is slow, unsatisfying, inflexible, and uncoordinated.

Picking group members

Whether the group is permanent (a department, say) or temporary (a task force), and whatever communication pattern it uses, you need to ensure that you select members to fill particular roles. This means more than making sure that different kinds of technical or professional competence are represented. According to team expert Murray Belbin, in most circumstances the fulfillment of eight key roles is essential to effective group performance.

The Eight Key Roles in a Group
1 Chairman: coordinates the group's work.
2 Shaper: drives the group and task forward.
3 Plant: comes up with the new ideas.
4 Monitor-evaluator: analyzes plans and performance.
5 Resource-investigator: provides internal and external contacts.
6 Company worker: organizes tasks and schedules.
7 Team worker: holds group together by providing support.
8 Finisher: makes things happen – and on time.

Make sure that every role is covered, but do not have too many people in the same role. Also, do not ask people to play roles to which they are unsuited by nature. Think carefully about your own role, too. If you are in charge, avoid combining the roles of chairman and shaper: you cannot perform both roles simultaneously. The chairman has to be objective, listen to everybody, and work through others; the shaper must be single-minded and forceful.

Testing effectiveness

Once your group is up and running, check its effectiveness (and your own), by testing it with the following questions:

- Do people share their information fully and freely?
- Do they tell the factual truth at all times?
- Do they face problems as a group, not as subgroups?
- Do they seek "Win/Win" solutions, with no losers?
- Are they always active and alert in group activities?
- Do they put contribution ahead of self-promotion?
- Do they display emotions as well as logic?

If the answers are negative, so will be the results. If there are faults, hold a team meeting and bring the defects into the open. Where individuals are at fault, confront them face-to-face. Publish an agreed code of conduct and insist that everybody adheres to it.

2 Organizing control

Lines of command are basic to organizational control. Whether you run the lines down through functions, territories, businesses, or products, each hierarchical layer is broader than its predecessor. For optimum efficiency and flexibility create as few layers as possible.

Increasing the span of control

As your unit grows, instead of adding hierarchical levels, increase the "span of control" at each existing level: in other words, increase the number of people who report to each superior. By creating maximum spans you give people maximum responsibility.

If the work of people reporting to you interlocks, you should not supervise more than six of them. If their work is independent, though, spans can be very much wider. Jack Welch at General Electric has built a fabulous management record with a dozen or more independent operating heads reporting directly to him.

Promoting flexibility and creativity

Handy quotes two experts who say that most organizations need only five hierarchical levels, seven if really large. But management guru James Champy says that three will suffice for any organization if you adopt a control structure that includes external expertise.

Champy's Structure	
Three-layer hierarchy	**Outside the hierarchy**
Enterprise managers People/process managers Self-managers	Expertise managers

In his ideal, enterprise managers make the final decisions. They are advised by the people-process managers, who implement the decisions and are responsible for the self-managers – the staff and line workers. The expertise managers outside the hierarchy provide the indispensable services, from finance to training. This structure depends on true delegation, and is inherently creative and flexible – which is what you want your unit to be for greatest effectiveness.

3 Beating the life cycle

Organizations tend to follow a life cycle in which their rise to achievement and wealth is followed by decline and fall. Avoid this fate by renewing your group while it is still strong and growing.

Renewing the organization

Timely renewal of an organization is rare. It does not have to be. To master the timing, apply the Sigmoid Curve (see p. 73) to your group.

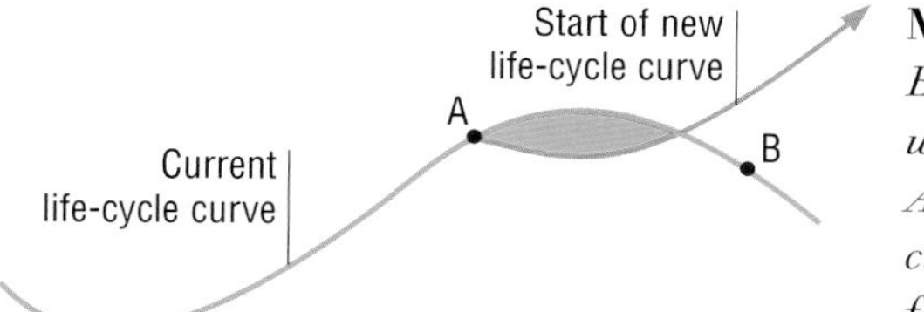

Master the curve
Begin a new iniative when you reach point A on your existing curve to avoid certain failure at point B.

Draw your own S-shaped life-cycle curve. Work out where you (or your organization) are along the curve by checking the validity of your key assumptions, and mark that position with an X. You will probably find you are further along than you would have thought.

Do not wait for bad results before instigating change. By the time you reach point B on the curve, resources will be depleted, energies will be low, and people will be depressed. Avoid decline completely by renewing your business or group on a regular basis.

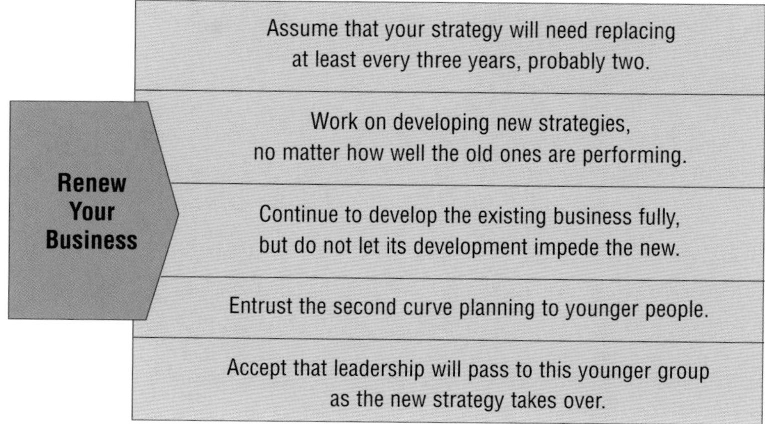

Adopting a portfolio career

Handy's discovery of the need for a new approach to work can be traced back to the early 1960s, when he was appointed to a job with Shell as the Regional Coordinator Marketing (Oil) Mediterranean Region.

Handy commented later: "My friends were impressed, but they did not know the reality. The reality was a three-page job description outlining my duties, but the hard truth was contained in the final paragraph: 'Authority to initiate expenditure up to a maximum of $15.'"

In the terms that Handy coined later – those of the "inside-out doughnut" – "the job was all core and no space." His role was predictable, planned, and controlled, and designed to spare the organization any surprises. Handy found his work dull and frustrating. He could not express himself, he could not make a difference, he was not empowered: "My memoranda went from my role – MK/32 – not from me. I was merely a 'temporary role occupant.'"

Switching to another of his metaphors, Handy remarks that he felt like an "empty raincoat." Leaving Shell as soon as he could, he resumed his search for the perfect job: interesting, exciting, rewarding him with money, travel, and pride, complete with pleasing colleagues and location. He never found it. But there was a doughnut solution:

> "If I adopted a 'portfolio' approach to life, meaning that I saw my life as a collection of different groups and activities, of bits and pieces of work, like a stock portfolio, I could get different things from different bits. A part of that portfolio would be 'core,' providing the essential wherewithal for life, but it would be balanced by work done purely for interest or for a cause, or because it would stretch me personally, or simply because it was fascinating or fun."

That meant saying goodbye to offers of 70-hour-a-week jobs that would have absorbed most of his time. Handy put together a package of different kinds of work, a work portfolio: "My life now is doughnut-shaped." He became a laboratory for testing

"The concept of balancing a core and a bounded space is crucial to a proper understanding of most of life.... It is a way of being an instrument of society but also a free individual."
The Empty Raincoat

his own theory, and it works: "I can now even specify the amount of days which I am prepared to allocate to core activities and the amount left over for personal space." Handy had discovered a new principle of organizing work for the new society.

The new principle, Handy originally thought, would be applied primarily in the Third Age, "the time for a second life." While this could be a continuation of the Second Age, "the time of main endeavor," it might be "something very different." Doing nothing, writes Handy, is no longer a realistic Third Age option. Having a portfolio is realistic, and many people in mid-life are now emulating Handy in this respect.

Even more interesting, Second Age people are also opting for plural careers, while companies are pluralizing and empowering their managers. Today's young managers would not be Regional Coordinator Marketing (Oil) Mediterranean Region, or an MK/2 – thanks partly to Handy.

5

Living in a doughnut

Applying the "Doughnut Principle" to jobs and organizations • The distinction between getting it wrong and not getting it right • **Developing the "portfolio career"** • Using different tasks and groups to bring out different talents • **Why the vertically integrated company is obsolete** • Laying out the doughnut organization • **How to avoid overdoing the core activities** • How organizations are structuring themselves into minimalist shapes • **Putting how you use time ahead of how much time you use**

Perhaps the greatest contribution in *The Empty Raincoat* is Handy's second pathway through paradox, the concept of the doughnut, the ring doughnut with a hole in the middle. He turns the doughnut (or "donut") inside out, with a core that "contains all the things which have to be done in (your) job or role if you are not to fail." The space around and beyond the core provides "our opportunity to make a difference, to go beyond the bounds of duty, to live up to our full potential."

This use of the doughnut metaphor for individuals has been less influential than its application to institutions. Organizations, just as Handy predicted, "have come to realize that they have their essential core... of necessary jobs and necessary people, a core which is surrounded by an open, flexible space which they fill with flexible workers and flexible supply contracts." Handy thus gives expression to a powerful corporate trend, in which companies "outsource" whatever they can.

The Doughnut Principle applies to jobs as well as to organizations. "In the past, jobs used to be all core, certainly at the lower levels, because too much discretion meant too much unpredictability." In such cases, the doughnut, because it is all core and no space, leaves no room for self-expression, no space to make a difference, no empowerment.

Handy experienced this discomfort in person when working for Shell as Regional Coordinator Marketing (Oil)

"The doughnut image is a conceptual way of relating duty to a fuller responsibility in every institution or group in society."
The Empty Raincoat

Mediterranean Region (see pp. 86–87). With a job that is "all core and no space," the result is dullness and frustration. But the opposite extreme, all space and no core, also has grave disadvantages. In a job such as that of a pastor, "there is no end, no way in which you can look back and say, 'It was a great year,' because it could always have been greater." But that must surely be true of any job.

Types of error

However, Handy wants to make the point that empowerment has gone too far, that being without a boundary is never enough. Even entrepreneurs need targets and limits: working all hours does not balance the doughnut. Another disadvantage of more space is having more room for "Type 2 error." Handy makes a vital distinction between getting it wrong (Type 1 error) and not getting it right (Type 2), which means that "the full possibilities have not been exploited or developed: enough was not enough."

Type 2 has become more important. Management, says Handy, was easier when the priority was to check for only Type 1 errors. Managing thus became merely administration, and managers never needed to explore the first statement in these familiar words from the old Anglican prayer book:

> "We have left undone those things which we ought to have done [Type 2]... and we have done those things which we ought not to have done [Type 1]."

Leaner and flatter organizations, in Handy's view, have given people more space at the price of a new Type 2 burden: "the things we could have done but didn't." The extra space in the doughnut brings extra responsibility. He sees acceptance of this truth as the way to "a truly free society." That is surely beyond man's reach. But the aspiration reveals the moral purpose underlying all Handy's work, and which clearly lies beneath the following question:

"Some people make their work the whole of their life. That necessary core of the job fills the whole doughnut, leaving little or no space for anything else. Are they right or wise?"

Handy does not provide a clear answer. Some people, he notes, suggest that those who seek personal fulfillment in demanding business jobs will be disappointed. Others think that the business of creating wealth can and should fulfill people's aspirations. Handy offers his doughnut as a bridge between the opposites: if your current job does not provide your "existential development," fill the empty spaces in your personal doughnut somewhere else.

The portfolio career

Here, Handy is developing perhaps his most famous idea: the "portfolio career." More and more people are following in his footsteps by leaving full-time employment, as Handy did at 50, and working for several employers, or clients, in different guises. The portfolio principle, however, is compatible with full-time employment, if you have the good fortune to work for an organization that provides different kinds of work within its walls. People can than join a number of different doughnuts:

"Wise organizations recognize the advantages of these internal portfolios. Different tasks and different groups bring out different talents in the individual; they confront him or her with different experiences."

This portfolio pattern is, in fact, appearing in large organizations. It is happening as a response to market and other trends, and to the demands of competition, rather than as a result of any sociological upheaval. Handy points to the death of the old organization chart: today's have "circles and amoebalike blobs where... boxes used to be." The boundaries have become fuzzy as well, "with customers, suppliers, and allied organizations linked into a varying 'network organization.'"

Handy was among the first observers to discern a "new shape of work." He saw it centering around small operations, mostly in services, which would use outsiders or portfolio workers to supplement a small core of key people. This is a "doughnut organization." The vertically integrated company which wanted to own and run everything internally is obsolete. Rather, every organization these days has its smaller core and its surrounding partnerships: traditional suppliers, independent professionals, joint venture partners, and so on.

Handy is always sharp-eyed about drawbacks. He sees a danger in bonding the partners so tightly that they become part of the core, and warns that the flexibility which is the whole point of the doughnut can disappear. He calls for flexible contracts, and recommends never tying more than 30 percent of capacity or requirements to a single partner. He also stresses that managing doughnuts is a new challenge for organizations:

> "It is a challenge because one is managing the doughnut and its different spaces, rather than the person... It is no longer the manager and the managed, but the designer of the doughnut and the occupant; a different relationship, built more on trust and mutual respect than on control."

Handy gives the example of Ricardo Semler, the president of Semco, a Brazilian engineering business, who has pioneered a form of doughnut organization. The company has a group of counselors in the middle of the business, while all the other employees, known as "partners" or "associates," live in the outer space. They all occupy smaller doughnuts, held together by coordinators. But what can be achieved at Semco, which is privately owned and relatively small, is obviously easier than it would be in larger, public organizations.

But larger organizations are trying. As Handy says: "Organizations everywhere are being 'reinvented' or 're-engineered'... breaking down, or rather blowing up their functions and their old ways of working, and... regrouping people, equipment, and systems around a particular task."

Ricardo Semler

Semler's maverick reorganization of his engineering business, Semco, into a participative venture company has made it one of the most advanced and best-known companies in Latin America.

He fits these new groupings into his doughnut metaphor by calling their specific objectives, rules, and duties the "core," with the surrounding space described as the discretionary freedom to complete the task "in the way they think best."

The doughnut organization may even be laid out physically to suit the metaphor. "The center no longer dominates from a headquarters tower block. It is smaller and more clublike, with outlying or satellite offices around the country." Handy believes that the present nomadic lifestyle of many modern executives, who spend little time in the office or at home, could be mirrored by corporate premises. He cites research by Frank Becker that envisions a central doughnut, a computer-equipped home office, and a satellite office in suburbia.

Overdoing the core

But these predictions are less important to Handy than a sermon. He believes that people and organizations overdo the core. Few individuals "need as much as they think they do, or as much security as they hanker after. Organizations build bigger cores than they need, and impose bigger cores on their internal doughnuts than are necessary." It is central to Handy's philosophy that: "If we do not allow people space, we cannot expect responsible behavior." Organizations must adapt to their needs.

> "For organizations the opportunity is now there to apply the doughnut principle to most of their work, devising a structure made up of muddy doughnuts, a system of interlocking double circles, in each of which the inner circle, the core, is tightly specified and controlled, as are the outer limits of authority, but where the space in the middle is to be developed."

Handy sees that anarchy can follow if the organization is lax, and its managers cannot handle the inevitable contradictions. What satisfies individuals and groups may not be advantageous to the organization. "The center cracks down, cores expand again, individuals resent the contraction of their space, and mutual resentment saps morale." The only remedy, in large doughnuts, is to develop a clear consensus about individual and corporate purposes and goals. But doughnut management is becoming an increasingly important skill because of the sheer proliferation going on inside organizations.

As Handy predicted, an increasing number of organizations are dividing their employees into "project teams, task forces, small business units, clusters, and work groups – smart words for doughnuts." The individual may even have multiple roles, say, in an operational doughnut, in an advisory one, and in another handling a temporary product assignment. Handy sees this as exciting for people, at the price of unpredictability. It is another nail in the coffin of the planned career. He notes that people are now being offered "career opportunities" instead of jobs.

Handy selects a real-life model – the advertising agency – to illustrate his view of "how we will be working tomorrow." People are organized into clusters of experts from whom task groups are selected for a particular account or campaign. "They may work on several different account groups, and the membership of the groups will flex with the demands of the work. It is a fluid-matrix organization." So is a consultancy, or the team at a medical center.

It is questionable whether these models are appropriate. How organizations arrange themselves is determined in a major way by the nature of their work. How else could you organize an advertising agency? As he says, "professionals have always worked on the principle of the doughnut." The work consists of related products, which call on some common services, but which are inherently distinct one-time projects: "flexibility and discretion had to be built in."

But if his model has weaknesses, his point does not. Such outfits, with their naturally flatter and looser structures, are being imitated, as far as possible, by larger organizations. Hierarchical ranks and disciplines are lessening in importance as flexibility and discretion become more critical for success. Organizational life is changing form. Slowly in most cases, fast in others, "organizations structure themselves into minimalist shapes."

The consequences have powerful effects outside firms. Organizations spin off insiders to join the ranks of outsiders, "most of them reluctant independents." As and when they find work, more and more spun-off individuals "are behaving as professionals always have, charging fees, not wages." In Handy's terms they are "going portfolio or going plural." He does not mean having several different kinds of work, but having several different clients.

What distinguishes these workers from in-house hired hands is that the price tag now goes on "their contribution, not their time." The value may vary from a $5 million commission, earned by a single introduction, to Handy's reward for writing *The Empty Raincoat*. As he notes wryly:

> "If I was paid by the hour at the average national wage for writing this book I would be counting my income in many tens of thousands of pounds. Sadly, the royalty advance takes no account of my time, but prices my produce at the level my publisher thinks it will fetch in the marketplace. I therefore sell my time cheaply to myself, in the hope that it will be an investment worth the making."

Knowledge workers

Applied intelligence, Handy argues, has become the crucial element, not time. Knowledge workers of all types "are obvious candidates for portfolio lives." They are no different, however, from the vast numbers of people whose members can be found all over the Yellow Pages: the fixers and makers, the craftsmen and craftswomen. Their work may be harder and longer than that of employees. "The difference is that they have more freedom to chunk their time in other ways, if they so choose."

Handy is emphatic that: "What matters now is *how* we use our time, not *how much* of that time we use." Charging by the hour is much less sensible than charging for the produce. "Those who charge for their produce can get richer by working smarter, not longer." This principle stretches beyond the individual portfolio worker. "Organizations are also latching on to the possibilities… extending the principle of produce not time to their own internal operations."

A unit, group, or person may be told: "Do this by this date; how you do it is up to you, but get it done on time and up to standard." Like the outsider, the insider gets more discretion in handling his or her time. The main difference remaining, says Handy, is that the full-time worker will have rights and entitlements that do not extend to the part-timer. He does not think that this distinction can or should last: "I have little doubt that we shall, increasingly, see both laws and best practice equalizing the benefits, proportionately, between full- and part-timers."

Another form of equalization concerns accommodation. The full-timer can go to an office. Portfolio workers, too, "need somewhere where they belong as of right." Handy is worried about the alienating effect of learning all by yourself, the loneliness of teleworking: "That asset which is yourself can atrophy in isolation." Companionship and gossip are required with people who are colleagues, not clients. Handy calls for: "Somewhere where we can exchange experience and contacts. We need a club." In the minimalist organization, the hub, he believes, "will be a clubhouse for the members of the dispersed core" – one that key portfolio workers also use.

Handy encourages portfolio workers to demand the use of a club facility as part of their fees. That deal can obviously be struck only with a company that takes a radically changed attitude to employment and to its own identity, and that regards insiders and outsiders as equally valuable. (The analogy is with a company like Dell Computer, which outsources much of its essential activity to suppliers who are regarded as part of the business.) Such an attitude is hard to avoid when, as Handy stresses, employment itself is changing, and with it the nature of organization.

For those offically inside, part of the personal doughnut will be the core, a job whose content may be written down in a job description; or, "if it's a classy organization," in a mission statement. But there is a snag. When those core activities have been completed, "you have not finished, for there is more." Handy remarks that in any job of any significance the jobholder is expected to do all that is required, and much more:

> "... to make a difference, to show responsible and appropriate initiative, to move into the empty space of the doughnut and begin to fill it up. Unfortunately, no one can tell you what you should do there because if they could they would make it part of the core. It is another organizational Catch-22. All they can tell you is the boundary of your discretion, the outer rim of the doughnut."

As Handy emphasizes, many organizations are now beset by the pressures of complexity, variety, and necessary speed of reaction. All this "makes the well-cored doughnut an impossible dream." Managers must struggle with the snag, be specific about core content, boundaries, and expected results, and follow a new philosophy of management that marks a major discontinuity. Among other things, they have to learn to forgive mistakes. Some, of course, are unforgivable, "but most are less critical than they seem at the time and can be the crux of important lessons."

The new manager

Forgiveness is asking a lot of organizations, which "are not by nature forgiving places." The organization itself, however, neither forgives nor blames: individual managers within the institution do that, heavily influenced by cultural norms, no doubt, but still acting as the final arbiters. The consequence is obvious: "The new manager must be a different manager," a person with a lot of learning to do. "The new manager must learn to specify the measures of success as well as the signs of failure, and must then allow his or her people to get on with it in their own way." The issue is whether he or she will.

In answer to such questions, Handy ends *The Empty Raincoat* with a large prophecy and a small prescription. He proclaims "the end of the age of the mass organization [which] has not been with us that long. We should not think of it as a law of nature." Nor is that necessarily bad news: "Maybe we shall be better off without it." Since Handy makes no secret of his distaste for mass organizations yet approves of so much contemporary and coming change, the cautious pessimism of his conclusion is surprising:

"We cannot wait for great visions from great people, for they are in short supply at *the end of history* [my italics]. It is up to us to light our own small fires in the darkness."

Readers who accompany Handy on what seems a hopeful journey must be puzzled to reach such a gloomy terminus. Has history really ended, and in darkness? Its trends, down the ages, have always rested on the collective, cumulative actions of individuals striving toward a brighter future. In *Beyond Certainty*, a 1995 collection of essays, Handy explains his position: "I remain optimistic about the possibilities of the future but pessimistic about our willingness to seize them." That is a final, personal paradox.

Ideas into action

- Seek and pursue the essential core of your personal and business activities.
- Unearth and prevent the unseen errors – the undone things you should have done.
- Help people to develop portfolio careers, either inside or outside the firm.
- Organize clusters of experts from whom you select task forces for specific projects.
- Employ and pay people for their results, not for the time they spend on getting them.
- Learn how to forgive mistakes and make them the crux of important lessons.
- Allow your people to get on with their work in their own way.

Organizing yourself

Charles Handy has approached his own life and career with the efficient planning of a truly modern manager. Even if you are not a "portfolio" worker, with a fee-paid, multiclient career, the portfolio principles are highly important in getting the most out of your work – and life. Learn to choose the work that suits you, and to plan your life around that choice.

Making personal choices

Developments inside companies mean that you have a wider choice than ever in the way in which you can serve an organization. Handy has identified three distinct working relationships between employees and employers.

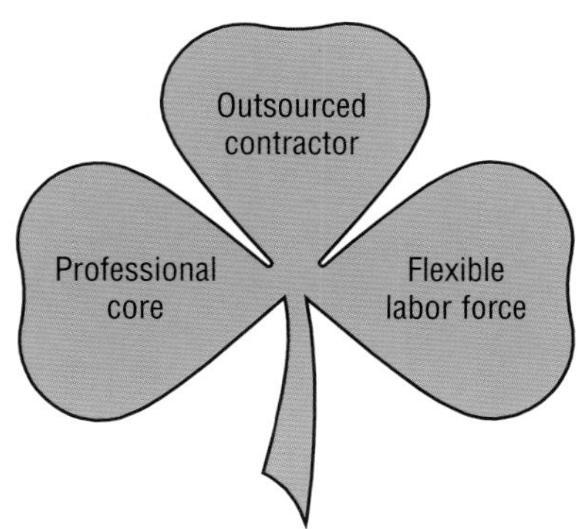

The three leaves of the shamrock

Today's organization is made up of three very different groups of people. To which group do you belong?

Choosing how to work

The choice for managers is between two leaves of the shamrock – being either a salaried member of the core or a fee-earning contributor of contracted skills. Weigh up the two options carefully before making your choice.

- As a contractor, you have the flexibility, variety, and upside potential of being your own man or woman. But your earning capacity is limited by the number of hours you can work and the fees you can charge, and you have very little security.
- As a salaried member of the core, you have greater security, considerable scope, and guaranteed rewards. But your freedom of movement and decision is outside your control.

Finding what suits

If you are undecided on your best way of working, look again at the questionnaires in Masterclass 1, and answer each proposition with yourself rather than an organization in mind.

- If you agree predominantly with the Zeus attitudes, you are either a born subordinate who needs a commanding boss, or a potential entrepreneur, a leader with the personal drive that can turn a business idea into profitable action.
- If you find you are an Apollonian, you will probably be happiest as a core professional, a salaried employee working within an organization.
- If you discover you have mainly Athenian attitudes, then you will be most suited to a highly decentralized, participative organization, or to your own consultancy-type operation.
- If you find you have primarily Dionysian characteristics, then you are a natural freelancer and heretic.

The ten commandments

If you believe after doing this exercise that you are in the wrong organization, think of moving. "Have skill, will travel" is the right motto to adopt. You should also consider moving if the company disobeys the 10 commandments of modern management.

Obey the 10 Commandments

1 Welcome new ideas – especially from below.

2 Insist that people need approval from only one level.

3 Praise when praise is due and only criticize constructively.

4 Encourage open debate ending in consensus.

5 Treat problems as opportunities.

6 Use trust, not supervision, as the main control.

7 Operate a "freedom of information" policy.

8 Institute change after consultation with those affected.

9 Take, announce, implement unpleasant decisions in person.

10 Share knowledge with others and share theirs.

1 Balancing your life

Handy bases his life on the Doughnut Principle. That means achieving a proper balance between mandatory and optional activities, between work and leisure. Getting the balance right is much more likely if you organize the doughnut efficiently.

Applying the doughnut

The inside-out doughnut is one of Handy's key ideas. The concept can be applied to your work alone, or to your life as a whole. Equally, it can be applied to organizations or units.

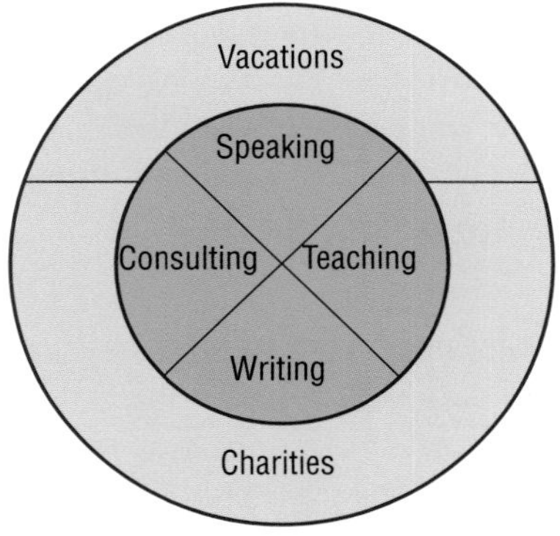

Handy's personal doughnut

At the core of Handy's doughnut are the various types of fee work to which he devotes about 200 days a year. In the outer space he has placed his charity work, which takes up approximately 100 days, and vacations, which claim 65 days a year.

Drawing your doughnut

Draw your personal version of the Handy doughnut. Place inside the doughnut your core activities – the tasks you must complete to earn a living and fulfill your career ambitions. The space around the core is where you place your other activities, the voluntary ones, the outside interests, the family, and so on. Now consider your personal doughnut. Is your life all core, or duty, and no personal space, or vice versa? Most people, says Handy, seem to like a balanced doughnut with about equal amounts of core and space.

Consider your work life, too. How much discretion do you have? Is your work doughnut all core – specific duties to perform – and no space for individual responsibility? Or do you work for an organization that gives individuals space outside the core in which to take initiatives and develop their strengths?

Creating your ideal

The principle of balance is well understood by people. Modern trends are making it much easier to obtain what you want at work – which is much more than money. When 2,000 employees were asked what mattered most in their work, the results showed clearly the greater importance of other factors.

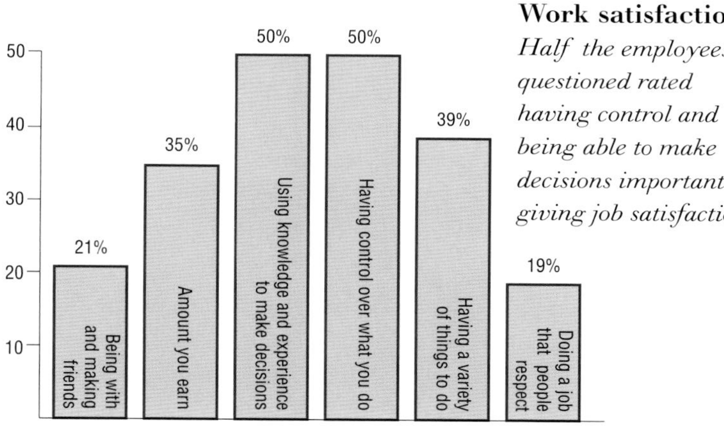

Work satisfaction

Half the employees questioned rated having control and being able to make decisions important in giving job satisfaction.

The portfolio career, in which you have several clients instead of one employer, provides the three prime needs in abundance. You may now be able to develop a portfolio career inside an organization: say, holding simultaneously a management role, a task-force function, and a planning position. That may well be an attractive option.

Optimizing your portfolio

You have an obligation to yourself to maximize your earning power. The portfolio career is a one-person company, and must be run efficiently. Work to a business plan that will generate a satisfactory financial return. Proper planning will almost certainly reveal gaps where you need new clients or more business from old ones. To win extra business, you will need to devote unpaid time to marketing.

You must also find unpaid time for education. Learning does not belong exclusively to your school days – it is important throughout your life. What you know represents your intellectual capital, the crucial asset. You must keep that capital in excellent condition.

2 Achieving excellence

Inside or outside an organization, if your results fail to satisfy an employer, insecurity will follow. Outside, whatever the quality of your work, continued employment is never guaranteed. Excellence is still the only insurance policy you can (and must) take out.

Playing to strengths

Achieving excellence is much easier if you are using your best talents, much harder if you are working in areas of weakness. Write down what you consider to be your best qualities and skills, and have them checked by somebody you can trust to be impartial and honest. Then make sure that your strengths match the work you plan to undertake. For example, do not become an independent consultant if you are shy or hesitant about selling yourself.

Learning to improve

Seek always to overcome your weaknesses and enhance your strengths by education and practice, by learning. That is where you not only maintain your intellectual capital, but expand it. Handy regards the learning process as having four parts:

- What is the question (problem to be solved, dilemma to be resolved, challenge to meet)?
- What are the possible answers?
- What does testing the possibilities tell me?
- What have I learned (reflection)?

This process neatly matches the PDCA approach to total quality management: Plan, Do, Check, Act.

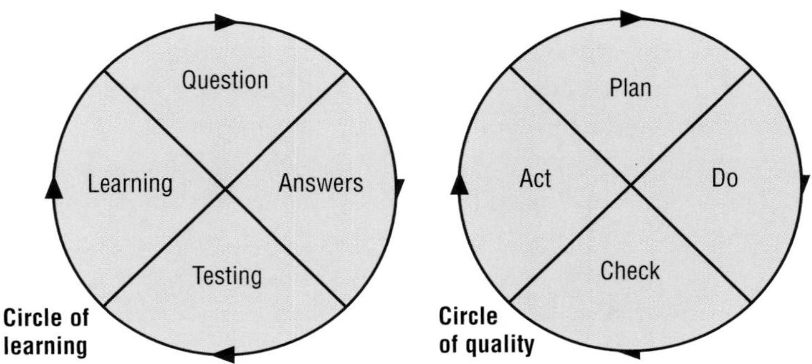

Supplying total quality

Use the PDCA process systematically to rethink and improve everything you do. Some of these improvements will be known only to you, like, say, meeting a standard of replying to all letters, e-mails, faxes, and phone calls on the day of receipt. Others will be all too obvious to the client, like delivering the work at the promised time. Set your standards at the highest level, and debrief clients on their assessment of your work – preferably face-to-face. That gives you the ultimate quality control and strengthens the relationship.

Going digital

Mastering the latest information technology will both enhance your efficiency and improve your communication with and service to clients. It will also help you manage your time more efficiently.

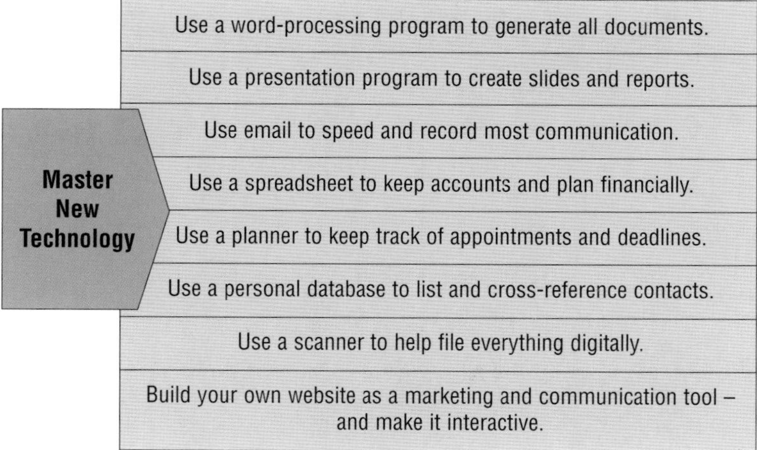

Sustaining excellence

Finally, sustaining excellence depends, not only on tools and techniques, but on having a long-term view. To achieve this, adhere to the following four rules recommended by Handy:

- Take responsibility for yourself and your future.
- Form a clear view of what you want that future to be.
- Determine to get that future.
- Believe that you can do so. You can.

andrew GROVE

Biography

Andrew S. Grove, known far and wide as "Andy," was born András Gróf in Hungary in 1936. When the Germans moved into Hungary during World War II, his Jewish family went into hiding and emerged only after the German defeat. Hungary remained inhospitable, though, under Soviet domination, which culminated in the savage repression of the 1956 uprising. Then a student, Grove had been active in the failed revolution, and he wisely fled to the United States.

An uncle living in New York took Grove in. He started studying chemical engineering at City College, and what followed was a typical story of self help and achievement, American-style. Working his way through college as a waiter, he finished at the top of his class. The honors degree opened the door to the University of California at Berkeley, where Grove earned his Ph.D. in 1963. He was by then married to Eva, a fellow Hungarian; they have two daughters.

Unusually, Grove has combined business and academic careers. While serving as one of America's most famous CEOs at Intel, he taught a class in strategic management at Stanford University's business school. Much earlier, as a young researcher at Fairchild Camera, he lectured at Berkeley. He had chosen his main employer well, though: Fairchild became, and rightly so, a legendary name in the history of microelectronics.

The roots of Fairchild Camera went back to the famous development of the transistor at Bell Laboratories in 1948 under William Shockley. After helping Schockley start his own lab, eight team members deserted him to launch their own venture. Nicknamed "The Traitorous Eight," they were given $1.5 million of financing by the playboy entrepreneur Sherman Fairchild and started making semiconductors. The new business prospered, but, in 1967, after a decade of increasing fame and internal troubles, the "traitors" started to go their separate ways. In 1968, two of the brightest and best, Robert Noyce and Gordon Moore, left the organization.

Grove's brilliant career is inseparable from the epochal achievements of these two men. Noyce is the father of the "integrated circuit" – the piece of silicon containing many transistors, which is at the heart of the electronic devices that have changed the world. He was general manager at Fairchild, and Moore was head of R&D. Another engineering genius, Moore became famous for "Moore's Law": that the performance of integrated circuitry would double every 18 months at constant prices; that is, the price of a given amount of power would halve. In hiring the 32-year-old Andy Grove, the pair formed the triumvirate whose breakaway, named Intel, became the king of Silicon Valley.

At that time, Grove sported gold chains and muttonchop whiskers, as well as frizzy brown hair and a Hungarian accent. The later, more conservative Grove has lost most of the accent, but still favors the Valley's shirtsleeved, tieless style. He is physically energetic, with the lean look of an enthusiastic mountain biker. Meticulous and a stickler for punctuality, enormously hardworking, and something of a control freak, Grove is clever, highly organized, and confident.

In 1968, however, he was not a manufacturing expert, and was hardly qualified to be Intel's "Director of Operations." But this was a man who would thrust himself and his company forward. In theory, Bob Graham, also from Fairchild, might have seized the number three position, but, by the time of Graham's delayed arrival to head marketing,

Grove had hired "dozens of engineers and managers... and to him... they established their first loyalty," as Tim Jackson notes in his book *Inside Intel* (1997).

"Grove took on more responsibility than he otherwise might have. Who does what is always vague in a start-up; an intelligent, energetic person with a eye for detail who is willing to do the things that others have left behind can become considerably more powerful than his job role would suggest. And Andy Grove was the ultimate detail guy."

The best manager in the world

The biography of Andy Grove from 1968 is the story of Intel and of how he developed into "the best manager in the world," according to *Fortune* magazine. By 1974 – the crucial year when Intel launched the 8008 microprocessor – Grove was executive vice president and official Third Man. Noyce had become chairman, and as the company's front man, he was now less involved in the strategic and technological decisions; Moore dominated these as CEO. Everything else came under Grove.

In 1979, Grove was promoted to president, and, in 1987, became chief executive. By then Noyce and Moore were pushing 60. They had masterminded an astonishing run of technological breakthroughs: the first memory chip, the first DRAM (dynamic random access memory), the first EPROM (erasable, programmable, read-only memory), and the first microprocessor. Just as important, all four innovations had been exploited commercially to lucrative effect; for this Grove deserves much of the credit.

As the devices poured out of his fabrication plants ("fabs," as they are known), so Intel's sales and profits soared.

It was not, however, a story of smooth progress; nor did it happen without strenuous effort or crisis. When it comes to effort or critical threats, though, Grove is in his element. Goading, challenging, bullying, shouting, he never relaxes the pressure for results or for relevance: in his office, a neat 8-ft by 9-ft (2.5-m by 2.7-m) cubicle surrounded by similar cubicles, there is a handheld wooden sign for use at meetings: IS THERE A QUESTION HERE OR IS IT A SPEECH?

Grove's driving, ambitious, take-no-prisoners personality is ideal for the highly combative climate of Silicon Valley.

Combining drive and vision
Grove applied his enormous energy and strategic thinking to steering Intel through the key crisis points in its history, as it capitalized on key advances in digital technology.

Intel under Grove won a near-monopoly of microprocessors that was (and is) every bit as strong as that of Microsoft in operating software. But while he is just as committed as Bill Gates to preserving his supremacy, Grove has navigated the rapids more adroitly.

Intel's dealings with rivals have been combative in the extreme. Negotiations with the antitrust authorities resulted in a 1998 consent decree that restrained Intel's competitive conduct, but which saved it from the legal embarrassments in which Microsoft became entangled. The company's unremitting enactment of Moore's Law, moreover, satisfied the PC makers with a continuous, dramatic improvement in microprocessor power, availability, and price/performance ratio, which, in turn, repeatedly spurred the PC market.

A practical intellectual

Throughout this rambunctious career, Grove not only retained his academic connections, but also wrote newspaper columns and books. His first book, *Physics and Technology of Semiconductor Devices* (1967), was a clear account, full of mathematics. *High Output Management*, published in 1983, broke new, nontechnical ground. The first chapter explains "The Basics of Production" by discussing and analyzing the serving of breakfast in a hotel (one of Grove's first jobs). How do you get a three-minute egg, buttered toast, and coffee to the customer simultaneously and hot? The answer was an analogy for developing "a clear understanding of the trade-offs between the various factors – manpower, capacity, and inventory" and how you "must reduce the understanding to a quantifiable set of relationships".

That passage gives an excellent picture of the special qualities of Grove's mind. He is the practical intellectual *par excellence*, as he demonstrated again with his 1996 book *Only the Paranoid Survive*, whose catchy title expresses a powerful idea: that, without unremitting vigilance and strenuous action, success will corrode into failure. That fear only reflects the realities of Intel's industry, and of the many major and minor threats that Grove has overcome.

In every difficult situation, Grove has combined necessary toughness with rare adaptability. His book, typically for Grove, turns insight into incisive, fact-based theory. The combination has helped to create vast wealth for Intel's investors. Grove has naturally shared in those proceeds: in a single year – 1996 – Grove pocketed nearly $95 million in stock options. The next year Grove became chairman as well as CEO, and in 1998 he relinquished his CEO title to Craig Barrett. This was doubly understandable: Grove was 62 and had suffered from prostate cancer.

The illness provided another demonstration of Grove's formidable personality. He thoroughly researched all the latest information available on the cancer before deciding on the appropriate treatment. Then he published a full and frank account of the entire experience in *Fortune*. To achieve such a degree of detachment when threatened with death shows enormous courage and much scientific curiosity.

These qualities were both essential in Grove's lifework. He was not the author of Intel's technological miracles, but he made them happen by taking and controlling the colossal risks and sums involved; one of his beloved "fabs" can cost as much as $2 billion. The methods and management philosophy that he describes so honestly and succinctly will leave generations of managers, as well as Intel investors, heavily in his debt.

1

Raising management output

Jsing delegation to achieve high nanagerial leverage • The three basics of business management • **Where the art of management comes in** • How to urn your calendar into a productivity ool • **Making meetings more effective as the key medium of managerial work** • The four conditions that must be met before a meeting is justified • **The hree-stage process – free discussion, larity, and full commitment – for good lecision-making** • Overcoming the “pee roup syndrome”

Andy Grove published *High Output Management* i 1983, when two decades of unprecedente turbulence lay ahead of both his company an ıanagement in general. Two developments in particul: ad profound impact on Intel: the upsurge of Japanes ›mpetition and the digital revolution, which gathere ıomentum as the applications of the new technolog ›nquered the world. The first drove Intel out of th ıemory industry, which it had founded; the secon ›nfronted the company with new opportunities and threat Yet, despite the upheavals, Grove found that, in the mi(990s, "most of the things that were useful [in 1983] ar ill useful now; the basics of management remain largel ıaffected." That applies to the three ideas on whic rove's book was founded:

The principles and discipline of manufacturing apply t other forms of business enterprise, including mos emphatically the work of managers.

The output of managers is the output of th organizational units under their supervision or influenc

A team will perform well only if peak performance i obtained from its individual members.

All three ideas are naturally based on Grove's experience Intel. They may read like statements of the obvious en the second, which Grove italicizes as "the single mos ıportant sentence of this book." But good managemen ›es largely consist of the practice of the obvious. The forc Grove's ideas lies in their clarity and in the practica gor with which he developed them, both in running Inte ıd in developing his "output-oriented approach t

Obvious or not, Grove's definition of management output is not shared by most executives. When he asked a group of middle managers at Intel what they understood by the term, they described activity, not output, which is "by no means the same thing." Their replies were:

- judgments and opinions
- direction
- allocation of resources
- mistakes detected
- personnel trained, subordinates developed
- courses taught
- products planned
- commitments negotiated

None of them talked about teamwork, although to Grove this is fundamental: "Business... is a team activity. And, always, it takes a team to win." Here Grove is discussing people contributing to a common output, not people working together in groups. As a CEO, he affected output by supervising his direct subordinates. He also influenced groups not under his direct supervision "by making observations and suggestions to those who manage them."

What managers do

Grove analyzed a day of his own in order "to find out what we managers really do." In a long day (over 12 hours), he spent an hour at lunch with Intel associates, three-and-a-quarter hours either alone or with one other person, six hours in meetings, and two hours giving an "orientation" lecture to professional employees (giving and gathering information, and acting as role model). The desk-time was devoted to garnering information, decision making, and "nudging" – Grove's gentle word for pushing people strongly in a certain direction.

The meetings, including lunch, were spent mostly on gathering information, with some decision making and nudging, not necessarily by Grove. He admits that the day shows no obvious pattern, but concludes that much of his day passed in acquiring information in every way possible:

> "I read standard reports and memos but also get information ad hoc. I talk to people inside and outside the company, managers at other firms or financial analysts, or members of the press. Customer complaints, both internal and external, are also a very important source of information."

Grove's guiding principle, though, is to shift his energy and attention to whatever will most increase the output of the organization. In his words, managers should move to the point where their "leverage will be the greatest."

Getting high leverage

Leverage is a central concept for Grove. He works by an equation that says that for every activity performed by a manager, the output of the organization should increase to some extent. The greater the increase, the higher the leverage. This has a direct link with productivity (output in a given unit of time), which can be raised by:

- increasing the speed at which a manager performs
- increasing the leverage associated with the various managerial activities
- shifting the mix of a manager's activities from those with lower leverage to those with higher leverage

Grove lists three basic ways in which high leverage can be achieved: first, when many people are affected by one manager; second, when somebody else's work or behavior over a long period of time is affected by a manager's brief and well-focused set of words or actions; third, when the work of a large group is affected by an individual who supplies a unique, key piece of knowledge or information.

The leverage concept is used to reinforce familiar instructions to managers: for instance, that they should prepare in advance of planning; act in a timely fashion; create a "tickler" file (to trigger inquiries into progress); and arrive fully prepared for meetings. "A manager can also exert high leverage by... an activity that takes... only a short time, but that affects another person's performance over a long time." An example here is a properly prepared performance review.

Examples of high negative leverage are numerous, including depressed, waffling, and meddling managers. With his scientific language ("leverage") and his equation, Grove seems to be constructing a scientific approach to management. But he also recognizes an "art of management," which "lies in the capacity to select from the many activities of seemingly comparable significance the one or two or three that provide leverage well beyond the others" and to concentrate on these. Paying close attention to customer complaints is one such high-leverage activity:

"Which one out of 10 or 20 complaints to dig into, analyze, and follow up is where art comes into the work of a manager. The basis of that art is an intuition that behind this complaint and not the other lurk many deeper problems."

Delegation has high leverage when it is effective, low when the delegator clings to the work. Grove insists that "delegator" and "delegate" must share "a common information base and a common set of operational ideas or notions on how to go about solving problems." He adds that this requirement is frequently not met, and that often emotion comes into play: "We all have some things that we don't really *want* to delegate simply because we like doing them and would rather not let go."

Monitoring delegation

Clinging to enjoyable tasks that could be delegated is permissible, in Grove's view, so long as that choice is conscious. He advises you to delegate familiar tasks before the unfamiliar. Doing so facilitates the essential task of monitoring to ensure that delegation is going according to plan. He draws an analogy between monitoring delegation and the principles of quality assurance:

- Monitor at the stage where least value has been added (thus, review rough drafts of requested reports, instead of waiting for the final version).
- Vary the frequency. Increase or decrease the incidence of monitoring based on delegate's experience with a specific task and their previous performance.
- Go into details only at random.
- Monitor delegated decisions by concentrating on the process the delegate has used in thinking them through.

Delegation is one way of increasing a manager's output per hour. Other methods include time management, which Grove treats in a perfunctory way, partly because he thinks his production principles are superior. First, he seeks the "limiting step," the element around which others have to revolve. In his own case, teaching duties have this role, because he must meet the class at the given time: "if we determine what is immovable and manipulate the more yielding activities around it, we can work more efficiently." You can also "batch" similar tasks to save on "setup time." If you have several reports to read, set aside a block of time and do a batch together. Another applicable production technique is forecasting, which is useful for much managerial work. The medium of a manager's forecast is the calendar, which most people use as repository of "orders" received. Grove calls this "mindless passivity." His calendar is a productivity tool:

- Use your calendar actively. Use your initiative to fill the holes between time-critical events with necessary activities that are not time-critical.
- Say "no" at the outset to any work beyond your capacity.

Grove advises that you should say "no" earlier rather than later. Remember, too, that time is your only finite resource: "when you say 'yes' to one thing you are inevitably saying 'no' to another." Moreover, your ability to say "no" will be needed in applying another production principle: "slack," or "a bit of looseness in your scheduling." Do not load your schedule beyond the optimum degree; then "one unanticipated phone call will not ruin your schedule for the rest of the day." Another of Grove's production principles is very nearly the opposite of allowing slack:

"What is 'nice' or 'not nice' should have no place in how you think or what you do. Remember, we are after what is most effective." *High Output Management*

"A manager should carry a raw material *inventory* in terms of projects... this inventory should consist of things you need to do but don't need to finish right away.... Without such an inventory of projects, a manager will most probably use his free time meddling in his subordinates' work."

If there are too many or too few subordinates, leverage is reduced, so Grove recommends six to eight for a supervisory manager, and suggests that half a day per week be allocated to each person. A similar calculation covers the "know-how manager," who supplies mainly expertise and information. Grove reckons that half a day spent in a planning, advisory, or coordinating group is equivalent to having one subordinate. If your job combines supervision and know-how, the number of subordinates should be reduced accordingly.

Handling interruptions

The more subordinates you have, the more interruptions you will experience. An experiment at Intel revealed that the output of supervisors and know-how managers was limited primarily by uncontrolled interruptions. Grove can only offer tips to deal with the problem: do not hide away; develop standard responses for standard interruptions; schedule an open hour when anybody can come in; batch interruptions and handle the issues at staff meetings and "one-on-ones."

Grove calls meetings "the medium of managerial work," where managers supply information and know-how, guide the groups under their control and influence, and make and help to make decisions. He says that these tasks can "only occur during face-to-face encounters and therefore only during meetings" – a generalization that is self-evidently untrue, but which reflects the specific culture at Intel.

Intel has three kinds of "process-oriented meetings," where knowledge is shared and exchanged. Grove is famous for his "one-on-ones" with subordinates, which are regularly scheduled, a practice that he believes "highly unusual outside of Intel." The habit sprang from his early days with the company, when he knew little about either memory chips or manufacturing techniques and therefore scheduled regular tutorials with two subordinates who could cure his ignorance. One-on-ones, lasting at least an hour, remain Grove's chief recommendation for learning, finding things out, and managing individuals.

Staff meetings

Grove believes that staff meetings are also "key to good management," because they allow peer interaction, including decision making; the supervisor can also learn from the exchange of views. Grove develops a much better understanding of an issue by listening to two people with opposing views than by hearing one side only. He prefers these meetings to work to an agenda but also includes an "open session." He asks a key question:

> "What is the role of the supervisor in the staff meeting – a leader, observer, expediter, questioner, decision-maker? The answer, of course, is all of them... A supervisor should never use staff meetings to pontificate, which is the surest way to undermine free discussion and hence the meeting's basic purpose."

Grove's third category of meetings – operation reviews – is "the medium of interaction for people who don't otherwise have much opportunity to deal with one another." The format here should include formal presentations in which managers describe their work to other managers who are not their immediate supervisors and to peers in other parts of the company. These are teaching and learning occasions, in which each of the players has a distinct role: the organizing manager, the reviewing manager, the presenters, and the audience. Grove is obviously aware of the boredom factor, and says sternly: "Regard attendance at the meeting for what it is: work."

There is also the mission-oriented meeting, which is "usually *ad hoc* and is designed to produce a specific output, frequently a decision." The problem here is an ineffective chairman who does not know what he wants. Only call a meeting if you know the answer to the first question listed below and can answer "yes" to the other three:

- What am I trying to accomplish?
- Is a meeting necessary?
- Or desirable?
- Or justifiable?

Grove is wary of these ad hoc meetings, which "a manager should never have to call... if all runs smoothly, everything is taken care of in regularly scheduled, process-oriented meetings." This ideal is surely unobtainable, and Grove concedes that 20 percent of problems and issues must be dealt with in *ad hoc* meetings; but spending more than 25 percent of your time this way is a "real sign of malorganization."

Three stages of decision

In practice, most organizations make key decisions in *ad hoc* meetings. The critical issue, though, is not the type of meeting, but the process used. Grove preaches (and practices) a three-stage process: genuinely *free discussion* (with no withholding of opinions), followed by a *clear decision* (taking care to achieve clarity of expression), and ending with *full commitment*: "everyone must give the decision reached by the group full support." If the decision proves wrong, you return to the start of the process: free discussion.

This "ideal decision-making model" is easy to follow in theory, but not, Grove finds, in practice. Middle managers "often have trouble expressing their views forcefully, a hard time making unpleasant or difficult decisions, and an even harder time with the idea that they are expected to support a decision with which they don't agree." Yet middle managers are vital in Grove's theory of management, in which rank ("position-power") does not confer "decision-power."

In a business such as Intel, knowledge-power people and position-power people have to make the decisions together: everybody involved in the free discussion stage must "voice opinions and beliefs as *equals* [his italics]." His company's overt signs of egalitarianism, such as informal dress and partitions instead of office walls, have a practical purpose. "Status symbols most certainly do not promote the flow of ideas, facts, and points of view," says Grove. "What appears to be a matter of style really is a matter of necessity."

Peer group syndrome

Another necessity is to overcome an awkward fact: anybody who makes a business decision also possesses "pride, ambition, fear, and insecurity." In this context, the most common problem is "peer group syndrome." At Intel's first-ever management training session, Grove discovered the "peer-plus-one" approach, meaning that equals need the leadership of a more senior manager; otherwise the peers will drift toward "group-think."

If no consensus emerges, "yet the time for a decision has clearly arrived," the senior person must make the decision. A balance must be struck between this necessity and the risk of bringing discussion to a premature halt by intervening too early. Grove repeats that all management activity has an output, "which in this case is the decision itself." The quality of the output is likely to be better, he writes, if expectations of quality and timeliness are made explicit by answering six important questions:

- What decision needs to be made?
- When does it have to be made?
- Who will decide?
- Who will need to be consulted before making the decision?
- Who will ratify or veto the decision?
- Who will need to be informed of the decision?

Grove "can think of no better way to make the decision-making process straightforward than to apply *before the fact* the structure imposed" by these six questions. The six also apply to the planning process. Planning's output is "the decisions made and the actions taken as a result of the process." He draws its structure from factory planning:

> "Step 1 is to establish projected need or demand: What will the environment demand from you, your business, or your organization? Step 2 is to establish your present status: What are you producing now? What will you be producing as your projects in the pipeline are completed? Put another way, where will your business be if you do nothing different from what you are now doing? Step 3 is to compare and reconcile steps 1 and 2. Namely, what more (or less) do you need to do to produce what your environment will demand?"

Grove also instructs planners to answer a key question: "What do I have to do *today* to solve – or better avoid – tomorrow's problem?" However, he hardly ever looks at the bound Intel volume called the Annual Plan. Rather, he is interested – passionately so – in how *operating managers* [my italics] carry out their planned tasks, "because the idea that planners can be people apart from those implementing the plan simply does not work." All that matters is their output and "the set of tasks it causes to be implemented."

Ideas into action

- Concentrate on the output of managers, not on their level of activity.
- Move your own activity to the place where your leverage is the greatest.
- Pay close attention to customer complaints and their underlying significance.
- Monitor activities at the stage where least value has already been added.
- Learn to say no as early as possible to work that is beyond your capacity to handle.
- Schedule one-on-one meetings with your subordinates on a regular basis.
- Ask what you must do today to solve or avoid tomorrow's problem.

2

Motivating the team to action

Why companies end up in hybrid forms combining functional organization with decentralization • Developing and mastering the technique of dual reporting • **How to control behavior inside teams** • Why the role of the team manager is that of the sports coach • **Using "task relevant maturity" to determine a management style** • Reviewing performance to develop skills and intensify motivation • **Why more time should be spent on improving star performers**

Andrew Grove's theories on management are based on the conviction that "the game of management is a team game." A manager's output is not the output of the individual, but that of the unit under the supervision or influence of that individual. Management "is a game in which we have to fashion a team of teams, where the various individual teams exist in some suitable and mutually supportive relationship with each other."

Most management texts concentrate on top management (to which, of course, Grove belongs), but his emphasis goes on teams of middle managers. As he notes, the middlemen and women and their teams are generally parts of larger organizations. He uses the "black box" analogy he applies to productive organizations in general (see p. 40). The black boxes that middle managers oversee are linked to other black boxes, and these linkages of smaller units determine how the organization operates as a whole.

Organizational extremes

Grove describes organizations in two extreme forms. In theory, they can be wholly mission-oriented or totally functional ("function" refers to corporatewide activities, such as marketing or production). In practice, the two extremes tend to be mixed. But where mission is dominant, the organization is the epitome of decentralization: "each individual business unit pursues what it does – its mission – with little tie-in to other units." This form is rarely found outside conglomerates, which are typically mission-oriented and have the minimum of corporate-level functions.

The entirely functional organization is centralized: the merchandising department looks after merchandising at every location, the human resources people hire, fire, and evaluate employees at every branch, and so on. Grove does not shy away from this centralization. On the contrary, he notes that "legitimate desire to take advantage of the obvious economies of scale and to increase the leverage of the expertise... in each operational area across the entire corporation [pushes] us toward a functional organization."

But decentralization is also strongly justified. "The desire to give the individual branch manager the power to respond to local conditions moves us toward a mission-oriented organization." Since neither alternative is likely to produce acceptable results on its own, the real-world solution is to seek a compromise between the two extremes.

The hybrid compromise

Grove refers to this compromise as the "hybrid organization," of which Intel is an excellent example. The company is organized as a mix of business divisions, which are mission-oriented, and functional groups "that can be viewed as if they were internal subcontractors." The subcontractor analogy is somewhat unconvincing, since about two-thirds of Intel's employees work in these functional units. Grove indeed describes "their enormous importance" and dwells on advantages that go well beyond the evident and valuable economies of scale. For example, "resources can be shifted and reallocated to respond to changes in corporatewide priorities."

A wholly decentralized company could never hope to manage its resources with equal efficiency. There is also the issue of "leverage" (see pp. 16–17). Grove finds that with a functional organization the "expertise of specialists – know-how managers, such as the research engineers who work in technology development – can be applied across the breadth of the entire corporation, giving their knowledge and work enormous leverage." Summing up, Grove makes Intel's functional groups sound almost benevolent: they "allow the business units to concentrate on mastering their specific trades rather than having to worry about computers, production, technology, and so forth."

The hybrid organization does not, however, have the best of both worlds. A functional group is hit with a flood of demands from the business units, which in turn must negotiate several management layers before they can influence the decisions made in the functional area. The obvious battleground is the distribution of shared resources, such as production capacity or computer time. "The bottom line here is that both the negotiation and competition waste time and energy, because neither contributes to the output or the general good of the company."

All the same, no company can afford to ignore the benefit of having much of its organization in a mission-oriented form. The argument is simple. Although there is only one advantage, according to Grove, that advantage is decisive: "... the individual units can stay in touch with the needs of their business or product areas, and initiate changes rapidly when those needs change. *That is it.* All other considerations favor the functional type of organization."

Grove's Law

Grove points out that even the conglomerates, mission-oriented as they are, have business units that are likely to be hybrids. His observations lead him to propound Grove's Law: *All large organizations with a common business purpose end up in a hybrid organizational form.* The corollary of that law is that all reasonably large companies must one day cope with the problems inherent in the workings of a hybrid organization. "The most important task... is the optimum and timely allocation of its resources and the efficient resolution of conflicts arising over that allocation." This task falls to middle managers, because, as Grove argues, only they are numerous enough to cover all of a company's operations. Moreover, they are very close to the problem of generating and consuming internal resources:

> "For middle managers to succeed at this high-leverage task, two things are necessary. First, they must accept the inevitability of the hybrid organizational form if they are to serve its workings. Second, they must develop and master the practice through which a hybrid organization can be managed. This is *dual reporting*."

Dual reporting is something that Intel "stumbled onto... almost by accident... when our company was young and small." It means that an employee has two bosses: one in the line role, say, and another in a functional capacity. Grove knows that what he is describing (and practicing) is not ideal: "Hybrid organizations and the accompanying dual reporting principle, like a democracy, are not great in and of themselves. They just happen to be the best way for any business to be organized" – and coordinated.

Make people responsible for coordination, taking them out of their regular daily work, and you create "a subtle variation of dual reporting." This is very similar in effect to what Grove calls "the two-plane concept," which is another everyday part of organizational life. "For instance, while people mostly work at an operating task, they also plan. The hierarchy of the corporation's planning bodies lies on a plane separate from the one on which you'll find the operating groups. Moreover, if a person can operate in two planes, he can operate in three."

Multiplane management

Status may well be turned on its head by the multiplane concept. Grove cites his own case. When president of Intel, he also belonged to a strategic planning group. In that capacity he came under the group's chairman, who was one of the division controllers, and who, in that role, reported ultimately to Grove. This reversal of the subordinate/supervisory relationship between planes is not only sensible but beneficial to the boss: "The two- (or multi-) plane organization is very useful. Without it I could only participate if I were in charge of everything I was part of. I don't have that kind of time, and often I'm not the most qualified person around to lead."

One key difference, however, is that the superior-leading-subordinate relationship is relatively permanent, while the subordinate-leading-superior nexus may well be temporary, because the group concerned has a finite life. It may be a task force, formed for a specific purpose, or an informal group set to work on a particular problem. These groups only last as long as the problem, but their use is growing fast. Making transitory teams effective is therefore crucial. Grove advises the same techniques that make hybrid organizations work: dual or multiple reporting and also decision making by peer groups.

Behavior inside the teams, and at work in general, says Grove, can be controlled by three invisible and pervasive means: free-market forces, cultural values, and contractual obligations. The (unwritten) contract gives the employer the right to monitor and evaluate and, if necessary, correct work. Both sides agree on other guidelines and work out rules that will be obeyed. When, for whatever reason, the guidelines and rules prove inadequate, you need another mode of control, based on cultural values.

Developing the culture

Management's cultural role is to "develop and nurture the common set of values, objectives, and methods essential for the existence of trust" by *articulation* ("spelling out... values, objectives, and methods") and, more important, by *example.* Fostering the development of a group culture promotes the reduction of "the CUA factor" – the degree of complexity, uncertainty, and ambiguity with which people must contend. The factor rises as their jobs become more involved with "the complex world of multiple bosses and peer decision making." Resolving the CUA factor, however, is ultimately down to the individual:

> "No matter how well a team is put together, no matter how well it is directed, the team will perform only as well as the individuals on it. In other words, everything we've considered so far is useless unless the members of our team will continually try to offer the best they can do."

What if the individual's best is not good enough? Grove sees clearly that there are only two possibilities: the person either cannot or will not do it. To determine which, he applies a simple test: if the person's life depended on doing the work, could he do it? If the answer is "yes," he is not motivated; if the answer is "no," he lacks competence. You have to tackle inability, however caused, by training and/or motivation, the two key weapons for the manager's most important task: to elicit peak performance from subordinates.

As a motivator, Grove relies heavily on behavioral scientist Abraham Maslow's theory that motivation is closely tied to needs, which cause people to have drives, which in turn motivate them. The highest need, according to Maslow, is self-actualization, which stems from personal realization that "what I can be, I must be." Some people are driven constantly to raise their level of competence, others to maximize their achievement. Either way, the drive to perform well has no limit and continues to motivate people to ever higher levels of performance.

Fear of failure

Grove recognizes that fear of failure can be a positive or negative source of motivation. "Given a specific task, fear of failure can spur a person on; but if it becomes a preoccupation, a person driven by a need to achieve will simply become conservative."

In writing about success and failure, Grove often uses sports analogies. He likens the role of the team manager to that of the sports coach. Like an ideal coach, the ideal manager takes no personal credit for the team's success. That earns the players' trust. The coach/manager, though, is tough on the team. Being critical is a strategy for eliciting the best performances. "A good coach," Grove concludes, "was likely a good player himself at one time. And having played the game well, he also understands it well."

One fundamental of the management game, Grove believes, is task-relevant maturity (TRM) – a variable that determines the style to adopt in a particular situation. The TRM referred to is that of subordinates. It is a combination, specific to the task at hand, "of the degree of their achievement, orientation, and readiness to take responsibility, as well as their education, training, and experience."

When the TRM is low, the effective management style is structured and task-oriented; you tell the subordinate "what," "when," and "how." With medium TRM, the appropriate style is oriented to the individual, with emphasis on two-way support and "mutual reasoning."

Football model
Knute Rockne (center), the tough American who built the Notre Dame college football team into a national icon, stands as a stern model for the "must win" team manager in business.

Where the TRM is high, the manager's involvement should be minimal, limited to establishing objectives and monitoring. Whatever the level, Grove is adamant on one point: do not deliberately let people learn from their own mistakes. "The responsibility for teaching the subordinate must be assumed by his supervisor, and not paid for by the customers of his organization, internal, or external."

Performance review

A key mechanism in teaching is the performance review, by which Grove sets great store: "giving such reviews is the *single most important form of task-relevant feedback* we as supervisors can provide." Not only is it the means of assessing performance and delivering that assessment, it is also how rewards – promotions, bonuses, stock options, and so on – are allocated. As Grove says, "the review will influence a subordinate's performance – positively or negatively – for a long time, which makes the appraisal one of the manager's highest-leverage activities."

Its fundamental purpose, Grove asserts, is *to improve the subordinate's performance*. Use it to discuss two things: "to determine what skills are missing and to find ways to remedy that lack," and "to intensify the subordinate's motivation in order to get him on a higher performance curve for the same skill level." This is the only time when a manager should act as judge and jury, which makes it doubly important to follow Grove's advice:

> "To make an assessment less difficult, a supervisor should clarify… in advance what [is expected] from a subordinate and then attempt to judge whether [the person] performed to expectations. The biggest problem… is that we don't usually define what… we want from our subordinates, and if we don't know what we want, we are surely not going to get it."

Grove draws attention to one big pitfall: the "potential trap." At all times you should "force yourself to assess performance, not potential." Although difficult, improving performance is fundamental:

> "No matter how well a subordinate has done his job, we can always find ways to suggest improvement… blessed with 20/20 hindsight, we can compare what

"With the few hours' work that a manager spends preparing and delivering the review, he can affect the work of the recipient enormously."
High Output Management

the subordinate did against what he might have done, and the variance can tell both of us how to do things better in the future."

Level, listen, and leave

According to Grove, three L's should always be kept in mind when delivering a review: Level, Listen, and Leave yourself out. "You must level with your subordinate – the credibility and integrity of the entire system depend on your being totally frank." The instruction "listen" speaks for itself. The third, "leave yourself out," needs explanation:

> "It is very important... to understand that the performance review is about and for your subordinate.... At issue are the subordinate's problems, not the supervisor's, and it is the subordinate's day in court."

This sounds as if the subordinate is on trial. If the appraisal is what Grove calls "the blast," that is certainly the case. "You have a subordinate who, unless turned around, could get fired." The initial trouble is that the poor performer "has a strong tendency to ignore his problem." You need facts and examples to cross the first barrier and move the person into active denial that a problem exists. Introduce more evidence, and the subordinate will go further, acknowledging the problem, but blaming others.

Committing to action

The next (and big) step is the assumption of personal responsibility. Once that has been achieved, says Grove, finding the solution to the problem is relatively easy. He feels very strongly that any outcome that commits the poor performer to action is acceptable. The process takes time and trouble, but may prove to be well worthwhile. But what about the excellent performer?

> "I think we have our priorities reversed. Shouldn't we spend more time trying to improve the performance of our stars?... these people account for a disproportionately large share of the work in any organization... concentrating on the stars is a high-leverage activity: if they get better, the impact on group output is very great indeed."

Other factors contribute to high output, of course, notably the quality of the interviews that select (or de-select) candidates for employment, and the reward system. Grove applies a simple test on rewards. If the relative pay (what you receive in relation to others) is what matters, and not the absolute amount (the size of a salary or pay increase), you are likely to be motivated in the best possible way – by self-actualization: "because money here is a measure, not a necessity." As Grove summarizes the issue:

> "... managers must be responsible and provide our subordinates with honest performance ratings and honest merit-based compensation. If we do, the eventual result will be performance valued for its own sake throughout our organization."

The final responsibility of the manager to the team is training, which Grove considers "one of the highest-leverage activities a manager can perform." He works out that it takes 12 hours of work to give four lectures to your subordinates. If the class numbers ten, they will do some 20,000 hours of work in a year. If the training improves their performance by only one percent, the company acquires the equivalent of 200 work-hours for the expenditure of just a dozen of yours.

Grove insists that what you teach must be closely tied to practice, and that "training needs to be a continuing process rather than a onetime event." Clearly, for that reason alone, "you and only you can fill the role of the teacher to your subordinates." But there is another reason. "Training must be done by a person who represents a suitable role model… a believable, practicing authority on the subject taught."

Training, Grove admits, is hard work: "Much deeper knowledge is required to teach the task than simply to do it." But when done well, "it is nothing short of exhilarating." The output of the team will benefit, but: "Guess who will have learned most… You."

Ideas into action

- Build an organization that is a team of teams and behaves like one.
- Leave the effective allocation of resources to the company's middle managers.
- Be prepared to serve more than one master – even if that means working under a subordinate.
- However high the level of performance, expect it to rise higher still.
- Foster group culture to reduce the "CUA factor" – the degree of complexity, uncertainty, and ambiguity.
- To determine competence, ask, "if this person's life depended on this work, could they do it?"
- To get what you want from subordinates, you must first define your requirement.

Optimizing management

Andy Grove equates his work with that in a production process. He does not measure his output by hours worked, or any other gauge of personal activity, but by the output of those he manages. Learn to use indicators to monitor progress and ensure that your "leverage" enhances everyone's output.

Understanding the production process

Grove explains general production principles with his early experience as a waiter, when he was working his way through college. He had to deliver to the table a boiled egg, buttered toast, and coffee "simultaneously, each of them fresh and hot." This routine exemplifies the PAT formula of process, assembly, and test.

The PAT Formula		
Process any activity that physically changes material	**Assembly** components are put together to create a new entity	**Test** components or the total are examined and evaluated

In Grove's breakfast task, the process includes boiling a three-minute egg and making the coffee, the assembly is setting out the tray, and the test could be checking on the browning of the toast.

The PAT formula applies to all kinds of productive work, such as training a sales force, developing a "compiler" for a computer, recruiting a graduate – or managing anything. Analyze your own work. How does the PAT formula apply?

Making the production process flow

All production processes have what Grove calls a limiting step – the "longest (or most difficult, or most sensitive, or most expensive) step." You construct your production flow by starting with the limiting step and building around it. In the case of Grove's breakfast, the limiting step is the three-minute egg. Grove works back from the time taken to boil the egg and staggers the other steps to ensure that every stage is completed in good time. Identify your own limiting step and organize the flow of work around that priority.

Focusing on the production essentials

There are five essential parts to every production process. Make these the basis of your approach to your own output, which is judged, remember, by its contribution to the output of others.

The Five Essentials of Production
Build and deliver products...
in response to customer demands...
at a scheduled delivery time...
at an acceptable quality level...
at the lowest possible cost.

Relate the five essentials to your own activities. Ask yourself:

- What are my "products"?
- Who are my customers and what do they want?
- What deadlines must I meet?
- How do I measure quality, and what quality is acceptable?
- What does my "production" cost, and how can that cost be cut?

Your effectiveness as a manager depends on knowing the answers to these questions and using the information to raise performance.

Using your time well

Time is your only finite resource. How well you use it is crucial. How do you divide your time between the three activities seen by Grove as the key functions of a manager?

The Three Activities of a Manager
1 Gathering information and giving it out
2 "Nudging" people to do what is required
3 Making decisions on what has to be done

Write down everything you do in a day under each heading. Are all your activities having a positive impact on the Five Essentials?

2 Managing by measurement

In management, what you measure is what you get. To run any operation really well you need good indicators or measurements, with each one focused on a specific operational goal.

Using indicators for forecasting

Grove envisions the production process as a "black box" that you can look inside. "Leading indicators" provide ways of measuring the process inside the box to see if problems are arising.

- A linearity indicator allows you to draw, for example, a month-by-month straight-line progress from the start of interviewing college graduates to the date when the number of graduates to be hired is supposed to be met. You plot actual progress against the straight line. If there is an adverse gap, act to close it.
- A trend indicator measures output against time (performance this month versus performance over a series of previous months), "and also against some standard or expected level."

A form of trend indicator that Grove has found effective in "getting a feel for future business trends" is the stagger chart. You forecast output over several months ahead and update the forecasts monthly. The chart presents your latest forecast alongside several earlier forecasts. It thus not only tests events against forecasts but also tests the quality of the forecasts themselves.

Optimizing performance

You also need indicators to help determine the most cost-effective way of deploying resources – of getting the most output from the least input. Grove suggests using five critical indicators here.

The Five Critical Indicators
1 The *sales forecast* for the day.
2 The *inventory* of material.
3 The condition of the *equipment.*
4 The *manpower* availability.
5 The *quality* of output.

Be careful: indicators tend to make you watch only what they monitor. Concentrating on one indicator at the expense of others can have bad results. For example, focusing on inventory levels might lead to cutting stocks to save money, without anybody realizing that this will create shortages and thus hamper production. Guard against such risks by pairing indicators, so that you simultaneously measure both effect and countereffect – in this instance, monitoring both inventory levels and the incidence of shortages.

Measuring output

Another mistake is to measure activity rather than output. Do not measure a salesman by his calls, but by his orders and his hit rate. What you measure should be physical and countable. These rules can be applied to administrative functions as well as production, through making the effort to find quantifiable indicators. Grove gives the example of output indicators for office work.

Output Indicators for Office Work

	Administrative function	Work output indicator
1	Accounts payable	Vouchers processed
2	Custodial	Square yards cleaned
3	Customer Service	Sales orders entered
4	Data entry	Transactions processed
5	Employment	People hired (by type of hire)
6	Inventory control	Items managed in inventory

Each of these output or quantity indicators needs to be paired with another indicator that stresses the quality of work: as well as measuring the area of office cleaned, for example, you need to measure the standards of cleanliness.

Draw up a similar list of output indicators for any functions for which you are responsible, and think of a quality indicator with which each of the output indicators might be paired.

3 Applying leverage

The manager's output is that of his subordinates and the unit. You can raise that output by how you use and impart information, get decisions made, and "nudge" people in the right direction.

Gathering the information

Information is the key to Andy Grove's management leverage. He gathers it from standard reports and memos, talking to people inside the company, talking to people outside the company (other managers, financial analysts, the media), and listening to customers.

Grove's most valued way of getting information ("much neglected by most managers") is the walkabout. Make a visit and talk to people as you walk. What takes two minutes on the factory or office floor would take at least half an hour in somebody's office. Do not feel awkward about making visits without any specific agenda. Your objective is to learn – which by definition means that you cannot know what you will discover in advance

Ad hoc communications are Grove's most useful sources of information because they tend to be both quick and timely. Written reports are secondary, but still important, for four reasons:

- They provide an archive of data.
- They help to validate *ad hoc* communications.
- They catch things that you might have missed.
- They force thinking discipline on the writer.

Grove says: "Writing the report is important; reading it often is not." He applies this view even to documents requesting authority to spend capital, when "people go through a lot of soul-searching analysis and juggling, and it is this mental exercise that is valuable."

Learning at Firsthand

Intel managers are asked to conduct "Mr. Clean" inspections in parts of the company they would not normally visit: the goal is simply to learn.

During the visit the managers check out the housekeeping, the way everything is laid out, the labs (if any), and the safety equipment. The browsing around takes an hour and acquaints them firsthand with processes and people about which they would otherwise know little.

Making the decisions

You need the best information you can obtain to make decisions – or to participate in them, which, says Grove, happens much more of the time. That applies to both kinds of decision: forward-looking (such as capital authorizations), or response to difficulties and crises (either people problems or technical ones). In order to make a correct decision that will result in a firm, clear directive you must know the answers to six important questions.

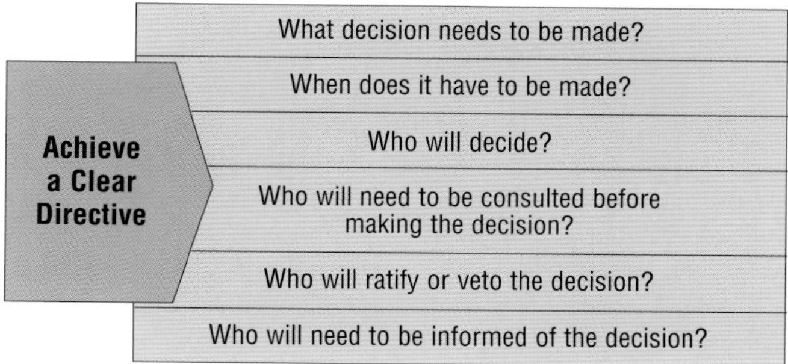

Nudging toward action

Giving information to subordinates and colleagues is equally important – especially in the form that Grove calls "nudging." You may nudge by phone call, note or memo, or making comments in meetings. "You may be advocating a preferred course of action," says Grove, "but you are not issuing an instruction or command." He reckons that "nudges" – pushing people where you want them to go – outnumber unambiguous commands a dozen-to-one.

Nudging is important in meetings as well as in one-to-ones. A meeting is a forum for gathering and giving information and for making participative decisions. Your job as its supervisor is to keep the discussion on track and to have your subordinates or colleagues (preferably all of them) do the work under your leadership. That is another clear example of management leverage.

Always work toward increasing leverage. Keep this key question in mind. Is what I am doing helping others to increase their contribution to the output of this enterprise? If the answer is No, stop doing it, and find something that really will achieve that end.

The loss of Intel's memory

Memory chips are the ubiquitous tools of the computer revolution. In the 1970s, Intel was the prime mover in memories – it had close to a one hundred percent share of the market – and prospered mightily from them.

As memory chips grew from 64-bit (meaning that they could store 64 numbers) to 256-bit, then 1,024, Intel remained king of the memories. But, in the 1980s, a cloud appeared in the east: the Japanese stormed Intel's citadel with ferocious and mounting efficiency.

Reports of Japanese quality results were "beyond what we thought were possible. Our first reaction was denial.... As people often do in this kind of situation, we vigorously attacked the ominous data." This only wasted time, during which the Japanese remorselessly added large and modern factories and slashed prices. Despite this pressure, Intel went on investing in R&D because, "Our priorities were formed by our identity; after all, memories were us."

For a while, the unchanged strategy seemed justified when the enormous impact of IBM's PC, born in 1982, created a surging demand for chips, including Intel's second-string product, the microprocessor. "Then in the fall of 1984 all of that changed. Business slowed down. It seemed that nobody wanted to buy chips anymore." Orders dried up, stocks soared. Unable to compete with the Japanese producers and their "high-quality, low-priced, mass-produced parts," Intel carried the memory losses on the back of profits elsewhere. Now a new strategy that would stem the losses was urgent.

Intel floundered through "meetings and more meetings, bickering and arguments resulting in nothing but conflicting proposals" and "just went on losing more and more money... We were wandering in the valley of death." In mid-1985, after a year of this aimless meandering, Grove was in his office with his chairman and CEO, Gordon Moore, and asked what proved to be a historic question. "If we got kicked out, and the board brought in a new CEO, what do you think he would do?" Moore answered without hesitation: "He would

“Had we not changed our business strategy, we would have been relegated to an immensely tough economic existence and, for sure, a relatively insignificant role in our industry.” *Only the Paranoid Survive*

get us out of memories.” Grove’s reaction was to stare at him numbly and say “Why shouldn’t you and I walk out the door, come back, and do it ourselves?”

This momentous decision – to abandon the very product that had created Intel – has cornered all subsequent attention. Yet what followed was even more important. Grove not only had to force through the decision against confused but serious opposition from senior executives, he had to find an alternative strategy and product. It took a year to implement the exit and throw all Intel’s energies into the microprocessor. Fortunately, the 386 was ready for production, and it “became very, very successful, by far our most successful microprocessor to that point.”

It took another year before the company became profitable once more. Intel the memory king was without a doubt dead. Intel the microprocessor emperor was on the high road to $29 billion of sales.

3

Management by confrontation

Using combative paranoia to drive management into a winning game • How to fit free and freely acting spirits into a regime of tight control • **"Ranking and rating" employees to exert pressure for improved performance** • The miraculous birth of the microprocessor which changed the world • **"Constructive confrontation" as a means of bringing problems into the open – and solving them** • The debate over the memory business • **How the psychology of threat leads to market domination**

Practicing managers demonstrate their philosophy in deeds, even if, like Andy Grove, they also commit their thoughts and experiences to books. They run a risk when they become authors: what they say and what they do may not be the same; how they behave may be a good deal less rational than how (and what) they write; how their companies work internally may differ from the text.

In Grove's case, inconsistency between words and deeds shows more in behavior than in the technicalities of management. His day-to-day style, and therefore that of the company, is confrontational. This is clear from the only full account of the man at work: Tim Jackson's *Inside Intel.* Published in 1997, this is a remarkable piece of reporting, written with the active noncooperation of Grove and the company. Although Jackson's account of Grove's ideas and personality is not meant to be flattering, the book provides essential evidence to support Grove's standing as one of the most brilliant managers of his or any other generation.

Combative paranoia

Even Grove's best-known and highly emotional remark, "only the paranoid survive," has a strong intellectual basis (see pp. 72–85): the company that is not constantly alert to threats automatically becomes vulnerable. The combative paranoia that he describes and uses as a management driver springs not only from his intellect, but also from secretive and aggressive elements in his personality. These explain why Intel went to some lengths to prevent Jackson, a reputable journalist, from gaining access to the sources he required.

Their efforts did not succeed. Jackson discovered strange tidbits, such as the stacks of paper next to Intel's photocopiers all preprinted with the legend "Intel Confidential." He found out about the three hours of legal training given twice a year to middle managers, during which they are warned never to say that the company "dominates" the world's microprocessor business, only that it "leads." He also learned about the role-plays in which Intel staff pretend to be law enforcement officers, invade an executive's office, seal it off, and cart away documents to check for incautious words.

Jackson concludes that paranoia works: "this culture helps to explain why the company has become what it is today." The culture reads like one of tight control, which is definitely one aspect of Grove's personality and his management methods. Yet he understands thoroughly that decisions in a highly technological industry must be devolved as far down as possible to people who have great discretion and freedom of action. The formula at Intel is to combine immense delegation with intense control.

The hierarchy that Grove established not long after becoming CEO in 1987 was designed accordingly. He prefers to have only a few people reporting directly to him. So he delegated substantial authority to four senior vice-presidents who headed the key activities: microcomponents, microcomponent operations, systems, and manufacturing. Beneath the quartet, a "management group" enjoyed great delegated powers, but within a framework of tight discipline.

Freedom and control

This results in a series of paradoxes. Managers at Intel are obliged to take the initiative, handling most issues themselves, with minimal upward passing of the buck. When issues affect the whole company, managers create an *ad hoc* group of peers, chaired by a "czar," to solve the problem. But all the free and freely acting spirits must obey the laws of a tough budgeting regime, which embraces all levels. Forecasts of costs and sales are regularly updated, and every deviation from plan must be fully explained.

Everybody at Intel, moreover, has an annual and demanding objective, and this includes the so-called "individual contributors," who have no subordinates and are responsible only for their own results. They, like everyone else, still get an "IMBOS," which stands for Intel Management by Objectives System. MBO is a management control and performance system, long out of fashion, which was introduced to the young Intel by a consultant. It suits Grove's temperament perfectly. MBO slots neatly into a management context whose strong flavor can be judged from this passage in a 1978 Grove memo entitled "Get Organized (Again) – Chapter 2":

> "For starters, the Executive Staff decided in reviewing progress against the specific milestones that we set for ourselves that our overall performance in this area rates a 'not done.' Basically, we have not achieved any of the detailed key results that we set in April. Because of that, and because of the continuing immense importance of this issue to both our short and long-term success as a company, we have again decided to adopt 'Getting Organized' as our top corporate objective for the third quarter, with an updated set of specific key results."

You might judge from these words that Intel had done badly. Far from it; shipments of products were much higher, and sales in the second quarter had risen by 17 percent to a new record. But Grove is relentless in pursuing better results, finding fault, demanding improvements, getting everything down firmly on paper, and expecting excellent performance from all people and all systems.

Ranking and rating

Jackson notes that: "Even before the days of client-server computing, Intel's finance function was so efficient that a detailed set of monthly management accounts was always available three days after the end of each month." The rigor of the financial system is matched by the human resources techniques. Intel has long operated a stiff system of "ranking and rating" employees. It initially had four ratings ("superior," "exceeds expectations," "meets expectations," or "does not meet expectations"). A later version had only three classes: "outstanding," "successful," and "improvement required."

Whether the label is "does not meet" or "improvement required," the implication is ominous. "Improvement required" results in a 60-day or 90-day program of "corrective action." If this "CA" fails to deliver the specified improvements, dismissal follows. The ranking part of "ranking and rating" is based on the employee's degree of improvement and is only revealed to individuals in general terms. Their managers, however, see the specific results. These compare employees to each other and obviously identify those whose services can most easily be lost.

"Ranking and rating" operates with no respect for previous achievements: at Intel you are only as good as your last performance, and you are kept only for as long as you perform well. Dismissal, however, is not the only sanction. Grove will also demote managers who perform badly, moving them to a lowlier job, which at least gives them the chance and incentive to haul themselves back. The whole organization, as well as individuals, can attract Grove's disapproval. In 1981, for example, he ordered the "125 percent solution": all staff, other than those paid by the hour, were asked to work an additional two hours per day.

Managing the hours

It seems strange that, in a company that can win only by brainpower, Grove should attach such importance to the quantity of hours worked rather than the quality. Ten years earlier, in 1971, the same obsession resulted in the saga of the "late list." Grove was annoyed by late starts to early morning meetings, and security officers were instructed to get signatures from all employees arriving after 8 a.m. The system was widely opposed, much resented, and often evaded (with false signatures, and so on). But Grove insisted on its retention for almost 17 years, finally ending the practice as part of a general liberalization and mellowing.

The whole approach to people and performance, with its emphasis on discipline and enforcement, reflects Grove's own attitudes. Jackson quotes him as saying to one executive that, "fundamentally, you believe that people left to their own volition will do good and not bad. I believe they'll do bad and not good." In Jackson's summary:

> "Grove was not a leader in the sense of someone who inspires the troops from the front, and relies on his own charisma to persuade them to follow. Instead, he was more like a shepherd – signaling with his crook where he wanted the flock to go, but keeping a team of dogs to bite the ankles of any sheep that strayed off...."

The principle of leaving people in charge of their own decisions and projects, but demanding and exacting excellent performance, fits the description "loose-tight controls." The phrase comes from *In Search of Excellence*, the best-seller written by Tom Peters and Robert Waterman and published in 1982. The meaning is obscure in the book – but not at Intel. However tightly everything else is controlled, innovation runs remarkably free. Important advances can be born anywhere in the company.

Microprocessor saga

The results are well illustrated by sagas such as that of the microprocessor, the device that literally transformed the world and saved Intel from extinction. Intel was supposed to be producing several logic chips for the Japanese company Nippon Calculating Machine Corporation, to be used in its Busicom desktop calculator. An engineer, Ted Hoff, proposed a design that would place all the circuitry on one chip. This product could be programmed like a computer, and slotted into any device, not only a calculator.

Hoff was taken away from his "computer-on-a-chip" to tackle other work, but Federico Faggin, a circuit designer, picked up the ball with a colleague. In three months, they produced a working prototype. Top management seems initially to have played no part in the development, nor to have sensed the huge importance of Hoff's brainstorm. The Japanese were no wiser.

Later, with the device plainly working, but the calculator market slumping, the Nippon people demanded a price cut. Chairman Bob Noyce joined the action, and his contribution proved to be a masterstroke: the Japanese could have a $60,000 refund if they surrendered their exclusive rights to the chip. The customer insisted only that Intel could not sell to other calculator makers. With that harmless proviso, the mighty microprocessor was Intel's for all time.

The irony was that Intel's marketing people saw no future in this low-priced, low-powered product, with no great market. It took desertion by two employees – to make microprocessors in a start-up company named Zilog – to spur Grove into action. He usually takes a belligerent stance toward people who leave Intel to set up new businesses or join a rival, and he has used Intel's full legal armory to protect its interests. In Zilog's case, the start-up was simply outgunned.

Shrewd business move
Bob Noyce, chairman of Intel from 1974 until 1979, sealed the company's future when he negotiated exclusive rights to the Intel device which developed into the mighty microprocessor families.

Belligerent style

In Grove's confrontational practice of management, belligerence is shown not only in legal and other corporate responses but in face-to-face ones as well. He has been known to behave aggressively at meetings, insulting and upbraiding an individual in front of his peers. According to Jackson, he can be "abrupt, aggressive, and interrogatory," relishing a fight and seeming "to take a positive delight in shouting at people." The war against underperformance is waged with memos, too. Grove's messages to staff are known as "Grovegrams" or "Andygrams." Woe betide any executive who does not respond swiftly to an Andygram that is marked "AR" – "action required."

There is a marked contrast between Grove's often emotional and explosive performance in meetings and the strict, rational controls by which Intel lives. The contrast is within Grove himself. On one hand, he is easily angered: on the other, he is highly cerebral. The same drive that makes his intellect so formidable, though, also results in a passion for detail. Jackson describes Grove as having a fetish for cleanliness and order, and as instituting regular (and unpopular) office inspections. An untidy desk or too many papers in the in-tray means a black mark.

Grove's personality thrives on confrontation. This personal bent has been intellectualized into a system called "constructive confrontation." Although it sounds like a contradiction in terms, it is regarded at Intel as a positive value. It is even taught in formal training and has a place in the company's statement of values. The idea is to bring problems out into the open, and to debate and resolve the issues pragmatically, without arousing personal animosities.

Agonized discussions

In fact, the defining moments in Intel's history, such as the crisis over the memories business (see pp. 46–7), or the decision not to back the more advanced RISC technology for microprocessors (see pp. 62–3), were marked by long and agonized discussions. On the memory issue, in Grove's own words from *Only the Paranoid Survive*:

> "We had meetings and more meetings, bickering, and arguments, resulting in nothing but competing proposals. There were those who proposed what they

called a 'go for it' strategy: 'Let's build a gigantic factory dedicated to producing memories and let's take on the Japanese.' Others proposed that we should get really clever and use an avant-garde technology... Others were still clinging to the idea that we could come up with special-purpose memories...."

Even when Grove and Moore, his CEO, produced a fourth alternative, abandoning memories altogether, many opposed this cutting of the Gordian knot. "The company had a couple of beliefs that were as strong as religious dogmas.... One was that memories were our 'technology drivers'.... The other belief was [that] our salesmen needed a full product line to do a good job in front of our customers." The twin beliefs made open-minded, rational discussion "practically impossible."

Note that, although two such strong personalities as Grove and Moore headed the firm, the issues were thrashed out thoroughly, even at the expense of high-priced delays in implementing what, in hindsight, proved to be a brilliantly correct decision. Grove is the opposite of indecisive, but "constructive confrontation" ensures that no alternatives are left unexplored, and that discussion, exhaustive and often exhausting, leads to the right choice, one that is understood – and fully endorsed – by the "management group." The alternative to endorsement is departure.

Confrontation is also a prominent feature of Intel's relationships with competitors. It has a host of mostly friendly alliances, which may include competitor partnerships, but they can turn unfriendly. Advanced Micro Devices (AMD), for example, was a partner in microprocessors, used as a "second source" for the supply of Intel designs. Second-sourcing was a precondition of winning the first, indispensable contract for the IBM PC:

the customer would not proceed otherwise. But the partnership had a most confrontational sequel. Three years of highly charged litigation followed when Intel dumped AMD and went ahead with production of the best-selling 386 chip on its own.

Keeping the market

Some alleged that Grove – not a man to antagonize – was getting his own back for various slights inflicted by Jerry Sanders, the flamboyant boss of the smaller company. But the dumping of AMD had far wider and weightier implications. Keeping competitors out of his markets is fundamental to Grove's strategy. The longer that Intel has a market to itself, the more money it can make from its often huge margins, which are well over 80 percent on microprocessors. Hence the ferocity with which Grove confronted Motorola in the marketplace, winning with the so-called "Operation Crush" sales campaign in 1978, despite a technically inferior product.

The sheer tenacity of Grove's drive can never be exaggerated. In September 1988, when Intel was deep into its program for the 486 chip, powerful-seeming rivals, including Sun Microsystems and Hewlett-Packard, were circling around. *Business Week* commented that "Japan is determined to break Intel's grip, as well," and quoted an American rival to the effect that, "This is a break in the action, where everybody gets the chance to play again." Play, yes: win, no. The 486 and its Pentium successor consolidated Intel's power and position, just as Grove had planned. Interviewed in *Business Week*, he said: "My hope and vision is that our technology is going to be the heart, spine, and framework of the entire computer industry."

Given all those circling rivals, Grove's paranoia becomes understandable. He uses it as a tool to make his managers as responsive to change as his engineers. The psychology of threat has been a driving force behind Intel's protection of its "intellectual property"; behind its investments in manufacturing capacity to make its dominant market share all but invulnerable; behind the acceleration in technology that has progressively made microprocessors and personal computers vastly more powerful and vastly cheaper.

Making model profits

In 1988, desktop computers containing the 486 chip were expected to cost $20,000. In 2000, Pentium-powered PCs cost a tenth or less of that amount. Such dramatic falls in prices might look calamitous, but Grove has developed the company's "business model" to a fine pitch of performance. A business model basically hinges on sales volume, realized prices, and gross margins. Intel's model has consistently generated higher and higher profits out of lower and lower prices, offset by higher and higher volumes.

In the decade to 1999, Intel rewarded its investors with a 44 percent annual growth in total return; only 13 companies in America's biggest 500 did better. Despite massive spending on R&D and capacity, its net margins were the eighth highest among the giants, while its growth in earnings per share hit an astonishing 32.2 percent per annum – that means doubling every two years, a most extraordinary rate of advance for a $30 billion company. This financial performance provides another key ingredient in Grove's practice of management: enriching staff.

Personal wealth is what makes Intel's confrontational style and hard manners palatable to people who, at any time, can walk out to an excellent job elsewhere. Stock options are very important in the organization's scheme of things. Employees who got in at the bottom when Intel went public in 1971 saw their shares rise from $23.50 to $4,385 in June 1993. The three-year gap between grant and ownership of option shares serves as a golden handcuff – and the higher the shares rise, the tighter the cuffs.

The continuing surge in Intel's shares has created many millionaires and multimillionaires, not least Grove. These rewards have cemented the executive and technical cadres, but crucial to their creation is the confrontational spirit exemplified and inspired by their leader.

Ideas into action

- Devolve decisions to people who get great discretion and freedom of action.
- Be relentless in pursuing better results, finding fault, and demanding improvements.
- Avoid any restriction that makes it harder for innovators to innovate.
- Operate "loose-tight controls" to combine essential freedom with necessary discipline.
- Debate and resolve issues pragmatically, without arousing personal animosities.
- Devote as much time and energy as necessary to thrashing out a consensus.
- Achieve the optimum combination of prices and volume to maximize profits.

Risking it all on RISC

In the late 1980s, many observers (and several competitors) believed that Intel had finally developed an Achilles heel in its mainline, near-monopoly business of microprocessors. The company itself felt vulnerable.

Intel's huge success had been founded on CISC technology (Complex Instruction Set Computing), which needed many more transistors than the newer RISC (the R stands for Reduced). Now, the 486 chip (right), using the older, slower technology, was deep into its development. Was Intel going to be leapfrogged?

Nobody knew the answer. But Grove was clear on one point. He regarded Intel's microprocessors as a family, with each new chip compatible with the same software as its predecessors. RISC chips were incompatible, so customers would need new software. All the same, with a somewhat heavy heart, Grove threw resources into developing an excellent and successful RISC chip, the i860. He now had two chips, but the company was torn apart by controversy over which one to back.

Development work on the RISC, while initially a necessary precaution, had grown to be "a very large force affecting the company," one that "eventually could have weakened our entire microprocessor thrust. In short, it created chaos."

Since Grove was not himself a computer scientist, he had to rely on his technical experts. But they "had all split into warring camps, each camp 100 percent convinced of its own chip's supremacy." The customers and partners were also divided: Compaq opted for the 486, and Microsoft the i860.

The turning point came in April 1989 when Grove introduced the 486 in Chicago. Everybody who was anybody in computers was there, and all announced their readiness to introduce 486-based products. "I remember sitting… and thinking, 'RISC or no RISC, how could we possibly not put all our efforts into supporting this momentum?'" Returning from Chicago, Grove ended the fierce debates, and Intel refocused on the 486, and on its equally successful descendants.

Looking back at those debates six years later, Grove was mystified at his indecision: "I shake my head about how I could have even considered walking away from our traditional technology that then had, and still has, phenomenal headroom and momentum." If the decision had gone the other way, Intel's whole marketing platform might have been undermined. The compatibility of its memory chips would no longer have been a massive advantage, and the rival RISC manufacturers would have started on level terms.

"The issue... didn't involve factors that might or might not arise a decade from now; it demanded a decision immediately, and the decision was crucial."
Only the Paranoid Survive

Moreover, wrote Grove in 1996, "the advantages of RISC technology over CISC technology are much smaller than they appeared then." The sacrifice would have been in vain. It was a false alarm, and one of the most expensive in history.

Driving performance

Andy Grove has demonstrated that, to flourish, the best and highest technology needs the best and highest standards of leadership. A manager's most important task is to get peak performance from staff. They need to be selected, motivated, trained, set stretching goals, appraised, and rewarded by leaders who set a powerful personal example.

Modeling the role

Motivation and training – the two key means to the end of peak performance – are both demanding tests of leadership. The more you participate as face-to-face motivator and trainer, the more effective your leadership will be. Every leader is a role model, for better or for worse. You must show the same drive for high achievement that you demand of others.

Above all, concentrate on creating an environment that values and emphasizes *output*. High motivation and training are useless if they do not advance the output of the unit and the individuals in that unit. Cross-examine yourself regularly with these three questions:

- Have my actions contributed to higher output?
- Is my contribution visible to others?
- Have I shown commitment to higher output still?

Getting your message across

Being a visible role model is easier in a small organization. But even in a small unit, where contacting people face-to-face is easy, you still need to find a way "to project your determination, will, and vision." You can never, says Grove, overclarify or overcommunicate.

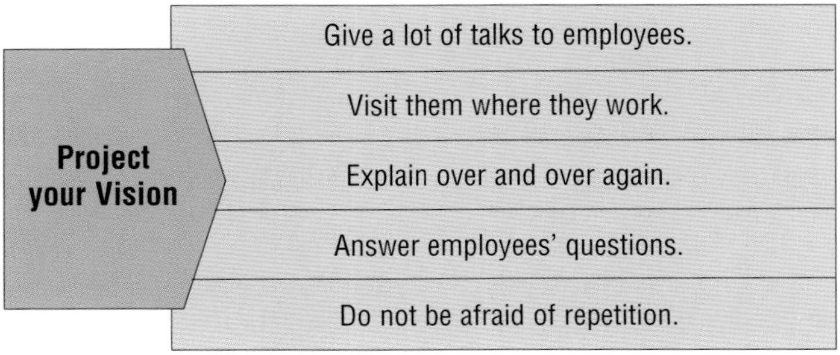

Project your Vision

- Give a lot of talks to employees.
- Visit them where they work.
- Explain over and over again.
- Answer employees' questions.
- Do not be afraid of repetition.

Working one-to-one

Personal interviews are crucial to leadership. Grove singles out two especially difficult tasks – selecting the right employee and keeping somebody who wants to leave. But one-on-one meetings are essential tools for other purposes, too, and the same three rules always apply.

The Three Rules of One-to-one Meetings
1 Have a clear purpose.
2 Use the interview to learn.
3 Make use of what you have learned to achieve your goal.

Applying the rules

In a job interview your purpose is to discover all you can: about the candidate's technical knowledge and skills; how well the person used those abilities in the past; any discrepancies, failures, and problems; how well the candidate will fit the organization and its needs. Get the candidate to speak for 80 percent of the time.

When someone you value says they want to quit, use the three rules to persuade them to stay. Follow Grove's approach:

- Drop what you are doing and deal with the issue at once. ("Your initial reaction… is absolutely crucial.")
- Let them talk – do not argue, lecture, or panic.
- Look for and learn the person's real motives.
- Buy as much time as you can and need.
- Seek help and advice as required.
- Make an offer that the person cannot refuse.

Giving Interviews Top Priority

To maximize the chances of hiring the right people, candidates at Intel may be interviewed by as many as six people, all of whom give interviews top priority.

One interviewer would not stop to take a phone call from the chairman, Robert Noyce, because "I have a candidate." Even Grove gets involved in hiring new graduates. When one star seemed likely to accept an offer from any of a dozen other would-be employers, Grove signed a personal letter telling the young man why he should join Intel – which he did.

1 Management by objectives

Andy Grove ardently practices Management by Objectives (MBO), an idea originally conceived by management guru Peter Drucker. He uses MBO as a control mechanism to raise everyone's performance.

Establishing the system

MBO is about setting yourself objectives and then breaking these down into more specific goals or key results. To get the whole process rolling, you need to answer only two questions:

- Where do I want to go? (What is the objective?)
- How will I pace myself to see if I am getting there? (What are my milestones, or key results?)

Make sure that the answers are precise. As Grove says, "The one thing an MBO system should provide is focus." So keep the number of objectives small. Most people disobey this rule; they try to focus on everything, and end up with no focus at all.

Start with a few well-chosen overriding objectives. Next, set your subordinates objectives that fit in with those objectives. Always allow your subordinates to set key results that will enable them to meet their objectives. At Intel Grove tells his managers to give "the key results very specific wording and dates, so that when deadline time arrives, there is no room for ambiguity."

MBO in Action at Intel

1 Intel manager adopts overriding objective to ensure that all plant expansion projects stay on schedule.

2 He gives subordinate executive particular objective: Obtain decision on Philippine plant expansion by October.

3 Subordinate sets four key results to attain:
- Study suitable land availability by June.
- Complete financial analysis of alternatives.
- Present results to steering group for decision.
- Get Grove to ratify by October.

4 Grove ratifies, and all objectives are met.

Aiming high

Grove uses MBO to drive exceptional performance by setting exceptionally high targets. He sets objectives at a point so high that even if individuals push themselves hard, they will still only have a 50–50 chance of hitting the target. He maintains that output will tend to be greater when everybody strives for a level of achievement beyond their immediate grasp.

A high-performance system will function best in an organization that consists mostly of people who are not easily deterred and want to maximize their achievement. To determine whether you are an achiever, place yourself in this situation. You are sent into a room where pegs are set around the floor. You are given a set of rings but no instructions. Which of the following would you do?

- Throw the rings at distant pegs (A).
- Walk up to the pegs and drop the rings over them (B).
- Walk back enough to find out your peak throwing skill (C).

If you chose A, you are a gambler, who takes high risks but does not control events. If you chose B, you are a conservative, who takes very little risk. If you answered C, you are an achiever, one of those who must always test and improve themselves.

Taking account of the CUA factor

Grove lays stress on the degree of complexity, uncertainty, and ambiguity, "the CUA factor," in a company, unit, or job. If CUA is high and individuals are motivated by self-interest, chaos will follow. Promote group interest and cultural values to cope with high CUA.

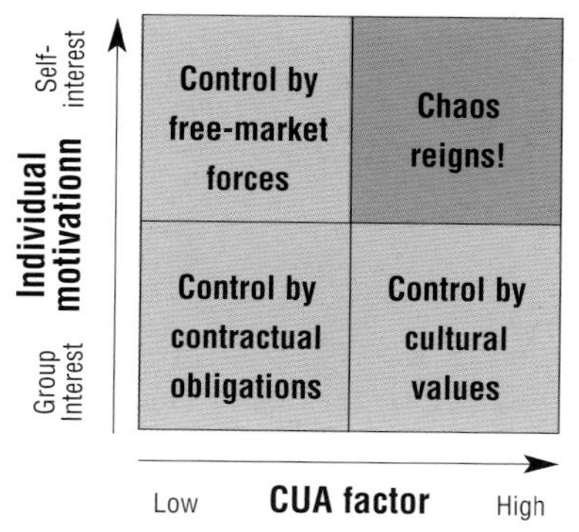

Modes of control

The chart shows how differing types of motivation and levels of CUA require different modes of control. When CUA is high, only group interest and control by cultural values will work.

2 Appraising achievement

Appraisals, or performance reviews, play a crucial role in improving the performance of subordinates. It has two key aspects: actually assessing performance and then delivering the verdict.

Making the assessment

Grove stresses that you should tie an employee's performance to the workings of the organization: "If performance indicators and milestones in a management-by-objectives system are linked to the performance of the individual, they will gauge his degree of success and will enhance his progress."

Use both output measures and internal measures to assess an individual's performance. Output measures "include such things as completing designs, meeting sales quotas, or increasing the yield in a production process." Internal measures survey what is being done to create output now and in the future. The relative significance of output and internal measures will vary from time to time, as will that of short-term and long-term needs.

Carrying out the appraisal

Choosing the right measures will not save you from having to make and deliver personal judgments – which is why most managers so dislike doing appraisals. You are very probably managing the subordinate wrongly if your comments during the review come as a surprise or shock. Follow seven principles of effective appraisal.

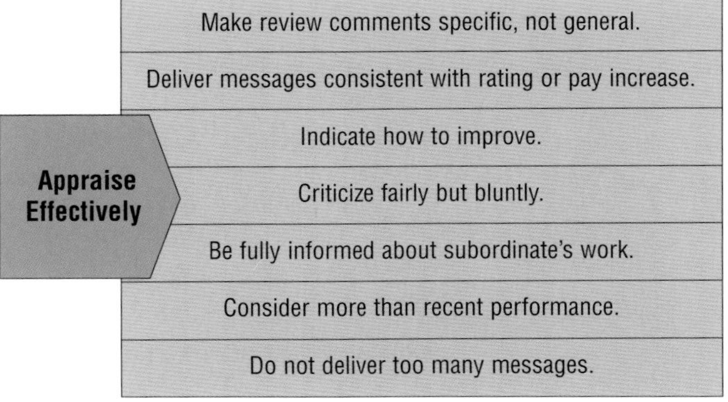

Rewarding performance

Andy Grove looks at money and other rewards as a key means of getting high performance. That means dispensing, allocating, and using money to deliver "task-relevant feedback" – the award tells the recipient how well he or she has performed.

Bonuses have to be linked to performance, although not necessarily to that of the individual alone. A bonus plan might base the payment on three separate factors, each of which would account for a third of the potential total payment.

The Three Bonus Factors
1 How well the individual has performed, as judged by the supervisor.
2 How well the team has done, as measured by objective results.
3 The overall financial performance of the company as a whole.

Grove suggests paying senior managers a bonus of up to half of base salary and middle managers between 10 to 25 percent.

Reviewing salaries and promotion

Under any system, there is a ceiling for the base salary of every job: what the job is worth. Do not pride yourself on paying below market rates: remember "the laborer is worthy of his hire," especially a good worker. You can set the base salary on the basis of experience only, merit only, or (as most companies do) on a combination of the two. Given Grove's basic principle – using pay to boost performance – merit must come into the computation.

Like it or not, any linkage of salary to merit means that you have to accept the need for a competitive, comparative evaluation of individuals. This is also inevitable in another vital means of reward: promotion. Do not consider people for promotion unless their performance exceeds the requirements of the present job: meeting the requirement is not enough. But do not leave an exceeder unpromoted for long. If you do "in time he will atrophy, and his performance will return to a 'meets requirements' level and stay there." That is bad for the employee – and for you.

10

4

Mastering strategic crisis

How the "strategic inflection point" drives companies into the turbulent waters of critical change • The six forces that impact on competitive strategy • **The two signs indicating that "10X" forces are changing an industry dramatically** • Why the most successful companies are the least likely to accept the need for dynamic change • **The inexorable trend toward "horizontal" industries** • Three tests to separate "signal" from "noise" • **How to achieve broad, intensive, and comprehensive debate**

Andy Grove's great contribution to strategic thought and practice centers around the "strategic inflection point." This technical phrase would have featured in the title of his 1986 book, had Grove had his way, but the publishers thought otherwise. They even rejected it for the subtitle, which now reads "How to Exploit the Crisis Points that Challenge Every Company and Career." But this message is far overshadowed by that of the book's main title: *Only the Paranoid Survive*.

Grove has no recollection of when, where, and why he said this, but it encapsulates his strategic approach to business. He is a world-class worrier. There is management method in what might otherwise seem mild madness. "Business success contains the seeds of its own destruction," he writes. "The more successful you are, the more people want a chunk of your business and then another chunk and then another until there is nothing left." The manager's prime responsibility is to protect the chunks, to defend success.

A world of worries

Grove guards constantly against other people's attacks and urges subordinates to share this guardian attitude. Fear of attack by no means exhausts the list of Grove's anxieties. He worries about products getting screwed up, or being introduced prematurely; about factories under-performing, or there being too many of them; about hiring the right people and falling morale; about competitors "figuring out how to do what we do better or cheaper" and stealing Intel's customers. "But these worries pale in comparison to how I feel about... a strategic inflection point... a time in the life of a business when its fundamentals are about to change."

While such a point can be caused by technological change, that is by no means all. Competitors may be the cause, but, again, more is involved. "Strategic inflection points are full-scale changes in the way business is conducted." You cannot rely on adopting new technology or battling the competition in the old way. The points "build up force so insidiously that you may have a hard time even putting a finger on what has changed, yet you know that something *has*." You also know that something of this fundamental order *will* happen:

> "Technological change is going to reach out and sooner or later change something fundamental in your business world... In technology, whatever *can* be done *will* be done. We can't stop these changes. We can't hide from them. Instead, we must focus on getting ready for them."

For Grove, that does not mean formal planning. You can plan to be ready to respond to any change, but a strategic inflection point is more than just any change. It compares to change in the same way that "deadly and turbulent rapids that even professional rafters approach gingerly" compare to ordinary waters. Grove calls these developments "10X" forces, suggesting that there has been a tenfold increase in one of the six forces that impact on competitive strategy:

1. Power, vigor, and competence of existing competitors
2. Power, vigor, and competence of "complementors" (other firms in the same business system, such as software suppliers vis-à-vis hardware firms)
3. Power, vigor, and competence of customers
4. Power, vigor, and competence of suppliers
5. Possibility that what your business is doing can be done in a different way
6. Power, vigor, and competence of potential competitors

These forces, based on Grove's reading of Harvard professor Michael Porter, tell you how "10X" phenomena may start, but not when or where the inflection point will occur. Technically, this point is where a curve stops curving in one direction and starts curving in another. The "old strategic picture dissolves and gives way to the new, allowing the business to ascend to new heights"; or, if the point is missed, "you go through a peak and after the peak the business declines."

Even in retrospect, it is difficult to tell exactly where a strategic inflection point occurred. So "how can you tell while going through one?" asks Grove. He highlights two signs. First, you are aware of "a troubling sense that something is different. Things don't work the way they used to." You notice changes in customer attitudes, less success in development work, rising competition from disregarded sources, and the "trade shows seem weird." Second, "there is a growing dissonance between what your company thinks it is doing and what is actually happening inside the bowels of the organization."

Division of opinion

The signs, however, will not be read in the same way by everybody concerned. The consequence – another indicator of strategic inflection, presumably – is division of opinion within the company: divergent views about what to do "will be held equally strongly, almost like religious tenets." As coworkers battle and long-term friends fight, management at all levels suffers:

> "Everything senior management is supposed to do – define direction, set strategies, encourage teamwork, motivate employees – all these things become harder,

The expert on competitive forces
Grove's "10X" forces – major changes affecting a business, for good or for bad – were based on Harvard professor Michael Porter's investigation of the competitiveness of companies.

almost impossible. Everything middle management is supposed to do – implement policy, deal with customers, train employees – also becomes more difficult."

But at some point the senior manager has "to take appropriate action, to make the changes that will save your company or your career." You do not know that the moment is right, yet you cannot wait until you do know. The only certainty is that the changes are best undertaken while the company is healthy. Act while cash and profits are still being generated and "you can save much more of your company's strength, your employees, and your strategic position."

Beyond that, says Grove, speaking as a believer in scientific management, unscientific instinct and personal judgment are the chief guides through strategic turbulence. History is also useful. Whether it is railroads changing transportation or superstores driving out small retailers, "The lessons and dynamics of what happens seem to be the same, no matter what the industry, no matter where it is located, and no matter which era it operates in."

Grove draws on his own industry, computing, to illustrate the process. Manufacturers, led by IBM, developed along vertical lines, with their own proprietary chips, computers, operating systems, and applications software. The "10X" force was the microprocessor, the core of the personal computer. "Over time this changed the entire structure of the industry, and a new horizontal industry emerged" with five different layers: distribution, applications software, operating systems, computers, and chips.

Missing the point

These PC developments are clear, but the exact timing of the strategic inflection point is uncertain, even in hindsight. The critical fact, though, is that all the leading players of the vertical era missed the inflection point – and that included IBM, the only one to launch a successful PC. Its managers were conditioned by the past: "Their long reign of success deeply reinforced and ingrained the thought processes and instincts that led to winning in the vertical industry." They were thus unsuited to the different rules of horizontal competition. Grove draws two lessons:

1. When a strategic inflection point sweeps through an industry, the more successful a player is, the more threatened it is by change and the more reluctant to adapt.
2. The cost of entry to an industry against well-entrenched competitors can be very high, but may become trivially small when the structure breaks.

The break will lead to a new structure that has its own rules. "Horizontal industries, for example, live and die by mass production and mass marketing" – and by their success in a "brutally competitive" environment. Grove lists three rules for brute competeting:

1. Do not differentiate without a difference; do not introduce improvements that provide an advantage over the competition but give no advantage to the customer.
2. Act first when a technology break or other fundamental change occurs. The first mover – and only the first mover – has a true opportunity to gain time over its competitors.
3. Price for what the traffic will bear, then "work like the devil on your costs" to make money at that level.

Grove's third rule leads to the economies of scale that make heavy investment effective and productive. The contrasting policy of fixing prices above your costs often leads only to a "niche position, which in a mass-production-based industry is not very lucrative." Although Grove is talking here of horizontal industries, like his own, he is undoubtedly correct in discerning a general trend toward the horizontal. "As an industry becomes more competitive, companies are forced to retreat to their strongholds and specialize in order to become world-class."

Going horizontal

Vertical companies, Grove points out, must be best in the class at everything. Horizontal ones have to be the best in only one field, which is self-evidently easier to achieve. Their functional specialization means that they should also be more cost-effective. Other industries will have to learn how to cope as they shift from being vertical to horizontal and encounter the strategic inflection point: "operating by these rules will be necessary for a larger and larger class of companies as time goes by."

Almost certainly, the changes propelling the shift to the horizontal will be "10X" forces, which, for practical purposes, always lead to strategic inflection points. Examples given by Grove include not only the arrival of superstores and the PC, but the coming of sound to the movies, container ships, and competition in the telecommunications industry. He is impressed both by the variety and the pervasiveness of the challenges. These always produce both winners and losers: "to a large extent, whether a company became a winner or a loser was related to its degree of adaptability."

Intel's adaptability was tested almost to breaking point in the 1984–85 crisis over memory chips (see pp. 46–7). The crucial incident came when Grove and his CEO, Gordon Moore, put themselves in the position of an incoming boss, an outsider completely new to the organization. "We figuratively went out the door, stomped out our cigarettes, and returned to do the job." The task was to exit from the company's founding product of memory chips, and the key to this wonderfully successful decision was "to adopt an outsider's intellectual objectivity."

Such objectivity is essential, says Grove, if "existing managers want to keep their jobs when the basics of the business are undergoing profound change." As he adds, managers who have no emotional stake in a decision can see what must be done (and do it) sooner. Outsiders have only one advantage, but it may be crucial:

"... unlike the person who has devoted his entire life to the company and therefore has a history of deep involvement in the sequence of events that led to the present mess, the new managers come unencumbered by such emotional involvement and therefore are capable of applying an impersonal logic.... "

The memory chip crisis taught Grove this lesson, together with the meaning and impact of a strategic inflection point. He describes how "small and helpless" you feel when confronted by a "10X" force, how confusion and frustration engulf you, how you want to avoid the new reality – but also how you experience "the exhilaration that comes from a set-jawed commitment to a new direction, unsure as that may be." He also learned some basic principles along the way:

- The strategic inflection point is not really a point, but a long, tortuous struggle.
- The points, however painful, "provide an opportunity to break out of a plateau and catapult to a higher level of achievment."
- Indecision magnifies the threat.
- What is happening lower down the organization, without direction from the top, can be crucial.

On the last point, Grove discovered that production resources had been increasingly diverted from memories to microprocessors, "not as a result of any specific strategic direction by senior management, but as a result of daily decisions by middle managers." These unsung heroes had begun to favor profitable microprocessors over money-losing memory chips. "By the time we made the decision to exit the memory business, only one out of eight silicon fabrication plants was producing memories. The exit decision had less drastic consequences as a result."

Bottom-up strategy

Devolved responsibility, in other words, had worked, not only tactically, but strategically. Grove had come across a vital truth. Salespeople know about shifts in customer demand first, before management; financial analysts, likewise, see the impact of fundamental change before anyone else. At Intel, middle managers acted while senior management was still dithering. The moral is clear: involve middle management in strategy and listen to its frontline information at all times.

Such information should help in trying to confirm that a change is really a strategic inflection point. Grove translates this into telling the "signal" from the "noise." In his business some loud noises have, nevertheless, proved to be poor signals. He gives the example of X-ray technology. Backed heavily by IBM but shunned by Intel, the technology proved not to be a "10X" factor in chip manufacture. Nor did another IBM innovation – RISC (Reduced Instruction Set Computing) – take over from Intel's CISC (Complex Instruction Set Computing); this story is told on pages 62–3. Grove suggests asking three questions to separate the signal from the noise:

- Is your key competitor about to change strategy? If people name a key competitor who previously was not one, that may signal a strategic inflection point.
- Is your key "complementor" about to change? If the company that mattered most to the business seems less important, that again may signal fundamental change.
- Do people around you seem to be "losing it"? Keep a lookout out for evidence that very competent people (including yourself) "have suddenly got decoupled from what really matters."

A fourth approach to the problem of identifying fundamental change is to listen to the "Cassandras," usually found among the middle managers mentioned previously. During the Trojan War, the prophetess Cassandra correctly foretold calamity for the Trojans, but nobody in a position of authority believed her. Such disbelief is also dangerously common in modern corporations. Grove points out that, being in the front line, the Cassandras "feel more vulnerable to danger than do senior managers in their more or less bolstered corporate headquarters. Bad news has a much more immediate impact on them personally. Therefore, they take the warning signs more seriously."

It follows that higher managers should take the middle Cassandras more seriously. You do not have to look for them: "they will find you [and] sell their concern to you with a passion." Grove advises you not to argue: "do your best to hear them out, to learn what they know, and to understand why it affects them." He adds that "news from the periphery is an important contribution to... sorting out signal from noise," but he makes a distinction between learning what goes on at the periphery and learning "what goes on in your business."

The latter phrase means getting information from your normal contacts, who will share much the same perspective. For a completely different viewpoint, advises Grove, talk to people who are geographically distant or are several levels below you in the organization. Instinct and experience will show you how to develop "a feel for those whose views are apt to contain gems of information and a sense of who will... clutter you with noise." But the overriding lesson is that, while you must limit the time spent on listening to random inputs, you should be open to them.

Appreciating "10X" forces

Another important lesson is that the first signs of "10X" forces may be distinctly unimpressive. Grove recalls the early days of the internet, when "getting from one place to another took forever." The Apple Macintosh looked to Grove like a "ridiculous toy," lacking a hard disk, painfully slow, and with a "graphical user interface," whose future seminal importance escaped him. Another big Apple innovation, the handheld computing device known as the personal digital assistant (PDA), was also a disappointment.

From today's perspective, handheld computing looks very different; indeed, it is vastly important. As Grove says, first versions of most things usually disappoint: "you can't judge the significance of strategic inflection points by the quality of the first version." His solution is to imagine what this first effort would be like if it improved by "10X." You might still think it uninteresting. "But if your instincts suggest that a '10X' improvement could make this capability exciting or threatening, you may very well be looking at the beginning of a strategic inflection point."

Managing by debate

The key management technique in this situation, writes Grove, is broad, intensive, and comprehensive debate. The more complex the issue, the more levels of management should participate. You need a variety of views, experience, and personality. Bring in outsiders, such as customers and business partners, too. Time and courage are required from all the debaters. Grove advises them as follows:

- Senior managers: take your time until people begin to repeat themselves and your own gut conviction builds up.

- Middle managers: give your most considered opinion clearly and forcefully, and ensure that you are listened to and understood.
- Specialists: be fully-fledged participants, contributing in hands-on experience what you may lack in perspective and breadth.
- All participants: accept that unanimity is neither the objective nor the likely outcome of the debate, and that the purpose is to enable senior management to come to a more informed and consequently correct decision.

Grove then proceeds to give the warning that fact-based management has real limitations here. He stresses that "data are about the past, and strategic inflection points are about the future." So, "you have to know when to hold your data and when to fold 'em," and when to argue against the data, turning to your experience and judgment, in dealing with emerging trends.

This advice is particularly powerful coming from a man who has little time for those who substitute opinions for fact and emotions for analysis. But Grove never denies the important role that emotions, particularly fear, play in management. "The most important role of managers," he asserts, "is to create an environment in which people are

"Debates are like the process through which a photographer sharpens the contrast when developing a print. The clearer images that result permit management to make a more informed – and more likely correct – call."
Only the Paranoid Survive

passionately dedicated to winning in the marketplace. Fear plays a major role in creating and maintaining such passion." Market victory, he adds, can be powerfully assisted by four different kinds of fear:

- fear of competition
- fear of bankruptcy
- fear of being wrong
- fear of losing

Grove describes fear as the opposite of complacency, as the force that makes him, "at the end of a long day," scan his email for "news of disgruntled customers, potential slippages in the development of a new product, rumors of unhappiness on the part of key employees," and so on. It is why he reads trade press reports on what competitors are doing, and tears out "particularly ominous articles to take to work for follow-up the next day." Fear makes him listen to Cassandras. But the fear he describes is not mere worrying. It expresses the knowledge, reinforced by Intel's own near-tragic experiences in 1984–85 (see pp. 46–7), that nothing fails like success, and that "a good dose of fear" may help to sharpen a company's survival instincts.

Living the culture

This type of fear is the good kind. However, "Fear that might keep you from voicing your real thoughts is poison.... If you are a senior manager... under no circumstances should you ever 'shoot the messenger' [who brings bad news], nor should you allow any manager who works for you to do so." That is a key element in "living the culture." Intel's culture, Grove says, is one in which holders of knowledge power and holders of organization power collaborate, risk-taking is rewarded, and values are incorporated in the management process. "Whatever success we have had in maintaining our culture," he concludes, "has been instrumental in Intel's success in surviving strategic inflection points."

Ideas into action

- Do not hide from major change: focus on getting ready for it.
- Embrace change while the existing business is still generating cash and profits.
- Regard strategic crisis, not just as a threat, but as a powerful opportunity.
- Confront major issues by adopting an outsider's intellectual objectivity.
- Involve middle management in strategy and closely observe its practical decisions.
- Listen to the Cassandras within the organization and take their bad news seriously.
- Do not rely on past data when deciding on the shape of the future.

The crash of the Pentium processor

On November 22, 1994, Andy Grove was assessing his students' performance at Stanford University, as their part-time teacher, when he received an urgent telephone call from Intel's head of communications.

The message was that CNN was sending a television crew to cover a sensitive story, that of the "floating paint flaw" discovered in Intel's flagship product, the Pentium processor.

It wasn't much of a story, and that was the problem. Grove did not believe that people could become very excited about a division error that one mathematics professor had encountered while working on some abstruse problem. Grove knew all about the design fault. It "caused a rounding error in division once every nine billion divisions." Thus "an average spreadsheet user would run into the problem only once every 27,000 years of spreadsheet use." Intel started to rectify the fault, and did nothing more about the problem, which was primarily aired on the internet.

The trade press picked up on the story, which was described "thoroughly and accurately... And that seemed to be that." The CNN filming, however, changed everything. The coverage was hostile, and the major newspapers joined in. The snowball grew into an avalanche. Users started to call Intel directly for replacement chips, and the company responded by replacing chips whose users appeared to have a real need.

This action seemed to bring the situation under control. But on December 12, the bombshell exploded: IBM stopped all shipments of Pentium-based computers. As the "most important player in the industry," IBM's move was particularly significant. Heavily back on the defensive, Grove found "all of a sudden" that "instead of predictable success, nothing was predictable... I felt we were under siege – under unrelenting bombardment."

What to do next was decided after a week of struggle. Grove made a U-turn: Intel would replace anybody's part as requested, regardless of "whether they were doing statistical analysis or playing computer games." With millions

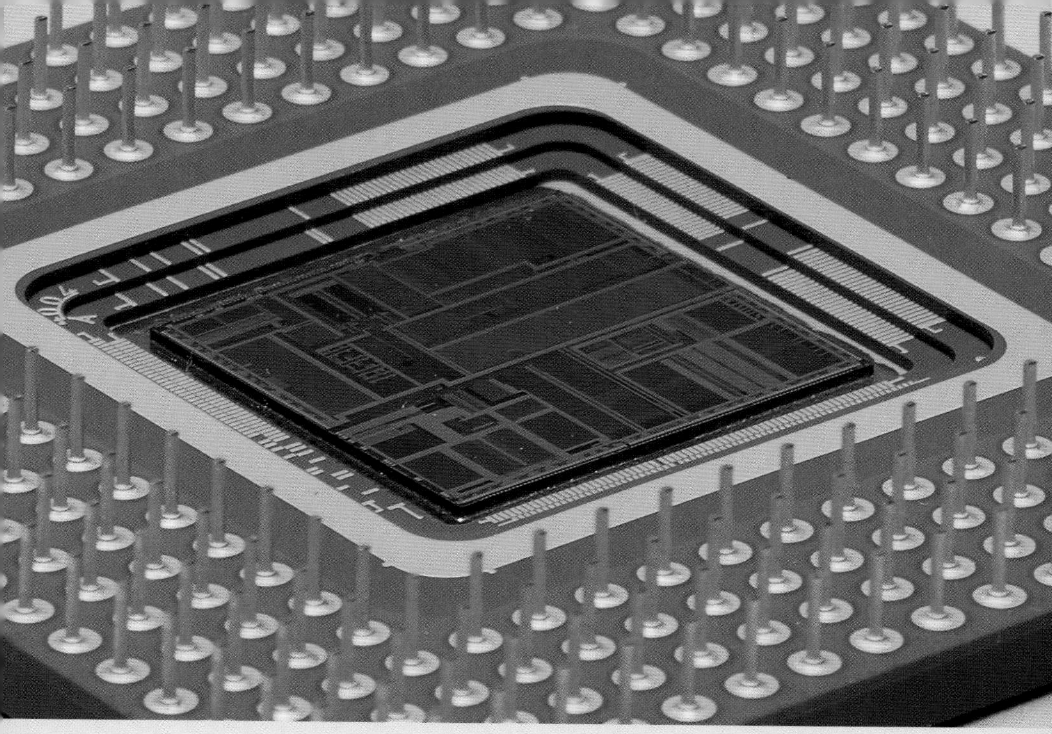

of chips on the market, Intel took "a huge write-off – to the tune of $475 million" as it speeded conversion of chip manufacture and scrapped old material. But, more important, Grove asked a question: "What happened here?"

"Something big, something different, something unexpected," was the answer. First, with its "Intel Inside" advertising policy, the company had identified itself to PC customers as the prime supplier of computing. Second, Intel had become much bigger – a giant – and was now perceived as such. "I was one of the last to understand the implications of the Pentium crisis," confesses Grove. "It took a barrage of relentless criticism to make me realize that something had changed." Intel had to do the same. As a newly fledged consumer powerhouse, it had to behave like a consumer company, not a high-tech temple – so "we embarked on a whole new way of doing business."

"What was the hardest to take was the outside world's image of us... now the world seemed to treat us like some typical mammoth corporation.... That outside image didn't jibe with my view of us."
Only the Paranoid Survive

5

Coping with change

The four approaches to experimentation and chaos • How and why managers loathe change, especially when it involves themselves • **The dangerous results of the "inertia of success"** • Falling into the dissonance trap of doing one thing and saying another • **Entering and escaping from "the valley of death"** • The difference between downsizing and fundamental transformation • **Why strategic plans fail, but strategic action succeeds** • The case for deciding and acting sooner rather than later

Although Grove's "strategic inflection points" are among the most momentous examples of change, there are others. He says flatly that "we managers loathe change, especially when it involves us." Like it or not, they are human beings, and "a lot of their emotions are tied up in the identity and well-being of their businesses." If the change is adverse, their reaction is likely to be emotional. Senior managers who have probably devoted much of their lives to their business feel the pain of sudden, sharp difficulties as a personal loss. They behave as in a real bereavement, but instead of the personal cycle of emotions (denial, anger, bargaining, depression, acceptance), they go through three stages when strategic inflection points occur:

1. Denial ("The Japanese can't possibly achieve these levels of quality.")
2. Escape or diversion ("When companies are facing major changes in their core business, they seem to plunge into... totally unrelated acquisitions and mergers.")
3. Acceptance and pertinent action

Handling change successfully therefore requires replacing denial with brutal realism, concentrating entirely on the front-line priorities, and closing down the gap between awareness and action. Grove actually reproduced a week's calendar for an unnamed CEO confronted by sweeping change. Did the man's allocation of "time, his most precious resource, reflect the strategic crisis?," asked Grove, rhetorically, of course. The answer was an emphatic "no." But Grove may have fallen into the same trap himself:

"Frankly... I have to wonder if it was an accident that I devoted a significant amount of my time in the years preceding our memory crisis, years during which the storm clouds were already very evident, to writing a book… I wonder what storm clouds I might be ducking now. I'll probably know in a few years."

Even if his self-doubt is justified, Grove's writing involved no major commitment of resources. The opposite is true of mergers and acquisitions. These have played a minor role in Intel's rise, which makes it easier for Grove to criticize what happens. The acquisition takes on greater importance than anything else, and the top management will have created "an infinite sink" for its attention.

Even a good leader can be caught in self-created traps, such as Intel's memory crisis (see pp. 46–7). The difference is that the bad leaders stay trapped, while the good ones "eventually emerge to the acceptance and action phases." Often, the inferior bosses are replaced by people who are not emotionally involved in what has gone before. For Grove, this is a key point: "The replacement of corporate heads is far more motivated by the need to bring in someone who has not invested in the past than to get somebody who is a better manager or a better leader in other ways."

Inertia of success

Grove describes the difficulty of the discharged executive as "the inertia of success." Nobody wants to abandon the methods and the strengths that have brought them to a high executive position. "So it's not surprising that they will keep implementing the same strategic and tactical moves that worked for them during the course of their careers…." As Grove says, this is extremely dangerous and can reinforce denial. People almost instinctively cling to the past, he writes, rather than acknowledge that their old skills and strengths are less relevant.

Even if inertia is overcome, "dissonance" can follow. Grove has seen many companies fall into the trap "of saying one thing and doing another." He is clear about what creates this divergence between actions and statements:

- Adapting to change starts with employees who, through their daily work, adjust to the new outside forces.
- Frontline employees and middle managers are therefore implementing and executing actions that say one thing.
- High-level pronouncements continue to say the opposite.

As Grove points out, dissonance is often a clear sign that major change is taking place and that the organization is not responding (see pp. 90–91). Moreover, while "this dissonance between what the company does and what management says is understandable, it accompanies a terribly unproductive and distressing phase." People become confused and uncertain. But light can emerge through the fog. The key process is what Grove calls "experimentation":

- Loosen up the organization: relax controls.
- Allow different techniques, products, sales channels, and customers to be tried.
- Tolerate the new and different.
- Adopt a new maxim: "let chaos reign!"

Here Grove is asking for a great deal. A conservative management will find it next to impossible to go through a phase of "experimentation and chaos." As he says, "you can't suddenly start experimenting when you realize you're in trouble unless you've been experimenting all along." For Intel, accustomed to experimenting in many fields, change is easier and more natural, as the microprocessor saga showed:

> "Intel experimented with microprocessors for over 10 years before the opportunity and imperative arose to make them the centerpiece of our corporate strategy... in fact, for a number of years we spent more money on developing and marketing them than they generated in revenue. But we kept at it... and, when our circumstances changed in a big way, we had a more appealing business to focus our resources on."

This sounds more simple than it was. Grove is emphatic that experimentation is not comfortable, especially for a company in trouble. Much better to switch when the existing business is strong. The strengths provide protection, under which "you can make changes far more easily than when the vital signs of your business have all turned south."

The key to avoiding crises like Intel's is to recognize the signs of change and to act promptly. The difficulty is mainly emotional: the "inertia of success" and other preconceptions stop most managers from acting in time. Grove quotes some often heard warning signs:

- "We shouldn't tinker with the golden goose."
- "How could we possibly take our best people away from the business that pays all our salaries and put them on some speculative new project?"
- "The organization can take just so much change; it's not ready for more."

As Grove points out, that last sentence really means, "*I'm* not ready to lead the organization into the changes that it needs to face." He draws a personal conclusion that no manager dare ignore: "*I have never made a tough change, whether it involved resource shifts or personnel moves, that I haven't wished I had made a year or so earlier.*"

Too little, too late

It is easier to see the need for "tough change" in somebody else's business than in your own. This was the stance that Grove and Gordon Moore took when deciding to exit from the memory business (see pp. 46–7). The problem, however, is not only seeing the need to change, but acting. As Grove observes: "very often we managers know that we need to do something. We even know what we should be doing." The strong manager trusts his or her instincts. Only self-discipline will conquer the "too-little-too-late" syndrome.

If the condition is not forestalled, the company enters what Grove calls "the valley of death." This is the hostile landscape through which the business and its managers must struggle or die. Grove advises that emerging from the valley requires you "to form a mental image of what the company should look like when you get to the other side." The image has to be short and sharp, otherwise it will not communicate to "your tired, demoralized, and confused staff." Grove illustrates the questions that must be answered by using another industry: "What exactly is your bookstore going to be about – will it be a pleasant place to drink coffee and read or a place where you go to buy books at a discount?"

Whatever the answer, it should come "in a single phrase that everybody can remember and, over time, can understand to mean exactly what you intended." The question for Intel in 1986 was whether to be a broad-based semiconductor company, a memory company, or a microprocessor company. The phrase that was "exactly what we were trying to achieve" was "Intel, the microcomputer company." This "mental image" equates with "vision," but Grove typically finds that management buzzword too lofty for the task of capturing "the essence of the company and the focus of its business."

Describing the compamy

Trying to define what the company will be, he stresses, must hinge on defining what it will *not* be. In Intel's case, memories were clearly the main no-go area. But it had significant businesses other than microprocessors. Grove admits that there is a danger of oversimplification, but declares that "it pales in comparison with the danger of catering to the desire of every manager to be included in the simple description of the refocused business... making that description so lofty and so inclusive as to be meaningless."

The short, sharp definition is an act of leadership. Grove recounts his impatience with very senior executives who are torn and indecisive and constantly change their strategic minds; he contemptuously calls this a "direction *du jour*" policy and asks rhetorically: "How can you motivate yourself... to follow a leader when he appears to be going around in circles?" Hesitant leaders are a puzzle to the usually decisive and incisive Grove. He sees, however, that much conviction and courage are needed to move to the front while everybody else is still arguing, and to "set an unhesitating course whose rightness or wrongness will not be known for years."

That is the real test of a leader's mettle. Grove contrasts this type of truly tough decision with the far easier adoption of downsizing. As he says, you need little self-confidence to close factories and fire workers, with short-term financial benefits that will delight Wall Street. Fundamental transformation not only takes longer to pay off, but also involves, as downsizing does not, escaping from the past that has shaped all parts of the organization. "If you and your staff got your experience managing a computer company, how can you even imagine what a microcomputer company might be like?"

Changing the people

You may well be unable to change the company without changing its people. Grove recalls Gordon Moore, his chairman, saying that "if we're really serious about this [becoming a microprocessor company] half of our executive staff had better become software types in five years' time." Among the converts, of course, was Grove himself; but he, too, needed to learn more about the software world:

> "So I deliberately started to spend a significant amount of time getting acquainted with software people. I set out to visit heads of software companies... met with them and asked them to talk to me about their business – as it were, to teach me."

This learning is easier said than done. Grove had to admit his ignorance and work hard at his self-appointed task. Managers at senior level are "accustomed to the automatic deference which people accord you owing to your position." They find it especially hard to admit that they need to learn new things. Grove was helped because Intel has long been what is now called a "learning company." Learning whole new sets of skills from time to time is part of the culture.

It follows that companies wishing to master change must acquire a similar willingness to learn. This always involves self-discipline, not just in studying, but in allocating time. There were problems at Intel because people accustomed to seeing Grove regularly saw him less often and wondered whether he still cared about their work. This proved a transitional stage, but it makes an important point. Top management cannot expect others and the company to change unless they are prepared to change themselves.

This is a shift of personal resources. Grove stresses that the knowledge, skills, and expertise of your best people are as valuable as material resources. Whenever you shift

Chairman of change
Gordon Moore realized that if Intel were to succeed as a microcomputer company, half of its executive staff would have to change their areas of know-how and become software types.

resources from one task to a new challenge, "you're putting more attention and energy into something, which is wonderful, positive and encouraging." But you are also subtracting production and managerial resources, and your own time, from other activities. Grove's advice is to redeploy all resources to accomplish a transformation; "without them, it turns out to be nothing but an empty cliché."

Strategic action

This commitment of resources to achieve strategic ends is "strategic action." Grove contrasts it with strategic planning, and is convinced that "corporate strategy is formulated by a series of such actions," far more than by the conventional, top-down plans. In his experience, these turn into "sterile statements, rarely gaining traction in the real work of the corporation." The differences are critical:

- Strategic *plans* are statements of intention.
- Strategic *actions* are already taken or being taken.
- Strategic *plans* sound like political speeches.
- Strategic *actions* are concrete steps.
- Strategic *plans* are abstract and usually have no concrete meaning except to management.
- Strategic *actions* immediately affect people's lives.
- Strategic *plans* deal with events far in the future and are thus of little relevance to today.
- Strategic *actions* take place in the present and thus command immediate attention.

The distinction that Grove draws here resembles that between culture and behavior. Concrete changes in behavior always change culture, but proposed changes in culture by no means always change behavior. According to Grove, "the most effective way to transform a company is through a series of incremental changes that are consistent with a clearly articulated end-result." He goes on: "Even if any one strategic action changes the trajectory on which the corporation moves by only a few degrees, if those actions are consistent with the image of what the company should look like... every one of them will reinforce every other."

Grove makes strategic actions sound quite simple, but is quick to point out the difficulties. Good timing is essential in switching resources. They should not be moved from the old task until the full benefit has been obtained. Hang on too long, however, and you may lose a new business opportunity, or lose momentum in a new product area. "Your tendency," warns Grove, "will almost always be to wait too long."

Advancing the pace

Moving too early is likely to be less harmful. Where major strategic change is required, "The risk is that if you are late you may already be in irreversible decline." If you are too early, however, the existing business is probably still healthy, and you are thus better placed to alter an erroneous course. Grove strongly recommends that you correct the tendency to delay: "Advance the pace of your actions and increase their magnitude. You'll find that you're more likely to be close to right."

Grove acknowledges that some companies, rapid in response and fast in execution, can operate a "taillight" strategy, traveling fast in the wake of the pioneers, before catching up and overtaking. The danger then is that, without any rear lights to follow, you may have no sense of direction. Another and increasingly great risk, which Grove does not mention, is that you may never catch up with the early movers. While their main risk is that of being wrong, either in the strategy or its timing, the risk is well worth running:

> "The early movers are the only companies that have the potential to affect the structure of the industry and to define how the game is played by others. Only by such a strategy can you hope to compete for the future and shape your destiny to your advantage."

The odds of accomplishing successful change are greatly improved, Grove argues, by adopting a highly focused approach. He quotes Mark Twain: "Put all of your eggs in one basket and WATCH THAT BASKET." Grove argues that all your energies are required to succeed with a single aim, "especially in the face of aggressive competition." The temptation is to try dodging the pursuers by having all kinds of alternative directions – by "hedging." Grove will not hedge, because it is expensive and dilutes commitment.

Clarity of direction

Meandering, moreover, has intolerable side effects. Managers are demoralized, and when that happens, nothing works, and every employee feels paralyzed. "This is exactly when you need to have a strong leader setting a direction. And it doesn't have to be the best direction – just a strong, clear one." Organizations in crisis, says Grove, are "very sensitive to obscure or ambiguous signals from their management." Conflicting messages also breed confusion. In an uncertain environment, facing an uncertain future, people need to know clearly where they are heading.

The need for clarity of direction, says Grove, increases as the change process develops. No longer do you need to let chaos reign as the alternatives are explored. "To lead your organization out of the resulting ambiguity and to energize your staff toward a new direction, you must rein in chaos." That requires five steps:

- Stop experimenting.
- Issue totally clear "marching orders."
- Commit the organization's resources.
- Commit your personal resources.
- Be a role model for change.

The ideal is to have an organization that can deal with the two phases: debate (where chaos reigns) and a determined march forward (where chaos is reined in). This, says Grove, is a powerful, adaptive organization with two key attributes:

- It tolerates and even encourages vigorous debates, devoted to exploring issues, indifferent to rank, and including individuals of varied backgrounds.

- It can make and accept clear decisions, which then receive unanimous support.

This is neither a "bottom-up" nor a "top-down" company. Grove identifies "bottom-up" with empowering middle managers, which seems unduly dismissive of other staff. However, the initiatives taken from below must meet halfway the actions generated by senior management. "The best results," says Grove, "seem to prevail when 'bottom-up' and 'top-down' are equally strong." Combine this dialectic with that between reigning chaos and chaos reined in, and change need bring no fears to any company.

Ideas into action

- If you get caught in a self-created trap, acknowledge it – and strive to escape.
- Start experiments with new methods or new business ideas as often as possible.
- Make tough changes, involving people or resources, earlier rather than later.
- Define what the company means in a short, incisive, and convincing statement.
- Set a firm and decisive course, even if the results will take time to appear.
- Once you have decided to act, make all necessary resources fully available.
- Concentrate your energies on a single goal, especially when facing aggressive competition.

Mastering change

Anticipating and exploiting change is the key to success in the 21st century. You need to recognize the signs of change early and then develop a timely strategy to cope with it. You must also make sure that you carry people with you in the transformation of the organization.

Profiting from paranoia

Whether or not you agree with Andy Grove's maxim "only the paranoid survive," the thought is a powerful tool for effective management of change. Strictly speaking, paranoia is a delusion: but the existence of competitive and other threats, whatever your industry, is likely to be only too real.

Take your guide from what is happening in the present and forget what has happened in the past in your business, which may be wholly irrelevant. Fight against the tendency to stick to the business and the methods that have sustained your fortunes for so long.

Avoiding denial

The opposite of healthy paranoia is unhealthy denial. Change that comes in the form of bad news tends to be denied. To avoid denial, analyze your response to such change honestly and rationally.

Dealing with Bad News
Do I want this news to be wrong?
Is that why I am denying it?
Have I conducted a thorough, dispassionate analysis that shows it to be wrong?
What will be the worst possible result if the news is right, and I have done nothing?
What action can and should I take if the news is right?
What is the worst possible result of that action?
What is the best possible result of that action?

Rational evaluation of a possibly threatening change as soon as it appears undermines false optimism and demonstrate what risks you are running through denial and inaction. Remember Andy Grove's words: "Looking back over my own career, I have never made a tough change, whether it involved resource shifts or personnel moves, that I haven't wished I had made a year or so earlier."

Look back over your career. Were there any events of which you would say the same as Grove? Ask yourself why you delayed. Almost always, the answer lies in your emotions; for example, fear of confrontation or fear of being wrong.

Shifting resources

The critical moment comes when you must commit resources to a new product or process. There are dangers in moving too early or too late, although acting too late incurs the greater penalties.

Resource Shift Dilemma		
Resource shift is premature	**Timing of shift is right**	**Resource shift is late**
Existing strategy not satisfactorily completed.	Momentum of existing strategy is still positive; new line builds steadily.	Opportunity for transformation is lost; decline may be irreversible.

The penalty of lateness is very possibly fateful. Proceed on the paranoid assumption that you will never catch up, which will almost certainly be true. Conversely, you probably can turn back and repair at least some of the damage done by shifting resources too early.

Playing Catch-up

The dangers of shifting resources too late are highlighted by IBM's late entry into the laptop market, in which it has yet to catch up with its main rivals.

IBM launched its minicomputer 14 years after Digital Equipment, and its PC four years after the launch of the Apple II. In both cases the IBM products were successful. But when IBM came five years late into the laptop market, Toshiba was the strong leader in a market already worth $6 billion a year. IBM thought it would again catch up. It never has.

1 Managing the change

Every organization, sooner or later, comes up against the "strategic inflection point" when past success levels off. Develop a new strategy before your existing products and markets begin to falter.

Exploiting the strategic inflection point

Do not regard the strategic inflection point as a threat. On the contrary, it is a great opportunity. When Intel at last responded to the crushing Japanese competition in memory chips, it soared to remarkable new heights by exploiting its microprocessors. The delay in leaving the memory chip market was overcome because the new business had been developed while the old one was still strong.

Intel's management of this particular strategic inflection point contains two essential lessons.

- Keep your existing business in the best possible condition. Your business is only as good as its latest results.
- Take all adverse trends in actual and forecast results as calls to action; that is, continually develop new products, new markets, new technologies, new processes, and new people.

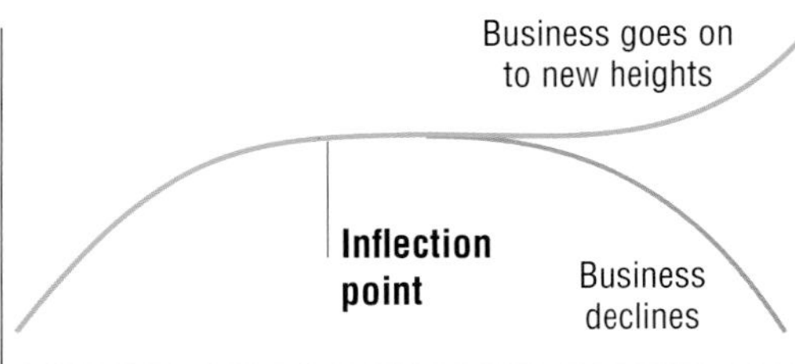

Inflection curve
To ensure business success in the face of an inflection point develop your new strategy while maintaining the old.

Developing the new

Use the "windows of opportunity" method to identify which new products and markets could be usefully developed or expanded.

- Draw a matrix with existing products on the left-hand side.
- Put your existing customers along the bottom.
- Extend the left-hand side upward with dotted lines for products under development.
- Extend the bottom line to the right with dotted lines for potential new customers.

- Check each square where you have a customer for an existing product.
- The empty squares are your "windows of opportunity."

Identifying the competition

You cannot develop a successful strategy in a vacuum. Who are your competitors? What are they doing or are likely to do? It is all too easy to concentrate on the rivals you have always faced, even though this may no longer be appropriate. Everybody in computers kept focused on IBM, for example, and ignored the rise of smaller PC makers who were, in fact, dramatically changing the industry. To avoid such dangers, Grove advises using the "silver bullet" test.

The Silver Bullet Test

Imagine that you and your colleagues have one gun and just one silver bullet each.

Ask everybody, including yourself, which competitor they would choose to shoot down by the silver bullet.

Expect a quick, unequivocal answer but follow up by asking, "Are you 100 percent sure?"

If either the first or second answers betray uncertainty, or come up with unexpected names, sit up and take notice.

Facing the future

"When the importance of your competitors shifts," says Grove, "it is often a sign that something significant is going on." Do not brush new competition aside, or concentrate on its weaknesses.

Making the Future Happen

With the microprocessor, Intel proved the validity of the words of the great PC pioneer, Alan Kay, who said: "The best way to predict the future is to invent it."

The untried, unfamiliar microprocessors started with only a few customers, an apparently tiny market and no profits; "in fact, for a number of years we spent more money on developing and marketing them than they generated in revenue." But when circumstances changed "in a big way," Intel had a new and far brighter future to pursue – and to make happen.

2 Turning the organization

Change cannot be managed without changing people, which means producing different and appropriate behavior. Achieve this by involving everybody in clear and clearly executed change strategies.

From planning to action

A plan is only as good as the actions that it generates. Many managers spend too much thought on planning and too little on the vital matter of implementation. Andy Grove tells you to test any plan with the following questions:

- Is it just a statement of intention?
- Does it sound like a political speech?
- Does it have concrete meaning only to management?
- Does it deal with events far in the future?
- Does it have little relevance to today?

If you answer Yes to any of these questions, the plan is likely to be as ineffective as most strategic planning. It will not achieve the object of change management, which is to alter people's behavior – what they do. Grove therefore gives much higher value to strategic actions. To earn his praise, your plan should contain actions.

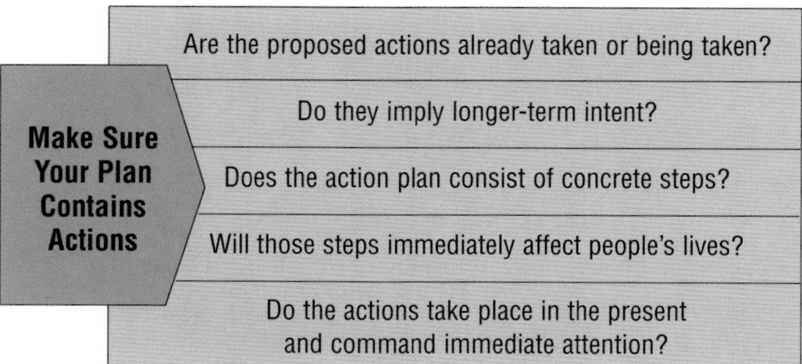

Communicating effectively

Make sure that everybody hears about your plan: the proposals, the intent, the concrete steps, what it will mean for them, and what is expected of them. However much you communicate, remember, it is never enough. And listen to your staff, often and hard. People all the way down the company are quite capable of seeing what needs to be done, and what needs to be done differently. They are simply unused to being heard, let alone to having their recommendations followed. They are an invaluable source of information and action.

As Grove says: "The process of adapting to change starts with employees who, through their daily work, adjust to the new outside forces." Hold a lot of discussions with employees in their workplaces. Ask questions of these experts. Repeat their answers back to them to be sure you have understood. Act on the valuable lessons you learn, and let them know that you have acted.

Achieving a synthesis

You want neither top-down management nor bottom-up, but a synthesis of the two. The chart shows what Grove calls a "dynamic dialectic." The best place by far is the top right-hand square, where both the actions coming down and the actions coming up are strong.

Top-down action ↑ / Bottom-up action →	weak	strong
strong	Sometimes copes with change	Copes well with change
weak	Fails to cope with change	Fails to cope with change

Dynamic dialectic

This matrix shows that organizations cope best with change when top-down and bottom-up actions are equally strong, balancing management direction with staff participation.

You can have a largely bottom-up system for strategic planning (Intel once did) but that will not cope with "big-time change." Managing such a change requires three elements:

- Vigorous debates in which everyone participates in discussing and arguing about the issues.
- Clear and timely decision making.
- Total support for the decision once made.

Merely adopting these elements, for most organizations, will represent enormous change. Trying to manage major change without them is unlikely to succeed.

GLOSSARY

Abandonment: The dropping of an organization's unproductive activities, after having questioned its business.
Abundance mentality: Belief that there is plenty of potential reward for everybody in any business relationship.
Activity-based costing: Obtaining more accurate cost data by allocating overheads and other indirect costs to specific activities required to make products or serve customer segments.
Affirmation: A statement that helps individual organizations to approach events with clear purposes and policies.
Amortization: Writing off a debt over time.
Apollonians: Natural bureaucrats who prefer rules, control, and order in their working lives over enterprise and operational freedom.
Arbitrage: Taking advantage of differences between prices for the same security or commodity.
Asterisk: Exceptional situation where the rulebook has failed and instinct and speed are required to achieve results.
Athenians: People who like to work in task forces and similar groups with a high degree of directed autonomy.
Atomization: The restructuring of an organization into small subunits headed by individual managers.
Balanced scorecard: Rating performance under headings.
Bandwidth: The measure of the number of bits that can be moved through a circuit in a second.
BASIC (Beginners All-purpose Symbolic Instruction Code): A standard coding method for programming computers.
Benchmarking: Examining the operating standards of other companies to improve performance.
Best practice: Top-of-the-class methods for every aspect of business.
Bit: The smallest amount of information, represented as binary numbers 0 or 1.
Black box: Grove's metaphor for all the processes in any disk operation that convert inputs into final output.
Book value: The value placed on a company's assets in the accounts.
Business engine: GE metaphor for a company driven by interaction between its various component parts.
Business x-ray: Determining how much innovation a company requires to stay competitive, in which areas, and within which time frame.
Character ethic: System of belief founded on enduring moral principles.
Chinese contract: Commercial agreement that provides the two sides with benefits.
Circle of concern: All issues that impinge on a person's life and work.
CISC (Complex Instruction Set Computing): Technology used for Intel's family of microprocessors from the beginning (see also RISC).
Completed staff work: Delegating an entire problem to staff, who return with a full and final recommendation.
Core: Businesses that are long-term corporate holdings and are not for sale.
Corporate IQ: Term used by Gates to refer to the intelligence, knowledge, and expertise of a company.
Crazy organizations: Organizations that are not built around continuity and routine, but vigorously promote "creativity and zest" as the drivers of profits, growth, and economic success.
Creation: The "first creation" is mental, forming a plan (leadership); the "second creation" is executing the plan (management).
Creative swiping: Taking innovative ideas from external sources.

CUA factor: The amount of Complexity, Uncertainty, and Ambiguity with which people most contend in their jobs.
Decentralization: Giving smaller units of an organization more responsibility and autonomy.
Digital Nervous System (DNS): A term Gates uses to refer to the electronic network binding together a company, its customers, and its suppliers.
Dionysians: Free-thinking, independent individualists who are much happier outside organizational life.
Doughnut: Division between core of essential activities and optional ones.
Economic goodwill: The value of the earnings of a business over and above its book value.
Economic Value Added (EVA): Deducting the total financing cost of equity and other capital from a business's recalculated profits to determine its true economic return.
Emotional bank account: Metaphor for the amount of trust built up or withdrawn in a relationship.
Feedback analysis: An exercise in which expectation is compared with outcome, and steps are taken to improve future performance.
Financial goodwill: The difference between the higher price paid for a company and its assets' book value (qv).
Flexilives: Careers that consist of several different jobs and employers.
Focus investment: The concentration of an investor's holdings in a few stocks.
Gods of management: Handy metaphor for cultures: Zeus/power, Apollo/role, Athena/task, Dionysus/free.
Goodwill accounting: *see* Economic goodwill; Financial goodwill.
Graphical user interface: Image-based operating system, where the user enters commands by clicking a mouse.
Hard, and hardware: Measurable processes and results and the physical assets required for them.
Horizontal management: Non-hierarchical structure of management.
Hybrid: Organization that is built neither wholly around corporate-wide functions nor on total decentralization.
IMBOS (Intel Management By Objectives System): Method of achieving collective performance by setting individual aims.
Incentive compensation: Paying for achievement to enhance performance.
Information Technology (IT): Any technology that can process, store, and transmit information.
Inside-out: Reversing the conventional logic to achieve breakthroughs in thinking (*see* Upside-down).
Integrated diversity: Concept of GE as a diverse set of businesses that support and learn from each other.
Intellectual capital: General and specific knowledge which a company possesses in its staff and databases.
Intrinsic business value: The true worth of a business, estimated by forecasting future cash inflows and working out their present value.
Java: A universal programming language devised by Sun Microsystems, used for internet applications.
Learning organization: One that mutates and develops to reflect new knowledge and experience.
Leverage: Achieving higher output than possible by the manager's direct contribution – for example, by delegation and motivation.
Look-through earnings: All the underlying profits in which the investor has an ownership.
Loose-tight controls: A mix of staff autonomy to encourage creativity and innovation, and centralized control over finance and reporting.

Mainframes: Large computers, capable of processing vast amounts of information, that are connected to a series of terminals.

Management by objectives: Technique for improving individual and group performance, in which all managers have goals that fit the overall goals of the organization.

Margin of safety: The difference between the purchase price of a company's stock and its higher intrinsic value, as advocated by Benjamin Graham and adopted by Buffett.

Maturity continuum: Successive development of habits to pass from dependence through independence to interdependence.

MBWA (Management By Wandering Around): Interventionist, out-of-the-office, hands-on top management.

Mission statement: Setting out priorities, values, and objectives.

Moore's law: Predicts that integrated circuits will double in power and speed at constant cost every 18 months.

MS-DOS (Microsoft Disk Operating System): The initial operating system used on the first IBM PC (1981).

Multi-plane concept: Having the same person work on two or more planes – for example, in both an operating and a planning role.

MVA (Market Value Added): The difference between the capital invested by a company and its quoted market value.

Operating system: The interface between the user and the computer that allows applications to be used.

Owner's manual: 13 owner-related business principles laid down by Buffett primarily for Berkshire Hathaway, but which can apply to other businesses.

P&L responsibility: Accountability for the financial results (profit and loss) of a unit.

Paradigm: Basic mental framework – the vision of the world of an individual or organization – that strongly influences ideas and actions.

Peer group syndrome: Tendency of meetings to degenerate into "group-think" in the absence of a senior discussion leader.

Portfolio career: Having several employers either for the same work or for a collection of activities.

P/PC balance: Balancing the highest possible production consistent with the fullest development of the means of production (production capability).

Price-led costing: When a company starts with what the customer is prepared to pay for the product or service, and then works backward to calculate what production costs must be targeted.

Process mapping: Procedure of describing and analyzing a business process from beginning to end with a view to streamlining the process.

Profit centers: Units within large companies that are responsible for minimizing costs and maximizing revenue for the products or services they provide for the organization.

Ranking and rating: Intel system for assessing employees, "rating" their performance and "ranking" them against others.

Relationship responsibility: The moral responsibility of every manager to communicate reasons and plans.

RISC (Reduced Instruction Set Computing): Rival, later chip technology. Advantages over CISC (q.v.) proved insufficient.

Scale economies: The reduction of production costs per unit of sale as numbers of units produced increase.

Scarcity mentality: Belief that one person's gain must of necessity be another person's loss.

Scientific management: Efficiency theory developed by Frederick Taylor in the late 19th and early 20th centuries, whose main application became known as "work study."
Seven-S Formula: McKinsey analysis of an organization, based on structure, strategy, systems, style of management, skills, staff, and shared values.
Shamrock organization: One divided into professional core, subcontractors, and flexible labor force.
Shareholder value: The worth of a company to its owners. Generally equated with its equity's market value.
"Sharpen the saw": Metaphor for exercise and practice to maintain and improve one's performance.
Sigmoid curve: The shape of the organizational life-cycle, which can be extended by timely action before it reaches the crest.
Six Sigma: Standard of quality performance in which no more than 3.4 defects per million parts or operations are acceptable.
Soft, and software: Management processes that are not measurable but which generate "hard" results.
Span of control: The number of people directly managed or controlled by one person.
Sticking to the knitting: The precept that companies should stay with the business they know.
Stock option: The right given to a company employee at an agreed date in the future to buy stock in that company at a price fixed (usually at the then current market level) when the option is awarded.
Strategic inflection point: Where 10X forces (q.v.) begin to impact an industry in what will become dramatic change.
10x force: A very great increase in one of the key forces that impact on competitive strategy.
Task-Relevant Maturity (TRM): Degree to which employees are equipped to take responsibility for the task.
Top-down policies: Policies dictated by top management.
TQM (Total Quality Management): A management system that trains all employees in the techniques and achievement of perfect quality.
Trinitarian: Also known as "third-angle" thinking, it adds an extra approach to resolving a conflict between two parties.
Triple I: Organization that uses intelligence, information, and ideas to add value.
Type 1 and 2 errors: Type 1 errors are doing things wrong; Type 2 errors are not doing the right things.
Upside-down: Reversing conventional logic to achieve breakthroughs in thinking (*see* Inside-out).
Utility power: The usual economic relationship in which individuals exchange their time, work, and talents for pay and benefits.
Value chain: The progress of a product from raw material to its final sale.
Windows: Microsoft's graphics-based operating system for the PC, which has been upgraded several times.
Wintel: A contraction that refers to computers that rely on a combination of Microsoft Windows operating system and Intel's microprocessors.
Win/win: Seeking or agreeing to a plan of action that promises equal satisfaction to both parties.
Zeus: The father-figure leader, typically found among companies still dominated by a founding entrepreneur.

BIBLIOGRAPHY

WARREN BUFFETT

The fullest account of Buffett's investment philosophy is contained in *The Warren Buffett Way* (1994, John Wiley & Sons, New York) and *The Warren Buffett Portfolio*, both by Robert G. Hagstrom. Mary Buffett and David Clark's *Buffettology* (1997, Scribner, New York) is another version, while Andrew Kilpatrick's *Of Permanent Value* (1994, Andy Kilpatrick Publishing Empire, Birmingham, Alabama) relates his life. Roger Lowenstein's contribution is *Buffett: The Making of an American Capitalist* (1995, Random House, New York).

Books that have inspired Buffett himself include *Developing an Investment Philosophy* (1991, Pacific Publishing Group, USA) by Philip A. Fisher.

WORKS CITED

Berkshire Hathaway Annual Reports.

Lawrence A. Cunningham (1997) *The Essays of Warren Buffett: Lessons for – Corporate America* (The Cunningham Group, USA).

Benjamin Graham (1985) *The Intelligent Investor: A Book of Practical Counsel* (HarperCollins, New York).

Robert G. Hagstrom (1999) *The Warren Buffett Portfolio: Mastering the Power of the Focus Investment Strategy* (John Wiley & Sons, New York).

BILL GATES

Bill Gates has written two books – *The Road Ahead* and *Business @ the Speed of Thought*. His stories and quotations have been compiled in *Bill Gates Speaks* by Janet C. Lowe (1998, John Wiley & Sons, New York).

The many books on Microsoft are led by Randall E. Stross's balanced if critical *The Microsoft Way*. And then there's the web, which abounds in unflattering, unofficial Gates sites.

WORKS CITED

Bill Gates (1995) *The Road Ahead*, Viking Books, New York.

– (1996) *The Road Ahead* (revised edition), Viking Books, New York.

– (1999) *Business @ the Speed of Thought: Using a Digital Nervous System*, Warner Books, New York.

Andrew S. Grove (1996) *Only the Paranoid Survive*, Bantam, Doubleday Dell, New York.

Geoffrey James (1997) *Giant Killers*, Orion, London.

Anthony Sampson (1995) *Company Man: the Rise and Fall of Corporate Life*, HarperCollins, London.

Peter M. Senge (1990) *The Fifth Discipline*, Doubleday, New York.

Alfred P. Sloan (1963) *My Years at General Motors*, Doubleday, New York.

Thomas A. Stewart (1997) *Intellectual Capital: the New Wealth of Organizations*, Doubleday, New York.

Randall E. Stross (1996) *The Microsoft Way: the Real Story of How the Company Outsmarts Its Competition*, Addison-Wesley, Longman, Reading, Massachusetts.

Peter Drucker

Peter Drucker has written some 30 books over seven decades, including two novels, *The Temptation to Do Good* (1984, HarperCollins, New York) and *The Last of All Possible Worlds* (1982, HarperCollins, New York).

Works cited

Jack Beatty (1997) *The World According to Drucker*, Simon & Schuster, New York.

Peter F. Drucker (1939) *The End of Economic Man*, John Day, New York.

– (1942) *The Future of Industrial Man*, John Day, New York.

– (1945) *Concept of the Corporation*, John Day, New York.

– (1954) *The Practice of Management*, Harper & Row, New York.

– (1969) *The Age of Discontinuity*, Harper & Row, New York.

– (1974) *Management: Tasks, Responsibilities, Practices*, HarperCollins, New York.

– (1984) *Innovation and Entrepreneurship*, HarperCollins, New York.

– (1985) *The Effective Executive*, Harper & Row, New York.

– (1986) *The Frontiers of Management*, Harper & Row, New York.

– (1986) *Managing for Results*, Harper Business, New York.

– (1989) *The New Realities*, HarperCollins, New York.

– (1990) *Managing the Non-Profit Organization*, HarperCollins, New York.

– (1992) *Managing for the Future*, Dutton, New York.

– (1993) *Post Capitalist Society*, Harper & Row, New York.

– (1995) *Managing in a Time of Great Change*, Dutton, New York.

– (1996) *The Pension Fund Revolution*, Transaction Publishers, New Brunswick.

(1999) *Management Challenges for the 21st Century*, HarperCollins, New York.

John Micklethwait and Adrian Wooldridge (1996) *The Witch Doctors*, Heinemann, London.

Alfred P. Sloan (1963) *My Years at General Motors*, John Wiley & Sons, New York.

Tom Peters

Tom Peters' latest book, *The Circle of Innovation* (1999, Random House, New York), is practical and innovative. Another practical series is *Reinventing Work* (1999, Random House, New York): each book lists 50 essential points for achieving success. There is also the *Tom Peters Business School in a Box* (1995, Alfred A. Knopf, New York), and a host of video and audio cassettes.

Works cited

Peter F. Drucker (1999) *Management Challenges for the 21st Century*, HarperCollins, New York.

Don Peppers and Martha Rogers (1995) *The One-to-One Future*, Doubleday & Co., New York.

Tom Peters (1982) *In Search of Excellence*, Harper & Row, New York.

(1987) *Thriving on Chaos*, HarperCollins, New York.

– (1989) *A Passion for Excellence*, Random House, New York.

– (1992) *Liberation Management*, Alfred A. Knopf, New York.

(1994) *The Pursuit of Wow!*, Random House, New York.

– (1994) *The Tom Peters Seminar*, Random House, New York.

Stephen Covey

The core of Stephen Covey's literary output is *The Seven Habits of Highly Effective People.* It has also provided the theme for many publications on Covey's second area of concern, the family and interfamilial relationships.

More of a business book than *Seven Habits* is *Principle-centered Leadership.* Business and workplace matters also account for a third of *Living the Seven Habits*, a collection of "stories of courage and inspiration." Another book, *The Nature of Leadership*, explores his principles through interviews and photographs.

Works cited

Sean Covey (1999) *The Seven Habits of Highly Effective Teens*, Simon & Schuster UK Ltd, London.

Stephen R. Covey (1989) *The Seven Habits of Highly Effective People*, Simon & Schuster UK Ltd, London.

(1990) *Principle-centered Leadership*, Simon & Schuster UK Ltd, London.

– (1994) *Daily Reflections for Highly Effective People*, Simon & Schuster UK Ltd, London.

– (1997) *First Things First Every Day*, Simon & Schuster UK Ltd, London.

– (1998) *Balancing Work and Family*, Covey Leadership Center, Utah.

(1998) *The Nature of Leadership*, Franklin Covey, Utah.

– (1998) *The Seven Habits Family Journal*, Covey Leadership Center, Utah.

– (1998) *The Seven Habits of Highly Effective Families*, Simon & Schuster UK Ltd, London.

(1999) *Living the Seven Habits*, Simon & Schuster UK Ltd, London.

Stephen R. Covey, A. Roger Merrill with Rebecca R. Merrill (1994) *First Things First*, Simon & Schuster UK Ltd, London.

Blaine Lee (1997) *The Power Principle*, Simon & Schuster UK Ltd, London.

Jack Welch

Although he has yet to write his own account of his life, time, and theories, there are plenty of words about this extraordinary business leader. *Jack Welch Speaks*, by Janet C. Lowe, draws extensively on his interviews and public speeches and gives an excellent account subject's life and ideas.

The author who has been closest to Welch, however, is Noel M. Tichy, who with his coauthor, Stratford Sherman, wrote *Control Your Destiny or Someone Else Will*, the title being a fundamental of Welch's management philosophy.

The GE Way Fieldbook, by former *Time* journalist Robert Slater, covers leadership, empowerment, organization, and customers; the book also looks at Welch as preacher, communicator, and strategist. Slater has written three other books on Welch. Thomas F. O'Boyle strikes a more critical note in *At Any Cost: Jack Welch and the Pursuit of Profit* (Random House, 1998).

Works cited

Janet C. Lowe (1998) *Jack Welch Speaks*, John Wiley & Sons, Inc., New York.

Robert Slater (2000) *The GE Way Fieldbook*, McGraw-Hill, New York.

Noel M. Tichy and Stratford Sherman (1993) *Control Your Destiny or Someone Else Will*, HarperCollins Publishers Inc., New York.

Charles Handy

Charles Handy's first book, *Understanding Organizations*, has become a standard textbook. He broke new ground with *Gods of Management*, with its powerful delineation of the four main management cultures. In *The Age of Unreason* he outlined the implications for society, and for individuals, of the dramatic ways in which technology and economics are changing workplaces and lives. *The Empty Raincoat* (called *The Age of Paradox* in the US) is the sequel to *Unreason*, and was named by both *Fortune* and *Business Week* as one of the ten best business books of the year.

Handy has won two McKinsey Awards for articles in the *Harvard Business Review* – "Balancing Corporate Power: A New Federalist Paper" (1992), and "Trust and the Virtual Organization" (1995). His *The Hungry Spirit* explores and explains his doubts about some consequences of free-market capitalism and questions the validity of material success. In 1999 Handy combined his skills with those of his wife Elizabeth, a portrait photographer, in *The New Alchemists* – a portrait of Londoners who have "created something out of nothing."

Works cited

Charles Handy (1992) *Understanding Organizations*, Penguin, London.
– (1995) *Gods of Management*, Arrow, London.
– (1995) *The Age of Unreason*, Arrow, London.
– (1995) *The Empty Raincoat*, Arrow, London.
(1995) *Beyond Certainty*, Arrow, London.
(1995) *Waiting for the Mountain to Move*, Arrow, London.
(1998) *The Hungry Spirit*, Arrow, London.
(1999) *The New Alchemists*, Hutchinson, London.

Andrew Grove

Andy Grove's two prime books on managing, *High Output Management* and *Only the Paranoid Survive* are genuine guides for practicing managers – and not the more typical tycoon memoirs. These two books bear the highly individual stamp of a top manager with the rare ability to intellectualize his activities. The books naturally draw on Grove's experiences at Intel, and contain much fascinating corporate material: but the latter is used strictly for illustrative purposes.

Grove's first book, *Physics and Technology of Semiconductor Devices*, is far less well known. It is a product of his early academic career, just as *Only the Paranoid Survive* reflects his later work teaching strategy at Stanford University. *High Output Management* is a guide to all aspects of running an effective business.

Intel, Grove's part-creation, has received surprisingly little literary attention considering its extreme importance in the digital revolution. The two books that do exist are *Creating the Digital Future*, a 1998 study by insider Albert Yu, and *Inside Intel*, by an outsider, the journalist and later e-entrepreneur Tim Jackson.

Works cited

Andrew S. Grove (1983) *High Output Management*, Random House, New York.
– (1996) *Only the Paranoid Survive*, HarperCollins, New York.
Tim Jackson (1997) *Inside Intel*, HarperCollins, New York.

Index

Page numbers in **bold** refer to main sections on business masterminds; those in *italics* refer to pictures or their captions.

D

E

F

G

M

N

Q

R

S

T

U

V

W

X

Z

Picture Credits

The publisher would like to thank the following for their kind permission to reproduce the following photographs:

AKG London: Erich Lessing 660; **Ardea London Ltd:** Francois Gohier 180, John Mason 138; **Associated Press AP:** 336, Stephan Savola 335, Toby Talbot 407, David Breslauer 790; **Camera Press:** Stuart Mark 760; **Corbis UK Ltd:** 504, 626, James L. Amos 106, Jeremy Homer 173, Kelly Harriger 158, Wolfgang Kaehler 137, Robert Holmes 467, E.O. Hoppe 555, Catherine Kamow 524, Robert Mass 5 (third from bottom), 531, 617, Bettmann 33, 207, 222, 647, Underwood and Underwood 769, Galen Rowell 804, Roger Ressmeyer 5 (fourth from top), 322, 831; **Courtesy of Franklin Covey Company:** 2 (bottom second from left), 5 (fourth from bottom), 426, 529; **Courtesy of GECrotonville:** 535, 539; **Garden Picture Library:** Ros Wickham 680; **General Motors Corporation:** GM Media Archives 226, 234; **Gidal:** 65; **Elizabeth Handy Portraits:** 2 (bottom second from right), 5 (second from bottom), 634, 639, 643, 696, 703; **Robert Harding Picture Library:** 359, 419, Nigel Francis 252, Andrew Mills 273; **Hulton Getty:** 81, 231, 286; **Image Bank:** Archive Photos 293, Steve McAlister 379, Patti McConville 401; **Katz Pictures:** John Abbot 2 (top left), Delluc/XPn 2 (bottom left), Jim Leynse/Sara Rea 449, Steve Labadessa 431, Nigel Parry/Cpi 5 (bottom), 738, William Mercer Mcleod/Outline 743; **Magnum:** Raghu Rai 195; **Popperfoto:** 438, Findlay Kember/Reuters 161, Reuters/Anthony Bolante 119, Peter Morgan/Reuters 551, Reuters 562, 578; **Rex Features:** 45, 50, Boulat-Jobard 2 (top second from left), Peter Brooker 132, SIPA 165, David Lomax 603, KMLA 577, R. Lawrence 574, 690; **Science & Society Picture Library:** 781, 797, 821; **Science Photo Library:** Erich Schrempp 822; **SIPA:** 89; **Frank Spooner Pictures:** Francis Apesteguy 5 (second from top), 114, Agostini 22, Brad Markel 10, 111, Nora Feller 93, Schwarz 5 (top), 16, 86, Halstead/Liaison 142, Wilson 213, Thierry Buccon-Gibod 414, Liaison 383, Wilson 397, John Rogers 494, Peter Smith/Liaison 809; **The Stock Market:** John Paul Endress 474; **Tony Stone Images:** Chuck Pefley 55, Doug Armand 105, Olney Vasan 76, Robert Mort 28, Andrew Errington 217, Christoph Burki 122, Cris Haigh 202, Frank Cezuz 267, 309, Mary Kate Denny 302, Walter Hodges 248, 355, Kaluzny/Thatcher 126, 267, G. Brad Lewis 404, Daniel J Cox 348, Howard Grey 340, Charles Gupton 372, Pal Hermansen 390, Ian Jackson 368, Terry Vine 347, Adam LuBroth 445, Christopher Thomas 514, Jon Gray 481, Lori Adamski Peek 450, Eric Sander 538, Grant Taylor 614, Jon Riley 330, 601, Wayne Eastep 717, Chris Everard 718, George Grigoriou 644, Aldo Torelli 695, Andy Sacks 746, Joe McBride 782; **Superstock Ltd:** J. Silver 100, James Gibson 18; **Telegraph Colour Library:** Gail Shumway 40, VCL 48, Michael Hart 146, Harry Bartlett 276, Robin Davis 264, G Germany 242, Jeri Gleiter 434; **Times Syndication:** 2 (top second from right, top right), 327, 497.

Front cover: Stone Images. Back cover: top (left to right): Katz Pictures/John Abbot, Rex Features/ Boulat-Jobard, Times Syndication (two pictures); bottom (left to right): Katz Pictures/Delluc/XPn, Courtesy of Franklin Covey Company, Elizabeth Handy Portraits.

Acknowledgements

Author's Acknowledgements

The many sources for this book have been acknowledged in the text, but I must now express my great debt to everybody, above all to the Masterminds themselves. Nor would the book exist but for the inspiration and effort of the excellent Dorling Kindersley team – to whom my warm thanks.

Publisher's Acknowledgements

Business Masterminds were originally produced for Dorling Kindersley by **Grant Laing Partnership**, 48 Brockwell Park Gardens, London SE24 9BJ.

Managing Editor Jane Laing
Project Editor Helen Ridge
Managing Art Editor Steve Wilson

Dorling Kindersley would also like to thank the following for their help and participation:

Editorial Josephine Bryan, Claire Ellerton, Nicola Munro, Daphne Richardson, Frank Ritter, Jane Simmonds, Lee Stacy;

Design Austin Barlow, Jamie Hanson, Christine Lacey, Caroline Marklew, Nigel Morris, Laura Watson, Sarah Williams;

DTP Rob Campbell, Jason Little, Louise Waller;

Index Kay Ollerenshaw;

Picture research Andy Sansom;

Production Elizabeth Cherry.

Robert Heller

Robert Heller is himself a prolific author of management books. The first, *The Naked Manager*, published in 1972, established Heller as an iconoclastic, wide-ranging guide to managerial excellence – and incompetence. Heller has drawn on the extensive knowledge of managers and management that he acquired as the founding editor of *Management Today*, Britain's premier business magazine, which he headed for 25 years. Books such as *The Supermanagers* and *In Search of European Excellence* address the ways in which the latest ideas on change, quality, and motivation are providing new routes to business success. In 1990 Heller wrote *Culture Shock*, one of the first books to describe how IT would revolutionize management. Since then, as writer, lecturer, and consultant, Heller has continued to tell managers how to "Ride the Revolution," the title of his 2000 book, written with Paul Spenley. His books for Dorling Kindersley's Essential Managers series are international bestsellers.